SEGUNDO NIVEL

¡Ya verás!

SECOND EDITION

JOHN R. GUTIÉRREZ
The Pennsylvania State University

HARRY L. ROSSER
Boston College

HH

Heinle & Heinle Publishers
An International Thomson Publishing Company • Boston, MA 02116 U.S.A.

I(T)P

Visit us on the internet http://www.thomson.com/heinle.html

TEACHER'S EDITION

The publication of *¡YA VERÁS! Segundo nivel* Teacher's Edition was directed by the members of the Heinle & Heinle School Publishing Team:

Editorial Director: Beth Kramer
Market Development Director: Pamela Warren
Production Editor: Mary McKeon
Developmental Editor: Regina McCarthy
Publisher/Team Leader: Stanley J. Galek
Director of Production/Team Leader: Elizabeth Holthaus

Also participating in the publication of this text were:

Manufacturing Coordinator: Barbara Stephan
Project Manager: Kristin Swanson
Interior Design: Susan Gerould/Perspectives
Composition: Perspectives and Pre-Press Company
Cover Art: Mark Schroder
Cover Design: Corey McPherson Nash
Photo/Video Specialist: Jonathan Stark

ISBN 0-8384-6214-6 Teacher's Edition

10 9 8 7 6 5 4 3 2 1

To the Teacher

"*The* greatest strength is that this is a student-oriented textbook. The students are required to participate, especially in pair work. The next greatest strength is the book's ability to recycle previously taught material. Very little content is not reviewed and there are always plenty of exercises for the teacher to use to reteach material if necessary. Lastly, I feel that the balance the book strikes between all five skills is wonderful–it makes for easy teaching as far as our curriculum goes. "

-Bartley Kirst, Ironwood High School, Glendale, AZ

"*The* contexts in *¡YA VERÁS!* help motivate students to learn Spanish because students put more effort into learning something which they can readily use. Students want to have the ability to 'say something in Spanish' at the end of the very first day of classes. If they see that they can understand something and say something in Spanish, then they will put forth more effort to learn. "

-Diane Henderson, S.P. Waltrip High School, Houston, TX

"*S*tudents acquire the language through a natural progression, and the recycling of the material reminds students that there is a focus and inter-relatedness of linguistic functions and patterns. *¡YA VERÁS!* is user friendly! It is very easy for me to plan as well as present new material. "

-Kristin Warner, Piper High School, Sunrise, FL

Contents

Why was the ¡YA VERÁS! program written?

As the preceding testimonials indicate, the *¡YA VERÁS!* program has had a major, positive impact on teachers and students. In large measure, our success is due to the fact that we have created a user-friendly program based on concerns expressed by you, the teachers. Before writing the first edition, we asked you to identify the most common problems you experience in the classroom and with the materials you have been using over the years. We then addressed each problem very specifically and provided solutions that have gone a long way in facilitating and enhancing your classroom experience.

Problem: Besides teaching my classes, I have many other assigned responsibilities. I don't have a great deal of time for preparation and I certainly don't have the time to reorganize the book, rewrite sections of it, or create a lot of new exercises. I also don't have time to create my own tests.

Our solution: We have organized our books in such a way that no time needs to be spent on reorganization or rewriting. Preparation time is reduced to a minimum because new and recycled materials have been carefully integrated, the four skills and culture complement each other, and there is a step-by-step progression from practice to meaningful communication.

Problem: My classes are very large and heterogeneous. Some students take a long time to learn something, others progress very quickly.

Our solution: We provide many opportunities for students to interact in small groups. This reduces anxiety in the more reticent students and allows slower students to learn from those who learn more quickly. Regular recycling provides numerous "passes" of the same material so that slower students have the time to assimilate it.

Problem: I should be able to express my own personality and teaching style. I should not be constrained by the textbook or by a particular method.

Our solution: We did not espouse one particular method in *¡YA VERÁS!* In an integrative approach such as ours, you are given a variety of options for working with the material. This allows you and your students to express your own preferences and teaching/learning styles.

Problem: Sometimes I feel that my teaching effectiveness is reduced by stress and fatigue. By the end of the day I feel completely drained because all of my students are totally dependent on me for all of their learning.

Our solution: In *¡YA VERÁS!*, we use small-group work to place more responsibility on students. Small groups give you regular "breathers" in each class period. Our student-centered approach does not, of course, remove you from the learning process. But it does teach students that they also need to look to each other and to the materials as resources for their learning.

Problem: No matter how hard I try, I have never been able to finish my textbook in one year. This is frustrating for me and for my students, and it causes real problems when we order textbooks because we have to order extra copies of one level to carry over to the next year. Not only is it an extra expense, but students become demoralized when they are using the same textbook two years in a row.

Our solution: The systematic recycling and review built into all levels of the *¡YA VERÁS!* program allows teachers to keep moving through the books because even if students have not yet "mastered" a particular vocabulary set or grammar point, they will get several more chances to practice. Additionally, each book was planned following a typical school calendar with time factored in for missed classes due to assemblies, snow days, sick days, and more. The *Capítulos preliminares* of Books 2 and 3 give an in-depth review of material from the previous level with a special emphasis on content from the last third of the previous book. If you do not complete a level in one year, you can rely on these review chapters without having to go back to the previous text. Many teachers using the first edition of *¡YA VERÁS!* have told us that with familiarity, they are now finishing a book in one year!

Problem: I'm held responsible for students' learning. I'm judged on how well my students communicate in Spanish and how well they perform on standardized tests. I'd also like to have the satisfaction of knowing that I've helped my students use the language effectively.

Our solution: In our integrative, communicative approach, students become very comfortable communicating in Spanish. The scope and sequence of grammar, vocabulary, and communicative functions over the three-year program provide students with ample time and opportunity to assimilate the material. Students are successful not only in the classroom, but on standardized tests as well. As the statements from students indicate, learning Spanish with *¡YA VERÁS!* is an enjoyable experience for them. Enjoyment is the greatest motivating factor that leads to the positive results you are looking for.

We believe that effective teaching and learning take place when textbooks accurately reflect teacher and student concerns. In our efforts to make *¡YA VERÁS!* very user friendly, we have succeeded, we believe, in creating a program that belongs to you and your students and that personalizes the Spanish language to the individual needs and interests of each learner.

Principles of the ¡YA VERÁS! Program

The *¡YA VERÁS!* program is an integrated learning system based on a number of principles and assumptions:

- It is possible for students to use the language creatively from the outset and, therefore, free expression can and should be encouraged.

- Student-student and student-teacher interaction should be based on tasks that simulate real-world situations.

- Trial and error are a necessary part of the language-acquisition process.

- Contexts should be selected according to the frequency with which they occur in real life so that students can readily relate to them.

- Everyday spoken Spanish does not include every vocabulary item and every grammar structure available in the Spanish language. Materials should therefore include the elements most frequently used by native speakers in daily life.

- Grammar should not be presented for its own sake but as a means of transmitting a spoken or written message as accurately as possible. Grammar is the means for effective communication.

- In a proficiency-oriented, integrative approach, the four skills and culture reinforce one another in an ever-widening spiral.

- Assimilation requires sufficient time and practice.

- Teaching techniques should be student-centered.

- The goal of teaching is to make students independent users of Spanish.

- The principles of the ACTFL Proficiency Guidelines can serve as the underpinnings of a proficiency-oriented curriculum in which students learn to function as accurately as possible in situations they are most likely to encounter either in a Spanish-speaking country or with Spanish speakers in the United States.

Use of English in ¡YA VERÁS!

Although we believe and advocate that English be used sparingly in class, we are using it in the program materials for very definite, pedagogically sound purposes. We also recognize that you, the teacher, and not the students, should decide when English is going to be used. Depending on the language-acquisition stage of your students, or the nature of a particular exercise, it will be up to you to decide whether activities can be done in Spanish (even if they are in English in the textbook). However, it would be unfortunate to inhibit students from demonstrating their aural and reading comprehension skills, as well as critical thinking abilities, because of unrealistic expectations of their speaking or writing skills. We have used the following research-supported guidelines in *¡YA VERÁS!:*

- English is used when developing comprehension skills. Since the receptive skills (listening and reading) develop more quickly than the productive skills (speaking and writing), it is important to allow students to demonstrate these skills with the least amount of frustration. For example, they may not have the speaking skills with which to demonstrate their comprehension of a reading text. Furthermore, it is unlikely that they will have the speaking skills with which to participate in discussions in Spanish, particularly early in the year.

- Throughout the textbook, the grammatical explanations are in English because it is essential that students clearly understand how the grammar structures will help them to do certain things with the language they are learning. Reading and listening comprehension exercises are largely in English in Level 1 of *¡YA VERÁS!*, although there is a gradual shifting to productive responses as the units progress. In Level 1 direction lines are in English, for the most part, until the last third of the book, when the more basic, repetitive direction lines are given in Spanish. Misunderstandings due to students' limited abilities in Spanish would be counterproductive and could lead to failure to do the homework, or even the classwork, properly. In Levels 2 and 3 of *¡YA VERÁS!* all simple direction lines are provided in Spanish. In addition, they reflect a gradual increase in the frequency of productive responses in Spanish in the listening and reading exercises.

- Using English judiciously in class tends to reduce the frustration that students often feel when learning a foreign language. Because they understand much more than they can express, they need to have the satisfaction of working occasionally at a more abstract level rather than always being confined to the simplest concrete expression level.

- When working with cultural topics, a Spanish-only approach tends to lead to generalizations and stereotyping simply because students are unable to express more complex ideas.

With limited proficiency in Spanish, they tend to reduce and simplify ideas to the point where culture becomes distorted. Using English in these instances allows you to have students discuss the risks of stereotyping and the more sophisticated cultural issues that arise through readings and cultural notes.

The Oral Proficiency Interview and ¡YA VERÁS!

The Oral Proficiency Interview is a face-to face test that assesses an individual's speaking ability in a foreign or second language. The interview can last from 5 to about 30 minutes, depending on the interviewee's level of language use. The resulting speech sample is rated on a scale from Novice (no functional ability in the language; limited use of words and phrases) through Intermediate, Advanced, and Superior levels to Native (able to speak like an educated native speaker), with Low, Mid and High ratings that distinguish among performances within levels. Some states are starting to require the administration of the Oral Proficiency Interview (also known as the OPI test) at the end of the third year of instruction, with the expectation that students should score in the low- to mid-Intermediate range. A less staff-intensive alternative test, called the Simulated Oral Proficiency Interview or SOPI is also used. The SOPI does not require a live interview, but rather provides a list of questions to which the student responds on tape.

The emphasis on real-life, task-based use of language in the OPI has several ramifications for students. If they have been learning Spanish from a more traditional, grammar-based program, the OPI could offer some difficulty. ¡YA VERÁS! , on the other hand, has several regular features that specifically prepare students for the OPI, such as the ¡Adelante! section (every *etapa* culminates in an open-ended situation) and the *Ya llegamos* feature at the end of every unit (provides several realistic, broad-based situations that encompass all the material covered in the unit). Most importantly, the testing program that accompanies ¡YA VERÁS! is proficiency based, so that students are always judged by what they can do, not by their mastery of discrete aspects of the language. After learning with ¡YA VERÁS! for three years, students will have received all the support they need to achieve an appropriate score on the OPI.

IMPLICATIONS FOR THE CLASSROOM

- What students "can do" is the primary focus of instruction oriented toward the development of functional proficiency. This is not to say that the grammar, pronunciation, syntax and cultural aspects of language study are not important, but rather that they should be viewed as tools used to accomplish various functional tasks. In ¡YA VERÁS! students are made aware of the task at hand and the functions that are needed to carry it out. Tasks are placed in a context that is culturally realistic, as well as meaningful and interesting for the students.

- For students to become proficient speakers of another language, they need time to engage in communicative oral activities. The more time students spend in small-group activities, the more oral practice each of them will have. ¡YA VERÁS! has been built around a progression of carefully planned and well-timed small-group activities, ranging from controlled to meaningful to open-ended.

- The curriculum in a proficiency-oriented program is spiral, not linear. The scope and sequence in ¡YA VERÁS! is based on the premise that for students to be able to use what they are learning, the curriculum cannot treat each topic or structure during only one segment of the course, but must return again and again to the same functions, the same contexts, and the same structures, each time reinforcing what has gone before while introducing some new elements.

- The development of oral proficiency cannot be isolated from the other language skills. The development of language proficiency can be enhanced by activities that integrate the skills, in which work in one skill can serve as stimulus material to activities in another skill. ¡YA VERÁS! develops all four language skills as well as culture, and in keeping with its real-life focus, provides realistic, multi-faceted activities in which students implement a cross-section of skills within a given context.

Components at a Glance

STUDENT MATERIALS

- Student Textbook
- Student Workbook
- *Atajo* Writing Assistant for Spanish

TEACHER MATERIALS

- Teacher's Edition
- Testing Program
- Critical Thinking and Unit Review Blackline Masters
- Tapescript

CLASSROOM MATERIALS

- Audiocassette Program
- Pronunciation Tape (for Levels 1 and 2)
- Teacher Tape or CD
- *¡YA VERÁS!* Video Programs
  (VHS cassettes or videodiscs) (for Levels 1 and 2)
- Video Guide/Activity Masters (for Levels 1 and 2)
- *Mosaico cultural* Video Program
  (VHS cassettes or videodiscs) (for Level 3)
- *Mosaico cultural* Video Guide (for level 3)
- Color Transparencies
- *¡YA VERÁS!* Software Program
- *Nuevas dimensiones* Interactive Multimedia Program
- *Mundos hispanos* Interactive Multimedia Program

Features of Each Component

STUDENT TEXTBOOK

- Colorful, high-interest content
- Drawings, realia, and photos to enhance activities and infuse cultural content
- Content relating to a wide variety of subjects
- Easy-to-follow format

- Abundant practice of grammar, vocabulary, and functions in a variety of situations
- Systematic progression from mechanical practice to communicative, open-ended activities
- Full integration of the four skills and culture
- Material presented in small, manageable segments
- Cumulative *Ya llegamos* section at the end of each unit
- Critical thinking and learning strategies called out in student text margins
- Interdisciplinary lessons included in each unit
- Systematic development of reading strategies

STUDENT WORKBOOK / LABORATORY MANUAL
(Reading, writing, and listening activities)

- Wide variety of exercises relating to each presentation in the Student Text
- Complete chapter *Vocabulario* reprinted at beginning of the workbook chapter so that students do not need textbook to do homework
- Recycling and reinforcement of vocabulary and structures
- Emphasis on reading and writing
- Systematic progression from mechanical practice to communicative, open-ended activities
- Systematic writing program (Level 3)

- Authentic texts and documents for reading comprehension development
- Emphasis on listening comprehension
- Support activities for the Audiocassette Program

TEACHER'S EDITION

- Introductory section that includes a program description, text organization, classroom techniques, and pedagogical principles
- Wrap-around margins for annotations (suggestions for each page). This new, expanded version of the margin notes is designed to lend increased flexibility in the selection of classroom activities, to focus teacher attention on cooperative learning activities, and to provide suggestions for the development of critical thinking skills. The annotations include:

  —Teaching suggestions for each segment of each chapter
  —Language and cultural notes for useful background information
  —Classroom management hints and strategies
  —Suggestions for grammar presentations
  —Expansion activities
  —Teaching suggestions for more- and less-prepared students
  —Reteaching ideas
  —Teaching suggestions for native speakers
  —An additional cumulative activity for each chapter
  —Homework assignments
  —Video and Teacher Tape indicators
  —Answers to selected exercises
  —Cues for use of transparencies
  —Cues for use of *Atajo*

  Note: The pacing schedule for *¡YA VERÁS!* was based on the core of material in the textbook. If you choose to try out some of the variations and additional activities suggested in the enlarged margins, you will want to keep pacing in mind. There are many inviting options from which to choose. Attempting to do *everything*, however, could keep you from completing the book in one year.

TESTING PROGRAM

- Quizzes and tests covering all four skills
- Quizzes for each *etapa*
- Tests for all chapters and units
- Cumulative exams for end-of-year
- Tests for the *Capítulos preliminares* for Levels 2 and 3 that can also be used as diagnostic tests
- Testing Manual with ideas for correction and grading

- Oral expression tests/activities accompanied by correction and grading strategies
- Portfolio assessment strategies

CRITICAL THINKING AND UNIT REVIEW BLACKLINE MASTERS

- Critical thinking activities from the student text with fill-in grids reproduced in blackline master format
- Additional set of exercises which reviews the vocabulary and structures presented in each unit

TAPESCRIPT

- Scripts for Audiocassette Program and Teacher Tape

AUDIOCASSETTE PROGRAM

- Set of 12 cassettes for use in classroom or language lab
- Controlled exercises to reinforce the grammar, vocabulary, and functions presented in the textbook
- Extensive practice in listening comprehension through dictations, simulated conversations, interviews, and a variety of exchanges in many different contexts
- Pronunciation exercises correlated to the pronunciation sections in the *¡YA VERÁS!* Level 1 and Level 2 texts

PRONUNCIATION TAPE
(for Levels 1 and 2)

- Pronunciation explanations and exercises from the Student Text recorded by native speakers and reproduced in one easy-to-use location

TEACHER TAPE

- Supplementary single audiocassette for extra listening practice
- Monologues and dialogues from the textbook
- Nonscripted situational conversations to begin and end each chapter

VIDEO PROGRAMS
(Videotapes and Videodiscs for Levels 1 and 2)

- Book-specific videos that contain segments for each chapter
- Authentic, real-life situations and conversations

VIDEO ACTIVITY MASTERS
(for Levels 1 and 2)

- Blackline masters that contain comprehension exercises and conversation activities based on each segment of the videos:
  —Exercises for understanding the gist
  —Exercises that require students to pay close attention to details of language, culture, and information
  —Expansion and role-playing activities
  —Video Script

TRANSPARENCIES

- Full-color transparencies for each unit of each Student Text
- Maps of Spain and Latin America

SOFTWARE PROGRAMS
(for Levels 1 and 2)

- Available in IBM and Mac platforms
- Segments that correspond to the chapters in the Student Texts
- Reinforcement of grammatical structures and vocabulary
- Independent student practice

Mundos hispanos is a complete, interactive multimedia program on CD-ROM that combines video, photographs, and exciting graphics in order to develop listening, speaking, reading, and writing skills and bring the culture of the Spanish-speaking world to life. Available for IBM and Mac platforms.

Atajo Writing Assistant for Spanish is a software program that facilitates the process of writing in Spanish. Students have access to a wide variety of on-line tools, including:

- a bilingual dictionary of some 8,000 entries, complete with examples of usage
- a verb conjugator that can call up over 500,000 conjugated verb forms
- an on-line reference grammar
- an index to functional phrases
- sets of thematically related vocabulary items

  Ya llegamos writing activities at the end of each unit of ¡*YA VERÁS!* are correlated to *Atajo*. *Atajo* is available for IBM (DOS and Windows) and Mac.

Nuevas dimensiones is an interactive multimedia program that combines software and video in order to develop listening and writing skills and bring Spanish culture to life. Students interact with the program as they listen, practice, test their comprehension, and complete writing exercises. Hardware requirements: IBM PS2 compatible; color VGA monitor; M-Motion Board; Mouse; Windows 3.1 with multimedia support for Toolbook; headphone or speaker. The program is also available for Mac platforms.

Text Organization at a Glance

PROGRAM ORGANIZATION

Each level includes some variations.

> **Level 1:** 6 units
> **Level 2:** 3 preliminary review chapters + 5 units
> **Level 3:** 1 preliminary review chapter + 4 units

The following observations are helpful in understanding the organization of the program:

- The number of units per book is reduced progressively as the material becomes more complex.
- The preliminary review chapters in Levels 2 and 3 highlight the major grammatical structures and vocabulary presented in Levels 1 and 2 respectively.
- The *Etapas preliminares* in Level 1 contain five preliminary lessons, one or more of which may be used as an introduction to Level 1.
- All three books integrate the four skills and culture.
- Each book also highlights one or more skills while continuing the development of the remaining skills:

Level 1: Speaking and listening
Level 2: Reading
Level 3: Writing

UNIT ORGANIZATION

Unit
    Chapter
        etapa
        etapa
        etapa
        Lectura cultural
    Chapter
        etapa
        etapa
        Lectura cultural
    Chapter
        etapa
        etapa
        Lectura cultural
    Aquí leemos
        Reading
    Ya llegamos
        Practice
    Conexión
        Interdisciplinary lesson

FEATURES OF THE UNIT ORGANIZATION

- Each unit consists of three chapters.

- The unit opens with photographs that illustrate the unit theme.

- The unit opener includes:

  a. the title
  b. the unit objectives
  c. chapter and *etapa* titles
  d. photographs of a young person from Spain or a Spanish-speaking country (Level 1) with questions

- This is followed by three chapters, each divided into *etapas*.

- The end of the unit includes:

  a. the *Aquí leemos* (reading section and review of the unit)
  b. the *Ya llegamos* (cumulative unit activities)
  c. *Conexión* interdisciplinary lesson

FEATURES OF THE CHAPTER ORGANIZATION

- Each chapter presents a subtheme of the unit theme

- Each chapter opens with a photo.

- Each chapter is divided into *etapas.*

- Each chapter ends with the *Vocabulario,* which includes the expressions and vocabulary presented in the chapter, and a *Lectura cultural,* a cultural reading and practice.

FEATURES OF THE ETAPA ORGANIZATION

- Each *etapa* presents one aspect of the chapter theme which, in turn, supports the unit theme.

- The *etapa* serves as the basic lesson plan for two or more class periods.

- Each *etapa* is self-contained, with an opening and a closing.

- Each *etapa* includes the presentation of new material, a review of the previous *etapa,* and a final review of the *etapa* being studied.

How to Use ¡YA VERÁS!, Segundo nivel

Level 2 of *¡YA VERÁS!* consists of five units preceded by three short *Capítulos preliminares,* designed to provide a review of previously studied material in order to provide a smooth transition into the second level of Spanish. The units are organized in the same way as those of Level 1— three chapters, each divided into two or three *etapas.* Since the basic organization by *etapas* remains the same, you as the teacher may choose, as in the first level, to proceed through the units in a linear fashion without having to reorganize material or worry about questions such as recycling, variety, or pacing of the material. However, you again have the flexibility to reserve parts of an *etapa* for a later date, and you, of course, may arrange the review of activities according to your own preferences and time constraints.

ORGANIZATION OF THE CAPÍTULOS PRELIMINARES

The three *Capítulos preliminares* (A, B, C) recycle the vocabulary, structures, functions, and cultural material from Level 1 in new combinations. Each chapter has two short *etapas.* The *etapas* all follow the same basic pattern.

- **Vocabulary review**— short paragraphs that can be read or listened to on the Teacher Tape, followed by comprehension exercises.
- **Grammar Review**— summary of major grammatical structures (*Repaso*) plus short reminders (*¿Recuerdan?*) of other points, followed by *Aquí te toca a ti* exercises.
- **Function Review**— four short *Situaciones* (usually in dialogue form) that can be read or listened to on the Teacher Tape, followed by comprehension and interactive communication exercises.
- *Actividades*— short interactive situations similar to the *¡Adelante!* section of Level 1.

Each *etapa* ends with vocabulary lists *(Tarjetas de vocabulario)* that allow students to find the words they need without having to go back to the Level 1 text.

The *Capítulos preliminares* allow students to practice and, if necessary, relearn the materials from Level 1 without duplicating exactly any exercises and activities they have already done. We would urge you to remember that, even though this is a review section, students will continue to make some errors. The objective still remains to communicate in Spanish. **While you can expect a higher degree of accuracy than when the material was presented for the first time, you should not overwork this material. Many of the structures, functions, and vocabulary sets will continue to be recycled in the course of Level 2.**

ORGANIZATION OF A UNIT

Unit objectives
- Three chapters (divided into *etapas*) with *Vocabulario* lists (key chapter vocabulary items)
- *Lectura cultural* (high-interest readings)
- *Aquí leemos* (reading section)
- *Ya llegamos* (cumulative end-of-unit activities)
- *Conexión* (interdisciplinary lessons)

HOW TO BEGIN A UNIT

The goal of the unit opener is to provide students with the cultural context and the main theme of the unit. You may use any of the following three methods to introduce the unit.

Teacher Tape
- Play the segment that corresponds to the unit.
- Have students do a basic comprehension activity (in Spanish or English, depending on the time of year).

- Have a short discussion about the context by comparing it to a similar situation in the United States.

Video
- Have students view the entire video segment that corresponds to the first chapter.
- Do some comprehension activities from the Video Activity Masters.

Unit Opener Pages
- Have students analyze the photographs and engage in a discussion about them based on the *¿Qué ves?* questions.
- Have students look at the second page while you review the unit objectives.

Once you've established the unit context, you can then proceed to the "Planning Strategy" found at the beginning of each unit in the Student Workbook. The purpose of the "Planning Strategy" is to have students match English words and expressions to the context in which they have just been introduced. As they then proceed through the unit, students will learn the equivalents of many of these expressions in Spanish.

If done on the first day of class, students brainstorm answers without prior preparation. If done on a subsequent day, this section should be assigned as homework for sharing in class.

HOW TO BEGIN A CHAPTER

Each chapter-opener page contains a photograph that features the main character of the chapter interacting with someone in the specific chapter context. A short conversational exchange is included.

- Have students engage in a short discussion analyzing the cultural content of the photograph. (See annotations in Teacher's Edition for suggestions.)

HOW TO DO AN ETAPA

The most important aspect of *¡YA VERÁS!* is the self-contained *etapas*, which serve as the basic lesson plans for class. Each *etapa* has a clear beginning and end and includes the presentation of new material, a review of the previous *etapa*, and a final review of the *etapa* being studied.

Each *etapa* contains the vocabulary, functions, and grammar necessary for the subtheme of the *etapa*. These, in turn, contribute to the functions and contexts of the chapter, which, in turn, illustrate the larger context of the unit.

Articulation within units and between units has thus been assured through the interplay and integration of functions, contexts, and accuracy features. (See pp. 30 – 32 for Function/Context/

Accuracy charts for each level.) As the teacher, you may therefore choose to proceed through the units in a linear fashion, without having to reorganize the material or worry about such questions as variety, the recycling of material, or pacing. You also have the flexibility, however, to reserve some parts of the *etapa* for a later date, and you may, of course, move the review activities according to your own preferences and time constraints.

Each *etapa* in Level 2 follows this pattern.

> *Preparación*
> Vocabulary Introduction
> > *¡Aquí te toca a ti!*
>
> **Comentarios culturales** (placement may vary)
> **Pronunciación** (in one *etapa* per chapter)
> > *Práctica*
>
> **Repaso** (in all *etapas* except the first one in each unit)
> **Estructura**
> > *Aquí practicamos*
>
> **Nota gramatical** or **Palabras útiles** (when needed)
> **Aqui escuchamos**
> **¡Adelante!**

The following sections define each segment of the *etapa* and suggest generic classroom techniques that may be used. Additional suggestions can be found in the annotations of the Teacher's Edition.

Preparación

Definition: This initial series of questions helps students to focus on the topic of each *etapa,* as well as serving to activate prior knowledge.

Classroom Techniques:

- Have students read and answer the questions in advance or in the beginning of class.
- If you have native speakers in your class, elicit more ample responses from them.
- Lead the class in a short discussion of the issues raised.

Vocabulary Introduction

Definition: This first section of the *etapa* introduces the vocabulary that is central to the theme of the *etapa*. The vocabulary is presented in a variety of ways: drawings with captions, narrations, dialogues.

Classroom Techniques:

1. Drawings with captions

- Point to real objects in class or to the drawings on the transparency (first without the captions).
- Pronounce the words and have students repeat them.
- Point randomly at the drawings on the transparency and have students provide the words.
- Use the caption overlay and have students repeat the words again while they look at the spelling.
- If the objects make it possible, intersperse some personalized questions during the presentation or add a series of questions at the end: *bicicleta—¿Tienes bicicleta? ¿Montas en bicicleta con frecuencia?* Tailor the questions according to the grammar that students have already studied. You may also use the objects to say something about yourself: *A mí me gusta montar en bicicleta. ¿Y a ti?*

2. Short narration

- Students have books closed.
- Read through the narration, one segment at a time.
- Illustrate each segment with gestures, visuals, or real objects from class.
- Read the narration again at a normal rate of speech.
- Ask some general comprehension questions.
- Have students open the book and follow the text as you read it again.
- Have students read through the narration silently.

3. Dialogue

- Students have books closed.
- Present main ideas in dialogue form while illustrating the new vocabulary through gestures, visuals, or objects from class.
- Act out the dialogue taking all the parts, or having one of the better students act it out with you. Alternative: Play the dialogue from the Teacher Tape.
- Ask students some general comprehension questions.
- Have students open their books and repeat the dialogue after you, one sentence or sentence segment at a time.
- Ask students to role-play the dialogue.

¡Aquí te toca a ti!

Definition: This set of exercises allows students to practice the vocabulary learned in the Vocabulary Introduction. In most cases, the exercises progress from controlled, to meaningful, to open-ended.

Classroom Techniques:

1. Controlled, mechanical exercises done with the whole class

- Books are closed.
- Have students repeat the model after you. In cases where there is no model, use the first item.
- Continue the exercise, calling on students randomly.

2. Controlled, mechanical exercises done in pairs

- Books are open.
- Have students repeat the model after you.
- Do the first item with the whole class.
- Then have students complete the exercise in pairs.
- When everyone is done, you may wish to spot-check items with the whole class.

3. Open-ended exercises

- Books are open.
- Begin by modeling the activity with a student.
- If necessary, remind students of key vocabulary and grammatical structures.
- Divide students into pairs or small groups as indicated by the activity.
- At the end of the activity, have several groups perform in front of the class.

COMENTARIOS CULTURALES

Definition: The *Comentarios culturales* contain cultural information that expands on the theme of the *etapa*. In Level 1, they are written in English to facilitate short discussions about culture.

Classroom Techniques:

- Have students read the cultural note at home or in class.
- Ask them basic questions about the content.
- Have them draw similarities and differences between the Spanish-speaking world and the United States.

Pronunciación and Práctica

Definition: In these sections (one per chapter), students learn the most common Spanish graphemes (letters or letter combinations) along with their phonemes (the sounds that the letters represent). The presentations always move from symbol to sound so that students are given the tools to pronounce the sounds in new words as they proceed through the program.

Classroom Techniques:

- Systematic correction should occur throughout the presentation and practice.
- Write several words on the board from the list provided.
- Underline the grapheme in question.
- Have students pronounce the words after you.
- Have students read the examples from the book (books open).
- Then have students do the *Práctica* exercise with books open.
- Finally, have them close the books and repeat the *Práctica* items after you.

Repaso

Definition: Found in all *etapas* except in the first of the initial chapter of a unit, these exercises provide consistent review of the structures, vocabulary, and functions of the previous *etapa*. They may be done as warm-ups at the start of a class period or as breaks in the middle of sessions.

Classroom Techniques:

1. Semi-controlled exercises done with the whole class

- Books may be open or closed depending on the level of difficulty.
- Make the directions clear to students (preferably in Spanish).

- Have students repeat the model.

- Proceed through the exercise, calling on students randomly.

- If students encounter difficulties with a particular item, the item may be used for a rapid transformation drill. For example, students are having trouble with *Ana quiere bailar*. Use this as the base sentence to make substitutions. You say *comer*. Students say *Ana quiere comer*. You say *estudiar*. Students say *Ana quiere estudiar*. After this brief break, resume the exercise items.

2. Semi-controlled exercises done in pairs

- Books are open.

- Make the directions clear.

- Have students repeat the model.

- Do the first item with the whole class.

- Have students divide into pairs and complete the exercise.

- After they are done, verify by spot-checking several items.

3. Open-ended activities

- Books are open.

- Make the directions clear.

- With a student, model the activity.

- Divide students into pairs or small groups according to the indications in the activity.

- When students are done, have several groups perform for the class.

ESTRUCTURA

Definition: Each *etapa* contains the presentation of a new grammatical structure. In *¡YA VERÁS!*, grammar is treated communicatively—that is, grammar is tied logically to the context of the *etapa*, chapter, and unit and to the tasks that students are expected to carry out linguistically. An *Estructura* section offers one of the following three types of presentations.

1. the introduction of a new verb

2. the introduction of a more complex grammatical structure

3. the introduction of a set of lexical items that has grammatical implications (e.g., days of the week, seasons, time)

Classroom Techniques:

In general, all structures can be presented either inductively or deductively, although it is recommended that, whenever possible, an inductive approach be used. In either case, students should have their books closed so that they pay close attention to your examples and explanations. It is generally preferable that you make grammatical presentations in simplified, tele-graphic-style Spanish, punctuated by examples. The following demonstrates the presentation of the **preterite.**

1. The inductive approach (from example to rule)

- Put some drawings on the board or use a transparency that show a person going through a series of actions (e.g., some of the things a person does on a typical day).

- Have students say what the person does typically, using the present tense.

- Then put the previous day's date on the board to signal *ayer*.

- Redo each action, using the **preterite.**

- Go through the actions again and have students repeat each item.

- Use yourself and the first person singular to transform each item.

- Then have students individually use the first person to go through the actions again.

- Finally, end your presentation (in Spanish, if possible) with a short, concise explanation about the formation.

- Return to the drawings and have students redo the sequence of actions using different pronouns.

2. The deductive approach (from rule to example)

- This approach is most appropriate for grammar points that do not merit prolonged class time, are particularly simple, have an exact equivalent in English, or do not lend themselves readily to an inductive presentation. Examples of this type of grammatical structure are demonstrative adjectives (*este, esta, ese, esa*), the interrogative adjective *cuánto* and its various forms, and so forth. Rather than devoting valuable class time to lengthy presentations, such grammatical topics are best dealt with as efficiently as possible to leave more time for practice. Whenever possible, presentations should be made in Spanish. Use a quick translation of the key element, if necessary.

- Put several examples on the board or on a transparency.

- Explain the rule in simple terms using the examples.

- Provide an additional series of examples by eliciting the grammatical structure through personalized questions and answers.

Aquí practicamos

Definition: A series of exercises follows each *Estructura* section. The exercises usually move from controlled or mechanical drills to bridging exercises to open-ended, communicative activities. The grammatical structures are practiced in a variety of contexts.

1. **Controlled or mechanical drills**

- provide structure and meaning
- usually require some type of transformation or substitution

2. **Bridging or meaningful exercises**

- provide structure and students provide meaning
- are generally contextualized

3. **Open-ended or communicative exercises**

- require students to provide structure and meaning
- are highly contextualized and usually personalized

Classroom Techniques:

1. **Controlled or mechanical drills**

- Correction should be systematic.
- You may do with the whole class or in pairs.
- Make the directions clear.
- Use the first item as a model.
- Continue with the whole class or have students complete in pairs.
- If done in pairs, follow-up with a spot check.

2. **Bridging or meaningful exercises**

- Do preferably in pairs or in small groups.
- Make the directions clear.
- Have students repeat the model.
- Divide the students into groups and have them complete the exercise.
- Spot-check some items with the whole class.

3. **Open-ended or communicative exercises**

- Do in pairs or small groups.
- Make the directions clear.
- Model the situation with a student.
- Divide the class into groups.
- When the activity is completed, have several groups role-play the situation for the class or report back the group results.

Important Note: Since small groups tend to progress through exercises at different rates, you can assign all three exercises or the last two as a chain. Make sure that students understand directions and instruct them to proceed to the next exercise when they are done with one. It is not necessary to wait until every pair has finished the entire chain. When the majority of pairs has reached the end of the chain, verify by doing some items with the whole class. This technique gives students the flexibility to progress at their own pace.

Nota gramatical
Palabras útiles
and Aquí practicamos

Definition: These follow-up sections to the *Estructura* present additional refinements to the main grammar point in the chapter or special uses of certain vocabulary items. If needed, the *Nota gramatical* (or *Palabras útiles* if the point is lexical) often comes directly after the mechanical exercise of the *Estructura* section and is followed by the meaningful and communicative exercises.

Classroom Techniques:

Use either an inductive or a deductive approach (see *Estructura* explanation), followed directly by the *Aquí practicamos* exercises.

Aquí escuchamos

Definition: In this section students will hear Spanish speakers carry out the function(s) that are being presented and practiced in the *etapa*. They are presented in dialogue or monologue form and also include the vocabulary introduced receptively at the beginning of each *etapa*. Students will be exposed to a wide variety of voices and accents. In order to provide a truly listening-oriented exercise, the script does not appear in the student edition of the textbook. These sections begin with pre-listening activities, designed to activate the students' background knowledge. They are followed by comprehension exercises that are meant be completed during or after listening to the recording. Both the pre-listening and the comprehension exercises are included in the student textbook.

Definition: These end-of-*etapa* exercises are designed to review the vocabulary, functions, and structures of the *etapa*. They will always consist of at least two exercises: an *Ejercicio oral* and an *Ejercicio escrito*. The *¡Adelante!* review may be done at the end of a class period or as a warm-up at the beginning of a class.

Classroom Techniques:

1. *Ejercicio oral*

- Books are open.
- Make the directions clear.
- Model the role play with a student

- Divide students into pairs or groups.
- As a follow-up, you may wish to ask some students to perform the role play for the class.

2. *Ejercicio escrito*

- Books are open.
- Make the directions clear.
- Have students brainstorm vocabulary they will need to carry out the exercise.
- Have students look at and comment on each others' work.

HOW TO END A CHAPTER

Each chapter culminates with a high interest, culturally oriented reading, called a *Lectura cultural.*

Definition: This reading section appears after each chapter. It is a short passage which provides information of cultural significance in the Spanish-speaking world. These sections are presented in two parts: *Antes de leer,* which contains pre-reading activities and is designed to activate the students' background knowledge, and *Guía para la lectura,* consisting of activities designed to help the student practice various reading strategies.

Conexión con...

Definition: Additional optional lessons that provide exposure to Spanish through an interdisciplinary or content-based approach. Some content areas included are mathematics, sociology, psychology, geography, and library science. Each lesson focuses on a piece of subject-area information in Spanish and includes warm-up and comprehension activities. Additional expansion activities are also available in the Teacher's Edition.

HOW TO END A UNIT

At the end of each unit is a cumulative review of the entire unit that consists of two components.

Aquí llegamos

Definition: This is a section-opening reading usually taken from authentic documents (newspapers, magazines, brochures,

advertisements), including literature. It is usually preceded by a reading strategy that helps students focus their reading. The *Aquí leemos* is always an expansion or illustration of the unit theme and is followed by activities that serve as a verification of students' understanding of the text.

Classroom Techniques:

- Have students read the text silently either for homework or in class.
- Impress upon them that they should not be reading word for word but rather should concentrate on the main ideas.
- Move directly to the activities.

Ya llegamos

(*Actividades orales y escritas*)

Definition: These cumulative, communicative activities are the culminating point of the unit. They combine the vocabulary, functions, structures, and cultural information presented in the unit. Everything in the unit leads up to this performance point, in which students can demonstrate their independence in using the Spanish language. The activities are done in pairs or in small groups. Instructions are given in English to avoid giving away the key structures and vocabulary, and to encourage students to use a variety of ways to express themselves. Using English in the direction lines also approximates the "real" situations in which students might find themselves. For example, if they were to enter a Spanish store, their reason for being there would exist in their minds in English.

The most important thing to remember is that the *Ya llegamos* activities demonstrate what language learning is all about. They show the tasks that students can accomplish with the language they know and in which contexts and with what degree of accuracy they can function. To sacrifice these activities to time constraints or to treat them as optional would be to subvert both the goals of the *¡YA VERÁS!* program and the goals of proficiency-oriented language instruction and learning. It is therefore imperative that the process be carried out fully and that students have the opportunity to demonstrate their accomplishments.

Classroom Techniques:

* Select the activities you wish your students to do and reserve the rest for another time or simply skip them.

* Make the directions clear.

* Model with one or more students, if necessary.

* If needed, have students brainstorm key vocabulary ahead of time.

* Divide the students into groups.

* When the activity is ended, have a few groups role play the situation for the class.

* If you wish, you may give these groups a grade. The rest of the students can get grades at other times when they perform in front of the class.

Once you've completed the end-of-the-unit section, you can complete the unit in one of two ways (or both)

1. Video

You can (re)play the video segments that correspond to the unit. At this point, students should understand much of what is being said and should grasp more cultural information than they did during the first viewing. This is generally a source of real satisfaction for them and demonstrates to them how much they have learned during the unit.

2. Teacher Tape

You can (re)play the conversations that correspond to the unit. Again, students' understanding should be considerably enhanced because of the work done in the unit. It should be remembered, however, that audiotaped material is always more difficult to understand than video because it does not provide additional visual support.

The Role of Culture in ¡YA VERÁS!, Primer nivel / Segundo nivel

It is important to note the various ways in which culture is integrated throughout the Level 1 and 2 texts. The role of culture in Level 3 will be discussed separately.

A variety of techniques is used to immerse students in the Hispanic cultures as they learn Spanish. Rather than isolating cultural phenomena from the language that students are learning, the culture is tightly integrated into every aspect of the textbooks.

1. Culture is ever present in that it is inseparable from language. As students learn to express themselves in various situations, the language they use and the behaviors that accompany this language are culturally authentic. This means that language in *¡YA VERÁS!* has not been doctored or modified for the sake of grammatical rules. For example, sentence fragments are acceptable because they are natural in speech. Communicative functions are taught from the outset.

2. The vocabulary in *¡YA VERÁS!* reflects the interests of young people in the Spanish-speaking world, as well as the interests of your students.

3. *¿Qué crees?* These short multiple-choice items placed in the margins at regular intervals throughout the units of Level 1 focus on interesting facts that are related to the *etapa* topics.

4. *Comentarios culturales* further student understanding of a particular topic.

5. The visual components of the program— the photos, art, realia, and video— contain a wealth of cultural material, both factual and behavioral. Their use should be fully integrated into classroom time to the greatest extent possible. Depending on facilities, the video may also be made available to students in a library or laboratory setting.

6. Reading units focus on important cultural topics and provide students with factual information about modern life and historical events.

7. Readings in the *Aquí leemos* section and throughout the Workbook expose students to a variety of texts for a multitude of purposes. Readings include ads, poems, magazine and newspaper articles, brochures, various types of guidebooks, recipes, classified ads, and literary sketches.

Spanish for Native Speakers

In the best of all possible worlds, schools would have two Spanish language tracks—one for monolingual speakers of English and another for native speakers of Spanish. Each group would be taught with materials specifically created for them. However, we do not live in a perfect world and many schools typically enroll native speakers alongside non-native speakers in Spanish language classes. What can you do if you find yourself in this situation? *¡YA VERÁS!* is a program that has been created to teach Spanish as a foreign language to non-native speakers of the language. We have, however, included suggestions for addressing the special needs of the Hispanic students who may be enrolled in your classes.

Who are Native Speakers?

Let us first begin by discussing the topic of what we mean by native speaker. By this we mean the broad spectrum of Hispanic students who have grown up in this country or immigrated here. If most of their education occurred in the United States, they have probably learned to speak and understand Spanish at home, but have never been taught to read or write it. Oftentimes, when they find themselves in a foreign-language classroom, native speakers feel unchallenged and/or resist the grammatical approach used to teach them a language whose grammatical structures they have already internalized. Many Hispanic students demonstrate a better command of both the listening and speaking skills in Spanish than their non-native classmates; yet too many teachers do not capitalize on the existing language proficiency of these students.

What do Native Speakers Bring to the Classroom?

The first order of business should be to capitalize on the linguistic skills these students already bring to the classroom. Assuming a student already speaks and comprehends Spanish, he or she must be taught to read and write the language. Students raised in a Spanish-speaking home bring a great deal of oral ability to the classroom, however few bring the knowledge of how that ability is expressed in a written mode. Contrary to popular belief, Spanish is not written just the way it sounds—it is not as phonetic as people think. While it may be more phonetic than English or French, it is certainly far from what linguists would term a phonetic language. For example, the sound of /k/ can be written with a number of symbols: qu (*que, queso*); c before a, o, u (*casa, cosa, cuna*); and even with the letter k (*kilo, kimono*). As Spanish-speaking students take their first steps toward becoming literate in Spanish, they must devote some attention to spelling. The following are some of the more problematic sound/symbol correlations they need to master.

Special attention should be paid to words with:

b	v	z + a	z + o
z + u	c + e	c + i	s + any vowel
h	x	ll	y
g + e	g + i	j	

Another area that can be addressed to improve literacy involves reading instruction. We have incorporated a number of reading activities in the *¡YA VERÁS!* program that reflect some of the latest research in this area. Hispanic students in foreign language classes generally already read English, for they have most likely been educated and learned to read in American schools. (Students who are not yet literate in English should be in ESL classes rather than foreign language classes.) However, as reading researchers have shown, the transfer of reading skills from one language to another is far from automatic. Students need support when learning to read an additional language. Special attention should be paid to having students go through all of the exercises and activities that accompany the readings in this program.

What about "Standard" Spanish?

As we have said earlier, many Hispanic students already speak Spanish; however, it may not be the variety of language that is taught in the typical classroom. In sociolinguistic terms, people in this group are termed diglossic. This means that while one language is used for all formal or what are termed "high" functions, the other is used in all informal or "low" functions. In the case of the United States, English is generally considered appropriate for formal exchanges (political rallies, business meetings, announcements, sermons, lectures, classrooms, etc.), and Spanish is used in informal situations within the home and among other members of the speech community. Because most of these students' education has taken place in English, they have seldom had the opportunity to hear Spanish as it is used for the high or formal functions of the language. Thus (except for radio and television, where available) they have had no models for this register of the language and have not developed this aspect of Spanish. Most students can expand their range of functions in Spanish. The Spanish that they speak is not wrong. The only mistake they may make is to use the their particular variety of Spanish in an inappropriate social situation. Part of these speakers' classroom learning, then, must involve getting acquainted with formal and academic Spanish.

Many, including members of the Spanish teaching profession, often refer to what these students speak as "dialect." Popular belief holds that dialects are substandard, even defective. In fact, any variety of a language is technically a dialect, even the educated standard. Again, drawing from the field of sociolinguistics, everyone speaks a dialect. The tremendous concern over "correct" speech is explicable only when the social functions of dialects are considered, even though it can be shown that no dialect is inherently better or worse than another. It is necessary for students to be able to command educated varieties of speech if they wish to be able to hold certain kinds of jobs. However, any attempt to teach a standard dialect to a nonstandard speaker must take into account the social reasons that explain why people speak the way they do.

With regard to listening, most students will be able to understand spoken Spanish. Even those students who might be third- or fourth-generation in this country (and who may have weak speaking skills) will probably comprehend the language. What they need to work on most is to gain exposure to the variety of ways that Spanish is spoken. Remember, there are a number of ways to speak Spanish correctly. We all know that a Spaniard does not sound like a Chilean, nor a Bolivian like a Mexican, nor a Puerto Rican like an Argentine, etc. The listening activities, including the video, that accompany the *¡YA VERÁS!* program have been created with this in mind; i.e., students will hear the language as it is spoken in many parts of the Spanish-speaking world.

Finally, it is important to remember that Spanish-speaking students are not beginning from ground zero. It is up to you, the teacher, to meet them where they are and take them as far as you can. Always endeavor to be sensitive to how they express themselves, for while it may be inappropriate to use certain vocabulary words and expressions in the classroom, it may be completely appropriate to do so within their speech community. Rather than "fixing" how they speak and write Spanish, it is up to you to capitalize on the linguistic strengths they bring to your classroom and help them increase their range of linguistic functions.

SPECIFIC SUGGESTIONS:

¿Qué ves?

Have students answer as much as possible in Spanish. Share some of this information with the rest of the class.

Etapa opener

Ask students for variations of new vocabulary. This is a good place to begin showing them that while what they say is quite correct in their particular speech community, in order to communicate with Spanish speakers from other parts of the world it is important for them to add this new vocabulary to their linguistic repertoire.

Estructura

Don't emphasize grammatical terminology. Students should use this section to familiarize themselves with the forms (not the names of the forms) of the Spanish language that may not be part of their linguistic repertoire. After all, it is not necessary to know the names of the 206 bones in the human body in order to walk, run, dance, etc. Have them skip some of the exercises that are very basic practice, which might be much too easy for them.

Aquí escuchamos

Again, ask students for variations. Emphasize that what they say in their speech community is correct, but in order to communicate with other Spanish speakers outside their speech community it is important that they learn other ways of expressing the same thing.

¡Adelante!

Ejercicio oral

You must be sensitive and accept how the students carry out this speaking activity. Don't label their use of vocabulary or certain expressions as wrong. Remember, don't penalize students for something that is sociolinguistically correct within their speech community. This is a good place to point out to the students where their Spanish differs from formal Spanish and to help them work on those elements of the language that are part of a more formal Spanish. Once this is done, have them expand and go beyond the basic instructions for this exercise.

Ejercicio escrito

Always have students complete this section. Have them focus on what and how the book is teaching them to write. Strongly encourage the inclusion of vocabulary from the book to enhance the vocabulary that they already know. Again, stress the idea that in order to communicate with other Spanish speakers outside their speech community it is important that they learn other ways of expressing the same thing. You may want students to edit each other's work so that they might help their fellow students with any spelling errors that might occur.

Comentarios culturales

Ask students how their specific cultural practices may be similar to or different from those expressed in this section. This is a good place to show them that while they might be a minority in this country, they are part of the vast majority of people who are living in the Western Hemisphere.

Vocabulario

Have students pay particular attention to how words are spelled. Make a concerted effort to point out to them the words that contain the more difficult sound/symbol correlations. You might have them keep a special notebook in which they write the vocabulary words. One category could be labeled: *Así lo dice el libro ...*

Another category could be used to allow them to write out those words that are already part of their linguistic repertoire and could be labeled: *Así lo digo yo ...*

Lectura cultural

Always have students go through each of the exercises in this section. Once they have completed the activities, they might be asked to summarize the reading in Spanish in order to give them additional writing practice. They might also be required to keep a notebook with a special list of new vocabulary they might find in the reading selections.

Pedagogical Considerations

A proficiency-oriented, integrative approach to teaching raises certain pedagogical issues that need to be addressed. In particular, these are questions dealing with the development of skills (listening, speaking, reading, writing, critical thinking) and culture as well as questions about classroom management (large, heterogeneous classes; cooperative learning; Total Physical Response, correction strategies, teacher behaviors).

DEVELOPING LANGUAGE AND CRITICAL THINKING SKILLS

Developing the Listening Skill

Through the Teacher Tape, the Video Program, the Laboratory Tapes, and appropriate teacher speech, *¡YA VERÁS!* seeks to develop the listening skill in a systematic way. The focus is on listening comprehension as it would occur in real life, using speech samples that are both scripted and unscripted and free of artificial grammatical and lexical manipulation. As you use these materials, several considerations should be kept in mind.

1. Students will not understand every word that they hear and this is not necessary. They should be encouraged to listen for gist. In real life, we do not necessarily hear every word that is said to us (noise interference, etc.) and students should become accustomed to this.

2. Students need to be able to demonstrate that they have understood something. At the beginning of the program this means that they will probably use English to indicate their comprehension. As they progress, an increased number of activities can be done in Spanish, although this will always depend on the complexity of the comprehension check.

3. Listening comprehension develops more quickly than speaking. It is therefore important to integrate listening activities fully into the learning process since it can serve as a confidence builder.

4. Since listening in real life is done for a variety of purposes, some comprehension activities are limited to understanding the main point while others require the comprehension of specific details.

5. General comprehension should usually be ascertained first, before an analysis of details is undertaken. The activities in the text and Listening Activity Masters follow this general to specific pattern.

6. Listening comprehension activities vary from simple multiple-choice and true/false items to more extensive summary-type exercises. In the *Aquí escuchamos* section, carefully designed pre-listening activities draw out students' background knowledge, which serves as a framework for comprehension. This helps students to acquire and organize new concepts. Follow-up activities check for accurate listening and the understanding of meaning in context.

7. You, the teacher, are one of the best sources for listening materials. Even your inductive presentations of grammatical structures contribute to the development of listening comprehension, providing, of course, that you speak at your normal rate of speech whenever possible.

Developing the Speaking Skill

If speaking is to become truly functional (i.e., students can accomplish real tasks with the language), a number of conditions must be met in the classroom. It is essential that learners be surrounded with interesting, age-appropriate materials if they are to acquire a new language in its cultural context. The *¡YA VERÁS!* program provides such material, including a range of oral practice from controlled to meaningful to open-ended that is necessary for the development of the speaking skill. When seeking to develop oral proficiency, the following pedagogical principles should be kept in mind.

1. Students should be corrected systematically when they're engaged in highly controlled exercises.

2. Correction should be delayed until after communicative, interactive activities have been completed. Real communication should not be interrupted with grammatical corrections.

3. The sequence of exercises in *¡YA VERÁS!* should be carried through completely whenever possible.

4. Students should be asked to speak in complete sentences when mechanical exercises require it, but sentence fragments are acceptable in communicative situations.

5. Small-group activities must be a regular part of classroom strategies. Students should work in pairs or small groups at least once and, if possible, more frequently during each class period.

6. Recognition must be given in grading for the message (content) as well as for grammatical accuracy. Students should feel that they get credit not just for how they say something but also for what they say.

When assessing spoken language, a procedure such as an oral proficiency interview or a modified version that elicits a speech sample through a somewhat standardized format, is generally quite helpful. An approach that takes into account ranges of performance at different levels allows for determining whether a student's proficiency meets or does not meet expectations. A sample of this kind of criterion-referenced scoring, which means that a speech sample should be held accountable to the criteria itself and not to other samples, is provided above. The overall evaluation should identify the sustained level of performance with regard to:

Syntactic control
Vocabulary usage and fluency
Pronunciation

9   VERY GOOD TO EXCELLENT
Very good to excellent command of the language. Very few errors of syntax. Wide range of vocabulary, including idiomatic usage. High level of fluency.

7–8   CLEARLY DEMONSTRATES COMPETENCE
Good command of the language. Few errors of syntax. Above-average range of vocabulary. Good idiomatic usage and little awkwardness of expression. Good fluency and intonation.

5–6   SUGGESTS COMPETENCE
Comprehensible expression. Some serious errors of syntax and some successful self-correction. Some fluency, but hesitant. Moderate range of vocabulary and idiomatic usage.

3–4   SUGGESTS INCOMPETENCE
Poor command of the language marked by frequent serious errors of syntax. Limited fluency. Poor pronunciation. Narrow range of vocabulary and of idiomatic usage. Frequent anglicisms and structure which force interpretation of meaning by the listener. Occasional redeeming features.

1–2   CLEARLY DEMONSTRATES INCOMPETENCE
Unacceptable from almost every point of view. Glaring weakness in syntax and pronunciation. Few vocabulary resources. Little or no sense of idiomatic usage.

0   IRRELEVANT SPEECH SAMPLE
Narrative irrelevant to task or assignment.

Developing the Reading Skill

Of all the language skills, reading is perhaps the most durable and should be developed systematically. The ¡YA VERÁS! program provides many opportunities for students to demonstrate their reading comprehension skills. As in listening, a number of factors have been taken into consideration in the development of the program.

1. Reading should be done in class as well as for homework.

2. Reading should be tested along with all the other skills.

3. In *Developing Reading Skills* (Cambridge: Cambridge University Press, 1981, p. 4) François Grellet points out that in real life our purposes for reading vary constantly. There also specific types of reading: (1) skimming, or quickly running one's eyes over a text to get the gist of it; (2) scanning, or quickly going through a text to find a particular bit of information; (3) extensive reading, or reading longer texts, usually for pleasure; and (4) intensive reading, or reading shorter texts to extract specific information. These different types of reading are not mutually exclusive. One often skims through a passage to see what it is about before deciding whether it is worth scanning a particular paragraph for the information one is seeking. The exercises that accompany the readings in this book have been created with this in mind, i.e., students are guided in their reading through specific reading strategies. Furthermore, reading sections include a diverse variety of text types, from menus to ads to magazine/newspaper articles to literary selections.

4. Since reading comprehension skills develop more quickly than speaking and writing skills, early comprehension checks should be done in English rather than Spanish. As students progress, these checks can be done in Spanish depending on the level of difficulty of the text and the exercise.

The reading selections are intended to further the development of students' reading skills. To this end, students work with cognates, words of the same family, and key words essential to the understanding of the texts.

In order to develop reading skills, students should be reading first for comprehension, second for detail, and finally for grammatical and/or vocabulary analysis (if you find such an analysis desirable). Vocabulary and unknown structures should be treated receptively without the expectation that students will be able to reproduce them in speaking. It is likely, of course, that they will retain some of the vocabulary for production, but this is not the aim of these lessons. As students work through the reading selections, they will become more and more comfortable with the idea of reading for meaning and for information. Since students will be timed as they read, they should also get used to reading without understanding every single word, thus increasing their reading rate. It might be helpful to point out to them that they should not be trying to decipher every word, but should look at the meaning of a whole sentence or paragraph.

Use of English

Because comprehension of information is the primary aim of the reading selections and because students' reading ability develops more quickly than their speaking ability, English is necessary at this stage if any meaningful discussion is to take place. This limited and clearly defined use of English will relieve students of the frustration they often feel when their ideas are at a higher level than their ability to verbalize them.

Developing the Writing Skill

Real-life writing involves many different tasks that are carried out for a variety of purposes. In *¡YA VERÁS!*, the writing skill is developed along similar lines as speaking. That is, students are required to move through a sequence of exercises, from mechanical to meaningful to communicative, at every stage of their language development. Additional writing practice is included in the *Ejercicio escrito* that appears in the *¡Adelante!* section at the end of each *etapa*.

In accordance with a proficiency orientation, the final stage of this sequence (communicative activities) is the goal of all writing tasks. Students are asked to make lists, write sentence-level notes, postcards, messages, and, finally, produce writing at the paragraph level. Since none of this writing will be error-free, it is important for you to recognize and give credit to the successful communication of the message before addressing the question of accuracy. This usually means that you assign a number of points for content and message, or you may decide simply to give two grades for each major writing assignment.

In Level 3 of *¡YA VERÁS!*, we have introduced a systematic writing program (along the lines of a freshman English composition course), that moves students through the basic levels of writing: from word to sentence to multiple sentences to paragraphs to multiple paragraphs. The writing done in Level 3 therefore serves as a capstone before students move to the types of writing required of them in Spanish 4 and 5 classes.

Encouraging risk-taking is an essential factor in developing the writing skill. Traditionally, students who wrote error-free compositions that showed very little innovation and imagination have been rewarded more than students who tried to express meaningful and personalized messages. The result has usually been that students used only grammatical structures and vocabulary of which they were absolutely certain, resulting in rather boring and artificial compositions. The traditional students had few red marks on the paper. The innovative students were faced with red-pen punishment. We suggest that this trend be reversed

by assigning points both for message and accuracy so that both types of students are rewarded for the efforts they have made. We would also suggest that correction techniques be modified to become less punitive. For example, comment first on what students do well before making suggestions and corrections. We further encourage you to consider underlining what is correct and to throw away the red pen! Furthermore, students can be given the opportunity to edit what they have written so that they receive two grades for their work—one grade for the first effort, another grade for their final writing sample.

Portfolios

A portfolio is any collection of student work. Most often, it is a folder containing some of the better work a student has produced. Instructionally, a portfolio allows students to examine the work they have produced, to select special pieces of work, and to reflect on what they have learned and how they learned it. In other words, a portfolio is a collection of work that exhibits a student's efforts, progress, and achievement in a given area, in this case, writing.

The purpose of a portfolio is to record student growth over time, allowing students to think about what they have learned and how they have learned it. Throughout the process, students gain a sense of pride and confidence in their abilities. The portfolio also provides a record of student achievement for teachers, parents, and other audiences. In this way, the portfolio becomes a window through which student learning and performance can be viewed.

The *Ejercicio escrito* that is found at the end of each *etapa* can serve as the piece of writing that could to be included in the students' portfolios.

Developing Cultural Awareness

The *¡YA VERÁS!* program integrates culture at all stages of language learning. Culture is not just dealt with in terms of facts, but includes cultural analysis and appropriate behavior in terms of language use. Authenticity of expression is an essential aspect of the program so that students develop a sense of social/contextual appropriateness. In the process, it is hoped that they become more accepting and non-judgmental of other cultures, that they become less ethnocentric about their own culture, and that they realize that the Spanish language represents peoples of various cultures.

Several factors come into play in the development of cultural awareness.

1. You should avoid judgmental or stereotypical statements.

2. You should challenge judgmental or stereotypical statements.

3. Students must understand that facts are important but that they are not the only definition of culture. Culture is embedded in the language. The language is a reflection of cultural attitudes.

4. Understanding another culture depends largely on one's ability to observe and analyze. As students look at the photographs in the textbooks or view the videotapes, they should be taught to become keen observers of behavior patterns.

5. Cultural awareness should not be developed solely through the observation of differences but also through the noting of similarities between one's own culture and the target culture. For example, students should note that Spanish-speaking youth tend to dress much the same way as American youth. Similarities and differences are pointed out in the cultural observation notes in the Teacher's Edition.

6. Students should be made aware that the words they use in commenting about other cultures may tend to be judgmental and should be avoided. Words such as "weird," "bizarre," "stupid," "nerdy," (or whatever words happen to be in vogue at a particular time) indicate that the speaker assumes that his or her own culture is somehow superior to the target culture. Perhaps this lesson will carry over into students' dealings with their peers and with adults!

Developing the Critical Thinking Skills

The foreign language class is an ideal place for developing critical thinking skills. As students acquire skills in a new language and information about a variety of cultures, they can also develop their ability to observe, analyze, synthesize, evaluate, and integrate new information in a variety of ways. In the *¡YA VERÁS!* program, activities which encourage students to practice analyzing, synthesizing, and evaluating information are labeled in the student margin. Additional critical thinking activities and strategies are suggested in the margin notes of the Teacher's Edition.

A number of general principles apply to the development of critical thinking skills.

1. Critical thinking involves a number of conditions and subskills, including the following.

   — flexibility of mind (the ability to change one's mind)
   — open-mindedness (sensitivity to multiple points of view)
   — the ability to evaluate various points of view without bias
   — the ability to observe and listen actively
   — the ability to analyze (to break down issues into their component parts)
   — the ability to synthesize (to combine separate elements to form a new unified, coherent whole)
   — the ability to evaluate (to determine worth, to judge)
   — the ability to integrate new information into what is known
   — the ability to apply knowledge to a new issue
   — the ability to make associations

2. The general categories of analyzing, synthesizing, and evaluating can be identified more explicitly. The following are examples and definitions of subheadings used in these groups.

Analysis
— **Analyzing** (examining an object or an idea, studying it from every angle to see what it is, how it works, how many similarities and differences it has from other objects or ideas, and how its parts relate or fit together)
— **Categorizing** (organizing information into groups with similar qualities or attributes)
— **Comparing and contrasting** (Looking for similarities and/or differences between ideas, people, places, objects, and/or situations)
— **Making associations** (using an idea, person, event, or object to trigger the memory of another; seeing relationships between two or more things)
— **Sequencing** (arranging details in order according to specified criteria)

Synthesis
— **Synthesizing** (pulling together pieces of information and ideas to create a new whole)
— **Drawing inferences** (guessing logical explanations or reasons for choices, actions, events, or situations).
— **Hypothesizing** (making an assertion as a basis for reasoning or argument)
— **Predicting** (expecting behavior, actions, or events based on prior experience and/or available facts)
— **Seeing cause-and-effect relationships** (anticipating a logical result from an action or event)
— **Creating** (producing an original product of human invention or imagination, originating, bringing about, dreaming up)

Evaluation
—**Evaluating** (determining worth, judging)
—**Determining preferences** (making personal value judgments)
—**Prioritizing** (establishing precedence in order of importance or urgency, determining relative value)

3. Critical thinking skills can be taught and should be inherent in foreign language teaching and learning. Teaching students to think critically is an ongoing process that is enhanced by directing student attention to the examination and understanding of their own thinking.

Developing Learning Strategies

In addition to listings of critical thinking skills, many of the activities in *¡YA VERÁS!* are labeled as to the specific learning strategies being emphasized in the activity. The learning strategies noted in the student margin can be considered to be in four different categories: **receptive strategies, productive strategies, organizational strategies,** and **multi-tasking strategies.**

The following lists provide sample entries in the four categories.

Receptive
- Active listening
- Reading
- Drawing meaning

Productive
- Describing
- Giving directions
- Listing

Organizational
- Brainstorming
- Interviewing
- Creating a chart

Multi-tasking
- Explaining
- Negotiating
- Summarizing from context

Cooperative Learning and Classroom Management

LARGE AND HETEROGENEOUS CLASSES

Two of the major problems in today's classrooms are the high number of students and, by definition, the varying levels of abilities represented. The *¡YA VERÁS!* program addresses these issues in a variety of ways.

1. Regular paired and small-group work maximizes student participation time and has the effect of turning a large class into many small classes.

2. In some parts of the program (e.g., *Aquí llegamos*), activities can be individualized in that different groups can be asked to work on different activities. If several weaker students are grouped together, for example, they can be given a less complex task to accomplish.

3. The *¡YA VERÁS!* program is highly motivating and thus gives the slower student a sense of accomplishment. Although some students will always learn more quickly than others, the program has a kind of leveling effect in that all students can be successful at different times.

4. Regular recycling and review of material helps weaker students "catch up" and gives stronger students the opportunity to reinforce what they know.

5. In the *¡YA VERÁS!* program, we do not expect students to learn all of the vocabulary about each topic. We assume that, for example, in lists of foods, students will focus on expressing their own likes and dislikes. In this instance, what one student likes is not necessarily the preference of another student. The same is true about vocabulary for family. Since every family has a slightly different configuration, students should first learn to speak about what applies to them, leaving the rest to be dealt with receptively. All of our

materials, including the testing program, give students the flexibility to express their own situations and preferences.

PRINCIPLES OF COOPERATIVE LEARNING

The major principles of cooperative learning techniques are inherent to the *¡YA VERÁS!* program. These principles help to define the roles of teachers and students in class and to acknowledge and utilize a variety of student learning styles. They are based on the idea that students can learn effectively from one another if their work is carefully detailed and assigned with specific information about the goal, the process, the timing, and the reporting of the results of their task. The foreign language classroom is an excellent setting for putting cooperative learning strategies into practice.

The following principles are central to cooperative learning.

- Teaching must be student-centered.

- Paired and small-group work is essential to engage students in frequent communication that is meaningful, based on real-world experiences, relatively free of anxiety, and challenging to various learner styles and abilities.

- Cooperative learning encourages multiple ways of expression.

- It promotes multiple points of view through the use of heterogeneous teams.

- It reduces dependence on the teacher and fosters linguistic independence and individual accountability.

- It promotes positive interdependence and creates a positive social atmosphere in which students learn to accept the contributions that others can make to their learning.

- It fosters the willingness to be helpful to others through shared responsibility.

- It promotes individual expression of likes, dislikes, and preferences rather than "cloned" behavior.

- It gives students a chance to raise language issues that are of interest to them and that might not surface in a teacher-centered classroom.

- It allows students to manipulate language in ways that are most suitable to them.

- It gives teachers the opportunity to relax and be the observers of student behavior, thus enhancing sensitivity to student needs and interests.

It is important to recognize that in order for an activity to be considered true cooperative learning, it must call for an outcome, such as a group product or decision, resulting from initial individual input and then a final negotiated consensus developed by all members of the team.

PAIR WORK AND SMALL-GROUP WORK IN THE ANNOTATIONS

This Teacher's Edition also contains annotations suggesting particular pair and group "structured" activities that can be used at logical places in a chapter. Each "structure" has a particular name, such as Jigsaw, Pairs Check, or Corners and is based on structures developed by researchers such as Johnson and Johnson, Slavin, and Kagan. Once you have learned to use these "structures" successfully, you can use them at other times in the course that seem appropriate to you.

Some structures are more useful for certain learning objectives than for others. For instance, Corners is particularly useful for warm-up activities because it gets students moving and communicating while setting the context for the chapter. Student Teachers (also known as Telephone) is good for pronunciation work because it forces students to listen carefully. Team Decisions (also called Numbered Heads Together) and Pairs Check are useful when your goal is mastery. Jigsaw works extremely well for reading comprehension, and Round Robin and Roundtable are useful for vocabulary practice.

Notice that in many group activities, you are asked to have students number off. This ensures that you call on students randomly to perform certain tasks or to give an individual response to a question already practiced with the group. In this way each student's individual accountability is guaranteed. Notice also that we often suggest doing warm-up activities in English. These activities appear at the beginning of the chapter in which the necessary contexts and skills to do the activity in Spanish will be taught. Students ought to be able to do a similar exercise in Spanish at the end of the chapter.

We suggest that before attempting a new and unfamiliar structure, you should (1) read through all of the directions, (2) be sure you can provide the materials, and (3) practice carrying out the activity (including saying the directions). When you become more familiar with the activities and structures, you will discover that they are not only simple and predictable, but that the results are very rewarding.

HOW TO DETERMINE GROUP SIZE

- In *¡YA VERÁS!*, group size is usually determined by the nature of the communicative activity. A symbol in the Teacher's Edition indicates the number of students per group.

- In cases where group size may be variable, it is important to make sure that every student has the opportunity to make a valuable contribution to the activity and that no one be allowed to sit on the sidelines while others do the work. Unless each student has a clearly defined role to play, it is not advisable to have groups larger than four students. Three or four students per group is probably the optimal

size unless an activity specifies paired work.

- The advantage of groups of three or four (particularly at higher levels in discussion activities) is that more than two points of view tend to eliminate the trap of "right" and "wrong." This is crucial when dealing with cultural topics.

HOW TO DETERMINE THE COMPOSITION OF THE GROUP

- Throughout the school year it is important to vary group composition so that students can regularly interact with different classmates.

- Various group combinations can be made: 1) stronger with weaker students; 2) groups of stronger students only, weaker students only; 3) random selection of students without concern for weaknesses and strengths. All of these combinations have merit and have their advantages and disadvantages.

HOW TO PUT STUDENTS INTO GROUPS

- If students are selected according to strengths and weaknesses, it is best to do this ahead of time during your lesson planning. Group selection wastes valuable class time which should be spent doing the activities themselves.

- Forming groups randomly can be accomplished in a variety of ways.

  1. As students enter the classroom, have them take a number out of a bowl or box. All students with the same number form a group. This can also be done with colors. Note that this may become chaotic as students try to find each other in order to do the assigned activity.

  2. Give students group assignments. Have them stay in the same groups for a couple of weeks. At the end of that period, change group assignments.

  3. Have students count off in Spanish before the activity begins. Either groups are formed from like numbers or in numerical order (e.g., 1–3, 1–4).

  4. Have students choose their own groups. Caution: This can lead to the exclusion of some students and the formation of cliques if used too often.

  5. Ask students to form groups with the people sitting closest to them.

  6. If students are given the option to work on different activities, they can group themselves according to the activity that interests them the most.

GUIDELINES TO SMALL-GROUP INTERACTION

As has already been noted, small-group interaction is essential for maximizing practice time and giving students a sense of linguistic independence and accomplishment. To avoid confusion in the classroom and make the best use of time, some basic guidelines should be followed.

Students should become used to pair and small-group work from the outset. They also need to learn the rules for this type of work very quickly. You, as the teacher, need to realize that you are not relinquishing control over the class: you make the rules, you give the direction lines, you expect accountability for the work done. For students, however, you are providing the illusion of freedom. This illusion very quickly becomes a reality because students find they can use language to communicate without the constant presence of a teacher.

The following are some guidelines for small-group classroom management.

1. The task that students are to accomplish has to be clearly defined and be relatively short. Students should not have to wonder what they are supposed to do once they have divided into groups.

2. A time limit should be placed on the activity and students should not be allowed to prolong it. Time to stop occurs when the groups finish the activity.

3. It should be made clear that students have to speak Spanish in their groups. They should be taught how to ask for information from other students: *¿Cómo se dice* star *en español?* Only if communication breaks down completely should students raise their hand to get your attention. With proper preparation, this should occur very seldom.

4. The ideal group sizes are two, three, or four students. With larger groups, some students tend to dominate while others will not participate at all or only minimally.

5. Unless the activity task is obvious, it should be modeled in front of the entire class before students work on their own. This model clarifies the task and provides linguistic suggestions.

6. It is usually advisable to have a couple of groups report back to the whole class, playing out the situation or giving the information they have gathered. Since students don't know which groups will be called upon to perform, this should be an added incentive to stay on task. You may wish to use the reporting back as a way to assign grades for different students on different days. Alternative: Create a couple of new groups to perform the activity in front of the class.

CORRECTION STRATEGIES

Students should learn very quickly that the goal of correction is not to punish them but to help them communicate more accu-

rately. It should be a confidence builder. This suggests that we should point out the things that were done well before we make comments on what needs to be corrected.

Error correction can occur at two different times during the class.

1. When students are engaged in a controlled, mechanical, or semi-mechanical exercise, correction should be systematic. Students need the immediate feedback so that they can work on their linguistic accuracy.

2. When students are in a communicative situation, i.e., in small groups or in meaningful interaction with you, error correction should be delayed until the communication can be completed. For example, students should not be interrupted for errors when they are working in pairs or small groups or when they are performing an activity for the class. Only when they have finished the task at hand should some of the errors be pointed out, with perhaps additional controlled practice by the whole class to correct the error. At this point, it is not necessary to identify the student who made the original error.

After the reporting-back stage, discuss with students some of the alternate language structures or vocabulary they could have used in the given situation. This short discussion raises cultural questions, grammar considerations, and communicative strategies that integrate and expand students group work.

TEACHER BEHAVIORS

Because a proficiency orientation has as its essential premise real-life linguistic behaviors, our interaction with students should mirror the interaction we have with strangers and friends in real life. In order to simulate such behaviors in a learning environment, we will probably have to modify some of our ways of dealing with students. These behaviors can be divided into four basic categories:

Speech and General Behavior

1. Our rate of speech should be our own. We should not slow down into artificial speech rates because we underestimate our students' ability to understand. Speech should be slowed down only when we have ascertained that there is, in fact, a comprehension problem, not because we anticipate such a problem.

2. We should limit or eliminate "teacher talk." Teacher talk *(muy bien, de acuerdo, bien)* is typically evaluative of grammatical accuracy. It rarely responds to the message. In communicative situations, i.e., when students say something personalized, the most positive feedback we can give them is to respond to the message naturally as we would in real life. This shows them that they were understood. *(¿Es verdad? ¡No me digas! ¿En serio? ¡Qué interesante!)* Then ask follow-up questions to keep the conversational ball rolling for a few seconds. The added advantage of natural speech is

that students gradually learn the many expressions you use and will eventually incorporate them into their own language.

3. We should not automatically repeat everything we say (*¿Qué hiciste ayer? ¿Qué hiciste ayer?*). Repetition underestimates students' ability to understand the first time. More importantly, it hinders the development of listening comprehension skills as students learn not to listen the first time we say something. Repetition should be used if students have truly not understood the first time, in which case the statement should probably be rephrased. If they did not hear what was said, students should be taught to say *Perdón, no comprendí.*

4. We should not finish students' sentences when they hesitate or grope for words. It is preferable to teach them to use some hesitation markers, such as, *este...* so that they can give themselves time to think. We should help out only if it becomes clear that communication has stalled completely.

5. We should not systematically repeat everything students say (Student: *El fin de semana pasado fui a una fiesta.* Teacher: *El fin de semana pasado fui a una fiesta.*) Because such repetition is often used as a correction strategy, it can become a behavior pattern even when no correction is needed. Again, repetition should be used as it would be in real life (*Ah, qué bien. ¿Fuiste a una fiesta? ¿Y qué tal la fiesta?*).

6. We should not interrupt real communication with grammatical correction. It is important for students to be able to complete their thoughts and to feel that the message is valued. Correction can occur after conversational exchange has ended.

7. The blackboard should be used sparingly. In order to foster the development of listening comprehension skills, students should not always see everything in writing. The blackboard is a teaching tool, not a substitute for communication.

Body Language

1. When addressing individual students, we should move as close to them as possible. Although this may be strategically more difficult in large classes, aisles can be created to reduce the space between the teacher and individual students.

2. We should keep eye contact with the student with whom we are interacting. As teachers, we are sometimes preoccupied with the next question we are going to ask the next student. Almost imperceptibly this can lead us to abandon eye contact with a student before the communication has been completed.

3. We should move around the entire classroom, not just stay at the front. Besides moving closer to students, this movement helps to maintain the energy level of the class.

4. We should avoid looking down on students physically. Since they are seated and we are standing, there is a tendency to hover over them. If we place some empty seats in different parts of the room, we can sit down for a couple of seconds and address students in that part of the room. We can also assume a half-stance by bending our knees and adjusting to students' eye level. Research has shown that eye-level interaction is less threatening and has a positive impact on student performance.

Silence

1. It takes the mind approximately three seconds to process information (e.g., a question). Given this fact, we should give students enough time to think of a response, allowing for enough silence so that the response can be formulated. Interfering too quickly by repeating, for example, the question in different ways in rapid-fire succession inhibits thinking and is likely to be very frustrating for students.

2. We need to be sensitive to silences that are constructive and those that become uncomfortable. Only when the discomfort stage sets in should we help the student out by reformulating the question.

General Attitude

1. We should always have a positive attitude toward students. This does not mean that we should underestimate them or teach them to rely on us in an unrealistic way. It does mean, however, that we have to have a fundamental belief that all students are able to learn Spanish, although some will learn more quickly and better than others.

2. Rather than being actors and actresses in class, we should be ourselves. We should be willing to share information about ourselves and not ask students questions we are not willing to answer ourselves. For instance, when dealing with leisure time, students are regularly put into the position of talking about their activities in detail. We should be prepared to do the same. This has the added effect of serving as a good linguistic model for students to imitate.

3. We must, at all times, be willing to give students the responsibility for their own language learning. We are essentially the facilitators for this process: in the final analysis, what matters is how well students learned what we taught. An example of this is the student who has been taught the imperfect in class but does not use it when he or she is examined in an oral test. Achievement in class in tests and classroom performance will only translate into proficiency if students have regularly been given the responsibility and the opportunity to accomplish linguistic tasks on their own.

Yearly Syllabus for ¡YA VERÁS!, Segundo nivel

The following is a suggested yearly syllabus based on 180 class days. The goal of our program is for you to be able to complete the material in Level 2 in one year. We have not, however, included specific time requirements for the completion of each *etapa* because we believe that you need to retain as much flexibility as possible in designing your own yearly plan. Some *etapas* will take longer than others, depending on the general ability of the students and the complexity of the material. For example, *Estructura* sections that are essentially vocabulary-based require less time than those that involve primarily grammatical structures.

Text content: three *Capítulos preliminares,* 5 units
Total number of class days: 180

* 20–25 days reserved for administrative details, review, testing, and class cancellations due to extracurricular activities

* 12–15 days for the *Capítulos preliminares*

* 25–30 days for each of the 5 units

The number of days for each category can be modified according to your particular school calendar and your own preferences. For example, you may prefer to allow fewer or more days for the *Capítulos preliminares,* testing, and other activities.

If you use the suggested maximum number of class days for the units, you will need to adjust the number of class days for the other components accordingly.

¡YA VERÁS! and Longer Class Periods (Block Scheduling/ Concentrated Curriculum)

The *etapa* structure of *¡YA VERÁS!* is uniquely well suited to the challenges and promises of longer class periods. The *etapa* is in fact a lesson plan for a 90- to 100-minute class, during which vocabulary and structures are introduced, practiced, and reinforced by student performance. The closely-integrated components provide for the variety of instructional approaches that longer class periods demand, while assuring that students' attention remains focused on developing language accuracy in specific functions and contexts. Moreover, the longer instructional periods allow students to receive immediate feedback from performance and other evaluations, a motivating experience which keeps them learning more efficiently and effectively.

The following suggested pacing for *¡YA VERÁS!* 1 includes presentation, practice, performance, evaluation, and enrichment.

> 6 units with 3 chapters per unit
> One unit presented every 15 instructional days
> One chapter presented every 5 instructional days
> First chapter of each unit (3 *etapas*): 1–1/2 instructional days per *etapa*, 1/2 day leeway
> Second and third chapters (2 *etapas* each): 2 instructional days per *etapa*
> *Ya llegamos:* 2 instructional days

The following suggested pacing for *¡YA VERÁS!* 2 includes presentation, practice, performance, evaluation, and enrichment.

> *Capítulos preliminares:* 7–8 instructional days
> 5 units with 3 chapters per unit
> One unit presented every 16 instructional days
> One chapter presented every 5–6 instructional days
> One *etapa* presented every 2 instructional days
> *Ya llegamos:* 2 instructional days

The following suggested pacing for *¡YA VERÁS!* 3 includes presentation, practice, performance, evaluation, and enrichment.

> *Capítulo preliminare:* 7–8 instructional days
> 4 units with three chapters per unit
> One unit presented every 18 instructional days
> One chapter presented every 6 instructional days
> One *etapa* presented every 3 instructional days
> *Ya llegamos:* 2 instructional days

THE ¡YA VERÁS! PROGRAM

Unit	Functions	Contexts	Accuracy
1	Meeting and greeting people Ordering something to eat or drink Discussing likes and dislikes Finding out about other people	**Café, bar de tapas,** restaurant Meeting and conversing with new people	**Gustar** + infinitive Indefinite articles **un, una** Present tense **-ar** verbs Subject pronouns Conjugated verb + infinitive Present tense **ser**
2	Identifying personal possessions Discussing preferences Talking about your family Finding out about other people Describing people and places	School, home, various other settings (museum, park, cinema, shopping)	Definite articles **Hay** + noun Possessive adjectives (1st, 2nd person) **Gustar** + noun **Ser** + **de** for possession **Ser** + adjective Present tense **-er, -ir** verbs Present tense **tener; Tener que** + inf.
3	Identifying and locating places / buildings in a city / town Expressing desires and preferences Taking about your age Giving and asking for directions Giving orders Suggesting activities Asking for and giving the time Discussing feelings	Downtown, festival	Present tense (continued) Contractions **al, del** Expressions of frequency (**rara vez,** etc.) Commands with **Ud., Uds.** Irregular commands Telling time **Estar** + adjective Possessive adjectives (3rd person) Prepositions, adverbs of place
4	Talking about the future Identifying what to do in town Giving directions for using the subway Buying tickets Taking a taxi Making plans for a trip	Downtown, subway station, travel agency	**Ir** + **a** for immediate future **Tener ganas de** Present tense **hacer, poder, esperar** Adverbs **hoy, mañana,** etc. Future with **pensar** Numbers 100–1,000,000
5	Discussing leisure time activities Talking about events / activities in the past, present, future Talking about sports	Leisure time activities	Preterite **-ar, -er, -ir** verbs Preterite **hacer, ir, andar, estar, tener** Adverbs, prepositions, etc. to indicate the past (**ayer,** etc.) **Hace, hace que** Preterite **-gar, -car** verbs Present progressive
6	Expressing likes and dislikes Making purchases Indicating quantities Asking for prices Making comparisons Pointing out places, objects, people Giving orders	Shopping mall, various stores (music, cards, sports, clothing, shoes) Grocery store, open-air market	**Gustar** (3rd person) Familiar commands Negative familiar commands Demonstrative adjectives **Cuál, cuáles** Demonstrative pronouns **Tan... como** to express equality

PRIMER NIVEL

Unit	Functions	Contexts	Accuracy
	Capítulos preliminares **A, B,** and **C** are a review of all major functions, structures, and vocabulary covered in *¡Ya verás! Primer nivel.*		
1	Describing the weather Understanding weather reports Describing objects Describing people	Using the weather to talk about a vacation site Meteorological maps Watching / reading / listening to weather reports	Months / seasons of the year / date Present tense of stem-changing verbs Present tense of **saber, conocer** Agreement and position of adjectives Plural forms of adjectives **Saber** vs. **conocer** Personal **a** **Ser para** + pronouns Shortened adjectives (**buen, mal, gran**)
2	Renting and paying for a hotel room Understanding classified ads / lodging brochures Describing a house or apartment Telling time using the 24-hour clock	**La Guía Michelín** (tourist guide) Hotels, apartments, houses Flight schedules, newspaper ads	Ordinal numbers Preterite **dormir** Present and preterite **salir, llegar, decir, poner** Time expressions / Parts of an hour The 24-hour clock Expressions with **decir**
3	Talking about one's daily routine Organizing weekend activities Discussing vacation plans	School, home Magazines with entertainment listings Various other settings (vacation sites)	Present tense of reflexive verbs **Ud., Uds., tú** commands of reflexive verbs Direct object pronouns Position of direct object pronouns Immediate future of reflexive verbs Reflexive vs. nonreflexive verbs Use of pronouns with the imperative
4	Taking about health / physical condition Referring to habitual actions in the past Using reflexive verbs in the past Indicating what you can and cannot do	Pharmacy, school Sports, pastimes	The imperfect and its uses Imperfect **ser, ver, ir** Preterite of reflexive verbs Present and preterite **dar, pedir** Present tense **doler** Indirect object pronouns Definite articles with parts of the body Expressions **desde cuándo, desde (que), cuánto tiempo hace, hace (que)**
5	Discussing leisure time activities Talking about sports Narrating and describing in the past	Home, school, public places, sporting events	Geographical names Preterite of some irregular verbs Uses of **ponerse** Imperfect and preterite: past actions, descriptions, interrupted actions, changes of meaning and translation

SEGUNDO NIVEL

The **Capítulo preliminar** is a comprehensive review of the materials presented in *¡Ya verás! Segundo nivel.*

Unit	Functions	Contexts	Accuracy
1	Purchasing clothing / shoes Asking for information Commenting on clothing / food Making restaurant plans Understanding a menu / recipe Ordering / paying for food	Department store, clothing store, shoe store Restaurant, grocery store / supermarket, open-air market	Posición de los pronombres de complemento indirecto y directo **Gustar** y otros verbos Usos de **se** **Estar** + adjetivos para estados y condiciones **Ser** y **estar** + adjetivo
2	Organizing a trip Using the telephone Talking about means of transportation Making travel arrangements Understanding a road map	Airport, train station, bus terminal, on the road	El tiempo futuro y sus usos Usos especiales del tiempo futuro Preposiciones para localizar Otras preposiciones útiles: **antes de, después de** Pronombres preposicionales Los tiempos perfectos: presente y pasado
3	Offering opinions Some abstract topics Dealing with symbolism Expressing emotions Expressing wishes, preferences	Travel in various Spanish-speaking countries	El subjuntivo para expresar la imposición indirecta de la voluntad El subjuntivo para expresar la emoción Expresiones impersonales para expresar la emoción
4	Understanding a variety of texts about the Spanish-speaking world Expressing doubt, uncertainty, improbability Talking about conditions contrary to fact Supporting an opinion	Cultural issues of the Hispanic world in the press, media, literature	El subjuntivo para expresar la duda, la incertidumbre, la irrealidad El subjuntivo con antecedentes indefinidos El subjuntivo con **creer** El condicional y sus usos Claúsulas con **si** + subjuntivo Claúsulas con **si** + indicativo El subjunctivo y la secuencia de tiempos

TERCER NIVEL

SEGUNDO NIVEL

¡Ya verás!

SECOND EDITION

JOHN R. GUTIÉRREZ

The Pennsylvania State University

HARRY L. ROSSER

Boston College

Heinle & Heinle Publishers

An International Thomson Publishing Company • Boston, MA 02116 U.S.A.

I(T)P

Visit us on the internet http://www.thomson.com/heinle.html

The publication of ¡Ya verás! Segundo nivel 2/e was directed by the members of the Heinle & Heinle School Publishing Team:

Editorial Director: Beth Kramer
Market Development Director: Pamela Warren
Production Editor: Mary McKeon
Developmental Editor: Regina McCarthy
Publisher/Team Leader: Stanley J. Galek
Director of Production/Team Leader: Elizabeth Holthaus

Also participating in the publication of this text were:

Manufacturing Coordinator: Barbara Stephan
Project Manager: Kristin Swanson
Interior Design: Susan Gerould/Perspectives
Composition: NovoMac Enterprises
Cover Art: Mark Schroder
Cover: Corey McPherson Nash
Photo/Video Specialist: Jonathan Stark

Gutiérrez, John R.
    Ya veras! segundo nivel / John R. Gutiérrez, Harry L. Rosser. — 2nd ed.
       p.   cm.
    Includes index.
    Summary: Continues study of the Spanish language by utilizing everday
    situations.
    ISBN 0-8384-6177-8
    1. Spanish language—Textbooks for foreign speakers—English.
   [1. Spanish language—Textbooks for foreign speakers—English.]
    I. Rosser, Harry L. II. Title.
    [PC4129.E5G89   1997]
    468.2'421—dc20   95-45122
                                      —CIP
                                          AC

Manufactured in the United States of America.

ISBN 0-8384-6177-8 Student

ii

To the Student

As you continue your study of Spanish, you will not only discover how much you can already do with the language, but you will also learn to build on what you know. By now, you know how to talk about yourself, your family, and your friends; you can get around towns, use the subway in Madrid, and give directions; you are able to make purchases in a variety of stores; you can talk about the diversity of the Spanish-speaking world, including parts of the United States; and you have learned to use appropriate language in a variety of social interactions.

As you move forward, your cultural knowledge will expand as you take a closer look at parts of the Spanish-speaking world, with its varied customs, traditions, landscapes, and points of interest. You will learn to describe people and things, know how to talk about your residence and be able to get lodging (in a hotel or hostel), interact with others about your leisure-time and vacation activities, and talk about health concerns. *Remember that the most important task ahead of you is NOT to accumulate a large quantity of knowledge about Spanish grammar and vocabulary, but rather to USE what you do know as effectively and creatively as you can.*

Communication in a foreign language means understanding what others say and transmitting your own messages in ways that avoid misunderstandings. As you learn to do this, you will make the kinds of errors that are necessary to language learning. DO NOT BE AFRAID TO MAKE MISTAKES! Instead, try to see errors as positive steps toward effective communication. They don't hold you back; they advance you in your efforts.

¡Ya verás! has been written with your needs in mind. It places you in situations that you (as a young person) might really encounter in a Spanish-speaking environment. Whether you are working with vocabulary or grammar, it leads you from controlled exercises (that show you just how a word or structure is used) to bridging exercises (that allow you to introduce your own personal context into what you are saying or writing) to open-ended exercises (in which you are asked to handle a situation much as you might in actual experience). These situations are intended to give you the freedom to be creative and express yourself without fear or anxiety. They are the real test of what you can DO with the Spanish you have learned.

Learning a language is hard work, but it can also be lots of fun. We hope that you find your experience with *¡Ya verás!* both rewarding and enjoyable.

Acknowledgments

reating a secondary program is a long and complicated process which involves the dedication and hard work of a number of people. First of all, we would like to express our heartfelt thanks to our Editorial Director, Beth Kramer, whose expertise and support were crucial for guiding the project through its realization. We are also grateful to our Developmental Editor, Regina McCarthy, who worked closely with us to facilitate our work each step of the way. Our Production Editor, Mary McKeon, managed the many facets of the process with skill, timeliness, and good humor. Vivian Novo-MacDonald flawlessly handled her typesetting responsibilities. Kristin Swanson was a particularly effective Project Manager and we greatly appreciate her keen eye, poignant comments, and excellent suggestions at every phase of the process. We would like to thank many other people who played a role in the production of the program: Susan Gerould, Mary Lemire, María Silvina Persino, Camilla Ayers, Sharon Inglis, and Esther Marshall.

Our thanks also go to others at Heinle and Heinle who helped make this project possible: Charles Heinle and Stan Galek, for their special interest and support; Vincent DiBlasi and Erek Smith for their marketing and technical knowledge; and Jeannette Bragger and Donald Rice, authors of *On y va!* We also wish to express our appreciation to the people responsible for revising the fine set of supporting materials available with the *¡Ya verás!* program. Many thanks to our Project Manager Esther Marshall, and to Greg Harris, Workbook; Chris McIntyre and Jill Welch, Teacher Edition; Joe Wieczorek, Laboratory Tape Program; Ken Janson, Testing Program; Jeff Morgenstein, Software; and Frank Domínguez, Ana Martínez-Lage and Jeff Morgenstein for creating the excellent *Mundos hispanos* multimedia program.

Finally, a very special word of acknowledgment goes to the authors' children:
— To Mía (age 12) and Stevan (age 9) who are always on their daddy's mind and whose cultural heritage is ever present throughout *¡Ya verás!*

— To Susan, Elizabeth, and Rebecca Rosser, whose enthusiasm and increasing interest in Spanish inspired their father to take part in this endeavor.

John R. Gutiérrez and Harry L. Rosser

The publisher and authors wish to thank the following writers for their contributions to *¡Ya verás!* second edition.

Critical Thinking Skills, Learning Strategies
Jane Harper
Tarrant County Junior College
Madeleine Lively
Tarrant County Junior College
Mary K. Williams
Tarrant County Junior College

Reading Strategies, Aquí leemos
Laura Martin
Cleveland State University

Interdisciplinary Lessons
Jessie Carduner
University of Pittsburgh
Charles Grove
University of Pittsburgh
Paul D. Toth
University of Pittsburgh

The publisher and authors wish to thank the following teachers who pilot-tested the *¡Ya verás!* program. They used the materials with their classes and made invaluable suggestions as our work progressed. Their feedback benefits all who use this final product. We are grateful to each one of them for their dedication and commitment to teaching with the program in a prepublication format.

Nola Baysore
Muncy JHS
Muncy, PA

Barbara Connell
Cape Elizabeth Middle
  School
Cape Elizabeth, ME

Frank Droney
Susan Digiandomenico
Wellesley Middle School
Wellesley, MA

Michael Dock
Shikellamy HS
Sunbury, PA

Jane Flood Clare
Somers HS
Lincolndale, NY

Nancy McMahon
Somers Middle School
Lincolndale, NY

Rebecca Gurnish
Ellet HS
Akron, OH

Peter Haggerty
Wellesley HS
Wellesley, MA

José M. Díaz
Hunter College HS
New York, NY

Claude Hawkins
Flora Mazzucco
Jerie Milici
Elena Fienga
Bohdan Kodiak
Greenwich HS
Greenwich, CT

Wally Lishkoff
Tomás Travieso
Carver Middle School
Miami, FL

Manuel M. Manderine
Canton McKinley HS
Canton, OH

Grace Angel Marion
South JHS
Lawrence, KS

Jean Barrett
St. Ignatius HS
Cleveland, OH

Gary Osman
McFarland HS
McFarland, WI

Deborah Decker
Honeoye Falls-Lima HS
Honeoye Falls, NY
Carrie Piepho
Arden JHS
Sacramento, CA

Rhonda Barley
Marshall JHS
Marshall, VA

Germana Shirmer
W. Springfield HS
Springfield, VA

John Boehner
Gibson City HS
Gibson City, IL

Margaret J. Hutchison
John H. Linton JHS
Penn Hills, PA

Edward G. Stafford
St. Andrew's-Sewanee
  School
St. Andrew's, TN

Irene Prendergast
Wayzata East JHS
Plymouth, MN

Tony DeLuca
Cranston West HS
Cranston, RI

Joe Wild-Crea
Wayzata Senior High
  School
Plymouth, MN
Katy Armagost
Manhattan HS
Manhattan, KS

William Lanza
Osbourn Park HS
Manassas, VA

Linda Kelley
Hopkinton HS
Contoocook, NH

John LeCuyer
Belleville HS West
Belleville, IL

Sue Bell
South Boston HS
Boston, MA

Wayne Murri
Mountain Crest HS
Hyrum, UT

Barbara Flynn
Summerfield
  Waldorf School
Santa Rosa, CA

The publisher and authors wish to thank the following people who reviewed the manuscript for the second edition of the *¡Ya verás!* program. Their comments were invaluable to the development of this edition.

Georgio Arias, Juan De León, Luís Martínez (McAllen ISD, McAllen, TX); **Katy Armagost** (Mt. Vernon High School, Mt. Vernon, WA); **Yolanda Bejar, Graciela Delgado, Bárbara V. Méndez, Mary Alice Mora** (El Paso ISD, El Paso, TX); **Linda Bigler** (Thomas Jefferson High School, Alexandria, VA); **John Boehner** (Gibson City High School, Gibson City, IL); **Kathleen Carroll** (Edinburgh ISD, Edinburgh, TX); **Louanne Grimes** (Richardson ISD, Richardson, TX); **Greg Harris** (Clay High School, South Bend, IN); **Diane Henderson** (Houston ISD, Houston, TX); **Maydell Jenks** (Katy ISD, Katy, TX); **Bartley Kirst** (Ironwood High School, Glendale, AZ); **Mala Levine** (St. Margaret's Episcopal School, San Juan Capistrano, CA); **Manuel Manderine** (Canton McKinley Sr. High School, Canton, OH); **Laura Martin** (Cleveland State University, Cleveland, OH); **Luís Millán** (Edina High School, Minneapolis, MN); **David Moffett, Karen Petmeckey, Pat Rossett, Nereida Zimic** (Austin ISD, Austin, TX); **Jeff Morgenstein** (Hudson High School, Hudson, FL); **Rosana Pérez, Jody Spoor** (Northside ISD, San Antonio, TX); **Susan Polansky** (Carnegie Mellon University, Pittsburgh, PA); **Alva Salinas** (San Antonio ISD, San Antonio, TX); **Patsy Shafchuk** (Hudson High School, Hudson, FL); **Terry A. Shafer** (Worthington Kilbourne High School, West Worthington, OH); **Courtenay Suárez** (Montwood High School, Socorro ISD, El Paso, TX); **Alvino Téllez, Jr.** (Edgewood ISD, San Antonio, TX); **Kristen Warner** (Piper High School, Sunrise, FL); **Nancy Wrobel** (Champlin Park High School, Champlin, MN)

Middle School Reviewers:

Larry Ling (Hunter College High School, New York, NY); **Susan Malik** (West Springfield High School, Springfield, VA); **Yvette Parks** (Norwood Junior High School, Norwood, MA)

CONTENTS

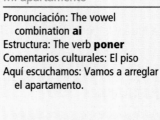

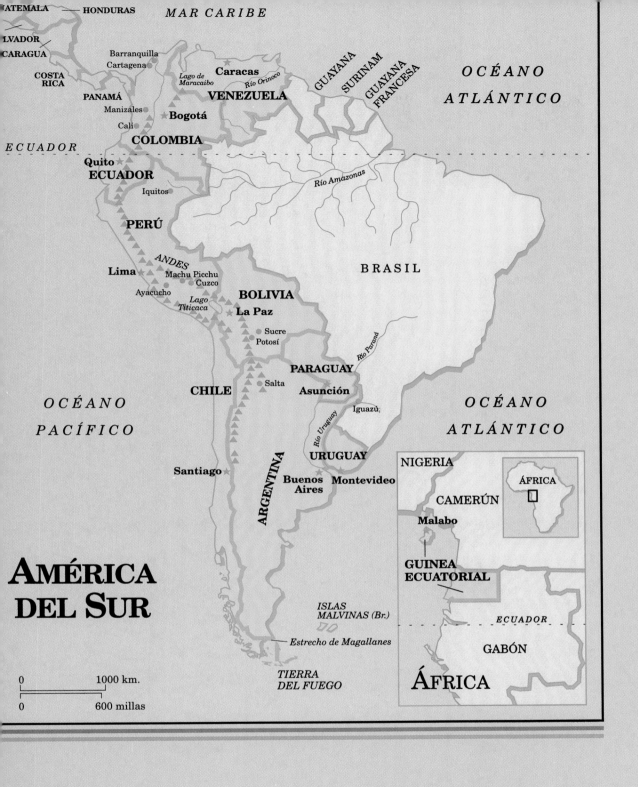

MAR CARIBE

ATEMALA — HONDURAS
LVADOR
CARAGUA

COSTA
RICA

PANAMÁ

Barranquilla
Cartagena

Lago de
Maracaibo

Caracas
Río Orinoco

VENEZUELA

GUAYANA
SURINAM
GUAYANA
FRANCESA

OCÉANO
ATLÁNTICO

Manizales

Cali

Bogotá

COLOMBIA

ECUADOR

Quito
ECUADOR

Iquitos

Río Amazonas

PERÚ

ANDES

Lima

Machu Picchu
Cuzco

Ayacucho

Lago
Titicaca

BOLIVIA

La Paz

BRASIL

Sucre
Potosí

Río Paraná

PARAGUAY

CHILE

Salta

Asunción

OCÉANO

PACÍFICO

Río Uruguay

Iguazú

OCÉANO

ATLÁNTICO

URUGUAY

Santiago

ARGENTINA

Buenos
Aires

Montevideo

NIGERIA

ÁFRICA

CAMERÚN

Malabo

AMÉRICA
DEL SUR

ISLAS
MALVINAS (Br.)

Estrecho de Magallanes

GUINEA
ECUATORIAL

ECUADOR

GABÓN

0   1000 km.

0   600 millas

TIERRA
DEL FUEGO

ÁFRICA

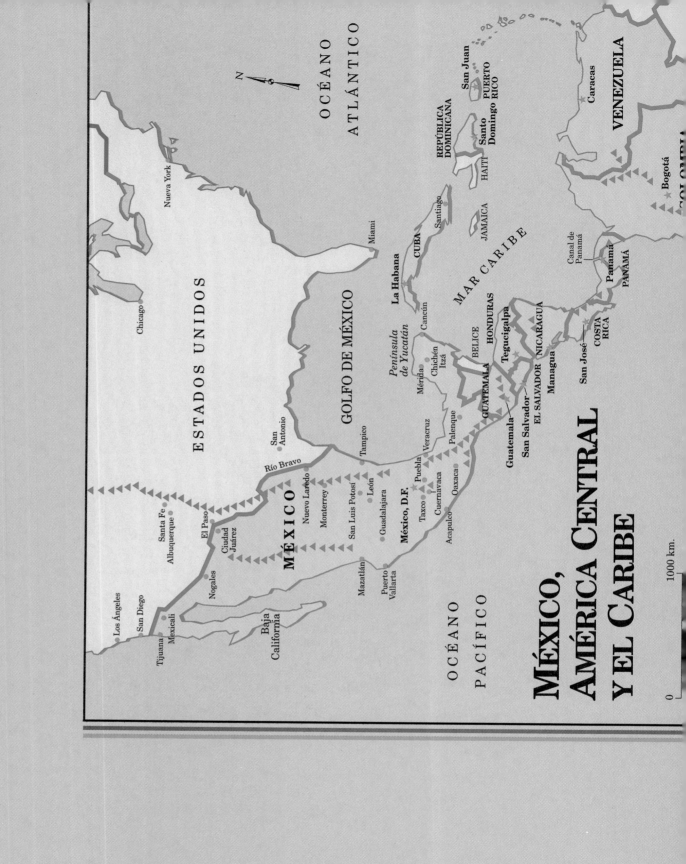

MÉXICO, AMÉRICA CENTRAL Y EL CARIBE

ESTADOS UNIDOS

OCÉANO ATLÁNTICO

OCÉANO PACÍFICO

GOLFO DE MÉXICO

MAR CARIBE

MÉXICO

N

Chicago

Nueva York

Miami

Los Ángeles
San Diego
Tijuana
Mexicali
Nogales

Santa Fe
Albuquerque
El Paso
Ciudad
Juárez

San
Antonio

Río Bravo

Nuevo Laredo
Monterrey
San Luis Potosí
León
Guadalajara

Mazatlán
Puerto
Vallarta

Baja
California

México, D.F.
Taxco
Cuernavaca
Acapulco
Oaxaca

Puebla
Veracruz
Palenque

Tampico

Península
de Yucatán

Mérida
Chichén
Itzá

Cancún

La Habana

CUBA

Santiago

HAITÍ

REPÚBLICA
DOMINICANA

Santo
Domingo

San Juan
PUERTO
RICO

JAMAICA

BELICE

GUATEMALA

Guatemala

San Salvador
EL SALVADOR

HONDURAS

Tegucigalpa

NICARAGUA

Managua

San José
COSTA
RICA

Canal de
Panamá

Panamá
PANAMÁ

Caracas

VENEZUELA

Bogotá
COLOMBIA

0   1000 km.

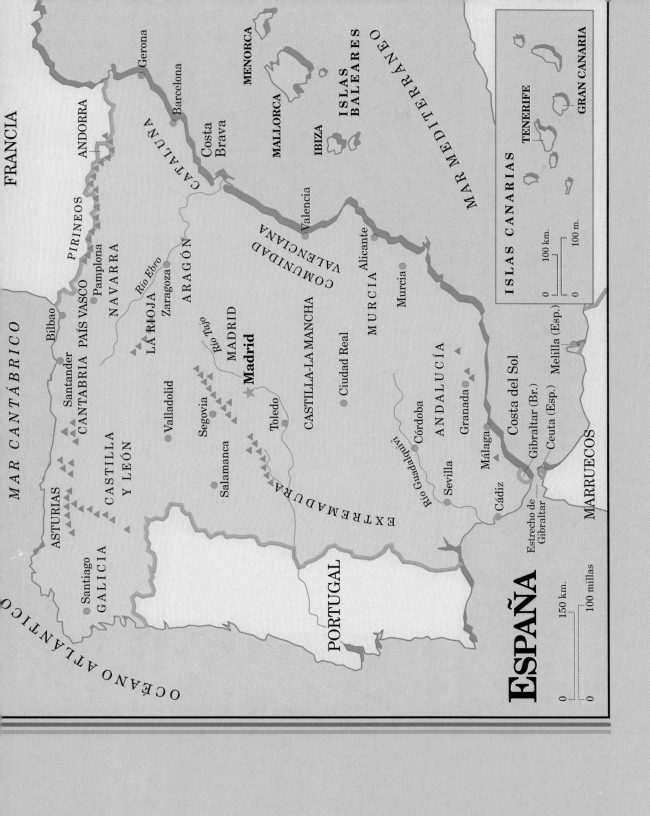

CAPÍTULO

A

¿QUIÉN SOY YO?

—Hola, ¿qué tal, Teresa?
—Muy bien. ¿Y tú?

Objectives:

>>> **R**eview words and expressions needed to talk about yourself and your family.

>>> **R**eview regular verbs ending in **-ar, -er,** and **-ir** and the verbs **ser** and **tener.**

>>> **P**ractice describing yourself and your family, greeting people, and making introductions.

Strategies:

>>> **T**aking notes

>>> **R**eporting

>>> **D**rawing conclusions

>>> **E**valuating

>>> **D**rawing inferences

1

Video/Laserdisc

Preliminary Chapter A Video Program and Video Guide

Planning Strategy

Have students become familiar with the layout of the text and its division into **Capítulos prelimi-nares** and **Unidades** (subdivided into **Capítulos** and further subdi-vided into **Etapas**). Explain how these are grouped according to topics and functional goals.

Chapter Objectives

The **Capítulos preliminares** (A, B, C) recycle the cultural situations, conversational functions, and grammatical structures of Level 1.
Functions: Meeting and greeting people; introducing oneself and others
Context: Describing yourself and your family
Accuracy: Review of regular **-ar, -er,** and **-ir** verbs; review of **ser, tener**

Cultural Observation

Look at the photo and discuss who the people may be and what their relationship may be to one another. Study their body lan-guage, and compare and contrast the appropriateness of the **besito** in Hispanic culture with the some-what more reserved manner of greeting in American culture.

Prereading

Have students look at the pictures of María and Esteban and guess their ages. Then have them scan the paragraphs to see if their guesses were accurate. Have them scan the reading a second time to see what other topics María and Esteban discuss. List these on the board (e.g., age, family, home, interests).

Then have students close their books and listen to the tape. Call on individuals to see if they recall any specific information about Esteban or María or both in regard to the topics on the board.

Learning Strategy:
Scanning

Postreading

Now have the students read the passages silently and answer the following comprehension questions. To truly test students' comprehension, follow-up questions should be in English. This way students cannot manipulate vocabulary and information provided in the questions without real comprehension. However, since many teachers have requested questions in Spanish, we have provided English and Spanish options throughout the book.

Possible questions, Yo me llamo: 1. Are María and Esteban from the same country? 2. Who is older? 3. Who has the bigger family? How do you know? 4. What is an interest that they have in common?

1. ¿Son del mismo país María y Esteban? 2. ¿Quién es mayor? 3. ¿Quién tiene la familia más grande? ¿Cómo lo sabes? 4. ¿Qué es un interés que tienen en común?

Learning Strategy:
Reading for details

Critical Thinking Strategy:
Comparing and contrasting

PRIMERA ETAPA

Yo me llamo...

Yo me llamo María Catarina Gutiérrez. Tengo dieciséis años. Soy española. Vivo en un apartamento en Madrid con mi padre y hermano. Me gustan los deportes de invierno — especialmente el esquí. También me gusta escuchar la radio. Me gusta mucho la música popular norteamericana.

María

Yo me llamo Esteban Méndez. Tengo quince años. Soy mexicano. Mi familia y yo vivimos en Guadalajara, la capital del estado de Jalisco. Tenemos una casa grande en las afueras de la ciudad. Me gusta mucho la música: toco el piano y la trompeta. También me gusta ir al cine con mis amigos.

Esteban

2

Etapa Support Materials

Workbook: **pp. 1–8**
Teacher Tape

Quiz: **Testing Program, p. 1**

Support material, **Yo me llamo: Teacher Tape**

Comprensión

A. *María y Esteban en los Estados Unidos*   Imagine that María and Esteban are delegates to an international meeting of young people being held in your region of the United States. You have met them both and would like to introduce them to your teacher. Prepare your introductions of both María and Esteban by answering the following questions: **¿Cómo se llama? ¿Cuál es su nacionalidad? ¿Cuántos años tiene él (ella)? ¿Dónde vive? ¿Con quién? ¿Vive en una casa o en un apartamento? ¿Qué hace en su tiempo libre?** Begin by saying, *"Señora (Señor), quiero presentarle a... Él (Ella) es..."*

Learning Strategy:
Describing

REPASO

Regular verbs ending in -ar, -er, and -ir

To conjugate regular **-ar** verbs in the present tense, drop the **-ar** from the infinitive and add the appropriate ending: **-o, -as, -a, -amos, -áis,** or **-an.**

hablar

yo	habl**o**	nosotros(as)	habl**amos**
tú	habl**as**	vosotros(as)	habl**áis**
él		ellos	
ella	} habl**a**	ellas	} habl**an**
Ud.		Uds.	

B. Replace the words in italics with those in parentheses and make the necessary changes.

1. *Ella* trabaja mucho. (nosotros / yo / él / tú / ellos / vosotros)
2. ¿Habla *él* francés también? (tú / Uds. / ella / ellos / vosotros)
3. *Ellos* viajan todos los años. (ella / nosotras / yo / él / ellas / vosotras)

3

Preparation, Ex. A: Before doing this exercise, solicit interrogatives from students and list them on the board. Also review the expressions often used in introductions (**Tarjetas de vocabulario, p. 10**).

Suggestion, Ex. A: Divide the class into two groups. Allow five minutes and have one group write an introduction of María, while the other group writes an introduction of Esteban. Then solicit contributions from each group and write out both introductions for all to see. Read the introductions aloud and together judge them for completeness, accuracy, and smoothness.

More-prepared students, Ex. A: More-prepared students can role play the parts of teacher, Esteban, María, and the student who introduces them to each other. Give students a few moments to organize, then have them perform the introductions, using varying expressions (**Tarjetas de vocabulario,** p. 10), for the class.

Ex. B: writing

Round Robin, Ex. B
- Put students into heterogeneous teams of three (mixed by ethnicity, age, gender, ability) and direct them to sit facing each other.
- Explain that they are going to do Ex. B together, taking turns from left to right.
- The first student will say: **Ella trabaja mucho.** The student to his or her left will say: **Nosotros trabajamos mucho.** The third student will say: **Él trabaja mucho,** and so on.
- Remind students that they need to take turns in order, so that every student gets an equal amount of practice. They should also give hints and encouragement when other team members hesitate.
- When they have finished, call on students at random to give verb forms.

More-prepared students, Ex. B: Alternatively, ask more-prepared students for other **-ar** verbs they remember and list them on the board. Have each group write a new sentence for one of these verbs, then have each group do the new sentence with the subjects suggested in the original exercise.

Answers, Ex. B: 1. Nosotros trabajamos / Yo trabajo / Él trabaja / Tú trabajas / Ellos trabajan / Vosotros trabajáis   2. Hablas tú / Hablan Uds. / Habla ella / Hablan ellos / Habláis vosotros   3. Ella viaja / Nosotras viajamos / Yo viajo / Él viaja / Ellas viajan / Vosotras viajáis

REPASO

To conjugate regular **-er** verbs in the present tense, drop the **-er** from the infinitive and add the appropriate ending: **-o, -es, -e, -emos, -éis,** or **-en.**

correr

yo	corr**o**	nosotros(as)	corr**emos**
tú	corr**es**	vosotros(as)	corr**éis**
él		ellos	
ella	corr**e**	ellas	corr**en**
Ud.		Uds.	

C. Replace the words in italics with those in parentheses and make the necessary changes.

1. *Yo* corro dos millas todos los días. (tú / ella / José y Roberta / nosotros / Uds. / vosotras)
2. *Ella* no bebe leche. (yo / él / Ud. / nosotras / tú / vosotros)
3. ¿Lee *él* el periódico *(newspaper)* todas las mañanas? (tú / Ud. / Uds. / ellos / tu papá / vosotros)

REPASO

To conjugate regular **-ir** verbs in the present tense, drop the **-ir** from the infinitive and add the appropriate ending: **-o, -es, -e, -imos, -ís,** or **-en.**

escribir

yo	escrib**o**	nosotros(as)	escrib**imos**
tú	escrib**es**	vosotros(as)	escrib**ís**
él		ellos	
ella	escrib**e**	ellas	escrib**en**
Ud.		Uds.	

4

D. Replace the words in italics with those in parentheses and make the necessary changes.

1. *Ellos* viven en un apartamento en el centro. (yo / ella / tú / nosotras / Ud. / vosotros)
2. *Él* no asiste a la escuela los sábados. (nosotros / ellos / Uds. / Ud. / tú / vosotras)
3. ¿Escriben *ellas* la composición ahora? (tú / ella / Ud. / Uds. / vosotros)

¿Recuerdan?

1. In order to express in Spanish what activities we like and do not like, the following structure is used:

   gustar + *infinitive*

   Me gusta estudiar, pero no **me gusta** trabajar.
   ¿Te gusta cantar o **te gusta** escuchar música?
   A Juan le gusta estudiar, pero **a Elena le gusta** hablar por teléfono.
   A nosotros nos gusta nadar, pero **a Uds. les gusta** correr.

2. This structure may also be used with singular and plural nouns:

   Me gusta la biología, pero no **me gusta** la física.
   Te gustan las ciencias, pero no **te gustan** las lenguas.
   A Marisol le gusta la música, pero **a Julia le gustan** los deportes.
   Nos gustan las clases, pero **a ellos les gustan** los profesores.

3. Remember that **gusta** is used with singular nouns and infinitives and **gustan** is used with plural nouns.

4. The definite articles in Spanish are: **el, la, los,** and **las.** They are often used after the verb **gustar** to indicate a general like or dislike of something:

   Sí, me gustan **los** deportes.   No me gustan **las** ciencias.
   ¿Te gusta **la** historia?   ¿Te gusta **el** fútbol?

E. Entrevista Find out about your classmate and his or her family and friends. Begin by preparing a set of at least 12 interview questions based on the expressions you have studied along with those in the **Tarjetas de vocabulario: Para indicar dónde vives** and **Para hablar de tus actividades**, pages 10–11. Sample questions include: **¿Te gusta**

//-//-//-//-//-//-//-//-//

Cooperative Learning

Learning Strategies:

Collecting information, taking notes, reporting

Critical Thinking Strategy:

Evaluating

5

Ex. D: writing

Answers, Ex. D: 1. Yo vivo / Ella vive / Tú vives / Nosotras vivimos / Ud. vive / Vosotros vivís
2. Nosotros no asistimos / Ellos no asisten / Uds. no asisten / Ud. no asiste / Tú no asistes / Vosotras no asistís   3. Escribes tú / Escribe ella / Escribe Ud. / Escriben Uds. / Escribís vosotros

Presentation: ¿Recuerdan?

After reviewing the rules, refer to the Workbook, p. 5, for a reiteration and clear listing of examples of these rules.

Ex. E: pair work

writing

Preparation, Ex. E: You may want to have the students review the **Tarjetas de vocabulario: Para hablar de tus actividades,** p. 11. Vocabulary review could be done as a "Pictionary" exercise if you wish. Divide students into teams and hand out prepared cards with appropriate items for each team to draw and have the other team guess. You can review regular verbs with students and by asking them to brainstorm sample questions as they go along. Then, in labeled columns for **-ar, -er,** and **-ir** verbs, write the infinitives for the verbs you want to encourage them to use.

Suggestion, Ex. E: Have students work in pairs to prepare their question lists; it might help to pair a more-prepared student with a less-prepared student. When ready, have students work in groups of four to compare and contrast facts about each other. Remind them that in real conversation, questions often elicit other questions, as well as responses from the asker, using words like **también** and **tampoco**. Have students report back to the class one interesting fact about each group member.

Implementation, Ex. E: Brainstorm with students to help them identify other regular verbs they have learned. Help them to focus on regular verbs by having them come up with sample questions as they brainstorm. Then, in labeled columns for **-ar, -er,** and **-ir** verbs, write the infinitives you want to encourage them to use.

Follow-up, Ex. E: Have students write up their notes in paragraph form and then have them edit each other's work. You may wish to collect a sample of their writing.

Answers, Ex. F: 1. Ella es / Nosotros somos / Yo soy / Ellos son / Tú eres / Vosotros sois   2. Es él / Son Uds. / Eres tú / Son ellos / Sois vosotros   3. Ella no es / Yo no soy / Ud. no es / Tú no eres / Ellas no son / Vosotros no sois   4. Uds. son / Él es / Tú eres / Ellos son / Vosotros sois

escuchar la radio? ¿Qué tipo de música te gusta? ¿Cantas bien o mal? ¿Dónde trabajan tus padres? ¿Dónde vive tu mejor amigo(a)? ¿Tú y tus amigos, comen en un restaurante de vez en cuando? ¿Qué comida les gusta?

Take notes on your classmate's answers, organizing the information in the following sections: **Mi compañero(a), Sus padres, Su mejor amigo(a), Mi compañero(a) y sus amigos(as).** Be sure to collect information for each of the four sections. Choose the most interesting information from each section to report to the class.

REPASO

The verb *ser* (present tense)

	ser		
yo	**soy**	nosotros(as)	**somos**
tú	**eres**	vosotros(as)	**sois**
él		ellos	
ella	**es**	ellas	**son**
Ud.		Uds.	

1. When **ser** is followed by an adjective (such as a description of nationality), the adjective must agree in gender (masculine or feminine) and number (singular or plural) with the subject of **ser:**

   Él es **mexicano; ellos** son **mexicanos.**
   Ella es **argentina; ellas** son **argentinas.**

2. Remember that **ser** + **de** can be used to express origin.

   Él **es de** México, pero ellas **son de** España.
   Nosotros **somos** de los Estados Unidos, pero tú **eres de** Francia.

F. Replace the words in italics with those in parentheses and make the necessary changes.

1. *Él* es de Argentina. (ella / nosotros / yo / ellos / tú / vosotros)
2. ¿Es *ella* rusa? (él / Uds. / tú / ellos / vosotros)
3. *Ellos* no son de aquí. (ella / yo / Ud. / tú / ellas / vosotros)
4. *Ellas* son españolas, ¿verdad? (Uds. / él / tú / ellos / vosotros)

6

G. *Los delegados*

At a reception being held as part of the international student congress, you point out some of the delegates, indicate their nationalities, and tell what cities they are from. Follow the model.

Learning Strategy:
Reporting

Modelos: Justo Alarcón / Guadalajara, México
Allí está Justo. Él es mexicano. Es de Guadalajara.

Linda Martín y Claudia González / Buenos Aires, Argentina
Allí están Linda y Claudia. Ellas son argentinas.
Son de Buenos Aires.

1. Inge Schnepf / Munich, Alemania
2. Joel Rini / Roma, Italia
3. Julian Weiss y Ralph Withers / Manchester, Inglaterra
4. Janet Maguire y Lisa Mullins / Boston, los Estados Unidos
5. Rosa Domínguez / México, México
6. Tashi Yokoshura (f.) / Tokio, Japón
7. Anne-Marie Pelliser y Jean Firmin / Ginebra, Suiza
8. Ivan Medchenko / Moscú, Rusia

Situaciones

Saludos y presentaciones

a) **En la calle**
—Buenos días, señora.
—Buenos días, señor. ¿Cómo está?
—Muy bien, gracias. ¿Y Ud.?
—Bastante bien, gracias. ¿Va Ud. al centro?
—No, yo voy a casa.
—Bien. Hasta luego, señor.
—Hasta luego, señora.

b) **En el centro**
—¡Hola, María!
—¡Hola, Linda! ¿Qué tal?
—Muy bien. ¿Y tú?
—Así, así. Estoy muy cansada. Mira, quiero presentarte a mi amiga, Isabel.
—Mucho gusto, Isabel.
—Encantada, Linda.
—¿Uds. van al centro?
—Sí. ¿Tú también? ¿Vamos juntas?
—De acuerdo. Vamos.

7

Ex. G: pair work

Preparation, Ex. G: Have students review the **Tarjetas de vocabulario: Para hablar de tu origen y tu nacionalidad,** p. 11.

Suggestion, Ex. G: To facilitate the review of nationalities, have students scan the exercise to identify the countries mentioned. Then, as a group, make two lists: **País** and **Nacionalidad/origen.** Using the information in Ex. G, match the countries with their corresponding nationalities (using the masculine singular form).

Answers, Ex. G: 1. ...Ella es alemana. Es de... 2. ...Él es italiano. Es de... 3. ...Ellos son ingleses. Son de... 4. Ellas son estadounidenses. Son de... 5. ...Ella es mexicana. Es de... 6. ...Ella es japonesa. Es de... 7. ...Ellos son suizos. Son de... 8. ...Él es ruso. Es de...

Vocabulary Expansion

Challenge students to identify which **nacionalidad** is the same as the **lengua** of the country. Contrast those with the ones that are not. **Modelo: ES IGUAL: español/español; francés/ francés NO ES IGUAL: argentino/español; americano/inglés**

Support material, Situaciones: Teacher Tape

Suggestion, Situaciones: Dialogues should be done as listening comprehension. Before beginning, have students review the **Tarjetas de vocabulario: Para saludar** and **Para hacer una presentación,** p. 10.

Ex. H: pair work

Implementation, Ex. H: Have students support their conclusions.

Answers, Ex. H: 1. b   2. c
3. a   4. d

Follow-up, Ex. H: Choose different groups of students to read / role play the **Situaciones.**

c) En casa de Juan Pablo
—Mamá, papá, quisiera presentarles al Sr. Lima. Es el padre de Francisco.
—Ah, sí. Buenos días, señor. Mucho gusto en conocerle.
—Igualmente. Francisco me habló mucho de Ud. y de su esposa. Encantado, señora.
—Mucho gusto, señor.

d) En la calle
—¡Martín! ¡Martín!
—¡Hola, Patricio! ¿Qué tal?
—Muy, muy bien. ¿Y tú?
—Muy bien. ¿Vas a la escuela?
—Ahora no. Tengo que hacer un mandado.
—¡Cuídate! Hasta luego.
—De acuerdo. Chao.

¡Aquí te toca a ti!

H. Match the preceding four conversations with the following drawings.

1.

2.

3.

4.

I. *Presentaciones y saludos*   For each of the following tasks give one greeting or introduction that would be appropriate and another that would be inappropriate. Be prepared to explain your examples.

1. Greet your teacher, whom you have just met while downtown.
2. Introduce a new classmate to your teacher. Imagine that it is the first time they have met.
3. Greet a classmate in the street.
4. Introduce a friend to your parents.
5. Introduce a friend's mother or father to your parents.

Learning Strategies:
Using culturally appropriate language, supporting opinions

Actividad

J. *Yo soy...*   You are planning to study abroad as a foreign exchange student. You know that you will be introducing yourself to a lot of different people and you want to be able to tell some interesting things about yourself. Drawing upon what you have studied along with ideas from the **Tarjetas de vocabulario** on pages 10–11, put together an introduction telling about (1) who you are, (2) where you are from, (3) your home, (4) your family, (5) your favorite activities, and (6) your likes and dislikes.

Then, working with a partner, take turns introducing yourselves to each other. Take notes on your partner's introduction so that you can introduce him or her to others.

Cooperative Learning

Learning Strategies:
Selecting and organizing information, listening for details

9

Tarjetas de vocabulario

Para saludar

Buenos días, señor (señora, señorita).
¡Hola!
¿Cómo está? (¿Cómo estás?)
¿Qué tal?
Muy bien, gracias. ¿Y Ud.? (¿Y tú?)

Para identificarte

Yo me llamo…
Mi nombre (apellido) es…

Para despedirte

Cuídate. (Cuídese.) Hasta luego.
Adiós.
Chao.

Para hacer una presentación

Quiero presentarte a… (Quiero presentarle a…).
Quisiera presentarte a… (Quisiera presentarle a…).
Te presento a… (Le presento a…).
Mucho gusto.
Encantado(a).
Igualmente.

Para indicar dónde vives

Yo vivo en… (ciudad o país).
Yo vivo en un apartamento.
          una casa.

10

Para hablar de tus actividades

Me gusta (mucho) bailar.	No me gusta descansar.
cantar.	viajar.
ir de compras.	esquiar.
mirar la televisión.	aprender español.
nadar.	estudiar.
pasar tiempo con mis amigos.	correr.
tocar el piano.	leer.
la trompeta. la flauta.	asistir a la escuela.
la guitarra. el violín.	a un concierto.
comprar discos compactos.	
trabajar.	

También me gusta el arte.		No me gustan las películas.
la naturaleza.	la música clásica.	los animales.
la política.	el jazz.	las ciencias.
la escultura.	la pintura.	las matemáticas.
la historia.	el rock.	las lenguas.
la literatura.	el teatro.	los deportes.

Para hablar de tu origen y tu nacionalidad

Yo soy de… (ciudad o país).
Yo soy alemán (alemana).

americano(a).	italiano(a).
chino(a).	japonés (japonesa).
español(a).	mexicano(a).
francés (francesa).	ruso(a).
inglés (inglesa).	

Yo soy de origen alemán (español, americano, mexicano, argentino, etc.).

11

Presentation: Mi familia

After students listen with their books closed, have them open their books and read the selection quietly. Then have them draw a simple family tree for María and for Esteban, including under each family member basic information such as age or occupation. Have them include information about María and Esteban on the tree, referring to page 2 of the text.

A variation of this would be to have the students sketch the members of each family, giving brief, but accurate, information under each picture.

SEGUNDA ETAPA

Mi familia

Mi mamá murió hace cinco años. Mi padre, mi hermano y yo vivimos en un apartamento en Madrid. Mi padre tiene cuarenta y cuatro años y trabaja en un banco. Mi hermano tiene ocho años y asiste a la escuela primaria. Yo soy estudiante de la escuela secundaria. Mi padre tiene un coche —es un Seat. Yo tengo una bicicleta. Nosotros tenemos un televisor y un estéreo. También tenemos un perro; se llama Chomsky.

María

Mi padre es abogado. Él trabaja en Guadalajara. Mi mamá no trabaja fuera de casa. Ella cuida a mi hermana que tiene tres años. Mis otras dos hermanas y yo somos estudiantes del Colegio Juárez. Mi hermano tiene veinticinco años y está casado. Él vive en la ciudad de México.

Mis padres tienen dos coches. Yo tengo una motocicleta. En casa nosotros tenemos una computadora y un vídeo. Mis hermanas y yo miramos la televisión todas las noches. También tenemos dos gatos.

Esteban

12

Etapa Support Materials

Workbook: pp. 9–16
Transparency: #1
Listening Activity masters: p. 1
Tapescript: p. 1
Teacher Tape

Quiz: Testing Program, p. 4
Chapter Test: Testing Program, p. 8

Support material, Mi familia:
Teacher Tape

Comprensión

A. *¿Quiénes son?*   Based on the comments made by María and Esteban on page 12, identify the following people or animals. Follow the model.

Learning Strategies:

Making associations, reporting

 Modelo: *Es la hermana de Esteban.*

1.   2.   3.

4.   5.   6.

REPASO

The verb tener *(present tense)*

tener			
yo	**tengo**	nosotros(as)	**tenemos**
tú	**tienes**	vosotros(as)	**tenéis**
él		ellos	
ella	**tiene**	ellas	**tienen**
Ud.		Uds.	

Ex. A: pair work

writing

Suggestion, Ex. A: Have students work in pairs to complete Ex. A. Go over the answers with the entire class.

Answers, Ex. A: 1. Es el perro de María. (Es Chomsky, el perro de María.)   2. Es María. 3. Es Esteban con sus hermanas. 4. Son los gatos de Esteban. 5. Es el hermano de María. 6. Es Esteban.

B. Replace the words in italics with those in parentheses and make the necessary changes.

1. *Ella* tiene un perro y dos gatos. (ellos / nosotros / Uds. / yo / él)
2. ¿Tienen *ellos* un coche? (tú / Ud. / Uds. / ellas / ella / vosotras)
3. *Él* no tiene un hermano. (ella / yo / Ud. / nosotras / ellos / tú)

REPASO

Possessive adjectives

Possessive adjectives in Spanish agree with the object possessed (not with the person who is the possessor). Here are the forms of the possessive adjectives:

Subject	Possessive adjective	English equivalent
yo	mi, mis	*my*
tú	tu, tus	*your*
él, ella, Ud.	su, sus	*his, her, your*
nosotros(as)	nuestro, nuestra, nuestros, nuestras	*our*
ellos, ellas, Uds.	su, sus	*their, your*

C. Replace the words in italics with those in parentheses and make the necessary changes.

1. Es mi *libro*. (lápiz / cintas / bolígrafo / llaves)
2. ¿Son tus *discos compactos*? (calculadora / amigas / cuadernos / estéreo)
3. Es nuestro *amigo*. (llaves / libros / casa / apartamento)
4. No es su *casa*. (libros / mochilas / cámara / apartamento)

¿Recuerdan?

Question words may be used to ask for specific information. Among the question words you know are:

dónde	**¿Dónde** vive tu amigo?	**quién**	**¿Quién** vive en la casa blanca?
cuántos	**¿Cuántos** libros hay en la mesa?	**qué**	**¿Qué** estudias?
cuántas	**¿Cuántas** muchachas hay en la clase?	**por qué**	**¿Por qué** comes pizza?

D. *La curiosidad* Work in pairs to find out about each other's families. Interview your partner to find out (1) how many people there are in the family and (2) whether he or she has brothers or sisters. If so, find out (3) their names, (4) their ages, and (5) what sports or activities they like. (6) Ask if the family has a dog or cat. If the answer is yes, find out (7) its name and (8) how old it is. (9) Ask if your partner's parents work. If they do, (10) find out where. As you exchange information, note similarities and differences in your families. Take notes on the information you collect, so that you can report on it later.

Use the following expressions in your interview:
**¿Cuántas personas hay en tu familia? ¿Cómo se llama(n)... ?
¿Cuántos años tiene(n)... ? ¿Qué deportes le gustan a tu hermana?
¿Dónde trabaja(n)... ?**

Learning Strategies:

Asking for and providing personal information, taking notes

Presentaciones

La familia

a) Yo me llamo Cristina Sáenz. Tengo una familia tradicional. Vivo con mis padres y mi hermano Raúl.

b) Me llamo Enrique Cuervo. Mi familia no es tradicional. Hace cinco años que mis padres se divorciaron. Mi madre se casó otra vez y vivo con mi madre, mi padrastro y su hijo.

c) Mi nombre es Pablo González. Soy de una familia grande. Vivo con mis padres. Tengo dos hermanos y cuatro hermanas. Mis abuelos, los padres de mi madre, también viven con nosotros.

d) Mi nombre es Catarina Landa. Soy hija única, es decir, yo no tengo hermanos. Vivo con mis padres.

¡Aquí te toca a ti!

E. *¿La familia de quién?* Match the preceding four descriptions with the following family portraits.

Critical Thinking Strategy:

Drawing conclusions

1.
2.
3.
4.

Ex. D: pair work

✎ writing

Suggestion, Ex. D: Have students consult the **Tarjetas de vocabulario**, p. 17, for this exercise.

Follow-up, Ex. D: In a follow-up discussion, have students supply information for their partner's family. Designate a secretary to write the information on the board. Poll the class to determine the average size of families, the average number of children, the average age of the children, and the ratio of cats to dogs among the pets. Have volunteers do the addition and the division in Spanish to figure the statistics.

More-prepared students, Ex. D: As an alternative, have more-prepared students do the polling and the figuring of classroom statistics.

Support material, Presentaciones: Teacher Tape 🎧

Suggestion, Presentaciones: After doing the **Presentaciones** as a listening activity, review the **Tarjetas de vocabulario: Para hablar de tu familia,** p. 17. Then assign Ex. E.

Support material, Ex. E: Transparency #1

Answers, Ex. E: 1. d   2. c
3. b   4. a

Ex. F: pair work

Preparation, Ex. F: Review the **Tarjetas de vocabulario: Para hablar de tus posesiones,** p. 17.

Suggestion, Ex. F: Have students work in pairs, taking notes on the family members of their partner. Then have them share three pertinent pieces of information with the class.

More-prepared students, Ex. F: Encourage more-prepared students to use their notes to draw their partner's family tree, or have them write up their notes as a report to be read to the class. In the latter case, you may have them edit each other's work first.

Ex. G: pair work

Preparation, Ex. G: Review the **Tarjetas de vocabulario: Para hablar de tu familia,** p. 17.

Variation, Ex. G: Have students bring in photographs of friends or family members, identifying and giving some information about them. Invite other students to ask questions to elicit more complete information about each photo. Students may work in pairs or groups of four for this activity. Have them report back on their findings.

More-prepared students, Ex. G: Have more-prepared students use their notes to draw their partner's family tree or give a summary description to the class. You may prefer to have them use their notes to write a report on their partner's family to be read to the class, after they edit each other's work.

Cooperative Learning

Learning Strategies:

Selecting information, reporting based on personal knowledge

Learning Strategies:

Interviewing, organizing information

Actividades

F. Mi amigo(a) Tell your partner about one of your friends. (1) Describe his or her family; tell (2) where he or she lives, (3) whether he or she lives in a house or an apartment. Tell about (4) some of his or her favorite activities and (5) some favorite possessions. (6) Finally, talk about what the two of you like to do together.

G. Mi familia Working with a partner, interview each other to do a profile of your families. Divide your interview into three sections: (1) First, find out about the immediate family. Get the names, ages, and relationship to your partner of each member of the household. (2) Next ask about his or her grandparents, aunts, uncles, cousins. (3) Ask about your partner's most interesting relatives. Try to find out what makes these relatives particularly interesting. Take notes so that you can give a summary description of your partner's family.

16

Tarjetas de vocabulario

Para hablar de tu familia

Yo soy de una familia pequeña.
            grande.
            tradicional.
Yo no soy de una familia tradicional.

Del lado de mi padre (mi madre),
  yo tengo un abuelo.
        una abuela.
        un tío.
        una tía.
        un primo.
        una prima.

Yo tengo padre.
        madre.
        un padrastro
        (stepfather).

una madrastra
   (stepmother).
un hermano.
una hermana.

Mi padre (mi madre) se llama…
Mi hermano(a) está casado(a).
                  divorciado(a).
Mi abuelo(a) está muerto(a).
Mi tío y mi tía tienen una hija.
                un hijo.
                no tienen hijos.

Para hablar de tu edad

¿Cuántos años tienes?
Yo tengo… años.

Para hablar de tus posesiones

Cuando voy a la escuela,
  llevo un bolígrafo.
      un borrador.
      una cartera.
      un cuaderno.
      una calculadora.
      un lápiz.

un libro.
una llave.
una mochila.
un portafolio.
un sacapuntas.

Voy al centro en coche.
          en bicicleta.
          en motocicleta.

En mi cuarto, yo tengo una alfombra.
        una cama.
        una cinta.
        una cómoda.
        una computadora.
        un disco compacto.
        un escritorio.

un estéreo.
una grabadora.
una máquina
  de escribir.
una planta.
un póster.

un radio
  despertador
una silla.
un televisor.
un vídeo.

17

Spanish speakers, Tarjetas de vocabulario:
Point out the words that have the problematic spelling combinations that were highlighted on p. 19 of "To the Teacher" in the Teacher's Edition. You may want to encourage students to keep a spelling notebook with categories such as: **Palabras con *ll*, Palabras con *v*, Palabras con *b***, etc. Another category might be headed **Así lo digo yo** for students to work on the spelling of words and expressions that they already know that might be variations of what has been presented in this book.

Chapter Objectives

Functions: Describing and locating various places in a town or city

Context: Giving and receiving information about places in a city or town; giving and understanding directions

Accuracy: Formal and informal commands; the verbs **ir, estar, pensar, querer,** and **preferir**

Cultural Context

Madrid, the capital of Spain (whose residents are called **madrileños**), has many places of historical and cultural interest. One of these is the **Puerta de Alcalá,** located in the **Plaza de Independencia.** The **Puerta de Alcalá** is a famous gate, which at one time marked a boundary of the city. The street leading to the **Puerta de Alcalá** runs from the **Puerta del Sol** and continues toward the city **Alcalá de Henares.**

CAPÍTULO

B

¿ADÓNDE VAMOS?

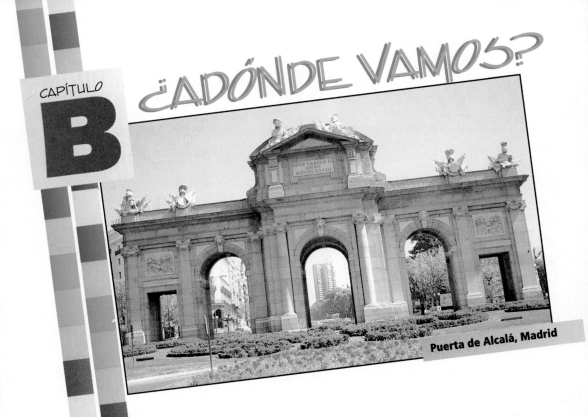

Puerta de Alcalá, Madrid

Objectives:

>>> **R**eview words and expressions needed to talk about your town or city.

>>> **R**eview formal and informal commands.

>>> **R**eview the verbs **ir, estar, pensar, querer,** and **preferir.**

>>> **P**ractice describing where places are located.

Strategies:

>>> **R**eading a map

>>> **D**escribing spatial relationships

>>> **P**olling

>>> **M**aking associations

>>> **C**omparing and contrasting

18

Video/Laserdisc

Preliminary Chapter B Video Program and Video Guide

PRIMERA ETAPA

Mi ciudad

Yo soy de Madrid, la capital de España. Madrid tiene aproximadamente tres millones de habitantes. Está situada en el centro del país. La parte central de la ciudad es la parte antigua. Allí está la Plaza Mayor, la Iglesia de San Pedro y el Palacio Real. Esta parte antigua está rodeada de barrios residenciales con edificios modernos y avenidas anchas. La avenida más animada es la Gran Vía. Allí hay muchos bancos, tiendas, restaurantes, hoteles, discotecas y cines.

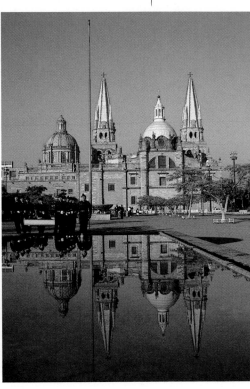

Yo soy de Guadalajara, una ciudad donde viven más de 1.800.000 habitantes. Es la segunda ciudad más grande de México. En el centro de esta linda ciudad hay cuatro plazas que forman una cruz. Éstas son: la Plaza de los Laureles, la Plaza de Armas, la Plaza de los Hijos Ilustres y la Plaza de la Liberación. En el centro de estas plazas está nuestra hermosa catedral. Cerca de aquí también están el Museo Regional de Guadalajara y el Palacio de Gobierno donde hay unos murales que pintó el artista mexicano José Clemente Orozco. Generalmente voy al centro para ir de compras o para visitar a amigos.

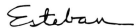

19

Presentation: Mi ciudad

Present using the Teacher Tape. Use Ex. A on p. 20 as a comprehension check.

Cultural Observation

Working as a class, students should list the places mentioned in the reading under two categories, **similar** and **differente,** comparing them to a chosen U.S. city or town. Focus especially on the cultural difference between the American and Hispanic connotations of a plaza.

Etapa Support Materials

Workbook: **pp. 17–24**
Critical Thinking masters: **Chapter B, primera etapa, activity J**
Tapescript: **p. 12**
Transparency: **#2**

Teacher Tape
Quiz: **Testing Program, p. 13**

Support material, **Mi ciudad:**
Teacher Tape

//-//-//-//-//-//-//-//

//-//-//-//-//-//-//-//

Comprensión

A. Name three major sights in Madrid and three major sights in Guadalajara. Tell which you would most like to visit. Be able to explain why.

B. Answer the following questions about the city or town where you live.

1. ¿Es tu ciudad (pueblo) grande (bastante grande, pequeña, muy pequeña)?
2. ¿Cuántos habitantes tiene?
3. ¿Está en el norte (el sur, el este, el oeste, el centro) de los Estados Unidos?
4. ¿Está cerca de una ciudad grande? ¿A cuántas millas está de esta ciudad?

C. For each of the following places listed, (1) tell whether or not there is such a place in your city or town; (2) tell whether you like to go there; (3) name an activity that you associate with each place.

Lugares en la ciudad

un hotel	una iglesia	un teatro	una estación de trenes
un restaurante	un estadio	una biblioteca	un aeropuerto
de servicio	una piscina	una tienda de música	un cine
rápido	una escuela	una panadería	una oficina de
un café	un museo	un supermercado	correos

REPASO

The verb *ir* (present tense)

ir

yo	**voy**	nosotros(as)	**vamos**
tú	**vas**	vosotros(as)	**vais**
él		ellos	
ella	**va**	ellas	**van**
Ud.		Uds.	

The verb **ir** is often used with adverbs such as **siempre, frecuentemente, de vez en cuando, a veces, raramente,** and **nunca.**

¿Recuerdan?

The preposition **a** combines with the article **el** to form **al.** There is no contraction between **a** and the articles **la, las,** and **los.**

Yo voy **al** banco y después voy **a la** tienda de música.
Nosotros vamos **a la** escuela y después vamos **al** centro.

D. ¿Adónde vas?   From the list in Activity C on page 20, choose four places that you enjoy. Then, following the model, interview at least four of your classmates to find out how often they go to these places. Make a chart like the one below to record their responses.

When you have completed your interviews, assign a value to each response: **nunca = 0, rara vez = 1, de vez en cuando = 2, frecuentemente = 3.** For each place on your list, add up the numbers to see which are most frequented by your classmates.

Modelo: **Estudiante 1:** *¿Tú vas frecuentemente al estadio?*
             Estudiante 2: *Sí, voy al estadio frecuentemente.*   o:
                               De vez en cuando voy al estadio.   o:
                               No, yo voy rara vez al estadio.   o:
                               No, nunca voy al estadio. No me gustan los deportes.

Lugares	Catarina	Roberto	Julia	Antonio
estadio	rara vez	de vez en cuando		
cine	frecuentemente	frecuentemente		
biblioteca	de vez en cuando	frecuentemente		
tienda de música	nunca	rara vez		

//.//.//.//.//.//.//.//.//.//

Cooperative Learning

Learning Strategies:

Polling, recording information on a chart, tallying results of a poll

E. ¿Y tú?   For each of the places listed, indicate (1) whether you like to go there, (2) how often you go, and (3) with whom you hope to go next time.

Modelo: a la biblioteca
            Me gusta bastante bien ir a la biblioteca.
            Voy de vez en cuando.
            La próxima vez espero ir con mi madre.

1. al cine   3. al museo   5. al aeropuerto   7. al teatro
2. al centro   4. a la piscina   6. al estadio   8. a la iglesia

//.//.//.//.//.//.//.//.//.//

Critical Thinking Strategy:

Evaluating

21

Ex. D: groups of four or more

writing

Preparation, Ex. D: Have students go over the **Tarjetas de vocabulario: Para indicar adonde vas,** p. 27.

Critical Thinking

After completing Ex. D orally, have the students look again at each sentence in the **Modelo** to focus on the position of the adverb in the sentence. Challenge them to come up with a rule governing the placement of the adverb. Lead them to conclude that the adverbs (with the exception of **nunca,** which as a negative must precede the verb) may be placed virtually anywhere; that is, adverbs are the most flexible part of speech of the language.

Ex. E: pair work

Implementation, Ex. E: Present alternative structures (**esperar** + inf. and **ir + a** + inf.) in the **¿Recuerdan?** section on p. 22 before doing this exercise. When students have prepared their responses, have them work in small groups to compare which places they like best, who goes where most often, and if there is some agreement about their favorite companions for certain places. Ask them to notice whether their favorite places are the same as the ones they visit most often. Have them report other students' information back to the class as a check.

More-prepared students, Ex. E: Have more-prepared students take notes on their partners' responses and report them back to the class.

¿Recuerdan?

The phrase **ir + a** + *infinitive* is used to indicate the immediate future—that is, what *is going to happen soon:*

Esta noche yo **voy a hablar** con Linda.
Mis padres **no van a comer** en un restaurante mañana.
El domingo Marirrosa **va a cenar** con nosotros.

Esperar + *infinitive* may also be used to talk about the immediate future:

Yo **espero ir** al centro esta tarde.
Mi amigo y yo **esperamos caminar** al centro mañana.

Learning Strategy:

Reporting based on visual information

F. Este fin de semana Miguel is talking to his sister Verónica about what she and her friends are planning to do this weekend. Based on the drawings below and on page 23, give Verónica's answers to her brother's questions.

Modelo: ¿Va a estudiar Miguel?
No, él va a mirar la tele.

1. ¿Va a jugar al fútbol Jorge?   **2.** ¿Va a cenar en casa Isabel?   **3.** ¿Va a jugar al básquetbol Federico?

4. ¿Va a tocar la trompeta Juan?

5. Verónica, ¿vas a trabajar en la computadora?

6. ¿Van a asistir al concierto Micaela y Teresa?

REPASO

The verb *estar* (present tense)

estar

yo	**estoy**	nosotros(as)	**estamos**
tú	**estás**	vosotros(as)	**estáis**
él		ellos	
ella	**está**	ellas	**están**
Ud.		Uds.	

The verb **estar** is used in Spanish to express the location of something or someone.

—¿Dónde **está** Boston?   —¿Dónde **están** Marcos y Elena?
—Boston **está** en Massachusetts.   —**Están** en la biblioteca.

—¿Dónde **está** el restaurante?
—**Está** detrás de la biblioteca.

¿Recuerdan?

The preposition **de** combines with the article **el** to form **del**. There is no contraction between **de** and the articles **la, las,** and **los.**

El hotel está al lado **del** banco.
El restaurante está cerca **de la** iglesia.

23

G. *En Guadalajara*   Esteban is trying to help you find your way around Guadalajara. Using the map below, play the role of Esteban and precisely describe the location of the following places.

1. Mercado Libertad
2. Plaza Tapatía
3. Antigua Universidad
4. Parque Morelos

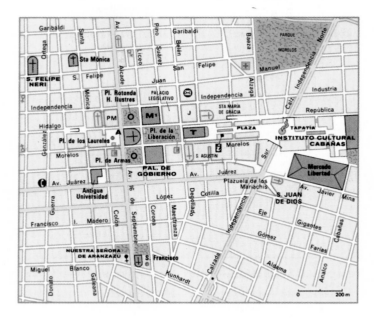

Situaciones

¿Dónde está…?

a) **En el centro**
—Perdón, señora. ¿Hay un banco cerca de aquí?
—Sí, señor, en la esquina de la Calle Galdós y la Avenida Meléndez.
—Muchas gracias, señora.
—De nada, señor.

b) **En la calle**
—¿Vas a la fiesta en casa de María esta noche?
—Sí, pero no sé dónde vive. ¿Sabes tú? Su casa está cerca del hospital en la Calle Chapultepec, ¿no?

—Sí, está en la Calle Chapultepec, pero no está cerca del hospital. Tienes que caminar por la Calle Chapultepec hasta el parque. Su casa está allí, cerca de la panadería.

c) En la esquina
—Perdón, señor. ¿Está el Hotel Juárez cerca de aquí?
—No, señora. Está al otro lado de la ciudad. Ud. tiene que tomar el autobús número 28 y bajar en la Plaza Juárez. Allí, al otro lado de la plaza, está el Hotel Juárez. Hay una estatua del Presidente Juárez delante del hotel.

d) Delante del banco
—¿Necesita otra cosa?
—Sí. Quisiera comprar un periódico.
—Bueno. Hay un quiosco en la Calle Colón, justo al lado del banco.
—Muy bien. Gracias.

¡Aquí te toca a ti!

H. Match the preceding conversations with the following drawings.

//-//-//-//-//-//-//-//-//
Critical Thinking Strategy:

Drawing conclusions

1.

2.

3.

4.

25

Follow-up, Ex. H: As a reinforcing listening activity, have students listen to the dialogue again with their books closed and quickly identify (1) what the person is looking for and (2) where it is.

Variation, Ex. H: The **Situaciones** may also be used as dictation exercises. Have the students close their books and listen one time. Replay the tape while students write down what they hear. Play the tape or segment again for final adjustments. Have different students write different segments on the board and have all students check their work against the written text with books open.

Answers, Ex. H: 1. d   2. a   3. b   4. c

Ex. I: pair work

role play

Implementation, Ex. I: You may want to brainstorm a list of five or six places your students commonly frequent and put these on the board as a guide for the paired conversation. When students finish, have various pairs present their question/answer dialogues before the whole class. Elicit variations on each dialogue.

Ex. J: pair work

Suggestion, Ex. J: Before having the students do this exercise, use the neighborhood around the school as an example. Draw a sample blank map on the board and model the exercise for the students, letting them tell you street names and writing in the names of places as you describe them.

Implementation, Ex. J: Remind students to keep their hands in their laps while they describe places on their maps in order to avoid the temptation to point.

Ex. K: pair work

writing

Suggestion, Ex. K: Have pairs of students research important cities in your state or region to use in their descriptions. You may want to work through these with them to encourage students to rely on the vocabulary and structures in the models. For each point in the assignment, have students identify corresponding components in the models (p. 19). Whenever possible, point out alternate ways of communicating the same information.

//-//-//-//-//-//-//-//
Learning Strategies:
Listing, making associations, describing spatial relationships

I. *Un peruano en...* Work with a partner. One of you will play the role of a Peruvian foreign exchange student who has just arrived in your city or town and who wants tips on places to go. The exchange student begins by making a list of at least four favorite activities. Examples include: **comer pizza, comprar discos compactos, alquilar vídeos, comprar libros, tomar refrescos, correr, ver un partido de fútbol, ver una película.** The exchange student asks where to go for each activity. The other student will think of an appropriate place for each activity and describe where the place is.

Actividades

//-//-//-//-//-//-//-//
Cooperative Learning
Learning Strategies:
Describing spatial relationships, active listening, verifying

J. *Tu pueblo o ciudad* Draw a map of the section of city or town where you live. Show—but don't label—five or six places where you or your family go from time to time and show the streets around them (at least five different streets). Label one of the streets. When you have completed your map, give it to your partner, who will label the streets and places as you describe them. Your partner can ask you if he or she is getting something right (e.g., **¿Cómo eso? / ¿Está aquí el cine Apollo? / ¿Está a la derecha o a la izquierda?**), and you can tell him or her there is a mistake (e.g., **No, el banco está más lejos de la farmacia. / No, la calle Lincoln está en frente de la piscina.**), but don't offer to help by pointing.

//-//-//-//-//-//-//-//
Learning Strategy:
Selecting and organizing information

K. *Otro pueblo o ciudad* Choose a town or city other than your own (for example, where you used to live or the town where your grandparents live). Briefly describe this town or city, mentioning (1) population, (2) what part of the state it is located in, (3) whether it is large or small, (4) what the downtown area is like (modern, old, busy), (5) some features that give it its character (buildings, monuments). Use the descriptions of Madrid and Guadalajara given by María and Esteban on page 19 as models.

26

For example, **Madrid** *tiene* **(...) habitantes** versus **Guadalajara, una ciudad donde** *viven* **(...) habitantes,** or **Guadalajara tiene** *más de* **1.800.000 habitantes** versus **Madrid tiene** *aproximadamente* **3.000.000 de habitantes.**

Tarjetas de vocabulario

Para indicar adonde vas

Yo voy a (al, a la)… frecuentemente.
　　　　　　　　　rara vez.
　　　　　　　　　de vez en cuando.
A veces voy a (al, a la)…
Nunca

Para localizar

Está al final de…　　　　en…
　　　al lado de…　　　　en frente de…
　　　cerca de…　　　　　en la esquina de… y…
　　　delante de…　　　　entre… y…
　　　detrás de…　　　　 lejos de…

Para hablar de tu ciudad

Mi ciudad es (muy, bastante) grande.
　　　　　　　　　　　　　pequeña.
Está situada en el norte de los Estados Unidos.
　　　　　　el sur　　 el este
　　　　　　el oeste　 el centro
En mi ciudad hay un aeropuerto.　　una farmacia.　　un parque.
　　　　　　　un banco.　　　　　una iglesia.　　　un restaurante.
　　　　　　　una biblioteca.　　　un hospital.　　　un estadio.
　　　　　　　una catedral.　　　　un hotel.　　　　un teatro.
　　　　　　　una discoteca.　　　 una librería.　　　una universidad.
　　　　　　　una escuela.　　　　un museo.

27

Spanish speakers, Tarjetas de vocabulario:
Point out the words that have the problematic spelling combinations that were highlighted on p. 19 of "To the Teacher" in the Teacher's Edition. You may want to encourage students to keep a spelling notebook with categories such as: **Palabras con *ll*, Palabras con *v*, Palabras con *b*,** etc. Another category might be headed **Así lo digo yo** for students to work on the spelling of words and expressions that they already know that might be variations of what has been presented in this book.

SEGUNDA ETAPA

Vamos al centro

Yo vivo cerca de la universidad de Madrid. Cuando quiero ir al centro, generalmente tomo el metro. Es muy fácil. Camino a la estación Moncloa que no está lejos de nuestro apartamento. Normalmente compro un billete de 10 viajes que cuesta 625 pesetas. Entonces tomo la dirección Legazpi y en 15 minutos estoy en Sol. Aquí es donde bajo si voy al Corte Inglés para ir de compras. O si quiero dar un paseo por el Parque del Retiro, cambio de trenes en Sol, dirección Ventas, y bajo en la estación Retiro.

María

Nuestra casa está cerca del Estadio Jalisco en la ciudad de Guadalajara. La escuela donde soy estudiante está en el centro. Para ir allí, tomo un autobús. Tarda media hora para llegar a la escuela. A veces, cuando tiene tiempo, mi papá nos lleva a la escuela en su coche. En esos días, tarda solamente cinco minutos para llegar de nuestra casa a la escuela. Durante el fin de semana, nos gusta dar paseos a pie por la ciudad.

Esteban

Comprensión

//-//-//-//-//-//-//-//-//
Learning Strategies:

Reading a map, giving directions

A. ¡Vamos en el metro! You have been staying in Madrid for some time and know the subway system very well. A friend of yours arrives from the U.S. and needs to go to the places listed on page 29. Explain to him or her how to get to these places on the **metro.** Your friend is staying near the **Plaza Castilla** station.

28

Presentation: Vamos al centro

Present using the Teacher Tape. Ask some comprehension questions before proceeding to Ex. A.

Possible questions,
Vamos al centro: 1. How does Esteban usually get to school —by bus, by car, or on foot? 2. Does it cost much to take the **metro** in Madrid? For María, how much does each trip cost? 3. María and Esteban mention one activity that they both like. What is it? 4. In your opinion, who can get to their destination more quickly, María or Esteban? Why?

1. **¿Cómo llega Esteban a la escuela normalmente—en autobús, en coche o a pie?** 2. **¿Cuesta mucho dinero tomar el metro en Madrid? Para María, ¿cuánto cuesta cada viaje? 3. María y Esteban mencionan una actividad que a los dos les gusta hacer. ¿Cuál es esta actividad? 4. En tu opinión, ¿quién puede llegar mas rápidamente a su destino—María o Esteban? ¿Por qué?**

Support material, Ex. A:
Transparency #3

Ex. A: pair work

Etapa Support Materials

Workbook: pp. 25–33
Transparencies: #3, #4, #5, #6
Listening Activity masters: p. 10
Teacher Tape

Quiz: Testing Program, p. 15

Chapter Test: Testing Program, p. 18

Support material, Vamos al centro:
Teacher Tape

Modelo: Museo del Prado (Atocha)
Para ir al Museo del Prado, tomas la dirección Portazgo.
Bajas en la estación Atocha.

1. Parque del Retiro   2. Plaza de España   3. Moncloa

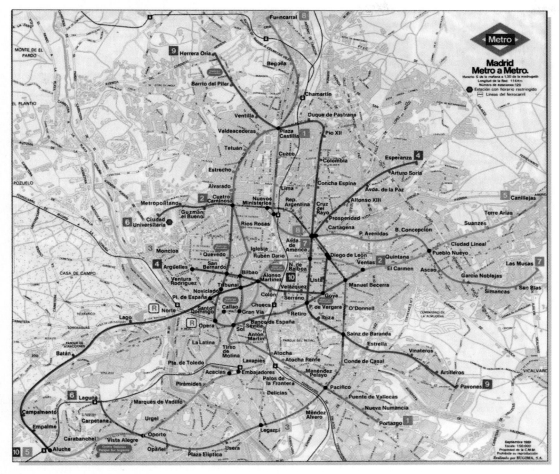

Ex. B: writing

Preparation, Ex. B: Have students review the **Tarjetas de vocabulario: Para indicar cómo vamos,** p. 38.

Presentation: Repaso

Remind students that to express *on* with the days of the week, they must use the definite article, never the preposition **en: El viernes voy a Chicago. Los sábados voy al centro.**

Now a family from Mexico is visiting Madrid. They are interested in seeing some of the sights. Using the map on page 29, explain to this family how to get to the following places. Remember to use **Uds.** when talking to the whole family. They are staying near the **Plaza del Cuzco.**

4. Puerta del Sol 　　　　　　 5. Ciudad Universitaria

Learning Strategy:

Providing personal information

B. ¿Y tú? Answer these questions about yourself and your family.

1. ¿Cómo vas a la escuela? ¿Vas a pie? ¿en el coche de tus padres? ¿Vas en tu bicicleta? ¿en el autobús?
2. ¿Tienen tus padres un coche? ¿Qué tipo de coche? ¿Van al trabajo en el coche? Si no van al trabajo en el coche, ¿cómo van?
3. ¿Tienes una bicicleta? ¿Adónde vas en tu bicicleta? ¿a la escuela? ¿al centro?
4. Cuando vas a casa de tus abuelos, ¿cómo vas? ¿a pie? ¿en coche? ¿Vas en tren? ¿en avión?

REPASO

Placing events in time

Days of the week

lunes martes miércoles jueves viernes sábado domingo

Remember that the definite article is often used with the days of the week:

el lunes = Monday, the upcoming Monday
los lunes = on Mondays, indicates a customary action on a specific day of the week

El viernes voy a una fiesta en casa de Jaime.
Los lunes voy a la escuela.

Time of day

Son las dos. 　　　　　　 Son las dos y diez. 　　　　　　 Son las dos y cuarto.

Son las dos y media. **Son las tres menos veinte.** **Son las tres menos cuarto.**

Twelve o'clock noon is **mediodía;** twelve o'clock midnight is **medianoche.** To indicate a.m. and p.m. with other times, add **de la mañana, de la tarde,** or **de la noche.**

C. ¿Dónde está Patricio?   Study the daily schedule of Patricio Fernández below; then answer the questions.

	lunes	martes	miércoles	jueves	viernes	sábado
9:30–10:25	historia	historia		historia	historia	historia
10:40–11:35	francés	francés	no	el gimnasio	francés	
11:40–12:35	matemáticas	arte	hay	el gimnasio	matemáticas	matemáticas
2:00–2:55	inglés	inglés	clases	inglés	inglés	inglés
3:00–3:55	biología	biología		biología	arte	
4:10–5:05	español	español		español	español	

1. ¿Qué días tiene Patricio su clase de francés?
2. ¿Qué días tiene su clase de matemáticas?
3. ¿Qué clases tiene Patricio por la tarde?
4. ¿A qué hora es su clase de biología?
5. ¿A qué hora es su clase de francés?
6. ¿Dónde está Patricio a las 11:00 de la mañana el jueves?
7. ¿A qué hora llega a la escuela si de costumbre él llega 15 minutos antes de su primera clase?
8. De costumbre, ¿a qué hora almuerza Patricio?

Learning Strategy:

Reading a schedule

31

Support material, Ex. C:
Transparency #4

Ex. C: writing

Cooperative Learning

Cooperative Pairs, Ex. C

- Put students into heterogeneous teams of four. Tell each group to divide into pairs.
- Explain that each pair of partners will take turns asking each other the questions listed. One student will answer, while the partner coaches or encourages as needed. Then they switch roles.
- Have each pair do two questions, one apiece. Then tell them to check with the other pair in their team to make sure their answers agree. If the answers do not agree, the group needs to figure out what the correct answer is before continuing. Students may check with another team if needed.
- Have students continue in the same manner until they have finished all the questions.
- To check for individual accountability, call on students at random to answer questions about Patricio's schedule.

Answers, Ex. C: 1. el lunes, el martes, el viernes   2. el lunes, el viernes, el sábado   3. inglés, biología, español, arte   4. a las tres   5. a las once menos veinte   6. en el estadio   7. a las nueve y cuarto (quince)   8. entre la una menos veinticinco y las dos de la tarde

Ex. D: pair work

Suggestion, Ex. D: Before students begin this exercise, show them an example of a page from an agenda on the board. Tell them to organize their notes in this manner as their partner describes her or his typical day.

Follow-up, Ex. D: Poll students to find the earliest and latest times for typical activities. Write these on the board and have the class determine the average times.

Presentation: Repaso

You may want to review the construction verb + infinitive with these verbs: **quiero + hablar, pienso + comer, prefiero + ir.**

Ex. E: writing

Answers, Ex. E: 1. Juan no quiere ir / Tú no quieres ir / Elena y Marta no quieren ir / Marirrosa y yo no queremos ir / Uds. no quieren ir / Vosotros no queréis ir 2. prefieres hacer tú / prefiere hacer Julián / prefieren hacer Ester y Roberto / prefieren hacer ellas / prefiere hacer Ud. / preferís hacer vosotros 3. Nosotros no pensamos ir / Tú no piensas ir / Marisol no piensa ir / Mari y Esteban no piensan ir / Uds. no piensan ir / Vosotras no pensáis ir

Cooperative Learning

Learning Strategies:

Providing personal information, active listening, organizing notes on a chart

Critical Thinking Strategy:

Comparing and contrasting

D. ¿Cómo pasas el tiempo?

Working in pairs, take turns describing your typical school day to your partner. Tell about when you arrive at school, your morning classes, when you have lunch, your afternoon classes, what time you leave school, when you get home. As your partner speaks, make a schedule of his or her day. When you have both schedules in hand, compare to see who arrives earlier, has lunch later, etc. Begin your description: **De costumbre, yo llego a la escuela a...**

REPASO

The verbs *querer, pensar,* and *preferir (present tense)*

yo	quiero pienso prefiero	nosotros(as)	queremos pensamos preferimos
tú	quieres piensas prefieres	vosotros(as)	queréis pensáis preferís
él ella Ud.	quiere piensa prefiere	ellos ellas Uds.	quieren piensan prefieren

Remember that the **e** of the stem of these verbs changes to **ie** in all verb forms except the **nosotros** and **vosotros** forms.

E. Replace the words in italics with those in parentheses and make the necessary changes.

1. *Yo* no quiero ir al centro ahora. (Juan / tú / Elena y Marta / Marirrosa y yo / Uds. / vosotros)
2. ¿Qué prefieren hacer *Uds.* esta noche? (tú / Julián / Ester y Roberto / ellas / Ud. / vosotros)
3. *Ella* no piensa ir a España el año próximo. (nosotros / tú / Marisol / Mari y Esteban / Uds. / vosotras)

32

REPASO

Formal commands

1. Formal commands in Spanish are created by dropping the **-o** of the **yo** form of the verb and adding an **-e** or an **-en** for **-ar** verbs and an **-a** or an **-an** for **-er** and **-ir** verbs.

cantar	comer	escribir
cant**o**	com**o**	escrib**o**
cant**e**	com**a**	escrib**a**
cant**en**	com**an**	escrib**an**

2. Verbs ending in **-car** change the **c** to **qu**. Those ending in **-gar** change the **g** to **gu**. Those ending in **-zar** change the **z** to **c**.

buscar	llegar	cruzar
bus**c**o	lle**g**o	cru**z**o
bus**que**	lle**gue**	cru**ce**
bus**quen**	lle**guen**	cru**cen**

3. Some other common verbs with irregular formal commands are:

ir	vaya	vayan
ser	sea	sean

F. Give both the singular and plural formal command forms for the following verbs.

1. estudiar
2. bailar
3. aprender español
4. correr 20 minutos
5. doblar a la izquierda
6. tener paciencia
7. no comer mucho
8. leer todos los días
9. cruzar la calle
10. buscar las llaves

REPASO

Informal commands

1. The informal command is used to address anyone whom you know well, such as friends and family members, and to address children. Unlike formal commands, the informal command has one form for the affirmative and a different form for the negative.

Cultural Expansion

An easy rule of thumb for students to remember is that the informal is used whenever one speaks to another on a first-name basis.

Language Enrichment

If students notice the spelling change and ask about it, point out that most spelling changes occur to maintain the original consonant sound of the infinitive. Therefore, the verb **buscar,** for example, will undergo a change only in the formal **busque** to maintain the original [k] sound; a spelling change is unnecessary in the informal command **(busca),** which naturally maintains the sound.

Ex. G: 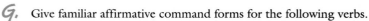 writing

Follow-up, Ex. G: For more practice, have students do the same exercise, changing the affirmative commands to negative, and vice versa.

Answers, Ex. G: 1. Haz las maletas.   2. Ten paciencia.
3. No dobles a la derecha.
4. Escribe tu lección.   5. No vendas tu bicicleta.   6. No vayas al centro.   7. Busca tus libros.
8. Sigue derecho.   9. Bebe leche.
10. No hables por teléfono.

To form the affirmative informal command, drop the **o** from the **yo** form and add **-a** for **-ar** verbs and **-e** for **-er** and **-ir** verbs.

doblo	→	dobla
corro	→	corre
escribo	→	escribe

2. To form the negative informal command, drop the **o** from the **yo** form and add **-es** for **-ar** verbs and **-as** for **-er** and **-ir** verbs.

doblo	→	no dobles
corro	→	no corras
escribo	→	no escribas

3. In the negative command, verbs that end in **-car** change the **c** to **qu**. Those that end in **-gar** change the **g** to **gu**. Those that end in **-zar** change the **z** to **c**.

buscar	busco	no busques
llegar	llego	no llegues
cruzar	cruzo	no cruces

However, none of these verbs change their spellings in the affirmative command:

buscar	busca
llegar	llega
cruzar	cruza

4. Other common verbs you know that have irregular informal commands are:

decir	**di**	no **digas**
hacer	**haz**	no **hagas**
ir	**ve**	no **vayas**
poner	**pon**	no **pongas**
salir	**sal**	no **salgas**
ser	**sé**	no **seas**
tener	**ten**	no **tengas**
venir	**ven**	no **vengas**

G. Give familiar affirmative command forms for the following verbs.

1. hacer las maletas
2. tener paciencia
3. no doblar a la derecha
4. escribir tu lección
5. no vender tu bicicleta
6. no ir al centro
7. buscar tus libros
8. seguir derecho
9. beber leche
10. no hablar por teléfono

Situaciones

Direcciones

a) A pie al banco

—Perdón, señora, ¿dónde está el banco?

—¿El banco? Está cerca de aquí, señor. Camine Ud. por la Calle Bolívar hasta la Avenida de la Paz. Doble a la derecha y camine tres cuadras y allí está la Plaza de la Revolución. Cruce la plaza y allí en la Calle Colón está el banco.

—Muchísimas gracias, señora.

—De nada, señor.

b) En coche en Valencia

—¿Hay un sitio para estacionar el coche en el centro?

—Sí, sí. Es muy fácil. Escucha. Toma la Calle San Vicente Mártir y dobla a la derecha en la Calle Xátiva. Sigue derecho dos cuadras y dobla a la izquierda en la Avenida Marqués de Sotelo. Pasa por delante de la Plaza del País Valenciano y sigue derecho tres cuadras más. Allí a la derecha hay un sitio para estacionar el coche. ¿De acuerdo?

—De acuerdo.

c) En coche al Alcázar de Segovia

—Perdón, señor, ¿dónde está la Calle Velarde? Queremos ir al Alcázar.

—Bien, sigan derecho por esta calle —la Calle Agustín. Pasen por delante de la Iglesia de San Esteban y después de una cuadra doblen a la izquierda. Allí está la Calle Velarde. Sigan la Calle Velarde derecho por más o menos diez cuadras. Allí van a ver Uds. el Alcázar.

—Muchas gracias, señor.

—De nada.

d) A pie a la farmacia

—¡Hola, Marirrosa! ¿Qué haces por aquí?

—Leira, yo estoy buscando una farmacia. ¿Hay una cerca de aquí?

—Sí, claro que sí. Hay una farmacia en la Calle Miramonte.

—¿La Calle Miramonte? ¿Dónde está? No conozco muy bien este barrio.

—Es muy fácil. Sigue esta calle —Calle Juárez— una cuadra hasta la esquina y dobla a la derecha.

—¿No está a la izquierda?

—No, no. A la izquierda está la Calle Cholula. Tú quieres la Calle Rivera. Sigue derecho y a la derecha vas a ver una plaza grande. Es la Plaza de Armas. Cruza la plaza y allí está la Calle Miramonte. ¿Comprendes?

—Sí, sí. Comprendo. Muchísimas gracias. Hasta luego.

—Hasta luego, Marirrosa.

35

Support material, *Situaciones:* Teacher Tape ⌒

Presentation: Situaciones

Have students review the **Tarjetas de vocabulario: Para dar direcciones,** p. 38. Present using the Teacher Tape. Use Ex. H on p. 36 as a comprehension check.

For additional practice, have students listen with their books closed in order to (1) determine whether the conversation is formal or informal and (2) identify some specific directions in each dialogue. A segment or segments of the **Situaciones** may also be used as dictation practice (see Variation, Ex. H, p. T25).

Support material, Ex. H:
Transparency #5

Answers, Ex. H: 1. a   2. b
3. d   4. c

Support material, Ex. I:
Transparency #6

Ex. I: pair work

Preparation, Ex. I: Have
students review **Tarjeta de
vocabulario: Para dar direcciones,** p. 38, before doing this
exercise.

//-//-//-//-//-//-//-//-//
Learning Strategy:

Listening for details

**Critical Thinking
Strategy:**

Making associations

¡Aquí te toca a ti!

H. Match the conversations on page 35 with the following drawings.

1.   2.

3.   4.

//-//-//-//-//-//-//-//-//
Learning Strategies:

*Reading a map, giving
directions, using
culturally appropriate
language*

I. *Por las calles de Madrid* Using the map of Madrid on page
37, give directions for each of the following situations. Pay attention to
where you are, where the other person wishes to go, and whether this
person is someone with whom you would use **tú** or **Ud.**

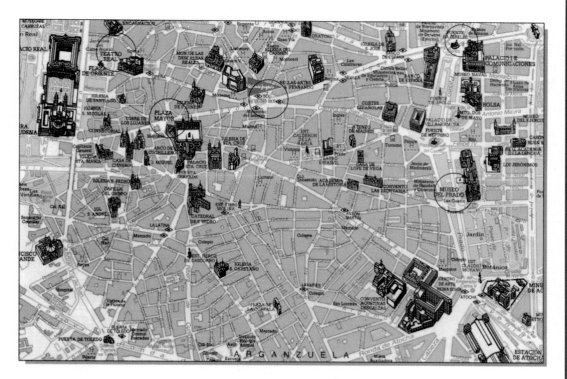

Answers, Ex, I: 1. Tome Ud. la Calle Alcalá y siga derecho hasta la Puerta del Sol.   2. Toma la Carrera de San Jerónimo hasta Fuente de Neptuno. Cruza la plaza y dobla a la derecha en el Paseo del Prado. Allí está el Museo del Prado en la izquierda.   3. Toma la Calle Mayor hasta la Calle Bailén; dobla a la derecha y sigue la calle hasta la Plaza de Oriente. Cruza la plaza, y allí está el Teatro Real.   4. Tome Ud. la Calle Arenal hasta la Puerta del Sol. Cruce la Puerta del Sol y tome la Carrera de San Jerónimo. Siga la Carrera San Jerónimo hasta la Fuente de Neptuno. Cruce la plaza y doble a la derecha en el Paseo del Prado. Allí está el museo en la izquierda.

There may be other routes to these destinations. If students use other routes, follow them on the map transparency to determine accuracy.

Ex. J: pair work

You are at the	You are speaking to	He or she wishes to go to
1. Fuente de la Cibeles	an older man	Puerta del Sol
2. Puerta del Sol	a person your age	Museo del Prado
3. Plaza Mayor	a person your age	Teatro Real
4. Teatro Real	an older woman	Museo del Prado

Actividad

J. *En tu ciudad* You and your partner want to get together after school to study for an exam. First, discuss your schedules to see when you can meet. Then, give each other directions to where you live and decide which home will be more convenient for meeting.

Cooperative Learning

Learning Strategies:

Scheduling, giving directions, reaching agreement

37

Tarjetas de vocabulario

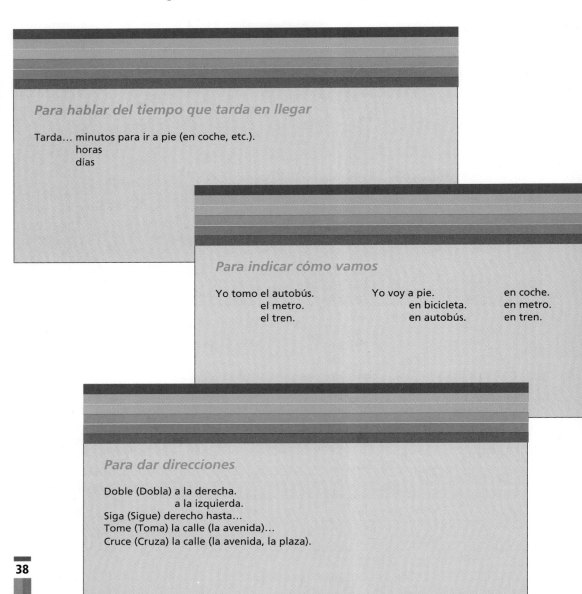

Para hablar del tiempo que tarda en llegar

Tarda... minutos para ir a pie (en coche, etc.).
      horas
      días

Para indicar cómo vamos

Yo tomo el autobús.	Yo voy a pie.	en coche.
el metro.	en bicicleta.	en metro.
el tren.	en autobús.	en tren.

Para dar direcciones

Doble (Dobla) a la derecha.
                a la izquierda.
Siga (Sigue) derecho hasta...
Tome (Toma) la calle (la avenida)...
Cruce (Cruza) la calle (la avenida, la plaza).

38

Para indicar qué día es

¿Qué día es hoy?
Hoy es lunes.
    martes.
    miércoles.
    jueves.

    viernes.
    sábado.
    domingo.

Para indicar la hora

¿Qué hora es?
Es la una.
    una y cuarto.
    una y media.
Son las dos menos cuarto.
¿A qué hora vienes?
Vengo a las diez y veinte de la mañana (10:20 a.m.).
                de la noche (10:20 p.m.).

39

Chapter Culminating Activity

An interesting activity for students would be some type of treasure hunt, where students are given a map of the inside of the school along with a set of directions as to where the imaginary treasure is hidden. They read the directions you give them and follow the route on the map. They then guess where the treasure is by placing an *X* on the map indicating the location. Students with the correct solution would receive some type of reward.

Chapter Objectives

Functions: Shopping; ordering food and drink
Context: Speaking about activities that are done downtown; comparing, indicating quantities; making purchases
Accuracy: Comparisons; the verbs **hacer** and **ir**

Cultural Context

The **Mercado Libertad** in Guadalajara is representative of a typical large market in Latin America. Although supermarkets are very practical and popular, many people still shop at the stands offering great varieties of fresh food, handmade artifacts, and other essentials at very reasonable prices.

CAPÍTULO

C

¿QUÉ HACEMOS?

Mercado Libertad, Guadalajara, México

40

Objectives:

>>> **R**eview words and expressions needed to shop and to order food and beverages.

>>> **R**eview the verbs **hacer** and **ir**.

>>> **P**ractice making comparisons.

>>> **P**ractice placing actions in the past, present, and future.

>>> **P**ractice shopping and ordering.

Strategies:

>>> **L**isting

>>> **M**aking plans

>>> **R**eaching agreement

>>> **C**ategorizing

>>> **E**valuating

Video/Laserdisc

Preliminary Chapter C Video Program and Video Guide

PRIMERA ETAPA

Vamos de compras

En Madrid, como en cualquier ciudad grande, hay muchos sitios para ir de compras. Hay tiendas pequeñas que se especializan en un sólo producto: zapaterías, joyerías, librerías, etc. También hay grandes almacenes donde hay de todo. Mi favorito es un almacén grande que se llama El Corte Inglés. Es una tienda donde puedes comprar cualquier cosa. Por ejemplo, en un piso venden comida, en otro venden ropa y aún en otro venden libros. También hay una joyería donde me gusta ir a ver los diamantes y las perlas. En otra sección de la tienda venden discos compactos y cintas. Allí es donde vamos mis amigas y yo cuando queremos comprar el disco compacto más reciente de Gloria Estefan o de Phil Collins porque tienen una selección buena.

María

En Guadalajara hay muchas tiendas y supermercados modernos, pero para ir de compras a veces vamos al Mercado Libertad. Éste es el mercado más grande del Hemisferio Occidental y allí puedes comprar cualquier producto imaginable. En una sección puedes comprar fruta fresca como sandías, melones, mangos, naranjas, limones y manzanas o vegetales como zanahorias, pepinos, chiles, aguacates, cebollas y tomates. En otra parte venden todo tipo de carne —res, puerco y pollo— y varios tipos de queso. En otra sección compramos tortillas de maíz o pan dulce. Después de hacer las compras, puedes pasar a otra parte del mercado donde hay muchos restaurantes pequeños. Allí puedes comer muchos de los platos típicos de esta región de México como el pozole, la birria, el cabrito asado o pollo en mole.

Esteban

41

Etapa Support Materials

Workbook: **pp. 34–40**
Tapescript: **p. 22**
Teacher Tape
Quiz: **Testing Program, p. 22**

Support material, **Vamos de compras:**
  Teacher Tape

Presentation: Vamos de compras

Have students listen to the Teacher Tape as they follow the text, concentrating on the spelling of words and their pronunciation. Point out that English and Spanish use the same alphabet, but pronounce the letters differently.

Critical Thinking

Prereading: Have students identify who the monologues are about and have them recall where María and Esteban are from. Then have students look at the photographs and infer the topic. Have them deduce that María will describe places in Madrid, and Esteban places in Guadalajara.

Skimming: Have students skim María's monologue. Have them point out which words or phrases suggest the monologue's subject.

Reading for organization: Point out that María's monologue has two sections. Tell students to glance through it again, focusing on the first words of each sentence. They should identify **Mi favorito...** as the turning point from her introduction on shops to her discussion of a specific place.

Elicit from more-prepared students or offer specific guidance, pointing out that **hay muchos sitios para ir de compras** announces her topic. Sentences that begin **Hay...** and **También hay...** give examples. **Mi favorito...** introduces a specific example and all of the succeeding sentences expand on her favorite place.

Reading for specific ideas: Ask students what two points María communicates. Point out that she splits the examples into two sentences in order to make a contrast. Have them identify the contrast and the vocabulary María uses to differentiate the two kinds of shopping places.

Suggestions, Vamos de compras: For additional practice, have more-prepared students work in pairs to read Esteban's monologue; have them follow the same method as for María's (see Critical Thinking, above); and then report back to the class. Go through Esteban's monologue with the less-prepared students, following the same method as for María's.

Comprensión

A. ¿Cierto o falso?
Based on the comments on page 41, indicate whether the following statements are true, false, or if there is not enough information to answer.

1. **El Corte Inglés** is a large open-air market.
2. María likes to shop at the specialty shops scattered throughout Madrid.
3. She and her friends buy CDs and tapes at a store near **El Corte Inglés.**
4. You can buy clothes at **El Corte Inglés,** but not jewelry.
5. Guadalajara has several open-air markets.
6. **El Mercado Libertad** is a huge department store.
7. You can get a good meal at **El Mercado Libertad.**
8. Along with fruits and vegetables, you can also buy meat at **El Mercado Libertad.**

B. ¿Tienes algo que hacer?
Answer the following questions, then ask them of a classmate. Compare your answers with those of your partner to decide if you would be compatible shopping companions. Be able to give reasons for your decision.

//-//-//-//-//-//-//-//-//

Learning Strategies:

Asking for information, providing personal information, supporting decisions

Critical Thinking Strategy:

Comparing and contrasting

1. ¿Hay un centro comercial cerca de tu casa? ¿Vas allí de vez en cuando? ¿Qué centro comercial prefieres?
2. ¿Prefieres comprar algo o solamente mirar?
3. ¿En general, qué compras en el centro comercial? ¿Qué tiendas prefieres?
4. ¿Vas tú con un(a) amigo(a) a hacer las compras de vez en cuando?
5. ¿Normalmente, quién hace las compras en tu casa? ¿Te gusta ir con él (ella)?
6. ¿Cuándo hace él (ella) las compras? ¿Todos los días? ¿Dos o tres veces por semana? ¿Una vez por semana?
7. ¿Adónde va él (ella) a comprar las frutas y vegetales? ¿a comprar carne? ¿Qué mercado prefieres tú?

El Rastro, Madrid

42

REPASO

The verb hacer (present tense)

hacer			
yo	**hago**	nosotros(as)	**hacemos**
tú	**haces**	vosotros(as)	**hacéis**
él		ellos	
ella	} **hace**	ellas	} **hacen**
Ud.		Uds.	

1. When the verb **hacer** is used in a question, the answer often requires a verb other than **hacer**, usually a form of a verb that expresses what you do.

—¿Qué **haces** tú los sábados por la mañana?
—Yo **juego** al fútbol con mis amigos.
—¿Qué **van a hacer** ellos el sábado por la noche?
—Ellos **van a ver** una película.

2. Expressions with **hacer.**

hacer las compras	(to do the shopping)	**hacer la cama**	(to make the bed)
hacer un mandado	(to run an errand)	**hacer un viaje**	(to take a trip)
hacer las maletas	(to pack)		

C. Replace the words in italics with those in parentheses and make the necessary changes.

1. ¿Qué hace *Juan* los viernes por la noche? (ella / tú / Ud. / Uds. / vosotros)

2. *Yo* no hago nada los domingos por la tarde. (tú / Uds. / ellos / ella / nosotros / vosotras)

D. La familia Lamas Tell your parents about a Hispanic family's weekly routine. Based on the drawings on page 44, answer your parents' questions.

Modelo: ¿Qué hace Miguel los lunes por la mañana?
Él va a la escuela.

> **Learning Strategy:**
> *Reporting based on visual information*

43

 **1.**

 **2.**

 **3.**

 **4.**

 **5.**

 **6.**

Answers, Ex. D: 1. Ella va al colegio.   2. Ellos van al trabajo.   3. Él va al cine.   4. Ellos miran la televisión.   5. Él va a la tienda de música con su amigo.   6. Ella visita a una amiga.

Ex. E: pair work

More-prepared students, Ex. E: Have more-prepared students take notes on their partner's answers and write them up in a short paragraph, comparing and contrasting them with their own answers. Students may be called on to summarize orally.

Less-prepared students, Ex. E: Have less-prepared students write the answers to the questions, then work with a partner, using their written text as a guide to ask and answer the questions orally. Have them put a star in their work where their partner has something in common with them, and an *X* where they differ in order to facilitate reference for summarizing.

1. ¿Qué hace Marirrosa los martes por la tarde?
2. ¿Qué hacen la Sra. y el Sr. Lamas los lunes por la mañana?
3. ¿Qué hace Miguel los viernes por la noche?
4. ¿Qué hacen la Sra. y el Sr. Lamas los sábados por la noche?
5. ¿Qué hace Miguel los domingos por la tarde?
6. ¿Qué hace Marirrosa los viernes por la tarde?

Learning Strategies:

Asking for information, providing personal information, supporting opinions

Critical Thinking Strategy:

Comparing and contrasting

E. ¿Y tú? Answer the following questions, then ask them of a classmate. Compare your answers with those of your partner to find out how many activities you and your families have in common. Summarize your findings with a statement like the following:

Tenemos mucho en común, por ejemplo... o:
Mi compañero(a) y yo no tenemos mucho en común porque él (ella)... y yo...

1. ¿Qué haces los viernes por la noche?
2. ¿Qué hacen tus padres?
3. ¿Qué hacen Uds. los sábados por la tarde?
4. Y tu hermano(a), ¿qué hace?
5. ¿Qué van a hacer Uds. esta noche?
6. ¿Qué van a hacer Uds. mañana?

Exs. F and G: pair work

Preparation, Exs. F and G:
Have students review the **Tarjetas de vocabulario**, pp. 50–51.

7. ¿Qué van a hacer Uds. el viernes por la noche?

8. ¿Qué van a hacer Uds. el sábado por la tarde?

F. ¿Qué haces en tu tiempo libre? What do the people in the following drawings do in their free time? What do you do in your free time?

1.   2.   3.   4.

5.   6.   7.

8.   9.   10.

G. ¿Qué deportes te gustan? Review the **Tarjetas de vocabulario** for sports on page 51 and indicate what sports you like and don't like. Ask a classmate what sports he or she likes and dislikes.

45

Preparation, Ex. H: Have students review the **Tarjetas de vocabulario: Para indicar la cantidad,** p. 50. Also suggest the use of the verb **necesitar.**

Answers, Ex. H: 1. Luisa necesita dos litros de leche. 2. Roberto necesita dos docenas de huevos.   3. Mi mamá necesita dos kilos de bananas (plátanos). 4. Alicia necesita quinientos gramos de arroz.   5. Marisol necesita cuatro latas de atún.

Cultural Expansion

Point out that many countries use the metric system of weights and measures. Here are some examples of the most commonly used weight equivalents: 1 kilo = **2,2 libras;** 50 grams = **2 onzas;** 1 liter = **0,26 galón** = **un poco más de un cuarto.**

REPASO

Expressing quantity and making comparisons

Some expressions of quantity in Spanish are:

Quantities	Comparisons	Equality
un kilo de	**más... que**	**tan** + *adjective* + **como**
medio kilo de	**menos... que**	**tanto(a)** + *noun* + **como**
una libra de		**tantos(as)** + *nouns* + **como**
50 gramos de	**bien → mejor(es)**	
un litro de	**mal → peor(es)**	
un atado de	**joven → menor(es)**	
una botella de	**viejo → mayor(es)**	
una docena de		
una lata de		
un paquete de		
un pedazo de		

H. ¿Qué necesita? Based on the drawings, indicate how much of each item the following people need to buy.

1. Luisa   **2.** Roberto   **3.** mi mamá

4. Alicia   **5.** Marisol

46

¿Recuerdan?

The demonstrative adjective is used to point out specific things. Its forms in Spanish are:

close to speaker	close to listener	far from both
este	ese	aquel
esta	esa	aquella
estos	esos	aquellos
estas	esas	aquellas

I. Las frutas y los vegetales You are in an open-air market. As you choose some fruit or vegetables that you like, your friend always points out others that are better. Follow the model.

Modelo: —Quiero estas manzanas.
—Pero esas manzanas son mejores.   o:
—Aquellas manzanas son mejores.

1. fresas
2. maíz
3. limones
4. peras
5. lechuga
6. cebollas
7. naranjas
8. zanahorias

Situaciones

Las compras

a) —Buenos días, señor.
—Buenos días. Mi hijo va a comenzar la escuela mañana y necesita varias cosas. ¿Dónde están los lápices y bolígrafos?
—Están por aquí. ¿Cuántos quiere?
—Quiero seis lápices y dos bolígrafos.
—¿Necesita algo más?
—Sí, necesito papel, también.
—El papel está allí.
—Bien, voy a llevar tres cuadernos.
—¿Algo más?
—Sí, busco una mochila buena.
—Las mochilas están por aquí.
—Muy bien, quiero esa mochila azul.

47

Variation, Situaciones:
You may want to use a segment or segments of the **Situaciones** to practice dictation. Remind students to listen with books closed the first time the tape is played, then to write the second, and correct and adjust the third time the tape is played. Finally, have them check their work against the written text.

—¿Es todo?

—Sí, es todo. ¿Cuánto es?

—Dos mil seiscientas setenta y ocho pesetas.

—Aquí tiene, señor.

—Muchísimas gracias. Hasta luego.

b) —¿En qué puedo servirle, señora?

—Busco un regalo para mi hijo. ¿Me puede sugerir algo?

—¿Qué deportes le gustan?

—¡Le gustan todos los deportes!

—Aquí están las raquetas de tenis.

—No, ya tiene una raqueta.

—Allí están las pelotas de fútbol.

—No, también tiene una pelota de fútbol y de básquetbol y de fútbol americano.

—¿Por qué no compra unos zapatos de tenis? ¡Éstos aquí están muy de moda!

—¡Estupenda idea! ¿Tiene ésos de allí, de color rojo, azul y blanco de tamaño 42?

—Voy a ver. Creo que sí.... Sí, aquí están. ¿Va a pagar en efectivo o con tarjeta de crédito?

—En efectivo. ¿Cuánto es?

—Dos mil quinientas pesetas.

—Aquí tiene.

—Muchísimas gracias.

—¡Gracias a Ud. por la magnífica sugerencia!

c) —Señores, señoras. Compren vegetales... fruta... tomates, guisantes, naranjas, manzanas.... ¿Señora, qué va a llevar?

—Quiero un kilo de tomates, por favor.

—¿Estos tomates?

—No, quiero esos tomates grandes de allí.

—Muy bien. ¿Qué más?

—Tres kilos de bananas. Es todo.

—Bien, vamos a ver... un kilo de tomates a treinta pesetas el kilo y tres kilos de plátanos a quince pesetas el kilo... sesenta pesetas por favor.

—¿Tiene cambio de quinientas pesetas?

—Sí, claro. Aquí tiene el cambio.

—Señores, señoras. Compren vegetales... fruta...

d) —¿Vas a comprar alguna cosa?

—Creo que sí. Si tengo suficiente dinero, voy a comprar un disco compacto.

—¿Qué vas a comprar?

—Quisiera comprar el nuevo disco compacto de Jon Secada.

—Ah, sí, dicen que es excelente.

—Te gusta la música de Miami Sound Machine, ¿verdad?

—Sí, me gusta muchísimo. ¿Sabes que tienen un disco compacto nuevo?

48

—Sí, pero no tengo suficiente dinero para comprar el disco compacto.
—Puedes comprar la cinta.
—Tienes razón. Voy a preguntar si tienen la nueva cinta de Miami Sound Machine aquí.

¡Aquí te toca a ti!

J. ¿Dónde están?   Indicate where each of the conversations on pages 47–49 took place. Possible locations: **la panadería, la papelería, la tienda de deportes, la tienda de música, el mercado, la carnicería, la tienda de ropa, el supermercado.**

Actividades

K. Al mercado   You and a classmate will play the roles of shopper and grocery store clerk.

One of you must prepare a large salad for a family dinner. That student should make a list of items (four or five, at least) needed for the salad. Your list should include how much of each item you will need and about how much you want to spend for each one.

The person playing the grocery store clerk should prepare two lists. On the first, write the names of six to eight items, including fruits and vegetables that you have in stock, indicating the price of each per bottle, kilo, etc. On the second list, write the names of five or six items that you do *not* have in your store.

Work on your lists separately. Before beginning your conversation look at the following five points which should be included in your conversation. Review the **Situationes** on pages 47–49 for ideas.

1. Greet each other at the market.
2. Discuss which produce items are needed and available.
3. Discuss the price of the items selected by the customer.
4. Conclude the purchase/sale.
5. Say good-bye.

L. De compras   Choose three stores and write down three items you need to buy at each. Work with a partner to role play the conversation you have at each store. Remember that there are several ways to indicate what you would like to buy: **Yo quisiera..., Yo necesito..., ¿Tiene Ud.... ?,** and **Yo voy a llevar....** Try to vary the expressions you use.

Critical Thinking Strategy:

Drawing inferences

Cooperative Learning

Learning Strategies:

Listing, making plans

Spanish speakers, Tarjetas de vocabulario:
Point out the words that have the problematic spelling combinations that were highlighted on p. 19 of "To the Teacher" in the Teacher's Edition. You may want to encourage students to keep a spelling notebook with categories such as: **Palabras con _ll_, Palabras con _v_, Palabras con _b_,** etc. Another category might be headed **Así lo digo yo** for students to work on the spelling of words and expressions that they already know that might be variations of what has been presented in this book.

Tarjetas de vocabulario

Lugares adonde vamos

la biblioteca	el parque zoológico
un restaurante	el gimnasio
la piscina	el concierto
el cine	la casa de un(a) amigo(a)
la fiesta	el centro
la playa	el médico
el museo	
el parque	

Para hablar de lo que hacemos en el centro

Yo voy al centro para ir al cine.
ir de compras.
hacer un mandado.
ver a mis amigos.

Para indicar la cantidad

un kilo de	50 gramos de	una botella de	una lata de
medio kilo de	un litro de	una docena de	un paquete de
una libra de	un atado de	un pedazo de	

En el mercado yo compré bananas.   melones.   guisantes.   papas.
el supermercado   fresas.   naranjas.   cebollas.   tomates.
limones.   peras.   lechuga.   zanahorias.
manzanas.   uvas.   maíz.

En la papelería yo compré una hoja de papel para escribir a máquina.
papel de avión.
un sobre.
una tarjeta de cumpleaños.
del Día de las Madres.
del Día de los Padres.

50

Para comprar alguna cosa

Yo quisiera…
¿Tiene Ud.…?
Aquí tiene…
¿Tiene Ud. cambio *(change)*
  de 500 pesetas?
Es todo.
¿Cuánto cuesta?
Un(a)… por favor.

Deportes

En mi tiempo libre me gusta jugar…
  al béisbol.
  al baloncesto.
  al fútbol americano.
  al fútbol.
  al tenis.
  al golf.
  al vólibol.

También me gusta…
  levantar pesas.
  patinar.
  patinar en ruedas.
  jugar al hockey.
  jugar al hockey sobre hierba.
  montar en bicicleta.
  hacer ejercicio aeróbico.

Deportes de verano

Durante el verano me gusta practicar…
  el esquí acuático.
  el windsurf.
  la vela.
  el alpinismo.
  el ciclismo.
  el surfing.

También me gusta…
  tomar el sol.
  nadar / la natación.
  bucear / el buceo.
  ir de pesca / la pesca.
  ir de camping.
  caminar en la playa.

  hablar por teléfono.
  escuchar música.
  alquilar vídeos.
  montar en bicicleta.
  escribir cartas.
  ir al cine.

En mi tiempo libre me gusta…
  desayunar en un restaurante.
  escuchar el estéreo.
  pasar tiempo con mi familia.
  mirar la televisión.
  cenar con un(a) amigo(a).
  caminar al centro.
  comprar un disco compacto.
  visitar a un(a) amigo(a).
  hacer ejercicio.
  hacer un mandado.

51

Cultural Expansion

Explain that **bocadillo** literally means a small mouthful, but in reality a **bocadillo** is a large, submarine-type sandwich. You might also ask students if they know what **calamares** are. They may be quite surprised to think of someone their age eating fried squid, but a **bocadillo de calamares fritos** is a very popular sandwich in Madrid! On the Mexican side of the Atlantic, ask students what **licuados** are. The idea of fresh fruit shakes will probably be very appealing, considering the tropical fruits, such as pineapple, mango, and papaya, that are so common there.

Presentation: Vamos a comer algo

Possible questions: 1. Does María like the same food as her father? 2. What type of sandwich does she prefer? 3. Which type of food is spicier, Spanish (from Spain) or Mexican? 4. What is a **taquería**? 5. What are some of the dishes served in Esteban's favorite **taquería**?

1. ¿Le gusta a María la misma comida que le gusta a su papá? 2. ¿Qué tipo de bocadillo prefiere ella? 3. ¿Qué tipo de comida es más picante, la comida de España o la comida de México? 4. ¿Qué es una *taquería*? 5. ¿Cuáles son unos de los platos que sirven en la taquería favorita de Esteban?

SEGUNDA ETAPA

Vamos a comer algo

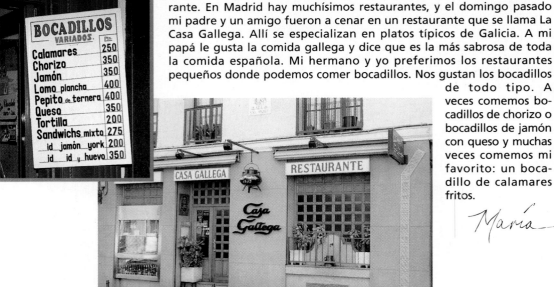

Cuando mi padre tiene hambre, le gusta comer en un buen restaurante. En Madrid hay muchísimos restaurantes, y el domingo pasado mi padre y un amigo fueron a cenar en un restaurante que se llama La Casa Gallega. Allí se especializan en platos típicos de Galicia. A mi papá le gusta la comida gallega y dice que es la más sabrosa de toda la comida española. Mi hermano y yo preferimos los restaurantes pequeños donde podemos comer bocadillos. Nos gustan los bocadillos de todo tipo. A veces comemos bocadillos de chorizo o bocadillos de jamón con queso y muchas veces comemos mi favorito: un bocadillo de calamares fritos.

María

El sábado por la tarde, como no hay escuela, normalmente voy con mis amigos al centro. Allí conversamos con otros amigos y, de costumbre, vamos a comer en nuestro restaurante favorito: El Farolito. El Farolito es una taquería donde puedes comer tacos de todo tipo: de carne o de pollo. También nos gustan las quesadillas. Tienen la mejor ensalada de guacamole de toda Guadalajara y también tienen varias salsas —unas picantes y otras que no son tan picantes. Para tomar hay limonada y varios tipos de licuados —de mango, melón y fresas. Después de comer allí, generalmente vamos al cine o damos un paseo por el parque.

Esteban

52

Etapa Support Materials

Workbook: pp. 41–49
Transparency: #7
Listening Activity masters: p. 18
Teacher Tape
Quiz: Testing Program, p. 26

Chapter Test: Testing Program, p. 29

Support material, Vamos a comer algo:
Teacher Tape

Comprensión

A. Mis gustos Scan the paragraphs on page 52 to find all the different foods that María and Esteban like. As you find them, add them to one of three lists. In the first, list all the foods mentioned that *you* have eaten. In the second, list foods that you have never eaten but that you would like to try. In the third, list foods that you don't think you would like.

When you have completed your lists, compare your categories with those of your partner. Make another set of the three lists, this time listing only the items that you have in common for each category.

B. Prefiero comer con... Based on their food preferences, decide whether you would rather go out to dinner with María or with Esteban. Be ready to explain your choice.

//-//-//-//-//-//-//-//-//
Learning Strategy:
Reading for specific details

Critical Thinking Strategies:
Evaluating, comparing and contrasting, categorizing

//-//-//-//-//-//-//-//-//
Learning Strategy:
Reading for ideas

Critical Thinking Strategy:
Evaluating

REPASO

The preterite of -ar, -er, and -ir verbs

hablar, comer, escribir

yo	hablé comí escribí	nosotros(as)	hablamos comimos escribimos
tú	hablaste comiste escribiste	vosotros(as)	hablasteis comisteis escribisteis
él ella Ud.	habló comió escribió	ellos ellas Uds.	hablaron comieron escribieron

53

Ex. A: pair work

writing

Reteaching, Ex. A: Remind students to use the verb **gustar** + infinitive, or **gusta** with a singular noun and **gustan** with plural nouns.

More-prepared students, Ex. A: Allow more-prepared students to expand on their lists by explaining their reactions and comments on foods. As a vocabulary expansion item, introduce the verb **probar (ue),** *to taste.*

Suggestion, Ex. A: Have all students report back to the class on the three food categories or on who they would prefer to eat with and why. If possible, bring in some of the food items for students to try. It would be very easy to create **licuados** as a class project. Students could carry out instructions, follow recipe directions, and determine amounts—all in Spanish. For example, **corta la fruta, pon la fruta en la licuadora, pon el azúcar y el agua**, etc.

Presentation: Repaso

As you review the conjugation of regular verbs in the preterite, you may want to have the students go over expressions for talking about the past in the **Tarjetas de vocabulario: Para hablar del pasado, presente y futuro,** p. 63.

C. Replace the words in italics with those in parentheses and make the necessary changes.

1. Yo *canté una canción* anoche. (mirar la tele / comprar unos libros / escuchar mi estéreo / tomar el autobús / caminar al centro / hablar por teléfono / bailar en una discoteca)
2. Ella *asistió a clase* ayer. (vender su bicicleta / escribir una carta / correr dos millas / aprender el vocabulario / salir de casa temprano / perder su libro / volver a casa tarde / compartir su bocadillo con un amigo[a])

¿Recuerdan?

The preterite of *ir*

yo	**fui**	nosotros(as)	**fuimos**
tú	**fuiste**	vosotros(as)	**fuisteis**
él ella Ud.	**fue**	ellos ellas Uds.	**fueron**

D. *El sábado de Marisol*   Based on the verbs and drawings provided below and on page 55, tell what Marisol did last Saturday. Follow the model.

 Modelo: hablar por teléfono
El sábado pasado Marisol habló por teléfono con Tomás.

1. salir de   2. caminar a un restaurante   3. comer con Tomás

4. ir al centro comercial   **5.** ir a la tienda de música   **6.** comprar un disco compacto

7. volver a casa de Marisol   **8.** escuchar discos compactos   **9.** mirar la televisión

E. Mi sábado Now imagine that you spent your Saturday much as Marisol did. Use the drawings in Activity D, but substitute names and places from your own life when appropriate. (If you would not normally do something that Marisol did, use **no** + the verb to indicate what you did not do.) Follow the model.

///-//-//-//-//-//-//-//-//
Learning Strategy:

Reporting based on personal knowledge

> **Modelo:** *El sábado pasado, hablé por teléfono con mi amiga Janet.*

F. Ayer: un día loquísimo (crazy) Imagine that yesterday nothing went as usual for you. Make a list of eight to ten things that usually happen in your daily routine. Include events such as (1) when you have breakfast, (2) what you eat for breakfast, (3) when you leave for school and what mode of transportation you use, (4) when your parents leave for work, (5) when you arrive at school, (6) what you do when you get there, (7) when you go to lunch, (8) what and how much you eat for lunch (e.g., **dos bocadillos y una ensalada**), (9) what time you leave school, (10) where you go, (11) with whom you go, (12) when and where you have dinner, (13) what you and your family do after dinner, and (14) how long you study.

///-//-//-//-//-//-//-//-//
Learning Strategies:

Listing, reporting based on personal knowledge, asking questions based on context

When you have completed your list, discuss with your partner what normally happens and how things didn't happen as usual yesterday. Follow the model.

> **Modelo:**
> **Estudiante 1:** *De costumbre, tomo el almuerzo en la cafetería, pero ayer no comí en la cafetería.*
> **Estudiante 2:** *¿No? ¿Dónde comiste?*
> **Estudiante 1:** *Comí en el restaurante con mi padre.*

Ex. E: writing

Suggestion, Ex. E: Do as an oral or a writing activity in paragraph form.

Ex. F: pair work

Suggestion, Ex. F: Before beginning the exercise, brainstorm with students by asking them questions in Spanish about what they normally do and what they did yesterday. Help them come up with sample sentences using the ideas, verbs, and preterite forms they have studied e.g., **¿De costumbre, a qué hora llegas a la escuela? ¿Y a qué hora llegaste ayer?**

Less-prepared students, Ex. F: Have less-prepared students list verbs and times for each event mentioned in the instructions. Then, have them use the list as a guide and go back and write complete thoughts or ideas. Brainstorm with them to come up with some ideas for the out-of-the-ordinary things that happened yesterday.

More-prepared students, Ex. F: Encourage the more-prepared students to be creative in their responses about why yesterday wasn't normal and to use as many different verbs as they can remember. You may want to encourage them to ask you or to consult a dictionary with your guidance for new verbs/expressions as they need them as vocabulary expansion items.

Presentation: Repaso

(1) As you discuss habitual actions, you may want students to review expressions for talking about these actions in the **Tarjetas de vocabulario: Para hablar de una actividad habitual,** p. 63.

(2) As you discuss the present progressive, you may want students to review expressions **(ahora, ahora mismo, en este momento)** that are used to emphasize that the action is going on at the moment of speaking.

(3) As you discuss the immediate future, you may want students to review the expressions for talking about the future in the **Tarjetas de vocabulario: Para hablar del pasado, presente y futuro,** p. 63.

(4) Point out to students that of the high frequency verbs that they have learned, most have regular present participles. The two notable exceptions are

leer	**leyendo**
dormir	**durmiendo**

More-prepared students,
Repaso: Have more-prepared students work in pairs to create questions contrasting the different time elements. Remind them to make up four questions for each verb and to vary adverbial time expressions. For example, **¿A qué hora comiste ayer? ¿A qué hora comes normalmente? ¿Estás comiendo en este momento? ¿A qué hora vas a comer mañana?** After the questions are edited, have them ask and their classmates answer the questions.

REPASO

Talking about past, present, and future events

1. Use the preterite to express a past action.

Ayer **nosotros fuimos** al centro.   Yesterday *we went* downtown.
Salió de la casa hace una hora.   *He left* the house an hour ago.

2. Use the present tense of the verb to indicate a habitual action or a present condition.

De costumbre yo ceno a las 6:00.   *I usually eat dinner* at 6:00.
Yo tengo 17 años.   *I am* seventeen.
Hoy es miércoles.   *Today is* Wednesday.

3. Use the present progressive (**estar** + **-ndo** *participle*) to emphasize that an action is going on at the moment of speaking.

Ahora ellos **están mirando** la tele.   Right now *they are watching* TV.
En este momento él **está leyendo** una revista.   At this moment he *is reading* a magazine.

4. Use the immediate future (**ir** + **a** + *infinitive*) to express a future action.

Esta noche **vamos a ver** una película.   Tonight *we are going to see* a movie.
Nosotros **vamos a trabajar** el lunes próximo.   We *are going to work* next Monday.

¿Recuerdan?

To express how long ago something happened or how long ago you did something, you would use:

> **hace** + *length of time* + **que** + *subject* + *verb in the preterite*
> **Hace** dos semanas **que** comí en un restaurante.

You may also use:

> *subject* + *verb in the preterite* + **hace** + *length of time*
> Yo comí en un restaurante **hace** dos semanas.

56

Some expressions for expressing length of time are:

un minuto, dos minutos, tres minutos, etc.
una hora, dos horas, tres horas, etc.
un día, dos días, tres días, etc.
una semana, dos semanas, tres semanas, etc.
un mes, dos meses, tres meses, etc.
un año, dos años, tres años, etc.

G. *La última vez que...*   Indicate the last time you did each of the following activities. Use expressions such as **el martes pasado, el año pasado, la semana pasada,** or **hace** + *length of time*. Follow the model.

 ¿Cuándo fue la última vez que comiste pizza?
Comí pizza el viernes pasado.   o:
Comí pizza hace dos semanas.

¿Cuándo fue la última vez que...

1. comiste en un restaurante?
2. fuiste al cine?
3. hiciste tu tarea?
4. visitaste a un(a) amigo(a)?
5. estudiaste para un examen?
6. fuiste a un partido de fútbol?
7. hiciste tu cama?
8. tomaste el autobús?
9. leíste un libro?
10. escribiste una carta?

Learning Strategy:
Reporting based on personal knowledge

H. *¿Cuándo vas a... ?*   Now indicate the next time you are going to do the following things. Use expressions such as: **mañana, mañana por la tarde, la semana próxima, el mes próximo, el año próximo.**

 ¿Cuándo vas a comer pizza?
Voy a comer pizza el viernes próximo.   o:
No voy a comer pizza.

¿Cuándo...

1. vas a hablar por teléfono con un(a) amigo(a)?
2. vas a viajar a Europa?
3. vas a hacer la tarea?
4. vas a nadar en la piscina?
5. vas a leer una revista?
6. vas a tomar un autobús?
7. vas a visitar a un(a) amigo(a)?
8. vas a comprar un disco compacto o una cinta?
9. vas a jugar al tenis?
10. vas a mirar la televisión?
11. vas a escribir una carta?
12. vas a ir de compras?

Learning Strategy:
Reporting based on personal knowledge

57

Back-to-Back Pairs, Ex. I

- Tell the students to form pairs and sit back-to-back so that only one student in each pair can see the overhead transparency.
- Explain that one student will ask a question about **el mes de Juan Robles** and the other student will answer the question according to the information on the calendar shown in the transparency.
- Tell them to begin. After five questions, have students reverse roles. They will need to change places to allow the student answering the questions to see the transparency.
- When they have finished, ask new questions about the calendar of all students at random to make sure that they understand the information in the calendar.

Answers, Ex. I: 1. Hoy es el 24.   2. Van a comer en un restaurante.   3. Fue a Madrid el primero. 4. Va a jugar al tenis.   5. Celebraron el cumpleaños de Juan el 16.   6. Fue al museo el 21 por la tarde.   7. El 11 corrió.   8. Va a nadar.   9. Fue al cine.   10. Va a la iglesia.

Learning Strategies:

Reading a calendar, reporting based on visual information

I. El mes de Juan Robles   This month has been, is, and will continue to be a very busy time for Juan Robles. Based on the drawings and the calendar that follows, answer the questions about his current, past, and future activities. Today is the 24th of the month.

L	M	M	J	V	S	D
1	2	3	4	5	6	7
8	9	10	11	12	13	14
15	16	17	18	19	20	21
22	23	24	25	26	27	28
29	30	31				

1. ¿Qué día es hoy?
2. ¿Qué van a hacer los padres de Juan esta noche?
3. ¿Cuándo fue el Sr. Robles a Madrid?
4. ¿Qué va a hacer Juan mañana por la tarde?
5. ¿Cuándo celebraron el cumpleaños de Juan?
6. ¿Cuándo fue Juan al museo?
7. ¿Qué hizo Juan el 11?
8. ¿Qué va a hacer el 29?
9. ¿Qué hizo el 13?
10. ¿Qué hace Juan los domingos por la mañana?

Situaciones

Vamos a comer algo...

a) Ángela y Mauricio
—Por favor, camarero.
—Sí, señorita, ¿qué desea?
—Quisiera un sándwich de jamón.
—¿Y para tomar?
—Quisiera una limonada.
—Y Ud., señor, ¿qué va a pedir?
—Yo quisiera una hamburguesa con queso y un licuado de mango.
—¿Alguna cosita más?
—No, es todo. Gracias.

b) Mario y Ernesto
—Ay, Mario. ¡Qué hambre tengo!
—Yo también. Vamos a la Taquería Mixteca. Está muy cerca de aquí.
—De acuerdo.

(Media hora después)
—Por favor, señorita. Tráigame dos tacos al carbón, una salsa picante y un té helado. ¿Tú, qué quieres, Mario?
—Tres quesadillas y un agua mineral sin gas, por favor.
—¿Es todo?
—Sí, señorita, es todo.

c) Antonio y Margarita
—Antonio, ¿tienes hambre?
—Sí, por supuesto. Tengo mucha hambre.
—¿Quieres comer alguna cosa?
—¡Claro que sí! ¿Por qué no vamos a la pizzería nueva que está en la esquina de la Calle Ocho y la Avenida Bolívar?
—Vamos, pues.

(Media hora después)
—Buenas tardes, ¿qué van a pedir?
—Por favor, quisiéramos una pizza grande con mucho queso, aceitunas y cebollas.

d) Carolina y Filomena
—Mira. Hay muchísima gente.
—Como siempre.
—¿Tienes suficiente dinero?
—Sí. Tengo 500 pesetas.

59

Support material, Situaciones: Teacher Tape

Presentation: Situaciones

Have students review the **Tarjetas de vocabulario: Para indicar adonde vamos a comer; Para indicar qué queremos beber o comer; Para pedir algo para comer o beber,** pp. 61–62.

Possible questions, Situaciones: 1. What do Ángela and Mauricio want to eat? What do they want to drink? 2. What do Antonio and Margarita order on their pizza? (What do you like on your pizza?) 3. What appetizers do Carolina and Filomena order?

1. ¿Qué quieren comer Ángela y Mauricio? ¿Qué quieren tomar? 2. ¿Qué piden Antonio y Margarita en su pizza? (¿Qué prefieres en tu pizza?) 3. ¿Cuáles son las tapas que piden Carolina y Filomena?

Variation, Situaciones: Use a segment or segments for dictation practice (see **Situaciones** in previous chapters).

—Yo también.
—¿Qué quisieras comer?
—¿Por qué no comemos unas tapas?
—Buena idea. Yo quisiera unas aceitunas y patatas bravas.
—Está bien. ¿Vamos a pedir unos calamares también?
—Sí, ¡cómo no!
—¿Qué vas a tomar?
—Agua mineral con limón. ¿Y tú?
—Agua mineral también, pero sin limón.

¡Aquí te toca a ti!

Learning Strategy:
Listening for specific details

J. *¿Dónde comen?*   Based on the four conversations on pages 59–60, indicate where each group of people are eating or planning to eat.

K. *En el restaurante*   You and two friends go to a restaurant for lunch. Discuss what each of you would like to eat and drink. Then call the waiter and place your order.

Actividad

Learning Strategy:
Reaching agreement, listing, verifying

L. *¿Qué vamos a comer?*
You and some friends are spending the afternoon together. Your friend's dad offers to pick up some carry-out lunches for you. Agree on what kind of food you all want (e.g., **tapas, tacos, pizza, sándwiches**), then make your individual decisions about what you want to eat and drink. One member of the group needs to write down what each of you wants.

Tarjetas de vocabulario

Para indicar adonde vamos a comer

Yo quiero ir a un restaurante.
Vamos a una taquería.
Quisiéramos ir a comer pizza.
¿Por qué no vamos a comer unas tapas?

Para aceptar

De acuerdo.
¿Por qué no?
¡Vamos!

Para indicar qué queremos beber o comer

En el restaurante, yo pido…
    café (con leche).
    chocolate.
    un licuado de fresas.
            de banana.
            de mango.
    una limonada.
    un agua mineral con (sin) gas (con limón).
    té (con limón).
    té helado.

En el restaurante, yo como…
    un sándwich de jamón con queso.
    un bocadillo.
    una pizza.
    una hamburguesa (con queso).

En una taquería yo como…
    tacos de carne.
            de pollo
    unas quesadillas.
    una ensalada de guacamole.
    una enchilada.
    frijoles.
    salsa picante.
            no muy picante.

En un bar de tapas yo como…
    unas aceitunas.
    unos calamares.
    patatas bravas.
    chorizo y pan.
    queso.
    tortilla de patatas.

61

Spanish speakers, Tarjetas de vocabulario:
Point out the words that have the problematic spelling combinations that were highlighted on p. 19 of "To the Teacher" in the Teacher's Edition. You may want to encourage students to keep a spelling notebook with categories such as: **Palabras con *ll*, Palabras con *v*, Palabras con *b*,** etc. Another category might be headed **Así lo digo yo** for students to work on the spelling of words and expressions that they already know that might be variations of what has been presented in this book.

Para pedir algo para comer o beber

Perdón señor (señorita),   Nosotros quisiéramos...
Yo quisiera...   Por favor, tráigame...
Mi amigo(a) quisiera...

Períodos de tiempo

un minuto, dos minutos, tres minutos, etc.
una hora, dos horas, tres horas, etc.
un día, dos días, tres días, etc.
una semana, dos semanas, tres semanas, etc.
un mes, dos meses, tres meses, etc.
un año, dos años, tres años, etc.

Para indicar la última vez que hiciste alguna cosa

hace tres días
hace tres meses
hace tres años

Para hablar de una actividad habitual

de costumbre   siempre
normalmente   todos los días
por lo general

Para hablar del pasado, presente y futuro

ayer	hoy	mañana
ayer por la mañana	esta mañana	mañana por la mañana
ayer por la tarde	esta tarde	mañana por la tarde
anoche	esta noche	mañana por la noche
el lunes pasado		el lunes próximo
la semana pasada	esta semana	la semana próxima
el mes pasado	este mes	el mes próximo
el año pasado	este año	el año próximo

Cultural Context

There are many ski resorts in Spain and Latin America. One such popular resort is Portillo in Chile. Located in the Andes mountains, it has a breathtaking view and spectacular trails. Since winter occurs in the Southern Hemisphere when it is summer in the Northern Hemisphere, July is a perfect time for U. S. skiers to enjoy Portillo.

Spanish speakers, ¿Qué ves?: Have Spanish speakers mention, in Spanish, what they see. Ask if they can share any specific information with the class about these photos and/or about such topics as the weather, seasons, or particular geographical features (e.g., mountain ranges, rivers, etc.).

¿Qué ves?

›› *¿Dónde está la gente en las fotografías?*

›› *¿Qué hacen las personas aquí?*

›› *¿Qué estación del año es y qué tiempo hace?*

›› *¿Qué hay en las montañas?*

›› *¿Qué piensas de este deporte? ¿Tú lo practicas?*

OBJECTIVES

IN THIS UNIT YOU WILL LEARN:
- To talk about the weather;
- To understand weather reports;
- To describe objects;
- To describe people.

64

Capítulo uno: ¿Qué tiempo hace?

Primera etapa: **¡Hace frío hoy!**
Segunda etapa: **¡Hoy va a nevar mucho!**
Tercera etapa: **¿Qué tiempo va a hacer mañana?**

Capítulo dos: ¿Cómo es?

Primera etapa: **Descríbeme…**
Segunda etapa: **¿Qué piensas?**

Capítulo tres: ¿Cómo es tu amiga?

Primera etapa: **Nuestros vecinos y nuestros amigos**
Segunda etapa: **El carácter**

UNIDAD

Descripciones

65

Planning Strategy

If you do not assign the Planning Strategy (Workbook, p. 51) for homework or if students have difficulty coming up with English expressions, you might ask several students to role play the situation: have one person play the student and another student play the conversation partner; or put students into groups to brainstorm as many answers as possible to one of the six conversational situations provided and then have each group share its responses with the entire class.

Functions: Describing the weather and understanding weather reports and meteorological maps

Context: Using the weather to talk about vacation sites; watching, reading, and listening to weather reports

Accuracy: Weather expressions with **hacer, estar, hay,** and specific verbs **(llover, lloviznar, nevar, tronar);** the months of the year, dates, and seasons; the verb **saber;** stem-changing verbs

Cultural Context

Chapultepec Park lies at the end of the **Paseo de la Reforma** in Mexico City. This immense park contains a huge variety of attractions, including a botanical garden, a zoo, an amusement park with rollercoasters, bridle paths, polo grounds, and a number of museums, including the **Museo de Antropología.** Also in the park are the remains of **El Sargento,** the famous **Árbol de Moctezuma.** This tree, which has a circumference of 14 meters and which was originally 60 meters high, has been cut off at a height of 10 meters.

CAPÍTULO

1

¿QUÉ TIEMPO HACE?

Unos amigos disfrutan del buen tiempo en el Parque de Chapultepec, México.

Objective:

>>> **D**escribing the weather and understanding weather reports and meteorological maps

Strategies:

>>> **R**eporting based on visual information
>>> **A**sking for information
>>> **M**aking associations

66

Video/Laserdisc

Chapter 1 Video Program and Video Guide

PRIMERA ETAPA

Preparación

>> **W**hat kinds of questions do you normally ask when talking about the weather?

>> **W**hat are some of the weather expressions used frequently in English to describe weather conditions?

>> **D**o you know where the equator is? What is the weather like there?

>> **W**here is the country of Ecuador located?

/-/-/-/-/-/-/-/-/-/-/-/
Learning Strategy:
Previewing

¡Hace frío hoy!

Hace sol.
Hace calor.
Está despejado.

Hace mal tiempo.
Truena. Hay tormenta.

Llueve.
Llovizna.

Hace buen tiempo.
No hace mucho frío.
No hace mucho calor.

Nieva.
Hace frío.

Está nublado.
Hay nubes.

Hace viento.
Hace fresco.

Hay niebla.
Hay neblina.

Hay hielo.
Está resbaloso.

67

Etapa Support Materials

Workbook: **pp. 53–58**
Tapescript: **p. 33**
Critical Thinking masters: **Chapter 1, primera etapa, activity J**
Transparencies: **#8, #8a**
Teacher Tape

Listening Activity masters: **p. 25**
Quiz: **Testing Program, p. 35**

Support material, ¡Hace frío hoy!:
Teacher Tape , **Transparencies #8, #8a**

Support material, ¡Hace frío hoy!: Transparencies #8, #8a

Presentation: ¡Hace frío hoy!

Show students the transparency with the captioned overlay. Say: **¿Qué tiempo hace?** Then point to the first symbol and say: **Hace sol. Hace calor. Está despejado.** You may need to use gestures to reinforce meaning. Have students repeat each statement you make. After practicing with the captions, remove them and have students make the statements according to the symbol you point out. Keep asking **¿Qué tiempo hace?** Finally, have students ask and answer the question as you continue to point to the symbols in random order.

Spanish speakers, ¡Hace frío hoy!: Ask Spanish speakers for variations of the weather expressions introduced here or for other expressions not listed here (e.g., **relámpago, tormenta, diluvio, nevada,** etc). They may know how to pronounce these variations, but may never have seen how they are written. Write the new expressions on the board or overhead. Remind students about the *c* and *h* in **hace,** the *ll* and *z* in **llovizna,** the *s* in **resbaloso.**

Vocabulary Activities

The **¡Aquí te toca a ti!** activities practice the new vocabulary in each **etapa**.

Ex. A: ✎ writing

Implementation, Ex. A: Have students give more than one comment. Remind them that they can use **no** before a verb in order to increase possible comments, for example: **hace sol, hace calor, está despejado, no hace frío, no llueve, no hace mal tiempo.**

Possible answers, Ex. A:
1. Está nublado. Nieva. Hace frío.
2. Hay nubes. Está nublado.
3. Hace fresco. Hace viento.
4. Truena. Hace mal tiempo. Hay tormenta.   5. Hay hielo. Hace frío. Está resbaloso.   6. Hace mal tiempo. Llueve. Llovizna.

Ex. B: 👥 pair work

Implementation, Ex. B: Do the **Modelo** with the whole class before students begin working in pairs. Have pairs give answers to the class to check accuracy.

More-prepared students, Ex. B: Ask more-prepared students to expand their answers: **No, no hace buen tiempo hoy. Hace mal tiempo. Llueve y hace frío.**

Answers, Ex. B: 1. No, no hace calor hoy. Hace frío.   2. No, no llueve hoy. Nieva.   3. No, no está nublado. Hace sol.   4. No, no hay tormenta. Hace buen tiempo.
5. No, no hace fresco. Hace mucho frío.   6. No, no hace calor. Hace viento.   7. No, no hace sol. Hay nubes.   8. No, no hace frío. Hace bastante calor.   9. No, no está despejado. Está nublado.

¡Aquí te toca a ti!

Learning Strategy:
Reporting based on visual cues

A. ¿Qué tiempo hace? Describe el tiempo en cada dibujo.

Modelo: *Hace sol.*
Hace mucho calor.
Está despejado.

1.　　　　2.　　　　3.　　　　4.　　　　5.　　　　6.

B. ¿Hace buen tiempo hoy? You're traveling around the United States with your friend's family. Each time you call home, your parents want to know what the weather is like. Answer their questions negatively. Then give the indicated weather condition. Follow the model.

Modelo: ¿Hace buen tiempo hoy? (mal)
No, no hace buen tiempo hoy. Hace mal tiempo.

1. ¿Hace calor hoy? (frío)
2. ¿Llueve hoy? (nieva)
3. ¿Está nublado? (sol)
4. ¿Hay tormenta? (buen tiempo)
5. ¿Hace fresco? (mucho frío)
6. ¿Hace calor? (viento)
7. ¿Hace sol? (nubes)
8. ¿Hace frío? (bastante calor)
9. ¿Está despejado? (nublado)

ESTRUCTURA

Los meses del año

enero	abril	julio	octubre
febrero	mayo	agosto	noviembre
marzo	junio	septiembre	diciembre

All the months of the year are masculine and are used without articles. They are not capitalized. To express the idea of *in* a month, use **en** or **en el mes de**.

En enero, nieva mucho.   *In January*, it snows a lot.
Hace calor **en el mes de agosto**.   It's hot *in the month of August*.

Critical Thinking

Have students make four lists of the weather expressions in Ex. B: **Expresiones del tiempo con *hace*, Expresiones del tiempo con *hay*, Expresiones del tiempo con *está*,** and **Verbos especializados para expresar el tiempo.**

Presentation: Estructura

(1) Have students name the months.
(2) Ask: **¿Quién nació en enero? ¿en febrero?,** etc.
(3) Ask: **¿En qué mes naciste?**

Spanish speakers, Estructura: Some Spanish speakers may not know how to spell the months. Point out any special spellings like the *z* in **marzo,** the *b* of **febrero, abril,** etc.

Aquí practicamos

C. *¿Qué tiempo hace donde vives tú?* Para cada mes, describe el tiempo.

Modelo: septiembre
En septiembre, hace fresco y hace viento.

1. enero
2. julio
3. marzo
4. noviembre
5. mayo
6. agosto
7. diciembre
8. junio

//-//-//-//-//-//-//-//-//
Learning Strategy:
Describing based on personal information

COMENTARIOS
CULTURALES

//-//-//-//-//-//-//-//
Learning Strategy:
Reading for cultural information

■ *El clima*

There is more variety in the weather patterns within very short distances in Latin America than in any other region of the world. Most Latin American countries north of the equator, such as Mexico, Costa Rica, and Venezuela, have a warm rainy season of about six months during the summer (April–October) and a dry, colder season the rest of the year during the winter months. In July, for example, the temperatures reach over 80° F or 27° C in most of the Latin American countries in the Northern Hemisphere, while 60° F or 16° C is the average during January.

South of the equator, however, the seasons follow the reverse pattern. Temperatures in January, for instance, climb to over 80° F or 27° C in the Southern Hemisphere, while July brings snow to the southernmost countries like Argentina and Chile.

69

Possible answers, Ex. C: (Answers will vary, depending on the region where you live.) 1. En enero, hace frío y nieva. 2. En julio, hace bastante calor y a veces está nublado. 3. En marzo, hace viento y hay tormentas. Hace mal tiempo. 4. En noviembre, hace fresco (frío). Nieva (Llueve). 5. En mayo, está despejado y hace buen tiempo. 6. En agosto, hace muchísimo calor. No llueve mucho. 7. En diciembre, hace mucho frío y nieva. No hace calor. 8. En junio, está despejado. Hace muy buen tiempo.

Suggestion, Comentarios culturales: After reading the **Comentarios culturales,** have students do Ex. C again, pretending they are from different Latin American countries and using the information from the **Comentarios** to formulate their answers. Afterwards, you may want to discuss in English weather/climate in Latin America and have students compare and contrast it to the climate in different regions of the United States.

Suggestion, Comentarios culturales: In English, ask students to tell you where similar climates are found in the United States.

Cultural Observation

You may want to see if students can guess which South American country is named after the Equator. Once Ecuador has been identified, have students bear in mind the location of the Equator when discussing the reverse seasons of the two hemispheres.

/I-/I-/I-/I-/I-/I-/I-/I-/I

Learning Strategy:

Reporting based on personal information

70

D. Yo nací (I was born) **en el mes de...**   Diles a tus compañeros de clase en qué mes naciste *(you were born)* y qué tiempo generalmente hace en ese mes. Sigue el modelo.

Modelo: *Yo nací en el mes de julio. Siempre hace mucho calor.*

Exercise Progression

The activities in each **¡Aquí te toca a ti!** and **Aquí practicamos** section progress from mechanical practice through meaningful or bridging practice, ending with open-ended expression.

Palabras útiles

La fecha

¿Cuál es la fecha de hoy?	
¿Qué fecha es hoy?	*What is today's date?*
¿A cuántos estamos?	
Hoy es el 5 de octubre.	*Today is October 5.*
¿Cuál es la fecha de tu	*What is the date* of your
cumpleaños?	birthday?
Yo nací **el primero de febrero**	I was born on *the first of*
de mil novecientos setenta	*February 1975.*
y cinco.	
Mi hermana nació **el once de**	My sister was born *on June 11,*
junio de mil novecientos	*1976.*
setenta y seis.	

To express the date in Spanish, use the definite article **el,** a cardinal number **(treinta, diez, cinco),** and the name of the month. The one exception is the first of the month, expressed by **el primero.** The day, the month, and the year of any date are connected by **de.**

Aquí practicamos

E. ¿En qué año? Lee las fechas que siguen. Sigue el modelo.

Modelo: July 4, 1776 — la independencia de los Estados Unidos
el cuatro de julio de mil setecientos setenta y seis — el día de la independencia de los Estados Unidos

1. October 12, 1492 — el descubrimiento de América
2. November 20, 1910 — la revolución mexicana
3. April 23, 1616 — las muertes *(deaths)* de Cervantes y Shakespeare
4. July 14, 1789 — la revolución francesa
5. September 16, 1821 — la independencia de México
6. November 22, 1963 — el asesinato del Presidente Kennedy
7. July 21, 1969 — el primer hombre en la luna *(moon)*
8. November 9, 1989 — la caída *(fall)* del muro *(wall)* de Berlín
9. ? — tu cumpleaños

71

Ex. E: writing

Suggestions, Ex. E: Point out that the day precedes the month when dates are given in Spanish. When Spanish speakers write dates, they place the numbers in the same order in which they state them. For example: **el primero de abril de 1990** (1/4/90), **el doce de enero de 1940** (12/1/40). You may want to guide students through the first items by writing a suitable response on the board. For example: **La fecha en que los Europeos llegaron a América es el doce de octubre de mil cuatrocientos noventa y dos.** To help students with the year, you may list on the side the word equivalents of 100–900, as well as 1000.

Follow-up, Ex. E: Have students categorize the events in Ex. E. Possible categories include: **literatura, ciencia, historia, personal.** Then brainstorm with them to come up with other important events and a broader range of categories, e.g., **música, sociedad.** You may want students to work in groups to create a timeline of the events, adding two or three other events on their own. In a full class discussion, you can create a timeline on the board, having students insert the new dates. As an alternative, have students create a timeline starting with their date of birth to the present.

Reteaching, Palabras útiles: Do a quick review of numbers in Spanish before working on dates. Have students count from 10 to 100 by tens, from 100 to 1,000 by hundreds, etc.

Presentation: Palabras útiles

(1) Write today's date on the board.
(2) Ask several students to give their birthdays.

Presentation: Palabras útiles

(1) Have students repeat the names of the seasons as they look at the drawings.
(2) Have them complete: **Los meses de otoño son...** etc.
(3) Ask: **¿En qué estación naciste?**
(4) Have students pretend they are from Uruguay, Argentina, or Chile and ask the same questions; everything will be reversed, i.e., **los meses del otoño son marzo, abril y mayo.** If a student was born here in the spring, it would be fall in the Southern Hemisphere.

Spanish speakers, Palabras útiles: Some Spanish speakers may not know how to spell the seasons. Point out any special spelling combinations like the *v* in **primavera, verano,** and **invierno.**

Palabras útiles

Las estaciones del año

la primavera

el verano

el otoño

el invierno

All the nouns for the seasons are masculine except **la primavera.** To express the idea of *in* a particular season, use **en** and the appropriate definite article.

En el otoño jugamos al fútbol.	*In the fall* we play soccer.
En el invierno hace frío.	*In the winter* it is cold.
Llueve mucho **en la primavera**.	It rains a lot *in the spring*.
Todos van a la playa **en el verano.**	Everybody goes to the beach *in the summer.*

72

Aquí practicamos

F. *Donde tú vives*   Describe el tiempo durante las estaciones del año en la región donde vives.

Modelo: ¿Qué tiempo hace en el invierno donde vives?
En el invierno nieva y hace mucho frío.

1. ¿Qué tiempo hace en el invierno donde vives?
2. ¿En el otoño?
3. ¿En el verano?
4. ¿En la primavera?

G. *¿Cuándo practicas... ?*   Indica la estación en que normalmente juegas a los siguientes deportes. Entonces, explica por qué el tiempo de esta estación es bueno para el deporte. Sigue el modelo.

Modelo: jugar al fútbol
Juego al fútbol en el otoño porque hace buen tiempo.   o:
... porque no hace demasiado calor en el otoño.   o:
... porque no llueve mucho en el otoño.

1. jugar al tenis
2. jugar al básquetbol
3. jugar al béisbol
4. nadar
5. jugar al golf
6. jugar al jai alai
7. practicar el alpinismo
8. patinar
9. ir de pesca
10. hacer proyectos de artesanía

73

Exs. F and G: pair work

Suggestion, Ex. G: Remind all students to use a variety of expressions for the second part by paraphrasing. Brainstorm an example or two with them, seeking alternative ways to say **hace buen tiempo;** answers might include **hace calor, está despejado, no hace frío, no llueve,** and so on.

More-prepared students, Ex. G: Have more-prepared students report back to the class, comparing and contrasting their partner's responses with their own.

Less-prepared students, Ex. G: After several other students have given examples, call on less-prepared students to contribute the responses they and their partners had for different items.

Possible answers, Ex. G:
1. Juego al tenis en la primavera (el verano).   2. Juego al básquetbol en el invierno.   3. Juego al béisbol en la primavera (el verano).
4. Nado en el verano.   5. Juego al golf en la primavera (el verano).
6. Juego al jai alai en la primavera (el otoño).   7. Practico el alpinismo en el otoño (la primavera / el verano).   8. Patino en el invierno.
9. Voy de pesca en el verano (la primavera / el otoño).   10. Hago proyectos de artesania en el invierno (la primavera / el verano / el otoño).

Cultural Expansion

Jai alai (or **cesta punta**) is a ball game that originated in the Basque region of northern Spain. It is a type of handball in which opposing individuals or teams bounce a hard ball off a wall and catch it in a special wicker contraption called a **cesta,** which is strapped to the player's wrist. **Jai alai** matches are played on a court (**la cancha**) in a large, auditorium-like area called a **frontón.** The ball reaches speeds of 200 mph, so it is a very dangerous game, requiring great skill.

Ex. H: writing

Possible answers, Ex. H:
1. Hay cuatro estaciones en un
año.   2. Los meses del verano
aquí son parte de junio, julio,
agosto y parte de septiembre.
3. Es posible esquiar en el invierno.
4. Vamos a la playa en el verano.
5. Jugamos al fútbol en la primavera y al básquetbol en el invierno.
6. Celebramos el día de Acción de
Gracias en el otoño.   7. Hoy es...
8. La fecha del primer día de las
vacaciones del verano es el _____
de junio.

*Support material, Aquí
escuchamos:* Teacher
Tape

Presentation: Aquí escuchamos

Begin by asking where students
prefer to vacation in the winter.
Then introduce the Valenzuela
family's conversation. Remind students that they will not understand
every word, but should listen for
the general idea.

*Variation, Aquí escu-
chamos:* You may want to use
part or all of the dialogue to practice dictation. Either read from the
tapescript or use the tape while students work with closed books.
Remind them only to listen the first
time, then to write the second and
third times the tape is played or you
read the material. Have them check
their work against the written text.

*Spanish speakers, Aquí
escuchamos:* The exercises
that accompany this section should
pose relatively little problem for
Spanish speakers. They should,
however, be directed to focus on
"listening in context" to any vocabulary that may be new for them.

H. ¡Preguntas, preguntas, tantas preguntas! Trabajas con
unos niños hispanos en los Estados Unidos. Te hacen muchas preguntas.
Contesta sus preguntas.

1. ¿Cuántas estaciones hay en un año?
2. ¿Cuáles son los meses del verano aquí?
3. ¿En qué estación es posible esquiar?
4. ¿En qué estación vamos a la playa?
5. ¿En qué estaciones jugamos al fútbol? ¿al básquetbol?
6. ¿En qué estación celebramos el día de Acción de Gracias?
7. ¿Cuál es la fecha de hoy?
8. ¿Cuál es la fecha del primer día de las vacaciones del verano?

Aquí escuchamos:
"¿El mar o las montañas?"

Learning Strategy:
Listening for details

Antes de escuchar

It's the month of July and the Valenzuela family, from Chile, has
eight days of vacation. But there is a problem. The mother and
father want to go skiing and the children prefer to go to the
beach. Look at the following questions and identify a few
things you expect to hear them talk about.

Después de escuchar

1. ¿Cuál es la estación del año donde vive la familia? ¿Qué tiempo hace?
2. ¿Adónde quieren ir los padres para las vacaciones? ¿Por qué?
3. ¿Adónde prefieren ir los hijos?
4. ¿Adónde va a pasar las vacaciones la familia, por fin?

74

Answers, Aquí escuchamos: 1. el verano; hace
frío   2. Portillo; esquiar   3. a la playa   4. Portillo

Cultural Expansion

You may want to explain to your students that in the Southern
Cone (Argentina, Uruguay, and Chile) students have a "winter
break" of one or two weeks of vacation in mid-July, the equivalent of our spring break—in reverse of course! The school year
begins early in March and ends in early to mid-December.

¡Aquí te toca a ti!

1. ¿Qué tiempo hace en... ? Usa la información que sigue para imitar la conversación del modelo.

Modelo: agosto / Portillo, Chile

Estudiante 1:   Yo quiero ir a Portillo en agosto.   o:
Yo no quiero ir a Portillo en agosto.

Estudiante 2:   ¿Por qué (no)? ¿Qué tiempo hace en Portillo en agosto?

Estudiante 1:   Hace frío. Nieva y hace viento.

1. agosto / Acapulco

2. febrero / Buenos Aires

3. octubre / Aspen

4. noviembre / Miami

75

Review of the Etapa

The activities in the ¡**Adelante!** section serve as **etapa** culminating activities and often involve role plays or other kinds of open expression.

Ex. J: pair work

role play

Preparation, Ex. J: In order for students to have more information on the climate of Peru, assign a group or groups of students to research this area. In fact, the most interesting aspect of Peruvian climate is the Andes mountains, because altitude rather than latitude determines climate. You can be in the tropics, but if you are high up in the mountains, the climate will be cold, not tropical. Theoretically, you could go swimming at the beach and skiing in the mountains all on the same day!

Suggestion, Ex. J: Brainstorm additional activity vocabulary with students, such as **dar un paseo; correr; leer; mirar videos; ir al cine, al parque, a un restaurante; hacer esquí acuático; tomar el sol;** and so on.

Spanish speakers, Ex. J: Remember that most Spanish speakers already have a command of a variety of Spanish that is used in informal very familiar contexts. This situation is an informal one, but have the students focus on using vocabulary that may be new for them. Emphasize that it may be necessary to use such vocabulary when talking to speakers who are from other parts of the Spanish-speaking world. Remember to be sensitive and accept how the students say it the first time. What they have said may be totally appropriate in their speech community. This is a good place to

¡Adelante!

EJERCICIO ORAL

J. Un(a) estudiante extranjero(a)   Un(a) estudiante extranjero(a) del sur de Perú acaba de llegar y te hace preguntas sobre el tiempo y las estaciones donde tú vives. Él (Ella) quiere saber cuales son los meses del invierno, verano, etc. y qué deportes y actividades tú haces en estos meses. Usando lo que sabes *(Using what you know)* del clima de Perú, trabaja con un(a) compañero(a) para comparar los dos climas. Hagan una tabla como la siguiente para tomar notas. Ahora imaginen que uno(a) de Uds. es el (la) estudiante extranjero(a) y conversen.

Las estaciones	Los meses		El tiempo		Los deportes y las actividades	
	En Perú	Aquí	En Perú	Aquí	En Perú	Aquí
primavera						
verano						
otoño						
invierno						

EJERCICIO ESCRITO

K. Las estaciones y mis actividades.   Write a paragraph of four or five sentences about the season of the year that you prefer. Describe its weather in detail as well as what you normally like to do during this particular season and why.

have them focus on the differences between how they say something in their speech community and how the book teaches them to express the same idea.

Ex. K: writing

Less-prepared students, Ex. K: Brainstorm alternate weather expressions with less-prepared students and have them associate the weather terms with the seasons. Remind them that they can use many of the same activities they used in Ex. J.

More-prepared students, Ex. K: Encourage more-prepared students to use as many alternate expressions as possible. Have students exchange papers, read and edit each other's work, and then write a short reaction (2–4 sentences) to their partner's paragraph.

SEGUNDA ETAPA

Preparación

>> **C**an you give some examples of when the weather makes the headlines in the newspaper or on television?

>> **D**oes the weather change much throughout the year where you live? Why or why not?

>> **W**hen you read or hear a weather report, what information do you expect to get?

/-/-/-/-/-/-/-/-/-/-/-/

Learning Strategy:
Previewing

Critical Thinking Strategy:
Making associations

¡Hoy va a nevar mucho!

¡Hoy va a nevar mucho!: Today it's going to snow a lot!

¡35°! ¡Calor increíble en la capital!

¡Los esquiadores están contentos!

Tormenta tropical localizada en el golfo

¡Seis semanas sin sol!

Accidente de dos barcos en el Lago de Chapala

El aeropuerto está cerrado

¡Aquí te toca a ti!

A. ¿Qué tiempo hace? Indica la descripción que corresponde a lo que dice el periódico *(what the newspaper says)*.

1. Hace mucho viento.
2. Hay niebla.
3. Nieva.
4. Está muy nublado.
5. Llueve mucho.
6. Hace calor.

77

Etapa Support Materials

Workbook: **pp. 59–64**
Teacher Tape
Quiz: **Testing Program, p. 38**

Spanish speakers, ¡Hoy va a nevar mucho!: Ask Spanish speakers if there is a Spanish-language newspaper in their community and, if so, if the weather is given any coverage. Ask them to bring in copies of the newpaper to share with the rest of the class.

Ex. A: pair work

Answers, Ex. A: 1. Tormenta tropical localizada en el golfo 2. El aeropuerto está cerrado / Accidente de dos barcos en el Lago de Chapala 3. ¡Los esquiadores están contentos! / El aeropuerto está cerrado / ¡Seis semanas sin sol! 4. ¡Seis semanas sin sol! / Tormenta tropical localizada en el golfo 5. ¡Seis semanas sin sol! / Tormenta tropical localizada en el golfo 6. ¡35°! ¡Calor increíble en la capital!

More-prepared students, Ex. A: Have more-prepared students create additional weather headlines. You may need to supply vocabulary as expansion items.

Less-prepared students, Ex. A: Have less-prepared students supply the possible weather conditions for the headlines created by their classmates, using Ex. A as a model.

Ex. B: pair work

writing

Suggestion, Ex. B: Supply students with, or ask them to bring, a weather map from a Spanish-language newspaper. Then have them repeat Ex. B using the weather conditions on that map. Students need not understand every word of the forecast. They will recognize some words that have been used previously. They can guess others because they are cognates, because of the context, or because of the symbols used. To facilitate this exercise, have students focus on Saturday's *maximum* temperature when determining the forecast, as well as the abbreviations (t, pc, s, c).

Possible answers, Ex. B:
1. Va a hacer fresco. Va a estar un poco nublado.   2. Va a hacer mucho calor. Va a estar un poco nublado.   3. Va a hacer calor. Va a estar un poco nublado.   4. Va a hacer mucho calor. Va a estar un poco nublado.   5. Va a hacer calor. Va a hacer sol.   6. Va a hacer muchísimo calor. Va a estar despejado.   7. Va a hacer fresco. Va a hacer sol.   8. Va a hacer calor. Va a estar un poco nublado.   9. Va a hacer muchísimo calor. Va a estar un poco nublado.   10. Va a hacer calor. Va a hacer sol.   11. Va a hacer mucho calor. Va a estar un poco nublado.   12. Va a hacer calor. Va a hacer sol.

B. Hoy va a hacer muy buen tiempo. Mira el pronóstico del tiempo *(weather forecast)* y contesta las preguntas. Sigue el modelo.

Modelo: ¿Qué tiempo va a hacer el sábado en Nueva York?
Va a hacer calor. Va a estar un poco nublado.

t = thundershower
pc = partly cloudy
s = sunny
c = cloudy

U.S. TRAVELERS' FORECAST

	FRI	SAT		FRI	SAT
Atlanta	94/74s	92/70t	Minneapolis	79/58s	85/62pc
Atlantic City	86/66t	76/60pc	New Orleans	93/72pc	93/72pc
Boston	81/64t	66/58pc	New York	84/65t	77/57pc
Buffalo	72/53c	70/54s	Orlando	94/74t	95/74pc
Chicago	75/55pc	79/59s	Philadelphia	88/66t	78/60pc
Cincinnati	89/65t	82/59pc	Phoenix	103/80pc	108/78s
Dallas	100/78s	100/78pc	Pittsburgh	80/60t	76/54pc
Denver	90/58pc	90/57s	Portland, OR	80/57pc	75/55s
Detroit	78/55c	77/57s	San Francisco	75/56s	75/58pc
Houston	96/76s	94/76pc	Seattle	72/56pc	70/55pc
Los Angeles	90/70pc	90/70pc	St. Louis	90/67t	87/67pc
Miami	92/76pc	90/75pc	Washington	93/70t	79/65pc

¿Qué tiempo va a hacer el sábado . . .

1. en Boston?
2. en Houston?
3. en San Francisco?
4. en Orlando?
5. en Detroit?
6. en Phoenix?
7. en Buffalo?
8. en Pittsburgh?
9. en Dallas?
10. en Denver?
11. en New Orleans?
12. en Chicago?

Learning Strategy:
Reading for cultural information

COMENTARIOS
CULTURALES

■ *La siesta*

The custom of taking an afternoon rest is often necessary in tropical countries where temperatures are hottest during the middle of the day. Seeking refuge indoors is practically a must, and the reference to the sixth hour of the day (**la sexta hora,** or high noon) as **la siesta** has become commonplace in Spanish-speaking cultures. In some countries, small businesses close for a few hours during the hottest part of the afternoon, extending store hours into the early evening. **Echar** or **dormir una siesta** means *to take a nap.*

78

Repaso

C. ¿Cuál es la fecha?
Working with your partner, make a list in Spanish of the 12 months of the year. For any ten months, name and give the date of a holiday or special event which takes place in that month. Some possibilities that you may want to include are **la Navidad** (Christmas), **la independencia de los Estados Unidos, el Año Nuevo, el Día de los Enamorados, tu cumpleaños, el Día de Acción de Gracias** (Thanksgiving). You might refer to Activity E on page 71 for other ideas.

Learning Strategy:
Listing

Critical Thinking Strategy:
Making associations

ESTRUCTURA

Stem-changing verbs in the present tense

—Yo siempre **juego** al fútbol por la tarde. ¿Y tú?
—Yo también. **¿Juegas** mañana?
—¿Mañana? Sí. Y Juan **piensa** jugar también.
—Bueno, **podemos** jugar juntos.

I always *play* soccer in the afternoon. What about you?
I do, too. *Are you playing* tomorrow?
Tomorrow? Yes. And Juan *is thinking about* playing also.
Good, *we can* play together.

As you learned in Level 1 of **¡Ya verás!**, some verbs change their stems in the present and preterite tenses. Stem-changing verbs are verbs that have a change in the vowels of the stem (everything before the **-ar, -er,** or **-ir** ending of the infinitive). All the endings, however, remain regular. There are three types of stem-changing verbs in the present: the stem vowels change to **ie, ue,** or **i.**

pensar (ie)		dormir (ue)		pedir (i)	
p**ie**nso	pensamos	d**ue**rmo	dormimos	p**i**do	pedimos
p**ie**nsas	pensáis	d**ue**rmes	dormís	p**i**des	pedís
p**ie**nsa	p**ie**nsan	d**ue**rme	d**ue**rmen	p**i**de	p**i**den

Other verbs of this type that you have seen include:

(ie) comenzar, despertar(se), empezar, querer
(ue) acostar(se), jugar, poder
(i)   servir

Stem-changing verbs are indicated in the glossary by the notation **(ie), (ue),** or **(i)** after the infinitive form.

79

Follow-up, Ex. C: After students complete their lists of months and holidays, make a master list on the board and poll the class to see which answers are the same and which are different. Ask students if they know any Hispanic holidays and add these to the list. Possibilities include: **el 5 de mayo, el 16 de septiembre, el 12 de octubre, el 6 de enero.**

Presentation: Estructura

Write an example of each type of stem-changing verb (**o–ue, e–ie, e–i**) on the board, underlining the stem changes and contrasting these forms with the **nosotros** forms. Brainstorm with students other verbs for each category and write these in the appropriate columns. Point to a verb and call on students at random to give the form for different subjects (**yo, tú, ella, Juan y yo,** etc.)

Spanish speakers, Estructura: Most Spanish speakers will be familiar with these verbs. A common variation in Spanish-speaking communities in the U.S. is to make the stem change in the **nosotros** form, i.e., **piensamos, duermimos, pidimos.** Have Spanish-speaking students focus on the difference between the Spanish they speak at home and the more formal Spanish that is being taught here.

Recycling Activity

The **Repaso** activity in the second (and third) **etapas** of each chapter recycles material from the previous **etapa.**

Ex. C: pair work

Answers, Ex. C: La Navidad es el veinticinco de diciembre. La independencia de los Estados Unidos es el cuatro de julio. El Año Nuevo es el primero de enero. El Día de los Enamorados es el catorce de febrero. Mi cumpleaños es el... .

Ex. D: pair work

writing

More-prepared students,
Ex. D: Have more-prepared students expand their answers by offering a contrast with a different subject and a reason for the contrast, using weather expressions or the verb **gustar.** For example: **Marisol piensa ir a la playa, pero nosotros no pensamos ir porque hoy hace mucho viento.**

Less-prepared students,
Ex. D: Have less-prepared students look at the verb column and identify the type of stem change in each verb. Make three columns on the board: **o–ue, e–ie,** and **e–i.** As students identify the stem changes, write the infinitives under the appropriate column and remind students to refer to this chart as they work. At the same time ask **¿Qué quiere decir pensar, volver?,** etc. in order to facilitate logical sentence writing.

Ex. E: groups of four or more

More-prepared students,
Ex. E: Encourage more-prepared students to ask each other follow-up questions, such as **¿Adónde quieres viajar los sábados?** or **¿Por qué duermes (no duermes) ocho horas cada noche?** When students have completed the exercise, call on them at random to report on their findings, e. g.: **María quiere viajar a la playa los sábados si hace buen tiempo.**

Aquí practicamos

D. Combina un elemento de cada columna para formar una oración lógica *(logical sentence)*. Sigue el modelo.

Modelo: Marisol   pensar   ir a la playa.
Marisol piensa ir a la playa.

A	B	C
mis hermanos	volver	ocho horas cada noche
Carlos	comenzar	hablar con los amigos
el (la) profesor(a)	pensar	café con leche
Alonso y Carmen	querer	al tenis
tú	pedir	a estudiar ahora
el camarero	jugar	a la casa después
vosotros	dormir	a los clientes
yo	servir	ir al cine

Learning Strategy:
Asking questions

Critical Thinking Strategy:
Making associations

E. Encuentra alguien que... (Find somebody who . . .) Ask questions of your classmates to find someone who fits each of the following descriptions. When you find someone, write a sentence in your notebook using that person's name.

Modelo: *Amy quiere viajar los sábados.*

1. querer viajar los sábados
2. dormir ocho horas cada noche
3. dormir mucho los sábados
4. jugar al básquetbol
5. pedir ayuda con la tarea
6. poder tocar la guitarra
7. pensar ir al cine mañana
8. acostarse después de las 11 de la noche
9. despertarse después de las ocho de la mañana los sábados
10. comenzar a jugar al tenis

80

Less-prepared students, Ex. E: Help less-prepared students write a list of questions with the correct forms of stem-changing verbs before they poll their classmates. Remind them to leave space to note their classmates' responses. When they are done, call on students at random to report on their findings.

F. ¿Qué haces después de las clases? Your new neighbor arrives home from school at the same time that you do. He (She) also happens to be in your Spanish class. (1) Greet each other. (2) Introduce yourselves. (3) Tell each other at least three activities that you typically do after school. (4) Find one activity in common that the two of you would like to do together this afternoon. Follow the model.

Modelo:
— *Buenos días. ¿Cómo estás?*
— *Muy bien. ¿Y tú?*
— *Bien, gracias. Tú estás en mi clase de español. Me llamo Juanita.*
— *Encantada, Juanita. Me llamo Sofía. Oye, ¿qué piensas hacer después de las clases?*
— *No sé. Generalmente vuelvo a la casa a las 3:30 y empiezo a hacer la tarea. A veces juego al béisbol; a veces miro la televisión.*
— *No quiero hacer la tarea ahora. No juego al béisbol, pero juego al tenis. Pienso ir al café para tomar un refresco y después ir al centro. ¿Quieres ir conmigo?*
— *Sí, Vamos. Tengo ganas de tomar un refresco.*

Cooperative Learning

Learning Strategies:

Asking and responding to questions, negotiating

Aquí escuchamos:
"¡Hace mucho frío!"

Antes de escuchar

The Valenzuela family is on vacation in Portillo, but the weather is bad and the children are unhappy. Look at the following questions to get an idea of what you will hear in their conversation.

START

Después de escuchar

1. ¿Por qué no están contentos los hijos?
2. ¿Qué tiempo hace en Acapulco, probablemente?
3. ¿Qué hizo la familia ayer?
4. ¿Hay música en el hotel?
5. ¿Qué cosa positiva dice el padre?

Learning Strategy:

Listening for details

Support material, Aquí escuchamos: Teacher Tape

Presentation: Aquí escuchamos

Begin by summarizing the conversation: **La familia Valenzuela está de vacaciones en Portillo. Hace mal tiempo y los hijos no están contentos. Pero por lo menos esquiaron un poco, todos comen bien y están de vacaciones en familia.**

Variation, Aquí escuchamos: Use this excerpt for dictation practice. Divide the class into three groups and assign a speaker to each group (Marcelo, Susana, and Mamá and Papá together for the third group). Remind students only to listen the first time the tape is played (perhaps with their desks cleared). Next have them take out paper and pencil, remind them to listen and write only for their group's speaker, then play the tape a second time. Finally, replay the tape for adjustments and corrections. Allow group members to consult with each other to check their work. Then assign a member of each group to read one of the parts and have them read through the whole conversation. You may also wish to assign secretaries to write the conversation on the board. Then do final corrections from the master on the board.

Spanish speakers, Aquí escuchamos: The exercises that accompany this section should pose little problem for Spanish speakers. They should, however, be directed to focus on "listening in context" to any vocabulary that may be new for them.

Answers, Aquí escuchamos: 1. Están aburridos / Hace mal tiempo. 2. buen tiempo, con mucho sol 3. esquió un poco 4. no 5. que están de vacaciones en familia

Ex. F: pair work

role play

More-prepared students, Ex. F: Remind more-prepared students to use as many stem-changing verbs as possible and to vary their greetings. Call on one or two pairs of students or create pairs to role play for the class.

Less-prepared students, Ex. F: Brainstorm possible greetings and normal daily activities with less-prepared students before they begin Ex. F. Have them follow the model closely on their first try, then have them use alternate greetings and activities on their second try. Call on several pairs of students to perform for the class.

Exs. G and H: pair work

Less-prepared students, Ex. G: Brainstorm a list of possible activities with less-prepared students. Quickly review months of the year and weather expressions. Remind them to use the preterite and have them recall how it is formed. Have them do the exercise twice, first following the model very closely, then substituting alternate expressions. Brainstorm a list of interrogative words with them before going on to Ex. H.

More-prepared students, Ex. G: Encourage variation and independence, reminding more-prepared students that they don't need to follow the model exactly. Have them invent vacations; for example, a dream vacation or the worst vacation of their life.

Follow-up, Exs. G and H: Have students report back on their vacations. Encourage them to compare and contrast their classmates' experiences.

Spanish speakers, Ex. H: Have the Spanish-speaking students practice using vocabulary that may be new for them. Emphasize that they may need such vocabulary when talking to people from other parts of the Spanish-speaking world. Be sensitive to the fact that what they say may be appropriate in their speech community. Have students focus on the differences between how they say something in their speech community and how the book teaches them to express the same idea.

Ex. I: writing

¡Aquí te toca a ti!

Learning Strategy:

Narrating in the past

G. Las vacaciones Tell your classmates about a vacation you took with your family or friends. Explain (1) where you went and (2) in which month. Then (3) describe the weather and (4) tell three activities that you did. Follow the model.

Modelo:

Dónde:	*Fuimos de vacaciones a Disney World.*
Mes:	*Fuimos en el mes de junio.*
Tiempo:	*Hizo calor. Hizo sol. Hizo muy buen tiempo.*
Actividades:	*Jugamos al tenis, bailamos por la noche y conocimos al Ratón Miguelito.*

¡Adelante!

EJERCICIO ORAL

H. Mis vacaciones Find out from one of your classmates about his or her last vacation. Ask (1) where he or she went, (2) with whom, (3) when, (4) what the weather was like, and (5) at least three activities that he or she did, including at least one activity done when the weather was bad. Prepare to report back to the class.

Learning Strategies:

Asking for information, organizing information

EJERCICIO ESCRITO

Learning Strategy:

Organizing information

I. Una postal Write a postcard to a friend, describing what you did during a vacation that you just had with your family. (You may refer to a real vacation or use your imagination.) Tell (1) where you went, (2) when, (3) with whom, (4) one interesting site that you visited, and (5) two other activities that you did, including one done when the weather was bad.

82

Suggestion, Ex. I: Have students write postcards to students in another Spanish class. Remind them to ask questions of the student to whom they are writing. Have the other class answer the postcards. You may want to continue periodic correspondence between students in different classes or different schools. Students enjoy these real communication activities.

Spanish speakers, Ex. I: Always have Spanish speakers fully carry out this activity. Although many of them speak and understand Spanish, they may not know how to write the language. This is a good place to start building basic literacy skills in Spanish. Have them pay special attention to the spelling of the vocabulary introduced in this **etapa.** Have them engage in peer-editing, focusing on the spelling in the written work of a partner.

TERCERA ETAPA

Preparación

》》 **W**hat do the weather symbols on the map mean?

》》 **W**hat temperature system is used in the United States?

》》 **W**hat temperature system is more commonly used in the rest of the world?

》》 **I**n what areas of the United States does it tend to be particularly hot? particularly cold?

》》 **W**hat do you know about weather patterns in the countries of Latin America?

/././././././././././

Learning Strategy:

Previewing

Spanish speakers, ¿Qué tiempo va a hacer mañana?: Ask Spanish speakers if they have traveled to Spanish-speaking countries where the Celsius scale is used. Have them give examples of hot and cold temperatures. (Is 17° C hot or cold?)

¿Qué tiempo va a hacer mañana?

83

Etapa Support Materials

Workbook: **pp. 65–69**
Transparency: **#9**
Teacher Tape

Quiz: **Testing Program, p. 41**
Chapter Test: **Testing Program, p. 43**

¡Aquí te toca a ti!

A. *La temperatura está en...*   Tell your new Spanish-speaking friend what the temperature usually is in your hometown during different months of the year, so that he or she may better understand climate in the U.S. Look at the **Comentarios culturales** below and use Celsius for the temperatures.

Modelo: *En octubre la temperatura en Boston está en cinco grados centígrados.*

B. *¿Qué tiempo va a hacer?*   Look at the temperatures given for the various cities on page 83. According to the temperature, say whether it will be warm (**calor**), cool (**fresco**), cold (**frío**), or very cold (**mucho frío**) on May 26, and give a second indicator of the weather in that city according to the icons on the map. Then choose one activity your friends in each location can plan to do outside (**afuera**) on that day.

Modelo: Lima
Va a hacer fresco y va a estar nublado. Mis amigos de Lima pueden jugar al fútbol, pero no deben nadar.

1. Asunción
2. Caracas
3. Santiago

4. San José
5. Buenos Aires
6. La Habana

7. Bogotá
8. La Paz
9. Montevideo

COMENTARIOS CULTURALES

La temperatura

Temperatures in Spain and Latin American countries are given on the Celsius (centigrade) scale. Here is a comparison of Celsius temperatures and their Fahrenheit equivalents.

C:	30°	25°	20°	15°	10°	5°	0°	-5°
F:	86°	77°	68°	59°	50°	41°	32°	23°

To convert from Celsius to Fahrenheit, follow these steps:
   a. Divide by 5   b. Multiply by 9   c. Add 32

For example, if the temperature is 34° Celsius, you would calculate as follows:
   a. 35 divided by 5 = 7   b. 7 x 9= 63   c. 63 +32 = 95° Fahrenheit

84

Cooperative Learning

Question-and-Answer Pairs

- Put the students into pairs of differing abilities. Explain that they are going to figure out together **¿Qué tiempo va a hacer el 26 mayo?** for various cities.
- Have them decide how to figure out the weather from the information in the map on page 83.

- Have them begin, taking turns telling about the weather for each city and encouraging and helping each other.
- Ask students at random where they would like to be on the map on **el 26 de mayo,** why, and what season it is there.

C. ¿Qué tiempo va a hacer mañana?

Indícale a un(a) compañero(a) el tiempo que crees que va a hacer aquí mañana. Pueden referirse a las posibilidades de la lista o añadir *(add)* otras. Sigue el modelo.

llover / hacer sol / estar nublado / estar despejado / hacer frío / hacer fresco / hacer calor

Modelo: ¿Va a hacer buen tiempo mañana?
No, va a llover.

1. ¿Va a nevar mañana?
2. ¿Va a hacer frío mañana?
3. ¿Va a hacer buen tiempo mañana?
4. ¿Va a estar despejado mañana?
5. ¿Va a llover mañana?

D. Ayer y mañana

Usa las pistas *(cues)* para hablar del tiempo de ayer y de mañana. Trabaja con un(a) compañero(a) y sigan el modelo.

Modelo: buen tiempo / también
—*¿Qué tiempo hizo ayer?*
—*Hizo buen tiempo.*
—*¿Qué tiempo va a hacer mañana?*
—*Va a hacer buen tiempo también.*

1. mal / también
2. calor / bastante frío
3. llover / también
4. viento / mucho calor
5. nublado / sol
6. muy buen tiempo / nevar
7. tormenta / buen tiempo
8. fresco / bastante calor

Critical Thinking Strategy:

Predicting

85

Ex. C: pair work

writing

Suggestion, Ex. C: After students have gone through the exercise, have them create their own questions for their partners, based on the models in the exercise, but using alternate expressions.

Ex. D: pair work

Preparation, Ex. D: Before beginning the paired work, have students recall and contrast the present, preterite, and future forms of the weather verbs **(hacer, haber, estar)**. Write **hoy, ayer,** and **mañana** at the top of three columns; under each have students supply the correct verb forms.

Expansion, Ex. D: When the pairs finish describing yesterday's and tomorrow's weather, have them redo the exercise, incorporating the present tense by describing (1) yesterday's vs. today's weather in numbers 1–4 and (2) today's vs. tomorrow's weather in numbers 5–8. Tell students they can use **y** to join and compare two like statements and **pero** to join and contrast two different statements. For example: 1. **Ayer hizo mal tiempo y hoy hace mal tiempo también.** 5. **Hoy está nublado, pero mañana va a hacer sol.**

Answers, Ex. D: 1. Hizo mal tiempo. Va a hacer mal tiempo también.   2. Hizo calor. Va a hacer bastante frío.   3. Llovió. Va a llover también.   4. Hizo viento. Va a hacer mucho calor.   5. Estuvo nublado. Va a hacer sol.   6. Hizo muy buen tiempo. Va a nevar. 7. Hubo tormenta. Va a hacer buen tiempo.   8. Hizo fresco. Va a hacer bastante calor.

Ex. E: ✎ writing

|/-/-/-/-/-/-/-/-/-//
Learning Strategy:

Describing based on visual cues

E. ¿Qué hacen?   Describe lo que hacen las personas en los dibujos. Usa los verbos *jugar* y *volver*, y otros verbos que sabes.

Modelo: *Juegan al fútbol.*

1.

2.

3.

4.

ESTRUCTURA

The verb *saber*

—¿**Sabes** quién es ese actor de cine?   *Do you know* who that movie actor is?
—Claro que **sé** quien es. ¡Es Rubén   Sure, *I know* who he is. It's Rubén Blades!
Blades! ¡Y además **sabe** cantar!   And he also *knows* how to sing!

Here is the way to form the present tense of the verb **saber:**

saber			
yo	**sé**	nosotros(as)	sab**emos**
tú	sab**es**	vosotros(as)	sab**éis**
él		ellos	
ella	} sab**e**	ellas	} sab**en**
Ud.		Uds.	

Saber is used to talk about knowledge of facts or something that has been learned thoroughly, as well as to say that you know how to do something. In this last instance **saber** is used before an infinitive form of another verb.

Rita **sabe bailar** bien.   Rita *knows how to dance* well.
Tú **sabes hablar** tres idiomas, ¿verdad?   You *know how to speak* three languages, right?

Aquí practicamos

F. *Sé hablar español*   Take turns talking with a classmate about what you know and do not know how to do. Refer to the possibilities on the list or add others. Follow the model.

Learning Strategies:
Selecting and giving personal information

 Modelo:
—*Yo sé nadar pero no sé esquiar. Y tú, ¿qué sabes hacer?*
—*Yo sé jugar al tenis pero no sé nadar.*

nadar	quién es el (la) mejor	manejar un automóvil
esquiar	estudiante de la clase	hablar español
jugar al tenis	el número de teléfono	tocar la guitarra
el nombre del	de la escuela	bailar el mambo
presidente de México	dónde está el estado	cuántos estudiantes
jugar al fútbol	de Iowa	hay en la clase hoy
	preparar tacos	de dónde es el (la) profesor(a)

G. *Preguntas*   Usa las pistas para hacerles cuatro preguntas a otros estudiantes. Usa el verbo *saber* y los sujetos *tú, Uds., él/ella* y *ellos/ellas*. Sigue el modelo.

Modelo: *¿Sabes tú hablar español?*
¿Saben Uds. hablar español?

1. hablar francés
2. los meses del año
3. cuándo va a hacer calor
4. si llueve mucho en marzo
5. quiénes son mis amigos
6. jugar al béisbol

87

H. Mi amigo(a) nuevo(a)   You are writing your Spanish-speaking pen pal about a classmate you would like to get to know better. Refer to the list of possible topics in Activity F if you need ideas for what your new friend knows and does not know how to do. Tell which things you know about your friend, such as age, telephone number, birthday, etc. Point out special talents (**Él/Ella sabe tocar el piano, patinar…**). Mention to your pen pal which facts you still do not know about this classmate. Use the verb **saber** as many times as you can along with other verbs you know.

Aquí escuchamos:
"¿Va a llover mañana?"

Antes de escuchar

Tomorrow is Saturday. Patricia and her friends talk about their plans for the weekend. Their plans depend on what the weather will be like. Look at the following questions and identify a few things you expect to hear them talk about.

Después de escuchar

1. ¿Qué tiempo va a hacer mañana por la mañana? ¿por la tarde?
2. ¿Cómo saben esto las amigas?
3. ¿Adónde quiere ir Margo?
4. ¿Qué van a hacer las amigas por la mañana?
5. ¿Adónde van por la tarde?

¡Aquí te toca a ti!

I. Planes para el fin de semana   You and two of your friends are making plans for the weekend. Each time one of you makes a suggestion, another uses the weather as a reason for not doing the proposed activity. Then the third person comes up with a suggestion of another activity more appropriate for the weather forecasted. Take turns being the first to suggest an activity. Follow the models.

Modelos: ir a la playa

Estudiante 1: *Vamos a la playa.*
Estudiante 2: *No, va a hacer frío mañana.*
Estudiante 3: *Entonces, vamos al cine.*

88

mirar la televisión

Estudiante 1: *Vamos a mirar la televisión.*
Estudiante 2: *No, va a hacer buen tiempo mañana.*
Estudiante 3: *Entonces, damos un paseo al parque.*

1. ir a las montañas
2. dar un paseo
3. ir al centro
4. nadar en la piscina
5. jugar al básquetbol
6. ir al cine
7. correr
8. estudiar en casa

¡Adelante!

EJERCICIO ORAL

J. *Una entrevista* Working with a partner, imagine that an exchange student from Latin America has just arrived on your campus. The school newspaper has asked you to interview him or her since you know Spanish. Use the following items as guidelines for organizing your interview and take notes on the information you receive. Switch roles and partners after the first interview.

Ask…

1. when he or she arrived in the United States
2. if he or she likes the United States
3. where he or she lives in Latin America
4. what the weather is like in his or her hometown
5. if he or she lives near the beach
6. when he or she was born
7. what his or her parents do
8. if he or she has any brothers or sisters
9. if he or she knows how to ski

> **Learning Strategies:**
>
> *Organizing, interviewing, asking for or giving personal information, taking notes*

EJERCICIO ESCRITO

K. *Los resultados de una entrevista* Ahora usa la información obtenida en la entrevista en el Actividad J para escribir el artículo para el periódico de tu escuela.

> **Learning Strategies:**
>
> *Compiling and organizing information in an article, paraphrasing, reporting*

89

Ex. J: pair work

role play

Less-prepared students, Ex. J: Before breaking the class into pairs, brainstorm with students a list of questions for eliciting the information needed for the exercise.

Spanish speakers, Ex. J: Have the Spanish-speaking students practice using vocabulary that may be new for them. Emphasize that they may need to use such vocabulary when talking to people from other parts of the Spanish-speaking world. Be sensitive to the fact that what they say may be appropriate in their speech community. Have students focus on the differences between how they say something in their speech community and how the book teaches them to express the same idea. Remember, your main objective is to expand the range of contexts in which these students can use Spanish.

Ex. K: writing

More-prepared students, Ex. K: Allow more-prepared students to edit and comment on each other's work.

Spanish speakers, Ex. K: Always have Spanish speakers fully carry out this activity. Although many of them speak and understand Spanish, they may not know how to write the language. This is a good place to start building basic literacy skills in Spanish. Have them pay special attention to the spelling of the vocabulary introduced in this **etapa.** Have them engage in peer-editing, focusing on the spelling in the written work of a partner.

Chapter Culminating Activity

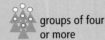 groups of four or more

Divide the class into groups of four or five students. Have each group create a ten-minute (approx.) TV show that includes a weather report with headlines and maps; an interview similar to Ex. J (p. 89), using an Hispanic celebrity; and a commercial, using formal commands, food items, and prices. Have the groups perform for each other or allow the students to videotape their shows and then have a viewing session.

Suggestion, Vocabulario: Many of these words and expressions lend themselves to "Pictionary" or "win-lose-or-draw" type games.

Spanish speakers: Vocabulario: Point out the words that have problematic spelling combinations that were highlighted on p. 19 of "To the Teacher" in the Teacher's Edition. You may want to encourage students to keep a spelling notebook with categories such as: **Palabras con ll, Palabras con v, Palabras con b,** etc. Another category might be headed **Así lo digo yo** for students to work on the spelling of words and expressions that they already know that might be variations of what has been presented in this book.

Vocabulario

Para charlar

Para hablar del tiempo

¿Qué tiempo hace?
Está despejado.
Está nublado.
Está resbaloso.
Hace buen tiempo.
Hace calor.
Hace fresco.
Hace frío.
Hace mal tiempo.
Hace sol.
Hace viento.
Hay hielo.

Hay neblina.
Hay niebla.
Hay nubes.
Hay tormenta.
Llovizna.
Llueve.
Nieva.
Truena.
La temperatura
  está en… grados
  (bajo cero).

Para preguntar y dar la fecha

¿A cuántos estamos?
¿Cuál es la fecha de hoy
  (de tu cumpleaños, etc.)?
¿Qué fecha es hoy?
Hoy es el 5 de abril.
En (el mes de) enero
  (febrero, marzo, etc.)…
Él (Ella) nació…

Temas y contextos

Los meses del año

enero	julio
febrero	agosto
marzo	septiembre
abril	octubre
mayo	noviembre
junio	diciembre

Las estaciones del año

la primavera
el verano
el otoño
el invierno

Vocabulario general

Sustantivos

el mar
la montaña
la neblina
la niebla
la nieve
la temperatura
la tormenta

Verbos

jugar
saber
volver

Otras palabras y expresiones

demasiado
depender de
echar (dormir) una siesta

Cooperative Learning

Paired Nerf Ball Toss

- Have the students form pairs and sit face-to-face in two concentric circles.
- Tell the pairs that they are going to review the **Vocabulario** together.
- Explain that you are going to start the exercise by making a statement. Say: **Hoy es el 5 de abril.** Direct the pairs to discuss all they can about **el 5 de abril,** making a particular effort to use the vocabulary they have recently learned.

Do not neglect this step, as it demands that all students think of a response before you call on particular students.
- Then throw the Nerf ball to a student in the circle. The student who catches the ball and his or her partner share their response.
- Make another statement and have all students confer on how to respond to it. Direct the pair with the ball to throw it to another pair to have them respond.
- Continue the exercise in the same manner. Keep it moving.
- You may want to give an individual or team quiz as a follow-up.

Lectura CULTURAL

EL TIEMPO ES RELATIVO

Antes de leer

1. What does the word **tiempo** mean in Spanish? Does it have more than one meaning? What do you think it will mean in this reading?
2. In a normal conversation between speakers of English, if the topic of weather comes up, at what point in the conversation does this usually happen?
3. What kinds of words or expressions do you usually find in articles dealing with the weather? Make a list of some of these in Spanish.
4. Do you have any of the following on your list? What do they mean?

condiciones atmosféricas	**hace calor**	**está lloviendo**
hace buen/mal tiempo	**hace frío**	**boletín meteorológico**

Guía para la lectura

A. Scan the passage on page 92 and find the expressions listed at the end of **Antes de leer**.

B. As you come upon the answers in each paragraph, indicate whether the following statements are true or false.

1. El tema del tiempo es de igual importancia en todas las culturas.
2. Cada cultura determina los usos y los significados de una palabra.
3. La palabra tiempo tiene varios significados en español.
4. Cuando hace buen tiempo en los países de habla española no se habla del clima.
5. Es una costumbre entre hispanohablantes iniciar una conversación con comentarios sobre el clima.
6. Hay muchas expresiones para preguntar sobre la salud de una persona.

//-//-//-//-//-//-//-//-//
Learning Strategies:
Scanning for cognates, previewing, reading for details

//-//-//-//-//-//-//-//-//
Learning Strategy:
Reading for details

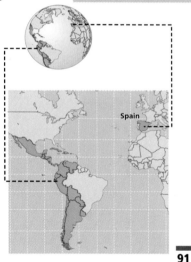

Spain

91

Lectura cultural

Postreading

After students have read and understood, you may want to open a general discussion in English on the topic, by asking some of the following questions. Why do people talk about the weather? What other topics do people make "small talk" about? What topics don't people discuss and why not? Judging from the article, what impressions does the Latin American author hold about North American people? Are these impressions realistic or not and why? What cultural information does he give about people in Latin America?

Spanish speakers: Lectura cultural: Have Spanish-speaking students go through each of the exercises in this section. We have incorporated a number of reading activities in the *¡Ya verás!* program that reflect some of the latest research. Spanish-speaking students who have been educated in American schools already read English. However, research on reading has shown that the transfer of reading skills from one language to another is far from automatic. Special attention should be paid to having Spanish-speaking students complete all of the exercises and activities that accompany the readings in this program. Once they complete the activities, you may want to ask them to summarize the reading in Spanish in order to give them additional writing practice. You may also suggest that they keep a notebook with a list of new vocabulary they find in the reading selections.

Answers, Guía para la lectura: **B.** 1.F 2.T 3.T 4.T 5.F 6.

El tiempo es relativo

José Juan Arrom

Para muchas personas que viven la mayor parte de su vida en Nueva Inglaterra, uno de los primeros temas de una conversación es el tiempo. Esta palabra tiene usos muy variados que dependen de su contexto cultural. Es decir, los significados y la importancia que tiene el tiempo en los países de habla española no siempre corresponden a los que tiene en los países de habla inglesa.

Es evidente que la palabra *tiempo,* tal como se acaba de usar, equivale a *condiciones atmosféricas.* También, como en inglés, es la idea que usamos para hablar de la distancia o la duración de algo que pasa, calculándolo por segundos, minutos, horas, días, meses, años y hasta siglos. Pero aquí vamos a limitar la discusión del tiempo, por ahora, a lo que también se llama *el clima.*

En este sentido de la palabra, en España y en América Latina de vez en cuando se dice que hace buen tiempo o que hace mal tiempo. Pero con más frecuencia, si el tiempo es bueno, se acepta como una realidad y no se dice más. Y si es malo, la gente puede decir que "hace un calor horroroso", que "está lloviendo a cántaros" o que "hace un frío de los mil diablos".

Aun así, hablar del tiempo es una manera poco usada para comenzar una conversación en español. Generalmente, el boletín meteorológico le interesa mucho menos a la persona de habla española que la salud de la persona con quien habla y la de su familia. Por eso el idioma español es tan rico en frases como: "¿Qué tal? ¿Cómo te va? ¿Cómo estás? ¿Qué cuentas? ¿Qué me dices? ¿Qué pasó? ¿Qué anda? ¿Qué hubo? ¿Cómo andan por tu casa? ¿Qué me dices de la familia?," etc. Y la persona que recibe la pregunta sabe que no es de mal gusto contestar con detalles. Al contrario, es importante dar esos detalles.

a cántaros: pitchersfull / *de mal gusto:* in bad taste

¿CÓMO ES?

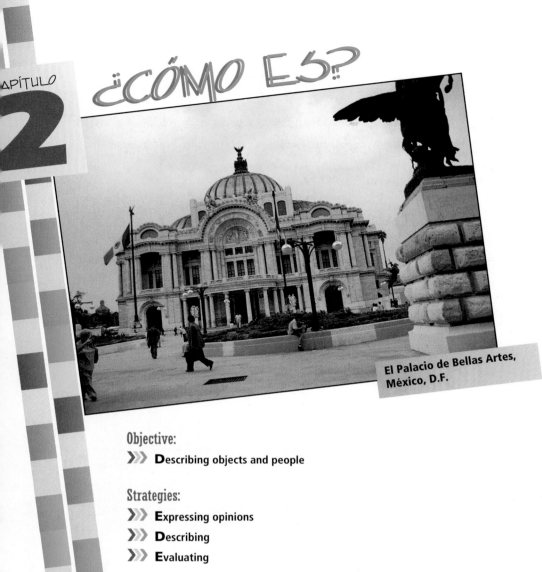

El Palacio de Bellas Artes,
México, D.F.

Objective:

>>> **D**escribing objects and people

Strategies:

>>> **E**xpressing opinions

>>> **D**escribing

>>> **E**valuating

Chapter Objectives

Functions: Describing objects and people

Context: Using descriptive adjectives to comment on people, places, and things

Accuracy: Agreement and position of adjectives; plural forms of adjectives; shortened adjectives

Cultural Context

Point out that this building is where the **Ballet Folklórico de México** performs on a regular basis. In addition, due to the weight of the building and the unstable nature of the ground beneath it (a lake bed at the time of the Aztecs), the **Palacio de Bellas Artes** sinks slightly each year. The effect can be seen by the way the paved area around the building angles down toward the building's base.

Video/Laserdisc

Chapter 2 Video Program and Video Guide

Presentation: Descríbeme...

Introduce the new adjectives using a question-answer format. **¿Este coche es grande o pequeño? Es pequeño. ¿Y ese coche? Es grande.** Reminder: **Este** is used to refer to an object close to the speaker. **Ese** refers to something farther away from the speaker.

Spanish speakers: Descríbeme...: Ask Spanish speakers for variations of the adjectives that are introduced here or other expressions that have not been listed (e.g., **chiquito, nuevo, asqueroso,** etc.). They may know how to pronounce these variations, but may never have seen how they are written. Help them with the spelling of these variations by writing them on the board or the overhead.

Support material, ¿De qué color es... ?: Transparencies #11, #11a

Presentation: ¿De qué color es... ?

Introduce colors using objects in the class. **Esta bolsa es azul. Ese lápiz es rojo.** Give the model: **Mi color preferido es azul.** Ask students: **¿Cuál es tu color preferido?** Ask students to give the school colors in Spanish.

Spanish speakers, ¿De qué color es... ?: Ask Spanish speakers for variations of the colors that are introduced here or other colors that have not been listed (e.g., **colorado, guinda, púrpura, vermejo, marrón,** etc.). Help them with the spelling of these variations by writing them on the board or the overhead.

PRIMERA ETAPA

Preparación

//./././././././././

Learning Strategy:
Previewing

>> **W**hen you describe an object, what details do you take into account?

>> **W**hich is easier to describe—an object, a place, or a person? Why?

>> **W**hat is your favorite color? Your least favorite?

Este coche es pequeño.
Este coche es bonito.
Este coche es moderno.
Este coche es bueno.

old

Ese coche es grande.
Ese coche es feo.
Ese coche es **viejo.**
Ese coche es malo.

Este libro es interesante.
Este libro es **fácil.**
Este libro es **ligero.**

easy / difficult
light / heavy

Ese libro es aburrido.
Ese libro es **difícil.**
Ese libro es **pesado.**

What color is it?

¿De qué color es... ?

blanco	morado	anaranjado	negro	azul	rojo
gris	verde	rosado	pardo, café	amarillo	violeta

94

Etapa Support Materials

Workbook: pp. 70–76
Tapescript: p. 42
Transparencies: #10, #10a, #11, #11a
Teacher Tape
Listening Activity masters: p. 31

Quiz: **Testing Program, p. 47**

Support material, **Descríbeme...:**
Transparencies #10, #10a

¡Aquí te toca a ti!

A. ¿Cómo es?   ¿Qué adjetivo describe mejor *(best describes)* cada dibujo?

1. ¿Es fácil o difícil el examen?   2. ¿Es grande o pequeño el auto?

3. ¿Es vieja o moderna la iglesia?   4. ¿Es aburrido o interesante el libro?   5. ¿Es bonita o fea la playa?

6. ¿Es buena o mala la película?   7. ¿Es ligera o pesada la maleta?   8. ¿Es bonito o feo el pueblo?

B. ¿De qué color es?   Escoge *(Choose)* el color que mejor describe el objeto.

1. ¿Es azul o verde el cielo *(sky)*?
2. ¿Son rojas o violetas las manzanas?
3. ¿Es negro o amarillo el sol?
4. ¿Es blanca o azul la nieve?
5. ¿Son grises o amarillos los plátanos?
6. ¿Son verdes o negros los guisantes?
7. ¿Son blancas o anaranjadas las papas?
8. ¿Son amarillas o grises las nubes?

95

/-/-/-/-/-/-/-/-/-/-/-/-/
**Cooperative
Learning**

Learning Strategies:
Listing, negotiating

*Critical Thinking
Strategies:*
Comparing and con-
trasting, evaluating

C. ***Reservaciones computarizadas***   Read the following advertisement for a computerized reservation system. As you read it, make a
list of the adjectives that you find, along with the nouns they modify. You
should be able to find at least ten adjectives. Remember that adjectives
give you information about the nouns they modify.

When you have completed your list, work with a partner to verify that
you have as many adjectives as possible. Then, together, decide which
two qualities of this service you consider most important.

Speedy

SU NUEVO SISTEMA DE RESERVACIONES COMPUTARIZADO

Ahora LACSA pone el mundo en sus manos con el
nuevo sistema computarizado de reservaciones-SPEEDY.
Este nuevo sistema nos permite ayudarle a organizar su viaje hasta
el más mínimo detalle y con mayor rapidez.
SPEEDY le brinda acceso al mayor banco de información sobre
disponibilidad de espacio en cualquier línea aérea, escoge y
organiza los más convenientes vuelos y conexiones para su viaje y le
indica las tarifas más económicas.
Con SPEEDY usted puede reservar hasta con 11 meses de
anticipación y escoger el asiento que prefiera de antemano.
Además, SPEEDY tiene capacidad para informar y reservar en

13,000 hoteles, 125 cadenas hoteleras y 26 compañías
de alquiler de automóviles en todo el mundo.
Y como si fuera poco, SPEEDY se encarga de informarle y
reservarle espacio en cruceros, excursiones y eventos
culturales,así como de darle información sobre su destino desde
los lugares de interés turístico hasta ¡qué tipo de ropa
llevar! Lo único que SPEEDY no puede hacer por usted
es...empacar.
Recuerde, ahora cada vez que viaje con LACSA,
usted cuenta con SPEEDY para ayudarle a organizar su viaje
hasta el último detalle y con mayor rapidez.

||Lacsa
nos encanta la gente

Pronunciación: *The vowel combination ia*

The combination **ia** in Spanish is pronounced in one single syllable, similar to
the *ya* in the English word *yacht.*

Práctica

D. Lee cada palabra en voz alta, pronunciando con cuidado la combinación *ia.*

1. sucia	4. gracias	7. democracia
2. familia	5. gloria	8. farmacia
3. estudia	6. patria	

Repaso

E. Comentando sobre (about) **el tiempo**   Un(a) reportero(a) *(A reporter)* informa sobre el tiempo. Comenta sobre la información. Sigue el modelo.

 Modelo: La temperatura está en 23 grados centígrados.
Hace buen tiempo.

1. Esta noche la temperatura va a bajar a cinco grados centígrados.
2. El cielo está despejado.
3. Por la tarde va a estar nublado con lluvias y tormentas eléctricas.
4. Mañana la temperatura va a estar en 29 grados centígrados al mediodía.
5. Hace sol, pero va a nevar *(to snow)* por la tarde.
6. Es un día perfecto para salir a jugar al tenis con los amigos.
7. La temperatura está en 15 grados centígrados bajo cero.

F. ¿Qué sabes del tiempo?   Alternando con un(a) compañero(a) de clase, pregunten y contesten las siguientes preguntas sobre el tiempo.

 Modelo: ¿Nieva mucho en la ciudad de Miami?
No, no nieva en Miami. Hace mucho calor.

1. ¿Dónde hace más calor en mayo, aquí o en Argentina?
2. ¿En qué meses hace mal tiempo en Seattle?
3. ¿Llueve mucho en Arizona?
4. ¿Qué tiempo hace en Ecuador en diciembre?
5. ¿Cuándo hace mucho viento en Chicago?
6. ¿Cuándo nieva en Chile?
7. Si la temperatura está en 20 grados centígrados, ¿cuánto es en Fahrenheit?
8. ¿Qué tiempo hace en Acapulco, en general?

ESTRUCTURA

Agreement of adjectives

1. As you have already learned, many adjectives end in **-o** if they are masculine and in **-a** if they are feminine. If the masculine form of an adjective ends in **-e,** the feminine form also ends in **-e.** To make these adjectives plural, you simply add **-s.**

El muchacho es **alto.**	La muchacha es **alta.**
El libro es **interesante.**	La pregunta es **interesante.**
Los hombres son **inteligentes.**	Las mujeres son **inteligentes.**

97

Ex. E:  writing

Suggestion, Ex. E: If necessary, have students refer to p. 84 **(Comentarios culturales)** for the Fahrenheit/Celsius conversion.

Expansion, Ex. E: Write the items from Ex. E and other similar ones on slips of paper and put them in a container. Divide the class into two or more teams; have a member of one team pull a slip from the container, read it, then comment on it, using a correct weather expression for one point. If another member of the same team can make an additional appropriate weather expression, the team gets another point. If not, the opposing team has the opportunity to comment on the first team's expression for one point and then takes its turn, and so on.

Possible answers, Ex. E:
1. Hace frío.   2. Hace buen tiempo. Hace sol.   3. Va a hacer mal tiempo.   4. Va a hacer buen tiempo.   5. Va a hacer mal tiempo.   6. Está despejado. Hace buen tiempo.   7. Hace mucho frío.

Ex. F: pair work

Expansion, Ex. F: To help students perceive some of the geographic conditions influencing weather, have them categorize the cities or countries by location. Point out that some places may fall into more than one category. Write category headings on the board, working with cognates as you do so: **está cerca del mar / está (bastante) cerca del polo norte / está (bastante) cerca del polo sur / está cerca del ecuador / está al sur del ecuador / está en un desierto.** When you have used all the items in the exercise, invite the students to contribute comments on the weather from other cities and countries they know (you may want to have them refer to the map on p. 83). Add these to the list.

Presentation: Estructura

(1) Remind students of the need for agreement by using **norteamericano.** Remind them that nouns have gender by recalling **el mes pasado** and **la semana pasada.**
(2) Establish the general rules for agreement in number and gender.
(3) Go through the in-text summary, pointing out examples that conform to the rules of agreement.

Vocabulary Expansion

Offer more examples of adjectives ending in a vowel in the singular form: **moderno, enorme, imposible, económico, físico, práctico, pesimista, simple, complicado;** and ending in a consonant in the singular form: **leal, particular, feroz, marrón, portugués, japonés.** Give students different subjects to go with each form of each adjective, and have the students write and/or say the correct forms. For example, **un hombre portugués/dos mujeres portuguesas,** etc.

Ex. G: writing

Answers, Ex. G: 1. aburrida
2. fácil   3. colombiana   4. alegre
5. deliciosa   6. feliz   7. normal
8. bonitas   9. activistas
10. blancas   11. inglesas
12. dominantes   13. formales
14. malas

Follow-up, Exs. G and H:
Using the same format, call out adjectives and have students respond with the other forms. Do this exercise at a brisk pace.

---

2. An adjective ending in **-sta** has the same ending for both the masculine and feminine forms. To make these adjectives plural, simply add an **-s.**

El abogado es **pesimista.**   Las abogadas son **pesimistas.**

3. If the masculine form of an adjective ends in **-l, -s,** or **-z,** the ending for the feminine form is also **-l, -s,** and **-z.** To make these plural, you add **-es.** Note that in the plural form, **z** changes to **c.**

El examen es **difícil.**   Las preguntas son **difíciles.**
El libro es **gris.**   Las faldas son **grises.**
El niño es **feliz.**   Las niñas son **felices.**

Remember: The exception to this rule is that when an adjective of *nationality* ends in **-s** in the masculine form, the feminine form then ends in **-sa.**

El profesor es **francés.**   La profesora es **francesa.**

Aquí practicamos

G. Da la forma femenina de cada adjetivo del 1 al 7 y la forma plural del femenino de cada adjetivo del 8 al 14. Sigue el modelo.

Modelo: caro *cara*
            negro *negras*

1. aburrido	5. delicioso	9. activista	12. dominante
2. fácil	6. feliz	10. blanco	13. formal
3. colombiano	7. normal	11. inglés	14. malo
4. alegre	8. bonito		

H. Ahora da la forma masculina de cada adjetivo del 1 al 10 y la forma plural del masculino para cada adjetivo del 11 al 20. Sigue el modelo.

Modelo: delgada *delgado*
            blanca *blancos*

1. interesante	8. católica	15. tranquila
2. famosa	9. larga	16. musical
3. bonita	10. real	17. baja
4. amable	11. japonés	18. grande
5. optimista	12. breve	19. realista
6. gorda	13. café	20. difícil
7. anaranjada	14. inglesa	

Ex. H: writing

Answers, Ex. H: 1. interesante   2. famoso   3. bonito
4. amable   5. optimista   6. gordo   7. anaranjado
8. católico   9. largo   10. real   11. japoneses   12. breves
13. cafés   14. ingleses   15. tranquilos   16. musicales
17. bajos   18. grandes   19. realistas   20. difíciles

1. Mi casa es...   Usa un adjetivo para hacer un comentario sobre cada objeto. Después hazle una pregunta a otro(a) estudiante. Sigue el modelo.

Modelo: mi casa
—*Mi casa es grande. ¿Y tu casa?*
—*Mi casa es grande también.*   o:
—*Mi casa no es grande. Es pequeña.*

1. mi casa (mi apartamento)
2. mi cuarto
3. mis libros
4. mi amigo(a)
5. mi coche
6. mis discos compactos
7. mi computadora
8. mi ciudad
9. mis padres
10. mi clase de…

Aquí escuchamos:
"¡Es feo este auto!"

Antes de escuchar

Felipe saved some money and finally was able to buy a used car. In this conversation, his friends will give their reaction to the car. Before listening, make a short list of adjectives commonly used to describe cars. Then look at the questions in the next section to anticipate for what information you should listen.

Después de escuchar

1. ¿Le gusta a la muchacha el coche?
2. ¿De qué color es el coche?
3. ¿Qué dice Felipe de su coche?

99

Ex. I:    pair work

Less-prepared students, Ex. I: Do the model and a few items with less-prepared students before dividing them into pairs. Brainstorm appropriate adjectives with them (see **Vocabulario, Para charlar** on p. 108 for suggested adjectives).

More-prepared students, Ex. I: Encourage more-prepared students to describe each object with more than one adjective if possible.

Preparation, Ex. K: You may suggest other categories based on your students' interests. Before students begin working, brainstorm with them the kinds of questions they might pose for the different categories. For example, for **una ciudad turística** they might ask about the size, the age, the weather, the location, and so on.

Less-prepared students, Ex. K: Brainstorm adjectives and other vocabulary, such as weather expressions, with less-prepared students before beginning.

Spanish speakers, Ex. K: Have Spanish-speaking students practice vocabulary that may be new for them. Emphasize that they may need such vocabulary when talking to people from other parts of the world. Be sensitive to the fact that what they say may be appropriate in their speech community. Have students focus on the differences between how they say something in their speech community and how the book teaches them to express the same idea.

Ex. L: ✏️ writing

Less-prepared students, Ex. L: This assignment lends itself to an outline that students can develop as they brainstorm ideas. You can help less-prepared students by working with them to come up with the basic shape of the outline on the board:

I. **Mi escuela**
  A. **adjetivo**
  B. **adjetivo**
  C. **adjetivo**
II. **Lugares favoritos**
  A. **lugar número 1**
    1. **adjetivo**
    2. **adjetivo**

¡Aquí te toca a ti!

J. *Acabo de comprar...* Describe to a classmate something you just bought. Tell him or her what it is, using the adjectives you've learned to describe its color, size, and other characteristics. Suggestions: **una bicicleta, un vídeo, una mochila, un coche, un televisor, una cámara, una computadora, un libro.** Follow the model.

Modelo: *Acabo de comprar una bicicleta. Es francesa. Es azul y gris. Es muy ligera. ¡Es muy rápida también!*, etc.

¡Adelante!

EJERCICIO ORAL

K. *¿Qué es?* (1) Choose someone or something from one of the following categories: **un monumento, una ciudad turística, un lugar en tu ciudad, una película, un programa de televisión popular.** (2) Write out five sentences that describe your choice without explicitly identifying it. These are your clues. Next, working in groups of four, (3) tell your group which category your choice is from (e.g., **Es una ciudad turística.**) and (4) give them one of your clues. (5) They will ask questions and try to guess what person, place, film, or television program you have in mind. (6) Give a new clue after each guess until your group guesses your choice or until you have used all of your clues.

EJERCICIO ESCRITO

L. *Un(a) amigo(a) quiere saber* A Spanish-speaking exchange student from Lima, Peru is coming to live in your community for a month, and it's your task to write a brief letter describing your school to him or her. (1) Begin by giving a general description of the school, telling whether it is large or small, modern or old, attractive or not, close to or distant from other places you like to go. (2) Then choose three places on your school's campus that you like. Tell what they are and describe them. Tell what you like about them, using a couple of different adjectives for each one. (3) Finally, tell about some part of your school that you would like to change using a couple of adjectives to tell what is wrong with it and a couple to describe how you would like it to be.

Some areas you may want to consider are **la cafetería, la biblioteca, la piscina, el estadio, la clase de inglés,** and **la clase de matemáticas.**

100

  B. **lugar número 2**
    1. **adjetivo**
    2. **adjetivo**
  C. **lugar número 3**
    1. **adjetivo**
    2. **adjetivo**
III. **Un lugar que no me gusta**
  A. **adjetivo**
  B. **adjetivo**
IV. **Opinión general de la escuela**

Spanish speakers, Ex. L: Always have Spanish speaker fully carry out this activity. Although many of them speak and understand Spanish, they may not know how to write the language. Have them pay special attention to the spelling of the vocabulary introduced in this **etapa.** Have them engage in peer editing, focusing on the spelling in the written work of a partner.

SEGUNDA ETAPA

Preparación

» **W**hat sort of entertainment is available in your town or city?

» **W**hen you are planning to go out for entertainment, where do you generally like to go?

» **I**f you are going to see a movie or a play, what information do you usually like to have?

» **H**ow do you get the information you need before going out?

Learning Strategy:

Previewing

¿Qué piensas?

NACIO USTED EN ESTE DIA

Es inventivo, nervioso y un poco sensible. Usualmente es talentoso en las líneas creativas. Para lograr sus habilidades tiene que aprender a controlar su temperamento. Tendrá éxito en cualquier carrera que mida sus ideales. Necesita autodisciplina. Tiene buena intuición en la cual debería aprender a confiar. Deje a un lado el escepticismo y la tendencia a ser muy sensitivo.

¿Es un horóscopo muy romántico?
¿Es un horóscopo demasiado pesimista?

Learning Strategies:

Reading for cultural information, reading for main ideas

Critical Thinking Strategies:

Analyzing, evaluating

¿Es una película interesante?
¿Es una película sensacional?
¿Es una película aburrida?

101

Etapa Support Materials

Workbook: **pp. 77–81**
Transparencies: **#12, #13**
Teacher Tape
Quiz: **Testing Program, p. 50**

Chapter Test: **Testing Program, p. 52**

Support material, ¿Qué piensas?:
   Transparencies #12, #13

Support material, ¿Qué piensas?: Transparencies #12, #13

Presentation: ¿Qué piensas?

Show students the transparency as you read the questions. You may need to reinforce some of the adjectives with gestures to make their meanings clear. If necessary, give translations of difficult adjectives.

Implementation, ¿Qué piensas?: Give students time to read each advertisement before asking questions about it or having students write out their answers. When they answer the questions, have them use the phrase or word(s) that support(s) their opinion. For example: —¿**El restaurante Luz de Luna es un buen restaurante? —Sí, es un buen restaurante porque tiene cuatro chefs internacionales.**

Spanish speakers, ¿Qué piensas?: Ask Spanish speakers what activities might be typical or special in their community (e.g., **bailes, fiestas,** celebrations for certain saints, etc.). Have them bring in information from Spanish-language newpapers or posters and fliers that announce these events.

left-margin note

Expansion, ¿Qué piensas?: After using the transparency and doing the exercises provided, you might divide the class into pairs and have students create their own advertisements in Spanish for an upcoming event (a school play, band concert, or sporting event), a video store, an amusement park, or anything of interest to your students. The best ads could be prepared as additional transparencies.

¿Es un lugar serio y formal?
¿Es un lugar alegre y divertido?

¿Es un libro difícil?
¿Es un libro histórico?
¿Es un libro infantil?
¿Es un libro bonito?

¿Es un programa teatral variado?
¿Es un programa teatral completo?
¿Es un buen programa teatral?
¿Es un programa teatral norteamericano?

102

¿Es un buen restaurante?
¿Es un restaurante nuevo?
¿Es un restaurante chino?
¿Es un restaurante elegante?
¿Es un restaurante caro?

RESTAURANTE

LUZ DE LUNA

Se complace en invitar al público en general a su

GRAN
INAUGURACION

Especialidad en comida china del
oeste a cargo de 4 cheffs internacionales.
Ofrecemos una bebida de cortesía por cada plato de comida.
Oferta válida durante la primera semana

¡Lo esperamos! Dirección: Sabana oeste 125 sur
de canal 7 Teléfono: 20-08-08

Horario:
De 11:00
a.m. a 3:00 p.m. y
de 6:00 p.m. a
11:00 p.m.

Ex. A: groups of three

writing

Expansion, Ex. A: After students complete the exercise, have each student go back and insert a new item of their own interest for each category with an appropriate description to match.

Possible answers, Ex. A:
1. Es una novela vieja (clásica, larga, aburrida, etc.).   2. Es un periódico español (viejo, interesante, etc.).   3. Es una obra teatral clásica (vieja, romántica, etc.).   4. Es un programa divertido (bueno, interesante, etc.).
5. Es un cuadro interesante (extraño, caro, moderno, etc.).
6. Es un vídeo formidable (largo, divertido, etc.).

¡Aquí te toca a ti!

A. ¿Qué piensas? Usa tres adjetivos para describir cada objeto o para dar tu opinión. Sigue el modelo.

 Modelo: *Es una novela buena.*
Es una novela interesante.
Es una novela sensacional.

Learning Strategy:
Expressing opinions

Critical Thinking Strategy:
Making associations

1. una novela

2. un periódico

3. una obra teatral

4. un programa

5. un cuadro

6. un vídeo

Pronunciación: *The vowel combination ie*

The combination **ie** in Spanish is pronounced in one single syllable, similar to the *ye* in the English word *yes*.

Cultural Expansion

Chichén Itzá is one of the most famous sites of Mayan ruins on the **Yucatán** Peninsula in Mexico. Early Mayan buildings date back to the fourth to ninth centuries. **El caracol** is an observatory from which astronomers kept careful track of the constellations and established a very accurate calendar system. About an hour's drive from **Mérida, Chichén Itzá** is a former Mayan religious center that tourists enjoy visiting.

Práctica

B. Lee cada palabra en voz alta, pronunciando con cuidado la combinación *ie*.

1. tiene	**3.** diente	**5.** siete	**7.** también
2. viene	**4.** cien	**6.** tiempo	**8.** cielo

Repaso

Learning Strategies:
Describing, expressing opinions

C. *Los monumentos* Usa dos adjetivos para describir cada uno de los siguientes monumentos en América Latina. Posibilidades: *pequeño, grande, alto, moderno, viejo, interesante, feo, bonito,* etc. Sigue el modelo.

Modelo: *Es alta y bella.*

arriba, izquierda: Chichén Itzá, México; *arriba, dere[cha]:* El Palacio Presidencial de la Moneda, Santiago de[?] Chile; *abajo, izquierda:* La Torre Latinoamericana, México, D.F.; *abajo, derecha:* La Catedral, México, D[?]

104

La Catedral (México, D. F.) is located in the **Zócalo (Plaza Mayor)** of the capital city. It was built on the site of the Aztec's **Templo Mayor,** using some of the same stones from the original building.

La Moneda, el Palacio Presidencial (Santiago, Chile), serves as the official residence and office of the President of Chile.

ESTRUCTURA

Position of adjectives

Acabo de comprar una motoneta **nueva.** I just bought a *new* moped.
Es una motoneta **linda.** It's a *beautiful* moped.

In Spanish, unlike English, an adjective is almost always placed *after* the noun it describes.

una película **japonesa** una lección **fácil** los libros **interesantes**

Adjectives indicating nationality always *follow* the noun.

Los automóviles **japoneses** son buenos. *Japanese* cars are good.

Aquí practicamos

D. Mi casa es tu casa. Your family is considering making a "home exchange" for a month with a family in Mexico City. With your partner, practice answering the questions that you expect to be asked about your residence. In order to make yourself clearly understood, give a complete response to each question. Follow the model.

Learning Strategy:
Asking for and providing information

Modelo: ¿Es nueva tu casa?
No, no es una casa nueva.

1. ¿Es grande tu casa?
2. ¿Es cómoda *(comfortable)* tu casa?
3. ¿Es bien equipada tu cocina?
4. ¿Son cómodos los cuartos?
5. ¿Es fácil la televisión?
6. ¿Es moderno el baño?

E. Cadenas (Chains) Form a spontaneous "chain" with your classmates. Start with a short sentence. The next person will use that sentence to form a new sentence by substituting a different word. Make any necessary changes as you go along. The process continues as quickly as possible, moving in turn from one association to the next. Follow the model.

Critical Thinking Strategy:
Making associations

Modelo: *La fiesta es estupenda.*
La ***película*** *es estupenda.*
Maricarmen *es estupenda.*
Maricarmen es ***simpática.***
El ***profesor*** *es simpático.*
El profesor es ***chileno.*** Etc.

Ex. D: pair work

More-prepared students, Ex. D: Encourage more-prepared students to expand their answers and combine information by using the conjunctions **y** and **pero.** For example, **No, no es una casa nueva, es vieja pero es muy cómoda.** Challenge them to come up with four more pertintent questions.

Implementation, Ex. E: If the class is very large, you might want to divide it into two or more teams. Time each team as the others listen to see who can finish fastest and most correctly.

Expansion, Ex. E: Keeping the same teams, do an add-on chain, with each student repeating what was said previously and adding one new element. For example, student one begins by saying: **La fiesta es estupenda.** Student two says: **La fiesta es estupenda y formidable.** Student three says: **La fiesta es estupenda, formidable y larga,** and so on. You may want to change the subect after four or five responses, varying between masculine and feminine and singular and plural nouns.

Presentation: Estructura

Remind students of expressions they already know that have adjectives following the nouns: **agua mineral, el año pasado, la música clásica, el estudiante norteamericano, la casa grande,** etc.

Presentation: Nota gramatical

To emphasize this rule, compare and contrast the expression *a big, beautiful house* with **una casa grande y bonita.** Point out that in English a comma is used to separate adjectives, while in Spanish **y** fulfills that function.

Suggestion, Ex. F: Point out that **e** is used instead of **y** when the word that follows begins with the same sound as **y.**

Ex. F: pair work

 writing

More-prepared students, Ex. F: Have students work in pairs. Instruct the more-prepared students that after one answers, the other should contradict her or him and offer different information. If student one answers, **tenemos una casa pequeña y amarilla,** the other would say, **no es verdad, tienen una casa grande y azul,** and so on.

Less-prepared students, Ex. F: Have less-prepared students concentrate on the agreement between nouns and adjectives. After they have finished, call on several pairs of students at random to perform a question or two.

Support material, Aquí escuchamos: Teacher Tape 🎧

Presentation: Aquí escuchamos

This dialogue describes paintings. Before presenting it, bring some Impressionist art books or prints to class as models. Then present the conversation, using techniques described in other **Aquí escuchamos** sections.

Variation, Aquí escuchamos: Use the **Aquí escuchamos** for dictation practice.

Nota gramatical

Position of two adjectives

When two adjectives modify the same noun, they are placed after the noun and connected to each other with **y.**

una escuela **buena y grande**
unos muchachos **inteligentes y responsables**

Learning Strategy:

Describing

F. ¿Qué tipo (kind) **de... tienes?** Escoge uno o dos adjetivos de la lista para contestar cada pregunta. Sigue el modelo.

alemán / azul / bonito / blanco / chino / difícil / español / fácil / feo / francés / grande / gris / inteligente / italiano / japonés / joven / largo / moderno / nuevo / pequeño / rojo / simpático / verde / viejo

Modelo: ¿Qué tipo de casa tienes?
Tenemos una casa pequeña y amarilla.

1. ¿Qué tipo de casa tienes?
2. ¿Qué tipo de coche tiene tu familia?
3. ¿Qué tipo de restaurante prefieres?
4. ¿Qué tipos de amigos(as) tienes?
5. ¿Qué tipo de tarea *(homework)* tienes para la clase de español?
6. ¿Qué tipo de viaje haces cuando vas de vacaciones?
7. ¿Qué tipo de bicicleta tienes?
8. ¿Qué tipo de exámenes tienes en la clase de español?

Aquí escuchamos:
"En el Museo de Arte Moderno"

Learning Strategy:

Listening for details

Antes de escuchar

Maricarmen and Ricardo are going to *El Museo de Arte Moderno.* What adjectives would you use in Spanish to describe modern art? Name some painters. Where are they from? Before listening, preview the questions in the next section.

START

106

Después de escuchar

1. ¿Cómo es el cuadro que admiran Ricardo y Maricarmen?
2. ¿Qué le gusta más a Ricardo del cuadro?
3. ¿Qué dice Maricarmen del pintor *(painter)*?
4. ¿De dónde es el pintor?

¡Aquí te toca a ti!

G. *Intercambio* Haga las siguientes preguntas a un(a) compañero(a) de clase. Él (Ella) las contesta.

1. ¿Vive en una casa o un apartamento tu familia? ¿De qué color es? ¿Es grande? ¿Es bonito(a)?
2. ¿Tienes un coche o una bicicleta? ¿De qué color es? ¿Es nuevo(a)? ¿Es americano(a)?
3. ¿De qué color es (son) tu(s)… camisa favorita? ¿pantalones? ¿zapatos?

Learning Strategy:
Asking for and giving information

¡Adelante!

EJERCICIO ORAL

H. *Vi una película.* Pick a film you've seen recently and describe it to a classmate. Tell whether you like or dislike the film, supporting your opinion by commenting on the content, the actors, the music, the cinematography, the kind of movie it is, and how it held your interest. Some adjectives that you may need in your description: **aburrido, bueno, malo, cómico, divertido, dramático, feo, interesante, sensacional, fantástico, largo, histórico, emocionante, romántico, triste, violento.**

Learning Strategies:
Giving details, describing, supporting an opinion

EJERCICIO ESCRITO

I. *Reseña de una película* Write a letter to your pen pal in Madrid in which you describe a movie that you have seen recently. Without giving away the plot, tell why you like or dislike the film. Describe the content, the actors, the music, the cinematography, the kind of movie it is, and how it held your interest. Advise your pen pal to see or not to see the film.

Learning Strategies:
Giving details, describing, supporting an opinion

107

Ex. G: pair work

Less-prepared students, Ex. G: Give less-prepared students time to answer the questions in writing, then have them pair up and exchange questions and answers.

More-prepared students, Ex. G: Challenge pairs of more-prepared students to come up with five more appropriate questions for each other. Point out that the question **¿Cómo es/son… ?** can be repeated for many items and will always elicit a description in response.

Ex. H: pair work

Less-prepared students, Ex. H: Have less-prepared students jot down a key word or phrase for each element of the movie. Then instruct them to use the key words to help them remember their ideas as they speak.

More-prepared students, Ex. H: Encourage more-prepared students to interrupt each other with appropriate questions or comments, using **también** and **tampoco,** as often occurs in real conversation. If one student says, **No me gustó Ace Ventura, Pet Detective,** the other might say, **¿Por qué no te gustó? Es una película cómica.**

Spanish speakers, Ex. H: Have Spanish-speaking students practice using vocabulary that may be new for them. Emphasize that they may need such vocabulary when talking to people from other parts of the Spanish-speaking world. Be sensitive to the fact that what they say may be appropriate in their speech community. Have students focus on the differences between how they say something in their speech community and how the book teaches them to express the same idea.

Ex. I: writing

Suggestion, Ex. I: Remind students to recycle their ideas from Ex. H here, especially the less-prepared students. Encourage more-prepared students to write about a different movie.

Spanish speakers, Ex. I: Always have Spanish speakers fully carry out this activity. Although many of them speak and understand Spanish, they may not know how to write the language. This is a good place to start building basic literacy skills in Spanish. Have them pay special attention to the spelling of the vocabulary introduced in this **etapa.** Have them engage in peer-editing, focusing on the spelling in the written work of a partner.

Chapter Culminating Activity

Cooperative Learning

Progressive Identifications

- Bring to class some identifiable items that lend themselves to the adjectives in the **Vocabulario.** Hide each item in a separate paper bag. If you ask students to bring the items, you should decide ahead of time which ones are appropriate for the activity.
- Divide the class into teams of five. Give each group an object (in its bag) and tell the students to work together to describe the item without actually saying what it is. Items should remain

Para charlar

Para hacer una descripción física

feo(a) / bonito(a)
largo(a)
ligero(a) / pesado(a)

moderno(a) / viejo(a)
pequeño(a) / grande

Para describir el color

amarillo(a)	gris	rojo(a)
anaranjado(a)	morado	rosado(a)
azul	negro(a)	verde
blanco(a)	pardo(a)	violeta
café		

Para evaluar cualquier cosa

aburrido(a) / interesante	formidable
alegre / triste	histórico(a)
bueno(a) / malo(a)	infantil
caro(a)	optimista / pesimista
clásico(a)	práctico(a)
completo(a)	regular
delicioso(a)	romántico(a)
divertido(a) / serio(a)	sensacional
económico(a)	teatral
elegante	variado(a)
formal	

Vocabulario general

Sustantivos	Otras palabras y expresiones
un cuadro	¿De qué color es... ?
un horóscopo	Descríbeme…
un período	pudo
una reacción	

concealed at all times. If you are using students' items, make sure that they are labeled with the student's name and that the student is in the group using his or her item.
- Have one group at a time sit at the front of the class with their hidden object as the center of attention. The remaining teams take turns asking questions about the object which the panel can only answer with *yes* or *no.*
- When questions have been exhausted, the teams are ready to guess what the object is. Each team must come up with one answer and write their guess on a sheet of paper. The panel then presents its description of the hidden object.

- At this point, the teams can revise their original answer on paper if they choose. Let all teams tell their guesses; then have the panel reveal the object. Grant 5 points for correct first answers and 3 points for correct revised answers. The team with the most points wins.

Lectura CULTURAL

EL CINE EN ESPAÑA Y AMÉRICA

Antes de leer

1. Based on the photos and the title, what do you think this article is about?
2. Who are some of the key people involved in the making of a movie?
3. List some words that you associate with movies and movie-making. Did you include some of the following?

| película | director | premio |
| cinematográficas | actor | filmar |

Learning Strategies:

Previewing, using cognates for meaning, reading for gist

Guía para la lectura

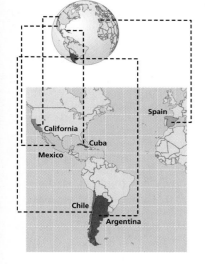

A. Scan the reading and find the words listed at the end of **Antes de leer.** From the context of the reading, what do you think these words mean?

Learning Strategies:

Reading for details, reading for main ideas

B. Now read the first sentence of each paragraph to get an idea of the overall meaning.
   1. Paragraph 1 includes information about . . .
   2. Paragraph 2 includes information about . . .
   3. Paragraph 3 includes information about . . .

C. Answer the following questions.
   1. ¿Cuáles son algunos de los países latinoamericanos conocidos por su industria cinematográfica?
   2. ¿Cuáles son dos ejemplos de películas de habla española que ganaron premios internacionales?

109

Answers, Guía para la lectura: **B.** 1. the films and film industries of Spain and Latin America   2. Two Spanish directors: Luis Buñuel and Pedro Almodóvar   3. Hispanic films and film-makers in the U.S.   **C.** 1. Argentina, Cuba, Chile, Mexico   2. *Como agua para chocolate, Bella época (El mariachi)*

Lectura cultural

Cultural Expansion

Many movies by and/or about American Hispanics have been produced recently and are available on video (*My Family* with Jimmy Smits and Edward James Olmos; *The Perez Family* with Marisa Tomei; *El mariachi; La Bamba; The Milagro Beanfield War; Zoot Suit,* based on the play by Luis Valdez and starring Edward James Olmos; and *La Pastorela* by Luis Valdez' theater company). You may want to view part of one of these movies with your class. Preview first for appropriateness, however.

Spanish speakers, Lectura cultural: Have the students go through each of the exercises in this section. We have incorporated a number of reading activities in the *¡Ya verás!* program that reflect some of the latest research. Spanish-speaking students who have been educated in American schools already read English. However, research on reading has shown that the transfer of reading skills from one language to another is far from automatic. Special attention should be paid to having Spanish-speaking students complete all of the exercises and activities that accompany the readings in this program. Once they complete the activities, you may want to ask them to summarize the reading in Spanish in order to give them additional writing practice. You may also suggest that they keep a notebook with a list of new vocabulary they find in the reading selections.

El cine en España y América

Luis Valdéz

La producción de películas cinematográficas tiene una larga tradición en España y en algunos países latinoamericanos como Argentina, Cuba, Chile y México. La primera película que se filmó este siglo en España fue en el año 1900. Muchas películas excelentes, como el reciente éxito mexicano *Como agua para chocolate* y *Bella época,* que ganó un Oscar para España en 1994, reciben premios en los festivales cinematográficos más prestigiosos del mundo. Uno de ellos es el famoso festival de cine de San Sebastián en el norte, que tuvo lugar por primera vez en 1952.

Edward James Olmos

Dos de los directores del cine español más conocidos internacionalmente son Luis Buñuel y Pedro Almodóvar. Buñuel vivió muchos años en México donde filmó películas sobre problemas de la sociedad, como en *Los olvidados* y *El ángel exterminador* entre otras. Almodóvar tiene fama por sus películas dramáticas pero que tratan ciertas situaciones con humor, como en *Mujeres al borde de un ataque de nervios* y *¿Qué he hecho para merecer ésto?* por ejemplo. Su nuevo proyecto se llama *Kika,* una película de intriga, pero cómica a la vez.

El cine hispano en los Estados Unidos se encuentra en un momento de gran vitalidad. Algunos de los directores más conocidos son Luis Valdéz, Edward James Olmos, Guillermo Varela y Robert Rodríguez.

El éxito de Rodríguez comenzó con su fenomenal película *El mariachi.* Este director mexicano-americano tiene 24 años y vive en Austin, Texas. Desde los 12 años hace películas en que sus nueve hermanos son los actores. Aunque *El mariachi,* una película filmada en español, recibió catorce premios internacionales, sólo costó 7.000 dólares. Robert escribió el guión en tres semanas y filmó la película en 14 días, con la cámara de un amigo.

Los actores de la película "Mujeres al borde de un ataque de nervios"

110

¿CÓMO ES TU AMIGA?

Todos ellos son amigos.

Chapter Objectives

Functions: Describing people's physical characteristics and personality traits

Context: Using descriptive adjectives to comment on physical features and personality characteristics of individuals

Accuracy: The verb **conocer;** the personal **a; ser para** + pronouns; shortened adjectives **(buen, mal, gran)**

Objective:

>>> **D**escribing people's physical characteristics and personality traits

Strategies:

>>> **L**isting

>>> **O**rganizing information

>>> **C**omparing and contrasting

Support materials, *Nuestros vecinos...:* Transparency #14

Presentation: *Nuestros vecinos...*

Show the transparency as you read the sentences. Begin with Sr. Salazar. Then describe Susana. Ask students personalized questions using the new adjectives: **¿Tienes los ojos azules, castaños o verdes?**, etc. Ask students about others in the class.

Spanish speakers, Nuestros vecinos...: Ask Spanish speakers to expand the descriptions presented here by including other details. They may know how to pronounce other expressions but may not know how they are written. Help them with the spelling of these expressions by writing them on the board or the overhead.

PRIMERA ETAPA

Preparación

>> **W**hen you describe how a person looks, what kind of information is useful to include?

>> **H**ow would you describe yourself over the telephone to someone who has never seen you before?

Learning Strategy:
Previewing

Nuestros vecinos y nuestros amigos

neighbor

a bit weak
eyes
hair / short
nose
moustache / beard

Aquí está nuestro **vecino**, el señor Salazar.
Es muy viejo; tiene 82 años.
Es pequeño y **un poco débil**.
Tiene los **ojos** azules.
Tiene el **pelo corto**.
Tiene una **nariz** grande.
Tiene **bigote** y **barba**.

granddaughter

strong
hazel

Aquí está su **nieta**, Susana.
Es joven; tiene dieciséis años.
Es alta y **fuerte**.
Tiene los ojos **castaños**.
Tiene el pelo rubio.
Tiene el pelo largo.
Tiene una nariz pequeña.
Es muy bonita.

112

Etapa Support Materials

Workbook: pp. 82–87
Tapescript: p. 52
Transparency: #14
Teacher Tape
Listening Activity masters: p. 36

Quiz: Testing Program, p. 57

Support material, **Nuestros vecinos...:**
Teacher Tape , **Transparency #14**

¡Aquí te toca a ti!

A. José y la señora Velázquez: retratos (portraits) físicos

Contesta las preguntas según lo que ves en los dibujos.

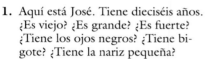

1. Aquí está José. Tiene dieciséis años. ¿Es viejo? ¿Es grande? ¿Es fuerte? ¿Tiene los ojos negros? ¿Tiene bigote? ¿Tiene la nariz pequeña?

2. Aquí está la señora Velázquez. Tiene sesenta y ocho años. Es vieja, ¿no? ¿Es grande? ¿Es delgada? ¿Tiene el pelo rubio? ¿Tiene la nariz grande?

B. Retrato de un(a) compañero(a)

Choose someone in your class to describe. Make a list of sentences presenting your description one feature at a time. Order your sentences so that each one identifies the person more specifically than the preceding one. For example, if your subject has short, brown hair and there are eight people with brown hair in your class, but only five people have short hair, tell the color before the length. Features that you will want to mention include: height (tall, short), color of eyes, color of hair, and length of hair. Use the descriptions of Sr. Salazar and Susana on page 112 as models.

Learning Strategies:

Selecting and organizing information, describing, sequencing

Pronunciación: *The vowel combination io*

The combination **io** in Spanish is pronounced in one single syllable, similar to the Spanish word **yo.**

Práctica

C. Lee cada palabra en voz alta, pronunciando con cuidado la combinación *io.*

1. rubio
2. Mario
3. adiós
4. acción
5. radio
6. comió
7. bebió
8. microscopio

113

Ex. D: pair work

writing

role play

Expansion, Ex. D: Have students brainstorm to come up with local tourist attractions and some adjectives to describe them. Then let them work in pairs to write a brief description of one place they think should be included in a tourist brochure. As a further expansion, role play the parts of tourist and guide, using the foregoing information.

Possible answers, Ex. D:
1. Estamos en un parque interesante.   2. Aquí hay muchos turistas norteamericanos.   3. El lago en este parque es muy bonito y popular.   4. Las estatuas son enormes.   5. El castillo de Chapultepec es un museo histórico mexicano.   6. Hay muchos cuadros viejos en el castillo.   7. El castillo tiene una terraza bella y alta.
8. Los patios del castillo de Chapultepec son elegantes y tranquilos.

Spanish speakers, Estructura: Most Spanish speakers will know this verb but may not know how to spell its forms. Stress to them the *z* in **conozco** and the *c* in the other forms.

/-/-/-/-/-/-/-/-/-/-/-/

Learning Strategies:
Reporting, paraphrasing

Repaso

D. *¡Vamos a visitar* (Let's visit) *el parque de Chapultepec!*
You're acting as a guide and showing your friends the Chapultepec castle and park in Mexico City. Use the shorthand notes below to give your descriptions. You may add to the description or change it, as long as you keep to the main idea. Follow the model.

Modelo: parque / inmenso
Es un parque inmenso.   o:
Es un parque muy grande.   o:
Estamos aquí en un parque inmenso.

El parque de Chapultepec	*El castillo de Chapultepec*
1. parque / interesante	5. museo / histórico / mexicano
2. turistas / norteamericano	6. cuadros / viejo
3. lago *(lake)* / bonito / popular	7. terraza / bello / alto
4. estatuas / enorme	8. patios / elegante / tranquilo

ESTRUCTURA

The verb *conocer*

—¿Quieres **conocer** a ese muchacho guapo?   Do you want *to meet* that good-looking boy?
—¡Cómo no! ¿Tú lo **conoces?**   Of course! *Do you know* him?
—¡Claro que lo **conozco!** Es mi hermano Raúl.   Sure I *know* him! He's my brother Raúl.

Here is the way to form the present tense of the verb **conocer:**

conocer

yo	cono**zco**	nosotros(as)	cono**cemos**
tú	cono**ces**	vosotros(as)	cono**céis**
él		ellos	
ella }	cono**ce**	ellas }	cono**cen**
Ud.		Uds.	

This verb is used to indicate an acquaintance or familiarity with someone, something, or someplace. It can also be used to talk about the act of meeting someone or visiting a place for the first time.

114

Aquí practicamos

E. *¿Lo conoces?* Forma una pregunta lógica con el verbo *conocer* y la información en cada columna. Sigue el modelo.

 **Modelo:**   *¿Ustedes conocen a Raquel?*

ustedes	la música española
Carlos	a esos actores de cine
yo	hablar español
Mario y Mercedes	al mejor mesero
mis padres	dónde está el restaurante
el (la) profesor(a)	la hora
la ciudad	quién es ella
vosotros	bailar el tango
el presidente	el número de teléfono
Carlos y tú	a Raquel

F. *Preguntas* Hazles preguntas a los otros estudiantes de tu grupo sobre la siguiente información. Usa una variedad de sujetos (tú, Uds., él/ella y ellos/ellas). Sigue el modelo.

 Modelo: México
¿Conoces tú México? / ¿Conocen Uds. México?

1. Buenos Aires
2. la comida mexicana
3. a Gloria Estefan
4. el castillo de Chapultepec
5. las mejores tiendas de esta ciudad

G. *¿Saber o conocer?* Cuando otro(a) estudiante te hace una pregunta sobre la información en la lista, contesta correctamente con *saber* o *conocer*. Sigue los modelos.

Modelos: la dirección de un hotel cerca de aquí
—*¿Sabes la dirección de un hotel cerca de aquí?*
—*Sí, sé la dirección del hotel.*

Maricarmen
—*¿Conoces a Maricarmen?*
— *No, no conozco a Maricarmen.*

1. el nombre del (de la) profesor(a)
2. los mejores libros de la biblioteca
3. cuántos habitantes tiene México
4. a las hermanas de tus amigos
5. usar la computadora
6. los meses del año
7. qué vamos a estudiar mañana
8. bailar el chachachá

115

Ex. E: writing

Ex. F: groups of four or more

Ex. G: pair work

Implementation, Ex. G: Point out the differences between **saber** (to know information or how to do something) and **conocer.** Skim the exercise with the class before pairing students. Together decide which verb would be appropriate in each situation and why. Have students refer to the information about **conocer** on the preceding page to help them decide.

More-prepared students, Ex. G: Have more-prepared students write up five new items for another pair to decide **saber/ conocer** usage.

Less-prepared students, Ex. G: After skimming with the whole class, go back over the exercise in more detail with less-prepared students. Have them point out which verb is correct and tell why. Then have them work with a partner.

Answers, Ex. G: 1. ¿Sabes el nombre del profesor (de la profesora)? Sí, (No, no) sé su nombre. 2. ¿Conoces los mejores libros de la biblioteca? Sí, (No, no) conozco los mejores libros.   3. ¿Sabes cuántos habitantes tiene México? Sí, (No, no) sé cuantos habitantes tiene. 4. ¿Conoces a las hermanas de tus amigos? Sí, (No, no) conozco a sus hermanas.   5. ¿Sabes usar la computadora? Sí, (No, no) sé usar la computadora.   6. ¿Sabes los meses del año? Sí, (No, no) sé los meses del año.   7. ¿Sabes qué vamos a estudiar mañana? Sí, (No, no) sé que vamos a estudiar. 8. ¿Sabes bailar el chachachá? Sí, (No, no) sé bailar el chachachá.

Ex. H: pair work

writing

Cooperative Learning

Pairs Check, Ex. H

- Put the students into heterogeneous teams of four. Have them form two pairs within their teams. The pairs will work simultaneously to perform a task and then compare their answers.
- Have one student in each pair describe the person in the first picture. The second student acts as a coach, directing and encouraging the first student as needed.
- Have students switch roles and do the second picture.
- Tell the pairs to share and compare their descriptions with the other pair on their team.
- Have pairs finish the exercise, describing the last two pictures, and comparing their descriptions with the other pair.
- Call on students at random to describe the pictures.

//-/-/-/-/-/-/-/-/-/-//

Cooperative Learning

Learning Strategies:

Describing, listing

Critical Thinking Strategy:

Comparing and contrasting

H. Retratos físicos   Prepare descriptions of three of the people in the photographs. Begin your description with a general statement such as **Es una mujer / un hombre / una chica / un chico.** Continue by guessing their ages (**Pienso que él / ella tiene...**) and giving other details about their appearance, including the length and color of their hair, the color of their eyes, their size, and other features you notice. (Consult the descriptions at the beginning of this **etapa.**)

Next, working with a partner, choose one of the five people in the photographs to compare with the other four. List as many different points of comparison and contrast as you can. When you have done your comparing and contrasting, decide which of the other four people has the most in common with your subject.

Sr. Mendoza

Sra. Álvarez

Miguel

Ana y Eduardo

116

I. Mi famila   Choose two or three members of your family to describe to your partner. Tell who they are, how old they are (if appropriate), and how they look. Finally, mention some of their interests. For example, what they do for work, their pastimes, likes, and dislikes.

As you listen to your partner's descriptions, ask questions to find out what the members in your two families have in common. As you discuss them, make two lists, one for similarities and one for differences.

 Modelo: *Mi hermano tiene diecinueve años. Es delgado y muy alto. Tiene el pelo negro y los ojos verdes. Tiene bigote pero no tiene barba. Es bastante guapo. El trabaja en un restaurante y es estudiante en la universidad. Mi hermano tiene una nueva motocicleta y le gusta mucho el cine.*

Nota gramatical

The personal a

¿Ves **a** Catalina?	Do you see Catalina?
¿Admiras **al** presidente?	Do you admire the president?
¿Ves **a** la mujer alta?	Do you see the tall woman?
¿Llevo **a** mi perro?	Shall I take my dog?
¿Ves el edificio grande?	Do you see the big building?
¿Admiras la inteligencia de Carlos?	Do you admire Carlos's intelligence?

The object of a verb is a person, a thing, or an idea that receives the action of that verb. When the direct object is a specific *human being* or *an animal that is personalized,* it is preceded by **a**. When the definite article in the masculine singular form follows the personal **a**, the contraction **al** is used.

Aquí practicamos

J.   Completa las oraciones, usando el modelo. Incluye la *a* personal cuando es necesario.

 Modelo: Miro… (la televisión / los estudiantes).
Miro la televisión. Miro a los estudiantes.

1. Buscamos… (el parque / los turistas / Roberto / el restaurante nuevo / mi perro).

117

Ex. I: pair work

Suggestion, Ex. I: Have students bring family pictures to class or give them the option of describing a make-believe family and bringing magazine photos to class for their descriptions.

Expansion, Ex. I: Have the pairs decide which one or two differences or similarities between families are most important to them and which are least important. List their answers on the board under columns labeled **más importantes** and **menos importantes**. Ask students if they see any classroom patterns or trends (number of siblings, mixed families, traditional families, one-parent families, number of cars, types and quantities of possessions such as TVs and VCRs, etc.) and discuss them.

Ex. J: writing

2. Voy a visitar... (el estadio / la señora Mendoza / mis amigos / Buenos Aires).
3. El presidente no comprende... (la gente / los jóvenes / la situación / la lengua japonesa).
4. ¿Necesitas... (el profesor / tu hermano / los libros / el dinero)?
5. Josefina piensa visitar... (el museo / México / su familia / los tíos).

K. De vacaciones en Hollywood   Imagine that you have won a trip to Hollywood. Your prize allows you to visit your favorite Hollywood per-sonalities and locations from movies or television shows (for example, **la escuela en 90210.**) Using at least four verbs from the list below, tell what you plan to do during your vacation. Mention both people and places in your plans.

ver	entender
visitar	conocer
mirar	buscar
escuchar	admirar

Learning Strategy:

Listing

Critical Thinking Strategy:

Imagining

Aquí escuchamos:
"¡Es muy guapo mi hermano!"

Learning Strategy:

Listening for details

Antes de escuchar

Cecilia is going to visit Manuel, her older brother, next week-end. She describes Manuel to her friend Cecilia. Look at the following questions to get an idea of what she will say.

Después de escuchar

1. ¿Dónde está el hermano de Cecilia?
2. ¿Para qué profesión estudia Manuel?
3. ¿De qué color tiene Manuel el pelo?
4. ¿Cómo reacciona Claudia?
5. ¿Cuál es el problema que menciona Cecilia?

118

¡Aquí te toca a ti!

L. Mi cantante (singer) preferido(a)   You are discussing your favorite singers with a classmate. Pick the one you like best and give a description of him or her. Tell the singer's name and nationality, and describe as many physical features as you can. Finally, give your general opinion of the singer and his or her music. (Refer to pages 94, 101–102, and 112 for ideas.)

Learning Strategies:

Describing, expressing opinions

Critical Thinking Strategy:

Evaluating

¡Adelante!

EJERCICIO ORAL

M. ¿Quién es?   Choose a famous person to describe to your classmates. They will try to guess who it is. Begin your description by telling what the person does (**es cantante, es actor/actriz, es profesor[a]**). Continue your description of physical features, nationality, and where the person lives. Prepare your description as a list of clues. (Write at least six sentences.)

Cooperative Learning

Learning Strategies:

Selecting information, describing, guessing

EJERCICIO ESCRITO

N. ¿Cómo soy yo?   Write a physical description of yourself on a piece of paper in six sentences. Then exchange descriptions with one of your classmates and read them to each other to see if either of you can add one more detail about the other person.

Learning Strategies:

Selecting information, providing personal information, reading for details, making suggestions

119

Ex. L: pair work

More-prepared students, Ex. L: Encourage more-prepared students to incorporate expressions from **Aquí escuchamos.** Remind them that in real conversations, people (politely) interrupt each other to ask a question, to seek clarification, or to make a comment using **también** and **tampoco.**

Less-prepared students, Ex. L: Have less-prepared students listen carefully to the way Cecilia describes her brother in the **Aquí escuchamos** section and then use her sentences as models for their descriptions of a singer.

Expansion, Ex. L: Allow students to bring in short selections of music and tell why they like that particular selection.

Ex. M: groups of four or more

Less-prepared students, Ex. M: Remind less-prepared students to recycle information, format, and ideas from Ex. L.

Suggestion, Ex. M: Have students prepare their lists of clues for homework. In class, group students in fours. One person will give clues while other group members try to guess the famous person. When they guess, or when all clues have been given, another member will give his or her clues. In a second round, the whole class could try to guess the famous people the groups couldn't identify.

Spanish speakers, Ex. M: Have Spanish-speaking students practice using vocabulary that may be new for them. Emphasize that they may need such vocabulary when talking to people from other parts of the Spanish-speaking world. Be sensitive to the fact that what they say may be appropriate in their speech community. Have students focus on the differences between how they say something in their speech community and how the book teaches them to express the same idea.

Ex. N: writing

Less-prepared students, Ex. N: Brainstorm with less-prepared students possible adjectives to use in their descriptions.

Spanish speakers, Ex. N: Always have Spanish speakers fully carry out this activity. Many who speak and understand Spanish may not know how to write the language. Have them pay special attention to the spelling of the vocabulary introduced in this **etapa.** Have them engage in peer-editing, focusing on the spelling in the written work of a partner.

Presentation: El carácter

Introduce the new vocabulary through personalized questions. Begin with cognates. **¿Eres optimista? ¿Eres idealista?**

Spanish speakers, El carácter: Ask Spanish speakers to expand the descriptions presented here by including other details about people's personalities and temperament. Help them with the spelling of the terms they introduce by writing them on the board or the overhead.

SEGUNDA ETAPA

Preparación

>> **W**hat are some of the personality traits that are taken into account when you talk about what someone is like?

>> **H**ow would you describe your personality to someone who does not know you?

/-/-/-/-/-/-/-/-/-/-//
Learning Strategy:
Previewing

El carácter: Personality

 **El carácter**

Aquí está mi amigo Eduardo. Él va a estudiar.

☐ Es pesimista.
☐ Es tímido.
☐ Es idealista.
☐ Es honesto.
☐ Es paciente siempre.
☐ Es intelectual.
☐ Es serio.

☐ Es **perezoso.**
☐ Es generoso.
☐ Es independiente.
☐ Es discreto.
☐ Es triste.
☐ Es **casado.**

Aquí está mi amiga Cecilia. Ella **da una vuelta** con su perro.
☐ Es optimista.
☐ Es valiente.
☐ Es realista.
☐ No es deshonesta.
☐ Es impaciente.
☐ Es atlética.
☐ Es simpática.

☐ Es **cómica.**
☐ Es activa y enérgica.
☐ Es generosa también.
☐ Es independiente también.
☐ Es indiscreta a veces.
☐ Es alegre.
☐ Es **soltera,** pero tiene **novio.**

perezoso: lazy / *casado:* married / *da una vuelta:* takes a walk /
cómica: funny / *soltera:* single / *novio:* boyfriend

120

Etapa Support Materials

Workbook: **pp. 88–94**
Transparencies: **#15, #16**
Teacher Tape 🎧
Quiz: **Testing Program, p. 60**

Chapter Test: **Testing Program, p. 62**

Support material, **El carácter: Transparency #15**

¡Aquí te toca a ti!

A. José y la Sra. Velázquez: retratos psicológicos

Contesta las preguntas sobre la personalidad de José y de la Sra. Velázquez.

|·|·|·|·|·|·|·|·|·|·|·|·|·|·|·|·|
Critical Thinking Strategy:

Making associations

1. A José le gustan mucho los coches rápidos y las actividades peligrosas *(dangerous)*. ¿Es valiente o tímido?
2. La Sra. Velázquez da dinero a los amigos que no son ricos. ¿Es generosa o tacaña *(stingy)*?
3. A José no le gusta trabajar. Prefiere mirar la televisión. ¿Es trabajador o perezoso?
4. La Sra. Velázquez encontró 25.000 pesos. Llamó por teléfono a la policía. ¿Es honesta o deshonesta?
5. A José no le gustan los libros, pero le encanta el fútbol y le gusta esquiar. ¿Es atlético o intelectual?
6. La Sra. Velázquez siempre escucha la radio. Le gustan la música clásica y las discusiones políticas. ¿Es seria o cómica?
7. A José le gusta la vida y tiene muchos amigos. ¿Es triste o alegre?
8. La Sra. Velázquez trabaja mucho. Va al teatro, al museo y al cine. ¿Es activa o perezosa?

B. Mi mejor amigo(a)

Tell one of your classmates about your best friend. Give a physical description first. Then describe his or her personality traits. Your classmate will respond by asking you two or more questions about your best friend.

|·|·|·|·|·|·|·|·|·|·|·|·|·|·|·|·|
Learning Strategies:

Listing, organizing information

Pronunciación: The vowel combination ua

The combination **ua** in Spanish is pronounced in one single syllable, similar to the *wa* in the English word *water.*

121

Ex. A: ✎ writing

Answers, Ex. A: 1. Es valiente.   2. Es generosa.   3. Es perezoso.   4. Es honesta.   5. Es atlético.   6. Es seria.   7. Es alegre.   8. Es activa.

Follow-up, Ex. A: Have students write three sentences comparing and contrasting the personality traits of José and Sra. Velázquez.

Ex. B: 👥 pair work

Suggestion, Ex. B: You may want to model this exercise for the class with personalized information. Have students listen carefully to your description so that they may ask a pertinent question about the person you describe. Then pair students and have them perform the activity. Have them refer to **Vocabulario, Para charlar** on p. 126 for supplemental vocabulary.

Less-prepared students, Ex. B: Ask individual less-prepared students to tell the class which five or six traits best describe their own personalities.

More-prepared students, Ex. B: Have more-prepared students compare and contrast their personalities with their best friends', using **y** and **pero**.

Presentation: Pronunciación

Remind students that *u* is pronounced separately only if there is an accent over it, e.g., **Raúl, yo continúo.** After doing Ex. C, have a short dictation exercise to contrast words like **suave** and **Raúl.**

Ex. D: pair work

 writing

Expansion, Ex. D: Give one partner a blank paper and the other a picture of someone. The student with the picture describes the person and the partner sketches based on the description. When they finish, have them compare the sketch to the picture.

Ex. E: pair work

Implementation, Ex. E: Encourage students to vary the pronouns.

Less-prepared students, Ex. E: Review **es** and **son** with less-prepared students. Have them skim the exercise and decide which verb form to use in each item before beginning.

Práctica

C. Lee cada palabra en voz alta, pronunciando con cuidado la combinación *ua*.

1. agua	3. cuanto	5. cuatro	7. cuaderno
2. cuadro	4. suave	6. guante	8. cuarenta

Repaso

Learning Strategies:

Listing, organizing information

D. Yo soy... If you had to meet someone at the airport who had never seen you before, how would you describe yourself over the telephone so that the other person would be sure to recognize you? Give as many details as possible.

ESTRUCTURA

Ser para + pronouns

Esta carta **es para ella.**   Estos cuadros **son para mí.**
Este dinero **es para ustedes.**   Estas camisas **son para ti.**

Pronouns used as objects of prepositions, following such phrases as **ser para**, have the same forms as subject pronouns, except for **mí** and **ti.**

The following object pronouns are used after a preposition such as **para.**

mí	*me, myself*	**nosotros(as)**	*us, ourselves*
ti	*you (fam.), yourself*	**vosotros(as)**	*you (fam.), yourselves*
usted	*you, yourself*	**ustedes**	*you, yourselves*
él	*him*	**ellos**	*them (masc.)*
ella	*her*	**ellas**	*them (fem.)*

Aquí practicamos

E. ¿Para quién es? A classmate will ask you if an object on the list on page 123 is for somebody. Answer by saying that it is not for the person in question but for somebody else. Follow the model.

Modelo: la cámara
—¿La cámara es para ella?
—¡Claro que no! Es para él.

122

1. el disco compacto	5. el dinero	9. los esquíes
2. la raqueta	6. las cartas	10. la tarjeta
3. las fotografías	7. la comida	11. la computadora
4. el coche	8. el refresco	12. la fiesta

F. *¡Qué generoso(a) eres!* As you point to people in the room, tell each person that you have something for him or her. Think of an object and indicate who it is for. Follow the model.

 Modelo: *Tengo un libro para ti.*
Tengo unas cintas para Uds.

Nota gramatical

Shortened adjectives: *buen, mal, gran*

Ramón es un **buen** muchacho.	Ramón is a good boy. (no emphasis on how good)
Ramón es un muchacho **bueno**.	Ramón is a *good* boy. (emphasis on how good)
Éste es un **mal** día para esquiar.	This is a bad day for skiing. (no emphasis on how bad)
Éste es un día **malo** para esquiar.	This is a *bad* day for skiing. (emphasis on how bad)
Plácido Domingo es un **gran** hombre.	Plácido Domingo is a *great* man.
Plácido Domingo es un hombre **grande**.	Plácido Domingo is a *big* man.

When the adjectives **bueno, malo,** and **grande** are used before a masculine singular noun, they are shortened to **buen, mal,** and **gran**. The meaning of **grande** is radically different when it precedes the noun, for then it means *great* instead of *large*.

Aquí practicamos

G. Usa los adjetivos sugeridos para modificar los sustantivos de la página 124 en dos maneras, cambiando las formas cuando es necesario.

 Modelo: Es un museo. (grande)
Es un gran museo.
Es un museo grande.

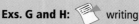

Exs. G and H: writing

Implementation, Ex. G: As students are writing, call on different pairs to put one of the items on the board. Do corrections with the whole class from these examples. On items 3, 7, and 8, ask students to explain the difference in what the sentence means when using **gran** and **grande.** You may ask students to draw a picture to illustrate these differences on the board next to the text itself.

Answers, Ex. G: 1. Es un buen libro. Es un libro bueno. 2. Son unos malos niños. Son unos niños malos.   3. Es un gran hombre. Es un hombre grande.   4. Son unos buenos amigos. Son unos amigos buenos.   5. Son unas buenas ideas. Son unas ideas buenas. 6. Es una mala situación. Es una situación mala.   7. Es un gran perro. Es un perro grande.   8. Son unos grandes libros. Son unos libros grandes.   9. Es una buena característica. Es una característica buena.   10. Son unos malos futbolistas. Son unos futbolistas malos.

Expansion, Ex. H: Ask students to name the 6–10 most important characteristics they would like to find in a friend. List these on the board. Then ask students to determine the four most important ones. Create a tick mark graph beside the list to determine the most important characteristics to the class as a whole.

You might also create a list of the characteristics that students would like to have in their best friend and another list of the characteristics they would like to have in a boyfriend or girlfriend. Create a tick mark graph for each, having the students compare and contrast similarities and differences beween the two lists.

---

1. Es un libro. (bueno)	6. Es una situación. (malo)
2. Son unos niños. (malo)	7. Es un perro. (grande)
3. Es un hombre. (grande)	8. Son unos libros. (grande)
4. Son unos amigos. (bueno)	9. Es una característica. (bueno)
5. Son unas ideas. (bueno)	10. Son unos futbolistas. (malo)

Learning Strategy:

Describing

H. *Descripciones* Escoge al menos cinco adjetivos de la lista para primero describirte a ti mismo(a) y después a las personas indicadas. Usa una gran variedad de adjetivos.

1. tú
2. tu amigo(a)
3. tu hermano(a)
4. tu madre o tu padre
5. tu profesor(a)

activo / alegre / antipático / bonito / bueno / cómico / cruel / delgado / discreto / dinámico / egoísta / enérgico / frívolo / fuerte / guapo / generoso / grande / honesto / idealista / imaginativo / impaciente / independiente / indiscreto / ingenuo / inteligente / joven / malo / optimista / paciente / pequeño / perezoso / pesimista / realista / serio / simpático / sincero / tímido / trabajador / triste / valiente / viejo

Learning Strategy:

Listening for details

Aquí escuchamos:
"¡Mi hermana es independiente!"

Antes de escuchar

Roberto is going to visit his sister Silvia next weekend. He describes what his sister is like to his friend Raúl. Look at the questions to get an idea of what Roberto will tell him.

Después de escuchar

1. ¿Cuál es la profesión de la hermana de Roberto?
2. ¿Dónde vive ella?
3. ¿Cuántos años tiene la mujer?
4. ¿Le gustan los deportes?
5. ¿Cómo la describe su hermano?
6. ¿Qué quiere Raúl cuando oye cómo es la hermana de su amigo?

124

Support material, Aquí escuchamos:
Teacher Tape

Presentation: Aquí escuchamos

This conversation is a model for students to practice describing people's personalities. You may wish to introduce the dialogue by describing someone you all know.

Variation, Aquí escuchamos: Use as a dictation exercise. Have less-prepared students write the part of Raúl and more-prepared students the part of Roberto.

Spanish speakers: Aquí escuchamos: Spanish speakers should be directed to focus on "listening in context" to any vocabulary that may be new for them.

Answers, Aquí escuchamos: 1. Es doctora. 2. en Chicago   3. veintinueve años   4. Sí, es atlética. 5. muy independiente, seria, atlética, muy feliz, símpatica, generosa   6. conocer a su hermana

¡Aquí te toca a ti!

I. Mi pariente (relative) preferido(a)

Describe your favorite family member to one of your classmates. Discuss both physical appearance and personality. Your classmate will ask you follow-up questions. Use **Aquí escuchamos** as a model.

Learning Strategies:

Listing, organizing information

¡Adelante!

EJERCICIO ORAL

J. Mi retrato

You want your friend to tell his or her cousin about you as a possible date. Use at least five of the adjectives listed in Activity H to describe yourself as you want your friend to tell his or her cousin. Give at least one example to explain or support your choice of each characteristic. For example, if you are **atlético(a),** tell what sports you participate in.

Learning Strategies:

Listing, elaborating, supporting an opinion

EJERCICIO ESCRITO

K. Una descripción

Write a brief description of a famous person who is visiting in your town or city. Describe the person's physical characteristics and personality, as well as what he or she does.

Learning Strategies:

Describing, organizing ideas in a paragraph

Jon Secada

125

Vocabulario

Para charlar

Para dar una descripción física de una persona

Tiene…
   los ojos azules / verdes / castaños / negros.
   el pelo corto / largo.
   la nariz grande / pequeña.
   bigote / barba.
Es…
   débil / fuerte.

Para describir la personalidad

Él (Ella) es…

activo(a) / perezoso(a).   idealista / realista.
ambicioso(a).   impaciente / paciente.
atlético(a).   independiente.
cómico(a).   intelectual.
deshonesto(a) / honesto(a).   perfecto(a).
discreto(a) / indiscreto(a).   tímido(a) / valiente.
generoso(a).

Vocabulario general

Sustantivos

un(a) nieto(a)   **Verbos**
un(a) vecino(a)   conocer

Adjetivos   ### Otras palabras y expresiones

casado(a)   dar una vuelta
soltero(a)

Chapter Culminating Activity

Cooperative Learning

Group Product

- Group students into heterogeneous teams of three and give them five minutes to review the items in the **Vocabulario.**

- Tell students to describe someone in school by using the expressions they have learned. Have them decide together who they are going to describe and how. Each student must make at least one statement about the person. Give them only a few minutes to plan.
- Call on the first team to describe their person. You may let other students call out a name as soon as they think they know who it is.
- Move on to the next team. Keep the exercise moving.
- Give the students a written quiz as a follow-up, asking them to describe themselves.

Lectura cultural

DIME QUÉ REGALO QUIERES Y TE DIGO QUIÉN ERES

Antes de leer

1. Look at the pictures on page 128 and the title and think about what this reading is going to be about. What do you think the word **regalo** means?
2. Look the passage over quickly. How is it organized?
3. What do you think the following words from the headings mean? Look at the picture that goes with each section to determine the meaning of the words that you may not know.

ajedrez	ropa	colección de
chandal	bicicleta	discos compactos

Guía para la lectura

A. Read the introduction. What do you think **prueba de personalidad** means? What do you think this phrase has to do with the rest of the reading?

B. On a separate piece of paper copy the headings. Read the passage, looking for descriptive words and phrases. Next to each heading make a list of the adjectives associated with the kind of person who wants each gift.

C. Work with a partner and decide which description best fits your personalities.

Dime qué regalo quieres y te digo quién eres

No importa a quién vas a pedir los siguientes regalos, a los Reyes Magos, a San Nicolás, a tus padres o a tus abuelos. Lo importante es que tienes que decidir qué quieres. Aquí te presentamos una prueba de personalidad para decirte cómo eres según tu selección. Pero ya sabes que solamente es un juego. ¡No te lo tomes muy en serio!

127

Un perro

Eres una persona cariñosa y responsable. Te gusta ayudar a otras personas pero a veces exiges mucho de tus amigos o familiares. Tienes que ser menos posesivo(a).

Una colección de discos compactos de tu cantante favorito(a)

Eres extrovertido(a) y dinámico(a). Te gusta divertirte y el futuro no te interesa demasiado. Debes pensar más en tus estudios.

Una colección de libros de historia

Eres una persona original. Piensas mucho en el pasado y no das tu opinión fácilmente. Tienes que tener más confianza en ti mismo(a).

Una cámara fotográfica

Eres introvertido(a) y creativo(a). También tienes mucha imaginación, pero tienes que ser un poco más realista.

Ropa

Te gusta ser el centro de atención. Generalmente tienes muy buen humor y te gusta estar con mucha gente. Eres muy popular, pero también un poquito frívolo(a). Debes pensar un poco más en las otras personas.

Un juego de ajedrez

Eres una persona muy lógica. Piensas mucho antes de y eso te quita naturalidad. Debes ser un poco menos rígido(a). Disfrutarás más de la vida.

Una bicicleta

Te gusta la naturaleza. Eres romántico(a) y apasionado(a). Tienes que ser menos impulsivo(a) y pensar antes de actuar; así vas a tener más amigos(as).

Un chandal

Eres independiente. Te gusta la aventura y todo lo nuevo. El riesgo es tu elemento. Siempre estás buscando nuevas metas. Un poco de calma en tu vida te va a hacer bien.

128

Aqui leemos

Estrategia para la lectura

Some kinds of writing are intended to create a particular mood in the reader. Writers use adjectives and other descriptive words to produce moods. (You can use adjective endings to help keep track of the nouns being referred to in such writing.) Some writing, such as poetry, is best read aloud because the author chooses particular words for their sounds and puts them together in ways that emphasize their rhythms. Reading aloud is a good technique to practice because it helps you improve pronunciation while learning how to be more expressive in Spanish.

/./././././././

Reading Strategies:

Use adjective endings to help you interpret meanings.
Pay attention to the mood of the reading.
Read aloud for pleasure and practice.

Antes de leer

This reading is a poem by a well-known Mexican poet, Amado Nervo (1870–1919). His work has two important themes: love and religion. Both are reflected in this poem in which the reader is invited to think about what a divine being might be like. Before reading the poem carefully, look at it to see how it is organized. Then answer these questions before going on to the **Actividades.**

> > **W**hat are some adjectives you might use to describe your idea of a supreme being?

> > **Y**ou can see that the poem is organized as a series of questions about the nature of God. What questions can you ask that might be answered by the adjectives you have thought of?

Read the poem through once to get the general idea and mood. Don't worry about every word. Notice especially how the organization of the poem changes from questions to statements in the last three lines. Then read the poem again, more carefully, making sure the meanings you guess fit the mood and content. Pay attention to the relationship between the title and the rest of the poem, and to the last three lines.

129

Support Materials

Workbook: pp. 95–97
Unit Review Blackline Masters: Unit 1 Review
Transparency: #16
Listening Activity masters: p. 41
Tapescript: p. 60
Atajo, Writing Assistant Software *supports* ATAJO

Cooperative Learning

Group Work: Peer tutoring

- Put students with differing abilities into groups of three.
- Explain that together each trio is going to answer the questions about the poem.
- Have students alternate roles. To begin, one student (the reader) reads the first question. Another student (the recorder) helps the other students find the answer (all the words that rhyme, for example) and then writes it down. The third student (the checker) makes sure the recorder has written down the correct answer(s). All students work together to find the answers for each question, but each student has a different role in the process. Have students rotate roles after each question.
- Have the teams continue this process for Exs. B and C. Watch for groups that need encouragement.
- Ask questions about the poem at random to check comprehension and to make sure all groups completed the activity.

Voluntad: Will

ley: law

fuera: beyond

Tiempo ha que: For a while now / *ya no:* no longer

¿Cómo es?

¿Es Dios personal?
¿Es impersonal?
¿Tiene forma?
¿No tiene forma?
¿Es esencia?
¿Es sustancia?
¿Es uno?
¿Es múltiple?
¿Es la conciencia del Universo?
¿Es Voluntad sin conciencia y sin fin?
¿Es todo lo que existe?
¿Es distinto de todo lo que existe?
¿Es como el alma de la naturaleza?
¿Es una ley?
¿Es simplemente la armonía de las fuerzas?
¿Está en nosotros mismos?
¿Es nosotros mismos?
¿Está fuera de nosotros?
Alma mía, hace tiempo que tú ya no te preguntas estas cosas.
Tiempo ha que estas cosas ya no te interesan.
Lo único que tú sabes es que Lo amas...

Actividades

A. Answer these questions by reflecting on the poem. Refer to it whenever you need to.

1. Which of the following statements is the best explanation of the relationship between the question section and the last three lines?
   a. The last three lines are the answers to the questions.
   b. The last three lines suggest that, in spite of all the questions, one thing is known with certainty.
   c. The last three lines are not related to the questions at all.
2. Which statement best describes the relationship between the title and the poem?
   a. The poem gives the answer to the title question.
   b. The last three lines give the answer to the title question.
   c. The title is a general question and the questions in the poem are specific ones included in it.

130

B. Read the poem again carefully. Next read it aloud, listening to how the words and lines go together. Then answer these questions about how Nervo uses words to create the mood and message of the poem.

1. Quickly list all the adjectives you find in the poem. What do they describe?
2. What rhyming words does the poet use?
3. Nervo uses many pairs of words with opposite meanings. An example is **personal** and **impersonal**. What other pairs like this do you see? What do you think the poet accomplishes with this technique?

C. Read the poem out loud, concentrating on the meaning. Then answer these questions about what the poem means.

1. What is the main question being asked in the poem?
2. What are some specific characteristics of a supreme being that Nervo wonders about? Why do you think Nervo does not actually give any specific answers to his questions?
3. What might be the reason why the poem is divided into so many short lines? Can you relate this pattern of lines to the message of the poem?
4. Who is the speaker in the poem? To whom are the last three lines addressed? What does the poet finally conclude about all his questions?

D. Writing that conveys a mood is intended to get a response from its readers. Read the poem again, thinking about your reaction to its message. The following questions will help you formulate your own response.

1. Do you think many people ask the questions that Nervo has asked? Have you ever wondered about these questions yourself?
2. Do you think there is a more specific answer than the one Nervo gives? Do you agree with his answer?
3. How do you feel when the poet switches from questions to statements? Can you feel the shift from doubt to certainty that he intends you to feel?
4. Do you enjoy the rhythm created by the pairs of oppositions in the questions? What feeling do you get when the pairs are interrupted by the longer statements in the last three lines? Do you think that's what the poet wanted you to feel?
5. Does the poem have more meaning after you work with it for a while? Do you like it better after reading it several times?

More-prepared students,
Ex. D: For homework or as an in-class assignment, more-prepared students could use their answers from the exercise as an outline for a composition in English. Have students underline or take notes on the parts of the poem that pertain to each question, so that they can insert some quotes to support their opinions.

Less-prepared students,
Ex. D: You may want to have less-prepared students concentrate on two or three of the questions in the exercise for their composition. Help them coordinate the corresponding lines or parts of the poem.

Ya llegamos

Spanish speakers, Actividades orales:

Spanish speakers already have a command of Spanish that is used in informal contexts. Have the students practice using vocabulary that may be new for them. Emphasize that they may need such vocabulary when talking to people from other parts of the Spanish-speaking world. Be sensitive to the fact that what they say may be appropriate in their speech community. Have students focus on the differences between how they say something in their speech community and how the book teaches them to express the same idea.

Ex. A:  writing

role play

Implementation, Ex. A:

This would be a good activity to videotape. Students could do a simple mock-up of a weather map and/or use regional geographic maps in their forecasts. They might also create icons (sunny face, partly cloudy sun face, etc.) to draw on the board when they do the weekend forecast. See also the Chapter Culminating Activity on p. T90.

Writing Activities

Writing suggestion: Remind students to refer for help in writing to the **Para charlar** and **Temas y contextos** sections of the chapter **Vocabularios,** as well as to the **Estructura** and **Nota gramatical** sections in each **etapa.** If you have access to **Atajo** software, students will find similar help there, both in the dictionary and in indexes labeled Functional vocabulary, Topic vocabulary, and Grammar. For instance, in Unit 1 students might refer to the following **Atajo** categories.

Actividades orales

Learning Strategies:

Organizing a report, sequencing

Critical Thinking Strategies:

Predicting, making associations

Learning Strategies:

Organizing ideas, describing, elaborating

Learning Strategy:

Making associations

A. *Una oportunidad*   Imagine that you are a weather forecaster and you have an opportunity to audition for a position on the Spanish-speaking television station in your area. Prepare a weather report for your region, including a mock-up of a weather map to use as a prop and to refer to during your audition.

Announce (1) the weather conditions for yesterday and last night, (2) what the weather is like today, and (3) what you forecast for tonight and tomorrow. Then (4) give your prediction for the upcoming weekend, suggesting appropriate weekend activities according to the weather conditions in your forecast.

B. *Un álbum de la familia*   While on a trip you meet two friends and show them pictures of your family.

Materials: Bring photographs of your family members to class. You might include pets and one or two of your best friends. If you are limited in the photographs you have available, you might borrow some, cut them from magazines, or draw them (stick-figure style is OK!), to represent your family and friends.

Scenario: You and two of your traveling companions are talking about people you know—friends and family. Show pictures and tell about the people in your photographs, elaborating on four of them. For the four people that you describe, tell (1) how they are related to you and (2) what they are like (naming at least two of their most outstanding physical traits and two personality traits). Tell also (3) where they live, and (4) two things or activities that they like and/or don't like **[(no) le gusta(n)]**. Finally, (5) mention for each person at least one of their possessions that is of interest to you (giving a description of that possession that includes at least two features).

Remember to speak conversationally, picking up the threads of discourse from each other, for example, "Oh, your grandfather likes fast cars? My Uncle Jim loves fast boats and waterskiing."

132

Atajo, Writing Assistant Software   supports ATAJO

Functional vocabulary: Describing people; describing weather; pointing to a person/object

Topic vocabulary: Calendar; clothing; days of the week; face; family members; hair; leisure; months; musical instruments; people; personality; seasons; time of day

Grammar: Adjectives: descriptive; adjectives: position; **jugar; volver;** comparatives; prepositions and dates; pronouns: object; verb summary; verbs: future; verbs **hacer;** verbs imperfect; verbs: **saber** and **conocer;** verbs: **ser** and **estar**

Actividades escritas

C. *El aviso meteorológico*
Write a brief weather report for your region. Indicate the weather and temperatures for today, tonight, and tomorrow.

D. *Una entrevista*
Pretend that you work on your school newspaper and that you're writing up an interview with a rock star who is performing in your town. Choose a rock star and imagine his or her answers to your questions about his or her personality, pastimes, favorite music and books, what sports he or she plays or watches, where he or she prefers to live, etc. Then write your article for the paper in interview format.

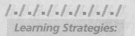

Learning Strategies:

Describing, organizing information, using appropriate journalistic style

Critical Thinking Strategy:

Making associations

133

Ex. B: groups of three

writing

role play

Implementation, Ex. B: Have students work in groups of three or four. They can pretend to be sitting at the same table in their hotel restaurant having a continental breakfast and discussing their families. They can improvise comments on foods (**El café es delicioso**, etc.) and indications to the waiter (**La cuenta, por favor**, etc.) as well.

Spanish speakers, Actividades escritas: Have Spanish speakers fully carry out this activity. Although many of them speak and understand Spanish, they may not know how to write it. Have them pay special attention to the spelling of the vocabulary introduced in this unit, especially those words with problematic spelling combinations. This is a good place to have them engage in peer-editing, focusing on the spelling and grammatical structures introduced in this unit as they are applied in the written work of a partner.

Ex. C: writing

 Atajo

Ex. D: writing

Suggestion, Ex. D: Have students prepare a list of questions for the rock star to help them focus on the assignment and to use in the final format.

The interdisciplinary lessons that have been included at the end of each unit provide a unique opportunity for teachers and students to study the Spanish language through the medium of another subject area (mathematics, science, or social studies), as recommended in the most recent draft of the National Standards for Foreign Language Education. These lessons are completely optional, and none of this material has been included in the Testing Program.

Each lesson centers around a short reading and includes warm-up and follow-up activities with ample support to walk students through the lesson. In some cases, additional extension activities are provided in the Teacher's Edition.

Conexión

La letra y la personalidad

AL EMPEZAR

>> Do you think that your handwriting reflects your personality? If so, how?

> Does your teacher's handwriting reflect his or her personality? If so, how?

The way we do things often says something about who we are. Graphologists make a study of our handwriting, claiming that the way we write tells something about our personalities.

ACTIVIDAD A

Listed below are adjectives used in the following reading. Working with a partner, select adjectives from the list which most closely describe your personality. Now select adjectives which most closely describe your partner's personality. Write the adjectives you choose in your notebook. How are you and your partner alike? How do you differ? Follow the model.

Modelo: *Soy independiente. Mi compañero(a) es sociable.*

extrovertido	introvertido	perfeccionista	motivado
suspicious (of others) — amigable	suspicaz	económico	extrovertido
sociable	independiente	organizado	entusiasta
compassionate — compasivo	meticuloso	agresivo	optimista
cautious — cauteloso	modesto	confidente	

LA LETRA Y LA PERSONALIDAD

handwriting
relative

characteristics
size

Cada persona tiene su **letra** particular. Por eso es fácil reconocer la letra de un buen amigo o un **pariente.** Pero hay gente que dice que la letra de una persona también expresa su identidad. Los grafólogos estudian los **rasgos** distintivos de la letra, incluyendo el **tamaño** de las letras individuales, y el grado y uniformidad de inclinación, ornamentación y curvatura. La grafología se basa en la teoría de que nuestra forma de escribir refleja las características elementales que forman la personalidad. Se mantiene, por ejemplo, que la persona que hace la letra grande tiene ambiciones. El siguiente esquema nos resume otras afirmaciones comunes de la grafología.

134

con la psicología

Estilo de letra	Características asociadas
Inclinación hacia la derecha	extrovertido, amigable, sociable, compasivo
Inclinación hacia la izquierda	cauteloso, introvertido, suspicaz, independiente
Letra pequeña	meticuloso, modesto, perfeccionista, organizado
Letra grande	agresivo, extrovertido, entusiasta, optimista

ACTIVIDAD B

Based on the information provided in the reading, make suggestions about the people who provided a handwriting sample below. Follow the model.

Modelo: *Damián Flores es muy extrovertido porque su letra es muy grande y está inclinada hacia la derecha.*

María Cubas   Mark T. Smith   Pedro Escobar

Javier Pinares   Damián Flores   Susana del Mar

ACTIVIDAD C

Paso 1: Find your name as you have written it on an old quiz or homework assignment. Answer the following questions.

1. ¿Es grande o pequeña tu letra?
2. ¿Está inclinada hacia la derecha o hacia la izquierda?
3. Según los grafólogos, ¿cuáles son los adjetivos que mejor describen tu personalidad?

Paso 2: Find the lists of adjectives that you and your partner chose to describe your personality before reading the passage. Do they match the ones predicted by the analysis of your handwriting in the previous **paso**?

Modelo: *Sí. Soy _____. Pero no soy _____.*

135

Answers, Actividad B:
María Cubas: agresiva, extrovertida, entusiasta, optimista **Mark Smith:** cauteloso, introvertido, suspicaz, independiente **Pedro Escobar, Damián Flores:** extrovertido, amigable, sociable, compasivo, agresivo, entusiasta, optimista **Javier Pinares, Susana del Mar:** extrovertido, amigable, sociable, compasivo, meticuloso, modesto, perfeccionista, organizado

Follow-up, Actividad C:
You may want to hold a class referendum and discussion around the question: *Is handwriting analysis a good way to predict personalities? Why or why not?* (**¿Cuántos estudiantes opinan que la grafología es una buena forma de predecir la personalidad de una persona? ¿Por qué?**)

Extension, Actividad C:
Ask students if they'd like to try analyzing the handwriting of a friend or family member. How accurate are the graphologists' predictions about others?

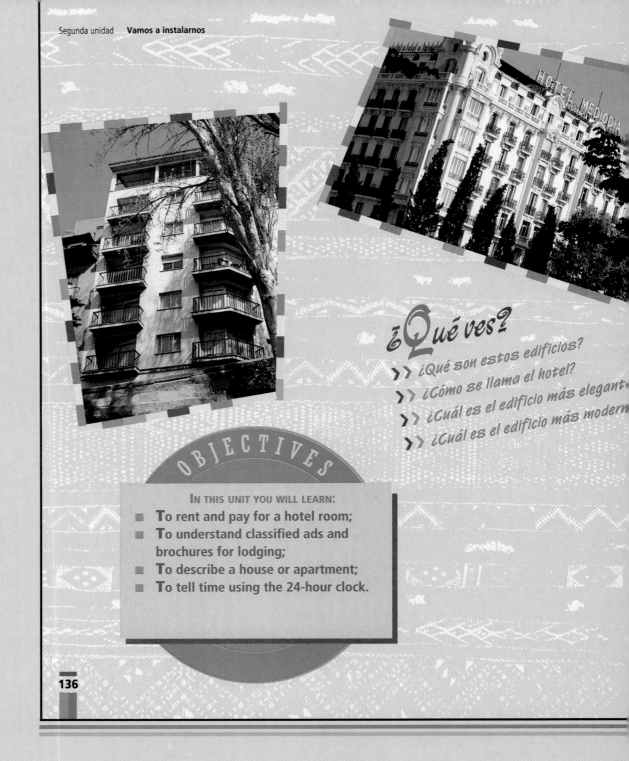

¿Qué ves?

>> ¿Qué son estos edificios?

>> ¿Cómo se llama el hotel?

>> ¿Cuál es el edificio más elegante?

>> ¿Cuál es el edificio más moderno?

OBJECTIVES

IN THIS UNIT YOU WILL LEARN:

■ **T**o rent and pay for a hotel room;

■ **T**o understand classified ads and brochures for lodging;

■ **T**o describe a house or apartment;

■ **T**o tell time using the 24-hour clock.

136

Capítulo cuatro: Buscamos un hotel

Capítulo cinco: Un año en casa de los Álvarez

Capítulo seis: Busco un apartamento

Vamos a instalarnos

sop UNIDAD

137

Planning Strategy

If you do not assign the Planning Strategy (Workbook, p. 99) for homework or if students have difficulty coming up with English expressions, you might try asking several students to role play the situation. One person can play the desk clerk and another student or students can play the customer(s). You can put students in groups to brainstorm as many answers as possible to the various questions.

Although some students may be too young to be renting a hotel room by themselves, this topic introduces them to travel and lodging. It engages them in inter-active activities while they practice vocabulary for rooms and furni-ture.

Cultural Context

Sevilla is considered by many to be one of Spain's most picturesque cities. Its white-washed **barrios** and its orange-blossom scented air charm native Spaniards and visi-tors alike. Among its many attrac-tions are its huge gothic cathedral (the largest gothic building in the world), the **Giralda** tower, the old **Barrio de Santa Cruz** with its twisting streets, and **el Parque María Luisa**. **Sevilla** is also associated with two festivals— **Semana Santa** and **La Feria de Sevilla.**

Chapter Objectives

Functions: Renting and paying for a hotel room; understanding classified ads and lodging brochures

Context: Using *La Guía Michelín* (tourist guide); renting hotel rooms, requesting amenities, paying the bill

Accuracy: Ordinal numbers; preterite of **dormir;** the verbs **salir** and **llegar** (present and preterite)

CAPÍTULO

4

BUSCAMOS UN HOTEL

—¿Qué te parece este hotel?
—Me parece muy típico. Me gusta mucho.

Objetives:

>>> **R**enting and paying for a hotel room

>>> **U**nderstanding classified ads and lodging brochures

Strategies:

>>> **R**eading for details

>>> **F**inding averages

>>> **C**ategorizing

138

Video/Laserdisc

Chapter 4 Video Program and Video Guide

PRIMERA ETAPA

Preparación

>> **D**o you like to travel?

>> **W**hen you travel, where do you stay?

>> **W**hen you plan a trip like a summer vacation, what types of information will you need to organize your trip?

>> **W**here will you get information on hotels?

>> **I**s there some publication that would have that kind of information?

>> **I**f you travel through Spain, the *Guía Michelín* might come in handy.

/-/-/-/-/-/-/-/-/-/-/-/

Learning Strategy:

Previewing

La Guía Michelín: The Michelín Guide

La Guía Michelín

La instalación

Las habitaciones de los hoteles que recomendamos poseen, en general, cuarto de baño completo. No obstante puede suceder que en las categorías 🏠, 🏠 y ☂ algunas habitaciones carezcan de él.

30 hab **30 qto**	Número de habitaciones
	Ascensor
	Aire acondicionado
TV	Televisión en la habitación
☎	Teléfono en la habitación directo con el exterior
🦽	Habitaciones de fácil acceso para minusválidos
	Comidas servidas en el jardín o en la terraza
	Fitness club (gimnasio, sauna...)
	Piscina : al aire libre – cubierta
	Playa equipada – Jardín
	Tenis – Golf y número de hoyos
🚗 25/150	Salas de conferencias : capacidad de las salas
℗	Garaje en el hotel (generalmente de pago)
	Aparcamiento reservado a la clientela
	Prohibidos los perros (en todo o en parte del establecimiento)
Fax	Transmisión de documentos por telefax
mayo-octubre *temp.*	Período de apertura comunicado por el hotelero
	Apertura probable en temporada sin precisar fechas. Sin mención, el establecimiento está abierto todo el año
✉ 28 012 ✉ 1 200	Código postal

139

Etapa Support Materials

Workbook: pp. 101–106
Tapescript: p. 63
Transparency: #17
Teacher Tape 🎧
Listening Activity masters: p. 43

Quiz: Testing Program, p. 71

Support material, *La Guía Michelín:*
Transparency #17

Presentation: *La Guía Michelín*

(1) Have students talk in English about hotel rooms in the United States. If they've never been in one, have them imagine what they are like.

(2) Have them look at the Spanish hotel classifications and use the symbols and cognates to deduce the meaning of each classification.

Presentation: *La Guía Michelín,* continued

Use Transparency #17 of the entry for the **Hotel Inglaterra.** As you read each descriptive sentence, have a student point to the appropriate symbol.

Ex. A: pair work

 writing

More-prepared students, Ex. A: More-prepared students can use the *Guía* itself and the reading information on p. 140 to write simple descriptions in Spanish.

Less-prepared students, Ex. A: When less-prepared students have identified the correct hotel classification in English, have them do a simple description in Spanish.

---

classifies

El gobierno español **clasifica** los hoteles en cinco categorías:

luxury / bathrooms / (bed)rooms

Hoteles de gran **lujo** —con **salas de baño** en todas las **habitaciones**

Hoteles **** (cuatro estrellas) —hoteles de primera clase; la mayoría de las habitaciones con sala de baño

comfort
elevator

Hoteles *** (tres estrellas) —gran **confort;** muchas habitaciones con sala de baño; **ascensor,** teléfono

Hoteles ** (dos estrellas) —buena calidad, muy confortables; 30 por ciento de las habitaciones con sala de baño

at least
sink / booth

Hoteles * (una estrella) —buena calidad, bastante confortables; **al menos** diez habitaciones con **lavabo; cabina** de teléfono

The following / what the *Michelin Guide* says

Si Ud. viaja a España, es muy útil usar la *Guía Michelín* roja (guía de hoteles y restaurantes). Esta guía usa un sistema un poco diferente de la clasificación oficial española. **Lo siguiente** es **lo que dice la *Guía Michelín*** del Hotel Inglaterra en Sevilla.

Comida (ver rest. *Florencia Pórtico*) – ⊡ 1200 – **228 hab** 18600/22000, 14 suites.   **s**

🏨 **Inglaterra,** pl. Nueva 7, ✉ 41001, ✆ 422 49 70, Fax 456 13 36 – 🛗 🖥 📺 ☎ 🚗 –
🏛 25/200. AE ⓘ E *VISA* JCB. ✂ rest   **r**
Comida (cerrado agosto) 2500 – ⊡ 1000 – **109 hab** 15600/19500, 4 suites – PA 5950.

🏰 **Los Seises,** Segovias 6, ✉ 41004, ✆ 422 94 95, Fax 422 43 34,   Instalado en el tercer patio del Palacio Arzobispal », 🛝 – 🛗 🖥 📺 ☎ – 🏛 25/100. AE ⓘ E *VISA* ✂   **f**
Comida (cerrado agosto) carta 3125 a 4475 – ⊡ 1500 – **37 hab** 15000/20000, 6 suites.

They do not permit
You don't have to go through the reception desk.

credit cards

El Hotel Inglaterra es un hotel de gran confort. Tiene restaurante y está en la Plaza Nueva. El número de teléfono es 422 49 70. Tiene ascensor y hay un televisor en cada habitación. **No permiten** perros en el restaurante. Hay un teléfono en cada habitación con línea directa al exterior. **No hay que pasar por la recepción.** En este hotel hay 109 habitaciones. Una habitación cuesta entre 15.600 y 19.500 pesetas. El desayuno cuesta 1.000 pesetas y no está incluido en el precio de la habitación. Aceptan cinco **tarjetas de crédito:** American Express, Diners Club, Eurocard, Visa y Japan Card Bank.

¡Aquí te toca a ti!

/-/-/-/-/-/-/-/-/-/-/
Learning Strategy:
Reading for details

A. *¿Qué significan los símbolos?*   In order to familiarize yourself with the symbols that the *Guía Michelín* uses to describe hotels, tell what each symbol on page 141 means. Then find an example of the symbol used in the *Guía Michelín* on pages 139 and 140. Follow the model.

Modelo: 🏛
Es un hotel con salas de conferencias.

140

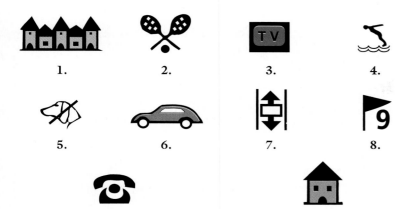

1. 2. 3. 4.

5. 6. 7. 8.

9. 10.

Answers, Ex. A: 1. This is a luxury hotel. It has a bathroom in each room and, most likely, a telephone, television, and other comforts. 2. The hotel has tennis facilities. 3. Each room has a television. 4. There is an outdoor pool. 5. No pets are allowed in the hotel. 6. The hotel has a garage. (Generally there is an extra charge.) 7. The hotel has an elevator. 8. There is a nine-hole golf course at this hotel. 9. Each room has a telephone from which you may dial directly without going through the main desk. 10. This is a one-star hotel. It is comfortable, but there is no bathroom or telephone in the room.

Ex. B: groups of three

Preparation and Implementation, Ex. B: Assign groups of three to decipher the information on individual hotels and report back to the class. Then have each group find the answer to one or two of the questions. Have each group explain their results to the rest of the class. Students may refer to p. 139 for the list of symbols. Encourage them to do as much as they can in Spanish.

COMENTARIOS CULTURALES

Los hostales

Learning Strategy:

Reading for cultural information

A convenient and economical place for students to stay when traveling in Spain is a youth hostel (**hostal**). **Hostales** are designed to accommodate young people up to the age of 26, primarily students. They offer modest rooms at unbeatable prices, and meals are often served for a nominal fee as well. There are both advantages and disadvantages to staying in **hostales**—there is usually an early curfew after which the doors are locked, and shared rooms are common practice. However, in addition to the economic advantages, you have the opportunity to meet young travelers from all over the world. The chance to make new friends and experience adventures you'll remember for a lifetime are the greatest advantages of the **hostal**.

B. Los hoteles de Sevilla Some friends of your parents are planning to visit Sevilla, a city in southern Spain. Because they don't speak Spanish, they ask your help in finding a hotel. Read the excerpt on page 142 from the *Guía Michelín*. Then answer their questions.

141

Alfonso XIII, San Fernando 2, ✉ 41004, ✆ 422 28 50, Telex 72725, Fax 421 60 33, « Majestuoso edificio de estilo andaluz » rest
Comida 4700 – 2300 – **129 hab** 29000/39000, 19 suites.

Príncipe de Asturias Radisson H. Sevilla, Isla de La Cartuja, ✉ 41092, ✆ 446 22 22, Fax 446 04 28, – 25/900.
Comida 3500 – **288 hab** 16800/21000, 7 suites.

Tryp Colón, Canalejas 1, ✉ 41001, ✆ 422 29 00, Telex 72726, Fax 422 09 38, – 25/240.
Comida (ver rest. *El Burladero*) 4100 – 1500 – **211 hab** 15500/19400, 7 suites – PA 7760.

Occidental Porta Coeli, av. Eduardo Dato 49, ✉ 41018, ✆ 453 35 00, Telex 72913, Fax 453 23 42, – 25/600.
Comida (ver rest. *Florencia*) – 1200 – **241 hab** 9500/16000, 3 suites.

Meliá Lebreros, Luis Morales 2, ✉ 41005, ✆ 457 94 00, Telex 72772, Fax 458 27 26, – 25/500.
Comida (ver rest. *La Dehesa*) – 1500 – **431 hab** 12250/16575, 6 suites.

Meliá Sevilla, Doctor Pedro de Castro 1, ✉ 41004, ✆ 442 15 11, Telex 73094, Fax 442 16 08, – 25/1000.
cerrado julio y agosto – Comida 3500 – 1500 – **361 hab** 14500/18100, 5 suites – PA 7225.

la Borbolla
25. 1000 – **77 hab** 10500/16000, 5 suites.

G. H. Lar, pl. Carmen Benítez 3, ✉ 41003, ✆ 441 03 61, Telex 72816, Fax 441 04 – 25/300.
Comida 2600 – 1000 – **129 hab** 12500/18000, 8 suites – PA 4900.

Husa Sevilla, Pagés del Corro 90, ✉ 41010, ✆ 434 24 12, Fax 434 27 07 – 25/220.
Comida 3250 – 1100 – **114 hab** 15500/21000, 14 suites – PA 6400.

NH Plaza de Armas, av. Marqués de Paradas, ✉ 41001, ✆ 490 19 92, Fax 490 12 32, – 25/250.
Comida 2200 – 1200 – **260 hab** 11200/14000, 2 suites.

Sevilla Congresos, av. Montes Sierra, ✉ 41020, ✆ 425 90 00, Telex 73224, Fax 425 95 00, – 25/270. rest
Comida 2750 – 1600 – **202 hab** 10500/15000, 16 suites – PA 5680.

Emperador Trajano, José Laguillo 8, ✉ 41003, ✆ 441 11 11, Fax 453 57 02 – 25/150.
Comida 2000 – 1000 – **77 hab** 13640.

San Gil sin rest, Parras 28, ✉ 41002, ✆ 490 68 11, Fax 490 69 39, Instalado parcialmente en un edificio típico sevillano de principios de siglo, patio ajardinado
800 – **4 hab** 11200/12800, 5 suites, 30 apartamentos.

Álvarez Quintero sin rest, con cafetería, Álvarez Quintero 9, ✉ 41004, ✆ 422 12 98, Fax 456 41 41 –
700 – **40 hab** 9500/13000.

Bécquer sin rest, con cafetería, Reyes Católicos 4, ✉ 41001, ✆ 422 89 00, Telex 72884, Fax 421 44 00 – 25/45.
800 – **120 hab** 10000/15000.

Giralda, Sierra Nevada 3, ✉ 41003, ✆ 441 66 61, Telex 72417, Fax 441 93 52 – 25/250.
Comida 2000 – 950 – **98 hab** 12650.

Derby sin rest, pl. del Duque 13, ✉ 41002, ✆ 456 10 88, Telex 72709, Fax 421 33 91 –
550 – **75 hab** 7000/9500.

1. Which is the largest hotel in Sevilla?
2. Which is the most expensive? What justifies the high prices?
3. Which hotels have swimming pools?
4. Which hotels don't have restaurants?
5. Which hotel is the least expensive?
6. Which hotels have meeting rooms?
7. How much does breakfast cost at the Hotel Giralda?
8. How many suites does the Alfonso XIII have?
9. Which hotels allow dogs?
10. Where will it be cheapest to eat breakfast?

142

ESTRUCTURA

Ordinal numbers

el primero, la primera	el quinto, la quinta	el noveno, la novena
el segundo, la segunda	el sexto, la sexta	el décimo, la décima
el tercero, la tercera	el séptimo, la séptima	
el cuarto, la cuarta	el octavo, la octava	

Ordinal numbers (such as *first, second, third*) are used to order and to rank items in a series. Notice the following special cases:

1. For *the first* use **el primero** or **la primera,** and for *the last* use **la última** or **el último.**
2. Note that ordinal numbers agree in gender with and precede the nouns they modify.
3. The shortened forms **primer** and **tercer** are used before masculine singular nouns: **el primer estudiante, el tercer piso.**
4. Beyond **décimo,** cardinal numbers are generally used. They follow the noun: **el siglo veinte, la Calle Setenta y Ocho.**
5. For dates, Spanish uses the ordinal numbers only for the first day of the month: **el primero de mayo, el primero de junio,** but **el dos de marzo, el tres de abril,** etc.
6. The abbreviated forms of the ordinal numbers are formed as follows:

primero	**1º**	primera	**1ª**	primer	**1er**
segundo	**2º**	segunda	**2ª**		
tercero	**3º**	tercera	**3ª**	tercer	**3er**
cuarto	**4º**	cuarta	**4ª**		
quinto	**5º**	quinta	**5ª**		
etc.					

Aquí practicamos

C. Lee los siguientes en voz alta *(out loud)*.

1. el 1º de abril
2. el 4º libro
3. la 1ª vez
4. la 3ª estudiante
5. el 8º lugar
6. el 1er lugar
7. el 2º año
8. la 5ª avenida
9. el 7º día
10. la 2ª clase
11. la 9ª semana
12. el 3er año

D. Contesta las siguientes preguntas.

1. ¿Cuál es el primer mes del año? ¿el tercer mes del año? ¿el octavo? ¿el último?

143

Presentation: Estructura

Before presenting the ordinal numbers, ask students to brainstorm their uses in English.
(1) Remind students of **el primero de enero, febrero, marzo,** etc.; **la primera clase, segunda clase,** etc.
(2) Have students repeat 2ª, 3ª– 10ª.
(3) Have students continue to generate ordinal numbers until the concept is established.

Learning Strategy: Brainstorming

Ex. C: writing

Answers, Ex. C: 1. el primero de abril   2. el cuarto libro   3. la primera vez   4. la tercera estudiante   5. el octavo lugar   6. el primer lugar   7. el segundo año   8. la quinta avenida   9. el séptimo día   10. la segunda clase   11. la novena semana   12. el tercer año

Ex. D: writing

2. ¿Cuál es el primer día de la semana en el calendario hispano? ¿el cuarto? ¿el último?
3. ¿A qué hora es tu primera clase? ¿tu segunda clase? ¿tu tercera clase? ¿tu última clase?

Aquí escuchamos:
"¿Tiene Ud. una reservación?"

Antes de escuchar

Linda and her friend Kelly are traveling through Spain on their own and have been using the *Guía Michelin* to organize their trip. They arrive at a hotel in Sevilla and go directly to the registration desk. Look at the following questions and identify a few things you expect to hear during their exchange at the hotel desk. What questions would you ask a clerk when checking into a hotel?

Después de escuchar

1. ¿Tenían Linda y Kelly una habitación reservada?
2. ¿Para cuántas personas?
3. ¿Cuánto costó la habitación?
4. ¿Tiene baño la habitación?
5. ¿El precio incluye el desayuno?

¡Aquí te toca a ti!

E. ¿Quisiera Ud. una habitación? Use the information given below and on page 145 to tell the desk clerk what kind of a room you want. Follow the model.

Modelo: dos personas / 5.500–7.000 pesetas (5.700 pesetas / sin baño)
—*Buenos días, señor. ¿Tiene Ud. una habitación para dos personas, entre 5.500 y 7.000 pesetas?*
—*Sí, tengo una habitación sin baño por 5.700 pesetas.*
—*Está bien.   o:*
—*Nosotros quisiéramos una habitación con baño.*

1. dos personas / 7.000–7.500 pesetas (7.300 / sin baño)

144

 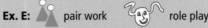

Ex. E: pair work   role play

Less-prepared students, Ex. E: Do one or two items with less-prepared students, making sure they understand and follow the model carefully. Then call on pairs of students to role play for the class.

More-prepared students, Ex. E: Encourage more-prepared students to expand on the model by asking other questions or making comments similar to those in the **Aquí escuchamos**. Then call on pairs of students to role play for the class, or create new pairs to role play.

2. tres personas / 9.000–9.500 pesetas (9.400 / con baño)
3. una persona / 4.500–5.000 pesetas (4.900 / con baño)
4. una persona / 4.200–5.500 pesetas (4.250 / sin baño)

¡Adelante!

EJERCICIO ORAL

F. Sí, yo tengo una reservación. You arrive at a hotel where you have made a reservation. Go to the front desk and talk to the employee (played by your partner). **Estudiante A** begins.

Estudiante A	Estudiante B
1. Greet the employee.	1. Greet the hotel guest.
2. Find out whether the hotel has a room for two people.	2. Find out whether the guest prefers a room with or without a private bath.
3. Say that you prefer a private bathroom and find out how much such a room costs.	3. Tell how much a room costs with bath (5,000 pesetas) and without bath (4,740 pesetas).
4. Ask whether breakfast is included.	4. Say that breakfast costs an additional 300 pesetas.
5. Thank the employee for the information. Tell which room you want and whether you want breakfast. **(Prefiero…)**	5. Give the guest the room key and welcome him or her to the hotel. **(Muy bien. Bienvenido al Hotel…)**

//-//-//-//-//-//-//-//-//

Learning Strategy:

Asking and answering questions

Critical Thinking Strategy:

Making decisions

EJERCICIO ESCRITO

G. El Hotel Montecarlo Imagine that you are Linda or Kelly **(Aquí escuchamos)**. Write a postcard to a friend describing the hotel where you're staying. Comment on (1) the location of the hotel, (2) how the hotel is classified by the *Guía Michelin*, (3) how many rooms the hotel has, (4) what floor your room is on, (5) one of the amenities in your room (such as television or telephone), and (6) how many days you are going to stay at the hotel. (7) Remember to date and sign your postcard.

//-//-//-//-//-//-//-//-//

Learning Strategies:

Organizing information, describing

145

Answers, Ex. E: 1. —Buenos días, señor. ¿Tiene Ud. una habitación para dos personas entre 7.000 y 7.500 pesetas? —Sí, tengo una habitación sin baño por 7.300 pesetas. —Está bien. o: —Nosotros quisiéramos una habitación con baño. 2. —Buenos días, señor. ¿Tiene Ud. una habitación para tres personas entre 9.000 y 9.500 pesetas? —Sí, tengo una habitación con baño por 9.400 pesetas. —Está bien. 3. —Buenos días, señor. ¿Tiene Ud. una habitación para una persona entre 4.500 y 5.000 pesetas? —Sí, tengo una habitación con baño por 4.900 pesetas. —Está bien. 4. —Buenos días, señor. ¿Tiene Ud. una habitación para una persona entre 4.200 y 5.500 pesetas? —Sí, tengo una habitación sin baño por 4.250 pesetas. —Está bien. o: —Quisiera una habitación con baño.

Presentation: En una habitación

As an introduction to the **etapa,** bring in hotel brochures (or newspaper ads) from your area. Have students talk about what is highlighted in American hotel advertisements. After they've read the brochure for the Madrid hotel, ask them to make comparisons. Have less-prepared students tell in English (then, in Spanish) what facts they get from the hotel brochure. Have more-prepared students give the information directly in Spanish.

SEGUNDA ETAPA

Preparación

As you begin this **etapa,** review the symbols used by the *Guía Michelín* on pages 139–140 for the various features of a hotel.

>> **W**hat information would you expect to see included in a hotel brochure?

>> **W**hich features do hotels usually highlight to attract customers?

>> **W**hat are some of the features you might expect to find in a highly rated hotel?

/-/-/-/-/-/-/-/-/-/-/-/

Learning Strategy:

Previewing

En una habitación

Hotel INGLES, situado en el corazón de Madrid, tan próximo a su tradición e historia monumental, como a sus núcleos comerciales y de diversión. En la capital de España, en el lugar preciso, siempre vecino a los puntos de interés.

Equipado con 58 habitaciones (Suites, Dobles, Individuales), disponiendo cada una de ellas de: Baño completo, Calefacción, Teléfono, así como de los servicios particulares del Hotel: Cafetería-Pub, Salón de TV (color), Hilo musical, Caja de Seguridad individual, Parking privado, Gimnasio.

UN PUNTO
IDEAL
EN EL CENTRO
DE LA CIUDAD

◇◇◇ **HOTEL INGLES**
ECHEGARAY, 8 - TELEF. (91) 429 65 51
28014 MADRID - ESPAÑA

146

Etapa Support Materials

Workbook: pp. 107–112
Transparencies: #18, #19, #19a
Teacher Tape 🎧
Quiz: Testing Program, p. 74

Support materíal, **En una habitación:**
Transparency #18

¡Aquí te toca a ti!

A. El gran hotel...
Basándote en el folleto (*brochure*) de la página 146, contesta las siguientes preguntas.

1. In what part of Madrid is the hotel located?
2. Near what tourist sights is the hotel located?
3. How many stars does the hotel have? What does that mean?
4. How many rooms does the hotel have?
5. What amenities does a typical room have?
6. Does each room have a television?

Learning Strategy:

Reading for details

la lámpara

la mesita de noche   el lavabo

el espejo   el bidé

la habitación   el pasillo

B. La habitación del hotel
Basándote en el dibujo de la habitación y el pasillo, contesta las siguientes preguntas. Usa las pistas entre paréntesis cuando aparecen (*when they appear*).

Learning Strategy:

Answering questions based on visual cues

1. ¿Cuántas camas hay en la habitación?
2. ¿Dónde está la mesita de noche? (cerca de)
3. ¿Dónde está el lavabo? (al lado de)
4. ¿Dónde está el bidé? (al lado de)
5. ¿Dónde está el ascensor? (al fondo de)
6. ¿Dónde está el WC? (en frente de)
7. ¿Dónde está la ducha (*shower*)? (al lado de)
8. ¿De qué color es la lámpara?

147

Variation, Ex. C: Have students pick, at random, cards containing the individual names of hotels. Then have them identify the hotel. (A student who picked a card with the name **San Gil** would say: **San Gil es el octavo hotel en la lista.**)

More-prepared students, Ex. C: More-prepared students can expand their discussion of hotels by commenting on each one. For example (after completing the **Modelo**), **No me gusta el San Gil porque no tiene piscina cubierta** or **Me gusta el San Gil porque las habitaciones tienen televisión.**

Expansion, Ex. C: Have student pairs ask each other questions about the hotels based on the information and symbols beside the hotel names.
Modelo: —¿Cuál es el sexto hotel de la lista? —El sexto hotel es el Sevilla Congresos. —¿Cuántas habitaciones tiene el hotel? —Tiene 202 habitaciones.

Learning Strategies:
Asking questions,
interpreting symbols
from a legend

COMENTARIOS CULTURALES

Los números de los pisos

In Spanish, the word **piso** is used for floors above the ground level. The term for *ground floor* is **la planta baja** (literally, the level of the pavement). This is abbreviated **PB** or sometimes **B** in elevators. Consequently, each **piso** is numbered one floor lower than its designation would be in English:

American hotel	Spanish hotel
4th floor	3er piso
3rd floor	2° piso
2nd floor	1er piso
1st floor	Planta baja (PB/B)

To indicate that a room is *on* a certain floor, use **en: en el segundo piso.**

Repaso

C. ¿Cuál es el primer hotel de la lista?   You and a friend are reviewing the list of hotels that follows. He or she asks you about a specific hotel, referring to it by its place on the list using ordinal numbers. You respond to the question. Follow the model.

 Modelo: —¿Cuál es el primer hotel de la lista?
—El primer hotel es el NH Ciudad de Sevilla.

```
╭─╮ NH Ciudad de Sevilla, av. Manuel Siurot 25, ✉ 41013, ✆ 423 05 05, Fax 423 85 39,
    - |♿| 🖩 TV ☎ 🐕 - 🅰 25/300. AE ⓓ E VISA                                      🛥
    Comida 3500 - 🍴 1400 - 90 hab 25400/31800, 3 suites.                          r
╭─╮ Pasarela sin rest, av. de la Borbolla 11, ✉ 41004, ✆ 441 55 11, Telex 72486, Fax 442 07 27,
    |♿| - |♿| 🖩 TV ☎ 🐕 - 🅰 25. AE ⓓ E VISA                                      n
    🍴 1000 - 77 hab 10500/16000, 5 suites.
╭─╮ G. H. Lar, pl. Carmen Benítez 3, ✉ 41003, ✆ 441 03 61, Telex 72816, Fax 441 04 52 - |♿| 🖩
    Comida 2600 - 🍴 1000 - 129 hab 12500/18000, 8 suites - PA 4900.                f
╭─╮ Husa Sevilla ⚓, Pagés del Corro 90, ✉ 41010, ✆ 434 24 12, Fax 434 27 07 - |♿| 🖩 TV
    Comida 3250 - 🍴 1100 - 114 hab 15500/21000, 14 suites - PA 6400.               a
╭─╮ NH Plaza de Armas, av. Marqués de Paradas, ✉ 41001, ✆ 490 19 92, Fax 490 12 32, 🛥
    Comida 2200 - 🍴 1200 - 260 hab 11200/14000, 2 suites.                          c
╭─╮ Sevilla Congresos, av. Montes Sierra, ✉ 41020, ✆ 425 90 00, Telex 73224, Fax 425 95 00,
    Comida 2750 - 🍴 1600 - 202 hab 10500/15000, 16 suites - PA 5680.      rest      a
╭─╮ Emperador Trajano, José Laguillo 8, ✉ 41003, ✆ 441 11 11, Fax 453 57 02 - |♿| 🖩 TV
    Comida 2000 - 🍴 1000 - 77 hab 13640.                                           a
╭─╮ San Gil sin rest, Parras 28, ✉ 41002, ✆ 490 68 11, Fax 490 69 39,   Instalado parcialmente
    en un edificio típico sevillano de principios de siglo, patio ajardinado , 🛥 - |♿| TV ☎. AE
    ⓓ E VISA 🐕
    🍴 800 - 4 hab 11200/12800, 5 suites, 30 apartamentos.
╭─╮ Álvarez Quintero sin rest, con cafetería, Álvarez Quintero 9, ✉ 41004, ✆ 422 12 98,
    Fax 456 41 41 - |♿| 🖩 TV ☎ 🐕 - 🅰 25/45. AE ⓓ E                               u
    🍴 700 - 40 hab 9500/13000.                                                      c
╭─╮ Bécquer sin rest, con cafetería, Reyes Católicos 4, ✉ 41001, ✆ 422 89 00, Telex 72884,
    Fax 421 44 00 - |♿| 🖩 TV ☎ 🐕 - 🅰 25/45. AE ⓓ E VISA 🐕
    🍴 800 - 120 hab 10000/15000.                                                    v
╭─╮ Giralda, Sierra Nevada 3, ✉ 41003, ✆ 441 66 61, Telex 72417, Fax 441 93 52 - |♿| 🖩 TV
    Comida 2000 - 🍴 950 - 98 hab 12650.                                             e
╭─╮ Derby sin rest, pl. del Duque 13, ✉ 41002, ✆ 456 10 88, Telex 72709, Fax 421 33 91 - |♿|
    🍴 550 - 75 hab 7000/9500.                                                       r
```

ESTRUCTURA

The preterite of the verb *dormir*

—¿**Dormiste** mucho anoche?
—Sí, **dormí** ocho horas.

Did you sleep a lot last night?
Yes, *I slept* eight hours.

dormir			
yo	**dormí**	nosotros(as)	**dormimos**
tú	**dormiste**	vosotros(as)	**dormisteis**
él		ellos	
ella	} **durmió**	ellas	} **durmieron**
Ud.		Uds.	

Ex. D: writing

Suggestion, Ex. D: Call on students at random to give possible answers.

Teacher's note, Ex. D: These column exercises are meant to provide controlled practice. One way to present them is through the creation of a "word web." On a separate piece of paper, students can draw a web and then connect elements from the columns in ways that form grammatically correct sentences. (They have to write the correct form of the verb in the middle column.) The drawing that follows is a sample word web format. Word web formats vary from exercise to exercise.

The verb **dormir** in the preterite is irregular only in the third person singular and plural. Notice that in these forms, only the **o** of the stem changes to a **u.**

A common expression with **dormir** is **dormir la siesta** *(to take a nap):*

—¿**Dormiste la siesta** ayer?   *Did you take a nap* yesterday?
—Sí, **dormí una siesta** de dos horas.   Yes, *I took* a two-hour *nap.*

Aquí practicamos

D. *¿Cuántas horas durmieron tus amigos?* Di hasta qué hora durmieron tú y tus amigos el sábado pasado.

A	B	C	D
yo	dormir	hasta las	8:00
tú			8:30
Elena			9:00
nosotros			9:30
?			10:00
			10:30
			11:00
			11:30
			12:00

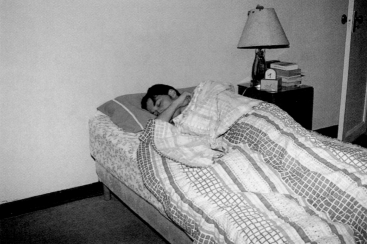

Ayer Eduardo durmió una siesta de tres horas.

E. Working in pairs, ask each other the following questions, noting both your answers and those of your partner. Determine which of you generally gets more sleep.

1. ¿Hasta qué hora dormiste ayer?
2. ¿Hasta qué hora dormiste el sábado pasado?
3. ¿Dormiste en una cama matrimonial *(double bed)* o en una cama sencilla *(twin bed)*?
4. ¿Cómo dormiste anoche? ¿Bien? ¿Mal?
5. ¿Cuántas horas dormiste anoche?
6. ¿Cuántas horas dormiste el sábado pasado?
7. ¿Dormiste la siesta ayer?
8. ¿Dormiste la siesta el fin de semana pasado?

F. *¿Duermen mucho Uds.?* Tú quieres saber más acerca de *(about)* cuántas horas duermen varios compañeros de clase. Hazle una pregunta a un(a) compañero(a) acerca de cuánto duerme él o ella y tres preguntas más sobre otros compañeros de clase.

Modelo: —¿Cuántas horas duermes en general?
—Duermo nueve horas cada noche.
—¿Cuántas horas duerme Susana?
…

Aquí escuchamos:
"¡Es una habitación bonita!"

Antes de escuchar

Linda and her friend Kelly get the key from the hotel clerk and go up to check out their room. Look at the questions below and identify a few things you expect to hear during their conversation in the room.

START

Después de escuchar

1. ¿Qué habitación tienen y dónde está?
2. ¿Dónde está el ascensor?
3. ¿Qué hay en la habitación?
4. ¿Dónde están el baño y la ducha?
5. ¿Qué piden para usar la ducha?

151

Ex. E: pair work   writing

Ex. F: groups of four or more

Less-prepared students,
Ex. G: Review questions with
dónde by doing a quick pattern
drill: **Ascensor —¿Dónde está**
el ascensor?, etc. Flash cards of
various places in the hotel would
help to move the drill at a steady
pace.

More-prepared students,
Ex. G: More-prepared students
can do the exercise as a role play
between the guest and the desk
clerk. Students can create answers
similar to those in the dialogue.
Have students switch roles and
give different information in their
answers.

Answers, Ex. G: 1. Perdón,
señor, ¿cuál es el número de mi
habitación? 2. Perdón, señor,
¿dónde está el WC? 3. Perdón,
señor, ¿dónde está la ducha?
4. Perdón, señor, ¿dónde está el
restaurante? 5. Perdón, señor,
¿está incluido el desayuno en
el precio de la habitación?
6. Perdón, señor, ¿tiene Ud. la llave
para la ducha?

Ex. H: pair work

role play

Less-prepared students,
Ex. H: Encourage less-prepared
students to recycle ideas and structures from Ex. G. Review vocabulary items as needed. Later, call on
students at random to play the
roles for each number.

More-prepared students,
Ex. H: Call on different students
to form pairs; make sure all students get to play both parts. Have
them perform for the class.

Ex. I: writing

¡Aquí te toca a ti!

G. *Perdón, señor*   Estás en un hotel y necesitas información. Usa las palabras entre paréntesis para hacer preguntas en la recepción. Sigue el modelo.

> **Modelo:**   the location of the elevator (**dónde está**)
> *Perdón, señor, ¿dónde está el ascensor?*

1. what your room number is (**cuál es**)
2. the location of the toilet (**dónde está**)
3. the location of the shower (**dónde está**)
4. the location of the restaurant (**dónde está**)
5. whether breakfast is included in the price of the room (**está incluido**)
6. if he has the key for the shower (**tiene Ud.**)

¡Adelante!

EJERCICIO ORAL

H. *En la recepción*   You are at the reception desk of a hotel.

1. Greet the hotel clerk.
2. Say that you would like a room with a bath.
3. The room is for one person for four nights.
4. You would like a room on the fifth floor, if there is an elevator.
5. Find out the price of the room.
6. Ask if breakfast is included.
7. Ask if there is a **metro** station nearby.
8. Thank the hotel clerk.

EJERCICIO ESCRITO

152

I. *Mi habitación*   Write a postcard to a friend in the U.S. describing your hotel room in Barcelona, Spain. Tell (1) the name of the hotel, (2) what floor your room is on, (3) whether there is an elevator, (4) whether there is a private bathroom, (5) how the room is furnished, (6) whether breakfast is included in the price, (7) whether you like the hotel and the room and why. (8) Remember to date and sign your card.

TERCERA ETAPA

Preparación

>> **W**hat types of information would you expect to find on a bill from a hotel?

>> **B**efore you proceed to **Activity A**, take a look at the bill below.

>> **W**hat information is included?

//-/-/-/-/-/-/-/-/-/-/-/
Learning Strategy:
Previewing

//-/-/-/-/-/-/-/-/-/-/-/
Learning Strategies:
Previewing, reading for details

La cuenta

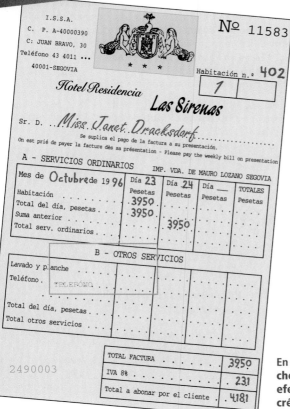

I.S.S.A.
C. P. A-40000390
C: JUAN BRAVO, 30
Teléfono 43 4011 ...
40001-SEGOVIA

Nº 11583

Habitación n.º 402

Hotel Residencia
Las Sirenas

Sr. D. ...*Miss Janet Dracksdorf*...

Se suplica el pago de la factura a su presentación.
On est prié de payer la facture dès sa présentation - Please pay the weekly bill on presentation

A - SERVICIOS ORDINARIOS
IMP. VDA. DE MAURO LOZANO SEGOVIA

Mes de *Octubre* de 19 96

	Día 23 Pesetas	Día 24 Pesetas	Día ___ Pesetas	TOTALES Pesetas
Habitación				
Total del día, pesetas	3950	3950		
Suma anterior	3950			
Total serv. ordinarios		3950		

B - OTROS SERVICIOS

Lavado y planche				
Teléfono	TELÉFONO			
Total del día, pesetas				
Total otros servicios				

2490003

TOTAL FACTURA	3950
IVA 8%	231
Total a abonar por el cliente	4.181

¡Aquí te toca a ti!

A. *La cuenta* Answer the questions based on the bill.

1. What is the name of the hotel?
2. In what city is the hotel located?
3. What are the dates of the hotel stay?
4. How many rooms is the bill for?
5. How many nights is the bill for? How much did the room cost per night?

En este hotel, se puede pagar la cuenta con **cheques de viajero** *(traveler's checks)* o **en efectivo** *(cash)*. No aceptan **tarjetas de crédito** *(credit cards).*

153

Etapa Support Materials

Workbook: pp. 113–117
Transparency: #20
Teacher Tape 🎧

Quiz: Testing Program, p. 76

Chapter Test: **Testing Program, p. 79**

Support material, **La cuenta:**
   Transparency #20

Ex. A: pair work

✎ writing

More-prepared students, Ex. A: Ask more-prepared students to write the equivalent questions in Spanish to ask the class.

Less-prepared students, Ex. A: After they have completed the exercise, less-prepared students should be able to answer other students' questions in Spanish, using the information they already know.

Answers, Ex. A: 1. (Hotel Residencia) Las Sirenas 2. Segovia 3. from Oct. 23 to Oct. 24, 1996 4. one 5. one; 3,950 pesetas per night

Teacher's note, Ex. A: Point out to the students that IVA means **Impuesto sobre el Valor Añadido** (value-added tax). In this case it is about 6% of 3,950 or 231 pesetas.

Repaso

B. ¿Cuántas horas dormiste tú? You have heard that high-school students have strange sleeping habits—some sleep a lot and some sleep very little. You want to conduct an informal survey on this. When your teacher gives the signal, circulate around the room and ask how much sleep several of your classmates got on various nights during the past week. Try to find out if there are differences between weekday and weekend nights.

C. En la recepción Go to the hotel desk and ask for a room. The student playing the role of the desk clerk will use the suggested information to answer your questions. Follow the model.

Modelo: una persona / con / 3.500 pesetas / 350 pesetas / 1er / 19
—¿Tiene Ud. una habitación para una persona con baño?
—Sí, tenemos una habitación por 3.500 pesetas la noche.
—¿Está el desayuno incluido en el precio?
—No... Tiene que pagar 350 pesetas más.
—Bien. Quiero la habitación.
—De acuerdo. Está en el primer piso. Es la habitación 19.

1. dos personas / sin / 3.900 pesetas / 250 pesetas / 2o / 24
2. una persona / con / 4.600 pesetas / 360 pesetas / 5o / 51
3. dos personas / con / 5.950 pesetas / incluido / 4o / 43
4. dos personas / sin / 6.250 pesetas / incluido / 3er / 16

ESTRUCTURA

The verbs salir and llegar

Mi hermano **sale con** María.	My brother *goes out* **with** María.
Salgo para Madrid mañana.	I *leave for* Madrid tomorrow.
Yo **salgo de** la escuela a las 4:00.	I *leave* school at 4:00.
¿A qué hora **llegas a** casa?	What time *do you get* home?
Yo **llego a** casa a las 4:30.	I *get* home at 4:30.
Mi papá **llega de** Nueva York el viernes próximo.	My father *arrives from* New York next Friday.

154

yo	salgo	llego	nosotros(as)	salimos	llegamos
tú	sales	llegas	vosotros(as)	salís	llegáis
él			ellos		
ella }	sale	llega	ellas }	salen	llegan
Ud.			Uds.		

In the present tense, only the **yo** form of **salir** is irregular. The verb **llegar** is completely regular in the present tense.

Mi hermano **salió con** María el viernes pasado.	My brother *went out* **with** María last Friday.
Yo **salí de** la escuela a las 4:00 ayer.	I *left* school at 4:00 yesterday.
¿A qué hora **llegaste a** casa?	What time *did you get* home?
Yo **llegué a** casa a las 4:30.	I *got* home at 4:30.
¿Cuándo **llegó de** Valencia tu amiga?	When did your friend *arrive from* Valencia?

yo	salí	llegué	nosotros(as)	salimos	llegamos
tú	saliste	llegaste	vosotros(as)	salisteis	llegasteis
él			ellos		
ella }	salió	llegó	ellas }	salieron	llegaron
Ud.			Uds.		

The **yo** form of **llegar** has a spelling change in the preterite. The verb **salir** is completely regular in the preterite.

Salir para means *to leave for* a place.
Salir de means *to leave from* a place.
Salir con means *to go out with* someone.
Llegar a means *to arrive at* a place.
Llegar de means *to arrive from* a place.

Aquí practicamos

D. ¿Cuándo llegaste? Di a qué hora tú y varios compañeros de clase salieron de la escuela y a qué hora llegaron a casa el miércoles pasado.

A	B	C
yo	salir de casa	a las 3:30
tú	llegar a casa	a las ?
?		
nosotros		
? y ?		

Presentation: Estructura

(1) Have students repeat the conjugation of **salir** while you write the pronouns in three groups—**yo, tú, él, ella, Ud. / ellos, ellas / nosotros, Uds.**
(2) Repeat in the negative.
(3) Add written verb forms to the pronouns.
(4) Repeat for **llegar.**

Ex. D: writing

Teacher's note, Ex. D: These column exercises are meant to provide controlled practice. One way to present them is through the creation of a "word web." On a separate piece of paper, students can draw a web and then connect elements from the columns in ways that form grammatically correct sentences. (They have to write the correct form of the verb in the middle column.) The drawing that follows is a sample word web format. Word web formats vary from exercise to exercise.

Expansion, Ex. D: Have students contrast when they usually leave and arrive with when they left and arrived last Wednesday (e.g., **De costumbre yo salgo de la escuela las 3:30 y llego a casa a las 4:00, pero el miércoles pasado salí de la escuela a las 5:00 y llegué a casa a las 6:00.**).

Unit 2, Chapter 4 **T155**

Preparation, Ex. E: Review time expressions with students before beginning. Have less-prepared students skim the exercise to determine the time frame, making a note of past, habitual present, or future.

Possible answers, Ex. E:
1. ¿A qué hora sales tú de casa por la mañana en general? (Responses for all answers will vary.)   2. ¿A qué hora salieron ellos del trabajo anoche?   3. ¿A qué hora salen Uds. (van a salir Uds.) para Miami este verano?   4. ¿A qué hora salieron tus padres para el cine el sábado pasado?   5. ¿A qué hora saliste tú del restaurante ayer?   6. ¿A qué hora salen ellos de Nueva York mañana?   7. ¿A qué hora sale ella de su clase de español todos los días?   8. ¿A qué hora salieron Uds. de la biblioteca el martes pasado?

Support material, Aquí escuchamos: Teacher Tape

Presentation: Aquí escuchamos

Make sure students refer to the **Antes** and the **Después de escuchar** sections. Have them predict the topic of the dialogue. After they listen to the tape, explain the difference between a continental breakfast (various breads, butter, jam) and a full American breakfast. Ask students what they prefer to eat for breakfast. This reviews some of the vocabulary from Unit 1 of Level 1.

Use the exercise for dictation practice if you wish.

Learning Strategies:

Asking questions, determining time frame

Critical Thinking Strategy:

Making associations

Learning Strategy:

Previewing

Learning Strategy:

Listening for details

156

E. ¿A qué hora?   Use the cues suggested to find out at what time your partner does certain routine activities (present time) or at what time he or she did a particular activity (past time). Your partner will answer by making up an appropriate time of day. Follow the model and be careful that the time used is appropriate for the activity being discussed.

Modelo: Ud. / salir para Chicago mañana
—*¿A qué hora sale Ud. para Chicago mañana?*
—*Salgo para Chicago a las 9:00.*

1. tú / salir de casa por la mañana en general
2. ellos / salir del trabajo anoche
3. Uds. / salir para Miami este verano
4. tus padres / salir para el cine el sábado pasado
5. tú / salir del restaurante ayer
6. ellos / salir de Nueva York mañana
7. ella / salir de su clase de español todos los días
8. Uds. / salir de la biblioteca el martes pasado

Aquí escuchamos:
"Arregle la cuenta, por favor."

Antes de escuchar

Linda and her friend Kelly are getting ready to check out of the hotel in Sevilla. Look at the following questions and identify a few things you expect to hear during Linda's conversation with the hotel clerk.

Después de escuchar

1. ¿Qué pide Linda?
2. ¿Qué toman para el desayuno?
3. ¿Cuántas noches estuvieron en el hotel?
4. ¿Cuántos desayunos tomaron?
5. ¿Cuánto y cómo pagaron?

Answers, Aquí escuchamos: 1. dos desayunos 2. un café con leche, un chocolate, dos tostadas   3. cinco noches   4. diez desayunos   5. en efectivo

¡Aquí te toca a ti!

F. *Por favor, señor(a).* Your tour group is checking out of the hotel. You need to settle your account. Greet the hotel clerk and find out…

1. if he or she has prepared the bill.
2. how much the bill is.
3. if they accept credit cards.
4. if the train station is far from the hotel.
5. if there is a restaurant at the train station.

Thank the desk clerk and say good-bye.

> **Learning Strategy:**
> *Asking and answering questions*

EJERCICIO ORAL

G. *Intercambio* You and your partner are sharing details about family vacations. Interview each other giving information about either a real or imaginary trip that you have taken or would like to take with your family. Include information about some of the following:

adónde / cuándo / dormir en hotel o en casa de amigos o parientes *(relatives)* / salir por la noche / museos / parque de atracciones / restaurantes / pagar en efectivo o con una tarjeta de crédito o con cheques de viajero / viajar en coche o en tren o en avión / escribir cartas o tarjetas postales

> **Cooperative Learning**
> **Learning Strategies:**
> *Interviewing, narrating in the past*
>
> **Critical Thinking Strategies:**
> *Comparing and contrasting, categorizing*

EJERCICIO ESCRITO

H. *Una comparación de hoteles* Choose any two of the hotels listed on page 149 and write a short comparison of the two. How are they similar? How are they different?

> **Critical Thinking Strategy:**
> *Comparing and contrasting*

157

Ex. F: pair work — role play

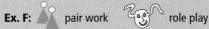

Suggestion, Ex. F: Since students do not have the text of **Aquí escuchamos,** ask for volunteers to come up with specific vocabulary items, such as *bill* or *credit card.* Then ask for volunteers to formulate each of the questions. Have a student secretary record these on the board for reference. Then divide the class into pairs. Make sure all students play both roles.

Ex. G: pair work

Less-prepared students, Ex. G: Invite less-prepared students to think about the time frame of the vacation. Did it happen already or not? If it did, what verb tense do they need to use? Once they have established the need for the preterite, help them formulate their questions before they interview each other.

More-prepared students, Ex. G: Encourage more-prepared students to use their imaginations and to use as wide a variety of appropriate expressions as possible in their work.

Expansion, Ex. G: Create a "tick mark" chart on the board, polling the class on the different categories of details about their trips. Follow-up discussion can be based on what the class profile looks like in such areas as: how many traveled; in which season; by what mode of transportation; where they stayed: in hotels or with relatives; what kinds of activities were the most popular; and which forms of payment were used.

Learning Strategy: Polling, reading a graph

Critical Thinking Strategy: Categorizing

Ex. H:  writing

Less-prepared students, Ex. H: Have less-prepared students make a chart with one-word categories (**habitaciones, garaje, desayuno, piscina,** etc.) along the top of the page and names of hotels down the side in order to facilitate comparison of different hotels. Students can put a check mark or number in each category, then refer back to the list as they write up their comparison.

- Put students into groups of four and tell them to brainstorm vocabulary items and expressions that would be useful in a hotel, including the expressions in the **Vocabulario.**
- Have each group form two pairs. Each pair will work together to plan their own hotel scenes. Tell the students that you will be the desk clerk. Each pair will rehearse their presentation with the other pair in their group before presenting it to the class.
- While they are rehearsing, circulate among the groups to act as the desk clerk.
- Call on pairs to present their hotel scenes to the class.
- Give a vocabulary quiz by having the students write about a hotel scene.

Vocabulario

Para charlar

Para hablar de una habitación en un hotel

Yo quisiera…	una habitación para dos personas.
Nosotros quisiéramos…	por tres noches.
Necesitamos…	con baño.
Buscamos…	sin baño.
Tenemos una reservación.	en el primer piso.
	con televisor.
	con teléfono.

Para pagar la cuenta

¿Puede Ud. arreglar la cuenta?
¿Tiene Ud. la cuenta para la habitación 38?
Yo voy a pagar en efectivo.
　　　　　con cheques de viajero.
　　　　　con una tarjeta de crédito.

Temas y contextos

En el hotel

una alfombra
un ascensor
un baño (una sala de baño)
un bidé
una cabina de teléfono
un corredor
una cuenta
el desayuno (incluido en el precio o no incluido en el precio)
una ducha

un espejo
una lámpara
un lavabo
una mesita de noche
el (primer, segundo, tercer, cuarto, quinto) piso
la planta baja
la recepción
el WC

Los números ordinales

el (la) primero(a) / el primer
el (la) segundo(a)
el (la) tercero(a) / el tercer
el (la) cuarto(a)
el (la) quinto(a)
el (la) sexto(a)
el (la) séptimo(a)
el (la) octavo(a)
el (la) noveno(a)
el (la) décimo(a)

Vocabulario general

Sustantivos	Adjetivos	Verbos	Otras expresiones
la calidad	confortable	clasificar	al menos
la categoría	incluido(a)	dormir (ue, u) (la siesta)	¡Claro que no!
el confort	simple	llegar de (a)	hay que pasar por…
el lujo	útil	salir con	lo que dice la
el sistema de clasificación		de	*Guía Michelín*
		para	lo siguiente
			no permiten

Lectura
CULTURAL

LOS PARADORES

Derecha: Un parador de lujo en Granada
Izquierda: El parador de San Francisco en Granada

Antes de leer

1. When people travel in the U. S., what are some of the places where they can stay overnight? Can you think of at least three types of places?
2. Look at the pictures that accompany this reading. What do you think the places featured are?
3. Look at the map that accompanies this reading. Where do you think these places are?
4. What do you think a **parador** is?

160

Guía para la lectura

A. Now read the first paragraph and answer the following:

1. Un parador es un tipo de _____.
   a. hotel
   b. restaurante
   c. viaje
2. ¿Qué hicieron el Marqués de la Vega-Inclán y el rey Alfonso XIII en 1926?
3. ¿Cuántos paradores hay en España?

B. Now read the second paragraph and answer the following question:
¿Dónde deciden en España establecer un parador?

Los paradores

a palabra *parador* aparece en muchos textos literarios españoles. Tradicionalmente en otros tiempos, el parador servía como un lugar donde los viajeros podían pasar la noche. Tomando esta tradición, en 1926 el Comisario Regio de Turismo, el Marqués de la Vega-Inclán, junto con el rey Alfonso XIII empezaron el proyecto de establecer una red de paradores en toda España. El primer parador se construyó en la Sierra de Gredos. Después se construyeron otros como el Parador de Manzanares y el Parador de Oropesa. Hoy día la red de paradores consiste en ochenta y seis establecimientos.

La filosofía básica es establecer un parador en una parte de España donde no hay muchos hoteles privados. Pero también hay un segundo punto importante en la concepción del Marqués de la Vega-Inclán. Y es que siempre que sea posible, se establezcan los paradores en antiguos monumentos como palacios, castillos o conventos.

Un viaje a los paradores no es sólo un viaje por las tierras de España. Es también un viaje por la historia. Usted puede dormir en la misma habitación en que durmió el Emperador Carlos V en el castillo de Jarandillo de la Vera. También puede comer en las salas que eran parte de la Universidad Complutense, fundada por el Cardenal Cisneros en Alcalá de Henares en 1498.

Spain

161

Chapter Objectives

Functions: Describing furniture and items in a room; telling time using the 24-hour clock
Context: Flight schedules, train schedules; official time vs. conversational time
Accuracy: Time expressions, parts of an hour; the 24-hour clock

Cultural Observation

The Alhambra, a famous palace of Moorish kings, is renowned for the beauty of its architecture and gardens. It is a popular tourist site in Granada, the last stronghold in Spain of the Moors, who were forced to abandon the Alhambra in 1492.

CAPÍTULO **5**

UN AÑO EN CASA DE LOS ÁLVAREZ

Vista de la ciudad de Granada desde la Alhambra, maravilla de la arquitectura árabe.

Objectives:

>>> **D**escribing furniture and items in a room
>>> **T**elling time using the 24-hour clock

Strategies:

>>> **C**alculating
>>> **N**arrating in the past
>>> **A**nalyzing

162

Video/Laserdisc

Chapter 5 Video Program and Video Guide

PRIMERA ETAPA

Preparación

In this chapter you will be focusing on an American student who is studying abroad.

>> **D**o you know of anyone who has studied in a foreign country? in which country?

>> **W**ould you like to study in a foreign country?

>> **I**n which one? What are your reasons for that choice?

>> **W**hat are other reasons that someone might have for wanting to study in another country?

//·//·//·//·//·//·//·//

Learning Strategies:

Previewing, supporting choices

Critical Thinking Strategy:

Hypothesizing

Un programa de intercambio

Un programa de intercambio: An exchange program

PROGRAMA DE INTERCAMBIO

Escuela _Santa Fe Capital High School_

Apellido _McGill_

Nombre _Patrick_

Edad _16_   *Edad:* Age

Dirección: Calle _1606 Jay St._

Ciudad _Santa Fe_

Estado _New Mexico 87502_   *Estado:* State

País _Estados Unidos_

Teléfono _(505) 555-4321_

Nombres de sus padres _Susan, Charles_

¿Ha vivido en el extranjero?   Sí _✓_ No____   ¿Ha visitado el extranjero? Sí _✓_ No____   *¿Ha vivido en el extranjero?:* Have you lived outside the country? / *Ha visitado:* Have you visited

País: _Canada_   Duración de la visita: _2 semanas_

Chile   _1 mes_

Presentation: Un programa de intercambio

As students look at the transparency, have one student ask a question and another answer for each item on the first part of the form. **¿A qué escuela asiste? Asiste a Santa Fe High School. ¿Cuál es su apellido? Su apellido es McGill.** Call on several students to read Patrick's essay (p. 164) out loud. Then have students do Ex. A, p. 164, as a comprehension check. As a follow-up, ask the questions below.

Possible questions, Un programa de intercambio: 1. How long has he studied Spanish? 2. What does he want to do someday? 3. What other languages does he study? 4. Does he like foreign languages? 5. What is his mother's nationality? 6. Who visited Spain? Why does he want to go to Spain?

 1. **¿Cuánto tiempo hace que estudia español? 2. ¿Qué quiere hacer algún día? 3. ¿Qué otras lenguas estudia? 4. ¿Le gustan las lenguas extranjeras? 5. ¿Cuál es la nacionalidad de su mamá? 6. ¿Quién visitó España? ¿Por qué quiere ir a España?**

Etapa Support Materials

Workbook: **pp. 119–123**
Tapescript: **p. 75**
Transparencies: **#21, #21a**
Teacher Tape 🎧
Listening Activity masters: **p. 50**

Quiz: **Testing Program, p. 84**

Support material, **Un programa de intercambio:**
Transparencies #21, #21a

Ex. A: writing

Less-prepared students, Ex. A: Have less-prepared students put an asterisk on the lines in the text that contain the answers to the questions, as a double check on comprehension.

More-prepared students, Ex. A: When they finish Ex. A, have the more-prepared students scan the reading and write at least three more questions about its content. (See p. T163, *Possible questions* for ideas.) Have them ask the class these new questions.

Answers, Ex. A: 1. Vive en Santa Fe, New Mexico. 2. Su madre es chilena. 3. Tiene 16 años. 4. Ha visitado el Canadá y Chile. 5. Pasó dos semanas en el Canadá y un mes en Chile. 6. Quiere conocer a unos españoles, perfeccionar su español y estudiar la cultura española. 7. Prefiere vivir con una familia.

Cooperative Learning

Turn to Your Neighbor, Ex. A

- Have students read the activity independently.
- Have them work in pairs to read the questions, find the answers, and then check with a neighboring pair to verify.
- Have students take turns answering each question first.
- Have the students answer all of the questions, turning to their neighbors to check on each one.
- Call on students at random to answer the questions.

Pensión: student lodging

sillón: armchair / *cajones:* drawers / *toallas:* towels / *jabón:* soap / *lavar la ropa sucia:* to wash dirty clothes

---

En Granada, prefiere vivir _____ ✓ _____ con una familia

_____ en una pensión con otros estudiantes norteamericanos.

Escriba un párrafo en que explique por qué quiere estudiar en una escuela española.

  Hace cinco años que estudio español y quiero ser profesor de español algún día. También estudio francés y alemán. Me gustan mucho las lenguas extranjeras y me encanta el español. Mi madre es chilena y mi hermana, Mía, visitó España el año pasado. Quisiera conocer a unos españoles de mi edad y quiero perfeccionar mi español. Un año en Granada va a darme la oportunidad para estudiar la cultura española. Creo que es importante conocer otras culturas y estoy seguro de que voy a beneficiar de este viaje.

PARA SU INFORMACIÓN:

Los cuartos en las pensiones y con las familias contienen una cama, un sillón, un escritorio, unos estantes para libros y una cómoda con tres o cuatro cajones. Los estudiantes tienen la responsabilidad de traer toallas y jabón para lavar la ropa sucia.

¡Aquí te toca a ti!

A. *Un retrato* (portrait) *de Patrick* Contesta las siguientes preguntas según *(according to)* la información que nos da Patrick en el formulario.

1. ¿Dónde vive Patrick?
2. ¿Cuál es la nacionalidad de su madre?
3. ¿Cuántos años tiene Patrick?
4. ¿Qué países extranjeros ha visitado Patrick?
5. ¿Cuánto tiempo pasó en cada país?
6. ¿Por qué va a Granada?
7. ¿Prefiere él vivir en una pensión o con una familia?

COMENTARIOS CULTURALES

▬ Vivir con una familia en el extranjero ▬

Many exchange programs offer students the possibility of living with a family during their stay in the country where they will be studying. Becoming a member of the family allows students to truly live the culture and isolates them from other American students with whom they would probably speak English. Generally, the families with whom students are placed speak little English, allowing students interaction with native speakers and plenty of practice speaking Spanish!

Patrick McGill

Pronunciación: The vowel combination ue

The combination **ue** in Spanish is pronounced in one single syllable, similar to the *we* in the English word *wet*.

Práctica

B. Lee cada palabra en voz alta, pronunciando con cuidado la combinación *ue*.

1. bueno	**3.** luego	**5.** después	**7.** fuerte
2. abuelo	**4.** cuerpo	**6.** puerta	**8.** nuez

165

Ex. C: writing

Repaso

C. Responde a las siguientes preguntas con la expresión que significa lo opuesto *(the opposite)* de la expresión en cursiva. Sigue el modelo.

Modelo: *¿Llega él al banco?*
No, él **sale del** banco.

1. *¿Llega* ella *de* Roma?   **2.** *¿Sale* él *de* la biblioteca?   **3.** *¿Llega* él *a* la escuela?

4. *¿Llegan* ellos *a* Madrid?   **5.** *¿Sale* ella *del* mercado?   **6.** *¿Llega* él *de* Oaxaca?

166

ESTRUCTURA

Some time expressions

No me gusta llegar **tarde,** y no me gusta llegar **temprano.** Me gusta llegar **a tiempo.**	I don't like to arrive *late,* and I don't like to arrive *early.* I like to arrive *on time.*
La clase comienza **en** cinco minutos.	The class begins *in* five minutes.
Yo salí de la escuela **hace** media hora.	I left school half an hour *ago.*
El profesor habló **por** una hora.	The professor spoke *for* an hour.

Here are some expressions associated with time.

1. **Temprano, a tiempo, tarde:** To express the ideas of *early* and *late* in relation to a specific moment in time (for example, an appointment or the departure time of a plane), use **temprano** and **tarde.** The expression a **tiempo** means *on time.*

   El concierto comenzó a las 8:00. Paula llegó a las 7:30; ella llegó **temprano.** Olivia llegó a las 8:30; ella llegó **tarde.** Santiago llegó a las 8:00; él llegó **a tiempo.**

2. **En:** To indicate when a future action will take place, use the preposition **en** as the equivalent of *in.*

   Son las 7:55. El concierto va a comenzar **en** cinco minutos.

3. **Hace, por:** As you have learned, **hace** is used with the preterite to indicate *how long ago* a past action occurred, and **por** is used to indicate *for how long* an action continued, continues, or will continue.

   Ahora son las 8:20. El concierto comenzó **hace** veinte minutos.
   El concierto terminó a las 10:00. La orquesta tocó **por** dos horas.

Aquí practicamos

D. *La clase de matemáticas comienza a las 9:00.*
Contesta las preguntas basándote en la información que tienes. (Recuerda que la clase comienza a las nueve.)

1. Ahora son las 8:50. Joaquín está durmiendo. Él vive lejos de la escuela. ¿Va a llegar a tiempo a su clase de matemáticas?
2. Ahora son las 7:30. Gabriela se está desayunando. Ella va a salir de casa en veinte minutos. Ella vive muy cerca de la escuela. ¿Va a llegar a tiempo para su clase de matemáticas?

Learning Strategy:
Calculating

Critical Thinking Strategy:
Analyzing time relationships

167

Presentation: Palabras útiles

Write a series of times on the board (2:30, 6:45, **mediodía,** 9:20, 10:35). Then point to the time and ask the following questions: **¿Qué hora va a ser en un cuarto de hora? En un cuarto de hora van a ser las 2:45.**

Ex. F: pair work

writing

/I-I-I-I-I-I-I-I-I-I-II

Learning Strategy:

Calculating

Critical Thinking Strategy:

Analyzing time relationships

3. Ahora son las 8:30. ¿En cuántos minutos va a comenzar la clase de matemáticas?

4. Ahora son las 9:15. ¿Cuánto hace que comenzó la clase de matemáticas?

E. En la Sierra Nevada   La temporada de esquí *(The ski season)* empieza *(begins)* en la Sierra Nevada el primero de diciembre. Basándote en esto, contesta las siguientes preguntas.

1. Hoy es el 1º de noviembre. ¿Cuándo va a comenzar la temporada de esquí?

2. Podemos esquiar hasta el 1º de abril. ¿Por cuántos meses podemos esquiar en la Sierra Nevada?

3. Hoy es el 1º de febrero. ¿Cuánto hace que comenzó la temporada del esquí?

4. Nos gusta esquiar el primer día de la temporada. Hoy es el 10 de noviembre. Tenemos dos semanas de clase antes de nuestras vacaciones. Necesitamos tres días para llegar a la Sierra Nevada. ¿Vamos a llegar tarde para el primer día de la temporada?

Parts of an hour

un cuarto de hora	*a quarter of an hour*
media hora	*half an hour*
tres cuartos de hora	*three quarters of an hour*
diez minutos	*ten minutes*
cuarenta minutos	*forty minutes*

/I-I-I-I-I-I-I-I-I-I-II

Learning Strategy:

Calculating

Critical Thinking Strategy:

Analyzing time relationships

F. Ahora son las 2:30.   Ahora son las 2:30. Contesta las siguientes preguntas.

1. Juan va a llegar en un cuarto de hora. ¿A qué hora va a llegar?

2. Eva salió de casa hace media hora. ¿A qué hora salió ella de casa?

3. Donaldo salió de su trabajo hace un cuarto de hora. Él trabajó por una hora. ¿A qué hora comenzó a trabajar?

4. Sara va a estar en el museo una hora y tres cuartos. Ella va a llegar al museo en media hora. ¿A qué hora va a salir del museo?

168

Aquí escuchamos:
"¡Aquí está tu habitación!"

Antes de escuchar

Patrick has just arrived at the home of the Álvarez family. Sra. Álvarez will show him his room. Look at the questions below and identify a few things you expect to hear during Patrick's conversation with Sra. Álvarez.

Learning Strategy:

Previewing, predicting

Después de escuchar

1. ¿Qué le muestra (show) la familia a Patrick?
2. ¿Qué hay en la habitación?
3. ¿Dónde está el baño y qué hay allí?
4. ¿Dónde puede dejar su ropa sucia?
5. ¿Cuándo lava la ropa la Sra. Álvarez?

Learning Strategy:

Listening for details

¡Aquí te toca a ti!

Learning Strategy:

Describing based on visual cues

G. ¿Qué hay en la habitación de Patrick? Describe Patrick's room according to what you see in the drawing.

169

Support material, Aquí escuchamos: Teacher Tape 🎧

Presentation, Aquí escuchamos:

Have students look closely at the corresponding materials to focus their listening. You may want to do as dictation the parts of the dialogue containing expressions students will need in later exercises. Preview the tapescript and make selections for dictation practice.

Answers, Aquí escuchamos: 1. su habitación 2. una cama, un sillón, un escritorio, una lámpara, unos estantes 3. en el corredor, a la derecha; toallas y jabón   4. en el baño 5. los sábados

Ex. G: pair work

 writing

Implementation, Ex. G: Have students list—orally or in writing—as many objects or pieces of furniture as they can in 60 seconds. Instruct them to include **un, una, unos,** or **unas** with the object mentioned. Have them start off by saying or writing **En la habitación de Patrick hay... .**

Answers, Ex. G: En la habitación de Patrick hay un clóset, un escritorio, una silla, unos estantes para libros y discos, un estéreo, una cama grande (matrimonial), una cómoda, una mesita de noche, una lámpara, un sillón, un espejo, unas cortinas, una alfombra y unos pósters (carteles).

Ex. H: pair work

Preparation, Ex. H: For homework, or before starting the activity, have students draw a floor plan of part of their house showing the location of the bathroom in relation to their own room and then a detailed plan of their room with all the furniture and other items of interest plotted on the plan.

To do the activity, have partners sit back to back as if on the phone and have the "host" student describe his or her floor plan to the "visiting" student. (You may want to review directional vocabulary ahead of time, i.e., **a la derecha de, cerca de**, etc.) While listening, the visiting student should draw the host's floor plan as he or she describes it and should also label the items in the room. Upon completion, partners should compare drawings, then switch roles and do the exercise again.

Cooperative Learning

Learning Strategies: Describing and interpreting spatial relationships based on visual cues, active listening

Ex. I: pair work

Suggestion, Ex. I: Have students refer to form on pp. 163–164 as a reference if they aren't sure about any particular line of the form in this exercise.

¡Adelante!

Learning Strategies:

Active listening, asking for information, describing and interpreting spatial relationships based on personal information

Learning Strategy:

Making associations

EJERCICIO ORAL

H. *Aquí está tu habitación.* Imagine that a Spanish-speaking friend is spending a semester at your home and you have volunteered to share your room with your guest. Tell him or her (1) where your room is located in the house and (2) where the bathroom is located in relation to the room. Describe (3) what is in the room and (4) where each item is located. A classmate will play the role of your friend and ask you follow-up questions to each one of your statements. Follow the model.

Modelo:
—*Mi habitación está en el segundo piso a la izquierda de la escalera y enfrente del cuarto de mis padres. El baño está al final del corredor.*
—*¿Cuántas habitaciones hay arriba?*

Learning Strategy:

Selecting information

EJERCICIO ESCRITO

I. *La hoja de inscripción* (Registration form) Following is a registration form for the summer program at the University of Salamanca. On a separate piece of paper, write information you'd need to fill out the form.

170

Cursos Internacionales

Reservado a Secretaría	FOTOGRAFÍAS 2
9 3	
Preinscripción:	Alojamiento:

Apellido

Nombre

Fecha de Nacimiento   Día   Mes   Año 1 9   Sexo: Fem.   Masc.

Pasaporte (Número)   Nacionalidad

Dirección

Teléfono (Número)   Fax (Número)

ALOJAMIENTO

VERANO: Señale con los números 1, 2, 3 y 4 su orden de preferencias, cubriendo todas las opciones.
RESTO DEL AÑO: Señale con los números 1 y 2 su orden de preferencia dentro del alojamiento en familia.

| **RESIDENCIA** (Sólo en verano) | | **FAMILIA** (Todo el año) | |
| Habitación doble (54.000 ptas. el mes) | Habitación individual (62.000 ptas. el mes) | Habitación doble (1.800 ptas. diarias) | Habitación individual (2.000 ptas. diarias) |

Expansion, Less-prepared students, Ex. I: After students have completed the form, have them write three or four sentences stating their reasons for wanting to participate in the program. They can refer to the personal essay on p. 164 for ideas and models.

More-prepared students, Ex. I: Have the more-prepared students write a personal essay to accompany the form. They should give their background in Spanish (how long they have studied), any experiences abroad in other Spanish-speaking countries, and their reasons for wanting to participate. This is a good real-life exercise, because many exchange programs require students to write such an essay.

SEGUNDA ETAPA

Preparación

At the beginning of this etapa, Patrick writes a thank-you note to the Álvarez family.

》》 Have you ever written a thank-you note?

》》 What sorts of information do you expect to find in a thank-you note Patrick would write after spending a year in the Álvarez home?

/-/-/-/-/-/-/-/-/-/
Learning Strategy:
Previewing

Una carta de agradecimiento

Santa Fe, 10 de julio de 1996

Queridos Sr. y Sra. Álvarez,

Hace quince días que salí de Granada y los extraño. Mi estancia en su casa fue inolvidable y les agradezco con todo el corazón su hospitalidad. Yo aprendí mucho en España y voy a continuar mis estudios de español en mi escuela y después en la universidad. Voy a hablarles a mis amigos de mi escuela de Granada y de mi familia española.

Mil gracias y espero que Uds. puedan visitar la ciudad de Santa Fe algún día. Mis padres quisieran conocerlos.

Un abrazo,

Patrick

*Una carta de agradeci-
miento:* A thank-you
letter

Queridos: Dear

los extraño: I miss you /
estancia: stay
inolvidable: unforgettable /
les agradezco: I thank you /
corazón: heart

hablarles a mis amigos: talk
to my friends

espero que Uds. puedan: I
hope that you can
conocerlos: to meet you

abrazo: hug

171

Presentation:
Una carta de
agradecimiento

Have students look at the form of the thank-you letter. Notice that the city from which it is written is given (Santa Fe). Also point out the organization of the date (day, month, year), the greeting, and the friendly closing. Ask students what they would expect Patrick to write in a thank-you letter. Have students name cognates and guess meaning from context using the glossed notes. Finally, see if students can give you additional information from the letter, not included in the comprehension questions.

Learning Strategies:
Previewing, using
cognates for meaning,
reading for details

Etapa Support
Materials

Workbook: pp. 124–127
Transparencies: #22, #23
Teacher Tape 🎧
Quiz: Testing Program, p. 87
Chapter Test: Testing Program, p. 89

Support material, **Una carta de
agradecimiento:**
Transparency #22

Ex. A: writing

Cultural Expansion

This is a photo of **los parques del Generalife,** one of many lush and beautiful gardens in the Alhambra, the Moorish palace in Granada.

¡Aquí te toca a ti!

//-//-//-//-//-//-//-//-//-//

Learning Strategy:
Reading for details

A. *Comprensión*   Contesta las siguientes preguntas según la información en la carta de Patrick en la página 171.

1. How long ago did Patrick leave Granada?
2. What is he going to do when he returns to school?
3. Is he going to continue studying Spanish? Where?
4. What does he hope the Álvarez family will do?

//-//-//-//-//-//-//-//-//-//

Learning Strategy:
Narrating in the past

B. *Hace... que*   Patrick is telling his friends at school about his stay in Spain and how long ago he did certain things. Follow the model and be sure to use the preterite of the verbs.

Modelo: dos semanas / salir
Hace dos semanas que salí de España.

1. quince días / salir de Granada
2. un mes / nadar en el Mar Mediterráneo
3. dos meses / visitar el Museo del Prado en Madrid
4. seis meses / ir a Barcelona
5. un año / conocer a la familia Álvarez
6. dos días / volver a la escuela aquí

Now imagine you are telling a friend about what Patrick did.

Modelo: dos semanas / salir
Hace dos semanas que salió de España.

//-//-//-//-//-//-//-//-//-//

Learning Strategy:
Narrating in the past

Los parques del Generalife en la Alhambra

172

Pronunciación: *The vowel combination uo*

The combination **uo** in Spanish is pronounced in one single syllable, similar to the English word *woe*.

Práctica

C. Lee cada palabra en voz alta, pronunciando con cuidado la combinación *uo*.

1. continuo
2. monstruo
3. antiguo
4. continuó
5. mutuo
6. cuota
7. arduo
8. actuó

Repaso

D. El día de Juan José   Describe el día de Juan Jose según los dibujos.

Ex. D: pair work / writing

Modelo: ¿Hasta qué hora durmió Juan José?
Él durmió hasta las 8:00.

Learning Strategies: Reporting based on visual cues, narrating in the present, past, and future

1. ¿En cuántos minutos comienzan sus clases?
2. ¿Va a llegar a tiempo para su primera clase?
3. ¿A qué hora sale de la escuela?

173

4. ¿Llegó tarde para el autobús?   **5.** ¿En cuántos minutos llega a casa?   **6.** ¿Qué hace hasta las 4:30?

7. ¿Va a llegar a tiempo para la cena?   **8.** ¿En cuánto tiempo hace su tarea *(homework)*?

//-/-/-/-/-/-/-/-/-/-/-//

Learning Strategy:

Reading for cultural information

ESTRUCTURA

The 24-hour clock

El partido comienza a las **19:00.**   The game begins at *7:00 p.m.*
Nosotros llegamos a las **20:45.**   We arrived at *8:45 p.m.*

You have already learned the conversational method of telling time in Spanish. But in airports and railroad stations, on radio and TV, and at concerts and movies, official time based on the 24-hour clock is used in the Spanish-speaking world. Note that military time in English is also expressed in official time. The basic differences between the two are as follows.

174

<table>
<tr><td colspan="2">**Conversational time**</td></tr>
</table>

Conversational time
- Is based on the usual 12-hour clock
- Divides the hour into two 30-minute segments (after and before the hour)
- Uses the expressions **y cuarto, y media, menos cuarto, medianoche, mediodía**

Official time
- Is based on the 24-hour clock (0 = midnight, 12 = noon)
- Treats the hour as a 60-minute whole (that is: only moves forward, never uses **menos**)
- Uses only cardinal numbers such as **y quince, y treinta, y cuarenta y cinco, veinte y cuatro horas, doce horas**

The easiest way to switch from official time to conversational time is to *subtract* twelve from the hour of official time, *unless* the hour is already less than twelve.

Conversational time		Official time	
9:45 a.m.	las diez menos cuarto	9:45	nueve horas y cuarenta y cinco
12:30 p.m.	las doce y media	12:30	doce horas y treinta
2:50 p.m.	las tres menos diez	14:50	catorce horas y cincuenta
11:15 p.m.	las once y cuarto	23:15	veintitrés horas y quince

Aquí practicamos

E. Cambia de hora oficial a hora conversacional.

Modelo: 15:00
las tres de la tarde

1. 13:00   3. 22:00   5. 3:15   7. 20:45
2. 9:00   4. 12:00   6. 15:30   8. 18:06

F. Horarios de avión   En clase conociste (**conocer** = *to meet*) a Pepe, un estudiante de Tenerife. Estás considerando la posibilidad de pasar una semana en su casa durante las vacaciones de Pascua *(Easter)*. Cada semana, Iberia y British Caledonia Airways (BCA) tienen cuatro vuelos *(flights)* de Madrid a Santa Cruz de Tenerife. Mira los horarios en la página 176 e indica si las afirmaciones a continuación son verdaderas o falsas *(true or false)*.

Learning Strategy:
Reading a timetable

Implementation, Exs. E, F, and G: The most common conversions that students will make in real life are from official time to conversational time. The exercises stress this function.

Ex. E: writing

Answers, Ex. E: 1. la una de la tarde   2. las nueve de la mañana   3. las diez de la noche   4. las doce (mediodía)   5. las tres y media de la mañana   6. las tres y media de la tarde   7. las nueve menos cuarto de la noche   8. las seis y seis de la noche

Madrid–Tenerife — Salidas del Aeropuerto Barajas

	Vuelo	Salida	Llegada
martes	Iberia 831	08:15	11:30
jueves	BCA 29	20:30	23:45
sábado	BCA 37	10:45	14:00
domingo	Iberia 867	21:15	00:30

Tenerife–Madrid — Llegadas al Aeropuerto de Barajas

	Vuelo	Salida	Llegada
lunes	Iberia 868	13:30	16:45
miércoles	Iberia 832	6:15	9:30
viernes	BCA 30	12:40	15:55
domingo	BCA 38	17:15	20:30

1. Los lunes el avión de Iberia llega a Madrid a las cinco menos cinco.
2. Los martes el vuelo de la BCA sale de Madrid a las ocho y media.
3. Los lunes el avión de Iberia 868 sale a la una y media y llega a las cinco menos cuarto de la tarde.
4. Los sábados el vuelo de BCA 37 llega a Tenerife a las dos de la tarde.
5. Los domingos el avión sale de Madrid a las nueve y cuarto de la mañana y llega a Tenerife a las 12 y veinticinco del mediodía.
6. La duración del vuelo es de tres horas y cuarto.

/-/-/-/-/-/-/-/-/-/-/-/

Critical Thinking Strategies:

Analyzing, solving problems

G. *Una pequeña prueba*   Para practicar cómo se usa el tiempo oficial, Pepe te hace las siguientes preguntas.

1. El avión de Madrid a Barcelona tarda una hora en llegar *(flight = 1 hour)*. ¿Quieres estar en Barcelona a las 9:00 de la noche. ¿Vas a tomar el avión de las 20:00 o el de las 21:00?
2. Quieres ir al cine pero tienes que volver a casa antes de las 6:00 de la tarde. La película es de dos horas y empieza a las 13:00, 16:00, 19:00 y 22:00. ¿A qué hora vas a poder ir al cine?
3. Vas a la estación de trenes para recoger *(to pick up)* a tus padres. El tren llega de Barcelona a las 17:30. Llegas a la estación a las 4:30 de la tarde. ¿Llegaste a tiempo?
4. Invitaste a un(a) amigo(a) a un concierto. El concierto empieza a las 21:00. Se tarda media hora en ir de tu apartamento al concierto. ¿A qué hora tiene que llegar tu amigo(a) a tu apartamento?

176

Aquí escuchamos:
"La salida"

Antes de escuchar

Patrick is getting ready to leave and will say good-bye to a friend. Later he will say good-bye to the Álvarez family at the train station. Look at the following questions and identify a few things you expect to hear during Patrick's conversations.

START

//-//-//-//-//-//-//-//
Learning Strategy:
Previewing

Después de escuchar

1. ¿Qué hace Patrick el día que sale?
2. ¿A qué hora sale su tren?
3. ¿Qué avión toma?
4. ¿Qué quiere hacer Miguel?
5. ¿Cuándo piensa volver Patrick a España?

//-//-//-//-//-//-//-//
Learning Strategy:
Listening for details

177

Support material, Aquí escuchamos: Teacher Tape 🎧

Presentation: Aquí escuchamos

Have students use the corresponding materials carefully. After they have listened to the tape twice, have them do the **Después de escuchar** exercise as a check on comprehension. Then play the tape once more, instructing them to listen for additional information not included in the exercise. Ask for volunteers to give these in Spanish; very short answers are acceptable, although you may want to expand, or have another student, expand them. Be sure to emphasize structures and expressions needed for further work, either through dictation practice or by practicing certain models from a prepared transparency or from the board.

Answers, Aquí escuchamos: 1. va a casa de un amigo para despedirse de él   2. a las 13:00 (una de la tarde)   3. el avión de la noche a Nueva York   4. visitar los Estados Unidos   5. el verano próximo

Exs. H and I: pair work

role play

Less-prepared students, Ex. H: Encourage less-prepared students to look carefully at each number to determine the time context, past or present, and necessary verb tenses. Ask students to supply individual vocabulary items. Ask for volunteers to formulate the questions. If students have difficulty here, provide models for them to refer to. Help them find and use the appropriate model. Then divide the class into pairs. Call on different pairs of students to role play each number.

More-prepared students, Ex. H: Call on students at random to form pairs to role play for the class.

Less-prepared students, Ex. I: Have less-prepared students convert conversational times to official ones before beginning. Have them skim the exercise to identify any words or expressions with which they need help. You may want to have another student provide the help.

More-prepared students, Ex. I: Have students make their dialogues as close to real conversation as they can, by repeating something before adding new information **(Quieres viajar por la mañana, está bien.)**, commenting, interrupting, or asking for a repetion or clarification **(Perdón, ¿cuántos días vas a estar allí?).** Have several pairs role play for the class.

Ex. J: writing

¡Aquí te toca a ti!

Learning Strategy:
Expressing past and future times

H. *Mil gracias* You have just spent a month with a Spanish family and are about to return to the United States. As your classmate plays a member of the family, enact the following conversation.

1. Thank him or her for everything.
2. Ask if he or she is going to visit the United States next summer.
3. Say that you would like to return to Spain very soon.
4. Tell him or her that you learned a lot and that you are going to tell your friends in the United States about Spain.

EJERCICIO ORAL

Learning Strategy:
Asking for and giving information

I. *Un viaje a las Islas Canarias* You are helping a friend plan a trip to the Canary Islands. He or she is starting from Valencia. Use official time to discuss the plans.

1. Ask if he or she wants to travel in the morning or afternoon.
2. Explain that the morning flight leaves Tuesday at 10:15 a.m. and arrives in Tenerife at 12:35 p.m. The afternoon flight leaves Saturday at 12:55 p.m. and arrives in Tenerife at 2:25 p.m.
3. Tell him or her that the cost of the ticket is 20,000 pesetas.
4. Find out in how many days your friend is going to leave for Tenerife.
5. Find out which flight your friend is going to take.
6. Find out how much time your friend will spend in Tenerife.
7. Explain that you would like to go to Tenerife too, but that you don't have enough money. You are going to spend the vacation at home.

EJERCICIO ESCRITO

Learning Strategy:
Organizing details

J. *Una carta de agradecimiento* Write a short thank-you note to an imaginary family with whom you spent the last year in Spain. Remember to (1) give the name of your town and today's date in the heading, (2) greet your host family by name, (3) tell how long you have been gone from their home, (4) comment on how much you learned while living with their family, (5) tell how your experiences in Spain will be important to you, (6) express your appreciation, and (7) include a friendly closing. (Use the letter on page 171 as a model.)

178

Less-prepared students, Ex. J: Have students study the model letter on p. 171 and note where information similar to that needed for items 1–7 is located. Then have them come up with their own information for items 1–7.

More-prepared students, Ex. J: Have more-prepared students edit, then write a reaction to another student's letter.

Vocabulario

Para charlar

Para hablar del horario

llegar a tiempo
llegar tarde
llegar temprano
en (veinte minutos, etc.)
por (una hora, etc.)
hace (un año, dos días, etc.)
un cuarto de hora
media hora
tres cuartos de hora
diez (etc.) minutos

Para decir que extrañamos a alguien

Te extraño
Los extraño

Para dar las gracias

Les agradezco.
Les agradezco con
   todo el corazón su
   hospitalidad.
Mil gracias por…
Muchas gracias
   por…

Temas y contextos

Los muebles de una habitación

una cama
un clóset
una cómoda con dos cajones
                cuatro cajones

un escritorio
un estante
una lámpara
una silla
un sillón

Vocabulario general

Sustantivos

la edad
un estado
un país
un programa de intercambio
una salida

Verbos

beneficiarse
extrañar
lavar
perfeccionar

Otras palabras y expresiones

un abrazo
durante
espero que Uds. puedan visitar
el jabón
prestar atención
querido(a)
queridos(as)
la ropa sucia
una toalla

Make flashcards for the **Vocabulario** with the Spanish on one side and the English on the other. You may also want to include some bonus cards with words from previous chapters. Divide the class into teams and have a vocabulary bee. If the card is in Spanish, students give the word's meaning in English and vice versa. The team with the most correct answers is the winner.

LA ALHAMBRA

Antes de leer

1. Look at the photos that accompany this reading. What kind of place do you think this is?
2. Where do you think it is located?
3. Have you ever heard about the Alhambra? It has been described in detail by Washington Irving in his famous book *Tales from the Alhambra*.
4. Note the arches in the photos. Are they different from other arches you have seen? In this reading, you will learn about their design.

**El patio de los Leones
en la Alhambra**

180

Guía para la lectura

A. Read the first paragraph to determine the following:

1. Who built the Alhambra with its beautiful arches?
2. When did this group of people invade Spain?
3. What part of Spain was influenced most by this group?

B. Now finish reading the passage and answer the following questions.

1. What does the phrase **"Calat Alhambra"** mean?
2. What illusion does the water and marble create?
3. How did they get the water to flow out of the lions' mouths?

Spain

ANDALUCIA
Granada ●

La Alhambra

n el año 711 los moros (también conocidos como árabes) invadieron la Península Ibérica y se establecieron en la parte del sur hasta 1492. Su influencia arquitectónica es evidente en toda esta región de España que también se conoce como Andalucía. Esta influencia se ve muy claramente en las tres ciudades principales de Andalucía: Sevilla, Córdoba y Granada. Pero de todos los monumentos que construyeron los moros en España, ninguno es tan espectacular como La Alhambra.

La "Calat Alhambra" o castillo rojo es una de las fortalezas más notables que ha construido el ser humano. Está situada en una colina desde donde se contemplan bonitas vistas de la ciudad. La mayor parte fue construida en el siglo XIV y es un conjunto de patios, salones y jardines extraordinarios. La mezcla del mármol con el agua de las fuentes causa una confusión entre lo líquido y lo sólido para el visitante. El famoso Patio de los Leones es una maravilla de la arquitectura medieval. El agua que sale de la boca de los doce leones es traída por una serie de canales y acequias desde las alturas de la Sierra Nevada. El agua sale sin la ayuda de una bomba—sale con la simple fuerza de gravedad que trae el agua desde las alturas de la sierra

Los arcos árabes de la Alhambra

181

Chapter Objectives

Functions: Understanding classified ads and lodging brochures; describing a house or apartment
Context: Apartments, houses; newspaper ads
Accuracy: Present and preterite of the verbs **decir** and **poner;** expressions with **decir**

Cultural Observation

You may wish to tell students that in large Spanish cities, as in large American cities, many new high-rise apartment complexes are located on the outskirts of the city because of space considerations. In Madrid, for instance, there are many such buildings to the south-west of the city (near **metro** stations Aluche, Carabanchel, Vista Alegre, Empalme, Batán, and Campamento. If you wish, refer to the **metro** map on p. 259 of Level 1).

CAPÍTULO 6

BUSCO UN APARTAMENTO

Muchos ciudadanos españoles viven en edificios grandes y modernos como éste.

Objectives:

>>> **U**nderstanding classified ads and lodging brochures
>>> **D**escribing a house or apartment

Strategies:

>>> **U**sing cognates for meaning
>>> **N**egotiating
>>> **I**magining

182

Video/Laserdisc

Chapter 6 Video Program and Video Guide

Support material, Anuncios del periódico:
Transparency #24. Use the transparency to familiarize students with how ads are written.

PRIMERA ETAPA

Preparación

>> **H**ave you ever looked at an apartment ad?

>> **W**hat kind of information would you expect to find in such an ad?

>> **B**elow are some ads for apartments in Madrid. How many ads are there?

>> **W**hat do you think the boldface words in each ad mean? (Hint: Think back to the Madrid **metro**. Remember the names of the **metro** stops?)

/-/-/-/-/-/-/-/-/-/-//
Learning Strategy:
Previewing

Anuncios del periódico

Anuncios del periódico:
Newspaper ads

Goya. Vacío. Dos dormitorios. 60 m². Cocina amueblada. Comedor. Baño. Teléfono. Terraza. 5º piso. Ascensor.
Tel. 2 43 94 54

Prado. Completamente amueblado. 225 m². Aire acondicionado. Piscina. Tres dormitorios. Garaje. Dos baños. Dos terrazas. 4º piso. Ascensor. Llamar después de las 20h.
Tel. 4 20 28 87

Lavapies. Un dormitorio. Baño. Teléfono. Cocina amueblada. Piscina. Jardín. Tenis. Llamar después de las 16h.
Tel. 5 31 67 06

Ventas. Vacío. 185 m². Cuatro dormitorios. Dos baños. Dos terrazas. Cocina grande. Estacionamiento. Comedor. 7º piso. Dos ascensores.
Tel. 5 73 34 30

Plaza de España. Completamente amueblado. Sala de estar grande. Dos dormitorios. 125 m². Cocina grande. Baño. 3er piso. Llamar mañanas.
Tel. 2 45 85 42

Centro. Tres dormitorios. Cocina amueblada. Garaje. Piscina. Jardín. Algunos muebles—mesa, sofá—para vender.
Tel. 4 52 58 24 noche.

Vacío: Vacant
Cocina amueblada: Furnished kitchen / *Sala de estar:* Livingroom / *Comedor:* Dining room / *Terraza:* Terrace / *Jardín:* Garden

Estacionamiento: Parking
muebles: furniture

183

Etapa Support Materials

Workbook: **pp. 128–134**
Tapescript: **p. 81**
Transparencies: **#24, #25, #26**
Teacher Tape
Listening Activity masters: **p. 55**
Quiz: **Testing Program, p. 92**

Sidebar (left column)

Ex. A: writing

Answers, Ex. A: 1. air conditioning (in apartment)   2. completely   3. bedroom   4. tennis (facilities available)   5. garage available   6. call (phone)

Ex. B: pair work

Expansion, Ex. B: Your students own apartments in Madrid and need to rent them. Have pairs of students write classified ads similar to those on p. 183. Or have them write want ads for different apartments in your city or town. You may want to post these on the bulletin board.

Possible answers, Ex. B:
1. **Lavapies.** El apartamento está cerca de la estación de metro Lavapies. Tiene un dormitorio y un baño. Hay un teléfono en el apartamento. Tiene una cocina amueblada. Hay una piscina, un jardín y puedes jugar al tenis allí también.
2. **Plaza de España.** El apartamento está cerca de la estación de metro Plaza de España. Está completamente amueblado. Tiene una sala de estar grande, dos dormitorios, una cocina grande y un baño. Tiene unos 125 metros cuadrados. Está en el tercer piso.   3. **Prado.** El apartamento está cerca de la estación de metro Prado. Está completamente amueblado. Tiene 225 metros cuadrados. Hay tres dormitorios, dos baños y dos terrazas. El apartamento tiene aire acondicionado también. Está en el cuarto piso, pero hay ascensor. El edificio tiene un garaje y una piscina.
4. **Ventas.** El apartamento está cerca de la estación de metro Ventas. Está vacío y tiene 185 metros cuadrados. Tiene cuatro dormitorios, dos baños, una cocina grande, un comedor y dos terrazas. Hay estacionamiento. Está en el séptimo piso y hay dos ascensores.
5. **Centro.** El apartamento está en el centro. Tiene tres dormitorios y una cocina amueblada. Hay un garaje y una piscina. Hay un jardín también.

Main content

¡Aquí te toca a ti!

Learning Strategy:
Using cognates for meaning

Learning Strategy:
Describing, paraphrasing

A. Lee los anuncios en la página 183 con cuidado *(carefully)*. ¿Qué piensas que significan *(mean)* las siguientes palabras?

1. aire acondicionado
2. completamente
3. dormitorio
4. tenis
5. garaje
6. llamar

B. *¡No comprendo!*   You are looking over the apartment ads in today's newspaper. Call one of your Spanish friends and describe one of the apartments to him or her. Base your description on one of the ads on page 183.

Modelo: *El apartamento está cerca de la estación de metro Goya. Está vacío y tiene dos dormitorios. Tiene unos 60 metros cuadrados (square meters) y la cocina está amueblada. También tiene un comedor, baño, teléfono y terraza. Está en el quinto piso y hay un ascensor en el edificio.*

> *Goya.* Vacío. Dos dormitorios. 60 m². Cocina amueblada. Comedor. Baño. Teléfono. Terraza. 5º piso. Ascensor. Tel. 2 43 94 54

Pronunciación: *The vowel combination ui*

The combination **ui** in Spanish is pronounced in one single syllable, similar to the English word *we*. Note that in the word **muy**, the same sound is spelled **uy**.

Práctica

C. Lee cada palabra en voz alta, pronunciando con cuidado la combinación *ui*.

1. fui
2. Luis
3. Ruiz
4. ruido
5. muy
6. fuimos
7. buitre
8. cuidado

Support material, Ex. D:
Transparency #25

Repaso

D. ¿A qué hora presentan los programas? Imagine that you and your friends are on a class trip in a Spanish-speaking country. Your roommate wants to watch TV but is having trouble figuring out the television schedule because the times are based on the 24-hour clock. As you and your partner look over a program listing taken from a Spanish newspaper, take turns expressing interest in certain programs and answering your partner's questions (page 186) using conversational time.

Ex. D: pair work

writing

Learning Strategies:
Calculating time conversions, reading for details

Modelo:
—*Me gustaría ver "Blossom" en el canal uno. ¿A qué hora lo (it) presentan?*
—*Lo presentan a las siete de la tarde.*

P R O G R A M A C I O N

tve1

07.30 Estamos de vacaciones.
11.30 Vacaciones de cine.
  "El hombre más fuerte del mundo"
13.00 McGyver.
14.00 Informativo territorial.
14.30 No te rías que es peor.
15.00 Telediario.
15.30 Alejandra.
16.30 Marielena.
17.30 Telefilme.
18.30 Vídeos de primera.
18.55 Noticias.
19.00 Blossom.
19.30 Justicia ciega.
20.30 Los problemas crecen.
21.00 Telediario-2.
21.27 El tiempo.
21.30 Pret a porter.
22.00 Cine español.
  "El tesoro"
24.00 Noches de gala.
01.15 Telediario 3.
01.45 Sobre mi cadáver.
02.35 Testimonio.
02.40 Dime luna.
03.30 Diga 33.
04.00 Despedida y cierre.

07.30 Euronews.
09.00 Epoca de cambios.

10.00 **La película de la mañana** .
  "Una mujer peligrosa"
11.35 Clip clip ¡hurra!
13.00 Pinnic.
15.00 Cifras y letras.
15.30 Grandes documentales.
17.00 Sueños de Olimpia.
17.30 **La película de la tarde.**
  "Entre la luz y las tinieblas"
19.10 Ruta Quetzal 94.
19.40 Planeta sur.
20.10 Habitación para dos.
20.35 El superagente 86.
21.00 Lingo.
21.30 Informa-2.
22.00 Fútbol.
  Bielorusia-España
24.00 Dudas razonables.
01.00 Los veranos de La 2.

TELEMADRID

07.15 Telenoticias (R).
07.35 La línea Onedin.
08.25 A saber.
08.55 Hermanas.
09.20 Gente casada.
09.45 Tele Empleo (R).
10.00 Avance informativo.
10.15 **Star Treck: la nueva generación.**
11.10 Primeros besos.
11.35 Dirty dancing.

12.00 La banda.
13.30 Los picapiedra.
14.00 Telenoticias.
15.00 Roseanne.
15.30 Cine de tarde.
17.15 Ole tus vídeos.
18.00 A través del tiempo.
18.45 Tele Empleo.
19.00 Madrid directo.
20.30 Telenoticias.
20.55 El tiempo.
21.00 Colegio mayor.
21.30 Cine: una de acción.
23.30 Un momento, por favor.
01.00 Telenoticias.
01.05 Tele Empleo .
01.20 Cine: sala de madrugada.
03.00 Información cultural de la CAM.

07.00 Programación.
07.30 Noticias.
08.00 Tras 3 Tris, vacaciones.
11.00 Punky Brewster.
11.30 Somos diez.
12.00 Colmillo blanco.
12.30 Aventuras en Africa.
13.00 Star Treck.
14.00 Un mundo diferente.
14.30 El príncipe de Bel Air.
15.00 Noticias.
15.30 Telecine.
17.30 Catwalk.
18.30 Salvados por la campana.
19.00 Paradise Beach.

19.30 Los vigilantes de la playa.
20.30 A toda página.
21.00 Noticias.
21.30 Cine.
23.30 Telecine.
24.00 Cine.
01.30 Noticias.
02.00 Línea América.
02.30 Cine de madrugada.
04.00 Televenta.
05.30 Cine de madrugada.

tele 5

07.15 Entre hoy y mañana (R).
07.45 Los periódicos.
08.00 La tele es tuya, colega.
10.55 Webster.
11.20 Grandullón.
11.45 Apartamento para tres.
12.15 Hotel.
13.15 La ruleta de la fortuna.
14.00 Veredicto.
14.30 Las noticias.
15.00 Veredicto (II)
15.30 Sensación de vivir.
16.30 Melrose Place.
17.30 Remington Steele.
18.30 Déjate querer.
19.30 Su media naranja.
20.30 Las noticias.
21.00 Telecupón.
21.10 Karaoke.
21.45 Cine.
23.45 Misterio para tres..

Expansion, Ex. D: After students complete Ex. D, have them look at the schedule, find three or four more programs of interest to them, and note what time they're on. Can they tell which programs are from the U.S. and which from Spain? Have them give examples.

Presentation: Estructura

(1) Have students repeat the present tense of **decir** while you write pronouns in three groups—**yo, tú, él, ella, Ud. / ellos, ellas, Uds. / nosotros.**
(2) Repeat in the negative.
(3) Add written verb forms to pronouns.
(4) Repeat for the preterite of **decir.**

Reteaching, Estructura:
You may want to review time expressions for present and past. Have students recall appropriate expressions and list them on the board near the corresponding tenses of **decir.**

00.45 Las pesadillas de Freddy.		14.30 Kate y Allie.	21.57 Primer piano.
01.45 Entre hoy y mañana.		15.00 Cine (Cod).	22.00 Estreno Canal Plus. (Cod).
02.15 Cine.	CANAL+	*"La novia del candidato"*.	*"Homicidio"*.
04.15 Novedades increíbles.	08.05 ABC World News.	16.28 Cine (Cod).	23.40 Cine. (Cod).
04.45 Los días y las noches de	08.30 Dibujos.	*"Juegos prohibidos de una	*"La ciudad de la alegria"*.
Molly Dodd.	08.55 Videominuto.	dama"*.	01.50 Piezas. (Cod).
05.15 Novedades increíbles.	09.52 Noticias.	18.07 Especial "Los jóvenes	02.17 Música noche. (Cod).
05.45 Cine.	10.00 Cine. (Cod)	flamencos"(Cod).	03.10 Sesión especial (Cod).
	"El beso del sueño"	19.35 Dibujos. (Cod).	*"Vivir por nada"*
	12.01 Cine. (Cod).	20.05 Los 40 principales.	04.37 Golf. (Cod)
	"El invitado".	20.30 Sigue soñando.	05.37 Cine (Cod).
	13.35 Los 40 principales.	21.00 Primos lejanos.	*"Más allá de la inocencia"*
	14.00 Noticias.	21.30 Noticias.	
	14.05 Mi viejo rockero.	21.53 Información deportiva.	

1. ¿A qué hora presentan "Star Trek: la nueva generación"?
2. ¿A qué hora presentan "Grandes documentales"?
3. ¿A qué hora presentan la película "El tesoro"?
4. ¿A qué hora presentan "Vídeos de primera"?
5. ¿A qué hora presentan "Hermanas"?
6. ¿A qué hora presentan el partido de fútbol entre Bielorusia y España?

ESTRUCTURA

The verb *decir*

—**¿Dicen Uds.** la verdad?   Are *you telling* the truth?
—Claro! Siempre **decimos** la verdad.   Of course! We always *tell* the truth.
—¿Qué **dijo Juan?**   What *did Juan say*?
—**Dijo que** no.   *He said* no.
—**Él dijo que** va a nevar.   *He said that* it is going to snow.
—**María dijo que** Juan no estudió.   *María said that* John didn't study.

The verb **decir** *(to say, to tell)* is irregular in both the present and the preterite tenses.

Present

yo	**digo**	nosotros(as)	**decimos**
tú	**dices**	vosotros(as)	**decís**
él		ellos	
ella	} **dice**	ellas	} **dicen**
Ud.		Uds.	

186

Preterite			
yo	**dije**	nosotros(as)	**dijimos**
tú	**dijiste**	vosotros(as)	**dijisteis**
él		ellos	
ella	**dijo**	ellas	**dijeron**
Ud.		Uds.	

Note that **decir que** can be used to report something.

Aquí practicamos

E. ¿Qué dicen ellos?   You're sitting inside a café with a large group of friends. Because of the street noise outside, you can't hear what some of your friends are saying; so you have to keep asking what's going on. Use the cues to ask your questions.

 Modelo: ellos
¿Qué dijeron ellos?

1. ella
2. tú
3. Uds.
4. él
5. ellas
6. ellos

F. Ellos dicen que...   Now that you've asked, the person sitting next to you at the table repeats everything that is said.

 Modelo: ellos / no hace buen tiempo hoy
Dijeron que no hace buen tiempo hoy.

1. ella / va a nevar
2. yo / hay niebla por las calles
3. nosotros / hace mucho frío
4. él / no hay escuela mañana
5. ellas / van a jugar en la nieve
6. ellos / van a esquiar

187

Presentation: Palabras útiles

Have students look at the meanings of the expressions as they proceed to Ex. G.

Ex. G: writing

Answers, Ex. G: 1. ¿Cómo se dice **apartment building** en español?   2. ¿Qué dijiste?
3. Para decir la verdad, no estoy seguro(a).   4. ¿Qué quieres decir?
5. Quiero decir que mi maestro(a) (profesor[a]) es muy difícil.   6. El maestro(a) (profesor[a]) dijo que no.

Support material, Aquí escuchamos: Teacher Tape 🎧

Suggestion, Aquí escuchamos: Emphasize expressions students will need for further work. Do as dictation practice. See other suggestions from previous chapters.

Palabras útiles

Expressions with *decir*

Para decir la verdad, no me gusta el francés.	*To tell the truth*, I don't like French.
¿Qué quiere decir esto?	*What does* this *mean*?
¿Cómo se dice "documentary" en español?	*How do you say* "documentary" in Spanish?

The verb **decir** is used in a variety of everyday expressions:

para decir la verdad	*to tell the truth*
decir que sí (no)	*to say yes (no)*
querer decir	*to mean*
¿Cómo se dice... ?	*How do you say . . . ?*
¿Qué dijiste?	*What did you say?*

Learning Strategy:

Applying appropriate expressions

G. Decide which of the **decir** expressions best fits the following situations.

1. You want to know how to say "apartment building" in Spanish.
2. You didn't hear what your brother said to you.
3. You explain that, to tell the truth, you are not sure.
4. You want to find out what someone means by what he or she said.
5. You explain that you mean that your teacher is very difficult.
6. You want to tell someone that the teacher said no.

Aquí escuchamos:
"Buscamos un apartamento"

Learning Strategy:

Previewing

Critical Thinking Strategy:

Predicting

Antes de escuchar

Patrick is looking at some apartment ads in the newspaper. Look at the following questions and identify a few things you expect to hear during Patrick's conversation with his friend. Is the rent (**el alquiler**) for apartments expensive in your town?

START

188

Después de escuchar

1. ¿Qué leen los dos amigos?
2. ¿Qué encuentra Patrick?
3. ¿Dónde está?
4. ¿Cómo es?
5. ¿Qué deciden buscar al final?

//-//-//-//-//-//-//-//-//-//
Learning Strategy:

Listening for details

¡Aquí te toca a ti!

//-//-//-//-//-//-//-//-//-//
Cooperative Learning

Learning Strategies:

Paraphrasing, supporting opinions, negotiating

Critical Thinking Strategies:

Comparing and contrasting, prioritizing

H. Buscamos un apartamento.   You and your friend are now college students and have just arrived in Madrid on a study abroad program from your university. Part of the experience is that you must find your own lodging. Look at the apartment ads from the classified section of the newspaper and carry out the following tasks: (1) Brainstorm together on the features that are most important to have in an apartment and rank your top three preferences; (2) Take turns describing the apartments in the ads to one another; (3) decide which apartments do not suit you both and give your reasons; (4) decide together which apartment you are going to rent (**alquilar**) and why.

Cuatro Caminos. Amueblado. Cuatro dormitorios. Dos baños. Comedor. Dos terrazas. Piscina. 95.000 ptas. Tel. 4 12 54 40

Argüelles. Tres dormitorios. Cocina grande. Comedor. Todo amueblado excepto salón. 50.000 ptas. Tel. 6 10 90 87

Lavapies. Amueblado. Comedor. Un dormitorio. Teléfono. Terraza. Piscina. Tenis. 70.000 ptas. Tel. 8 14 23 85

Delicias. Un dormitorio grande. Cocina amueblada. Aire acondicionado. Jardín. 45.000 ptas. Tel. 7 21 40 89 noche.

Legazpi. Vacío. Dos dormitorios. Comedor. Baño. Cocina. 30.000 ptas. Tel. 4 50 17 76

Goya. Amueblado. Dos dormitorios. Comedor. Cocina. Baño. Terraza. 60.000 ptas. Tel. 3 15 41 55

189

Answers, Aquí escuchamos: 1. los anuncios del periódico 2. un apartamento 3. cerca de la universidad 4. con dos dormitorios y está amueblado 5. un apartamento más pequeño

Ex. H: pair work

  role play

Support material, Ex. H: Transparency #26

Less-prepared students, Ex. H: Brainstorm possible vocabulary expressions with less-prepared students. Have them skim the ads for these terms before beginning the exercise.

Suggestion, Ex. H: Make sure different groups of students report back on their final decisions, and compare their conclusions with those of other students. Do an informal poll to see which choice was most popular and why.

Ex. I:  pairwork

Suggestion, Ex. I: Have students draw a sketch or schematic as homework or preparation for the activity. Then have them sit back to back with a partner (similar to Ex. H, p. T170). As one describes the home, the listener should draw the sketch as he or she hears it. Have students compare the two sketches for accuracy.

Cooperative Learning

Learning Strategies: Active listening, verifying

Ex. J: writing

Suggestions, Ex. J: Have students brainstorm a list of features for their ideal apartment before beginning. Publish a "newsletter" of these ads for students to read. Have students role play the parts of apartment hunter and owner. Have the hunters call the owners to ask follow-up questions based on the information in the ads.

/-/-/-/-/-/-/-/-/-/-//

Learning Strategies:

Describing, asking questions

Critical Thinking Strategies:

Imagining, making associations, prioritizing

/-/-/-/-/-/-/-/-/-/-//

Learning Strategy:

Summarizing

Critical Thinking Strategy:

Imagining, creating

EJERCICIO ORAL

I. Mi casa / Mi apartamento Describe your dream house or apartment to one of your classmates. Where is the house or apartment located? How do you get from there to school? How many rooms does it have? Name the rooms. How big are the rooms? On what floor are the rooms located? Is there a garden? Do you have a garage? Is there an elevator? Your classmate will ask you questions to get more information.

EJERCICIO ESCRITO

J. Mi apartamento ideal Write an ad for your ideal apartment. Base it on those that appear on pages 183 and 189.

SEGUNDA ETAPA

Preparación

>> If you were to rent an unfurnished apartment, with what sorts of items would you need to furnish it? Make a list of them.

>> What are the basic necessities?

>> What are some of the luxury items?

>> Look at the drawings for some basic apartment furnishings.

/-/-/-/-/-/-/-/-/-/-//

Learning Strategies:

Previewing, listing

Critical Thinking Strategies:

Categorizing, evaluating

Mi apartamento

el sofá el cuadro la ventana las cortinas

el sillón

la lámpara la alfombra

191

Etapa Support Materials

Workbook: **pp. 135–140**
Transparencies: **#27, #27a**
Teacher Tape
Quiz: **Testing Program, p. 94**

Chapter Test: **Testing Program, p. 98**

Support material, **Mi apartamento:**
Transparencies #27, #27a

Exs. A and B: pair work

 writing

Suggestion, Ex. A: Show Transparency #27 or #27a as students do the exercise.

More-prepared students, Ex. A: Have students imagine that they can have only one television, one desk, one telephone, one compact disc player, and one lamp in their new apartment. Ask where they would put each of these items: living room, parents' bedroom, their bedroom, the kitchen, or the bathroom. Create a separate tick-mark graph on the board for each household item and chart the students' responses.

Afterwards, you may want to determine which rooms were chosen to contain the most items. Students can then draw inferences about the results, for example: **Hay más cosas en el salón porque más miembros de la familia pasan tiempo allá.**

Learning Strategy: Reading a graph

Critical Thinking Strategies: Prioritizing, drawing inferences

Suggestion, Ex. B: As a model, give a description of your own house or apartment. Then divide the class into pairs. To verify work, have some students report to the entire class what they have learned from their partners.

Expansion, Ex. B: Have student pairs decide on one piece of furniture from each of their homes that they would consider trading with each other.

Learning Strategy: Negotiating

¡Aquí te toca a ti!

A. Un apartamento nuevo You and your family are about to move into a new apartment. Using words you already know and the new vocabulary in the drawings, imagine how you'll furnish each room. Use the verb **poner** *(to put)* in the infinitive form, according to the model.

 el dormitorio
En el dormitorio voy a poner una cama, un televisor, etc.

1. la cocina
2. el dormitorio
3. la oficina
4. la sala de estar

B. Donde yo vivo Describe los muebles en cada cuarto (in each room) de la casa o apartamento donde vives.

Pronunciación: *The vowel combination ai*

The combination **ai** in Spanish is pronounced in one single syllable, similar to the English word *eye*. Note that it can also be spelled **ay,** as in the Spanish words **hay** and **ay.**

192

Práctica

C. Lee cada palabra en voz alta, pronunciando con cuidado la combinación *ai*.

1. aire	3. paisaje	5. hay	7. caimán
2. baile	4. habláis	6. ¡ay!	8. compráis

Repaso

D. ***¿Qué dijiste?*** You are talking about what you and some of your classmates did last night. One of your classmates, who didn't hear, will ask you what you said. You will respond using the verb **decir**. Follow the model.

 Modelo: ella / estudiar
—*Ella estudió para un examen.*
—*¿Qué dijiste?*
—*Dije que ella estudió para un examen.*

1. ella / hablar por teléfono	5. nosotros / ir al partido
2. yo / ir al cine	6. ellas / mirar la televisión
3. ella / estudiar para un examen	7. ellos / comer pizza
4. él / salir con una amiga	8. él / alquilar un vídeo

E. ***Su casa está...*** Describe the homes of the people listed below to a group of your classmates. In addition to saying where each home is located, be precise about what it is like (rooms, furnishings, etc.). Use sentences like: **Su casa está...** and **Su casa tiene....**

1. a teacher	3. a professional athlete
2. a famous actress	4. a famous rock star

/-/-/-/-/-/-/-/-/-/-/-/-//
Learning Strategies:

Listing, describing

Critical Thinking Strategies:

Imagining, comparing and contrasting, making associations

 **ESTRUCTURA**

The verb poner

Voy a poner el sofá en la sala de estar.	*I'll put* the couch in the living room.
Ella puso el televisor en el dormitorio.	*She put* the television in the bedroom.
Yo puse el estante en mi oficina.	*I put* the bookcase in my office.
Yo pongo la mesa.	*I set (I'm setting)* the table.

193

 **Ex. D:** pair work

Follow-up, Ex. D: Once this activity has been done in pairs, have students form groups of three. Have Student 1 make the statement, Student 2 ask Student 3 what was said, and Student 3 respond appropriately.

Modelo: ella / aprender
—**Ella aprendió español en la escuela.**
—**¿Qué dijo?**
—**Dijo que ella aprendió español en la escuela.**

More-prepared students, Ex. D: More-prepared students can work in groups of three, per instructions for the Follow-up, creating their own statements. Have all students rotate positions in the group, so that everyone does all three tasks.

Answers, Ex. D: 1. —Ella habló por teléfono. —¿Qué dijiste? —Dije que ella habló por teléfono.   2. —Yo fui al cine. —¿Qué dijiste? —Dije que fui al cine.   3. —Ella estudió para un examen. —¿Qué dijiste? —Dije que ella estudió para un examen.   4. —Él salió con una amiga. —¿Qué dijiste? —Dije que él salió con una amiga.   5. —Nosotros fuimos al partido. —¿Qué dijiste? —Dije que nosotros fuimos al partido.

---

6. —Ellas miraron la televisión. —¿Qué dijiste? —Dije que ellas miraron la televisión.   7. —Ellos comieron pizza. —¿Qué dijiste? —Dije que ellos comieron pizza.   8. Él alquiló un vídeo. —¿Qué dijiste? —Dije que él alquiló un vídeo.

Ex. E: groups of four or more

Expansion, Ex. E: Have students read their descriptions to the class without identifying whose house it is. Have the class guess the owner and tell why. **Pienso que es la casa de un(a) profesor(a) (maestro[a]) porque tiene muchos libros, una mesa con muchos papeles y una computadora.**

Variation, Ex. E: Compare students' expectations for a teacher's house with their ideas about the home of a famous rock star. Make two lists on the board: (1) items expected in the rock star's house, but not in the teacher's house and (2) items expected in the teacher's house, but not in the rock star's house.

Critical Thinking Strategies: Drawing inferences, comparing and contrasting

Presentation: Estructura

Place various objects on top of, under, or next to other objects. (List these prepositions on the board for student reference.) Describe what you're doing using the verb **poner**. **Yo pongo los libros en la mesa.** Proceed through the conjugation as you've done with other irregular verbs. Finally, have some students place objects around the room while others describe what they're doing.

Cultural Observation

Compare the use of **piso** here with the formerly learned use of the word to describe a floor or level of a building.

The verb **poner** has several meanings. It may mean *to put* or *to place* something somewhere. It can also be used in the idiomatic expression **poner la mesa** *(to set the table)*.

Present

yo	**pongo**	nosotros(as)	**ponemos**
tú	**pones**	vosotros(as)	**ponéis**
él		ellos	
ella	**pone**	ellas	**ponen**
Ud.		Uds.	

Notice that, like **decir**, only the **yo** form of **poner** is irregular in the present, but all preterite forms are irregular.

Preterite

yo	**puse**	nosotros(as)	**pusimos**
tú	**pusiste**	vosotros(as)	**pusisteis**
él		ellos	
ella	**puso**	ellas	**pusieron**
Ud.		Uds.	

Learning Strategy:

Reading for cultural information

COMENTARIOS CULTURALES

El piso

In large cities like Madrid, because of the way space is used, it is rare to find suburbs as we know them in this country. What happens is that large apartment-like buildings are constructed that contain units with several rooms each. A unit, called **un piso**, can consist of a kitchen, living room, dining room, bathrooms, and bedrooms. People in Madrid buy **pisos** (similar to our condominiums) the same way we would buy houses in the suburbs.

194

Aquí practicamos

F. *¿Dónde pones los libros?* Di donde tú y tus compañeros de clase ponen sus libros cuando llegan a casa. Usa las pistas *(cues)*.

A	B	C
yo	poner en	la mesa
tú		el estante
?		el escritorio
nosotros		
? y ?		

G. *¿Dónde pusiste... ?* All the new furniture for your apartment arrived while your sister or brother was spending the weekend with a friend. You decided where to put the new items and rearranged the apartment while your sibling was away. Now telephone him or her. When asked, tell where you put each item.

> **Modelo:** la cómoda
> —¿Dónde pusiste la cómoda?
> —Puse la cómoda en el dormitorio.

/-/-/-/-/-/-/-/-/-/-/-/-/

Learning Strategy:

Asking and answering questions

Critical Thinking Strategy:

Making associations

Aquí escuchamos:

"Vamos a arreglar el apartamento."

Antes de escuchar

Patrick and his friend are looking at their new apartment and deciding where they are going to put their furniture. Look at the following questions and identify a few things you expect to hear during Patrick's conversation with his friend.

 START

/-/-/-/-/-/-/-/-/-/-/-/-/

Learning Strategy:

Previewing

195

Ex. F: writing

Teacher's note, Ex. F: These column exercises are meant to provide controlled practice. One way to present them is through the creation of a "word web." On a separate piece of paper, students can draw a web and then connect elements from the columns in ways that form grammatically correct sentences. (They have to write the correct form of the verb in the middle column.) The drawing that follows is a sample word web format. Word web formats vary from exercise to exercise.

Ex. G: pair work

Suggestion, Ex. G: Have students sketch a house with all the rooms mentioned in the exercise. Then have partners sit back to back. One describes where he or she put the furniture and the other draws each piece in the appropriate room. Have them switch roles halfway through the exercise. Check for accuracy when done.

Support material, Aquí escuchamos: Teacher Tape

Ex. H: groups of four or more

Preparation, Ex. H: Before doing this exercise, give students a blank apartment plan and have them place furniture according to your directions. Match what you told them to their results. This serves as a listening comprehension exercise and as a quiz.

Learning Strategies: Active listening, interpreting spatial relationships

Suggestion, Ex. H: You may wish to distribute copies of the floor plan to all. Instruct students to draw in the furniture, but nothing else. They must be able to explain orally, using the drawing as reference.

Ex. I: writing

Suggestion, Ex. I: Have students write a letter to someone describing their dream apartment or house. Have them accompany the letter with a labeled schematic or floor plan showing the location of the rooms and furniture. This would serve as an appropriate Chapter Culminating Activity.

Learning Strategy:

Listening for details

Cooperative Learning

Learning Strategies:

Negotiating, describing

Critical Thinking Strategies:

Creating a floor plan, making associations, comparing and contrasting

Learning Strategies:

Listing, describing

Critical Thinking Strategy:

Making associations

196

Después de escuchar

1. ¿Qué hacen?
2. ¿Qué ponen en la cocina?
3. ¿Quién sabe cocinar?
4. ¿Cómo arreglan *(arrange)* la sala de estar?
5. ¿Qué deciden hacer al terminar?

EJERCICIO ORAL

H. *¡Vamos a arreglar el apartamento!* Using the furniture names you have learned, work with several classmates to create a floor plan for an apartment and decide how you're going to arrange your furniture. When your group has finished, compare your arrangement with that of another group. Use the present tense of **poner** when you make your plans. (**Pongo las dos camas en el segundo dormitorio.**) Then use the *preterite* to explain to the other group what you did. (**Pusimos las dos camas en el segundo dormitorio.**)

EJERCICIO ESCRITO

I. *Mi apartamento ideal* Write a description of your dream apartment. Tell what furniture is in at least four of the rooms. Place a minimum of twelve pieces of furniture.

Vocabulario

Temas y contextos

Los anuncios en el periódico para una casa o un apartamento

aire acondicionado
(completamente) amueblado(a)
la cocina
el comedor
el dormitorio
el estacionamiento

el garaje (para dos coches)
el jardín
la sala de estar
la terraza
vacío(a)

La cocina y los muebles

las cortinas
el cuadro
la cuchara
el cuchillo
la estufa
el horno (de microondas)
el plato

el refrigerador
la servilleta
el sofá
la taza
el tenedor
el tostador
el vaso

Vocabulario general

Sustantivos	Verbos	Adjetivos
el alquiler	arreglar	increíble
el periódico	cocinar	
el plan	decir	
la ventana	poner	

Otras palabras y expresiones

¿Cómo se dice… ?
decir que sí (no)
m^2 (metros cuadrados)
para decir la verdad
¿Qué dijiste?
querer decir

Cooperative Learning

Vocabulario: Group Move

- Have all students review the **Vocabulario** list and look at the exercises that involved moving and arranging furniture.
- Tell the students to close their books.
- Have the students form five heterogeneous groups. Assign rooms to each group. Each group is responsible for arranging a different room in a house.
- Have groups make a poster with pictures of the items they want to put in the room. Explain that they have a lot of furniture and they need to put as much of it as possible in their room. Remind the students that all of the students in each group need to contribute equally.
- Once the items are placed, each group should make up a story about their move and their room, using as many of the words from the **Temas y contextos** and **Vocabulario general** sections as possible.
- Have each group tell its story to the class, using the pictures of their rooms as visual aids.

Lectura
CULTURAL

MACHU PICCHU

Los jardines en terrazas de Machu Picchu

198

Antes de leer

1. Look at the photos that accompany this reading. What do you think this place is?
2. Where do you think this place is? Who do you think lived there?
3. Are you familiar with the major indigenous civilizations that existed in the Americas long before the arrival of the Spaniards? Which ones do you know about?
4. Look at the title. Have you ever heard of this place?

Guía para la lectura

A. Read the first paragraph and answer the following questions.

1. ¿En qué país está Machu Picchu?
2. ¿Quién construyó esta ciudad?
3. ¿Por qué era tan importante Cuzco?
4. ¿En qué montañas está Machu Picchu?

B. Now finish the passage and answer the following questions.

1. ¿Por qué fue difícil encontrar esta ciudad?
2. ¿Quién era Hiram Bingham y por qué es importante?

Machu Picchu

n un lugar de privilegiada belleza y difícil accesibilidad de los Andes peruanos, se levantan las ruinas de Machu Picchu. En tiempos antiguos, la ciudad fue ciudad-fortaleza de los incas. Hoy es uno de los principales atractivos turísticos del Perú. Los restos arqueológicos están situados en una de las zonas más elevadas de los Andes, muy cerca de Cuzco, la antigua capital del imperio inca. Machu Picchu fue construida en un altiplano situado a unos 2.400 metros de altitud.

En cierto momento fue abandonada por sus antiguos pobladores y quedó cubierta por la vegetación durante siglos. Aunque los habitantes de la región creían en la mítica existencia de esta ciudad nadie la podía encontrar. Es que las ruinas estaban muy aisladas y eran accesibles a través de un camino muy difícil y montañoso. En el año 1911 una expedición encabezada por el profesor Hiram Bingham, de la Universidad de Yale, por fin encontró esta ciudad maravillosa.

Peru

199

Prereading

Show students similar ads in English so they can become familiar with layout and vocabulary before working with this reading.

Answers, Ex. A: The largest type in each ad gives the name and location (2). The next most important information usually has to do with price—the down payment or term of payments (3).

Estrategia para la lectura

Reading Strategies:

Read first for main ideas, then for details. Use titles, subtitles, and words that stand out as clues to the topic or main idea. Pay attention to the contexts of words you are guessing.

As you know, most of the time, you do not need to understand every word in a reading. It is more important to figure out the main idea, then go on to the details, since you look for details only when you need them. Main ideas are usually given in the titles or subtitles and in the first (and sometimes the last) sentence or paragraph. You should concentrate on these parts of a reading first. When you need to guess the meaning of a word, remember that surrounding context is extremely important, especially for false cognates. Be sure the guess you make fits the context.

Antes de leer

Here are some ads for vacation chalets in Spain. Before reading them, answer these questions.

>> **W**hat kind of information is typically included in house ads?

>> **W**hat information is usually highlighted?

>> **W**hat are some words you know are used in real estate ads?

Read the ads carefully, noticing what they have in common. Then go on to the **Actividades.**

Actividades

A. Based on the way the ads here and on page 201 highlight different words, what do you think the person who placed the ads most wants to stress? Choose two of the following features.

1. amount of space in the chalet
2. name of development or neighborhood where chalet is located
3. price of chalet
4. description of individual rooms
5. lot size

200

Support Materials

Workbook: **pp. 141–145**
Unit Review Blackline Masters: **Unit 2 Review**
Listening Activity masters: **p. 61**
Tapescript: **p. 90**
Unit Exam: **Testing Program, p. 103**
Atajo, **Writing Assistant Software**

should be able to get close.)
9. remainder (of the loan)
10. term (of the loan) (The last two are hard for anyone who doesn't know much about mortgages. Use them as examples to emphasize the importance of individual background knowledge in understanding what we read.)

Answers, Ex. C: 1. five
2. **Los Gamos** and **El Mirador de Coimbra** 3. **Los Gamos**
4. All ads mention a garage, but only **Los Gamos** and **El Mirador** specify room for two cars.

Ex. D: writing

Less-prepared students, Ex. D: Brainstorm a list of important features for a luxury vacation home with less-prepared students first.

More-prepared students, Ex. D: Have more-prepared students compare ads for luxury homes in their region with the ones in the book. Do they emphasize and/or include the same features as the Spanish homes or different ones (i.e., the period of the mortgage)? Can they draw any cultural conclusions from them? Share any cultural observations with the rest of the class. Have them choose between designing an ad for a home in Spain or in their region and ask them to explain their choice.

B. These words are cognates. Try to figure out their meanings from context as well as by thinking of the English words they resemble.

1. chimenea   3. estudio
2. parcelas   4. fase

These words are not cognates. Use context and background knowledge to guess what they mean.

5. sala de juegos   7. bodega
6. aseo   8. entrada

These words are false cognates. You will have to depend completely on context and your background knowledge to help you guess them. Here's a hint: Like **entrada**, these words have to do with the way people pay for houses.

9. facilidades   10. resto

C. Use the vocabulary you learned in this unit to help you answer the following questions.

1. How many bedrooms will you have at **Los Juncos**?
2. Which chalets are on more than one floor?
3. Which ad advertises a separate dining room?
4. Do all the chalets have a double garage?

D. Using these ads as models, design an ad for a house in your region of the country.

201

Teacher's note, Ex. B: Parts of this activity are difficult. It [is be]st done as a class exercise. Emphasize that students are [pra]cticing guessing and deduction skills. They are not expected [to g]et every answer correct. Even incorrect answers, however, [pro]vide opportunities for vocabulary building.

Answers, Ex. B: 1. chimney (Point out that this word actually refers to the fireplace itself, not just the chimney.)
2. parcels (Lots of land are often referred to as parcels in English.) 3. study or studio (Both English words are cognates of the same Spanish word.) 4. phase (Remind students of any local construction projects they may know about that are being built in stages or phases.) 5. game room 6. powder room
7. storeroom (For those students who know the American usage "small store," point out the meaning relationship.)
8. down payment (This one may be especially difficult. If students are asked to think about what might be an "entrance" in such a context and pay attention to the amounts given, they

Ex. A: pair work

 role play

Ex. B: pair work

 role play

 writing

Ex. C: pair work

 role play

Implementation, Ex. C: You might play the role of the apartment rental agent in this exercise.

Learning Strategy: Negotiating

Follow-up, Exs. A, B, and C: Divide the class into pairs and assign each pair one of these activities to perform in front of the class.

Writing Activities

Atajo, Writing Assistant Software supports ATAJO

Functional vocabulary: Asking / telling the time; describing objects; greeting and saying good-bye; inviting; linking ideas; thanking; writing a letter

Topic vocabulary: Bathroom; bedroom; furniture; house; kitchen; living room; time expressions; traveling

Grammar: Adjectives: numbers; verbs: preterite; verbs: summary; **salir; llegar; decir; poner**

Ya llegamos

Actividades orales

A. *Una habitación de hotel* You and your family are checking into a hotel. With a partner who will play the clerk, enact the following situation.

1. Greet the desk clerk.
2. Tell him or her you have reservations for two rooms for five nights.
3. You want two rooms with bathrooms.
4. Say you want the first floor. You don't like elevators.
5. Ask how much the rooms cost.
6. Ask if they take traveler's checks.
7. Thank the desk clerk and say good-bye.

B. *Adiós... Hasta luego.* You've just spent some time at the home of some Spanish friends and are about to return home. Thank your friends for everything they did for you, ask them to visit you in the United States, tell them you plan to return to Spain next summer, and say good-bye. Work with a partner.

C. *Yo busco un apartamento.* You have gone to an apartment rental office in Spain to rent an apartment for you and your friend during your semester-long stay. With a partner who will play the role of the rental agent, negotiate the following.

Cooperative Learning

Learning Strategies: Describing, negotiating

Critical Thinking Strategy: Prioritizing

Rental Agent	**Client**
1. Greet the new client.	1. Return the greeting.
2. Ask how you can help him or her.	2. Say you want an apartment with two bedrooms.
3. Ask how many rooms are wanted.	3. Say you want a living room and a small dining room.
4. Ask what is wanted in the kitchen.	4. Say you need a kitchen equipped with a refrigerator and stove, etc.
5. Ask what floor is preferred and if an elevator is needed.	5. Say you want to live several stories off the street level so it will be quieter. You want to have an elevator.
6. Ask what special amenities are desired.	6. Say you prefer an apartment with a swimming pool.
7. What part of town is preferred?	7. You prefer to live downtown.

202

The rental agent should decide on one element on the client's list that cannot be provided, and the client should decide on two elements he or she cannot give up. An agreement then should be negotiated with an acceptable price.

Actividades escritas

D. Muchas gracias Write a thank-you note to someone you visited recently.

E. Un hotel en España Write a postcard describing the hotel you are staying in on your vacation in Spain. Use the *Michelin Guide* descriptions on pages 142 and 149 for inspiration.

F. Una carta You've just moved into an apartment. Write a letter to your Spanish family describing the apartment and your furniture.

Less-prepared students, Exs. D and E: Remind less-prepared students to recycle ideas and expressions for these exercises from Exs. A and B. Have them refer to the letter on p. 171 as model for Ex. D.

More-prepared students, Ex. E: Ask the more-prepared students to write two different descriptions. Have them pretend they are going on a luxury vacation and describe what hotel they would stay in if money were not a problem. In the next scenario, they are students with very little money, traveling on a shoestring. Have them describe the hotel that fits this budget.

203

Conexión

Los inmigrantes en los Estados Unidos

AL EMPEZAR

ancestors
native Northamericans
Because of
roots

Casi todos los norteamericanos tienen **antepasados** que salieron de otros paises para vivir en los Estados Unidos. Hace quinientos años, sólo los **indígenas norteamericanos** vivieron en este continente. **A causa de** la inmigración, somos un país de personas con diversas **raíces** étnicas y culturales.

ACTIVIDAD A

Abajo hay una lista de las regiones principales del mundo. ¿Cuáles regiónes representan el origen de tus antepasados?

- África
- Asia
- Australia y las islas del Pacífico

- Europa
- Norteamérica (los indígenas)
- Latinoamérica

La tabla en la página 205 tiene los principales grupos étnicos que salieron para los Estados Unidos. ¿Cuántos de estos nombres reconoces? ¿Tienes antepasados que llegaron con uno de estos grupos?

ACTIVIDAD B

Primero, mira el esquema en la página 205. Después, contesta las preguntas.

1. ¿Cuáles grupos de inmigrantes llegaron a los Estados Unidos antes de 1820?
2. ¿Cuáles grupos de inmigrantes llegaron recientemente?
3. ¿Quiénes llegaron primero, los africanos o los alemanes? ¿los cubanos o los polacos? ¿los irlandeses o los ingleses?
4. ¿Durante cuantos años llegó el grupo principal de judíos?
5. ¿Cuántos italianos llegaron entre 1880 y 1930?
6. ¿Hace cuánto tiempo que llegó el primer grupo de mexicanos?
7. ¿Con cuáles grupos llegaron tus antepasados?

con la sociología

GRUPOS DE INMIGRANTES PRINCIPALES EN LOS ESTADOS UNIDOS

¿Quiénes llegaron?	¿Cuándo?	¿Cuántos?	¿Quiénes llegaron?	¿Cuándo?	¿Cuántos?
africanos	1700-1810	400.000	ingleses, franceses y escoceses	1700-1810	500.000
alemanes	1840-1890	4 millones			
austriacos, húngaros, checos y eslovacos	1880-1930	4 millones	irlandeses	1840-1860	1,5 millones
			italianos	1880-1930	4,5 millones
chinos, coreanos y filipinos	1960-1990	1 millón	judíos de Europa oriental	1880-1930	2,5 millones
cubanos	1960-1990	700.000	mexicanos	1910-1990	3 millones
daneses, noruegos y suecos	1870-1910	1,5 millones	polacos	1880-1930	1 millón
dominicanos, haitianos y jamaiquinos	1970-1990	900.000	vietnamitas	1970-1990	500.000

Source: World Book Encylcopedia, Vol. "I", p. 82, 1994.

ACTIVIDAD C

Work with a partner to put the following immigrant groups in order according to when they arrived in the United States. You will need to refer to the immigration table to complete this activity. One person should cover the table and ask questions, while the other should look at the table and provide the necessary information.

 Modelo: **Estudiante 1**: *¿Quiénes llegaron hace doscientos años?*
Estudiante 2: *Los ingleses llegaron hace doscientos años.*

africanos	chinos	cubanos	mexicanos	polacos
judíos	irlandeses	alemanes	ingleses	

LLEGARON...

... hace 200 años	... hace 150 años	... hace 100 años	... hace 30 años
_____	_____	_____	_____
_____	_____	_____	_____

205

Answers, Actividad C:
hace 200 años: africanos, ingleses; hace 150 años: alemanes, irlandeses; hace 100 años: judíos, polacos, mexicanos; hace 30 años: chinos, cubanos

Extension activities:
You may want to put the table below on the board, and ask students to match the nationalities to country names. (You may want to have them review country names first.)

Nacionalidad	País o región de origen
africanos	
alemanes	
chinos	
coreanos	
cubanos	
dominicanos	
franceses	
húngaros	
ingleses	
irlandeses	
italianos	
mexicanos	
polacos	
suecos	
vietnamitas	

¿Qué ves?

> ¿Dónde está y qué hace la gente
> se ve en cada foto?

> ¿Crees que hacen lo mismo todo
> los días? ¿Por qué?

> ¿Cuáles de las fotos muestran
> vida diaria? ¿Cómo sabes?

OBJECTIVES

IN THIS UNIT YOU WILL LEARN:
- To talk about your daily routine;
- To organize weekend activities;
- To discuss vacation plans.

206

Capítulo siete: ¿Qué haces de costumbre?

Primera etapa: Una mañana en la casa de Cristina Gallegos
Segunda etapa: Una tarde con Enrique Castillo
Tercera etapa: Una noche en la casa de Marilú Méndez

Capítulo ocho: ¿Qué haces este fin de semana?

Primera etapa: La revista *Cromos*
Segunda etapa: Te invito a una fiesta

Capítulo nueve: ¿Cuándo son las vacaciones?

Primera etapa: Las vacaciones con la familia
Segunda etapa: Una visita a un parque nacional

Nuestro día

207

Planning Strategy

If you do not assign the Planning Strategy (Workbook, p. 147) for homework or if students have difficulty coming up with English expressions, you might put students into groups of four, working in cooperative pairs, to answer each question. The group that comes up with the most usable responses for each question in the time allotted (10–15 minutes) wins. You might ask various pairs of students to role play in English several of the situations outlined in the Planning Strategy.

Chapter Objectives

Functions: Talking about daily routines; organizing weekend activities; discussing vacation plans

Context: Home, school, town, city; vacation sites; advertisements

Accuracy: Present tense of reflexive verbs; **usted, ustedes, tú** commands of reflexive verbs; direct object pronouns; immediate future of reflexive verbs; reflexive vs. nonreflexive verbs; pronouns with the imperative

Cultural Context

Approximately one and a half million people live in Quito, which lies within 25 km of the equator, at an altitude high enough to create a temperate climate. The second highest capital in Latin America, Quito lies nestled in a hollow at the foot of the Pichincha volcano. Originally an Inca city, Quito was refounded in 1534 by Sebastián de Benalcázar, Francisco Pizarro's lieutenant, and the old section of the city still reflects its colonial past. The **Calle de la Ronda,** located in old Quito, is one of the oldest streets in the city. Visitors marvel at the "living museum" quality of its historic buildings, homes, and narrow cobblestone streets.

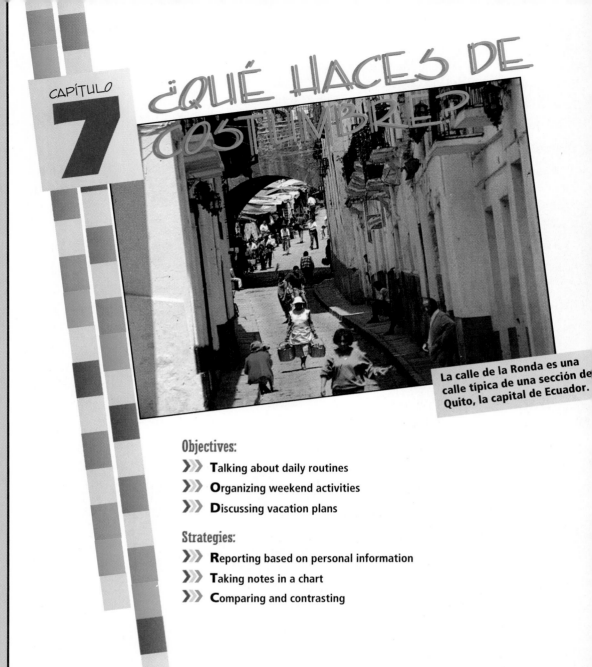

CAPÍTULO 7

¿QUÉ HACES DE COSTUMBRE?

La calle de la Ronda es una calle típica de una sección de Quito, la capital de Ecuador.

Objectives:

>>> **T**alking about daily routines
>>> **O**rganizing weekend activities
>>> **D**iscussing vacation plans

Strategies:

>>> **R**eporting based on personal information
>>> **T**aking notes in a chart
>>> **C**omparing and contrasting

208

Video/Laserdisc

Chapter 7 Video Program and Video Guide

PRIMERA ETAPA

Preparación

>> **W**hat do you usually do on weekdays? on weekends?

>> **W**hen and with whom do you talk about your daily activities?

>> **H**ow is a typical day different from an extraordinary one?

//-//-//-//-//-//-//-//

Learning Strategy:
Previewing

Critical Thinking Strategy:
Contrasting

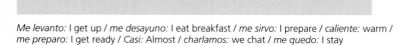

Una mañana en la casa de Cristina Gallegos

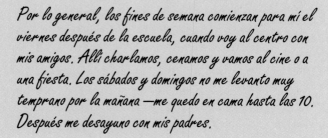

Me levanto a las 7:20 y me desayuno. Siempre me sirvo un chocolate bien caliente y luego me preparo para ir a la escuela. Esto tarda tres cuartos de hora, más o menos. Salgo para la escuela a las 8:10. Voy a pie porque el autobús no va directamente a la escuela. Llego en un poco menos de 20 minutos. Generalmente mis clases comienzan a las 8:30. Casi siempre llego a tiempo.

Por lo general, los fines de semana comienzan para mí el viernes después de la escuela, cuando voy al centro con mis amigos. Allí charlamos, cenamos y vamos al cine o a una fiesta. Los sábados y domingos no me levanto muy temprano por la mañana —me quedo en cama hasta las 10. Después me desayuno con mis padres.

Me levanto: I get up / *me desayuno:* I eat breakfast / *me sirvo:* I prepare / *caliente:* warm / *me preparo:* I get ready / *Casi:* Almost / *charlamos:* we chat / *me quedo:* I stay

209

Etapa Support Materials

Workbook: pp. 149–153
Tapescript: p. 93
Transparencies: #28, #29
Teacher Tape

Listening Activity masters: p. 67
Quiz: Testing Program, p. 109

Support material, Una mañana en la casa... :
   Transparency #28

Presentation: Una mañana en la casa...

Have students listen with their books closed as you read the paragraphs. Ask general comprehension questions such as: **¿A qué hora se levanta Cristina? ¿Va ella en autobús?** Then have students read the paragraphs to prepare for Ex. A.

Chapter Warm-up: Corners

- To set the context for this chapter, play Corners in English. Each corner of the room represents the amount of time students need to prepare themselves for school in the morning. For example, the first corner might represent fifteen minutes, for those who do only the essentials. The second corner could represent a half hour, which might include washing up and getting coffee. The third corner might represent an hour, for those students who take a shower and eat breakfast. The fourth corner might be an hour and a half or more, for those who do their hair, shave, put on makeup, read the newspaper, etc.
- Tell students to go to the corner that most closely fits their style.
- Have students discuss in pairs what they do in that amount of time each morning.
- Have pairs share their thoughts with another pair, until all people in each corner have heard how each student uses his or her time.
- Call on one student from each corner to summarize what all of the students in that corner do each morning.

Ex. A: ✎ writing

Cultural Expansion

You may want to mention that the expression **mañana** is commonly used to mean "I'll do it tomorrow." Note that **la tarde** can refer to hours that non-Hispanics think of as evening, such as 6–8 P.M. Point out that dinner usually takes place about 9–10 P.M.

Cultural Brainstorming

Point out to students that in the U.S. we also have varying "comfort zones" regarding time. Ask students if they would feel it was important to arrive at the time scheduled in each of the following cases: to go to their best friend's house, to meet a first-time date, to visit relatives, to go to the doctor, to go to a party on a Friday night, to attend a wedding, etc. What seems to be the determining factor that makes it acceptable to arrive late in some cases and important to be on time in others?

Learning Strategy: Brainstorming

Critical Thinking Strategies: Analyzing, making associations, evaluating

¡Aquí te toca a ti!

///-//-//-//-//-//-//-//-//
Learning Strategy:
Reading for details

///-//-//-//-//-//-//-//-//
Learning Strategy:
Reading for cultural information

A. ¿Verdad o falso?   Basándote en la descripción de Cristina en la página 209, indica si los siguientes comentarios son verdaderos (V) o falsos (F). Si es falso, di *(say)* por qué.

1. Cristina se levanta muy temprano todas las mañanas.
2. Se queda en cama tarde los sábados y los domingos.
3. Se desayuna, después se prepara para ir a la escuela.
4. Se prepara para ir a la escuela en menos de una hora.
5. Vive cerca de la escuela.
6. Toma el autobús para llegar allí.
7. Su primera clase es a las 8:30.
8. Los fines de semana de Cristina son parecidos a *(are similar to)* los fines de semana norteamericanos.

COMENTARIOS
CULTURALES

■ *Actitudes hacia el tiempo*

The word **mañana** means both *morning* and *tomorrow*, but is also commonly used in Spanish-speaking cultures to mean at some indefinite future time, rather than specifically the next morning or the next day, as might be assumed. It is also important to understand that references to **la mañana, la tarde,** and **la noche** are often much broader in meaning than they are in English. There is a different attitude on the part of Spanish speakers regarding the amount of time in which they allow themselves and other people to do things.

When used specifically, **la mañana** is viewed as any time before noon. After that, **la tarde** can go on into what is considered "evening" to a person from an English-speaking culture.

La noche begins after 8:00 or 9:00 p.m. or thereabouts. There is not a big concern with dividing the day into precise, inflexible units of time.

This is good to know because it also means that people in Spanish-speaking cultures often function according to a general time range when it comes to social occasions. It is perfectly acceptable, and even expected, for example, for someone to agree to meet at 7:00 and then arrive 30–45 minutes after that. This is not viewed as rude behavior, but rather as dealing in a kind of "comfort zone" in which everyone is assumed to live. When it comes to business or medical appointments, however, sticking to a precise hour is understood to be the agreement.

210

The present tense of reflexive verbs

Me levanto temprano.	*I get up* early.
Mi amiga Isabel **se levanta** temprano también.	My friend Isabel *gets up* early, too.
Nos llamamos por teléfono todas las mañanas.	*We call each other* on the telephone every morning.

Reflexive verbs can be used to express two different meanings:

1. an action that reflects back on the subject

Yo me lavo.	*I wash (myself).*
Ella se levanta.	*She gets up.* (Literally, *she gets herself up.*)

2. an action in which two or more subjects interact

Nosotras nos reunimos por la tarde.	*We get together* in the afternoon.
Ellas se miran.	*They look at each other.*

In either case, the subject (noun or pronoun) is accompanied by a corresponding reflexive pronoun (**me, te, se, nos, os, se**).

---

bañarse (to bathe)

yo	**me baño**	nosotros(as)	**nos bañamos**
tú	**te bañas**	vosotros(as)	**os bañáis**
él		ellos	
ella	**se baña**	ellas	**se bañan**
Ud.		Uds.	

To express that the subject does something to himself/herself/themselves, the reflexive pronoun must agree with the subject of the verb with which it is used. When the verb is conjugated, the pronoun usually precedes it; with an infinitive, the pronoun is normally attached to it.

Yo **me levanto** temprano todos los días.
Yo quiero **levantarme** temprano mañana.

Presentation: Estructura

(1) Begin by asking, **¿Cómo te llamas? ¿Cómo se llama tu hermano(a)? ¿Cómo se llaman tus padres?**
(2) Write pronoun combinations on the board.
(3) Ask, **¿Te llamas Enrique?** (**No, nos llamamos Laurie y Kim.**)
(4) Have students conjugate **llamar** while you point to the subjects. Point to yourself: **Yo me llamo.** Point to a student: **Tú te llamas.** Point to another student: **Ella se llama.**, etc.

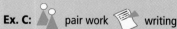
Here is a list of some frequently used reflexive verbs. (The pronoun **se** attached to an infinitive means that the verb is reflexive.)

acostarse (ue)	to go to bed
afeitarse	to shave
cepillarse (el pelo, los dientes)	to brush (one's hair, teeth)
darse prisa	to hurry up
desayunarse	to eat breakfast
despertarse (ie)	to wake up
divertirse (ie, i)	to have a good time
dormirse (ue, u)	to fall asleep
ducharse	to take a shower
lavarse (las manos, el pelo, los dientes)	to wash (one's hands, hair; to brush one's teeth)
maquillarse	to put on makeup
peinarse	to comb one's hair
ponerse	to put on
quedarse	to stay, to remain
sentarse (ie)	to sit down
vestirse (i, i)	to get dressed

Aquí practicamos

B. Usa la información entre paréntesis para crear oraciones nuevas.

1. *Yo* me despierto a las nueve. (Juana / nosotros / tú / tus amigos / vosotros)
2. *Él* se viste antes de desayunarse. (María y Carlos / yo / Uds. / ella / tú)
3. *Ellas* se llaman mucho por teléfono. (Uds. / mis hermanas / nosotros / ellos)
4. *Ud.* se ducha después de levantarse. (yo / Uds. / Marta / ellos / tú / vosotras)
5. *Tú* te acuestas muy temprano. (nosotros / él / mis padres / Carlos y tú / ella)

C. *Pedro o Ana María y yo* Compare your activities with those, on page 213, of Pedro (if you are male) or those of Ana María (if you are female).

Los muchachos

Modelo: Pedro se despierta a las siete.
Yo me despierto a las siete menos cuarto.

 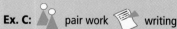

1. Pedro se queda en cama por media hora y se levanta a las siete y media.
2. Pedro no se baña por la mañana de costumbre.
3. Pedro se lava los dientes una vez al día.
4. Pedro se afeita de vez en cuando.

Las muchachas

Modelo: Ana María se despierta a las siete.
Yo me despierto a las seis y media.

1. Ana María se queda en cama por un cuarto de hora.
2. Ana María se levanta a las siete y cuarto.
3. Ana María se baña todas las mañanas.
4. Ana María se cepilla el pelo y se maquilla.

D. *Una familia* Tu compañero(a) describe la rutina diaria de su familia. Tú le haces algunas preguntas usando la información entre paréntesis.

Modelos: Mi madre se baña todas las mañanas. (cepillarse el pelo)
¿Se cepilla el pelo también?

Mi padre siempre se queda en cama. (a qué hora / levantarse)
¿A qué hora se levanta?

1. Mi hermano se despierta a las seis. (a qué hora / levantarse)
2. Yo no me quedo en cama por la mañana. (por qué / levantarse inmediatamente)
3. Mi hermana se cepilla el pelo todas las mañanas. (maquillarse)
4. Yo me baño todas las mañanas. (lavarse el pelo)
5. Mi padre se baña, se viste y sale de la casa. (cuándo / afeitarse)
6. Yo me levanto, me baño y me desayuno. (cuándo / vestirse)

E. *¿Y tú?* You and two of your friends are discussing the morning routines of your families. First, name the members of your family. Then use the suggested verbs to tell something about the members of your family and to ask your partners about theirs. Follow the model.

Modelo: despertarse muy temprano
Estudiante A: *Mi padre se despierta muy temprano.*
Estudiante B (a Estudiante C): *¿Tu padre se despierta muy temprano también?*
Estudiante C: *Sí, se despierta muy temprano también.* o: *No, de costumbre se despierta a las nueve.*

1. despertarse
2. levantarse antes de… (la hora)
3. quedarse en cama hasta… (la hora)
4. cepillarse / lavarse los dientes… veces por día
5. ducharse todas las mañanas
6. afeitarse todos los días / a veces
7. maquillarse todos los días / a veces
8. vestirse antes / después del desayuno

213

Sidebar

Learning Strategy:
Reporting based on personal information

Critical Thinking Strategy:
Comparing and contrasting

Learning Strategy:
Asking questions

Learning Strategies:
Reporting based on personal information, asking questions

Answers, Ex. C, Los muchachos: 1. Yo (no) me quedo en cama... y me levanto... 2. Yo no me baño... (Yo me baño...) 3. Yo me lavo... (Yo me cepillo...) 4. Yo me afeito...
Las muchachas: 1. Yo (no) me quedo... 2. Yo me levanto... 3. Yo (no) me baño... 4. Yo me cepillo... y me maquillo...

Ex. D: pair work

Answers, Ex. D: 1. ¿A qué hora se levanta? 2. ¿Por qué te levantas inmediatamente? 3. ¿Se maquilla también? 4. ¿Te lavas el pelo también? 5. ¿Cuándo se afeita? 6. ¿Cuándo te vistes?

Ex. E: groups of three

More-prepared students, Ex. E: Ask the more-prepared students to add four or five other verbs and questions about family members and friends.

Answers, Ex. E: Answers will vary, but they should follow this pattern: **Mi padre (madre, hermano, hermana) se despierta... ¿Tu padre (madre, hermano, hermana) se despierta... también? Sí, se despierta... también (No, de costumbre se despierta...)**

Aquí escuchamos:
"Una mañana en casa de Juan Manuel y Cecilia"

Antes de escuchar

Juan Manuel, 18, and Cecilia, 14, are brother and sister. Both are students at the **Escuela Simón Bolívar.** For each of them every morning is the same. What do you typically do each morning? Look at the following questions in order to help you listen for the details of Juan Manuel's and Cecilia's schedule.

■ START

Después de escuchar

1. ¿Qué dice Juan Manuel que Cecilia hace por las mañanas?
2. ¿Qué hace Juan Manuel cuando se despierta?
3. ¿A qué hora dice Cecilia que se levanta su hermano?
4. ¿Qué no tiene tiempo de hacer Juan Manuel?
5. ¿Siempre se desayunan los hermanos?

¡Aquí te toca a ti!

F. *En casa de Victoria* Mornings at Victoria's house are very different from those at Juan Manuel's and Cecilia's. Based on the drawings below and at the top of page 215, describe what Victoria and her brother Miguel do in the morning. Use the following verbs and expressions: **despertarse, levantarse, quedarse en cama, ducharse, lavarse, cepillarse, maquillarse, vestirse, peinarse, desayunarse, irse.**

Miguel

214

Victoria

G. *¿Y tú?* Now describe your own morning activities. Talk about the same topics as mentioned in the conversation with Juan Manuel and Cecilia, but fit the information to your personal situation.

Modelo: *De costumbre, yo me despierto a las 6:30…*

//-//-//-//-//-//-//-//-//
Learning Strategy:
Reporting based on personal information

¡Adelante!

EJERCICIO ORAL

H. *Intercambio* Conversa con un(a) compañero(a) usando las siguientes preguntas.

1. ¿A qué hora se levantan en tu casa?
2. ¿Quién se levanta primero?
3. ¿Quién se ducha?
4. ¿Quién se lava el pelo por la mañana?

//-//-//-//-//-//-//-//-//
Learning Strategy:
Providing personal information

EJERCICIO ESCRITO

I. *Una mañana típica* Your family has registered to host an exchange student from a Spanish-speaking country. In preparation for the visit, the student has written you asking for an idea of your family's daily routine.

Write a letter to him or her. (1) Give the names of your family members with a brief description of each. (2) Describe the early morning routine of your family, (3) commenting on specific times when certain family members do certain things. In the next paragraph, (4) tell where everyone goes during the day and (5) two facts about each one's day. In the final paragraph, describe the family's evening at home, (6) telling what you do together and (7) what you do individually, including preparation for bed and what time you go to sleep. Don't forget to (8) use appropriate letter format with date, salutation, and closing.

//-//-//-//-//-//-//-//-//
Learning Strategies:
Organizing ideas, describing, reporting based on personal information

215

Ex. H: pair work

Less-prepared students, Ex. H: Give less-prepared students time to answer the questions silently for themselves before they interview their partner. Have them jot down a few notes for each of their partner's answers to use when they report back to the class.

More-prepared students, Ex. H: More-prepared students may include other appropriate questions for their partners. Remind them to speak conversationally, commenting (**Yo también me levanto primero**), interrupting (**Perdón, ¿a qué hora se levantan en tu casa?**), or asking another question (**¿Se maquilla tu hermana en el baño?**).

Ex. I: writing

Less-prepared students, Ex. I: Review with less-prepared students the adjectives for physical description and personality traits. Remind them to recycle ideas and expressions from Ex. H in their work. You may want them to make an outline for each family member by jotting down notes under the person's name for items 2–5. They can repeat this process for each family member, then use the notes to write the paragraph. For items 6 and 7, students could make two columns with appropriate notes.

Ex. G: pair work

More-prepared students, Ex. G: Have more-prepared students compare their morning with their partner's, e.g., **De costumbre, mi compañero se despierta a las 7:00 y no se queda en la cama. Yo también me despierto a las 7:00, pero me quedo en la cama hasta las 7:30.** Another alternative would be to have students compare their habitual actions with what they did yesterday, e.g., **De costumbre me despierto a las 7:00, pero ayer me desperté a las 9:00.** You may want to have students report on their partners as well.

Presentation: Una tarde con Enrique Castillo

Let students read the paragraphs out loud, then have them do Ex. A on page 217 as a comprehension check. Discuss in English some cultural information about school schedules in Spanish-speaking countries. Point out that Enrique has a typical two-hour break at lunch time. In many countries students who live close enough to school go home for the family **comida.** You may bring in another schedule or use the one in the Workbook (p. 154), or, if you have or have had Spanish exchange students, tell about or show students their schedules.

Cultural Expansion

Have students compare the length of Enrique's schoolday with their own. What disadvantages does his day have in comparison with theirs? Can they think of any advantages to a longer schoolday? Possible answers include more time for lunch, the day starts later, the pace is less hectic, etc.

Learning Strategy: Brainstorming

Critical Thinking Strategies: Comparing and contrasting, seeing cause-and-effect relationships

---

SEGUNDA ETAPA

Preparación

>> **W**hat is a typical afternoon like for you?

>> **W**hat do you do on Fridays after school that you don't do on other days of the week?

Learning Strategies: Previewing, listing

Una tarde con Enrique Castillo

Las clases comienzan a las 9:00 y duran 55 minutos. Los lunes, mi primera clase es el latín. Después, tengo una hora de español y una hora de francés. ¡A veces no sé qué lengua estudio!

Al mediodía tengo una hora para comer: de las 12:00 hasta la 1:00. Almuerzo en la cafetería de la escuela y hablo con mis amigos. Después del almuerzo, tengo una hora libre (para hacer la tarea) o salgo de la escuela para dar un paseo con mis compañeros.

Las clases comienzan de nuevo a las 2:00. Por la tarde, tengo ganas de echar una siesta, pero no puedo porque tengo una hora de historia y geografía, luego siguen las clases con una hora de matemáticas, luego una hora de física y química. ¡Es mucho! Después de las clases estoy cansado. Siempre me quedo un buen rato en frente de la escuela para charlar con mis amigos. Luego regreso a casa. Llego en muy poco tiempo porque vivo cerca de la escuela.

Esta tarde sólo es un ejemplo, porque tengo un horario diferente para cada día de la semana. Por ejemplo, los martes, comienzo a las 8:30, almuerzo de las 11:30 a las 12:30 y termino a las cuatro. Y los cursos mismos son diferentes: estudio también inglés y ciencias naturales, y tengo dos horas de deportes por semana.

duran: last / *tarea:* homework / *de nuevo:* again / *siguen (seguir):* continue / *un buen rato:* a good while / *sólo:* only / *ejemplo:* example / *mismos:* themselves

216

Etapa Support Materials

Workbook: **pp. 154–158**
Critical Thinking masters: **Chapter 7, segunda etapa, activity J**
Transparency: **#30**
Teacher Tape 🎧

Quiz: **Testing Program, p. 111**
Support material, **Una tarde con Enrique Castillo:**
   Transparency #30

¡Aquí te toca a ti!

A. *Los cursos de Enrique*
Here are some of the courses offered in **escuelas secundarias** or **colegios** in Spanish-speaking countries. Indicate which courses are part of the **programa** Enrique just described on page 216 and which are not.

el español	la física	la geografía
el alemán	la química	la economía
el inglés	las ciencias naturales	la música (instrumento,
el francés	(la biología, la geología)	canto, baile)
el griego *(Greek)*	la educación física	las artes plásticas
el latín	la historia	(pintura, escultura)
las matemáticas		

B. *Enrique y tú*
Compare your school day with the one Enrique describes. For each statement Enrique makes, either say that your situation is similar (**Para mí, es lo mismo...**) or explain how it is different (**Para mí, es diferente...**). Follow the model.

Modelo: Generalmente, mis clases comienzan a las 9:30.
Para mí, es diferente. Mis clases comienzan a las 8:45.

Learning Strategy:
Identifying

Critical Thinking Strategy:
Comparing and contrasting

1. Las clases en mi escuela duran 55 minutos.
2. Los lunes por la mañana tengo tres clases.
3. En nuestra escuela tenemos una hora y media para comer.
4. Yo almuerzo en la cafetería de la escuela.
5. Después de almorzar, salgo de la escuela para dar un paseo con mis amigos.
6. Las clases terminan a las tres de la tarde.
7. Después de las clases, me quedo un buen rato en frente de la escuela.
8. Siempre llego a casa en cinco minutos porque vivo muy cerca de la escuela.
9. Tomo cursos de español, inglés, francés, latín, historia, geografía, física, química, biología, geología y matemáticas.

C. *No es verdad...*
Indicate that the statements on page 218 are incorrect. For at least three items, provide more accurate statements based on the drawings. Follow the model.

217

Learning Strategy:
Reporting based on visual information

 Modelos: Pablo se levanta antes de las siete. *No es verdad. No se levanta antes de las siete. Se levanta a las ocho y media.*

Yo me levanto muy temprano. *No es verdad. Tú no te levantas muy temprano. Te levantas después de las diez.*

1. Jorge se lava los dientes una vez al día.

2. Consuelo y su hermano se dan prisa para ir a la escuela.

3. Yo me afeito todas las mañanas.

4. Juana se viste antes de desayunarse.

5. Después de las clases, nos gusta dar un paseo por el parque.

Repaso

Learning Strategy:
Giving personal information

D. ¿Qué hago y qué no hago? Para cada actividad en la página 219, indica si es verdad para ti o no. Sigue el modelo.

Modelo: despertarse muy temprano
Yo me despierto muy temprano. o:
Yo no me despierto muy temprano.

218

Actividades: despertarse muy temprano / levantarse inmediatamente / quedarse en cama / ducharse por la mañana / lavarse el pelo todos los días / afeitarse / maquillarse / vestirse rápidamente / desayunarse antes de ir a la escuela / salir para la escuela antes de las siete y media / darse prisa para llegar a tiempo / cepillarse los dientes después de la comida

Suggestion, Ex. E: Compare a regular day with a day of vacation. Model it first: **De costumbre me levanto a las seis y media, pero los días de vacaciones, yo me levanto a las ocho. ¿Y tú?**

E. ¡Dime! (Tell me!)   Habla con un(a) compañero(a) de clase sobre su rutina diaria. Usa la información entre paréntesis.

Learning Strategy:
Requesting and giving personal information

1. ¿A qué hora… ? (levantarse durante la semana / levantarse el sábado por la mañana / levantarse en el verano)
2. ¿Cuántas veces al día (a la semana)… ? (lavarse los dientes / lavarse el pelo / ducharse)

Learning Strategy: Comparing and contrasting

Expansion, Ex. E: As an interesting (mis-)communication or listening exercise, divide the class into two groups and have them sit in a circle to play a version of "rumor" or "telephone". One student begins by whispering one item of information about his/her partner to the person on the right, for example: **Juan se levanta a las 7:00 durante la semana.** This person whispers this information to the next, and so on. The last person in the circle states the information out loud. Then the originator gives the first statement again. It's always interesting to see how things change from beginning to end, or to see if students can accurately keep relaying the same message. This process can be repeated several times.

ESTRUCTURA

Ud. and Uds. command forms of reflexive verbs

Levántese Ud. ahora mismo, por favor.	*Get up* right now, please.
Levántense Uds. antes de las 10:00, hijos.	*Get up (all of you)* before 10:00, children.
Póngase la camisa azul.	*Put on* the blue shirt.
Pónganse los zapatos, niños.	*Put on* your shoes, kids.
No **se duerma** en clase.	Don't *fall asleep* in class.
No **se duerman** aquí.	Don't *(all of you) fall asleep* here.

Reflexive verbs form their command forms the same way that other infinitives do. The only difference is that command forms for reflexive verbs must also include reflexive pronouns.

Presentation: Estructura

This might be a good time to play "Simon says", or **Simón dice.** Have students mime actions of other verbs, e.g., **lávense las caras, lávense las manos, cepíllense los dientes, cepíllense el pelo, aféitense, maquíllense.** This is a good example of total physical response (TPR) learning.

219

Ex. F: pair work

Answers, Ex. F: 1. Sí, levántese temprano.   2. Sí, báñese ahora.   3. Sí, siéntense aquí.   4. Sí, lávese los dientes.   5. Sí, llámense por teléfono.   6. Sí, péinese antes de salir.   7. Sí, maquíllese para la fiesta.   8. Sí, póngase el abrigo.   9. Sí, acuéstense a las 7:00.   10. Sí, diviértanse con la música.

To form the **usted** affirmative formal command of reflexive **-ar** verbs, add **-e** to the stem of the **yo** form of the verb in the present tense. For **-er** and **-ir** verbs, add **-a** to the stem of the **yo** form of the verb. Then attach the reflexive pronoun **se** to this command form.

yo qued**o**	qued-	qued**e**	qué**dese**
yo pong**o**	pong-	pong**a**	pón**gase**
yo duerm**o**	duerm-	duerm**a**	duér**mase**

The negative formal command is formed the same way, except that the reflexive pronoun **se** is used *before* the command form. Notice that **no** is placed *before* the reflexive pronoun.

yo qued**o**	qued-	qued**e**	**no se** quede
yo pong**o**	pong-	pong**a**	**no se** ponga
yo duerm**o**	duerm-	duerm**a**	**no se** duerma

The plural formal affirmative and negative command forms add **-n** to the singular command forms. The reflexive pronoun **se** is positioned the same as it is in each singular form.

yo qued**o**	qued-	qued**e**	qué**dense**
			no se qued**en**

Note that a written accent appears on the third syllable from the end of all command forms when the reflexive pronoun is attached. This indicates that the original stress remains despite the changes to the word.

quédese   **qué**dense   **pón**gase   **pón**ganse   **duér**mase   **duér**manse

Aquí practicamos

F. **¡Órdenes, órdenes!** (Orders, orders!)   Using a reflexive verb, a classmate will ask you if he or she or everyone should do something. You respond by using the same verb in the appropriate **Ud.** or **Uds.** affirmative command forms. Follow the models.

Modelos: ¿Me quedo aquí?
Sí, quédese aquí.

¿Nos lavamos las manos?
Sí, lávense las manos.

1. ¿Me levanto temprano?
2. ¿Me baño ahora?
3. ¿Nos sentamos aquí?
4. ¿Me lavo los dientes?
5. ¿Nos llamamos por teléfono?
6. ¿Me peino antes de salir?
7. ¿Me maquillo para la fiesta?
8. ¿Me pongo el abrigo?
9. ¿Nos acostamos a las 7:00?
10. ¿Nos divertimos con la música?

220

G. ¡No, no, no y tres veces que no!

This time, respond to questions asked by your classmate by using the appropriate **Ud.** or **Uds.** *negative* command forms of the reflexive verbs. Follow the models.

Modelos:
¿Me quedo aquí?
¡No, no, no! No se quede aquí.

¿Nos levantamos tarde?
¡No, no, no! No se levanten tarde.

1. ¿Me siento en la mesa?
2. ¿Nos ponemos tres suéteres?
3. ¿Me afeito en la cocina?
4. ¿Me cepillo los dientes con jabón *(soap)*?
5. ¿Nos acostamos a la una?
6. ¿Me divierto con el coche nuevo de papá?
7. ¿Me duermo en la clase de español?
8. ¿Nos bañamos a la medianoche?
9. ¿Me afeito en la biblioteca?
10. ¿Me levanto a las 4:00 de la tarde?
11. ¿Me peino en la iglesia?
12. ¿Nos quedamos en tu casa por dos meses sin salir?

H. El (La) director(a)

Pretend you are directing a commercial for personal hygiene products. You must tell the actors exactly what to do or not to do during the filming of scenes typical of a family's routine early in the morning. Give at least six orders, using the **Ud.** and **Uds.** forms of reflexive verbs in affirmative or negative command forms. Suggested verbs to use: **afeitarse, peinarse, sentarse, maquillarse, acostarse, levantarse, cepillarse, lavarse, despertarse, ponerse,** etc. Each actor/actress will act out what the director asks him or her to do.

//-//-//-//-//-//-//-//-//

Learning Strategies:

Organizing, sequencing

Aquí escuchamos:
"La tarde de Juan Manuel y Cecilia"

Antes de escuchar

Juan Manuel and Cecilia talk with their Uncle Pedro about their life in school. Look at the questions on page 222 to help you anticipate what they might tell him about a typical school day.

START

221

Ex. G: pair work

Answers, Ex. G: 1. No, no se siente en la mesa.   2. No, no se pongan tres suéteres.   3. No, no se afeite en la cocina.   4. No, no se cepille los dientes con jabón. 5. No, no se acuesten a la una. 6. No, no se divierta con el coche nuevo de papá.   7. No, no se duerma en la clase de español. 8. No, no se bañen a la medianoche.   9. No, no se afeite en la biblioteca.   10. No, no se levante a las 4:00 de la tarde.   11. No, no se peine en la iglesia.   12. No, no se queden en mi casa por dos meses sin salir.

Ex. H: groups of four or more

role play

Suggestion, Ex. H: This could be a good basis for a skit. You may also want to have the students videotape each other. Students might use props or make poster-props of the products they're advertising, using other commands, such as **compren** or **usen este producto.**

Support material, Aquí escuchamos: Teacher Tape

Suggestion, Aquí escuchamos: Have students take out paper and pencil and make two columns on the page, one for Cecilia and one for Juan Manuel. As they listen to the tape, have them jot down activities associated with each person. Each time they listen, they should be able to add more to the list. After listening three times, check and compare results by asking for volunteers to give different pieces of information. Make a master list on the board, perhaps having a student secretary do the recording.

Answers, Aquí escuchamos: 1. si van a la escuela juntos por la mañana   2. no   3. Juan Manuel estudia las lenguas modernas (el frances y el inglés).   4. en dos restaurantes diferentes   5. entre las cuatro y las cinco; después de las seis   6. el Colegio Simón Bolívar

Ex. I: pair work

//-/-/-/-/-/-/-/-/-/-/-//
Learning Strategy:

Listening for details

Después de escuchar

1. ¿Qué quiere saber el tío Pedro?
2. ¿Van a la escuela juntos Juan Manuel y Cecilia?
3. ¿Qué estudia Juan Manuel?
4. ¿Dónde almuerzan los dos?
5. ¿A qué hora regresa Juan Manuel a casa? ¿y Cecilia?
6. ¿Cómo se llama la escuela?

//-/-/-/-/-/-/-/-/-/-/-//
Learning Strategy:

Reading for cultural information

COMENTARIOS
CULTURALES

▪ *La cortesía*

The use of direct commands is usually avoided in Spanish except in specific instances when the speaker wishes to be quite firm, express a degree of anger or impatience, or is in an "ordering about" or agitated frame of mind. Gentler, more indirect ways of getting people to do things are preferred by most Spanish-speaking people in everyday social situations. For example, **¿Quiere abrir la puerta?** or **¿No me abre la puerta?** are used as kinder alternatives to a direct **Abra la puerta,** even if this affirmative command is used with **por favor.**

In other words, basic courtesy is an important characteristic of the Spanish language as most people around the world speak it. They don't think it is overly polite or "flowery" to use the higher frequency expressions that convey wishes instead of using command forms. In fact, to some Spanish speakers who do not know the English language well, the normal and acceptably frequent use of commands in English often seems brusque and even rude.

¡Aquí te toca a ti!

1. ¿Y tú? With a partner, ask and answer the questions on page 223 about your school routine.

222

1. ¿A qué hora sales de casa por la mañana?
2. ¿Tu colegio está lejos de tu casa?
3. ¿Cómo vas a la escuela?
4. ¿A qué hora comienzan las clases?
5. ¿Hasta qué hora tienes clases por la mañana?
6. ¿Cuánto tiempo tienes para comer?
7. ¿Dónde almuerzas?
8. ¿A qué hora vuelven a comenzar tus clases por la tarde?
9. ¿A qué hora sales de la escuela?
10. ¿A qué hora regresas de costumbre a casa?

Learning Strategy:

Requesting and giving personal information

¡Adelante!

EJERCICIO ORAL

J. ¿Tú, no?   Identify five things in Activity D on page 219 that you do *not* do. Then question your classmates until, *for each activity*, you find at least two other people who do not do it either. In order to report back to the class, create a chart of your findings. Follow the model.

Cooperative Learning

Learning Strategies:

Taking notes in a chart, interviewing

Modelo:

NO	Yo	Mi amigo(a)	Mi amigo(a)
1. lavarse el pelo todos los días	X	*Carmen*	*Jaime*
2. maquillarse	X	*Juan*	*Carlos*
3.	X		
4.	X		
5.	X		

EJERICIO ESCRITO

K. Por la tarde...   Write six to eight sentences describing what you normally do in the afternoon. Don't forget to include weekends as well. Make a calendar of the week to illustrate your afternoon activities.

Learning Strategy:

Taking notes on a calendar

223

More-prepared students, Ex. I: Have more-prepared students interview two others and report back, comparing and contrasting their days. You may also want to have them write their findings in a paragraph.

Ex. J: groups of four or more

More-prepared students, Ex. J: Ask the more-prepared students to tell why at least two classmates don't do these activities. For example, **María no se lava el pelo todos los días porque no tiene tiempo en la mañana.**

Ex. K: writing

Presentation: Una noche en la casa...

After the students read the paragraphs, have all but one close their books. This student should read Marilú's words, stopping after each main idea while you question other students to see if their experiences are similar or different, e.g., **¿Hasta qué hora duran sus clases? ¿Tomas el autobús?**

TERCERA ETAPA

Preparación

》》 **W**hat do you do in the evening during the week? on weekends?

》》 **W**hat time do you go to bed when you have school the next day?

》》 **W**hat do you like to do on Sunday evenings?

/-/-/-/-/-/-/-/-/-/-/-//
Learning Strategy:
Previewing

Una noche en la casa de Marilú Méndez

Normalmente mis clases duran hasta las 5:00. Entonces regreso a mi casa. Vivo bastante lejos del colegio. Por eso tomo el autobús. El autobús hace el viaje en 40 minutos, más o menos.

Ya en casa, hago mi tarea para el día siguiente. En mi casa cenamos a eso de las 7:45. Mi madre se encarga de preparar las comidas. Después de la cena, yo quito la mesa y lavo los platos. Después hay más tarea que hacer y tengo que ocuparme de los animales —tengo un gato y un perro. Por lo general, me acuesto a las 10:30. Es un poco aburrido, pero nadie tiene la culpa. ¡Siempre hay tanto que hacer!

Por eso prefiero el fin de semana. Los sábados por la noche voy al centro con mis amigos. Vamos al cine o vamos a bailar. Los domingos por la noche casi siempre miro la televisión porque generalmente hay buenas películas esa noche.

bastante: rather, pretty / *Ya en casa:* Once I'm home / *a eso de:* at about, around / *se encarga de:* she's in charge of / *quito la mesa:* I clear the table / *ocuparme de:* to take care of / *tiene la culpa:* is to blame

224

Etapa Support Materials

Critical Thinking masters: Chapter 7, tercera etapa, activity J
Workbook: pp. 159–163
Transparency: #31
Teacher Tape 🎧

Quiz: Testing Program, p. 114
Chapter Test: Testing Program, p. 117

Support material, Una noche en la casa... :
Transparency #31

¡Aquí te toca a ti!

A. ¿Dónde está Marilú? ¿Qué hace ella?
On the basis of what you have read on page 224, indicate for each day and time where Marilú probably is and what she is doing. Follow the model.

> **Modelo:** martes a las 15:00
> *Marilú está en la escuela. Está en clase.*

1. martes a las 18:15
2. miércoles a las 20:00
3. jueves a las 21:00
4. viernes a las 23:00
5. sábado a las 21:00
6. domingo a las 21:00

Learning Strategies:
Reading for information, answering questions

B. Una entrevista
Radio Futuro quiere entrevistarte *(interview you)* sobre tu rutina diaria. Contesta las siguientes preguntas.

1. ¿Generalmente, hasta qué hora duran tus clases?
2. ¿Vives cerca del colegio?
3. ¿Cuánto tiempo tarda para regresar a la casa?
4. ¿Qué haces, ya en casa?
5. ¿A qué hora cenan ustedes en tu casa?
6. ¿Quién prepara la comida? ¿Quién quita la mesa? ¿Quién lava los platos?
7. ¿Qué haces los fines de semana?
8. ¿Qué haces los domingos por la noche?

Learning Strategy:
Answering questions based on personal information

Repaso

C. Durante las vacaciones...
During vacations, people want to get away from their daily routines. Use the **Uds.** command form of the verbs suggested to indicate to your friends what they should or should not do when they are on vacation. Follow the model.

> **Modelo:** *Durante las vacaciones acuéstense tarde y no se levanten temprano.*

Possible verbs: acostarse / despertarse / dormirse / divertirse / levantarse / ducharse / lavarse / vestirse / desayunarse / darse prisa / comer / descansar / estudiar / bailar / dormir

225

Reteaching, Ex. A: Briefly review the 24-hour clock. You may want to use the following format: **Si el reloj de la hora oficial dice que son las 23 horas, ¿qué hora es? ¿Si son las 16 horas?**

Ex. A: writing

Suggestion, Ex. A: Have students convert official time to conversational time as they give their answers.

Answers, Ex. A: 1. Marilú está en casa. Hace la tarea. 2. Marilú está en casa. Cena. 3. Marilú está en casa. Hace la tarea. 4. Duerme. No estoy seguro(a). 5. Marilú va al centro. Va al cine. 6. Marilú está en casa. Mira la televisión.

Ex. B: pair work

Cooperative Learning

Three-Step Interview

Learning Strategies: Interviewing, answering questions based on personal information, selecting and reporting information

Critical Thinking Strategies: Making associations, expressing preferences

- Put students into teams of four and have each team divide into pairs.
- Explain that each pair will interview each other, with one person portraying the Spanish radio interviewer and the other a famous young actor.
- Have the students interview each other, asking all of the questions in the exercise.
- Have them reverse roles.
- Have the pairs share with their teams the most interesting or unusual fact they learned from their partner and one fact that they share in common.
- Finally, have each group of four select the most unusual fact reported by one of the group members to report to the class.

Ex. C: writing

More-prepared students, Ex. C: Ask more-prepared students to add four commands to their lists.

Answers, Ex. C: ¡Acuéstense tarde! ¡No se despierten temprano! Duérmanse inmediatamente! ¡Diviértanse bien! ¡No se levanten temprano! ¡Dúchense, lávense, no se vistan como de costumbre! ¡Desayúnense tarde! ¡No se den prisa! ¡(No) Coman demasiado! ¡Descansen! ¡No estudien! ¡Bailen! ¡(No) Duerman mucho!

ESTRUCTURA

Tú command form of reflexive verbs

¡Levántate, Marisa! Ya es tarde.	*Get up*, Marisa! It's late.
¡Muévete, por favor!	*Move (yourself)*, please!
¡No **te duermas** otra vez!	Don't *fall asleep* again!
¡No **te acuestes** tan tarde mañana!	Don't *go to bed* so late tomorrow!

The affirmative **tú** command form of most reflexive and nonreflexive verbs, whether they are **-ar, -er,** or **-ir** verbs, is exactly the same as the third person singular of the present indicative tense.

él, ella **habla**	**¡Habla** (tú)!	*Speak!*
él, ella **come**	**¡Come** (tú)!	*Eat!*
él, ella **escribe**	**¡Escribe** (tú)!	*Write!*

When the verb is reflexive, the familiar reflexive pronoun **te** and an accent are added to the command form.

levanta (tú)	¡Levánt**ate** (tú)!	*Get up!*
duerme (tú)	¡Duérm**ete** (tú)!	*Go to sleep!*

The negative **tú** command form of most reflexive and nonreflexive verbs is the same as the **Ud.** command form, except that an **-s** is added to it and **no** goes before the word.

habl**e** Ud.   **no** habl**es** (tú)   com**a** Ud.   **no** com**as** (tú)   escrib**a** Ud.   **no** escrib**as** (tú)

When the verb is reflexive, the reflexive pronoun **te** is used *before* the verb. Notice that **no** is placed *before* the reflexive pronoun.

no levantes   **no te** levantes (tú)   no duermas   **no te** duermas (tú)

Aquí practicamos

D. Give the affirmative **tú** command form of the following verbs.

 Modelo: lavarse
¡Lávate!

1. levantarse	**4.** quedarse	**7.** maquillarse
2. ducharse	**5.** acostarse	**8.** dormirse
3. vestirse	**6.** moverse	

226

¡Aquí te toca a ti!

A. ¿Dónde está Marilú? ¿Qué hace ella?
On the basis of what you have read on page 224, indicate for each day and time where Marilú probably is and what she is doing. Follow the model.

 Modelo: martes a las 15:00
Marilú está en la escuela. Está en clase.

1. martes a las 18:15	4. viernes a las 23:00
2. miércoles a las 20:00	5. sábado a las 21:00
3. jueves a las 21:00	6. domingo a las 21:00

Learning Strategies:

Reading for information, answering questions

B. Una entrevista
Radio Futuro quiere entrevistarte *(interview you)* sobre tu rutina diaria. Contesta las siguientes preguntas.

1. ¿Generalmente, hasta qué hora duran tus clases?
2. ¿Vives cerca del colegio?
3. ¿Cuánto tiempo tarda para regresar a la casa?
4. ¿Qué haces, ya en casa?
5. ¿A qué hora cenan ustedes en tu casa?
6. ¿Quién prepara la comida? ¿Quién quita la mesa? ¿Quién lava los platos?
7. ¿Qué haces los fines de semana?
8. ¿Qué haces los domingos por la noche?

Learning Strategy:

Answering questions based on personal information

Repaso

C. Durante las vacaciones...
During vacations, people want to get away from their daily routines. Use the **Uds.** command form of the verbs suggested to indicate to your friends what they should or should not do when they are on vacation. Follow the model.

 Modelo: *Durante las vacaciones acuéstense tarde y no se levanten tarde.*
temprano.

Possible verbs: acostarse / despertarse / dormirse / divertirse / levantarse / ducharse / lavarse / vestirse / desayunarse / darse prisa / comer / descansar / estudiar / bailar / dormir

Presentation: Estructura

(1) Have students stand up and sit down on command: **¡Levántense! ¡Siéntense!** Then vary commands: **¡Levántate, Jorge! ¡Siéntate, Betsy! ¡No te sientes, Helen!**
(2) Have students give each other commands.
(3) Ask students to generate the **ustedes** forms for different verbs, based on the preceding practice.
(4) Then expand to the use of the **tú** forms.

Ex. D: writing

Answers, Ex. D: 1. ¡Levántate! 2. ¡Dúchate! 3. ¡Vístete! 4. ¡Quédate! 5. ¡Acuéstate! 6. ¡Muévete! 7. ¡Maquíllate! 8. ¡Duérmete!

ESTRUCTURA

Tú command form of reflexive verbs

¡Levántate, Marisa! Ya es tarde.	*Get up*, Marisa! It's late.
¡Muévete, por favor!	*Move (yourself)*, please!

¡No **te duermas** otra vez!	Don't *fall asleep* again!
¡No **te acuestes** tan tarde mañana!	Don't *go to bed* so late tomorrow!

The affirmative **tú** command form of most reflexive and nonreflexive verbs, whether they are **-ar, -er,** or **-ir** verbs, is exactly the same as the third person singular of the present indicative tense.

él, ella **habla**	**¡Habla** (tú)!	*Speak!*
él, ella **come**	**¡Come** (tú)!	*Eat!*
él, ella **escribe**	**¡Escribe** (tú)!	*Write!*

When the verb is reflexive, the familiar reflexive pronoun **te** and an accent are added to the command form.

levanta (tú)	**¡Levántate** (tú)! *Get up!*
duerme (tú)	**¡Duérmete** (tú)! *Go to sleep!*

The negative **tú** command form of most reflexive and nonreflexive verbs is the same as the **Ud.** command form, except that an **-s** is added to it and **no** goes before the word.

hable Ud.   **no** habl**es** (tú)   coma Ud.   **no** com**as** (tú)   escriba Ud.   **no** escrib**as** (tú)

When the verb is reflexive, the reflexive pronoun **te** is used *before* the verb. Notice that **no** is placed *before* the reflexive pronoun.

no levantes   **no te** levantes (tú)   no duermas   **no te** duermas (tú)

Aquí practicamos

D. Give the affirmative **tú** command form of the following verbs.

 Modelo: lavarse
¡Lávate!

1. levantarse	**4.** quedarse	**7.** maquillarse
2. ducharse	**5.** acostarse	**8.** dormirse
3. vestirse	**6.** moverse	

226

E. Give the negative **tú** command form of the following verbs.

> *Modelo:* afeitarse
> *¡No te afeites!*

1. peinarse
2. mirarse
3. moverse
4. desayunarse
5. dormirse
6. darse prisa
7. sentarse
8. acostarse

F. *Díle a ella* (Tell her)   First tell your friend Ana María to do each of the activities suggested. Then change your mind and go through the list again, telling her *not* to do them. Follow the model.

> *Modelo:* levantarse
> *¡Ana María, levántate!*
> *¡Ana María, no te levantes!*

1. despertarse
2. darse prisa
3. cepillarse los dientes
4. acostarse
5. lavarse el pelo
6. divertirse
7. maquillarse
8. peinarse

G. *Díles a ellos* (Tell them)   Tell the small children you are taking care of to do each of the activities suggested. Then go through the list again, telling them *not* to do those things.

> *Modelo:* levantarse
> *¡Levántense!*
> *¡No se levanten!*

1. cepillarse los dientes
2. darse prisa
3. acostarse
4. peinarse
5. dormirse
6. lavarse las manos
7. ducharse
8. despertarse

H. *Diálogos para completar*   Complete each mini-conversation with the affirmative or negative command of one of the following: **levantarse, acostarse, darse prisa, lavarse, vestirse, despertarse.**

> *Modelo:* —¡Andrés! ¡Andrés! *¡Despiértate!*
> —¿Cómo? ¿Qué pasa?
> —Tienes que levantarte para ir a la escuela.

1. —¿Qué hora es, Francisco?
   —Son las 9:55, papá.
   —¿Cómo? ¿Las 9:55? ¿Por qué estás todavía en la cama? ¡_____!

2. —¡Maricarmen! ¡Maricarmen!
   —¿Sí, mamá?
   —Vamos a cenar, mi hija. _____ las manos y siéntate.
   —Sí, mamá.

//.//.//.//.//.//.//.//.//.//

Learning Strategies:

Reading for main ideas, selecting appropriate meaning from context

Critical Thinking Strategy:

Making associations

227

3. —¡Carlos! ¡Ya son las 7:30!
   —¿Qué pasa, mamá?
   —¡La película comienza dentro de media hora! ¡_____!

4. —¡Luis! ¡Anita! ¿Qué hacen ustedes?
   —Ehhh, una cosa, mamá.
   —Ya es medianoche. ¡_____, hijos!
   —Un momento más, mamá.

Aquí escuchamos:
"La noche con Juan Manuel y Cecilia"

Antes de escuchar

The parents of Juan Manuel and Cecilia are on a trip. Their aunt
and uncle are spending the weekend with them at their house.
When Juan Manuel and Cecilia arrive home from school, their
Aunt Margarita is waiting for them. What are some of the household tasks you do in the afternoon and evening at your house?
Look at the following questions in preparation for listening to
their conversation.

///-///-///-///-///-///
Learning Strategy:
Listening for details

Después de escuchar

1. ¿Qué trabajo va a hacer Juan
   Manuel?
2. ¿Quién va a preparar la
   comida?
3. ¿A qué hora comen Juan
   Manuel y Cecilia?
4. ¿Quién dice que va a quitar la
   mesa?
5. Como ya terminó su tarea,
   ¿qué quiere hacer Juan
   Manuel para divertirse?
6. ¿A qué hora se acuesta Juan
   Manuel? ¿y Cecilia?

///-///-///-///-///-///
Learning Strategy:
*Requesting and giving
personal information*

¡Aquí te toca a ti!

1. ¿Y tú? Alternando con otro(a) estudiante, hagan y contesten las preguntas abajo y en la página 229 sobre su rutina en casa.

   1. ¿A qué hora regresas del colegio?

2. ¿Cuándo haces tu tarea generalmente?
3. ¿Ayudas *(Do you help)* con los quehaceres *(chores)* de la casa?
4. ¿Quién se encarga de lavar la ropa en tu casa?
5. ¿Quién lava los platos en tu casa?

EJERCICIO ORAL

J. Encuentra a alguien que... (Find someone who . . .) Make a chart like the following one. In the second column (1) fill in the information about how you will ask certain questions of your classmates. (2) Then add the appropriate information about yourself in the third column. (3) When your teacher gives the signal, circulate around the classroom asking questions of your classmates to find out information about their routine and home life. (4) When you find a student with an answer that matches one of your own, enter the person's name in the appropriate cell in the last column. *Note:* you cannot use the same person's name more than once.

¿Qué tenemos en común?			
	La pregunta que voy a hacer en español	Mi información	Nombre de amigo(a) con quien tengo algo en común
time you get home from school			
time you do your homework			
time your family has dinner			
which household chores you do			

EJERCICIO ESCRITO

K. Un día típico Write a description of a typical day for you. First tell what you usually do on a weekday. Then describe what you do on weekends as well.

229

Chapter Culminating Activity

writing

Conduct a "protocol recall" with the class in which you present a narration of your own typical day, week, teaching activities and schedule, and other routine information, using the 24-hour clock. Before you start, you may review vocabulary by listing three categories on the board: **por la mañana, por la tarde, por la noche.** Review telling time on the 24-hour clock as well. While you talk, have students take brief notes, but do not slow down or pause for them during your narration.

groups of four or more
After you finish, have students form groups of four or five in which to prepare a timetable of your typical day using the 24-hour clock and listing (in Spanish) your daily routine as you have described it.

Have each group post their timetable on the board so that they can check their accuracy against the timetables of other groups.

Cooperative Learning

Learning Strategies: Active listening, taking notes, negotiating, completing a chart

Critical Thinking Strategy: Sequencing

Suggestion, Vocabulario:
Have students review the vocabulary list, then repeat in Spanish the Corners activity that you did in English at the beginning of the chapter (p. T209). You may also want to play vocabulary "charades" or "Pictionary".

Vocabulario

Para charlar

Para hablar de las actividades de todos los días

acostarse (ue)	divertirse (ie, i)	ponerse
afeitarse	dormirse (ue, u)	prepararse
bañarse	ducharse	quedarse en cama
cepillarse el pelo, los dientes	lavarse (las manos, el pelo, los dientes)	sentarse (ie) servirse (i, i)
darse prisa	levantarse	tardarse
desayunarse	maquillarse	vestirse (i, i)
despertarse (ie)	peinarse	

Temas y contextos

Los quehaceres de la casa

encargarse de	lavar la ropa	poner la mesa
lavar los platos	ocuparse de	quitar la mesa

Vocabulario general

Sustantivos	Verbos		
la culpa	comenzar (ie)	irse	regresar
un ejemplo	charlar	llamarse	reunirse
el latín	durar	mirarse	
una tarea	encargarse de	moverse (ue)	

Adjetivos	Adverbios	Preposiciones	Otras palabras y expresiones
caliente	bastante	en frente de	a eso de
conveniente	casi		un buen rato
mismo(a)	directamente		de nuevo
	sólo		¡Dense prisa!
	ya		los espera
			ya en casa

Lectura CULTURAL

ESPAÑA JOVEN

Antes de leer

1. Look at the photo and the title to help you decide what this reading is about.
2. What do you think young teenagers do in Spain in their spare time?
3. What sorts of things do you think they like?
4. How do you think they like to dress in general?
5. Do you think their interests are fairly similar to or very different from yours?

Learning Strategy:
Previewing

231

Lectura cultural

Guía para la lectura

A. Look at the five headings to determine what the content of each section will be. What are they?

B. What sorts of information does the introduction suggest will be covered in the reading?

C. Find out what Spanish young people do in their free time on weekdays and weekends.

D. According to the next paragraph, what do they spend their money on?

E. Read the fourth paragraph and tell what kinds of clothes they wear. What do you think a **pendiente en la oreja** means?

F. Read the last paragraph and point out a problem that they worry about.

España joven

oy hay más de tres millones de españoles entre los doce y los dieciséis años de edad. ¿Cómo son estos jóvenes? ¿Qué hacen normalmente? ¿Qué les interesa? ¿Qué les preocupa? La siguiente información viene de entrevistas que se hicieron con varios grupos de estos jóvenes que representan el futuro de España.

Vida diaria

Durante la semana los adolescentes españoles casi no salen. Generalmente dividen su tiempo entre la casa y el colegio. Cuando están en casa, además de estudiar, pasan mucho tiempo hablando por teléfono y escuchando música. Pero los fines de semana nadie se queda en casa. Normalmente todos salen con sus amigos, sobre todo a bailar. A veces van a comer en grupo en un restaurante o café.

Sus gustos

Los jóvenes gastan su dinero en lo que más les apasiona: la música, la ropa de marca y los videojuegos que, junto con el "walkman", son sus juguetes favoritos. Van bastante al cine y ven todo tipo de películas.

La ropa

A los chicos les gusta llevar vaqueros y un pendiente en la oreja. Las chicas también llevan vaqueros durante la semana, pero para ir a la discoteca prefieren las faldas cortas o los vestidos largos.

Cómo ven el futuro

A muchos adolescentes les preocupa la crisis económica en su país. Saben que hay mucha gente sin trabajo en España y temen que la situación vaya a afectar su futuro. Muchos opinan que los ecologistas son las únicas personas que se preocupan por salvar el planeta.

Spain

232

¿QUÉ HACES ESTE FIN DE SEMANA?

Buenos Aires es una ciudad importante en la costa atlántica de Argentina. Es la capital, con más de diez millones de habitantes.

Objetives:

>>> **I**ssuing invitations for leisure-time activities
>>> **O**rganizing and coordinating plans for various activities

Strategies:

>>> **R**eading for cultural information
>>> **N**egotiating
>>> **D**etermining preferences

Chapter Objectives

Functions: Issuing invitations for leisure-time activities; organizing and coordinating plans for various activities

Context: Reading schedules and listings for movies, plays, and television; party invitations

Accuracy: Direct object pronouns; position of double object pounouns; the immediate future with reflexive verbs

Cultural Context

Buenos Aires is considered the second largest city in the Southern Hemisphere and among the twelve largest cities in the world. Almost the entire city has been rebuilt since the beginning of the twentieth century, and very few old buildings remain. Buenos Aires's many theaters host world-class theatrical and musical performances. The city's abundant nightlife, cultural events, flourishing publishing businesses, and arts scene have earned it the nickname "the Paris of South America."

233

Video/Laserdisc

Chapter 8 Video Program and Video Guide

Presentation: La revista Cromos

Begin with a prereading exercise. Have students talk about where to look for information about movies and what kinds of information newspaper listings provide. Have them bring in an example. Ask them what is different about the English and Spanish listings (in Spanish the times are given in the 24-hour clock). Then have them look at the **Cromos** listings here and on page 235.

PRIMERA ETAPA

Preparación

›› **W**hat plans do you have for the weekend?

›› **D**o you read a particular magazine or a newspaper entertainment section to decide what you are going to do on weekends?

›› **W**hat kind of information does the newspaper give you about possible activities for the weekend?

/-/-/-/-/-/-/-/-/-/-/

Learning Strategies:

Previewing, brainstorming

La revista Cromos

Cromos es una revista popular en Bogotá, Colombia, que se vende cada semana en los quioscos de periódicos. Contiene artículos sobre varios temas, entrevistas con personas interesantes y también información sobre el teatro, el cine y la televisión, entre otras cosas.

TEATRO

El *Teatro Esquina Latina* comienza a partir del 11 de junio, todos los domingos y lunes festivos del resto del año, la programación para niños. Teatros, títeres y marionetas con los grupos más representativos de la región llevan a los niños realizaciones artísticas de alta calidad.

El *Teatro Santa Fe* presenta "*Yerma*" con Waldo Urrego y Natalia Giraldo en los papeles de los protagonistas. Después de mucho éxito esta temporada, la inmortal obra de Federico García Lorca se despide en dos semanas de los bogotanos para visitar otras ciudades del país. "*Yerma*", a cargo del grupo Teatral Actores de Colombia y bajo la dirección de Jaime Arturo Gómez. Calle 57 No. 17-13, Tel. 255 05 92.

En el *Auditorio Crisanto Luque,* durante los próximos días, se estará presentando la obra *"Outside Okey"* del grupo Teatro Quimera, dirigida por Carlos Alberto Sánchez. La obra tiene como tema central las relaciones entre el fútbol, la música, el teatro y la filosofía. Se presentará en escena hasta el 17 de junio. Calle 20 No. 9-45.

TELEVISIÓN

viernes 9

Quinceañera (15:00, cadena uno). Beatriz, a causa de un accidente, pierde a su hijo. Por eso entran en discusiones amigos y parientes.

The Monsters (16:30, cadena uno). Lily descubre que la cuenta bancaria de Herman no tiene dinero y decide trabajar en un salón de té para ayudar a la familia.

La naturaleza de las cosas (18:30, cadena tres). El oso polar, estudios científicos sobre su vida y campañas para salvar este animal de la extinción.

234

Etapa Support Materials

Workbook: pp. 165–169
Listening Activity masters: p. 72
Transparency: #32
Teacher Tape 🎧

Tapescript: p. 101
Quiz: **Testing Program, p. 122**

Support material, **La revista Cromos:**
Transparency #32

TELEVISIÓN

sábado 10

El túnel (20:00, cadena uno). Película basada en la novela del escritor argentino Ernesto Sábato. Un pintor se obsesiona con una tímida mujer casada.

La bella y la bestia (20:30, cadena dos). Muere su padre y Catherine se va "abajo" a vivir con Vincent para siempre.

Cómo casarse con un millonario (22:00, cadena tres). Película. Tres chi-

cas deciden, cada una, "pescar" un millonario. Actúan las cómicas y guapas Marilyn Monroe, Lauren Bacall y Betty Grable.

domingo 11

El espíritu de Asia (18:30, cadena tres). Mundo de sombras: El Ganges, sagrada fuente de la primera religión del mundo, el hinduísmo.

Matar o morir (19:30, cadena uno). Vicente Fernández en una película de pasiones y emoción.

Crónica de una muerte anunciada (21:45, cadena dos). Película basada en la novela de Gabriel García Márquez, narra la triste historia de un pequeño pueblo colombiano y su reacción al crimen de Santiago Nassar.

¡Aquí te toca a ti!

A. *¡Dínos!* (Tell us!)   Contesta las preguntas sobre *Cromos* en inglés.

1. How many movies are being shown on television over the weekend? On which network(s) *(cadena)* are they presented? What time(s) are they on?
2. Which documentary programs are listed? What are they about? Which one seems to be the most serious?
3. What other programs are mentioned in these listings? What kind are they?
4. Which theater listing mentions what the play is about? Which theater seems to have booked the most successful show? How do you know this?
5. If you had to pick just one of these productions to see, which one would you choose? Why?

> **Learning Strategies:**
> Reading for details, reading for cultural information, supporting an opinion
>
> **Critical Thinking Strategy:**
> Determining preferences

Pronunciación: *The vowel combination ei*

The combination **ei** in Spanish is pronounced in one single syllable, similar to the *a* in the English word *date*. Note that in some words, such as **rey** and **mamey**, this sound is spelled **ey**.

Práctica

B. Lee las siguientes palabras en voz alta, pronunciando con cuidado la combinación *ei*.

1. peine
2. veinte
3. reina
4. aceite
5. ley
6. buey
7. afeitar
8. vendéis

235

Ex. A: ✎ writing

More-prepared students, Ex. A: Have more-prepared students give or write their responses in Spanish, even if only a word or phrase.

Less-prepared students, Ex. A: Encourage less-prepared students to match the number of each question to the portion of the text containing the appropriate information.

Answers, Ex. A: 1. 4: uno, 8:00 P.M.; tres, 10:00 P.M., uno, 7:30 P.M.; dos, 9:45 P.M.   2. *La naturaleza de las cosas* (polar bear); *El espíritu de Asia* (Hinduism); (Students should support their opinions.)   3. *Quinceañera* (soap opera); *The Monsters* (comedy); *La bella y la bestia* (suspense / romance)   4. **Auditorio Crisanto Luque; Teatro Santa Fe;** mentions its success 5. (open-ended question to elicit personal opinions)

Follow-up, Ex. A: Bring in a guide from another Spanish-speaking country or from a newspaper. Photocopy it for each student and then ask similar questions. This can be a written or oral assignment. Another alternative is to transform an English-speaking TV / leisure activity guide into Spanish, listing programs with a 24-hour clock, categorizing them (vocabulary expansion), creating new names for the programs, etc.

Presentation: Pronunciación

After students have repeated the words with the **ei** sound, ask them if they can think of any others, e.g., **treinta, peinar, reinar,** any other **-er vosotros** verb in the present tense, or any **-ir, -er,** or irregular verb using the preterite of **vosotros**.

Ex. C: pair work

writing

More-prepared students,
Ex. C: More-prepared students
can create an additional scenario
with an accompanying list of verbs.
Have pairs exchange scenarios and
make appropriate commands.

Less-prepared students,
Ex. C: Have less-prepared students scan the exercise to decide
which scenarios are formal (**Ud.**),
informal (**tú**), or plural (**Uds.**)
before beginning to work.

Answers, Ex. C: 1. ¡Estudia
hasta las diez de la noche!   2. ¡No
te acuestes tarde!   3. ¡Levántate
temprano!   4. ¡Desayúnate!
5. ¡Dúchate primero!   6. ¡Lávate
el pelo!   7. ¡Péinate!   8. ¡Vístete
elegantemente!   9. ¡Come antes
de ir al baile!   10. ¡No miren la
televisión!   11. ¡Cepíllense los
dientes!   12. ¡Acuéstense temprano!   13. ¡No se levanten
durante la noche!

/-/-/-/-/-/-/-/-/-/-/-/
Critical Thinking
Strategy:

Seeing cause-and-
effect relationships

Repaso

C. *Los consejos* (Advice)   In each of the following situations, advise the
person or people involved to do or not to do each of the actions mentioned. First, give advice to a friend who has a difficult exam tomorrow.

 acostarse temprano
¡Acuéstate temprano!

estudiar hasta las tres de la mañana
¡No estudies hasta las tres de la mañana!

1. estudiar hasta las diez de la noche
2. acostarse tarde
3. levantarse temprano
4. desayunarse

Now talk to a friend who is planning to go to a semiformal
dance.

5. ducharse primero
6. lavarse el pelo
7. peinarse
8. vestirse elegantemente
9. comer antes de ir al baile

Finally, talk to the *three* children for whom you are babysitting.

10. mirar la televisión
11. cepillarse los dientes
12. acostarse temprano
13. levantarse durante la noche

ESTRUCTURA

Direct object pronouns

—¿El policía mira **mi coche?**   Is the police officer looking at *my car?*
—Sí, el policía **lo** mira.   Yes, he's looking at *it.*

236

—¿María quiere **la cámara japonesa?**
—Sí, **la** quiere.

Does María want the *Japanese camera?*
Yes, she wants *it.*

—¿Ven **a los muchachos?**
—No, no **los** ven.

Do they see *the children?*
No, they don't see *them.*

—¿Prefiere José **novelas de aventura?**
—Sí, **las** prefiere.

Does José prefer *adventure novels?*
Yes, he prefers *them.*

A direct object is the person or thing that is directly affected by a verb; it tells whom or what is acted upon. In the Spanish sentences you just read, **mi coche, la cámara japonesa, los muchachos,** and **novelas de aventura** are all direct objects.

Whenever possible, speakers take shortcuts by using pronouns. Direct objects can be replaced by direct object pronouns. The pronouns agree with the direct object they stand for in both number (singular and plural) and gender (masculine and feminine).

masculine singular: lo
El niño no ve **mi cuaderno.**
El niño no **lo** ve.

The child doesn't see *my notebook.*
The child doesn't see *it.*

feminine singular: la
Escuchamos **música clásica.**
La escuchamos.

We listen to *classical music.*
We listen to *it.*

masculine plural: los
Despierto **a mis hermanos.**
Los despierto.

I wake *my brothers.*
I wake *them.*

feminine plural: las
No compramos **las entradas.**
No **las** compramos.

We don't buy *the tickets.*
We don't buy *them.*

Aquí practicamos

D. *En pocas palabras*   Shorten each sentence on page 238 by replacing the direct object noun or noun phrase with the corresponding direct object pronoun. Follow the model.

 Modelo: Ruth llama a Francisco por teléfono.
Ruth lo llama por teléfono.

237

Begin by establishing the idea of substitution. **¿Tienes el libro? Sí, lo tengo.** Then add the idea of people as well as things. **¿Ves a José? Sí, lo veo.**

To continue practice, give each student something in the classroom, trying to keep the vocabulary familiar. Ask: **¿Quién tiene mi cuaderno? (Lo tengo.) Roberto, ¿tienes mi bandera? (No, no la tengo. Juan la tiene.)** After you ask a few questions, have students begin asking the questions.

Preparation, Ex. D: Before doing Ex. D, give a few more examples where you replace a whole phrase with one pronoun, e.g., **Compré una falda bonita con rayas. La compré.** Ask students what happened to the rest of the words. Have them do a similar example in English to be sure they understand the substitution principle.

Ex. D: writing

1. Hago la tarea ahora.
2. Los estudiantes no leen el libro.
3. No como carne.
4. Compramos los cuadernos en la librería.
5. Invitan a las muchachas.
6. Dan una película después de la clase.

Learning Strategy:

Reporting based on personal information

E. ¿Sí o no? You and a classmate take turns asking each other the following questions. Answer them briefly and use a direct object pronoun for the noun or phrase provided. Follow the model.

Modelo: ¿Hablas alemán?
Sí, lo hablo.   o: *No, no lo hablo.*

1. ¿Miras la televisión por la noche?
2. ¿Tomas el autobús a la escuela?
3. ¿Tus profesores dan mucha tarea?
4. ¿Tienes tiempo de practicar deportes?
5. ¿Quién prepara la comida en tu casa?
6. ¿Lees el periódico cuando te desayunas?

Nota gramatical

Position of direct object pronouns

¿El edificio? **Lo** conozco.	The building? I'm familiar with *it*.
¿El número? Es importante saber**lo.**	The number? It's important to know *it*.
¿Las cartas? Puedes poner**las** allí.	The letters? You can put *them* there.
¿Los libros? **Los** quiero comprar ahora.	The books? I want to buy *them* now.

238

The direct object pronoun is placed immediately *in front of* the conjugated verb.

Leo **la revista.**	I read *the magazine.*
La leo.	I read *it.*

When used with an infinitive, the direct object pronoun is *attached* to it.

Es posible vender **el coche.**	It's possible to sell *the car.*
Es posible vender**lo.**	It's possible to sell *it.*

When a conjugated verb and an infinitive are used together, the direct object pronoun can be placed *either* in front of the conjugated verb or it may be attached to the end of the infinitive. Attaching the pronoun to the infinitive is probably the more common practice.

Prefiero comprar **la cámara.**	I prefer to buy *the camera.*
La prefiero comprar.	I prefer to buy *it.*
Prefiero comprar**la.**	

F. *¡Ya lo hice!*   When your mother tells you to do something, you indicate that you have already done it. Follow the model.

Modelo: ¡Lava los platos!
            ¡Ya los lavé!

1. ¡Compra el pan!
2. ¡Prepara el desayuno!
3. ¡Come tus vegetales!
4. ¡Quita la mesa!
5. ¡Lava el coche!
6. ¡Termina tu tarea!
7. ¡Escucha mi nuevo disco compacto!
8. ¡Busca mis llaves!

G. *No quiero hacerlo… no voy a hacerlo…*   You are in a particularly bad mood one evening. Whenever you are asked if you are going to do what you normally do, you indicate that you don't want to do it and, moreover, you are not going to do it. Follow the model.

Modelo: preparar la cena
            —¿Vas a preparar la cena esta noche?
            —No, no quiero prepararla esta noche.
            —Pero, vas a prepararla de todas maneras (anyway)*, ¿no?*
            —No quiero prepararla y no voy a prepararla.

1. lavar la ropa
2. ayudar a tu hermano
3. quitar la mesa
4. leer el libro
5. terminar tu tarea
6. mirar la televisión
7. escribir tu composición
8. lavar los platos

239

Answers, Ex. G: 1. ¿Vas a lavar la ropa esta noche? No, no quiero lavarla esta noche. / Pero, vas a lavarla de todas maneras, ¿no? / No quiero lavarla y no voy a lavarla.   2. ¿Vas a ayudar a tu hermano esta noche? / No, no quiero ayudarlo esta noche. / Pero, vas a ayudarlo de todas maneras, ¿no? / No quiero ayudarlo y no voy a ayudarlo.   3. ¿Vas a quitar la mesa esta noche? / No, no quiero quitarla esta noche. / Pero, vas a quitarla de todas maneras, ¿no? / No quiero quitarla y no voy a quitarla.   4. ¿Vas a leer el libro esta noche? / No, no quiero leerlo esta noche. / Pero, vas a leerlo de todas maneras, ¿no? / No quiero leerlo y no voy a leerlo.   5. ¿Vas a terminar tu tarea esta noche? / No, no quiero terminarla esta noche. / Pero, vas a terminarla de todas maneras, ¿no? No quiero terminarla y no voy a terminarla. 6. ¿Vas a mirar la televisión esta noche? / No, no quiero mirarla esta noche. / Pero, vas a mirarla de todas maneras, ¿no? / No quiero mirarla y no voy a mirarla. 7. ¿Vas a escribir tu composición esta noche? / No, no quiero escribirla esta noche. / Pero, vas a escribirla de todas maneras, ¿no? / No quiero escribirla y no voy a escribirla.   8. ¿Vas a lavar los platos esta noche? / No, no quiero lavarlos esta noche. / Pero, vas a lavarlos de todas maneras, ¿no? / No quiero lavarlos y no voy a lavarlos.

Reteaching, Ex. F: Briefly review preterite verb forms before students do Ex. F.

Answers, Ex. F: 1. ¡Ya lo compré!   2. ¡Ya lo preparé! 3. ¡Ya los comí!   4. ¡Ya la quité!   5. ¡Ya lo lavé!   6. ¡Ya la terminé!   7. ¡Ya lo escuché!   8. ¡Ya las busqué!

Ex. G: pair work

Suggestion, Ex. G: Call on different pairs of students to perform each of the responses with lots of expression.

Support material, Aquí escuchamos: Teacher Tape 🎧

Preparation: Aquí escuchamos

After students have previewed the materials, have them take out paper and pencil and make a chart with two headings at the top: **le gusta** and **no le gusta.** Down the left margin, list the boys names: **Juan Manuel, Mario, Enrique.** Have students jot down each boy's likes and dislikes as they listen to the tape two or three times. Create a master list on the board, having students volunteer the information as a check. Students may use this list to help them complete the comprehension questions. Create dictation practice, using all or parts of the dialogue, if you wish.

Pairs Check, Aquí escuchamos

Learning Strategies: Paraphrasing, peer tutoring

- Have students form pairs with students of their choice. (In this way, they may continue to work with each other outside of class.)
- Tell students to listen to the segment together, without stopping the tape, to get the general idea.
- Then have them listen to the tape again for the main ideas.
- Have them paraphrase for each other in English what they think the main ideas of the passage are. (Stress that they are not to translate, but to use what they know, combined with their knowledge of cognates, to understand generally what is being said.)
- Once they have the general idea, give them some general questions focusing on the main idea to discuss and agree upon with each other. Then they can listen for details together.
- Call on students at random to answer your questions.

//-//-//-//-//-//-//-//
Learning Strategy:
Previewing

//-//-//-//-//-//-//-//
Learning Strategy:
Listening for details

//-//-//-//-//-//-//-//
Learning Strategy:
Reading for cultural information

240

Aquí escuchamos:
"¡Vamos a ver la nueva película!"

Antes de escuchar

Juan Manuel and Cecilia work hard during the week, so they like to have a good time on weekends. Juan Manuel likes to go to the movies. Look at the following questions before you listen to the conversation he has with his friends Mario and Enrique.

Después de escuchar

1. ¿Cuántas personas hablan aquí?
2. ¿Cuál es el problema que tienen?
3. ¿Qué ideas tienen para divertirse?
4. ¿Qué dice Mario de las películas de horror?
5. ¿A qué hora deciden reunirse los amigos?
6. ¿Dónde van a reunirse?

COMENTARIOS
CULTURALES

■ *El cine*

Going to the movies is a very popular activity for people of all ages and backgrounds in Spanish-speaking countries. Movie theaters abound in the cities and towns and show a variety of films, particularly those that are produced in the U.S. These movies are generally dubbed in Spanish. Newspapers always carry several pages of movie advertisements. In some countries, like Mexico, box-office prices are kept within a certain range by the government so that practically anyone can afford to buy a ticket. Many times the ticket lines wind around the block!

Answers, Aquí escuchamos: 1. tres   2. no pueden decidir qué hacer   3. dar un paseo, alquilar un vídeo, ver una película   4. las odia   5. a las 8:30   6. en frente del Cine Variedades

¡Aquí te toca a ti!

H. ¿Qué van a ver?   Using the listings from *Cromos* on pages 234–235, recommend shows for your friends. (1) First, they will tell you what kind of programs, films, or plays they like. (2) Respond with a suggestion. Your friends will then ask you questions about (3) what time a program is on television, (4) where a play is being presented, and (5) which country the show represents. Suggested types of shows: **película (de aventuras, de ciencia-ficción, de terror, policíaca** *[police story]***), comedia, drama psicológico, obra teatral, programa documental, telenovela,** etc.

Modelo: películas cómicas
—*A mí me gustan las películas cómicas.*
—*Debes ver "Cómo casarse con un millonario".*
—*¿A qué hora la dan* (are they showing it)?
—*A las 10:00 de la noche en el canal tres.*
—*¿Es una película mexicana?*
—*No, es una película norteamericana.*

¡Adelante!

EJERCICIO ORAL

I. ¿Qué hacemos esta noche?   Using the listings from *Cromos* on pages 234–235, make arrangements with another student to watch a program on television or go to a play. Imagine that you are talking on the telephone. Be sure to discuss the kind of program, movie, or play you would like to see, make a selection, and arrange where and when you will meet.

EJERCICIO ESCRITO

J. Más programas de televisión   Write descriptions of two different television programs (real or imagined) in Spanish to be included with the other entries in *Cromos*. Include time, channel, and a few sentences that give an idea of the content of each of the programs.

241

Learning Strategies: Expressing preferences, reading for information, providing information

Cooperative Learning
Learning Strategies: Active listening, expressing preferences, negotiating, making plans

Learning Strategies: Describing, organizing

and create a sample question about each one. Put one or two mini-dialogues together with them before having them work on their own. Call on different pairs afterwards to perform for the class.

Suggestion, Ex. H: You may wish to adjust the model to use the 24-hour clock rather than having students change hours into regular time.

Cultural Observation

Explain to students that when American movies are marketed in Spanish-speaking countries, their titles are not always translated directly into Spanish, but may change to reflect cultural differences. See if students can match the following movies with their Spanish titles.
1. National Velvet (b)
2. Uncle Buck (a)
3. It's a Wonderful Life (d)
4. Mr. Smith Goes to Washington (c)
   a. Solos con nuestro tío
   b. Fuego de juventud
   c. Caballero sin espada
   d. ¡Qué bello es vivir!

Ex. I: pair work

Less-prepared students, Ex. I: Remind less-prepared students to recycle ideas from Ex. H for their work here.

More-prepared students, Ex. I: Have more-prepared students arrange for different nights with other friends, using a variety of programming and meeting places.

Ex. J: writing

More-prepared students, Ex. J: Challenge more-prepared students to create new Spanish names for English programs, based on the information from the Cultural Observation above.

Ex. H: groups of four or more

Less-prepared students, Ex. H: Remind less-prepared students that the model will change according to the type of program being discussed. This is especially true in the case of direct object pronouns. You may want to model a few substitutions and appropriate answers. (—**A mí me gustan los programas documentales. —Debes ver "La naturaleza de las cosas". —¿A qué hora lo dan?**)
Have students look at the categories suggested in bold type. Then, have them find examples in the *Cromos* listings

SEGUNDA ETAPA

Preparación

>> **W**hat kind of information does a written invitation contain?

>> **W**hat are some social events that require an invitation?

Te invito a una fiesta

dentro de: within

aprovechar: to take advantage of / *darles:* to give them / *despedida:* send-off / *desearles:* to wish them

¿Te parece bien?: Does that sound O.K.? / *Cuento contigo:* I'm counting on you. / *Contéstame cuanto antes:* Answer me as soon as possible. / *no les digas nada:* don't say anything to them / *será una sorpresa:* will be a surprise / *No te preocupes:* Don't worry / *traer:* to bring

Querida amiga,

Eduardo y Carmelita salen para los Estados Unidos dentro de quince días. Queremos aprovechar la ocasión para darles una despedida y desearles un buen viaje. Estoy organizando una pequeña fiesta en casa… el viernes, 4 de septiembre, a las 20:30.

¿Te parece bien? Cuento contigo. Contéstame cuanto antes. Y sobre todo… ¡no les digas nada a nuestros invitados de honor! La fiesta será una sorpresa para ellos.

No te preocupes —no debes traer nada. Sólo queremos pasar un rato agradable con los amigos en casa.

Afectuosamente,
Mercedes

242

Etapa Support Materials

Workbook: pp. 170–173
Transparencies: #33, #34
Teacher Tape 🎧
Quiz: Testing Program, p. 125

Chapter Test: Testing Program, p. 128

Support material, Te invito a una fiesta:
Transparencies #33, #34

Estimada señorita:

En la ocasión de la quinceañera de nuestra hija Marisol, la familia está organizando una fiesta en nuestra casa, Calle Sur Nº 112, el sábado 17 de julio a las 21:00.

Nos daría mucho gusto tenerle a usted y a su hermano Carlos entre nosotros esa noche para la celebración.

Tenga la bondad de responder tan pronto como le sea posible.

Sin más por ahora, reciba los mejores deseos de,

Teresa Camacho Del Valle

quinceañera: fifteenth birthday

Nos daría mucho gusto: It would give us great pleasure

Tenga la bondad de responder: Please be kind enough to answer / *como sea posible:* as possible

---

El señor y la señora Rafael Bolaños de la Garza

invitan cordialmente a Rosario Vega Arroyo a disfrutar de

la celebración del segundo aniversario de su boda que

ofrecerán en su residencia el sábado 17 de febrero

a las 20:00

R.S.V.P.

Calle Jardín 87   Tel. 28 03 94

disfrutar: to enjoy

boda: wedding

ofrecerán: they will offer

Cultural Expansion

Point out that the custom of celebrating the **quinceañera** is more popular in Central and Latin America than in Spain. Along with Sweet Sixteen, which has lost some of its popularity in our country, what other occasions can the students think of that would be similar? (Confirmation, Bar/Bat Mitzvah)

Ex. A: writing

Learning Strategies:

Reading for cultural information, reading for details

Critical Thinking Strategy:

Comparing and contrasting

¡Aquí te toca a ti!

A. Las tres invitaciones   Contesta en inglés las preguntas sobre las tres invitaciones en las páginas 242 y 243.

1. Which invitation is the most formal? the least formal? What words and expressions in Spanish support your answer?
2. What is the occasion for each invitation?
3. Except when writing to close friends, Spanish-speakers tend to use formalized expressions in making invitations. Find in Sra. Camacho Del Valle's note the Spanish equivalent of the following expressions:
   a. Dear   c. R.S.V.P.
   b. for Marisol's fifteenth birthday   d. Very truly yours
4. In what situations might Americans send similar invitations?

Learning Strategy:

Reading for cultural information

COMENTARIOS CULTURALES

La quinceañera

In most Spanish-speaking countries, it is still a popular tradition to have an extra special birthday party when a girl reaches the age of fifteen. The celebration is called **la quinceañera** and includes all extended family members and many friends. It is the equivalent of the "sweet sixteen" party that marks the beginning of a new phase in the life of a teenager.

Generally, the party includes dinner, music, dancing, and, of course, gifts. It may be a lavish affair held at a family club or a smaller party that takes place in the home. In either case, it is a dress-up occasion that people enjoy attending and celebrating.

Pronunciación: The vowel combination oi

The combination **oi** in Spanish is pronounced in one single syllable, similar to the *oi* in the English word *oink*. Note that in the words **voy, doy, hoy, estoy,** and **soy,** among others, the sound is spelled **oy.**

244

Cultural Expansion

Have students make up invitations in Spanish to an American party, e.g., Sweet Sixteen, bridal or baby shower, or graduation.

Critical Thinking Strategy: Creating

Presentation: Pronunciación

This might be a good time for a spelling dictation using the tv types of diphthongs studied in this chapter (see p. 235). You could list the words or make up silly sentences like **Veinte reinas tienen veintidós peines. Soy muy heróico en mi boina.**

Práctica

B. Lee las siguientes palabras en voz alta, pronunciando con cuidado la combinación *oi*.

1. oigo
3. heróico
5. doy
7. estoy
2. boina
4. voy
6. hoy
8. soy

Repaso

C. **En casa de Raúl y en casa de Graciela** Raúl, his parents, and his sister lead a very traditional life. Guess who probably does the following household chores in Raúl's family: **su papá, su mamá, su hermano, su hermana,** or **Raúl.** Use a direct object pronoun in your answer.

> **Modelo:** ¿Quién lava la ropa?
> *Su mamá (Su hermana) la lava de costumbre.*

1. ¿Quién prepara las comidas?
2. ¿Quién quita la mesa?
3. ¿Quién lava los platos?
4. ¿Quién hace los mandados?
5. ¿Quién lava el coche?

Graciela, on the other hand, lives in a nontraditional family. Household chores are not assigned by gender. Guess who did the following chores last week at her house: **su padre, su madre, su hermano,** or **Graciela.** Use a direct object pronoun in your answer. Follow the model.

> **Modelo:** ¿Quién lavó la ropa?
> *Su padre (Su hermano) la lavó.*

6. ¿Quién preparó las comidas?
7. ¿Quién quitó la mesa?
8. ¿Quién lavó los platos?
9. ¿Quién hizo los mandados?
10. ¿Quién lavó el coche?

D. **En tu casa** Ask a classmate who in his or her house usually takes care of the household chores on page 246. Then ask if that person *is going to do* that chore at the indicated time. Use a direct object pronoun when possible. Follow the models.

> **Modelo:** lavar los platos / esta noche
> —¿Quién lava los platos de costumbre en tu casa?
> —Mi hermana los lava.
> —¿Ella va a lavarlos esta noche?
> —Sí, ella va a lavarlos esta noche.   o:
> —No, mi padre va a lavarlos esta noche.

Learning Strategy:
Expressing present and past time

Critical Thinking Strategy:
Making associations

Learning Strategy:
Expressing present and future time

Critical Thinking Strategy:
Making associations

245

Ex. C: writing

Less-prepared students, Exs. C and D: Have less-prepared students identify direct object nouns or phrases before beginning.

Answers, Ex. C: 1. Su mamá las prepara.   2. Su hermana la quita.   3. Su mamá los lava. 4. Su mamá los hace.   5. Su papá lo lava.   6. Su padre las preparó. 7. Su hermano la quitó.   8. Graciela los lavó.   9. Su padre los hizo.   10. Su hermano lo lavó.

Ex. D: pair work

More-prepared students, Ex. D: Have more-prepared students create original questions about household chores to ask their partners.

1. preparar la cena / esta noche
2. quitar la mesa / esta noche
3. lavar la ropa / esta semana

4. hacer los mandados / esta semana
5. lavar el coche / este fin de semana

ESTRUCTURA

The immediate future of reflexive verbs

—Mi hermana y yo **nos vamos a levantar** a las seis de la mañana.
—**¿Te vas a lavar** el pelo?
—Sí, **voy a lavarme** el pelo.
—Nuestros padres **van a reunirse** en el centro.

My sister and I *are going to get up* at six in the morning.
Are you going to wash your hair?
Yes, *I'm going to wash* my hair.
Our parents *are going to get together (meet)* in town.

The immediate future of reflexive verbs is formed in the same way as the immediate future of any other verb—that is, with **ir** plus **a** and an infinitive. The reflexive pronoun that accompanies the reflexive verb agrees with the subject of **ir.** This pronoun can be placed immediately before the conjugated form of **ir** or attached to the infinitive.

Aquí practicamos

/-/-/-/-/-/-/-/-/-/-/

Learning Strategy:

Expressing present and future time

Critical Thinking Strategy:

Making associations

E. Hoy y mañana   Di lo que tienes que hacer hoy y lo que vas a hacer mañana. Usa una de las sugerencias de cada columna de una manera lógica. Sigue el modelo.

Modelo: yo   darse prisa   divertirse
Yo tengo que darme prisa hoy pero mañana voy a divertirme.

A	B	C
yo	dormirse	llamarse por teléfono
ustedes	quedarse	reunirse en el centro
mis amigos(as) y yo	ducharse	levantarse
el (la) profesor(a)	prepararse	lavarse el pelo

/-/-/-/-/-/-/-/-/-/-/

Learning Strategy:

Expressing present and future time

F. El sábado próximo   Next Saturday is a special day. Consequently, you are not planning to follow your usual weekend routine. Use the first cue to describe what you normally do on Saturday. Then use the cue in parentheses to tell how next Saturday is going to be different.

Possible answers, Ex. D:
1.¿Quién prepara la cena de costumbre en tu casa? Mi mamá la prepara. ¿Ella va a prepararla esta noche? Sí, ella va a prepararla esta noche.   2. ¿Quién quita la mesa de costumbre en tu casa? Yo la quito. ¿Vas a quitarla esta noche? No, mi hermano va a quitarla esta noche.   3. ¿Quién lava la ropa de costumbre en tu casa? Mi mamá la lava. ¿Ella va a lavarla esta semana? Sí, ella va a lavarla esta semana.   4. ¿Quién hace los mandados de costumbre en tu casa? Mi papá los hace. ¿Él va a hacerlos esta semana? Sí, él va a hacerlos esta semana.   5. ¿Quién lava el coche de costumbre en tu casa? Mi papá lo lava. ¿Él va a lavarlo este fin de semana? No, yo voy a lavarlo este fin de semana.

Presentation: Estructura

Begin by telling students about how tomorrow is going to be different for you. **De costumbre, me levanto a las 7:00, pero mañana voy a levantarme a las 6:00. Voy a lavarme el pelo. Voy a...** , etc. Have them compare the present and the immediate future. Then, ask students questions about their routine tomorrow morning. **¿A qué hora te levantas de costumbre? ¿Vas a levantarte a las... mañana?** Continue until they are familiar with where to put the reflexive pronoun.

Ex. E: writing

Suggestion, Ex. E: These column exercises are meant to provide controlled practice. One possible way to present these is by creating a "word web". On a separate piece of paper, students draw a web, and then connect elements from the columns in ways that form grammatically correct sentences. (They write in the correct form of the verb.) A sample word web format follows. Word web formats will vary from exercise to exercise.

Ex. F: writing

Modelo: quedarse en casa (pasearse con los amigos por el campo)
Normalmente me quedo en casa los sábados. Pero el sábado próximo, me voy a pasear con mis amigos por el centro.

1. despertarse tarde (despertarse temprano)
2. quedarse en cama (levantarse inmediatamente)
3. bañarse (ducharse)
4. no lavarse el pelo (lavarse el pelo)
5. vestirse después del desayuno (vestirse antes del desayuno)
6. cepillarse los dientes después del desayuno (no cepillarse los dientes)

G. *El lunes próximo*   On the other hand, next Monday promises to be a perfectly ordinary day. Imagine that you and the other members of your family are going to do what you normally do every Monday. Describe your activities. Follow the model.

 Modelo: *El lunes próximo, mi papá y mi mamá van a levantarse como a las 7:00. Mi hermana y yo vamos a quedarnos en cama hasta las 7:30, etc.*

Learning Strategies:

Organizing, sequencing, describing

Critical Thinking Strategy:

Imagining

Aquí escuchamos:
"Una fiesta en la casa de Cecilia"

Antes de escuchar

Cecilia wants to give a party. Saturday night is a perfect time because her brother will not be there; he'll be in town. What are some of the things she'll need to think about when organizing the party? Look at the following questions in preparation for the conversation she has with her parents about her plans.

START

Después de escuchar

1. ¿Quién va a organizar la fiesta?
2. ¿Cuántas personas van a ir a la fiesta?
3. ¿Dónde va a ser la fiesta?
4. ¿A qué hora comienza? ¿Cuándo va a terminar?
5. ¿Qué dice Cecilia que van a hacer durante todo este tiempo?

Learning Strategies:

Listening for details, listening for cultural information

247

More-prepared students, Ex. F: Ask more-prepared students to include what they did last Saturday, e.g., **Normalmente me quedo en casa los sábados, pero el sábado pasado me paseé con mis amigos. Y el sábado próximo voy a pasearme también.**

Ex. H: groups of four or more

Preparation, Exs. I and J: Have students organize a mini-fiesta for the class as a way to end the chapter, before or after the test. They could ask **¿Quién va a traer los nachos (los chips, la fruta)? ¿Quién va a hacer un pastel? ¿Quién va a comprar platos (utensilios, vasos)? ¿Quién va a traer jugo (zumo, gaseosas)?** Everyone would have to bring something and say what he/she is bringing and what one other person is bringing.

Learning Strategy: Brainstorming

Ex. I: pair work

Less-prepared students, Ex. I: If you choose to do this along with Ex. H, remind less-prepared students to recycle ideas and models from Ex. H.

Ex. J: writing

Less-prepared students, Ex. J: Remind less-prepared students of the model invitations on pp. 242–243 if they need help.

¡Aquí te toca a ti!

H. ¿Qué vas a hacer tú? You and your friends have decided to organize a party. In groups of four, decide how each one of you will participate in the preparations. Using the following list as a starting point, determine all the necessary activities to assure the success of the party. Agree on a list of responsibilities for each member of your group.

Modelo: *Yo voy a preparar una ensalada. ¿Y tú?*

Actividades: comprar la fruta / comprar jugo de fruta / comprar la comida / preparar una ensalada / traer las cintas / traer el estéreo y la grabadora / tocar la guitarra / invitar a los amigos / arreglar la comida / hacer un pastel / lavar los platos

¡Adelante!

EJERCICIO ORAL

I. ¡Organicen una fiesta! You and a friend decide to organize a party. Decide when and where you will have it. Then talk about the preparations. Share the responsibilities as follows:

You: invite the guests (talk about how many and who to invite) and arrange the location

Your friend: take care of the food (three things to eat and two kinds of beverages) and provide activities

EJERCICIO ESCRITO

J. Una invitación escrita Write an informal invitation to the members of your Spanish club to a surprise birthday party for an exchange student from Bolivia. Give the important details about time, place, food to be served, and the fact that it is a surprise for the guest of honor. Also indicate some of the activities that are planned, such as a movie, dancing, or other entertainment.

248

Vocabulario

Para charlar

Para hacer invitaciones

Nos daría mucho gusto…
Tenga la bondad de responder
  tan pronto como sea posible.
Cuento contigo…
Contéstame cuanto antes.

Será una sorpresa; no les digas nada.
¿Por qué no?
Nos vemos a / en…
¿Te parece bien?

Vocabulario general

Sustantivos	Verbos	Otras palabras y expresiones
una boda	aprovechar	darles la despedida
una quinceañera	seguir (i, i)	dentro de
una respuesta	traer	desearles
		disfrutar de
		Espero que no sea…
		Exacto.
		No se preocupen.
		tal vez

Chapter Culminating Activity

Cooperative Learning

Vocabulario: Group Poster

Learning Strategies: Negotiating, describing

Critical Thinking Strategies: Imagining, creating

- Divide the class into six groups and assign each group a topic related to the unit vocabulary.
- Explain that each group is going to make a poster about their topic. Every student in the group must agree on the topic and must have input into the poster. You may want to give the assignment one day and have the students make the posters the following day.
- Give students materials and allow them about 15 minutes to make the posters.
- Have the groups practice describing their topic and poster, using the items from the **Vocabulario.** Remind them that all students must have equal time to talk.
- Have the six teams present their posters to the class.

Lectura cultural

Lectura CULTURAL

LOS CANALES DE TELEVISIÓN EN ESPAÑA

//-//-//-//-//-//-//
Learning Strategies:
Previewing

Antes de leer

1. Look at the reading's photo and the title. What do you think it is about?
2. What does the word **canales** in the title mean?
3. Look at the layout of the reading. Of what does it remind you?
4. What sorts of words do you expect to find in a reading about television?

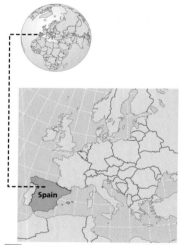

Spain

250

Guía para la lectura

Learning Strategies:

Scanning, taking notes in a chart, reading for details

A. Now scan the reading and find the following words. According to the context, what do you think they mean?

canales	programa	noticias	caja
cadenas	tele	programación	el mando
transmitiendo	documentales	alboroto	

B. How many "speakers" are there in the passage and what are their names?

C. Make a chart with the following headings. Read the **mini-drama** and fill in the information about each speaker.

Los chicos   Los canales que prefieren   Tipo de programación

Los canales de televisión en España

n el siguiente mini-drama unos jóvenes andaluces hablan sobre los programas de las cadenas nacionales y los de Canal Sur, la cadena regional.

Son las ocho de la noche y está lloviendo, así que Juan, Pedro, Borja y Javier se reúnen en casa de Borja para ver la "tele".

Juan: Vamos a ver qué hay en la "tele". ¡Ah! en Tele 5 ponen ese concurso tan cómico, con esas chicas guapas…

Pedro: No puedo creer que te gusta la Tele 5. ¡Es una cadena tan superficial! A mí me parece que la 2 es la única cadena con un poco de inteligencia.

Javier: No exageres, Pedro. La 2 sólo tiene documentales, noticias y deportes. Puede ser un poco aburrida… Antena 3 es una cadena seria e interesante.

Borja: ¡Que no!, ¡que no! que Canal Plus es la que tiene mejores películas. Tienes que pagar, pero te ofrecen una programación de calidad…

Juan: ¡Dame el mando, que me pierdo mi programa favorito en Tele 5!

Pedro: ¡Sobre mi cadáver! ¡La 2 sí que está bien!

Javier: ¡Antena 3 o me voy!

Borja: Pero Canal Plus está transmitiendo este programa tan interesante…

Todos terminan peleándose por el mando y arman gran alboroto en la casa.

Madre de Borja: ¡Chicos! ¿Por qué no dejáis ya de ver la caja tonta? Acaban de llamar unas amigas para ir al cine…

Borja: Bueno… la verdad es que es un poco tonto el discutir por los canales de la "tele".

Los demás: Pues sí, tienes razón. ¿Y si nos vamos al cine?

Juan: Sí, vamos al Astoria, que tiene "pelis" muy de moda.

Pedro: ¡Ni lo pienses! ¡Yo sólo voy a ver películas de calidad… !

Los demás: ¡Oh no! ¡Otra vez!

251

Chapter Objectives

Functions: Talking about vacation routines as opposed to normal daily routines; advising people where to go and not to go for vacation; describing vacation activities

Context: Family vacations; going to the beach; camping in national parks

Accuracy: Reflexive versus nonreflexive verbs; commands with pronouns

Cultural Context

Located on the northern coast of Colombia, Cartagena is one of the most picturesque cities in Latin America. The city was founded in 1533 by Pedro de Heredia and became a storage point for goods received from Spain and for treasure en route to Spain from the New World. This shipping industry made Cartagena an attractive target for pirates, and the old city was protected by a series of forts blocking all approaches by water—from the Caribbean on the west, the Bay of Cartagena on the south, and various lakes and lagoons on the north and east. The result was a completely walled city, now the old section of Cartagena, that seems to float on the waters that surround it. Walking its crooked, narrow streets with their high white walls is a favorite pastime of visitors from all over the world. Today the modern Cartagena is still an important port; it is also known for its beautiful beaches.

CAPÍTULO

9

¿CUÁNDO SON LAS VACACIONES?

Situada en la costa del Caribe en el norte de Colombia, Cartagena tiene un clima ideal para ir a la playa.

Objectives:

»» **T**alking about vacation routines as opposed to normal daily routines

»» **A**dvising people where to go and not to go for vacation

»» **D**escribing vacation activities

Strategies:

»» **L**istening for details

»» **S**upporting an opinion

»» **E**valuating

252

Video/Laserdisc

Chapter 9 Video Program and Video Guide

PRIMERA ETAPA

Preparación

» **W**hat do you do when you are on vacation from school?

» **W**hat did you do last summer?

» **W**hat are some of the activities you enjoy most during the summer?

/./-/./-/./-/./-/./-/.//
Learning Strategies:

Brainstorming, previewing

Las vacaciones con la familia

Me llamo Natalia Romero y vivo en Bogotá. Todos los veranos voy de vacaciones con mi familia a Cartagena, una ciudad que está en la costa. En mi familia a todos nos gusta mucho nadar. Además, mi hermano Andrés practica **la navegación a vela.** Tiene un pequeño **velero** y **una tabla vela.** Mi hermana Victoria **se dedica** al **esquí acuático.** Cuando no estoy en la playa, mi deporte **preferido** es **la equitación.** Mi madre y yo **montamos a caballo** en un **centro ecuestre.** Además, nos gusta salir a correr. Por la tarde, cuando ya no hace mucho sol, jugamos al vólibol con Andrés y Victoria. ¿Cómo? No hablé de mi padre. ¡Ah, pues él no es muy atlético! ¡Prefiere leer, descansar y tomar el sol!

sailing / sailboat / sailboard
devotes herself / waterskiing
favorite / horseback riding /
  ride horses /
  equestrian center

253

Presentation: Las vacaciones con la familia

Begin by talking about summer vacations in the United States. Have students read or listen to the recording of Natalia's description of her family's vacation. Use Ex. A as a comprehension check, following up each answer with personal questions. **¿Te gusta nadar? ¿Sabes esquiar en agua?**

Etapa Support Materials

Workbook: pp. 175–178
Listening Activity masters: p. 78
Transparency: #35
Teacher Tape 🎧
Tapescript: p. 109
Quiz: Testing Program, p. 133

Ex. A:
pair work

writing

role play

Ex. C:
pair work

writing

Reteaching, Ex. C: Brainstorm reflexive verbs with students. Have them recall different verbs. Call on students or have the whole class give the correct verb form and pronoun for a given subject (**yo, tú, nosotros,** etc.). Have students refer to p. 211 if necessary.

Less-prepared students, Ex. C: Do two or three of these items with less-prepared students first. Have them read the items out loud. To check comprehension ask them in English to consider what they would do in those circumstances. After they respond, ask them in Spanish for possibilities in a choice format. In the first item, for example: **¿Tú te quedas en la cama o te levantas rápidamente? ¿Y Cecilia?** In the second, **¿Tú te das prisa o te duermes otra vez? ¿Y Juan Manuel?,** etc.

More-prepared students: Have more-prepared students incorporate more than one possibility in their answers. For example, in the first item: **Cecilia no se levanta rápidamente, se queda en la cama.**

Possible answers, Ex. C:
1. Va a dormirse otra vez, quedarse en cama, no va a levantarse.
2. Va a darse prisa, levantarse rápidamente.   3. Vamos a divertirnos, sentarnos en el parque.   4. Vas a ducharte, lavarte el pelo.   5. Van a divertirse, reunirse.   6. Va a lavarse los dientes.

¡Aquí te toca a ti!

A. *La familia de Natalia*
Based on Natalia's description of her family vacations on page 253, play the role of each family member and explain what that person does during the summer.

1. su hermano Andrés   3. su hermana Victoria   5. Natalia
2. su madre   4. su padre

Pronunciación: *The vowel combination au*

The combination **au** in Spanish is pronounced in one single syllable, similar to the *ou* of the English word *ouch.*

Práctica

B. Lee las siguientes palabras en voz alta, pronunciando con cuidado la combinación *au.*

1. aula   3. autor   5. aunque   7. pausa
2. causa   4. auto   6. gaucho   8. jaula

Repaso

Critical Thinking Strategy:

Seeing cause-and-effect relationships

C. *Consecuencias lógicas*
Usa verbos reflexivos para decir lo que probablemente van a hacer, o no van a hacer, las siguientes personas en las situaciones que siguen. Sigue el modelo.

 Modelo: Enrique sale con Beatriz. Ella está cansada; está triste.
No van a divertirse. o:
Van a aburrirse.

1. Son las 6:00 de la mañana. Cecilia se despierta. No tiene clases antes de las 9:00.
2. Son las 8:45 de la mañana. Juan Manuel se despierta. Tiene una clase a las 9:15.
3. Hace buen tiempo. Tenemos dos horas libres *(free)*. Hay un parque muy bonito cerca de la casa.
4. Tienes el pelo sucio *(dirty)*. Vas a salir con tus amigos esta noche.
5. Cecilia tiene mandados que hacer en el centro. Isabel también. Van a ver una película en el Cine Palacio.
6. Cecilia comió muchos dulces y helado. No le gusta ir al dentista.

254

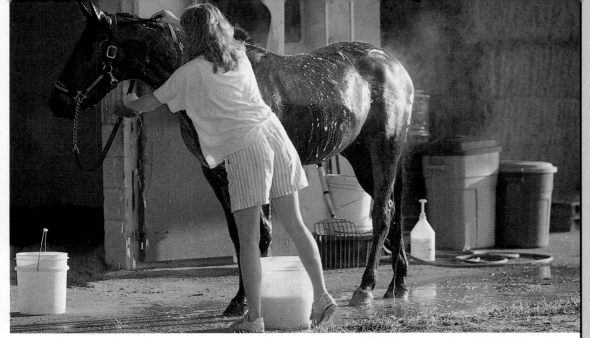

Ella lava el caballo porque el caballo no puede lavarse.

ESTRUCTURA

Reflexive versus nonreflexive verbs

Many Spanish verbs have both a reflexive and a nonreflexive form. In some cases, the meanings of the verbs change when they are used with reflexive pronouns:

Siempre **duermo** ocho horas.
I always sleep eight hours.

Casi siempre **me duermo** cuando estudio en la biblioteca.
I almost always fall asleep when I study in the library.

Me pongo los zapatos.
I put on my shoes.

Pongo los zapatos afuera.
I put the shoes outside.

In other cases, the meaning of the verbs is the same, but the meaning of the sentence changes. The nonreflexive verb expresses an action that goes from the subject to the object. The reflexive verb expresses a reciprocal action (the idea of *each other*):

Llamo a Claudia por teléfono a menudo.
I call Claudia on the telephone often.

Claudia y yo **nos llamamos** por teléfono a menudo.
Claudia and I call each other on the telephone often.

255

This section is designed to help students grasp the difference between reflexive and nonreflexive forms of the same verb. You may wish to present the idea by using corresponding expressions such as **lavar / lavarse** and miming the actions. You may use Ex. D on page 256 to underscore the differences. Ask students when reflexive verbs would be nonreflexive, e.g., the waiter seats the patrons, I wake up my children. You could give examples that combine the two, e.g., **Despierto a mi hijo porque él tiene que levantarse.**

Suggestion, Estructura:
Remind students that they should be careful not to make every verb reflexive. Tell them that most of the time they will be using nonreflexive verbs, that a reflexive verb or the reflexive form of a verb is used only in fixed expressions (such as **llamarse**), to express a reciprocal action (to each other), or to indicate a reflexive action (to itself).

Exs. D and E: pair work

Suggestion, Ex. D: Have students draw or sketch an illustration to accompany each of their answers (stick figures are acceptable!). You may want to have students do this at the board. Be sure to have contrasting drawings next to each other.

Similarities and Differences, Exs. D and E

Critical Thinking Strategies: Analyzing, comparing and contrasting

- These exercises contain expressions that may be confusing because of the differences between English and Spanish. Put students of differing abilities into pairs to discuss what is similar and what is different in the Spanish and English expressions.
- Explain to students that they are to discuss each sentence, with students taking turns starting the discussion each time.
- Call on students at random to give similarities and differences.

Answers, Ex. D: 1. Maricarmen gets dressed (dresses herself). 2. Maricarmen dresses the children.   3. My brother listens to the radio.   4. My parents don't listen to each other.   5. You don't get up early.   6. You don't get your brother up early.

Suggestion, Ex. E: Pair a less-prepared and a more-prepared student together to do this exercise for student-to-student learning and teaching.

In most cases, however, the nonreflexive verb indicates an action that the subject does to someone or something else, and the reflexive verb expresses an action that the subject does to itself.

Yo **lavo** el coche.	I *wash* the car.
Yo **me lavo.**	I *wash myself.*
Yo **me lavo** las manos.	I *wash my* hands.

Aquí practicamos

D. *En inglés*   Give the equivalent in English of the following sentences.

1. Maricarmen se viste.
2. Maricarmen viste a los niños.
3. Mi hermano escucha la radio.
4. Mis padres no se escuchan.
5. No te levantas temprano.
6. No levantas a tu hermano temprano.

Learning Strategy:

Reporting based on visual cues

E. *Se lava la cara* (face).   Use the verbs provided to describe the activities of the people portrayed in the drawings. For each pair of drawings, decide which activity requires the reflexive form of the verb and which activity can be expressed with the nonreflexive form.

Modelo: lavar
Miguel se lava la cara.
La Sra. Pérez lava el coche.

Miguel

Sra. Pérez

Sr. Jiménez

Sr. Jiménez / Jaime

1. despertar

256

Sra. Galindo

2. mirar

Juan José

Sra. Fernández

3. hablar

ella / los jóvenes

Aquí escuchamos:
"¡Siempre vamos a la costa!"

Antes de escuchar

Cecilia talks with her friend Isabel about her summer vacation. Based on your own experience, anticipate what she might say. Look at the following questions before you listen to what Cecilia tells her friend.

Después de escuchar

1. ¿Adónde va la familia de Isabel todos los veranos?
2. ¿Dónde vive la familia durante las vacaciones?
3. ¿Se aburre Isabel?
4. ¿Qué hace la familia durante el día por lo general?
5. Por la noche, ¿cómo se divierten todos?

//·//·//·//·//·//·//·//·//

Learning Strategy:

Listening for details

257

Answers, Ex. E: 1. El Sr. Jiménez se despierta a las siete. El Sr. Jiménez despierta a Jaime.
2. La Sra. Galindo mira la television. Juan José se mira en el espejo.
3. La Sra. Fernández se habla. Ella habla a los jóvenes.

Support material, Aquí escuchamos: Teacher Tape 🎧

Presentation: Aquí escuchamos

Have students look at the **Antes de escuchar** paragraph first to focus their listening. Then instruct them to take out pencil and paper and divide their paper into three columns headed **dónde, día,** and **noche.** Have them jot down any information that fits into these categories as they listen. Be sure to replay the tape two or three times. Have students use their notes to complete the **Después de escuchar** questions. Then correct by having student volunteers give possible answers.

Answers, Aquí escuchamos: 1. a la costa
2. alquilan una casa a la orilla del mar   3. no   4. deportes
5. comen y van al cine o bailan

Learning Strategy:
Reporting based on visual cues

¡Aquí te toca a ti!

F. *Las vacaciones de verano* Describe un día típico, para Isabel y para sus hermanos según los dibujos. Sigue el modelo.

Modelo: *Por la mañana Isabel se levanta a las ocho y media.*

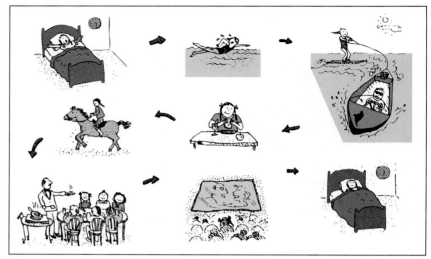

258

¡Adelante!

EJERCICIO ORAL

G. Mis vacaciones   Tell a classmate about your family's usual summer vacation or about your ideal summer vacation. (1) Say where you go and what activities you do. (2) Describe a typical day, giving the time of day you get up and go to bed as well as at least five activities during the day. (3) Then listen to your partner's description. (4) Decide on the one most interesting activity that each of you does during your typical vacation day.

EJERCICIO ESCRITO

H. ¿Adónde fuiste y qué hiciste?   Write a letter to a Spanish-speaking friend about where you went and what you did during a recent vacation. (1) Describe the location and the weather. (2) Describe the hotel or other place(s) that you stayed. (3) Name at least five activities in which you participated. (4) Tell which one you liked the best and why. (5) Describe the most interesting meal that you ate. (6) Tell whether you want to return to the same place again. Then, in groups of four, read one another's letters. Decide which one of the location spots the four of you will choose for a vacation together next summer. Give three reasons for your choice.

Cooperative Learning

Learning Strategies:

Active listening, describing, reporting based on personal knowledge

Critical Thinking Strategy:

Sequencing

Cooperative Learning

Learning Strategies:

Organizing information, listing, describing, commenting on preferences, reading for main ideas, negotiating, supporting an opinion

Critical Thinking Strategies:

Comparing and contrasting, evaluating

Ex. G: pair work

Less-prepared students, Ex. G: Have less-prepared students make small sketches without words of the points they want to tell their partner and use these to help them remember what they want to talk about.

Ex. H: writing

Reteaching, Ex. H: Quickly review verbs in the preterite for students to use in their letters, as well as weather expressions, descriptive adjectives, and hotel and food vocabulary. Have students recall and give vocabulary items. You may want to limit reteaching to less-prepared students, according to your class composition.

259

Cultural Observation

Camping has become popular all over Europe, as well as in Latin America. If you have access to any brochures from travel agencies that highlight camping, show them.

Costa Rica is perhaps best known for its extensive system of national parks, which encompass an amazing variety of vegetation and wildlife. A visitor to these parks may encounter virgin rain forest, dry tropical forest, cloud forest, caves, lagoons, volcanos, hot springs, mudpots, marshes, mountains, beaches, and a wide variety of flora and fauna including butterflies, bats, tropical birds, monkeys, turtles, crocodiles, and jaguars.

Reading Strategies

Previewing: Find out how many students have gone camping and how many have camped in an organized campground. Discuss briefly the facilities that you find there. Also ask if anyone has camped outside the United States and how camping in another country might differ. Then have the students read the brochure and do Ex. A.

Reading for the main idea: Tell students they do not need to understand every word. They should try to get the general idea as well as some of the more important messages rather than every detail. Remind them to use their prior knowledge of camping and park services to help them infer these ideas and messages.

Scanning for cognates: Emphasize how first scanning for cognates helps students to infer the main idea of the document before they read for details.

SEGUNDA ETAPA

Preparación

›› **D**o you know the name of a national park?

›› **H**ave you ever been to a national park? When? What did you do there?

›› **W**hat kind of information is usually contained in a brochure about a national park?

/-/-/-/-/-/-/-/-/-/-/-/
Learning Strategy:
Previewing

Una visita a un parque nacional

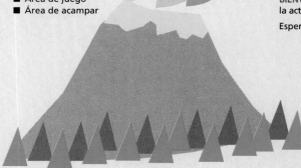

SERVICIOS
■ Información a cargo de guías y guardaparques
■ Servicios sanitarios
■ Agua potable
■ Estacionamiento
■ Refugio para almorzar
■ Área de almuerzo
■ Centro de visitantes
■ Sendero
■ Mirador
■ Área de juego
■ Área de acampar

Parque Nacional Volcán Poás

PARQUE NACIONAL: VOLCAN POÁS

El servicio de Parques Nacionales de Costa Rica administra veintidós áreas silvestres entre parques nacionales y otras reservas afines. Estas áreas cubren 425.329 hectáreas, lo que equivale a un ocho por ciento del territorio nacional.

El principal objetivo del Servicio de Parques Nacionales es preservar áreas naturales para beneficio y disfrute de las generaciones futuras.

El Parque Nacional Volcán Poás, área de gran interés geológico, es importante también porque en él nacen varios ríos que alimentan a otros que dan origen a las cuencas hidrográficas: río Grande de Tárcoles y río Sarapiquí.

BIENVENIDO al Parque Nacional Volcán Poás, una muestra de la actividad geológica y de la belleza del paisaje de Costa Rica.

Esperamos que su visita sea agradable y provechosa.

HORARIO
De 8:00 A.M. a 4:00 P.M.
Agradecemos su colaboración en el mantenimiento del aseo.

DATOS DE INTERÉS
Punto más alto: 2.708 metros
Altura del mirador del cráter: 2.560 metros
Altura del mirador de la Laguna Botos: 2.675 metros
Profundidad del cráter: 320 metros
Diámetro de la Laguna Botos: 400 metros
Superficie de la Laguna Botos: 12 hectáreas
Extensión del parque: 53.173 hectáreas

Etapa Support Materials

Workbook: **pp. 179–183**
Transparency: **#36**
Teacher Tape 🎧
Quiz: **Testing Program, p. 135**
Chapter Test: **Testing Program, p. 137**

¡Aquí te toca a ti!

A. *Un parque nacional de volcanes*   Some friends of your parents are going to visit the national parks of Costa Rica, famous for their volcanos, rare birds, and plant life. They bring you a brochure for the **Parque Nacional Volcán Poás** (on page 260) and ask for your help in reading it. You don't know many of the words, but you are able to read enough to get the general idea. Answer the friends' questions about the national park.

Learning Strategies:

Scanning for cognates, reading for main ideas, reading for details

1. How big is the national park system?
2. Is there a place to camp?
3. Is there parking?
4. Are there toilet facilities?
5. Is there a restaurant there?
6. What are some of the other facilities?
7. How high up (**altura**) is the volcano?
8. How deep (**profundidad**) is the crater?
9. What time does the park close?
10. What is the main objective of this national park service?

Pronunciación: *The vowel combination eu*

To pronounce the combination **eu**, start with your lips spread, positioned to smile, as you pronounce the Spanish vowel **e**. Bring them slowly to a rounded position as though you were going to whistle. All this should be done in one smooth motion—in one single syllable.

Práctica

B. Lee las palabras en voz alta, pronunciando con cuidado la combinación *eu*.

1. Europa	**3.** neutro	**5.** seudo	**7.** ceuta
2. deuda	**4.** neurosis	**6.** seudónimo	**8.** neurótico

Repaso

C. *Un día en la playa*   En el verano vas a la playa con tu hermana los sábados. Usa la información en la página 262 para decir que hacen Uds. típicamente. Sigue el modelo.

   yo / levantarse a las 7:30
Yo me levanto a las 7:30.

261

Ex. A: pair work
writing

Reading Partners

Learning Strategy: Peer tutoring

Critical Thinking Strategies: Imagining, creating

- Pair students who have not worked together recently. (The reading may seem difficult to some students and you can ease them into it by having them work together.)
- Have students read the brochure about the **Parque Nacional Volcán Poás** together. Tell them to take turns answering the questions, so that both students get equal practice. The student who is not answering should encourage the other student and guide him or her as needed.
- Ask follow-up questions at random.
- For homework, you may want to have each pair design a similar brochure about a local park, another well-known park, or a park that they make up.

Answers, Ex. A: 1. 425.329 hectáreas 2. yes 3. yes 4. yes 5. no   6. information, drinking water, shelter, visitor center, trail, playing field 7. 2.560 meters 8. 320 meters 9. 4:00 p.m. 10. to preserve natural areas for future generations

Presentation: Pronunciación

It may be a good time to do a spelling dictation quiz after you've done this second pronunciation section of the chapter.

Ex. C: writing

Unit 3, Chapter 9   **T261**

1. mi hermana / levantarse a las 8:00
2. ella / ducharse
3. yo / bañarse
4. nosotros(as) / desayunarse juntos(as)
5. nosotros(as) / vestirse
6. ella / navegar en la tabla vela
7. yo / jugar al vólibol
8. nosotros(as) / reunirse a las 6:00 de la tarde
9. nosotros(as) / comer mariscos
10. nosotros(as) / regresar como a las 9:00
11. yo / acostarse en seguida *(right away)*
12. ella / acostarse a eso de la medianoche

ESTRUCTURA

The use of pronouns with commands

¡Cálma**te**!	Calm *yourself*! (Take it easy!)
¡Levánten**se**!	Get *(yourselves)* up!
¡No **te** preocupes!	Don't worry *(yourself)*!
¡No **se** despierten!	Don't wake *each other* up!

You have already learned that the reflexive pronouns for **Ud., Uds.,** and **tú (se, se, te,** respectively) are attached to the end of the affirmative command and are placed *before* the verb form in the negative command.

The direct object pronouns **lo, la, los, las** follow the same pattern with command forms.

¡Lléva**lo**!	Take *it*!
¡Láven**la**!	Wash *it*!
¡Tráe**los**!	Bring *them*!
¡No **la** mires!	Don't look at *her*!
¡No **los** compren!	Don't buy *them*!

Aquí practicamos

D. Use the cues on page 263 to form affirmative commands.

Modelo: tú / levantarse
¡Levántate!

Ex. D: writing

1. tú / llevarla
2. tú / mirarlo
3. Uds. / llamarse
4. Ud. / comprarlos
5. tú / despertarse
6. Uds. / levantarse
7. tú / acostarse
8. Ud. / comerlos
9. tú / traerla
10. Uds. / lavarse

E. Now use the cues in Activity D to form negative commands.

 Modelo: tú / levantarse
    ¡No te levantes!

F. ¡Buena idea!... ¡No, no, no!   Cecilia and Isabel are talking about the plans for their party. Two of their friends respond to their comments—the first positively and the second negatively. Follow the model.

 Modelo: Voy a comprar el nuevo disco compacto de Rubén Blades.
    —*¡Buena idea! ¡Cómpralo!*
    —*¡No, no, no! ¡No lo compres!*

1. Voy a invitar a Ricardo Núñez.
2. Voy a preparar la ensalada esta tarde.
3. Voy a acostarme a descansar.
4. Voy a llevar a mis primos.
5. Voy a traer el nuevo disco compacto de Los Lobos.

Modelo: Vamos a invitar a Mario y a su hermano.
    —*¡Buena idea! ¡Invítenlos!*
    —*¡No, no, no! ¡No los inviten!*

6. Vamos a invitar a Ana María y a su amiga.
7. Vamos a servir la carne primero.
8. Vamos a lavar los platos mañana por la mañana.
9. Vamos a preparar la comida esta tarde.
10. Vamos a darnos prisa.

Aquí escuchamos:
"¡Vamos a acampar!"

Antes de escuchar

Cecilia and Juan Manuel talk about their upcoming vacation with their parents. Look at the questions on page 264 in preparation for their conversation.

START

263

Less-prepared students, Ex. D: Encourage less-prepared students to scan the exercise first to distinguish between reflexive and nonreflexive constructions. Then have them use appropriate pronouns.

More-prepared students, Ex. D: Invite more-prepared students to invent the direct object nouns for items 1, 2, 4, 8, and 9. For example, the **la** in item 1 could refer to **la comida.**

Answers, Ex. D: 1. ¡Llévala!   2. ¡Míralo!   3. ¡Llámense!   4. ¡Cómprelos!   5. ¡Despiértate!   6. ¡Levántense!   7. ¡Acuéstate!   8. ¡Cómalos ! 9. ¡Tráela!   10. ¡Lávense!

Ex. E: writing

Answers, Ex. E: 1. ¡No la lleves!   2. ¡No lo mires!   3. ¡No se llamen!   4. ¡No los compre!   5. ¡No te despiertes!   6. ¡No se levanten!   7. ¡No te acuestes!   8. ¡No los coma!   9. ¡No la traigas!   10. ¡No se laven!

Ex. F: pair work

More-prepared students, Ex. F: Have more-prepared students work with a partner and invent three new, real-life situations to which their partner should react.

Answers, Ex. F: 1. ¡Buena idea! ¡Invítalo! ¡No lo invites! 2. ¡Buena idea! ¡Prepárala esta tarde! ¡No la prepares!   3. ¡Buena idea! ¡Acuéstate a descansar! ¡No te acuestes! 4. ¡Buena idea! ¡Llévalos! ¡No los lleves!   5. ¡Buena idea! ¡Tráelo! ¡No lo traigas!
    6. ¡Buena idea! ¡Invítenlas! ¡No las inviten!   7. ¡Buena idea! ¡Sírvanla primero! ¡No la sirvan! 8. ¡Buena idea! ¡Lávenlos mañana por la mañana! ¡No los laven! 9. ¡Buena idea! ¡Prepárenla esta tarde! ¡No la preparen! 10. ¡Buena idea! ¡Dense prisa! ¡No se den prisa!

Support material, Aquí escuchamos: Teacher Tape

Presentation: Aquí escuchamos

Ask students about their family's vacation plans. **¿Cómo va a pasar las vacaciones tu familia? ¿Quién va a la costa? ¿a las montañas? ¿Quién va a visitar a sus abuelos?**

Después de escuchar

1. ¿Qué idea tiene el padre para las vacaciones este año?
2. ¿Qué piensan los hijos de la idea de su padre?
3. ¿Qué quiere hacer Juan Manuel?
4. ¿Qué cosas tiene el coche-caravana *(camper)*?
5. ¿Qué dice el padre al final de la conversación?

¡Aquí te toca a ti!

G. *El camping tradicional... el camping moderno...*

"Traditional" campers often make fun of "modern" campers. Compare the activities of traditional and modern campers, using the suggested expressions. Divide these expressions into two lists: one of activities unique to traditional campers and the other of activities unique to modern campers. Would you identify yourself as traditional or modern? Why?

Actividades: acampar / ir al bosque *(woods)* / dormir bajo las estrellas *(under the stars)* / dormir en el coche-caravana / dormir en una tienda de campaña *(tent)* / hacer una fogata *(bonfire)* con leña *(firewood)* / guardar *(to keep, to store)* las bebidas en el refrigerador/en el agua fría / preparar las comidas en una estufa / ducharse / bañarse en el río

H. *Las vacaciones de primavera*

Discuss with two classmates where to go for spring vacation. (1) Choose possible destinations from the list in Column A. (2) Select appropriate activities for each site, one from Column B and one from Column C. (3) Add any other activities that you

264

would like to do in each of these locations. (4) Finally, agree on a destination for spring vacation this year. Follow the model.

A	B	C
ir a las montañas	tomar el sol	patinar
acampar	esquiar	ver a la Casa Blanca
ir a la costa	alquilar un coche-caravana	descansar
ir a España	visitar el Senado	esquiar en agua
ir a Washington	alquilar un coche	visitar las provincias
	nadar	dormir en una tienda de campaña

Modelo:

Estudiante A:	*¿Cómo vamos a pasar las vacaciones este año?*
Estudiante B:	*Yo quiero ir a la costa.*
Estudiante C:	*Es una buena idea. Podemos nadar.*
Estudiante A:	*Y podemos descansar.*

¡Adelante!

EJERCICIO ORAL

I. *Las vacaciones de la familia* Discuss with another student your family's vacation plans for the summer. Talk about (1) where you are going, (2) when you are going to leave (**salir**), and (3) what you are going to do. (4) Discuss at least four activities, including one that you can do when the weather is bad. (5) If some people in your family would like to do something different, talk about their wishes, too. Each of you will take notes on the plans of each other's family in order to make a report to the class. Be sure to ask questions of your partner about anything that you do not clearly understand.

/-/-/-/-/-/-/-/-/-/-//

Learning Strategies:

Requesting and giving personal information, taking notes, expressing future time

EJERCICIO ESCRITO

J. *Mis planes para las vacaciones* Write a letter to your pen pal about your plans for an upcoming vacation. Describe (1) when and (2) where you will go, (3) with whom, (4) for how long, and (5) what you will do during the vacación. (6) Describe at least four activities that you hope to participate in, including at least one plan for a rainy day. (7) Don't forget to date and sign your letter. (Remember to use **ir a** + *infinitive* and verbs like **pensar** and **querer** in your letter.)

/-/-/-/-/-/-/-/-/-/-//

Learning Strategies:

Expressing future time, listing, organizing ideas, writing a letter

Critical Thinking Strategy:

Making associations

265

Chapter Culminating Activity

Cooperative Learning

Vocabulario: Group Vacations

Learning Strategy: Describing, narrating in the present and in the past

Critical Thinking Strategies: Creating, evaluating

- The day before you wish to do this activity, put the students into heterogeneous groups of three. Explain that they are going to plan and present a skit about a vacation involving the activities listed in the **Vocabulario.** Have them use as many of the expressions from each category as they can, but do not allow them access to notes. They should try not to memorize what they are going to say, because it will not seem natural.
- Give students time in class to talk about what they'd like to do on their group vacations.
- The next day, have the groups share their vacations with the class. You may want to have the students grade the skits, based on criteria such as creativity, comprehensibility, linguistic skills, and vocabulary.
- For follow-up, have the students talk or write about a memorable holiday.

Vocabulario

Para charlar

Para organizar las vacaciones

¿Por qué no...   acampamos en una área de acampar?
           alquilamos un coche-caravana?
           dormimos en una tienda de campaña?
           pasamos las vacaciones en... ?
           tomamos el sol?
           vamos a la costa / a las montañas?
           visitamos un centro ecuestre para hacer equitación?

Temas y contextos

Las actividades deportivas

esquiar en agua   montar a caballo
                         practicar la navegación a vela / tabla vela
                              el esquí acuático
                              la equitación

Vocabulario general

Sustantivos	Otras palabras y expresiones
un pueblo	en seguida
	¡Magnífico!

Verbos	Adjetivos
costar (ue)	anterior
dedicarse	

ℒectura CULTURAL

LLEGARON LAS VACACIONES

Antes de leer

/-/-/-/-/-/-/-/-/-/-/-/
Learning Strategy:
Previewing

1. Look at the photos and title to learn what the reading is about.
2. What do you usually like to do during vacation months away from school?
3. What might you expect young people in a Spanish-speaking country to talk about when referring to activities during vacation?

Abajo: A Eva le gusta acampar durante las vacaciones.
Derecha: Vicente disfruta el clima gallego.

267

Lectura cultural

//-/-/-/-/-/-/-/-/-/-/-/

Learning Strategies:

Reading for cultural information, reading for details, recording information in a chart

Critical Thinking Strategy:

Categorizing

Guía para la lectura

A. When does summer vacation start in Spain?

B. Now read each description and record the information using a chart with the following headings:

Name	Age	Destination	Activities

C. Based on the information you recorded in your chart, answer the following questions.

1. ¿Qué piensa hacer la chica que va al campamento de verano?
2. ¿Quiénes van a ser más activos en cuanto a deportes durante sus vacaciones?
3. ¿Cuáles de las tres vacaciones te gustan más? ¿Por qué?

Llegaron las vacaciones

Spain

finales de junio los colegios de toda España cierran sus puertas. Chicos y chicas comienzan a hacer sus maletas para irse a la playa, a las montañas o a un campamento juvenil.

Tres jóvenes españoles hablan de lo que van a hacer durante sus vacaciones de verano.

Eva Lamas (15 años): Este verano voy a ir a un campamento de verano. Allí vamos a estar al aire libre todo el día, incluso vamos a dormir en tiendas de campaña. Vamos a hacer excursiones, queremos practicar montañismo, vamos a encender hogueras por las noches y vamos a cantar canciones alrededor del fuego. Espero divertirme igual este año.

Vicente Pazuelos (16 años): Yo soy de Madrid y en verano hace muchísimo calor, así que todos los veranos mis padres alquilan una casita en un pueblo de Galicia, en el norte de España, donde no hace tanto calor. Allí hay mucha gente joven de todas partes de España. Durante el día vamos a la playa, nadamos, navegamos en tabla vela y por las tardes vamos de paseo en motocicleta. Me lo paso fenomenal.

Sara Ramírez (18 años): Voy a ir a un campo de trabajo en Valencia, en el este de España, a recoger naranjas durante el mes de agosto. Es un trabajo voluntario, así que no voy a ganar dinero, pero como pienso vivir con la familia dueña de la finca, tampoco lo necesito. Estoy segura de que va a ser una experiencia inolvidable.

268

Aquí leemos

Estrategia para la lectura

The reading techniques you have learned so far work in longer passages, even about topics that are somewhat unfamiliar. Usually, the main idea is found at the beginning and may be summarized again at the end. Even if there are some words you don't know, you will be able to recognize many others. By using cognates, word families, context, and your background knowledge, you will be able to guess even more. This information is often enough to give you the general idea. A good approach is to treat a reading as a puzzle to be solved, but in order to do so, you must focus on what you do understand rather than on what you do not. Read for details only when you need to.

Reading Strategies:

Look for main ideas in the first and last sentences or paragraphs of a reading.

Pay more attention to what you understand than to what you don't.

Look for details only when you need to.

Antes de leer

People of all ages are fascinated by mountain climbing, a very popular sport in much of Latin America. The degree of difficulty can range from a casual hike up a gradual slope to a demanding and daring assault on unbelievably high peaks. The article on page 270, reproduced in part from the Peruvian newsmagazine *Caretas,* reports on four young Peruvian men who recently climbed to the top of the spectacular snow-capped Alpamayo peak in the Andes. Before reading it, think about the following questions.

>> **W**hat do you already know about hiking and mountain climbing?

>> **W**hat kinds of people do you think are likely to be mountain climbers?

>> **W**hat, if anything, do you already know about the Andes in Peru? Try to find Alpamayo on a map.

>> **T**hink about vocabulary you might need to read about a mountain-climbing adventure: words related to mountains (peak, summit, etc.); words related to climbing (e.g., base camp); words for snow or weather; words for equipment and supplies.

Prereading

Have students read the **Estrategia para la lectura,** and then write down their answers to the questions in the **Antes de leer** section. Alternately, the questions can serve as the basis for a class discussion about mountain climbing. You may want the class to brainstorm in English a list of words related to mountain adventures and to write the list on the board as a reference.

269

Support Materials

Workbook: **pp. 184–188**
Unit Review Blackline Masters: **Unit 3 Review**
Listening Activity masters: **p. 85**
Tapescript: **p. 115**
Unit Exam: **Testing Program, p. 141**

Atajo, Writing Assistant Software *supports*

Cultural Observation

Alpamayo has been called "the most beautiful mountain in the world" and is found in the **Cordillera Blanca** of the Andes, northwest of Lima. The nearby town of Huarás is the mountain climbing center of Peru and is the headquarters of the Huascarán National Park. From Huarás one can see more than 23 peaks higher than 5,000 m, crowned by Huascarán (6,768 m), the highest mountain in Peru. The **Cordillera Blanca** contains the world's largest concentration of glaciers in a tropical zone and is the most popular backpacking and climbing location in Peru. Its network of trails is also used by the local people for day-to-day transportation. Most circuits can be hiked in five days, but the trails are rugged, with high passes between 4,000 and 5,000 m. Although it is a beautiful setting, it is also a dangerous one. In 1941, one-third of Huarás was swept away when the **Laguna Palacoche** above the city ruptured, killing 6,000 people.

Read over the article quickly. Don't worry about words you don't understand. Just try to see how it is organized, figure out what kinds of information it contains, and identify the main idea.

Una expedición de alpinistas peruanos logró conquistar la cima del Alpamayo, nevado de 5.947 metros de altura en la Cordillera Blanca de los Andes, una de las montañas más bellas del mundo. Lo notable es que son los primeros en subir por la ruta llamada "francesa" que, según explican, es la más larga y la más difícil. "Nadie creía que lo podíamos hacer", dice, riendo, Renzo Uccelli, uno de los miembros de la exitosa expedición Alpamayo Suroeste 87.

A pesar del escepticismo general, Uccelli, fundador y presidente de la Asociación de Andinismo de la Universidad de Lima, junto con Antonio Rodríguez Verdugo, 24 años, Hugo Mugling, 32 y Ronald Bottger, 23, dice que siguieron un plan de entrenamiento no muy profesional, pero con el que tuvieron éxito. Durante meses, todos los días, corrieron un par de horas e hicieron muchos ejercicios abdominales. Al mismo tiempo, preparaban el temperamento para estar mentalmente listos para la dura aventura.

Y así, la noche del 16 de julio, los cuatro compañeros viajaron en ómnibus a Huarás, con 45 kilos de equipos y comida, "miles de paquetes de tallarines, porque no hay plata para comprar otras cosas". Dos días más tarde, alquilaron unos animales de carga y caminaron hasta que llegaron al campamento base, a 3.900 metros de altura.

Una vez al pie de la montaña, se dieron cuenta de que podían subir por la "ruta francesa", la más larga y peligrosa de la Cordillera Blanca. Durante los dos días siguientes, transportaron el equipo hasta el campamento, avanzando a 4.500 metros de altura.

Al despertarse el 24 de julio, los cuatro alpinistas estaban impacientes por atacar la cumbre porque las condiciones climatológicas eran perfectas. La nieve tenía una consistencia ideal para seguir adelante, pero los esperaban un par de días muy largos.

los tallarines: noodles

Por el lado suroeste del Alpamayo hay una famosa pared de hielo y nieve, prácticamente vertical, de 450 metros de alto y una inclinación de 55 a 65 grados. Es el último gran reto para conquistar la cima del Alpamayo, y los alpinistas que se atreven a afrontarla deben tener una excelente técnica "y los cinco sentidos listos".

Afortunadamente, los miembros de la expedición tienen mucha experiencia, pues han escalado juntos muchos nevados en Europa y América del Sur. ¿Qué se siente cuándo se trepa por una pared? "Te sientes bien", comenta Uccelli. "Hay que tener calma y serenidad. Tienes que hacer todos tus movimientos con mucho cuidado."

Así, durante 19 horas, 16 de las cuales estuvieron en la pared, escalaron por la peligrosa "ruta francesa". A cinco metros de la cima perdieron una mochila llena de equipo y comida que cayó rodando centenares de metros más abajo. "Pero eso ya no era tan importante", dice Uccelli. "Subimos a la cumbre y al llegar arriba uno puede sentir mil cosas… ¡Como estamos tan contentos a veces hasta lloramos!"

Lo más importante de esta conquista del Alpamayo es que estos cuatro hombres han demostrado que el alpinismo peruano está mejorando su nivel técnico, y con esto se abren las puertas hacia el camino de las grandes y difíciles escaladas.

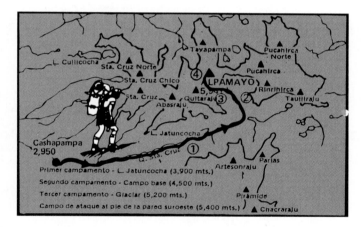

reto: challenge / *escaladas:* climbs

Actividades

A. 1. Read the first and last paragraphs. Based only on the information you find there, write a one-sentence summary of the article.

2. Look for these names mentioned in the article. Use immediate context to identify why they are important. The ones marked * occur more than once.
   a. **Alpamayo***
   b. **Alpamayo Suroeste 87**
   c. **Renzo Uccelli***
   d. **Asociación de Andinismo de la Universidad de Lima**
   e. **ruta francesa***

3. This article is mostly a chronological account of the progress of the expedition. By following the dates and the activities, you get the general idea about the most important content. Here is a list of dates. The ones in parentheses are not mentioned directly in the article but can be deduced from it. Match each date with the activity associated with it during the expedition.

___ **16 de julio**   a. move equipment and advance 600 meters
___ **(18 de julio)**   b. weather is perfect and climb begins
___ **(20 de julio)**   c. arrive at the summit (5947 meters)
___ **24 de julio**   d. travel by bus to Huarás
___ **(26 de julio)**   e. arrive at base camp (3900 meters)

B. 1. What are some new cognates that you can identify immediately?
2. List the adjectives that are applied to each of the following:
   a. the climbers
   b. Alpamayo peak
   c. the **ruta francesa**
3. How many synonyms can you find for **la cima**? for the four climbers?
4. Find at least three reflexive verb forms. What are the best English equivalents?
5. Uccelli is quoted three times in the article (Paragraphs 1, 7, and 8). Each time his quotes refer to emotions associated with aspects of the expedition. What words (in the quotes or in their contexts) express these emotions?

C. Answer the following questions by referring to the article. Pick out a key word or phrase that provides the answer. (You may not understand a word exactly but can still recognize it as the answer.)

1. What makes the four mountain climbers' accomplishment a "first"?
2. What sort of training program (**entrenamiento**) did they use to prepare for this particular climb?
3. What did the men take with them to the base camp?
4. What was the final obstacle the climbers had to face near the top?
5. Did all four men have a lot of previous climbing experience?
6. What does one climber say is required to climb up a sheer wall?
7. How many hours did they spend scaling the most dangerous part of the mountain?
8. What fell during the very final stage of the climb?
9. How does Uccelli describe the feeling of reaching the very top?
10. According to the article, what is the most important thing about this conquest of Alpamayo overall?

D. 1. Imagine that a book is being written based on the conquest of Alpamayo. Design a book jacket using adjectives, quotes, and other material from this article to highlight the excitement of mountain climbing.
2. With another student, play the roles of Uccelli and a newsmagazine writer. Conduct the interview that would have resulted in this article.
3. Imagine that you are a participant in this expedition, and you are keeping a diary of your adventures. Be sure to include some entries that describe the training, the shopping, the travel, the early stages of the climb, and the arrival at the summit itself. Use everything you have learned so far—descriptions, actions in the past, expression of emotions—to make your writing as vivid as possible.

Ya llegamos

Exs. A and B: groups of
four or more

Suggestion, Ex. B: Assign
the exercise as homework. Remind
students to bring in visuals and to
review and then use preterite verbs
in their description.

Ex. C: groups of three

 role play

Actividades orales

/·/·/·/·/·/·/·/·/·/·/·/

**Cooperative
Learning**

Learning Strategies:

*Negotiating, describing,
making an oral presen-
tation, active listening,
taking notes*

*Critical Thinking
Strategies:*

*Analyzing, sequencing,
making associations*

A. *¿Qué es la telenovela?* In groups of three or four, agree among
yourselves on the television soap opera that you want to describe for the
class. Have each member of your group select a main character in the
soap opera and prepare a description of (1) at least two physical characteristics and (2) two personality traits of that character, as well as (3) a
detailed description of that person's daily routine, naming four specific
activities typical for that character. Do not give any names or titles that
would give away which soap opera or character you are describing.

While each group is giving its presentation, the other members of the
class should take notes. Record at least (1) two descriptive facts about
each character and (2) two details in each character's daily routine. The
small groups should then get together to compare notes, try to name the
soap opera, and then ultimately the individual characters. Each group
can turn in a written group report for each presentation.

/·/·/·/·/·/·/·/·/·/·/·/

**Cooperative
Learning**

Learning Strategies:

*Describing in the past,
organizing ideas*

*Critical Thinking
Strategies:*

*Sequencing, evaluating,
categorizing*

B. *Mis vacaciones favoritas* Think back on past vacations you
have spent either on a trip or at home, or even in your imagination.
Prepare a description of the vacation before coming to class, and bring in
some photos that were taken during that time. (If you have none available,
cut some appropriate pictures from a magazine or draw some yourself.) In
groups of three or four, describe your vacation to your other group members, (1) showing pictures, (2) describing the people you spent time with,
including their physical and personality traits, (3) explaining the daily routine you kept during that vacation time, and finally, telling (4) two positive
features and (5) one negative feature of the vacation.

After all members of your group have made their presentations, decide
together, (1) the person who got the most rest (**la persona que descansó
más**), (2) the person who was the busiest (**que estaba la más ocupada**),
(3) the one who was the most athletic during that vacation time (**que era
la más atlética**), and (4) two other similar features that apply to your
group. Be prepared to report these results to the class.

C. *En el restaurante* You and some friends meet downtown in a
restaurant. Greet each other, order something to drink and/or eat, and
then use the *Cromos* listing on pages 234–235 to decide on a television
program or a play to see.

274

Actividades escritas

D. Las vacaciones Write about one of your favorite vacations. If possible, bring in photos and describe your activities and those of the other people who were with you.

E. Un día feriado (A holiday) You and your friends are making plans for a one-day holiday from school. Write out your schedule of activities, including sports, movies, and the like. Be detailed in your plans—determine times, places to meet, etc.

F. Una invitación a una fiesta You and your friends are planning a party. Write an invitation indicating who is giving the party, the time, place, and reason. Look at the invitations on pages 242–243 for ideas if you need them.

Writing Activities

Atajo, Writing Assistant Software supports ATAJO

Functional vocabulary: Persuading; planning a vacation; sequencing events; talking about daily routines

Topic vocabulary: Geography; household chores; leisure; toilette

Grammar: verbs: reflexives; pronouns: direct objects; verbs: imperative

Ex. D: writing

Exs. E and F: pair work

 writing

275

Los sueños: dreams

>> ¿Do you dream?

>> ¿What images are usually in your dreams?

>> ¿Do you know how to interpret your dreams?

Los sueños

AL EMPEZAR

In the passage below you will read about dreams and what they mean.

LA INTERPRETACIÓN DE LOS SUEÑOS

Todos nosotros soñamos 4 o 5 veces cada noche aunque no siempre recordamos nuestros sueños. Los sueños son importantes para nuestra salud mental y física. Pero, ¿qué significan los sueños?

Nuestras experiencias, **recuerdos**, emociones, **temores** y esperanzas forman la base de nuestros sueños. Pero a veces no los comprendemos fácilmente porque soñamos con símbolos. Se ha escrito mucho sobre la simbología de los sueños. Todos tenemos experiencias y recuerdos diferentes. Por eso, soñamos con diferentes cosas. Sin embargo, hay ciertos símbolos universales. Se presentan algunos en la siguiente tabla.

recuerdos: memories, *temores:* fears

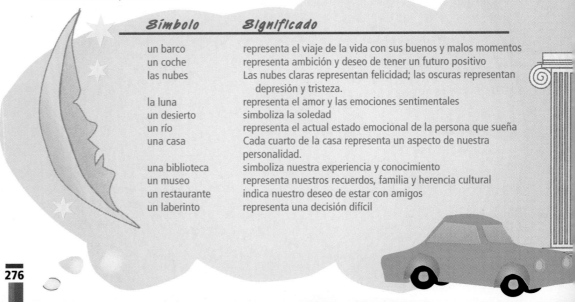

Símbolo	Significado
un barco	representa el viaje de la vida con sus buenos y malos momentos
un coche	representa ambición y deseo de tener un futuro positivo
las nubes	Las nubes claras representan felicidad; las oscuras representan depresión y tristeza.
la luna	representa el amor y las emociones sentimentales
un desierto	simboliza la soledad
un río	representa el actual estado emocional de la persona que sueña
una casa	Cada cuarto de la casa representa un aspecto de nuestra personalidad.
una biblioteca	simboliza nuestra experiencia y conocimiento
un museo	representa nuestros recuerdos, familia y herencia cultural
un restaurante	indica nuestro deseo de estar con amigos
un laberinto	representa una decisión difícil

276

con la psicología

Expansion activity: Have the students keep a log of the things they dream about for a month. You may want to provide them with a list of common dream topics with a space for the date next to each topic.

ACTIVIDAD A

Paso 1: We all have good dreams, bad dreams, and neutral dreams. What type of dreams do the symbols you have read about represent?

Write the symbols down in your notebook. Indicate whether they are positive (**positivo**), negative (**negativo**) or both (**los dos**). Compare your responses with a partner.

Expresiones útiles:

Creo que <u>la luna</u> es un símbolo positivo.   I believe
Creo que <u>un río</u> puede ser un símbolo positivo o negativo.

Paso 2: With a partner, think of other common symbols which appear in dreams.

lugares: _____

la naturaleza: _____

medios de transporte: _____

otro: _____

¿Creen Uds. que son positivos, negativos o neutrales estos símbolos?

¿Representan felicidad, tristeza, enojo, **paz**, estrés o soledad?   peace

ACTIVIDAD B

How often do you dream about the symbols you read about? Write the symbols in your notebook. Next to them indicate how often you dream about them: **nunca, a veces, frecuentemente.**

When you are done, compare your answers with a partner. Do you dream about the same things or different things?

Expresiones útiles:

¿Con qué frecuencia sueñas con <u>la luna</u>?
Sueño con <u>la luna</u> frecuentemente.

277

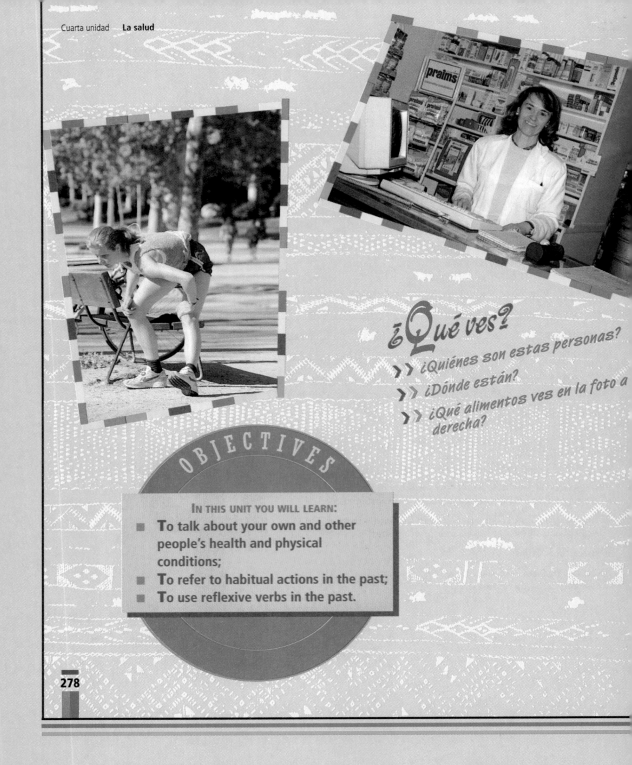

¿Qué ves?

> » ¿Quiénes son estas personas?

> » ¿Dónde están?

> » ¿Qué alimentos ves en la foto a derecha?

OBJECTIVES

IN THIS UNIT YOU WILL LEARN:

- **T**o talk about your own and other people's health and physical conditions;
- **T**o refer to habitual actions in the past;
- **T**o use reflexive verbs in the past.

278

cuatro UNIDAD

La salud

279

Planning Strategy

If you do not assign the Planning Strategy (Workbook, p. 189) for homework or if students have difficulty coming up with English expressions, you might ask several students to role play the situations. Have them play the pharmacist, the doctor, and the patients. You can also put students in groups to brainstorm as many answers as possible to the questions.

Chapter Objectives

Functions: Talking about parts of the body and physical complaints; talking about past routines and habitual activities

Context: School; leisure time

Accuracy: The formation and uses of the imperfect; the imperfect of **ver, ser,** and **ir;** the preterite of reflexive verbs

CAPÍTULO

10

¿CÓMO TE SIENTES?

Patinar en ruedas es un excelente ejercicio y una manera muy divertida para pasearse.

Objectives:

>>> **T**alking about parts of the body and physical complaints

>>> **T**alking about past routines and habitual activities

Strategies:

>>> **I**nterviewing

>>> **R**eporting in the past

>>> **C**omparing and contrasting

280

Video/Laserdisc

Chapter 10 Video Program and Video Guide

PRIMERA ETAPA

Preparación

>> **D**o you know the words for any body parts in Spanish?

>> **W**hen would you need to refer to various body parts?

//-/-/-/-/-/-/-/-/-/-//
Learning Strategies:

Previewing,
brainstorming

El cuerpo humano

El cuerpo humano: The human body

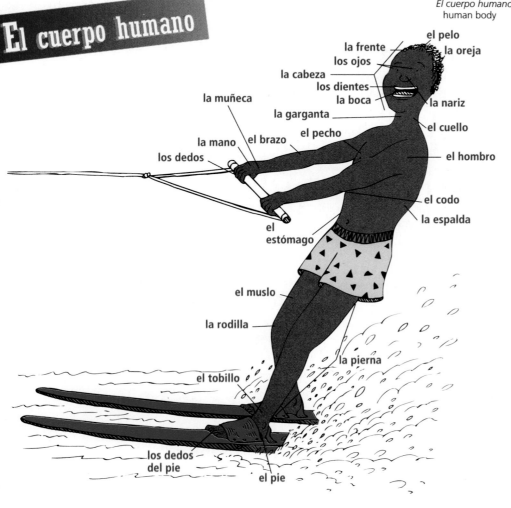

- el pelo
- la frente
- la oreja
- los ojos
- la cabeza
- los dientes
- la boca
- la nariz
- la muñeca
- la garganta
- el cuello
- la mano
- el brazo
- el pecho
- los dedos
- el hombro
- el codo
- la espalda
- el estómago
- el muslo
- la rodilla
- la pierna
- el tobillo
- los dedos del pie
- el pie

281

Presentation: El cuerpo humano

Body parts are an excellent topic for TPR (total physical response). First have students repeat the various parts of the body as you say them. Then ask them to point to the parts of the body you name. If you wish, you can divide the vocabulary into sections—the head, the upper body, the lower body—thus reducing the amount of vocabulary to be presented each time. Or you could play "Simon says". **Simón dice: Toquen los dedos. Toquen la cabeza.**

Etapa Support Materials

Workbook: **pp. 192–197**
Listening Activity masters: **p. 89**
Critical Thinking masters: **Chapter 10, primera etapa, activity I**
Transparencies: **#37, # 37a**
Teacher Tape
Tapescript: **p. 119**

Quiz: **Testing Program, p. 147**

Support material, **El cuerpo humano:**
Transparencies #37 and #37a. Use students or the transparency to demonstrate parts of the body.

Answers, Ex. A: 1. Yo tengo dos... Mi amigo tiene un... 2. Yo tengo dos... Mi amigo tiene tres... 3. Yo tengo treinta y dos... Mi amigo tiene cuatro... 4. Yo tengo dos... Mi amigo tiene tres... 5. Yo tengo diez... Mi amigo tiene doce... 6. Yo tengo dos... Mi amigo tiene una... 7. Yo tengo dos... Mi amigo tiene una... 8. Yo tengo dos... Mi amigo tiene un...

Follow-up, Ex. A: (1) Have students draw their own monsters, label their parts, and hang the pictures in the room. (2) Ask students which body parts they associate with Big Bird (**las piernas**), Dumbo (**las orejas**), Pinocchio (**la nariz**), the Tin Man (**el corazón**), or a popular actor or sports figure.

Possible answers, Ex. B:
1. los dedos, las manos 2. las piernas, los pies 3. la nariz 4. la mano, la cabeza

Presentation: Estructura

The imperfect is discussed in three sections. This presentation concentrates on the forms of the imperfect. Later in this **etapa** and the next, exercises will demonstrate the most frequent uses of this tense. The use of the imperfect here is limited to *what one used to do.*

- Start off by telling students about what you used to do: **Cuando tenía siete años, vivíamos en Nueva Jersey.** Ask students: **Cuando tú tenías siete años, ¿dónde vivías?**
- Ask students what fruits and vegetables they like. Then ask them if they liked those fruits and vegetables when they were 4 or 5 years old.

¡Aquí te toca a ti!

A. *Un amigo extraterrestre* Describe el cuerpo de tu amigo extraterrestre *(your extraterrestrial friend)*. Compara su cuerpo con tu cuerpo, basándote en el dibujo. Sigue el modelo.

Modelo: la cabeza
Yo tengo una cabeza.
Mi amigo tiene una cabeza también.

1. los ojos
2. las orejas
3. los dientes
4. los brazos
5. los dedos
6. las piernas
7. las rodillas
8. los pies

B. *Las partes del cuerpo* Identifica la(s) parte(s) del cuerpo que asocias con *(that you associate with)* las siguientes actividades.

1. playing the piano
2. jogging
3. testing perfume
4. eating

ESTRUCTURA

The imperfect

¿Dónde **vivías** cuando tenías 10 años?	Where *did you used to live* when you were 10 years old?
Yo **vivía** en Indiana.	I *used to live* in Indiana.
¿Qué **hacías** durante el verano?	What *did you used to do* during the summer?
Yo **nadaba y jugaba** al tenis todos los días.	I *used to swim and play* tennis every day.

You have already learned to express actions in the past by using the preterite. Now you will learn a second past tense, the imperfect, which will allow you to describe what you *used to do.*

To form the imperfect, begin by dropping the **-ar, -er,** or **-ir** of the infinitive and adding the imperfect endings **-aba, -abas, -aba, -ábamos, -abais, -aban** for **-ar** verbs, and **-ía, -ías, -ía, -íamos, -íais, -ían** for **-er** and **-ir** verbs.

The imperfect tense has three equivalents in English:

Ella vivía en España. { *She lived* in Spain.
She used to live in Spain.
She was living in Spain.

282

	hablar habl-	comer com-	vivir viv-
yo	hablaba	comía	vivía
tú	hablabas	comías	vivías
él, ella, Ud.	hablaba	comía	vivía
nosotros(as)	hablábamos	comíamos	vivíamos
vosotros(as)	hablabais	comíais	vivíais
ellos, ellas, Uds.	hablaban	comían	vivían

Aquí practicamos

C. ¿Qué hacían Uds.? Di lo que hacían tú y tus amigos(as) *(what you and your friends used to do)* durante el verano cuando tenían diez años.

A	B	C	D
yo	(no)	nadar	todos los días
tú		estudiar	
?		jugar…	
nosotros(as)		beber…	
Uds.		montar en bicicleta	

Nota gramatical

The imperfect of ver, ser, and ir

The verbs **ver, ser,** and **ir** are conjugated in this way:

	ver	ser	ir
yo	veía	era	iba
tú	veías	eras	ibas
él, ella, Ud.	veía	era	iba
nosotros(as)	veíamos	éramos	íbamos
vosotros(as)	veíais	erais	ibais
ellos, ellas, Uds.	veían	eran	iban

283

Ex. C: writing

Less-prepared students, Ex. C: Have less-prepared students give the English equivalent for each of their Spanish answers as a comprehension check.

More-prepared students, Ex. C: More-prepared students can work up their sentences into a short paragraph about their elementary school days, adding any extra vocabulary as needed (**mirar la tele, andar en bicicleta, comer caramelos, tomar helado, acostarse / levantarse temprano,** etc.)

Suggestion, Ex. C: These column exercises are meant to provide controlled practice. One way to present them is through a "word web." On a separate piece of paper, students draw a web and then connect elements from the columns in ways that form grammatically correct sentences. (They have to write the correct form of the verb in the middle column.) The drawing that follows is a sample word web format. Word web formats vary from exercise to exercise.

Presentation: Nota gramatical

Model **ir** and **ser** with a personal sentence, e.g., **Cada verano cuando yo era joven, íbamos a la playa.** Then ask students where they used to go or have them ask each other.

Presentation: Estructura (cont.)

- Have students repeat the conjugation of **hablar** or **estudiar** in the imperfect while you write pronouns in three groups: **yo, tú, él, ella, Ud. / nosotros, vosotros / ellos, ellas, Uds.**
- Contrast the imperfect forms with those of the present and the preterite.
- Write out the verb forms.
- Repeat with **-er** and **-ir** verbs.
- Have each student conjugate a verb or part of a verb on the board. Ask if it is correct; if it is, have the student pass the chalk to the next person until everyone has been to the board.

Exs. D and E: pair work

Suggestion, Exs. D and E:
Send student teams to the board to do these exercises. Time each team and declare the winner at the end. After all work is on the board, ask volunteers to give some English equivalents for the Spanish sentences as a comprehension check.

Answers, Ex. D: 1. Yo iba, Ellas iban, Nosotras íbamos, Tú ibas, Juan y su familia iban, Vosotras ibais 2. Yo no veía, Uds. no veían, Ellas no veían, Mirta y Guillermo no veían, Tú no veías, Vosotros veíais 3. ¿Eras tú, Eran ellas, Era Mario, Era Ud., Era ella, Eran Uds., Erais vosotras?

Answers, Ex. E: 1. El año pasado, Carlos nadaba cada jueves por la tarde. 2. El año pasado, Dina y su novio estudiaban cada jueves por la tarde. 3. El año pasado, Jaime hablaba por teléfono cada jueves por la tarde. 4. El año pasado, Mónica esquiaba cada jueves por la tarde. 5. El año pasado, Olga y Lucía miraban la televisión cada jueves por la tarde. 6. El año pasado, Alberto leía cada jueves por la tarde. 7. El año pasado, Miguel y Patricio corrían cada jueves por la tarde. 8. El año pasado, Isabel escribía cada jueves por la tarde.

D. Sustituye las palabras en cursiva con las palabaras entre paréntesis y haz los otros cambios necesarios.

1. *Ellos* iban a la playa cada verano. (yo / ellas / nosotras / tú / Juan y su familia / vosotras)
2. *Nosotros* no veíamos a Juan a menudo. (yo / Uds. / ellas / Mirta y Guillermo / tú / vosotros)
3. ¿Era *él* de España? (tú / ellas / Mario / Ud. / ella / Uds. / vosotras)

Learning Strategy:
Reporting based on visual cues

E. *El año pasado... cada jueves por la tarde* Di lo que hacían *(used to do)* cada jueves el año pasado las personas en los siguientes dibujos. Sigue el modelo.

Modelo: El año pasado, Carmen corría cada jueves por la tarde.

Carmen

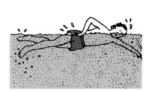

1. Carlos

2. Dina y su novio

3. Jaime

4. Mónica

5. Olga y Lucía

6. Alberto

7. Miguel y Patricio

8. Isabel

284

F. El año pasado, mi amigo y yo... Now imagine that every Saturday afternoon, you and a friend did what the people in the drawings in Activity E did. Repeat each item following the model.

> *Modelo:* El año pasado, corríamos cada jueves por la tarde.

Aquí escuchamos:
"¡Pobre Martín!"

Antes de escuchar

Dina and Felipe run into their friend Martín who doesn't feel too well. Look at the following questions and identify a few things you expect to hear during their conversation.

Después de escuchar

1. ¿Cómo se ve Martín según Dina?
2. ¿Qué tiene Martín?
3. ¿Cómo se ve Martín según Felipe?
4. ¿Qué dice Dina que debe hacer Martín?
5. ¿Qué va a hacer Martín?

¡Aquí te toca a ti!

G. No te ves muy bien. (You don't look very good.) Talk to a classmate about his or her state of health. Follow the general pattern of the models while varying the health expressions that you use.

> *Modelos:*
> —¿Qué tal?
> —No me siento muy bien. (I don't feel very well.)
> —¿Qué te pasa? (What's wrong?)
> —Tengo dolor de cabeza (estómago, etc.).
>
> —¡Hola, amigo! No te ves muy bien.
> —¿Verdad? Tengo dolor de cabeza (espalda, etc.).
> —Pobre. Debes descansar.
> —Tienes razón. (You're right.) Voy a volver a casa.

285

Support material, Aquí escuchamos: Teacher Tape

Presentation: Aquí escuchamos

(1) Discuss with students the social convention of asking people how they are when they meet.
(2) Have students listen to the dialogue on the recording.
(3) After playing the tape once, divide the class into groups and assign parts **(Felipe, Martín, Dina)** to each. Instruct students to listen for their part and to write it out. Play the tape at least twice more. Finally, correct from master. You may want to organize students to write the final version on the board, underlining expressions needed for future work.

Answers, Aquí escuchamos: 1. no se ve muy bien 2. los ojos rojos 3. está muy pálido 4. volver a casa y descansar 5. acostarse y descansar

Ex. G: pair work

Ex. F: writing

More-prepared students, Ex. F: Have more-prepared students include some of their own activities as well as those in the drawings.

Answers, Ex. F: 1. Mi amigo y yo nadábamos. 2. ...estudiábamos. 3. ...hablábamos. 4. ...esquiábamos. 5. ...mirábamos la tele. 6. ...leíamos. 7. ...corríamos. 8. ...escribíamos.

Presentation: Estructura

Ask students about a typical day and/or week during summer vacation when they were younger. **¿A qué hora te levantabas? ¿A qué hora te acostabas?** Work into your questions the expressions from the **Estructura,** most of which students already know. You could also model this with a personal statement, e.g., **Cuando tenía ocho años e íbamos a la playa, me levantaba cada día a las nueve y frecuentemente nadaba con mi padre.**

Ex. H: writing

Answers, Ex. H: 1. nosotros nos despertábamos   2. yo me quedaba   3. mi hermano se levantaba   4. nosotros nos duchábamos   5. nosotros nos desayunábamos

Ex. I: pair work

ESTRUCTURA

The imperfect: habitual actions

Todos los veranos **íbamos** a la playa.   Every summer *we used to go* to the beach.
Cada noche **escribíamos** postales.   Every evening *we used to write* postcards.

The imperfect tense is used to describe something that happened over and over again in the past. Certain adverbs and expressions that convey the idea of a routine often accompany the imperfect tense. They reinforce the idea of habitual actions and of things that *used to be done* repeatedly. You already have learned some of the following adverbs and expressions.

a menudo	*often*
a veces	*sometimes*
cada día (viernes, sábado, tarde, mañana, noche, semana, mes, etc.)	*every day (Friday, Saturday, afternoon, morning, night, week, month, etc.)*
con frecuencia / frecuentemente	*frequently*
con regularidad	*regularly*
de vez en cuando	*from time to time*
muchas veces	*many times*
normalmente	*normally*
siempre	*always*
todos los días (lunes, martes, etc.)	*every day (Monday, Tuesday, etc.)*
una vez al día (a la semana, mes, año, etc.)	*once a day (week, month, year, etc.)*

Aquí practicamos

H. *El verano pasado* Last year Silvia's parents went away for a couple of weeks. Use the suggested elements and the imperfect to tell what Silvia and her brother did while their parents were gone.

> **Modelo:** Cada sábado por la noche / yo / salir con mis amigos
> *Cada sábado por la noche salía con mis amigos.*

1. cada día / nosotros / despertarse temprano
2. muchas veces / yo / quedarse en cama una hora o dos
3. de costumbre / mi hermano / levantarse en seguida
4. todos los días / nosotros / ducharse
5. normalmente / nosotros / desayunarse juntos

I. *Cuando tú tenías siete años...* Create a chart like the one on page 287. Decide if each item on the list was true for you when you were seven and mark it to the left of the items. Then interview your part-

286

ner about his or her situation at the same age. Mark his or her responses in the columns on the right. Follow the model.

Modelo: ir a la escuela
—*Cuando tú tenías siete años, ¿ibas a la escuela?*
—*Sí, iba a la escuela.*

Yo			Mi amigo(a)	
Sí	No		Sí	No
X	___	ir a la escuela	X	___
___	___	vivir aquí	___	___
___	___	tener hermanos y hermanas	___	___
___	___	ir a la playa	___	___
___	___	dormir una siesta	___	___
___	___	comer mucho	___	___
___	___	ser travieso(a) *(mischievous)*	___	___
___	___	jugar con los compañeros	___	___
___	___	levantarse temprano	___	___
___	___	beber mucha leche	___	___

¡Adelante!

EJERCICIO ORAL

J. ¿Qué hacías el verano pasado?   Think back to what you used to do last summer. (1) Make a list of at least eight activities that you did repeatedly. (2) Using the expressions on page 286, mark down how often each week you participated in each of the activities. (3) Get together with a partner and interview each other about last summer. (4) Compare your partner's activities with yours, noting two similarities and one difference.

EJERCICIO ESCRITO

K. Cuando yo era niño...   After spending an afternoon with your ten-year-old niece, you recall your own life at that age. Write a short description in your diary about things that you used to like to do when you were ten or twelve years old. (1) Include at least five activities in which you liked to participate. (2) Tell how often you were involved in these activities. (3) Tell which of these activities was your favorite.

//-//-//-//-//-//-//-//-//-//
Cooperative Learning

Learning Strategies:

Interviewing, recording information on a chart

Critical Thinking Strategy:

Comparing and contrasting

//-//-//-//-//-//-//-//-//-//
Cooperative Learning

Learning Strategies:

Listing, reporting based on personal knowledge, interviewing

Critical Thinking Strategy:

Comparing and contrasting

//-//-//-//-//-//-//-//-//-//
Learning Strategies:

Listing, describing, organizing ideas, commenting on preferences

287

Presentation: El ejercicio ideal

Treat this section as a reading exercise. Have students discuss activities that help people stay in shape. Then, have them scan the reading and pick out cognates. Next, have them read the article, reminding them that they need not understand every word but encouraging them to use their reading skills to understand as much as they can.

SEGUNDA ETAPA

Preparación

›› **W**hat do you do for exercise?

›› **L**ook at the photograph. What do you think the reading will be about?

›› **W**hat does the title of the reading suggest to you?

//-/-//-/-//-/-//-/-//
Learning Strategy:
Previewing

El ejercicio ideal: The ideal exercise

El ejercicio ideal

Ventajas: Advantages
peso: weight
tonificarte: to tone up / *lastimarse:* to hurt oneself

las coyunturas: the joints
ponerte en forma: to get in shape / *Aseguran:* Assure

sencilla: simple / *los pulmones:* the lungs

sudando: sweating / *levantar pesas:* to lift weights / *trotar:* to jog

Tírate: Throw yourself

En el agua vas a bajar de peso y vas a tonificarte el cuerpo. No hay manera más eficiente y divertida de ponerte en forma.

¿Buscas una manera **sencilla** y agradable de ponerte en forma? ¿Te gusta la idea de pasar horas **sudando** en un gimnasio? ¿No? Entonces, la solución para ti puede ser la natación. Además de ser un excelente deporte, la nata-

ción puede ser un divertido evento social. En la piscina puedes reunirte con tus amigos… a la vez que trabaja tu sistema cardiovascular.

¿Por qué?

Porque cuando tú nadas, el corazón y **los pulmones** trabajan a su capacidad máxima porque tu cuerpo demanda una gran dosis extra de oxígeno. El movimiento continuo hace de la natación un excelente ejercicio aeróbico.

Ventajas

Una de las grandes ventajas de este deporte es que es difícil **lastimarse** porque cuando tu cuerpo flota en el agua, no hay presión en **las coyunturas. Aseguran** los expertos que la persona que nada 15 minutos consecutivos todos los días va a mantenerse en condiciones óptimas sin tener que **levantar pesas** o **trotar.**

¿Quieres ponerte en forma? **Tírate** al agua y nada, nada, nada…

288

Etapa Support Materials

Workbook: pp. 198–203
Critical Thinking masters: Chapter 10, segunda etapa, activity H
Transparency: #38
Teacher Tape 🎧
Quiz: Testing Program, p. 150

¡Aquí te toca a ti!

A. Contesta las siguientes preguntas sobre la lectura en la página 288.

1. What does the headline say are two benefits of this exercise?
2. In the first paragraph, what is another benefit of this activity, in addition to its being a good sport in general?
3. Why is it a good aerobic exercise?
4. Why is it difficult to injure yourself while doing this activity?
5. How often should you do this activity in order to stay in good shape, according to the experts?

Learning Strategy:

Reading for details

Repaso

B. Tiene dolor de... Indica dónde tiene dolor cada persona.

Learning Strategy:

Reporting based on visual cues

1. Sara   2. mi papá   3. mi mamá   4. Magda

C. Recuerdos Marcos and Lucila remember the days when they were students in elementary school. They talk about what they used to do on days they had to go to school. If you are a boy, play the role of Marcos and if you are a girl, play the role of Lucila. Use the imperfect for all verbs.

Learning Strategy:

Expressing past time

Modelo: Marcos y Lucila / despertarse / 7:00
Marcos: *Cada día, mi hermana y yo nos despertábamos a las siete.*
Lucila: *Cada día, mi hermano y yo nos despertábamos a las siete.*

1. Lucila / levantarse / 7:15
2. Marcos / levantarse / 7:30
3. Lucila / ducharse
4. Marcos / afeitarse
5. Marcos / beber leche
6. Lucila / beber jugo de naranja
7. Lucila y Marcos / lavarse los dientes
8. Marcos y Lucila / ir a la escuela / 8:00

Presentation: Estructura

Have students describe what is going on in the classroom. **Nosotros estamos en la clase de español. Son las 10:15. El profesor habla. Diana escucha al profesor, pero Roberto mira su libro. Él está aburrido.** Then have students give the same description in the imperfect by leaving the room for a minute and coming in and asking **¿Qué pasaba cuando yo entré?**

ESTRUCTURA

The imperfect: additional uses

Mientras **hablábamos,** ella **leía** una revista.	While *we were talking*, she *was reading* a magazine.
Ella **tenía** los ojos azules.	She *had* blue eyes. (Her eyes *were* blue.)
Yo **creía** que **era** bonita.	I *thought she was* pretty.

In addition to indicating habitual past actions, the imperfect tense is used to talk about several other kinds of situations in the past.

1. To indicate actions that *were going on* at the time about which you are speaking.

Mientras **hablábamos,** ella **leía** una revista.	While *we were talking*, she *was reading* a magazine.

2. To describe the physical attributes of people you are remembering.

Ella **tenía** los ojos azules.	She *had* blue eyes.

3. To express attitudes and beliefs that were held at that time in the past, using verbs such as **creer, pensar,** etc.

Yo **creía** que era bonita.	I *thought* she was pretty.

4. To express how old someone was in the past.

Él **tenía** cincuenta años.	He *was* fifty years old.

5. To describe past states of health.

Yo **no me sentía** bien.	I *didn't feel* well.

6. To set the background or context for a story that takes place in the past.

Eran las nueve de la noche.	*It was* 9:00 at night.
Yo **estaba de visita** en Phoenix.	I *was visiting* Phoenix.
Era invierno, pero **hacía** muchísimo calor allí. **Estábamos** en un pequeño restaurante.	*It was* winter, but *it was* very hot there. *We were* in a tiny restaurant.

290

Aquí practicamos

D. *La fiesta de Cecilia* Daniel llegó tarde a la fiesta de Cecilia. Basándote en el dibujo, usa el imperfecto *(the imperfect tense)* para describir lo que hacían sus amigos cuando llegó a la fiesta.

//-//-//-//-//-//-//-//-//-//
Learning Strategy:
Reporting based on visual cues

Cecilia
Mónica Liliana
Sr. Castañeda
Jorge Verónica
Óscar
Joaquín
Enrique
Jaime

Modelo: Óscar
Óscar escuchaba discos compactos.

1. Jaime, Enrique y Joaquín
2. Mónica y Liliana
3. Jorge y Verónica
4. Cecilia
5. Sr. Castañeda
6. todo el mundo

E. *Anoche a las 8:00* You are going to tell a story about something that happened to you. Set the scene by explaining where you were and what you were doing when the story's action began. For the first situation, you are given questions to help you. For the other situations, give similar descriptions on your own.

//-//-//-//-//-//-//-//-//-//
Learning Strategy:
Expressing past time
Critical Thinking Strategy:
Creating

1. Ayer por la noche a las 8:00 —¿Dónde estabas? ¿Qué hacías? ¿Qué tiempo hacía? ¿Cómo te sentías? ¿Estabas solo(a) *(alone)* o con otras personas? ¿Qué hacían ellas?
2. Esta mañana a las 7:30
3. El sábado pasado a las 10:00 de la noche
4. El viernes pasado por la noche
5. Un momento importante de tu vida

291

Cultural Observation

Guide students to observe the diversity of races at the party pictured on page 291. Explain that in Hispanic cultures parties are not limited to people of the same age group, as they tend to be in the U.S., but may include family members of all ages, family members' friends and their friends' children, neighbors, business associates, and others.

Support material, Ex. D: Transparency #38

Ex. D: writing

Possible answers, Ex. D:
1. Jaime, Enrique y Joaquín comían, bebían.   2. Mónica y Liliana hablaban, charlaban.   3. Jorge y Verónica bailaban.   4. Cecilia cantaba.   5. El Sr. Castañeda sacaba fotos.   6. Todo el mundo se divertía.

Follow-up, Ex. D: Have students recount orally or in writing what was happening yesterday evening when they got home, e.g., **Mi padre preparaba la comida, mi madre leía el periódico, mis hermanos jugaban,** etc.

Ex. E: writing

Follow-up, Ex. E: Pick special days for which to set the scene: Halloween night, Christmas and/or New Year's Eve, the Fourth of July, **los reyes magos, el 5 de mayo,** etc.

Presentation: Aquí escuchamos

Discuss what teenagers do to keep physically fit. (Cultural commentary: Tell students about the rising consciousness regarding fitness in Europe. There are more aerobics, gymnastics, and dance classes, and more people jogging, etc.) You may want to use suggestions from previous **etapas** for this exercise.

Answers, Aquí escuchamos: 1. correr o jugar al tenis   2. que no se ve bien, que come mucho, que siempre está cansada, que tiene que bajar de peso   3. porque hace gimnasia   4. tres   5. una

Ex. F: pair work

writing

Follow-up, Ex. F: Have students ask each other which of these activities they participate in. Have one student keep track and report the responses.

Answers, Ex. F: 1. Dina juega al tenis.   2. María Teresa nada.   3. Carmen levanta pesas.   4. Virginia practica yoga.

Aquí escuchamos:
"¡Tú siempre estás en forma!"

//-//-//-//-//-//-//-//-//

Learning Strategy:
Previewing

Antes de escuchar

Magda and Sofía are talking about what they do to stay in shape. Look at the following questions and identify a few things you expect to hear during their conversation.

//-//-//-//-//-//-//-//-//

Learning Strategy:
Listening for details

Después de escuchar

1. ¿Qué desea hacer Magda?
2. ¿Qué piensa Madga de Sofía?
3. ¿Por qué está Madga siempre en forma?
4. ¿Cuántas veces por semana hace gimnasia (*work out*) Magda?
5. ¿Cuántas veces por semana va Magda a una discoteca?

//-//-//-//-//-//-//-//-//

Learning Strategy:
Reporting based on visual cues

¡Aquí te toca a ti!

F. *Ellas hacen gimnasia.* Look at the pictures of young women and how they stay in shape. Then answer the questions that follow to match the names of the appropriate activities with the women who do them.

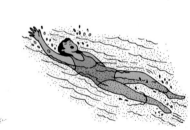

Dina   Virginia   María Teresa   Carmen

1. ¿Quién juega al tenis?
2. ¿Quién nada?
3. ¿Quién levanta pesas?
4. ¿Quién practica yoga?

292

G. Intercambio Hazle las siguientes preguntas a un(a) compañero(a). Tu compañero(a) va a responderte según su experiencia personal.

1. ¿Eres activo(a)? ¿Te gusta practicar un deporte o mirar los partidos en la tele?
2. ¿Haces ejercicios aeróbicos? ¿Practicas yoga?
3. ¿Nadas de vez en cuando?
4. ¿Te gusta bailar? ¿Ballet o rock?
5. ¿Estás en forma? ¿Tus amigos piensan que tú eres fuerte o débil? ¿Levantas pesas? ¿Quisieras levantar pesas?

EJERCICIO ORAL

H. ¿Estás en forma? Ask several classmates what they used to do a couple of years ago and what they do now to stay fit. Create a chart like the following one to record their responses and to prepare for class discussion. Start your conversation with: **¿Qué hacías hace dos años para estar en forma? Y ahora, ¿qué haces?** Share with the class some of the common responses as well as the most unusual response.

Hace 2 años	Compañero(a) de clase	Ahora
nadaba	*Cecilia*	*juega al tenis*

EJERCICIO ESCRITO

I. Soy muy activo(a). ¿Y tú? Write a note to your Spanish-speaking pen pal in Argentina telling him or her what you do to stay in shape. (1) Tell at least three things that you do and describe your usual diet. (2) Compare your current activities to what you used to do two or three years ago. (3) Then ask what people your age in Argentina do for exercise. (4) Request photographs of people engaged in popular sports or activities.

Learning Strategies:

Requesting and providing personal information, taking notes in a chart

Critical Thinking Strategies:

Comparing, evaluating

Learning Strategies:

Expressing present and past time, asking questions, making requests

Critical Thinking Strategy:

Comparing and contrasting

293

Ex. G: pair work

Less-prepared students, Ex. G: Allow less-prepared students time to formulate answers to these questions before pairing them up.

More-prepared students: Have more-prepared students create two or three more appropriate questions for each other.

Ex. H: groups of four or more

Suggestions, Ex. H: You may wish to have students do a physical fitness survey of the entire class and report back. You could also take Spanish out of the classroom and have students survey other members of the school.

Follow-up, Ex. H: Do a "tick mark" graph on the board as a follow-up activity. Have the class look for similarities among students' choices, both two years ago and now. Guide them to generalize from their findings. Help them make inferences about changes in lifestyles of the students. Can any changes be attributed to age, popularity of sports (in-line skating, for example), moving of students from one climate to another, etc.?

Critical Thinking Strategies: Drawing inferences, hypothesizing, generalizing

Ex. I: writing

Less-prepared students, Ex. I: Have less-prepared students make a chart like the one in Ex. H where they can take notes and compare their activities then and now. Have them use their charts to prepare their paragraphs.

Presentation: Dos accidentes

Treat this section as a reading exercise. As a prereading activity, bring in a local newspaper and read a short news item dealing with a car, bike, or motorcycle accident. Have students identify the types of information given. Or assign each student, or groups of them, to bring in their own newspapers. Then have students read the two articles and do Ex. A. Once they have done Ex. A, ask students to reread the articles and do Ex. B on page 295. After doing Ex. B, students can write an article of their own, using the questions in Ex. B as a base.

Ex. A: writing

Answers, Ex. A: 1. atropellada 2. chocaron 3. motociclista 4. pasajero 5. se lastimaron (lastimados)

TERCERA ETAPA

Preparación

As you start this **etapa**, think about physical ailments. How would you express such things as:

//-//-//-//-//-//-//-//
Learning Strategy:
Previewing

>> a hurt knee?

>> a stomachache?

>> a headache?

>> a sprained ankle?

>> other aches and pains?

Dos accidentes

Niña atropellada

Nívea Lucero, una niña de 7 años, fue atropellada por un automóvil ayer a las 9:30 de la mañana en la Calle Cervantes. La niña caminaba a la escuela y el coche la atropelló cuando cruzaba la calle. En el accidente la niña se quebró un brazo y una pierna y se cortó la frente. Fue transportada al Hospital Santa Cruz en una ambulancia de la Cruz Roja.

Dos lastimados

Un accidente ocurrió ayer a las 2:30 de la tarde en la Avenida Bolívar. Dos jóvenes que andaban en motocicleta chocaron con un automóvil. El motociclista, Alejandro Bernal, 14 años, y su pasajero, Tomás Ferrer, 14 años, se lastimaron en el choque. Fueron transportados al Hospital San Juan en una ambulancia de la Cruz Roja.

¡Aquí te toca a ti!

A. Estudio de palabras   Based on the context of the two newspaper articles, answer the following in order to figure out the meanings of some of the words you may not know.

1. Find a word that means *to be struck, banged into,* or *knocked down*.
2. Find a word that means *collided*.
3. Find a word that means *driver*.
4. Find a word that means *passenger*.
5. Find a word that means *to be injured*.

294

Etapa Support Materials

Workbook: pp. 204–210
Critical Thinking masters: Chapter 10, tercera etapa, activity E
Transparencies: #39, #40
Teacher Tape ∩

Quiz: Testing Program, p. 152
Chapter Test: Testing Program, p. 155

Support material, Dos accidentes: Transparency #39

B. Artículos cortos (Short articles)   Los dos artículos de periódicos en la página 294 dan mucha información en pocas líneas. Contestan para cada artículo estas preguntas: ¿quién?, ¿qué?, ¿dónde?, ¿cuándo?

Repaso

C. El comienzo de un cuento   Aquí tienes el comienzo de un cuento. Cambia los verbos del presente al imperfecto.

Es una noche del mes de diciembre. Hace mucho frío y nieva. Mi hermana y yo estamos en el coche de mi papá. El coche no funciona porque no tiene gasolina. Al lado de la carretera está una mujer vieja. Ella tiene el pelo blanco y una nariz muy larga. Ella camina con un gato negro y canta una canción de Counting Crows. *Mi hermana y yo pensamos que todo eso es muy extraño.*

Now invent the beginning of a second story, based on the drawing to the right. Instead of telling the whole story, establish the scene by using the imperfect to describe the setting, the situation, and the characters.

Learning Strategies:

Describing based on visual cues, narrating in the past

Critical Thinking Strategy:

Creating

ESTRUCTURA

The preterite of reflexive verbs

Yo **me acosté** a las nueve anoche.	I *went to bed* at 9:00 last night.
Mi hermana **se levantó** a las 7:30 ayer.	My sister *got up* at 7:30 yesterday.
Nos encontramos en el centro.	We *met each other* downtown.

295

B: writing

ggestion, Ex. B: Have students do this in Spanish, n if they only give one-word answers.

pport material, Ex. C: Transparency #40

C: writing

Cooperative Learning

Simultaneous Creation Pairs, Ex. C

Learning Strategies: Describing, narrating in the past, negotiating

Critical Thinking Strategies: Creating, evaluating

- Have students work in pairs to do the first part of Ex. C, taking turns performing and encouraging.
- Then have them think independently about how they would begin their story.
- Ask them to share their beginnings with their partners. Instruct them to listen carefully to their partner's beginning.
- Once they have heard each other's idea, have them create a new beginning that is better than each student's initial beginning, by building on and synthesizing their thoughts.
- Have them follow the same procedure for describing the setting, the situation, and the characters.
- Call on students at random to evaluate their collaborations.
- Then call on a few students to share the beginnings of their stories with the class.

Answers, Ex. C: Era, Hacía, nevaba, estábamos, funcionaba, tenía, estaba, tenía, caminaba, cantaba, pensábamos, era

Expansion, Ex. C: Choose a well-known fairy tale for each group of students. Have each group prepare the story's set-up, as in Ex. C. You may want to tell students that one Spanish equivalent for "Once upon a time" is **Había una vez.**

Presentation: Estructura

Review the present tense of reflexive verbs covered in Unit 3 (pp. 211–212). Ask students to recall as many verbs as they can before turning back to Unit 3.

In **Capítulo 7**, you learned about reflexive verbs in the present tense. As they do in the present tense, these verbs may have two meanings in the preterite:

1. an action that reflects back on the subject

Mi hermana **se levantó** a las 7:30 ayer.	My sister *got up* at 7:30 yesterday.

2. an action in which two or more subjects interact

Nos encontramos en el centro.	*We met each other* downtown.

In both cases, the subject (noun or subject pronoun) is accompanied by its corresponding reflexive pronoun (**me, te, se, nos, os, se**).

Aquí practicamos

D. *Ayer me levanté a las...*   Indica algunas actividades que tú y tu hermano(a) hicieron ayer. Sigue el modelo.

Modelo: yo / levantarse / 7:30
Me levanté a las 7:30 ayer.

1. yo / despertarse / 6:30
2. mi hermano / despertarse / 7:00
3. yo / levantarse / 7:30
4. mi hermana / levantarse / inmediatamente
5. yo / ducharse / 7:45
6. mi hermano / bañarse / 7:15
7. mi hermana / maquillarse
8. yo / afeitarse (maquillarse)
9. mi hermana y yo / cepillarse los dientes
10. mis hermanos y yo / desayunarse juntos

Learning Strategies:

Interviewing, reporting in the past, recording information on a chart

296

E. *Ayer, anoche y esta mañana*   (1) Make a chart like the following one and fill in information about your own activities yesterday, last night, and this morning (following the model information shown). (2) Interview three other members of your class to determine if they did some of those activities. For each one they did, (3) find out some additional detail about it, as suggested in the chart on page 297.

¿Qué hicimos ayer y esta mañana?				
Actividad	Yo	Nombre de amigo(a)	Nombre de amigo(a)	Nombre de amigo(a)
llegar a casa tarde (¿a qué hora?)	*sí; a las cinco*			
hacer deporte (¿por cuánto tiempo?)	*jugué al tenis dos horas*			
salir anoche (¿dónde y hasta qué hora?)	*salí a la casa de Pete hasta las 10*			
acostarse (¿a qué hora?)	*a las once y media*			
cepillarse los dientes (¿cuántas veces?)	*dos veces*			
dormir bien o mal (¿por cuántas horas?)	*bien; por siete horas*			
despertarse (¿a qué hora?)	*a las seis y media*			
levantarse en seguida (¿a qué hora?) o quedarse en la cama (¿hasta qué hora?)	*no, quedé en la cama hasta las siete*			
maquillarse o afeitarse (¿por cuánto tiempo?)	*me maquillé por quince minutos*			
desayunarse con la familia o solo	*con mi hermana*			

Aquí escuchamos:
"¡No me digas! ¿Te rompiste la pierna?"

Antes de escuchar

Carlos and Felipe are talking on the telephone about an accident that Felipe had yesterday. Look at the questions on page 298 and identify a few things you expect to hear during their conversation.

Learning Strategy:
Previewing

Critical Thinking Strategy:
Predicting

297

Suggestion, Ex. E: Have students include appropriate preterite verb forms in their lists.

Support material, Aquí escuchamos: Teacher Tape

Presentation: Aquí escuchamos

Tell students that they are about to hear about an accident. Have them listen to the dialogue. Ask them to answer the basics about any accident report (refer to Ex. B, p. 295): who, what, where, and when. You may want to write on the board: **¿Quién? ¿Qué? ¿Dónde? ¿Cuándo?** As students listen several times, they should be able to add one or two details to the basic information. You may also want to do a dictation exercise with this material.

//-//-//-//-//-//-//-//-//
Learning Strategy:
Listening for details

Después de escuchar

1. ¿Por qué no fue Felipe a la escuela?
2. ¿Qué parte del cuerpo se lastimó Felipe?
3. ¿Cómo pasó el accidente?
4. ¿Qué hacía Felipe?
5. ¿Se lastimó otra persona también? ¿Dónde se lastimó?

¡Aquí te toca a ti!

//-//-//-//-//-//-//-//-//
Learning Strategy:
Identifying based on visual cues

F. Un accidente   In Spanish, you often use the verbs **lastimarse** *(to hurt oneself)*, **torcerse** *(to twist)*, **romperse** *(to break)*, and **cortarse** *(to cut)* with parts of the body to describe the results of an accident. Use the following expressions and those on page 299 to indicate what happened to you. Follow the model.

Modelo: Yo me lastimé…
Yo me lastimé la mano.

1. Yo me lastimé…

2. Yo me torcí…

3. Yo me rompí…

298

After determining the most common injuries, guide the class in drawing inferences about why those injuries happen more often (sports participated in by students in this sampling, such as skiing, football, in-line skating, etc.)

4. Yo me corté …

G. ¿Qué pasó? Identify three people you know who have had an accident that resulted in an injury at one time or another. (You may use yourself as one of those people, if appropriate.) Then share that information with a partner. At the end of your conversation, identify together: (1) any acquaintances who have had the same injury and (2) the person who had the most serious injury.

Cooperative Learning

Learning Strategies:

Selecting and providing information, reporting in the past, negotiating

Critical Thinking Strategy:

Evaluating

Ex. H: pair work

role play

Less-prepared students, Ex. H: Allow less-prepared students time to formulate the questions before beginning to work with a partner.

Suggestion, Ex. H: After the activity has been done as a telephone call, have partners change roles. Then have each pair team up with another pair. Each student should report to the small group the details of his/her partner's accident report.

Then have each group of four plan a portion of a news broadcast. They should select the accident report to be featured on the broadcast, select the person to play the role of anchor person, and help the reporter to organize and embellish the details. The news broadcasts can be delivered to the whole class.

EJERCICIO ORAL

H. Tuve un accidente. Think of a time when you or a close acquaintance was hurt in an accident. Imagine that the accident just happened. Call up a friend on the telephone to report the news of the accident. Your partner will express appropriate concern, asking about the circumstances of the accident. Discuss (1) when it happened, (2) where, (3) what the injured person was doing before and when the accident occurred, (4) who the person was with, and (5) what the specific injury was.

Learning Strategies:

Asking for and providing information, reporting in the past

EJERCICIO ESCRITO

I. Un accidente Imagine that your local newspaper wants to include some articles in Spanish in its weekend edition as a service to the Spanish-speaking population of your city. An editor has asked your Spanish class to submit some articles to be judged for determining who would be offered a position as freelance reporter in Spanish. Using the clippings on page 294 as models, write a short article about an accident (either imaginary or real) that happened recently. Include who, what, where, and when in your article.

Learning Strategies:

Selecting information, organizing details in a sequence, selecting appropriate journalistic tone

299

Learning Strategies: *Negotiating, peer tutoring, organizing details in a report, selecting appropriate journalistic tone*

Critical Thinking Strategy: *Evaluating*

G: pair work

Suggestion, Ex. G: Have students create a chart to condense their information. They can use the following column headings: **Persona / Tipo de accidente / Cuando / Serio no.** They may refer to the chart as they relay information in a more complete form to their partner. They may also keep a similar chart of their partner's information. The charts should facilitate final comparisons and conclusions.

Learning Strategy: Polling

Critical Thinking Strategies: Drawing inferences, generalizing

Follow-up, Ex. G: Create a "tick mark" graph on the board by listing the different types of injuries suffered by the members of the class (use the expressions in Ex. F.). By each injury, place a tick mark to represent each student in the class who has suffered that injury.

Ex. I: writing

Less-prepared students, Ex I: Remind less-prepared students to recycle ideas from Ex. H for their work here.

Vocabulario

Para charlar

Para hablar de tu estado físico

bajar de peso
cortarse
lastimarse
mantenerse en condiciones óptimas
ponerse en forma
romperse
(no) sentirse bien (mal)
sudar
tener dolor de…
tener un accidente
tonificarse
torcerse (ue)

Para hablar del estado físico de otra persona

¿Cómo te sientes?
¿Te sientes bien (mal)?
No te ves muy bien.
¿Estás en forma?
¿Qué te pasa?
¿Qué te pasó?
¿Te lastimaste?
¿Tuviste algún accidente?

Temas y contextos

Las actividades físicas

hacer gimnasia
levantar pesas

El cuerpo

la boca
el brazo
la cabeza
la cara
el codo
el corazón
la coyuntura
el cuello
el dedo (de la mano)
el dedo del pie

el diente
la espalda
el estómago
la frente
la garganta
el hombro
la mano
la muñeca
el muslo
la nariz

el ojo
la oreja
el pecho
el pelo
el pie
la pierna
el pulmón
la rodilla
el tobillo

Vocabulario general

Sustantivos

la capacidad
una dosis
un evento social
un gimnasio
una manera
un movimiento
el oxígeno
la presión
el sistema cardiovascular
una solución
una ventaja

Verbos

asegurar
demandar
flotar
tirarse

Adjetivos

agradable
consecutivo(a)
continuo(a)
eficiente
experto(a)
grave
máximo(a)
sencillo(a)

Adverbios

normalmente

Otras palabras y expresiones

a menudo
a veces
cada día (viernes, sábado, tarde, mañana, noche, semana, mes, etc.)
con frecuencia
con regularidad
de vez en cuando
muchas veces
tener razón

Chapter Culminating Activity

Cooperative Learning

Vocabulario: Team Charades

- Have students form teams of five to plan and present charades using chapter vocabulary.
- Give each group ten minutes to plan their charade. Remind them that every student needs to contribute equally to the idea for the charade and play an equal part in its execution.
- Have the teams perform their charades. Call on students from the other teams to guess what the performing team is doing.
- When all of the teams have performed, you may want to ask for volunteers to perform further charades, or you might want to do one yourself and have the students write down what you are doing (as a quiz).

Suggestion, Vocabulario: Use either the Bingo game (p. T300) or charades (above) as Chapter Culminating Activities.

Lectura cultural

Lectura CULTURAL

EL CICLISMO EN ESPAÑA

Antes de leer

Learning Strategies:

Previewing, brainstorming

1. Look at the title of this reading. What do you think **ciclismo** means?
2. What do we do in the U.S. to stay in shape? Do you do anything in particular?
3. Look at the photographs that accompany the reading. Do you know who some of these people are? Where do you think they are from?

Arriba: La bicicleta es mi ejercicio favorito.
Derecha: Miguel Induráin

302

Un muchacho en bicicleta en el Retiro, Madrid

Guía para la lectura

 Read the first paragraph and answer the following questions.
1. ¿Qué dice el artículo sobre la popularidad del ciclismo en España?
2. Según el artículo, ¿qué no hay en las ciudades para los ciclistas?

B. Now read the second paragraph and answer the following questions.
1. ¿Quién es Miguel Induráin?
2. ¿Qué se necesita para ser un gran ciclista?
3. ¿Cuál es la carrera que Induráin ganó cuatro veces?
4. ¿Qué información sabemos sobre el corazón de Induráin?

//-//-//-//-//-//-//-//

Learning Strategies:

Reading for cultural information, reading for main ideas, reading for details

El ciclismo en España

unque las carreteras españolas no son un paraíso para los ciclistas, el número de los aficionados a este deporte crece cada día. Cada día hay más y más jóvenes que van a la escuela en bicicleta, a pesar de que no hay carriles-bici en las ciudades. Mucha de esta popularidad se debe al éxito del gran ciclista español Miguel Induráin.

Induráin es el mejor ciclista del mundo en la actualidad y probablemente uno de los mejores ciclistas en la historia de este deporte. El ganó el prestigioso Tour de France en los años 1991, 1992, 1993 y 1994 y en 1992 y 1993 también ganó el Giro de Italia. Para ser un ciclista como Induráin se necesita estar en forma excelente. Para darles un ejemplo de la forma en que está Induráin vamos a hablar de los latidos del corazón humano. Cuando una persona está en forma, el corazón late más o menos 72 veces por minuto. El corazón de Induráin es tan fuerte que cuando está descansando, el corazón le late 28 veces por minuto.

Spain

303

Chapter Objectives

Functions: Describing illnesses and complaints; suggesting medical remedies; giving advice about health-related topics

Context: The pharmacy; the doctor's office

Accuracy: The verb **doler;** indirect object pronouns; the verb **dar**

Cultural Expansion

Explain to students that outside the U.S. pharmacies are specifically health related and do not carry the wide range of office products, stationery items, cosmetics, soft drinks, etc., that are found in most U.S. drugstores. Refer students to the **Comentarios culturales** on p. 314 for more information on Hispanic pharmacies.

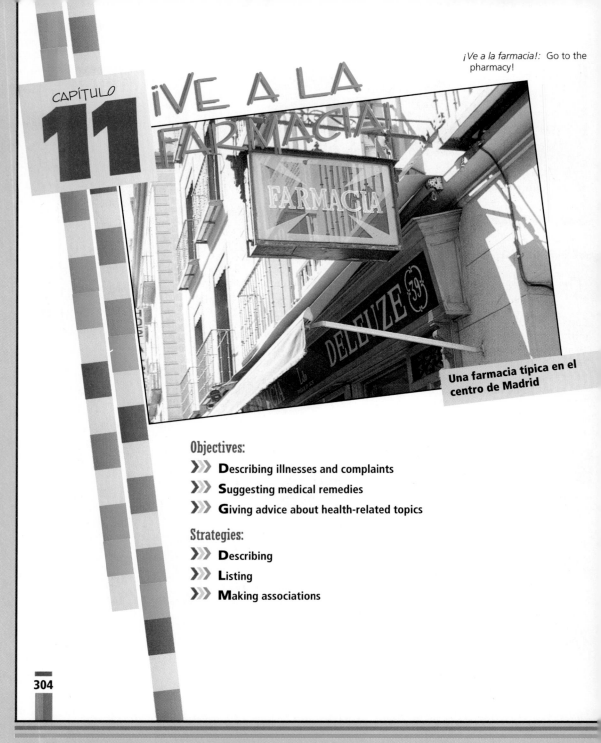

CAPÍTULO

11

¡VE A LA FARMACIA!

¡Ve a la farmacia!: Go to the pharmacy!

Una farmacia típica en el centro de Madrid

Objectives:

>>> **D**escribing illnesses and complaints
>>> **S**uggesting medical remedies
>>> **G**iving advice about health-related topics

Strategies:

>>> **D**escribing
>>> **L**isting
>>> **M**aking associations

304

Video/Laserdisc

Chapter 11 Video Program and Video Guide

PRIMERA ETAPA

Preparación

Think about the various common illnesses we tend to get in the winter.

》》 **W**hat are some of these illnesses? What are the symptoms?

》》 **W**hat are some of the medicines we take for these illnesses? Are these over-the-counter medicines? Do you need a prescription?

Learning Strategies:

Previewing, brainstorming

La gripe: un virus anual

Cada invierno los microbios cruzan **las fronteras**. Llegan de todas partes del mundo. Es la temporada del **catarro** y de la gripe. La epidemia de la gripe **alcanza** su **punto** más alto en diciembre, enero y febrero. El Sr. Valdés está enfermo. Tiene la gripe. Noten los síntomas que tiene.

La gripe: un virus anual: The flu: an annual virus

borders

cold

reaches / point

Él tose.

Él estornuda.

Él tiene dolor de garganta.

Él tiene escalofríos.

Él tiene dolor de estómago.

Él tiene fiebre.

Él tiene dolor de cabeza.

305

Etapa Support Materials

Workbook: **pp. 212–217**
Listening Activity masters: **p. 95**
Transparencies: **#41, #41a**
Teacher Tape
Tapescript: **p. 126**

Quiz: **Testing Program, p. 160**

Support material, **La gripe:**
   Transparencies #41, #41a

Presentation: La gripe

Have students read the introduction and then the captions. Ask them if they have heard their parents or grandparents use the old-fashioned word *grippe* when talking about a bad flu.

Reteaching, La gripe:
Review body vocabulary before beginning. Point to a part of your body and have students give the word in Spanish.

¡Aquí te toca a ti!

A. ¿Qué tienen? Describe los síntomas de las personas en los dibujos. Sigue el modelo.

 *El Sr. González tiene dolor de estómago.*

Sr. González

1. Sra. López   **2.** Simón   **3.** Beatriz   **4.** Sr. Torres   **5.** Srta. Martín   **6.** Isabel

Repaso

B. Mi hermana y yo Paula Ramírez describes how she and her sister Luisa spent the day yesterday. Use the preterite to recreate her sentences, making sure to distinguish between reflexive and nonreflexive verbs.

 Luisa y yo / despertarse temprano
Luisa y yo nos despertamos temprano ayer.

1. Luisa / levantarse en seguida
2. yo / quedarse en cama por media hora
3. ella / hacer gimnasia
4. ella / ducharse / lavarse el pelo
5. yo / ducharse / no lavarse el pelo
6. nosotras / desayunarse juntas
7. yo / ir al centro
8. ella / quedarse en casa
9. nosotras / cenar / las 6:30
10. ella / mirar un programa de televisión
11. yo / leer una revista
12. nosotras / lavarse los dientes
13. nosotras / acostarse a las 10:45

306

C. ¿Se lastimó... ?
A friend is asking you about slight accidents that friends of yours had yesterday. You explain what happened. Work with a partner, use the cues, and follow the model.

Modelo: Juan / cortarse / la frente
—¿Se lastimó Juan?
—Sí, se cortó la frente.

1. Alicia / romperse / brazo
2. Roberto / torcerse / tobillo
3. Carlos / cortarse / mano
4. Bárbara / romperse / pierna
5. Elena / torcerse / muñeca
6. Horacio / cortarse / pie

ESTRUCTURA

The verb *doler*

—¿Cómo estás?
—No muy bien. **Me duele** la garganta.
—**¿Te duele la cabeza?**
—Sí, y **me duelen la espalda y las piernas** también.

How are you?
Not too well. *My* throat *hurts.*

Does your head ache?
Yes, and *my back and legs hurt* also.

The verb **doler** is like the verb **gustar** in that it is used with the pronouns **me, te, le, nos, os,** and **les.** Furthermore, like **gustar,** only the third person singular and plural forms are used, depending on whether what hurts is singular or plural. Notice in the examples that Spanish uses definite articles for body parts where English uses possessives.

Aquí practicamos

D. Sustituye las palabras en cursiva con las palabras entre paréntesis y haz los otros cambios necesarios.

1. Me duele *la garganta.* (la cabeza / los ojos / la mano / la espalda / el tobillo / las piernas)
2. ¿Te duele *el hombro?* (la cabeza / la mano / los pies / la muñeca)
3. Nos duele *el estómago.* (los pies / las piernas / la rodilla / la espalda)
4. A Juan le duelen *los pies.* (la cabeza / el brazo / la rodilla / los ojos)
5. A ellas les duele *el estómago.* (la cabeza / los ojos / los pies / la espalda / las piernas)

Nos duelen los pies.

307

Left margin column

Support material, Aquí escuchamos: Teacher Tape

Presentation: Aquí escuchamos

Discuss with students when people may have symptoms such as sneezing, runny nose, sore throat, etc., other than when they have the flu. Then have students take out paper and pencil and make two columns headed **hace o tiene / no hace o no tiene.** Have them listen to the tape several times, each time adding information on **Andrés** in the appropriate columns. Students can use this material as they do the comprehension questions.

Answers, Aquí escuchamos: 1. no se siente bien; le duele la garganta   2. no tiene catarro; tiene una alergia   3. no tose; estornuda   4. estornuda sin parar   5. Va a la farmacia (para comprar un antihistamínico y unas gotas para los ojos).

Ex. F: 　 writing

Sick Trios, Ex. F

Learning Strategies: Providing personal information, describing, reporting

- Have students form groups of threes with people with whom they have not worked recently.
- Have them take turns telling about their physical ailments in round robin fashion, from left to right.
- When they have finished, tell them to discuss how they feel and what symptoms they have or do not have.
- Call on students at random to report how their teammates feel.

Main column

E. ¿Qué les duele?   When your teacher gives the signal, circulate around the room asking several of your classmates if some part of their body hurts. After you finish, tally your responses as a class to find the results of your survey.

Aquí escuchamos:
"Andrés, ¿qué te pasa?"

Learning Strategy:
Previewing

Antes de escuchar

Emilio runs into Andrés who doesn't look very well. Look at the following questions and identify a few things you expect to hear during their conversation.

Learning Strategy:
Listening for details

Después de escuchar

1. ¿Qué le pasa a Andrés?
2. ¿Qué tiene y qué no tiene?
3. ¿Qué hace y qué no hace?
4. ¿Cómo estornuda?
5. ¿Adónde va?

¡Aquí te toca a ti!

Learning Strategy:
Listing

Critical Thinking Strategy:
Making associations

F. ¿Qué te pasa?   Here are some expressions used to talk about minor physical ailments. Choose the symptoms that would be most likely in each situation.

Síntomas: Me duele(n) la garganta (la cabeza, la espalda, el estómago, los ojos). Toso. Estornudo. No tengo apetito. Estoy mareado(a) *(dizzy)*. No puedo dormir.

1. Tú tienes catarro.
2. Tú comiste mucho.
3. Tú tienes la gripe.
4. Tú tienes una alergia.
5. Tú tienes un examen muy importante y estás muy nervioso(a).

308

Possible answers, Ex. F: 1. Me duele la garganta. Toso. Estornudo. No puedo dormir. Tengo los ojos rojos.   2. Me duele el estómago. No tengo apetito.   3. Me duelen la garganta, la cabeza, la espalda y el estómago. Toso. Estornudo. No puedo dormir. Tengo fiebre. Tengo escalofríos.   4. Me duele la garganta. Toso. Estornudo. No puedo dormir. Tengo los ojos rojos. 5. Me duele la cabeza. Me duele el estómago. No puedo dormir. No tengo apetito.

¡Adelante!

EJERCICIO ORAL

G. No me siento muy bien.   Think back to the last time you were sick and imagine that you now have the same symptoms. Tell a classmate that you are not feeling well. Answer his or her questions about your symptoms. After having heard the symptoms, he or she will give you some advice: **Tú debes ir a la farmacia (quedarte en casa, ir al médico,** etc.).

EJERCICIO ESCRITO

H. Mis síntomas   Write a letter to your grandmother. (1) Tell her that you are not feeling well. (2) Describe at least three symptoms that you are having. (3) Tell her whether or not you have been to see a doctor. (4) Tell her what kinds of medication you are taking. (5) Explain that you cannot visit her this weekend because of the illness. (6) Tell her when you will plan another trip to her house. (7) Remember to date and sign your letter.

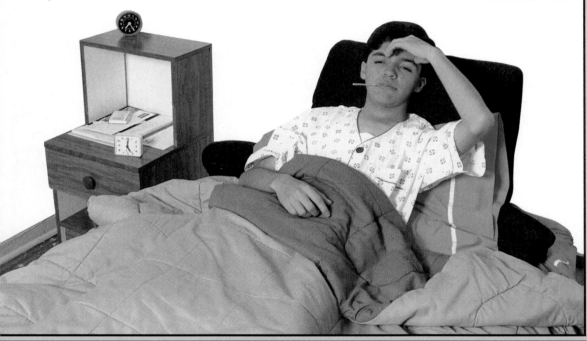

Learning Strategies:

Listing, reporting based on personal knowledge, describing

Critical Thinking Strategy:

Analyzing

Learning Strategies:

Listing, describing, providing information, organizing ideas

Critical Thinking Strategy:

Making associations

Ex. G:  pair work

Variation, Ex. G: Have students role play the parts of doctor and patient, greeting each other appropriately, etc. The patient decides ahead of time what symptoms he/she will have. Then the doctor must correctly diagnose the illness and perhaps recommend a treatment or medication. You may want to have students perform these for the class.

Ex. H: writing

Variation, Ex. H: Have students write an absence excuse to the principal, using this same information and saying what days they will be absent from school and when they plan to return.

Presentation: Los remedios

Treat this section as a reading exercise. As a prereading activity, ask students who cares for them when they are sick. Ask what happens when they go to the doctor. You could also have them scan for cognates. Have students read aloud.

Cultural Expansion

In many Spanish-speaking countries, as in parts of the U.S., **remedios caseros** or home remedies are very popular as an alternative to prescription drugs. They often involve herbs and foods that are prepared especially for specific complaints, such as hot pepper held under the nose to relieve congestion, camomile tea for an upset stomach, garlic to ease arthritis pains, and rosemary to relieve tension headaches.

SEGUNDA ETAPA

Preparación

Think about the last time you were sick.

›› **D**id you go to the pharmacy and get an over-the-counter medicine? What was it?

›› **D**id you go to the doctor?

›› **D**id the doctor give you a prescription?

//-//-//-//-//-//-//-//
Learning Strategy:
Previewing

Los remedios

Los remedios:
Treatments

she buys me

cough syrup

gives me
chamomile

examines me / takes my
temperature

prescription

she takes care of me

Cuando no me siento bien, mi mamá va a la farmacia y **me compra** medicina. Cuando sufro un ataque de alergia y estornudo constantemente, ella me compra un antihistamínico. Cuando toso mucho, ella me compra un **jarabe.** Si tengo la gripe y me duele todo el cuerpo, me acuesto para descansar. Mi mamá **me da** mucha agua o jugo y aspirinas para el dolor. A veces mi mamá prefiere darme los remedios caseros. Ella me da un té de **manzanilla** cuando me duele el estómago.

Cuando estoy muy enferma, tengo que ir a la doctora. Ella **me examina** y **me toma la temperatura.** Si tengo una infección y si tengo fiebre, ella me da una **receta.** Con la receta mi mamá va a la farmacia y me compra un antibiótico. Mi mamá es muy amable y **me cuida** muy bien cuando estoy enferma.

310

Etapa Support Materials

Workbook: **pp. 218–222**
Teacher Tape 🎧
Quiz: **Testing Program, p. 163**
Chapter Test: **Testing Program, p. 166**

¡Aquí te toca a ti!

A. Cuando estoy enferma... Answer the questions based on the information given on the previous page.

/-/-/-/-/-/-/-/-/-/-/-/
Learning Strategy:
Reading for details

1. What does this person do when she has an allergy attack?
2. What does this person do when she has a cough?
3. What about when she has the flu?
4. When does this person go to the doctor?
5. When does the doctor give this person a prescription?

B. ¿Qué recomiendas? You are traveling in Uruguay with your family. Whenever someone is not feeling well or needs some medicine, he or she asks you for help. You go to the pharmacy. Based on the information in **Los remedios** on page 310, make the recommendations you think the pharmacist will make to you in each of the following cases.

/-/-/-/-/-/-/-/-/-/-/-/
Learning Strategies:
Reading for details, recommending

1. Your sister has a very bad cough.
2. Your father has a backache.
3. Your mother's allergies are acting up and she can't stop sneezing.
4. You have a fever and ache all over.

Repaso

C. ¿Qué le duele? Describe qué le duele a cada persona en los dibujos en la página 312. Sigue el modelo.

/-/-/-/-/-/-/-/-/-/-/-/
Learning Strategy:
Reporting based on visual cues

A Jorge le duele la rodilla.

a Jorge

311

Ex. A: writing

Answers, Ex. A: 1. She takes an antihistamine. 2. She takes cough syrup. 3. She goes to bed to rest, drinks plently of fluids, and takes aspirin. 4. when she is very ill 5. if she if has an infection or a fever

Suggestion, Ex. A: Have students answer the questions in Spanish.

Ex. B: writing

Possible answers, Ex. B: 1. Ud. necesita un jarabe. 2. Ud. necesita acostarse para descansar y tomar aspirina para el dolor. 3. Ud. necesita un antihistamínico. 4. Ud. necesita esta receta para un antibiótico y también necesita descansar y tomar aspirina para el dolor.

Ex. C: writing

1. a Sara

2. al Sr. Lamas

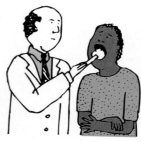

3. a Ricardo

4. a Rita y a Guillermo

ESTRUCTURA

Indirect object pronouns

Él **me** escribió una carta.	He wrote a letter *to me*.
Ella **te** compró un disco compacto.	She bought a CD *for you*.
Tú **nos** vendiste el coche.	You sold the car *to us*.
¿Le escribió ella una carta **a Juan?**	Did she write a letter *to Juan*?
No, ella **les** escribió una carta **a sus amigas.**	No, she wrote a letter *to her friends*.

The indirect object pronouns in Spanish are listed below.

me	*to (for) me*	**nos**	*to (for) us*
te	*to (for) you*	**os**	*to (for) you*
le	*to (for) him, her, you*	**les**	*to (for) them, you*

Indirect object pronouns are used to indicate what person or thing receives the direct object.

Aquí practicamos

D. Sustituye las palabras en cursiva con las palabras entre paréntesis y haz los otros cambios necesarios.

1. Ella *me* escribió una carta la semana pasada. (te / nos / le / les / os)
2. Yo le escribí una carta *a Juan*. (a ellos / a Elena / a Margarita y a Marcos / a Ud. / a mi novia / al director / a la profesora)
3. Ellos te enviaron *a ti* una postal de Madrid. (a nosotros / a mis padres / a Ud. / a Ricardo / a Felipe y a Carolina / a mí)

312

Presentation: Estructura

You may want to review direct object pronouns and point out that they differ from indirect object pronouns only in the third person singular and plural forms, or you could ask students how they differ. Point out that the greatest difference is in meaning (even though many of the direct and indirect object pronouns look the same) and that indirect object pronouns always have a translatable meaning of *to* or *for* (or sometimes another preposition) included in the pronoun itself. For example, **lo veo** (I see him) versus **le escribo** (I write *to* him).

Ex. D: writing

E. *¿Dijo la verdad?* Your friend is a very naive person and often cannot tell whether people are telling the truth or not. As you watch a mystery story on television, your friend asks you questions about what the main character said to other characters in the program. Follow the model.

Modelo: a María
            ¿Le dijo la verdad a María?

1. a Juan	**3.** a los extranjeros	**5.** a su esposa	**7.** a sus hijos
2. a la policía	**4.** a su novia	**6.** a sus padres	**8.** al Presidente

Nota gramatical

The verb dar

Yo le **doy** el libro a la profesora.	I *give* the book to the teacher.
Ella me **da** la llave.	She *gives* me the key.
—¿Le **diste** la carta a tu novia?	*Did you give* the letter to your girlfriend?
—Sí, le **di** la carta a ella.	Yes, *I gave* the letter to her.
Mi papá nos **dio** dinero para comprar libros.	My father *gave* us money to buy books.

Present

yo	**doy**	nosotros(as)	**damos**
tú	**das**	vosotros(as)	**dais**
él		ellos	
ella	**da**	ellas	**dan**
Ud.		Uds.	

Except for the **yo** form, the verb **dar** is conjugated in the present tense in the same way as other **-ar** verbs.

Preterite

yo	**di**	nosotros(as)	**dimos**
tú	**diste**	vosotros(as)	**disteis**
él		ellos	
ella	**dio**	ellas	**dieron**
Ud.		Uds.	

Ex. F: ✎ writing

Ex. G: 🔺 groups of four or more

Cultural Expansion

Before having students read the **Comentarios culturales,** ask them to indicate where they would go in the U.S.—to a pharmacy, a doctor's office, or an emergency room—for each of the following medical problems. Then have them read the cultural information in the textbook and say where they would go in a Spanish-speaking country for each of the same problems.

Although **dar** is an **-ar** verb, it is conjugated in the preterite with the endings that you use for **-er** and **-ir** verbs. The forms **di** and **dio** do *not* take an accent mark.

The verb **dar** is often used with indirect object pronouns that indicate to whom something is being given.

Other verbs commonly used with indirect object pronouns are **hablar, decir, mandar** *(to send),* and **escribir.**

/./././././././././././
Learning Strategy:
Expressing past time

F. *El médico le dio la medicina a...*   Indica a quién le dio el médico cada cosa. Sigue el modelo.

Modelo: el jarabe / Mario
Le dio el jarabe a Mario.

1. la medicina / Laura	6. la receta / la profesora
2. el jarabe / mis hermanos	7. la aspirina / mi padre
3. el antihistamínico / Ud.	8. las gotas para los ojos / tú
4. el antibiótico / yo	9. la medicina / mis padres
5. el jarabe / tú	10. las aspirinas / mis primos

/./././././././././././
Learning Strategy:
Asking and answering personal questions

Critical Thinking Strategy:
Making associations

G. *¿Qué te da tu mamá cuando... ?*   Ask several classmates what their mothers give them when they have various illnesses. Suggestions: **la gripe, un catarro, un dolor de cabeza** (**estómago,** etc.), **una alergia.**

/./././././././././././
Learning Strategy:
Reading for cultural information

COMENTARIOS
CULTURALES

■ *La farmacia en el mundo hispano*

In the Spanish-speaking world, people often consult their local pharmacist when they are not feeling well. If the pharmacist considers the illness to be serious, he or she will advise the customer to see a doctor. In the case of a cold, flu, or minor accident, the pharmacist will recommend over-the-counter medicines and drugs that often require a prescription in the U.S. Many cities and towns in the Spanish-speaking world have at least one pharmacy that remains open all night. Many other pharmacies have signs on their doors indicating that the pharmacy remains open long hours each day.

314

---

1. They have a stomach virus. (U.S.: doctor's office; Hispanic country: pharmacy)
2. They cut their finger. (U.S. and Hispanic country: doctor's office or emergency room)
3. They have a rash on their legs. (U.S.: doctor's office; Hispanic country: pharmacy)
4. They need an allergy shot. (U.S.: doctor's office; Hispanic country: doctor's office or pharmacy)

Learning Strategy: Brainstorming

Critical Thinking Strategies: Making associations, seeing cause-and-effect relationships

Here is some useful vocabulary to use in pharmacies throughout the Spanish-speaking world.

Quisiera algo para la garganta.
         los ojos.
         el estómago.

Quisiera algo para la tos.
         la alergia.
         la fiebre del heno.
         el dolor de cabeza.
         la gripe.

Quisiera unas aspirinas.
         un antihistamínico.
         unas pastillas para la garganta.
         unas gotas para los ojos.
         un jarabe para la tos.

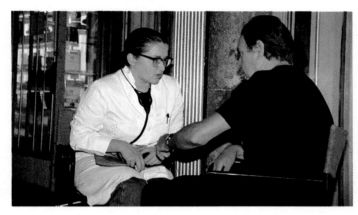

Aquí escuchamos:
"En la farmacia"

Antes de escuchar

Alicia is not feeling well and goes to the pharmacy to get advice from the pharmacist about her symptoms. Look at the following questions and identify a few things you expect to hear during their conversation.

Después de escuchar

1. ¿Cómo se siente Alicia?
2. ¿Qué le pasa a ella?
3. ¿Cómo la ve el farmacéutico?
4. ¿Cuánto tiempo hace que está así?
5. ¿Qué le da el farmacéutico?

Learning Strategies:
Previewing, predicting

Learning Strategy:
Listening for details

315

Support material, Aquí escuchamos: Teacher Tape

Presentation: Aquí escuchamos

Discuss drugstores in the United States and in the Spanish-speaking world if you have not yet done so. Have students listen to the dialogue after they have previewed corresponding materials. You may want to use all or part of the dialogue as dictation practice. As students listen, have them jot down some notes or key words for each of the comprehension questions.

Answers, Aquí escuchamos: 1. no se siente muy bien 2. estornuda sin parar y le duele la garganta 3. con los ojos rojos 4. ocho horas, más o menos 5. un antihistamínico y unas pastillas

Sidebar (left column)

Ex. H: writing

Ex. I: pair work

role play

Suggestion, Ex. I: Have students alternate playing the customer and the pharmacist.

Ex. J: writing

Less-prepared students, Ex. J: Point out that there are two different time contexts presented here. Have students identify each one and tell what verb tense they need for each. Ask less-prepared students if they have any questions before beginning.

More-prepared students, Ex. J: After all students have written their letters, have them exchange papers. Using the cultural information on p. 314, have more-prepared students write the Spanish-speaking student's answer to the letter, explaining a similar situation and how it would be treated in his or her country.

¡Aquí te toca a ti!

H. *Quisiera...* You are traveling in Spain with a group of people who do not speak Spanish. Serve as their interpreter at the pharmacy and make an appropriate request in each situation. Follow the model.

 **Modelo:** your friend / sore throat
A mi amigo le duele la garganta. Quisiera unas pastillas para la garganta.

1. your friend / headache
2. your sister / stomachache
3. your brother / cough
4. your father / cold symptoms
5. your mother / allergy
6. your friend / flu symptoms

¡Adelante!

EJERCICIO ORAL

I. *En la farmacia* Explain to the pharmacist that you have the symptoms that usually accompany the following medical problems. For each problem, name at least three symptoms. Then the pharmacist (your partner) will recommend at least two possible medicines or ways to treat each problem.

1. catarro
2. la gripe
3. la fiebre del heno

EJERCICIO ESCRITO

J. *Cuando me enfermo* A friend of yours from a Spanish-speaking country wants to know more about what we do in this country when we get sick. Write a note to him or her in which you (1) name at least three common ailments and a typical treatment for each. Then (2) describe the symptoms that you had the last time that you were sick enough to miss school. Tell (3) what medicines you took and (4) what you did to get well.

316

Vocabulario

Para charlar

Para describir los síntomas

Estornudo.
No puedo dormir.
Me duele(n)…
Tengo una alergia.
    catarro.
    dolor de cabeza.
        espalda.
        estómago.

Tengo escalofríos.
    fiebre.
    fiebre del heno.
    la gripe.
    una infección.
    la tos.
    un virus.
Toso.

Para comprar medicina en la farmacia

Quisiera… (remedio)
Quisiera algo para…
Quisiera alguna cosa para… }   (parte del cuerpo)

Temas y contextos

Los remedios

un antibiótico
un antihistamínico
una aspirina

unas gotas para los ojos
un jarabe
unas pastillas

una taza de té de manzanilla

Vocabulario general

Sustantivos	Verbos	Adjetivos	Adverbios
una epidemia	alcanzar	anual	constantemente
una frontera	cuidar		
un microbio	dar		
un punto	mandar		
	sufrir		

Otras palabras y expresiones

tomar la temperatura

- Have the groups agree on a problem. Distribute cards and tell the groups to write the problems on one side of the card and to mark that side *Q*. Remind the groups to proofread for errors.
- Instruct the group to talk about possible solutions to the problem. Tell them that they need to agree on the solution(s) and then write the solution(s) on the back of the card, which they will mark *A*. Remind them to proofread.
- Have each group send its card, with the question on one side and the solution on the other, to the group to their left.
- The groups will read the new problem, discuss its solution, and then compare their solution with the one on the back of the card.
- If time permits, have groups write additional problems and solutions.
- Call on students at random to relate the problem their group received and its solution.

Chapter Culminating Activity

Use the Cooperative Learning exercise on this page or have students create some kind of medical board game with cards for ailments, symptoms, etc. The board could have different places to visit, such as the pharmacy, a clinic, a hospital, and a health food or natural remedy store. Let students use their imaginations.

Cooperative Learning

Vocabulario: Send-A-Problem

Learning Strategies: Proofreading, making recommendations, negotiating, reporting

Critical Thinking Strategy: Seeing cause-and-effect relationships

- Have students form groups of four or more.
- Tell the groups that they are to figure out a medical problem that someone has, using the **Vocabulario** words and expressions.

Lectura cultural

Lectura CULTURAL

LA MEDICINA EN ALGUNAS PARTES DEL MUNDO HISPANO

Antes de leer

Learning Strategies:

Previewing, brainstorming

Critical Thinking Strategy:

Making associations

1. Look at the pictures and the title that accompany this reading. What do you think the people are selling?
2. What connection do you think there is between these items and illness?
3. Are you familiar with any kind of traditional home remedy? If so, what?

Guía para la lectura

Learning Strategies:

Reading for cultural information, reading for details

A. Read the first paragraph and decide which of the following statements best summarizes the main idea it contains.

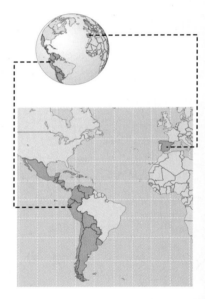

1. En general, la gente en países de habla hispana paga por sus visitas al médico.
2. En general, hay programas de medicina muy modernos que el gobierno paga.
3. En general, los remedios en algunas partes del mundo hispano son sólo tradicionales.

318

B. Read the second paragraph and answer the following questions.

1. ¿Qué solución hay para un(a) enfermo(a) cuando no hay médico?
2. ¿Qué usa esta persona para curar a la gente?
3. ¿Qué tienen en común las medicinas naturales y medicinas producidas por compañías farmacéuticas?

La medicina en algunas partes del mundo hispano

a medicina en algunas partes del mundo hispano es una rara combinación de influencias indígenas, africanas y europeas. Claro que al lado de estas influencias también existen programas de medicina que son tan modernos como los que tenemos en este país, pero a veces, a causa de la historia cultural es muy difícil cambiar las prácticas tradicionales de la gente. Hay países hispanos con programas de medicina muy completos. Si la gente se enferma, va al médico y el gobierno paga la visita. También paga servicios como cirugía, que se hace en un hospital, y visitas del médico a la casa del paciente. En ciertas ocasiones, el gobierno también paga parte de las medicinas.

En las regiones rurales de estos países donde no hay muchos médicos ni grandes hospitales modernos, a veces la gente va a ver al curandero o curandera local. Ésta es una persona que tiene un gran conocimiento de las hierbas y otros ingredientes naturales y sabe cómo usarlas para hacer remedios que curan a la gente. Éstas son medicinas que tienen mucha tradición entre la gente rural. El proceso no parece ser muy científico, pero muchas de las medicinas naturales tienen los mismos ingredientes que las medicinas que recomiendan los médicos en los grandes hospitales modernos.

319

Answers, *Guía para la lectura:* **A.** 2   **B.** 1. ir al curandero local   2. hierbas y otros ingredientes naturales   3. los ingredientes

Chapter Objectives

Functions: Describing dietary and sleeping habits; advising others what to eat and what not to eat; asking for advice

Context: Diet; sleep routines

Accuracy: The verb **pedir;** the time expressions **desde cuándo, desde (que), cuánto tiempo hace,** and **hace (que)**

Cultural Observation

Have students look at the picture and identify the different kinds of fruit in English. Have them name some fruits and vegetables that come from Central and South America that are not grown in the U.S., e.g., guavas, papayas, etc.

Cultural Expansion

Many of the tropical fruits grown in the Hispanic world have a high nutritional value. Pineapple **(la piña, el ananás)** is rich in fiber, iron, potassium, and vitamins A, B, and C. The mango contains vitamins A and K, calcium, iron, and as much vitamin C as an orange. The papaya has large quantities of vitamin A and more vitamin C than an orange. Because of this, many nutritionists predict an increase in the popularity of these fruits here in the U.S.

LA SALUD: MEJOR QUE LA RIQUEZA

La salud:
la rique
better

Para la buena salud hay que comer frutas y vegetales y así obtener la fibra, la vitamina C y los minerales necesarios al cuerpo.

320

Objectives:

>>> **D**escribing dietary and sleeping habits

>>> **A**dvising others what to eat and what not to eat

>>> **A**sking for advice

Strategies:

>>> **R**eading for relevant information

>>> **A**ctive listening

>>> **S**eeing cause-and-effect relationships

Video/Laserdisc

Chapter 12 Video Program and Video Guide

PRIMERA ETAPA

Preparación

>> **A**s you begin this **etapa**, think about the interest in healthful food this country has experienced in the past few years. Think about your own eating habits. Do you eat health food? Do you eat junk food? What about red meat? Do you know any vegetarians?

//-/-/-/-/-/-/-/-/-/-/-//
Learning Strategy:
Brainstorming

Los cinco grupos alimenticios

*Los cinco grupos alimenti-
cios:* The five food groups

1		**Leches y productos lácteos**	calcio, proteína, **grasa,** vitamina B, vitamina A
2		**Carne, pescado, huevos**	proteína, grasa, **hierro,** vitamina A, vitamina B
3		**Frutas y vegetales**	vitamina C, fibra, minerales
4		**Pan, cereales, papas, vegetales secos**	**almidón,** proteína, vitamina B
5		**Grasa**	lípidos, vitamina A en la mantequilla y la crema

grasa: oil, fat / *hierro:* iron / *almidón:* starch

321

Etapa Support Materials

Workbook: pp. 224–228
Listening Activity masters: p. 100
Critical Thinking masters: Chapter 12,
   primera etapa, activity G
Transparency: #42
Teacher Tape 🎧

Tapescript: p. 133
Quiz: Testing Program, p. 169
Support material, Los cinco grupos
   alimenticios: Transparency #42

Presentation: Los cinco grupos alimenticios

Using the transparency, have students identify the foods in each group. Then, as a class, read the functions of the food groups (p. 322). Ask students in English (or Spanish) if they eat from the five food groups daily and what they eat.

As homework, have students bring in pictures of foods and identify from which groups they come. You could use this activity as the basis for a small project where you divide the class in half and divide the alphabet in half. Have students find a food or drink that starts with every letter of the alphabet. The idea is to find healthy foods, but this may not always be possible.

Possible answers, Ex. A:
1. Debe comer alimentos de los grupos 1 y 2 y también alimentos de los grupos 3, 4 y 5.   2. Debe comer alimentos de los grupos 4 y 5.
3. Debe comer alimentos de los grupos 1 y 2.   4. Debe comer alimentos del grupo 3.   5. Debe comer alimentos de los grupos 1 y 2.

Ex. B: pair work

Ex. C: writing

Funciones de los cinco grupos alimenticios

Develop / renew / tissues
bones / healthy

Grupos 1 y 2:   **Desarrollan,** mantienen y **renuevan** los **tejidos** del cuerpo. Forman los **huesos** y los dientes; mantienen **sanos** los nervios y los músculos; regulan el tono muscular y el ritmo cardíaco.

Grupo 3:   Facilitan la digestión; mejoran la vista nocturna; ayudan al movimiento muscular.

Grupos 4 y 5:   Le dan energía al cuerpo (calorías).

¡Aquí te toca a ti!

/-/-/-/-/-/-/-/-/-/-/-/-/
Learning Strategies:

Reading a chart, reading for relevant information

Critical Thinking Strategies:

Analyzing, making associations, seeing cause-and-effect relationships

A. Debes comer los alimentos del grupo...   Diet has a strong influence on your physical condition. The following people want to supplement their medical treatment with good nutrition. Based on the information at the beginning of the **etapa,** recommend what the following people should eat. Follow the model.

> *Modelo:*   Paula Lerma tiene problemas cuando maneja *(drives)* el coche de noche; ella no puede ver muy bien.
> *Debe comer los alimentos del grupo 3, las frutas y los vegetales.*

1. Mateo Torres se prepara para una competencia deportiva.
2. Virginia Estrada siempre está cansada.
3. Adela López empieza a echar los dientes *(to teethe).*
4. Pablo Chávez tiene problemas después de comer; le molesta el estómago.
5. Juan José Cisneros se rompió el brazo tres veces.

/-/-/-/-/-/-/-/-/-/-/-/-/
Learning Strategies:

Listing, reporting based on personal knowledge

Critical Thinking Strategy:

Evaluating

B.   ¿Comes bien?   Discuss the food that you ate yesterday in terms of the five basic food groups. Your classmate will then tell you whether you ate well or not. Follow the model.

> *Modelo:*   —*Del primer grupo comí queso para el almuerzo y bebí leche para la cena. Del segundo grupo...* etc.
> —*Comiste muy bien.*   o: *Comiste muy mal.*

Repaso

C.   Tú eres el (la) farmacéutico(a).   Usa el verbo *deber* y un infinitivo para recomendarles a tus clientes *(to recommend to your clients)* lo que deben hacer *(what they should do)* en cada situación en la página 323.

> *Modelo:*   Tengo dolor de cabeza.
> *Debes tomar dos aspirinas.*

322

1. Estornudo sin parar.
2. Tengo la gripe.
3. Tengo una tos terrible.
4. Me duele la garganta.
5. Siempre estoy cansado(a).
6. Tengo fiebre.
7. Me duele el estómago.
8. Me duele todo el cuerpo.

D. ¿Qué les dio la doctora?   Indica lo que el médico les dio a tus amigos la última vez que estaban enfermos. Usa pronombres de complemento indirecto *(indirect object pronouns)* con el verbo *dar*. Sigue el modelo.

Modelo: a ella / un jarabe
La doctora le dio a ella un jarabe.

1. a ellos / dos aspirinas
2. a él / una pastilla para la garganta
3. a nosotros / una receta
4. a ti / un antihistamínico
5. a mí / unas gotas para los ojos
6. a Ud. / un jarabe para la tos

The verb *pedir*

¿Le **pides** permiso a tu padre cuando quieres salir?

No, yo le **pido** permiso a mi mamá.

¿Le **pediste** permiso al profesor para ir al concierto?

Sí, le **pedí** permiso.

Do you ask your father for permission when you want to go out?

No, I *ask* my mother for permission.

Did you ask the teacher for permission to go to the concert?

Yes, I *asked* him for permission.

Pedir means *to ask for something* as opposed to **preguntar,** which means *to ask questions.* Here are the conjugations of **pedir.**

Present

yo	**pido**	nosotros(as)	pedimos
tú	**pides**	vosotros(as)	pedís
él		ellos	
ella	} **pide**	ellas	} **piden**
Ud.		Uds.	

323

Notice that the **e** in the stem of **pedir** changes to **i** in all forms of the present except **nosotros** and **vosotros**.

Preterite			
yo	pedí	nosotros(as)	pedimos
tú	pediste	vosotros(as)	pedisteis
él		ellos	
ella	**pidió**	ellas	**pidieron**
Ud.		Uds.	

Notice that the **e** in the stem of **pedir** changes to **i** in the third person singular and plural preterite forms. Other verbs conjugated like this are

servir   **repetir** *(to repeat)*   **reírse**
medir *(to measure)* **sonreír** *(to smile)*

Aquí practicamos

E. Sustituye las palabras en cursiva con las palabras entre paréntesis y haz los otros cambios necesarios.

1. *Yo* le pido permiso al profesor. (tú / ella / nosotras / Uds. / Francisco / vosotros)
2. *Yo* le pedí permiso al profesor. (tú / ella / nosotros / Uds. / Francisco / vosotras)
3. ¿Cuánto mide *Francisco*? (tú / tu hermano / Uds. / ella / Ud. / vosotros)
4. *El profesor* repitió la respuesta. (yo / ellos / Ud. / nosotras / Uds. / vosotras)

F. **¿Qué le pidieron al camarero?**   You and several friends are in a busy restaurant and the waiter makes several mistakes when he brings you your food. Follow the model.

Modelo: Marta / ensalada / sopa
Marta le pidió ensalada, pero el camarero le sirvió sopa.

1. Francisco / una hamburguesa / un sándwich de jamón con queso
2. Carolina / sopa / ensalada
3. Carlos / té / café
4. Berta / agua mineral / leche
5. Jorge / una pizza / una hamburguesa con queso
6. Laura / pastel / helado

324

G. ¿Qué pediste?

Create a graph like the following one to record your responses and those of your classmates.

Think about the last time that you ate in a restaurant with a group of your friends when everyone paid his or her own bill. What did you order? Put your name in the appropriate space in the graph. Now ask this question of five of your classmates; put their names in appropriate spaces in the graph to chart their responses.

	Hamburguesa	Pizza	Pollo	Pescado	Tacos	Ensalada
yo						
5						
4						
3						
2						
1						

Now draw another graph. This time think about the last time that you ate out in a restaurant with family or friends when someone else paid the bill. What did you order? Put your name in the appropriate space in the graph. Now ask this question of five of your classmates; put their names in appropriate spaces in the graph to chart their responses.

COMENTARIOS CULTURALES

■ Metros y kilos

In Spanish-speaking countries, height and weight are expressed in **metros** and **kilos**.

One meter (**metro**) is equivalent to 3.281 feet (a little over 39 inches). Conversely, one foot equals 0.305 meters, and one inch equals 2.5 centimeters. To convert your height to meters and centimeters, multiply your height in inches by 2.5. For example, if you are 5'8" tall, you would be 170 centimeters tall (68" x 2.5). Since there are 100 centimeters in a meter you would say that you are 1 meter 70 centimeters tall, or **"Mido un metro setenta."**

325

One kilogram (**kilo**) is the equivalent of 2.2 pounds, and one pound equals 454 grams. To convert pounds to kilograms, divide your weight in pounds by 2.2. For example, if you weigh 145 pounds, you would weigh 65.9 kilograms (145 ÷ 2.2) and you would say, **"Peso casi sesenta y seis kilos."**

Aquí escuchamos:
"¿Cuánto mides?"

/-/-/-/-/-/-/-/-/-/-/
Learning Strategy:
Previewing

Antes de escuchar

Héctor and Felipe are talking about how tall they are and how much they weigh. Review the **Comentarios culturales,** look at the following questions, and identify a few things you expect to hear during their conversation.

/-/-/-/-/-/-/-/-/-/-/
Learning Strategy:
Listening for details

Después de escuchar

1. ¿Cuánto mide Felipe?
2. ¿Cuánto pesa?
3. ¿Cómo guarda la línea?

4. ¿Qué le sirve su mamá?
5. ¿Qué le pide a ella a veces?

¡Aquí te toca a ti!

H. *¿Qué les pides a tus padres?* Your friend asks if you ask your parents for certain foods that are normally not considered good for you. You respond by saying that you do, but that your parents serve you other food instead. Work with a partner and follow the model.

Modelo: dulces / fruta
—*¿Les pides dulces a tus padres?*
—*Sí, les pido dulces, pero me sirven fruta.*

1. pasteles / yogur
2. papas fritas / zanahorias y apio *(celery)*
3. dulces / pasas *(raisins)*

4. helado / manzanas o peras
5. galletas / bananas
6. torta / fruta y queso

326

I. ¿Qué pides en la cafetería? Tell what kinds of exotic foods you ask for in the school cafeteria and what you actually get served. Use the phrases: **Pido… pero me sirven… .**

¡Adelante!

EJERCICIO ORAL

J. Una encuesta (survey) Survey some of your classmates about the eating habits and physical conditions of their family members. Then, without naming names, report to the class your general conclusions about the physical condition of people in your town.

EJERCICIO ESCRITO

K. La semana pasada comí… Create a food journal for one week. (1) For each day, list everything that you ate. (2) Using the chart of the five food groups on page 321, indicate from which group each item comes. (3) Then place a check mark beside all the foods that are considered healthy for you. (4) Name two changes that you could make in your regular diet that might improve your physical condition and health. (5) Read the food journal of your partner. Add one suggestion for your partner to improve his or her eating habits.

//-//-//-//-//-//-//-//-//
Learning Strategy:

Asking for and reporting information based on personal knowledge

Critical Thinking Strategies:

Making associations, drawing inferences, seeing cause-and-effect relationships

//-//-//-//-//-//-//-//-//
Cooperative Learning

Learning Strategies:

Listing, reporting based on personal knowledge, compiling information, recommending

Critical Thinking Strategies:

Categorizing, sequencing, hypothesizing, seeing cause-and-effect relationships

Ex. I: writing

Suggestion Ex. I: If you don't have this type of cafeteria, substitute **Quiero…, pero me sirven…**

Less-prepared students, Ex. I: Brainstorm two lists with less-prepared students, one with foods they like, and one with foods from the cafeteria. Have them refer to the lists as they talk to their partners.

Ex. J: groups of four or more

Ex. K: writing

Suggestion, Ex. K: Have students subdivide the day by meals (**desayuno, almuerzo, cena, merienda** [snack]). You may want students to keep the food journal for a few days. Whatever the time frame, give them some time each day to record entries in their journals, perhaps first thing in the morning. You may also want to ask them to write down what they eat at home each day.

327

Presentation:
Los jóvenes
duermen mal

Ask about students' sleeping habits—what time they go to bed and get up, how many hours they sleep, and if they dream. Model by telling your habits: **Me acuesto usualmente a las once y media y me levanto a las seis y media. Duermo por siete horas y sueño en español.**
Then have students read the article silently and do Ex. A.

Ex. A: ✎ writing

SEGUNDA ETAPA

Preparación

>> **H**ow much sleep do you get in a typical night?

>> **D**oes the amount differ on weekends?

>> **D**o you think getting enough sleep is important for good health?

Learning Strategy:

Previewing

Los jóvenes duermen mal

Learning Strategy:

Reading for information

A group of doctors carried out a survey **(una encuesta)** and determined that young people between the ages of 15 and 19 don't sleep enough. The following article reports the results of this survey.

Los jóvenes duermen mal

majority / the same

at least in part

nightmares

snore
try to

Aparentemente, los jóvenes se acuestan muy tarde y no duermen lo suficiente. El 75% dice que no duermen más de siete horas cada noche durante la semana. La gran **mayoría** se acuesta a eso de las 22 o 23 horas. La televisión es la causa, **en parte al menos**, por no dormir lo suficiente. Casi el 25% admiten estar muy cansados durante el día y otro 25% duermen la siesta cuando es posible.

Durante el fin de semana, los jóvenes **tratan de** recuperar las horas de

dormir que perdieron durante la semana. La mayoría dice que duerme dos horas adicionales los sábados y domingos. Durante las vacaciones también hacen **lo mismo**.

El 25% de estos jóvenes tiene dificultades durmiéndose. Esto es una señal de ansiedad y sin duda una indicación de una vida no muy saludable. Las jóvenes tienen más **pesadillas** que los jóvenes pero los muchachos **roncan** más que las muchachas.

Learning Strategy:

Reading for details

¡Aquí te toca a ti!

A. ¿Verdad o falso? Basándote en la información en la lectura, indica si las frases en la página 329 son verdaderas o falsas.

328

Etapa Support Materials

Workbook: pp. 229–233
Teacher Tape 🎧
Quiz: Testing Program, p. 173
Chapter Test: Testing Program, p. 176

1. Los jóvenes típicos duermen ocho horas cada noche durante la semana.
2. Los jóvenes típicos duermen siete horas durante el fin de semana.
3. Los jóvenes típicos se acuestan generalmente a eso de las 10:00 de la noche.
4. El 50% de los jóvenes duermen una siesta durante las vacaciones.
5. Durante las vacaciones los jóvenes de 15 a 19 años duermen poco.
6. El 25% de los jóvenes tiene dificultades durmiéndose.
7. Las muchachas nunca roncan.
8. Los muchachos tienen más pesadillas que las muchachas.

B. ¿Y tú? Contesta las preguntas sobre tus hábitos de dormir *(sleeping habits)*.

1. Generalmente, ¿a qué hora te acuestas?
2. ¿Miras la tele antes de acostarte?
3. Generalmente, ¿cuántas horas duermes cada noche?
4. ¿Duermes una siesta?
5. Cuando te despiertas, ¿estás cansado(a)?
6. ¿Cuándo te duermes tarde?
7. ¿Te acuestas más tarde durante el fin de semana?
8. ¿Sueñas *(Do you dream)* de vez en cuando?
9. ¿Tienes pesadillas de vez en cuando?
10. ¿Roncas tú?

Learning Strategy:

Reporting based on personal experience

A Cristina le gusta dormir tarde.

Repaso

C. ¿Cuánto mide... ? ¿Y cuánto pesa? Tú quieres saber cuánto miden y cuánto pesan varias personas. Trabaja con un(a) compañero(a). Sigue el modelo.

Modelo: José / 1.79 / 68
—*¿Cuánto mide José?*
—*Mide un metro setenta y nueve.*
—*¿Y cuánto pesa?*
—*Pesa sesenta y ocho kilos.*

1. Marisol / 1.66 / 51
2. Lidia / 1.45 / 48
3. Oscar / 1.96 / 82
4. Verónica / 1.89 / 76

329

Ex. D: pair work

Presentation: Estructura

To introduce students to this structure, make some personal statements. **Yo soy profesor(a) desde hace... años. Estamos en la clase desde hace... minutos.** Then lead students to answer, **¿Desde cuándo vives en... ? ¿Desde cuándo sabes nadar (esquiar, jugar al fútbol)? ¿Desde cuándo trabajas a... ?** Make the questions as personal as you can and ask each student. Write some of the answers on the board, using a time line with statements such as, **Tú comenzaste a estudiar español en septiembre de 19.... La clase comenzó a las...** Show two different ways to express these ideas: **desde cuándo / cuánto tiempo hace.** You may want to use their English equivalents.

D. *Les pedí..., pero me sirvieron...*   You and your friends asked your parents for certain snack foods. Because your parents thought the foods weren't good for you, they served you something they thought was better. Work with a partner and follow the model.

Modelo: Bárbara / helado / yogur
    —*¿Qué les pidió Bárbara a sus padres?*
    —*Bárbara les pidió helado, pero le sirvieron yogur.*

1. Lorenzo / pastel / una manzana
2. Rebeca / papas fritas / zanahorias y apio
3. tu hermanito / dulces / pasas
4. ellas / torta / fruta y queso
5. tus amigos / helado / ensalada de fruta
6. ellos / galletas / yogur

ESTRUCTURA

The expressions desde cuándo, desde (que), cuánto tiempo hace, and hace (que)

—**¿Desde cuándo** estudias español?   *How long (Since when, Since what point in time) have you been studying Spanish?*

—Estudio español **desde que** tenía 15 años.   *I have been studying Spanish since I was 15.*

—Estudio español **desde** el año pasado.   *I have been studying Spanish since last year.*

—**¿Cuánto tiempo hace que** estudias español?   *For how long have you been studying Spanish?*

—**Hace** tres meses **que** estudio español.   *I have been studying Spanish for three months.*

Desde cuándo, cuánto tiempo hace, desde, desde que, and **hace** can be used to ask and answer questions about something that started in the past and is *continuing in the present.*

Question	Answer
¿Desde cuándo + *present tense verb . . . ?*	*Present tense verb* + **desde** + *specific point in time.*
	Present tense verb + **desde que** + *subject + past tense verb.*
¿Cuánto tiempo hace que + *present tense verb . . . ?*	**Hace** + *length of time* + **que** + *present tense verb.*

330

Remember that in Unit 5 of *¡Ya verás!, Primer nivel,* you learned to use a similar construction with the preterite tense to express *ago* in Spanish.

Hace cinco años que viví en Indiana.	*I lived* in Indiana *five years ago.*
or	
Viví en Indiana **hace cinco años.**	*I lived* in Indiana *five years ago.*

Aquí practicamos

E. *La señora Cortina va al médico.*   Your friend Cristina's mother, who has been ill for several days, goes to see the doctor. Before she is examined, the nurse asks her some questions. Use the cues in parentheses to give Sra. Cortina's answers. Follow the model.

Learning Strategy:

Expressing past and present time

Modelo: ¿Desde cuándo vives en Madrid? (1982)
Vivo en Madrid desde 1982.

1. Muy bien, entonces, ¿hace tres años que vive en Madrid? (no / ... años)
2. ¿Cuánto tiempo hace que trabaja en el Banco de Bilbao? (diez años)
3. ¿Desde cuándo consulta al Dr. Pérez? (1985)
4. ¿Cuánto tiempo hace que no va al médico? (seis meses)
5. ¿Cuánto tiempo hace que tiene catarro? (tres o cuatro días)
6. ¿Tiene fiebre? ¿Sí? ¿Desde cuándo? (ayer)
7. ¿Qué medicina toma Ud.? ¿Aspirina? ¿Cuánto tiempo hace? (dos días)
8. ¿Durmió bien anoche? ¿No? ¿Cuánto tiempo hace que no duerme bien? (dos días)

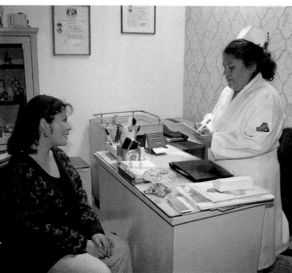

331

Ex. E: writing

Less-prepared students,
Ex. E.: As students do each item, have them note whether they are expressing an amount of time gone by **(hace + ...)** or a point of time at which something started in the past **(desde)**. Have them pick one or two items to express in an alternate fashion. For example, **Hace 10 años que vive en Madrid** means **Vive en Madrid desde 1986,** and so on.

More-prepared students,
Ex. E: Have more-prepared students give alternate expressions wherever possible. For example, **Hace seis meses que no va al médico = No va al médico desde el noviembre pasado.** (The month will vary depending on when your class does this exercise.)

Answers, Ex. E: 1. No, vivo en Madrid hace... años.   2. Hace diez años que trabajo en el Banco de Bilbao.   3. Consulto al Dr. Pérez desde 1985 (mil novecientos ochenta y cinco).   4. No voy al médico hace seis meses.   5. Tengo catarro hace tres o cuatro días.
6. Tengo fiebre desde ayer.
7. Hace dos días que tomo aspirina. (Tomo aspirina hace dos días.)
8. Hace dos días que no duermo bien. (No duermo bien hace dos días.)

Ex. F: writing

Answers, Ex. F: 1. Hace dos semanas que me siento mal. Tengo fiebre desde el lunes pasado. 2. Hace un mes que Mía tiene catarro. Hace cinco días que ella tose. 3. Mis padres tienen dolor de garganta desde el principio de la semana. 4. ¿Cuánto tiempo hace que te duele el estómago? 5. ¿Desde cuándo no duermes bien? (¿Desde cuándo duermes mal?) 6. Hace un mes que no duermo bien.

Follow-up, Ex. F: Have students write these sentences for homework after you have done them orally. You could use them as a dictation to familiarize students with this sometimes difficult concept.

Support material, Aquí escuchamos: Teacher Tape 🎧

Presentation: Aquí escuchamos

Ask students to brainstorm reasons for having a bad night's sleep. Then have them look at the pre-listening materials and listen to the tape, concentrating on details about Rebeca's night. Afterwards, ask students how many of them have a baby brother or sister or have had a friend or relative's baby keep them awake.

Answers, Aquí escuchamos: 1. un poco cansada 2. no durmió bien anoche 3. su hermana y su esposo con su bebé 4. hasta el sábado 5. bien; durmió hasta las 10:00

Ex. G: pair work

Less-prepared students, Ex. G: Allow less-prepared students time to formulate the questions and their own answers before working with a partner. Review the preterite of **dormir** with them as well.

Learning Strategy:
Expressing past and present time

F. ¡Traducciones! (Translations!)
Give the Spanish equivalents of the following sentences.

1. I have been feeling poorly for two weeks. I've had a fever since last Monday.
2. Mía has had a cold for a month. She has been coughing for five days.
3. My parents have had sore throats since the beginning (**el principio**) of the week.
4. How long has your stomach been hurting?
5. Since when have you been sleeping badly?
6. I haven't slept well for a month.

Learning Strategy:
Previewing

Learning Strategy:
Listening for details

Aquí escuchamos:
"¿Dormiste bien?"

Antes de escuchar

Claudia and Rebeca are talking about how much sleep they got last night and why. Look at the following questions and identify a few things you expect to hear during their conversation. ▣ START

Después de escuchar

1. ¿Cómo ve Rebeca a Claudia?
2. ¿Por qué está cansada Rebeca?
3. ¿Quiénes están de visita en casa de Rebeca?
4. ¿Cuánto tiempo van a estar con Rebeca?
5. ¿Cómo durmió Claudia?

¡Aquí te toca a ti!

Learning Strategy:
Requesting and giving personal information

G. ¿Dormiste bien anoche?
Question a classmate about his or her sleeping habits and experiences.

Haga las preguntas para saber…

1. si él (ella) durmió bien anoche.
2. a qué hora se acostó.
3. cuántas horas durmió.
4. cuántas horas duerme generalmente durante la semana.
5. cuántas horas duerme generalmente durante el fin de semana.

332

More-prepared students, Ex. G: Remind more-prepared students that **dormir** is an irregular verb in the present and preterite. Have them tell you how it works. Then have them interview two other students and compare and contrast the two interviews. **(Miguel durmió bien anoche, pero Susana durmió mal. Sólo durmió 4 horas.)**

¡Adelante!

EJERCICIO ORAL

H. ¿Cuánto dormiste?   Work with a partner to compare how much each of you slept during the last week. Create a weekly calendar for each of you to report your sleep for each night. Calculate the average amount of sleep per night that each of you got. For any nights that you slept at least one hour more or less than the average, indicate why on your calendar. Prepare to report to the group for each of you (1) the average amount of sleep per night, (2) the least amount of sleep in any one night, (3) the longest you slept in any one night, (4) and the most interesting reason that you had a "short" night.

EJERCICIO ESCRITO

I. Una encuesta   Working with several students, create a survey to find out about the sleeping habits of your classmates and those of their families. Find out information that will either confirm or dispute the following statements. Once you have completed the survey, compile the results, and compare them to the results reported in the article at the beginning of this **etapa.**

1. High school students don't get enough sleep (that is, they go to bed too late and/or get up very early).
2. High school students catch up on lost sleep on weekends and during vacations.
3. Young people fall asleep more easily than older people.
4. Females have nightmares more often than males do.
5. Males snore more often than females do.

Ex. H:  pair work

Suggestion, Ex. H: Have students create a blank calendar ahead of time. Then, give them a small amount of time each morning to record the previous night's sleep on the calendar. After the specified number of days, have students work in groups to do Ex. I.

Ex. I: groups of four or more

writing

Suggestion, Ex. I: Have students work in groups of five. Have each team or group give an oral report to the class on its findings. You may want to compile all of these into a whole-class profile.

Cooperative Learning

Vocabulario: Team Word-webbing

Learning Strategies: Listing, brainstorming

Critical Thinking Strategies: Categorizing, making associations

- Put the students into heterogeneous teams of four.
- Give each team a set of colored pencils or markers and a sheet of paper. Each student may use only one color.
- Tell all students to close their books and then one student to write **La salud** in the center of his or her team's sheet of paper.
- Divide the vocabulary into four categories and assign one category to each teammate. Have each student write the name of his or her category on the paper, with a line connecting it to the title of the chapter. Then have each student write down all the words he or she can think of to fit his or her own category.
- Next, tell students that they are going to write in round robin fashion, from left to right, all the words and expressions they can think of to fit their teammates' categories. The point of the exercise is to recall vocabulary by linking concepts together and to show teammate contributions to each list.
- When they are done, have each team show and decribe its word web.

Vocabulario

Para charlar

Para hablar del aspecto físico

Mido un metro…   Tengo que subir de peso.
Peso… kilos.   bajar de peso.

Para hablar de un período de tiempo

¿Desde cuándo?   desde (que)
¿Cuánto tiempo hace?   hace (que)

Temas y contextos

Los alimentos

el almidón	el hierro	las papas
el calcio	la leche	los productos lácteos
el cereal	los lípidos	la proteína
la fibra	los minerales	los vegetales
la fruta	el pan	las vitaminas
la grasa		

El sueño

roncar
tener una pesadilla

Vocabulario general

Sustantivos

la ansiedad	una indicación
un artículo	la mayoría
un(a) bebé	un movimiento muscular
unas calorías	un músculo
una causa	un nervio
una dificultad	un resultado
la digestión	el ritmo cardíaco
una duda	la salud
la energía	una señal
una falta	el tono muscular
un hueso	la vista nocturna

Verbos

admitir	regular
desarrollar	renovar
facilitar	repetir (i, i)
formar	sonreír(se) (i, i)
mejorar	tratar de
presentar	
recuperar	

Adverbios

aparentemente
exactamente

Otras palabras y expresiones

en parte al menos
estar de visita
lo mismo
¡Qué envidia!

Adjetivos

adicional
balanceado(a)

Chapter Culminating Activity

Have students bring in a healthful food from each food group for a review **fiesta.** Have students say what they are bringing and which group it represents. Have them write up their menu. You may also want to bring in samples of fruits like papayas and mangoes for students to try. These are now available fresh or prepared in many stores.

Lectura CULTURAL

TRES ALIMENTOS INDÍGENAS

Antes de leer

Learning Strategy:

Previewing

1. Look at the photos and title that accompany the reading. What do you think the reading will be about?
2. Can you identify the foods in the photos? Have you ever seen any of these foods before?
3. Can you name some dishes that contain these ingredients?

Guía para la lectura

Learning Strategy:

Reading for details

A. Read the first paragraph to answer the following question: ¿Qué tienen en común el tomate, el maíz y la papa?

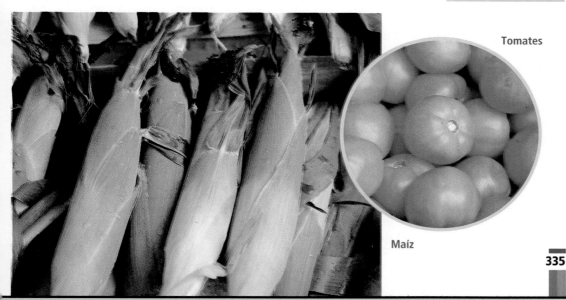

Tomates

Maíz

335

Lectura cultural

Expansion, Lectura cultural: Ask students what other foods they know of that originated in the Americas. For example, pineapple and papaya, mentioned earlier in this chapter. Others include chile peppers, squash, chocolate, and avocados. You may want to have students research particular food items and report their findings to the class.

Papas

B. Now read the second paragraph and answer the following questions.

1. ¿Qué información tenemos sobre el tamaño *(size)* y el color del tomate?
2. ¿Desde cuándo se cultiva esta fruta en las Américas?

C. Read the third paragraph to obtain the following information.

1. ¿De dónde viene la palabra *maíz*?
2. ¿Cuál es una comida importante que se hace con el maíz?

D. Now read the last paragraph and answer the following questions.

1. ¿Por qué no podían cultivar el maíz los incas?
2. ¿Qué inventó la gente de los Andes?

Tres alimentos indígenas

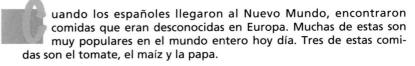

uando los españoles llegaron al Nuevo Mundo, encontraron comidas que eran desconocidas en Europa. Muchas de estas son muy populares en el mundo entero hoy día. Tres de estas comidas son el tomate, el maíz y la papa.

Xitomatl es la palabra para tomate en náhuatl, el idioma de los aztecas. Hoy día en México se usa la palabra *jitomate* en vez de *xitomatl*, pero en otras partes del mundo hispano se usa la palabra *tomate*. Hay muchos tipos de tomates —grandes, pequeños, rojos, amarillos y anaranjados. Se cree que esta fruta se cultiva en México y en partes de la América Central desde hace más de 5.000 años. Los exploradores españoles introdujeron esta fruta en Europa. ¿Pueden imaginar la cocina italiana sin el tomate?

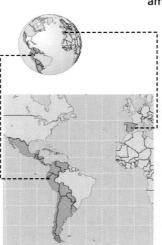

El maíz, conocido como *mahiz* en la lengua de los indios del Caribe, es un producto importantísimo que se originó en las Américas también desde hace más de 5.000 años. En la época precolombina se cultivaba desde lo que hoy es Chile hasta el sur de Canadá. El maíz es el ingrediente esencial de muchas comidas de la América Latina, entre ella la tortilla.

En las altas montañas de los Andes no podían cultivar maíz porque hace mucho frío. Allí los indios cultivaban la patata, conocida como *papa* en el quechua, la lengua que hablaban los incas y que hoy todavía se habla en los países andinos. Se cosechaban varios tipos de papa y los indios de los Andes inventaron una manera de conservarlas por medio del frío y el calor, o sea el proceso de conservarlas y deshidratarlas a la misma vez. ¿Se imaginan un mundo sin estas tres comidas?

336

Aqui leemos

Estrategia para la lectura

Certain kinds of prose give advice or teach us how to do something. In passages like this, not every word is equally important, but the verb forms that tell what to do are usually especially significant. Sometimes, the order in which information is given is crucial. As always, read first to get an overall idea of content and organization. Then look for the main ideas or topics. Finally, read for specific details either for your own information or because you need them.

Antes de leer

The following article is from *El Regional*, a Puerto Rican newspaper. The article is full of advice for people who want to exercise but have trouble keeping at it. Answer these questions before you read it.

>> **W**hat do you already know about the value of physical exercise for good health?

>> **W**hy do people usually start an exercise program?

>> **W**hat are some reasons people stop exercising?

>> **W**hat are some techniques you use or have heard of that can help make exercise a habit?

Before reading the article, look to see how it is organized. Notice the section titles and the numbered subsections. Look closely at any subsection to see what kinds of verb forms are used. Then go on to the **Actividades.**

Reading Strategies:

When reading instructions, look for main categories of activities, then for details.

Notice whether the order in which activities are to be done is important.

337

Prereading

Have students read the **Estrategia para la lectura** and answer the questions in the **Antes de leer** section. Students can answer these questions individually or as part of a whole class discussion. After taking a quick look at the reading (no more than a minute), students should proceed to the activities.

Support Materials

Workbook: pp. 234–236
Unit Review Blackline Masters: **Unit 4 Review**
Listening Activity masters: **108**
Tapescript: **p. 143**
Unit Exam: **Testing Program, p. 180**

Atajo, Writing Assistant Software *supports* **ATAJO**

Exs. A and B: pair work

Acerca de los dolores musculares

Por Robert P. Sheldon

MANTÉNGASE

Mientras innumerables cantidades de personas comienzan un régimen de ejercicios cada año, otro tanto "tira la toalla" antes de ver algún resultado positivo. Y la cesación de la actividad no está limitada a los principiantes: veteranos, también, frecuentemente abandonan su deporte. La falta de interés y de tiempo y las lesiones son algunas de las razones para renunciar. Los científicos especialistas en comportamiento humano, John Martin, Ph.D. y Patricia Dubbert, Ph.D., de Veteranos y el Centro Médico de la Universidad de Mississippi tienen estos consejos para los deportistas novatos y los no tan novatos, lo mismo que para los profesionales y amigos alentadores:

1) Vaya paso a paso. Comience de una manera fácil, de baja intensidad y gradualmente aumente su ritmo de ejercicios.

2) Control del refuerzo. Siéntase orgulloso de usted mismo. Mantenga una lista que le recuerde sus logros. Cuéntele a sus amigos lo mucho que ha avanzado. Envuélvase en desafíos motivacionales de premios ganados o separe cierta cantidad de dinero por cada milla que corra, nade o corra en bicicleta.

3) Control estimulante. Saque la ropa que va a utilizar en la corrida mañanera la noche anterior, o por la mañana si es que va a correr en la tarde después del trabajo. Evite las amistades que no aprecian el ejercicio. Lleve un historial de su millaje, tenga a la vista carteles y fotografías de personas ejercitándose, programe sus ejercicios semanalmente por adelantado y escriba notas sobre usted mismo.

4) Contratos de comportamiento humano. Escríbase un contrato a usted mismo, y sea realista acerca de sus metas. Guárdelo y cuando haya logrado su meta, celébrelo.

5) Estrategias congénitas. Establezca metas, visualícese logrando éstas, y sea positivo. La gente comienza a ejercitarse por que es bueno para su salud y quiere hacerlo bien. Con un poco de empuje mental y premeditación, usted puede mantenerse en un programa de ejercicios o ayudar a otros a continuar el suyo.

Actividades

A.
1. Read the first and last sentences. Based only on the information you find there and what you learned from the title, subtitles, illustration, and so on, what seems to be the main idea of the article? In English, write a one-sentence prediction of what you expect the rest of the article to be about.
2. Read the opening paragraph rapidly. According to this paragraph, what are two reasons people give up on their exercise programs? Were these the reasons you had predicted?

338

3. Read the first few words of each subsection. Based on the subtitle and the first few words, what is the likely content of each subsection?
4. Go to the subsection you previewed in **Antes de leer**. Read it carefully, looking for how each piece of advice relates to the section heading.

B. 1. Return to the opening paragraph and read it more carefully. List all the cognates you see.
2. Go to a numbered paragraph you have not yet read carefully. Read it and list all the command forms you see in it.
3. Based on the content of the reading and the contexts in which the following words and phrases occur, what is the best English equivalent for each one?
   a. **régimen**
   b. **principiantes**
   c. **lesiones**
   d. **novatos**
   e. **refuerzo**
   f. **logros**
   g. **evite**
   h. **semanalmente**
   i. **metas**
   j. **empuje mental**

C. Answer the following questions in English, based on the reading.

1. Who are John Martin and Patricia Dubbert? Why are they qualified to give advice about exercise?
2. According to number 5, why do people begin exercising?
3. According to number 1, how should you begin an exercise program?
4. According to number 2, how can you reward yourself?
5. What are some suggestions to help maintain a routine when exercising?

D. 1. Imagine you have a friend on an exercise program who is having trouble sticking with it. She has written to ask you for some advice. Using what you learned from this article, write your friend a note in Spanish, giving her some suggestions. Be sure to explain why the things you suggest are important.
2. With a partner, design a flyer that could be posted in your school gym to encourage more people to exercise. Use the information from this article to help you think of important points to emphasize.
3. Prepare a motivational poster for some sport or physical activity that you enjoy. Use the suggestions in number 3 from the article as a starting point. Write slogans and captions in Spanish.

339

Presentation, Ex. B: This activity helps focus attention on vocabulary. Students will not be able to guess every word accurately. Going over the word list in class can help them see how to think about the contexts of words in order to increase accuracy. Emphasize the importance of the entire context in which any word appears.

Answers, Ex. B, number 3:
a. program b. beginners
c. injuries d. novices e. reinforcement f. achievements
g. avoid h. weekly i. goals
j. mental effort

Exs. C and D: pair work

More-prepared students, Ex. C: Have more-prepared students do as much of their work as possible in Spanish.

Less-prepared students, Ex. C: Make sure less-prepared students note a key word or words in Spanish from the text for each of their answers in English.

Answers, Ex. C: 1. specialists in human behavior; they understand the psychological aspect of maintaining an exercise program 2. for good health 3. gradually 4. remind yourself and your friends of your accomplishments, give yourself a prize, or pay yourself per mile 5. plan ahead, avoid nonexercising friends, keep records, use motivational materials

Ex. D: pair work

 writing

Ex. A:

pair work

role play

Ex. B:
groups of four
or more

Ex. C:
pair work

role play

Variation, Ex. C: If you have videotaping capabilities, students may rehearse and tape their skits. Then you may show the finished product to other Spanish classes.

Ya llegamos

Cooperative Learning

Learning Strategies:

Asking for and providing information, organizing ideas, paraphrasing

Critical Thinking Strategies:

Making associations, seeing cause-and-effect relationships

Cooperative Learning

Learning Strategies:

Providing personal information, organizing ideas, active listening, negotiating

Critical Thinking Strategies:

Analyzing, making associations, seeing cause-and-effect relationships, evaluating

Actividades orales

A. *Un amigo te ayuda.* You and your friend are traveling in a Spanish-speaking country. One of you begins to feel ill. The friend notices this and expresses concern. Thus encouraged, the one who is ailing sets about describing his or her symptoms. Since the friend must seek help from the pharmacist, he or she carefully repeats the symptoms to be sure that they are well understood. In addition, he or she inquires about other possible symptoms (for example, **Dices que tienes escalofríos. ¿Tienes fiebre también?**)

Together you should (1) list five symptoms and/or possible causes and (2) think of at least one medication or possible treatment.

B. *Yo no estoy en forma.* Your group of four is comparing notes to determine who is in the worst physical condition. Take turns mentioning facts about your health that could be improved upon and discussing sleeping, eating, and exercise habits. Every time one of the group mentions a reason he or she is not in great shape, try to come up with an even better excuse.

The group should then determine (1) which member needs the most improvement in each of the three areas of sleeping, eating, and exercise (that could be three different students, or one, or two); (2) which of you has the best habits overall; and (3) which one is in the worst overall physical condition. Finally, the group should make recommendations for each of the four members, prescribing what changes each one should make in his or her personal habits in order to improve his or her physical condition.

C. *Voy al médico.* Prepare a skit based on a visit to a doctor's office. One student will play the doctor and the other will play the patient. Be sure to include symptoms, how long the patient has had them, and what medicine the doctor recommends.

340

Ex. D: pair work

writing

Exs. E and F: writing

Actividades escritas

D. ¿Qué hacías cuando eras niño(a)? You and your friends are comparing what you used to do during summer vacations when you were children. Make a list of at least five activities that reflect how you spent a typical summer day. Then, in pairs, combine your list with a class-mate's and write a description of a typical day in the life of a child.

E. ¿Cómo comen los jóvenes? Your family is hosting a foreign exchange student for the year. In order to make your guest more com-fortable, you draw up a calendar showing meal times and sleep schedules. Be sure to include weekends, altering meal times and sleep schedules as appropriate.

F. ¿Cómo duermen los jóvenes? Write a letter to a friend in a Spanish-speaking country in which you provide details about your sleep-ing habits and inquire about theirs.

Writing Activities

Atajo, Writing Assistant Software

Functional vocabulary: Ask-ing for an opinion; asking for help; asking for / giving advice; com-plaining; describing health; express-ing an opinion; expressing time relationships; reassuring; sequenc-ing events; thanking; warning

Topic vocabulary: Body; medi-cine; quantity, sickness and dis-eases; time expressions

Grammar: Verbs: imperfect; verbs: preterite; verbs: reflexives; verb summary; pronouns: indirect objects; **doler; dar; pedir;** adverbs of time

341

we become

Conexión

Las enfermedades respiratorias

AL EMPEZAR

Usamos las vías respiratorias para respirar. Cuando inhalamos y exhalamos el oxígeno que nuestros cuerpos necesitan, el aire pasa por las vías respiratorias. A veces los microbios infectan las vías y **nos ponemos** enfermos.

ACTIVIDAD A

¿Cuáles de las siguientes partes del cuerpo forman las vías respiratorias?

la nariz	la boca	los ojos	los brazos
el estómago	la garganta	la tráquea	las rodillas
el cuello	los pulmones	las orejas	
la espalda	el muslo	el corazón	

TRES ENFERMEDADES DE LAS VÍAS RESPIRATORIAS

a bronquitis, la gripe y el resfrío son tres de las enfermedades más comunes de las vías respiratorias. Normalmente los microbios que causan estas enfermedades son víruses. La siguiente tabla tiene una descripción de cada enfermedad.

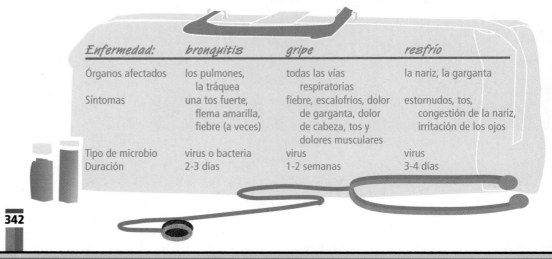

Enfermedad:	bronquitis	gripe	resfrío
Órganos afectados	los pulmones, la tráquea	todas las vías respiratorias	la nariz, la garganta
Síntomas	una tos fuerte, flema amarilla, fiebre (a veces)	fiebre, escalofríos, dolor de garganta, dolor de cabeza, tos y dolores musculares	estornudos, tos, congestión de la nariz, irritación de los ojos
Tipo de microbio	virus o bacteria	virus	virus
Duración	2-3 días	1-2 semanas	3-4 días

342

con las ciencias

Contesta las siguientes preguntas.

1. ¿Cuántos tipos de enfermedades respiratorias hay en la tabla?
2. ¿Cuáles de las enfermedades pueden afectar los pulmones?
3. ¿Cuáles pueden afectar la nariz?
4. ¿Cuáles afectan partes del cuerpo que no están en las vías respiratorias?
5. ¿Cuáles nos dan fiebre? ¿escalofríos? ¿estornudos? ¿tos?
6. ¿Cuál enfermedad dura más tiempo?
7. ¿Hace cuánto tiempo que estuviste enfermo(a) con una de estas enfermedades? ¿Qué tuviste?

ACTIVIDAD C

Think of the last time that you had a respiratory infection and describe the symptoms by answering the following questions.

	Sí	No
¿Tenías fiebre?	_____	_____
¿Tosías?	_____	_____
¿Te dolía la garganta?	_____	_____
¿Tenías escalofríos?	_____	_____
¿Te dolían los ojos?	_____	_____
¿Tenías dolor de cabeza?	_____	_____
¿Estornudabas con frecuencia?	_____	_____
¿Tenías congestionada la nariz?	_____	_____
¿Te dolían los músculos?	_____	_____

¿Otros síntomas? _____

¿Cuánto tiempo duró la enfermedad? ¿Dos o tres días? ¿Cuatro días? ¿Una semana?_____

ACTIVIDAD D

Work with a partner to see if you can correctly diagnose the respiratory infection each of you had. Take turns describing your symptoms using the list in Actividad C. Then complete a medical report like the one below.

Síntomas de mi compañero(a): _____

Mi diagnóstico: _____

343

Expansion Activity: At the bottom of this page is a list of remedies commonly taken to alleviate the symptoms of respiratory infections. You may want to share this with students and have them check the boxes next to the remedies they used the last time they were sick. Then ask students to work with a partner to find out what remedies were used when the partner was sick. Have students follow the model provided.

Model:
Student 1: *Cuando estabas enfermo(a), ¿dormiste?*
Student 2: *Sí, dormí.*
Student 1: *¿Tomaste jarabe?*
Student 2: *No, no tomé jarabe.*

Remedio	Yo	Mi compañero(a)
dormir		
tomar jarabe		
quedarse en cama		
beber líquidos		
pedirle medicina al médico		
tomar antihistamínicos		
respirar vapor		
tomar aspirinas		
descansar		
otras posibilidades:		

Cultural Context

Many of the same sports that are popular in the U.S. are also popular in the Spanish-speaking world. Popular sports in both cultures include baseball, tennis, basketball, and cycling. The most popular sport in the U.S. is football, while in the Hispanic world, soccer is the favorite.

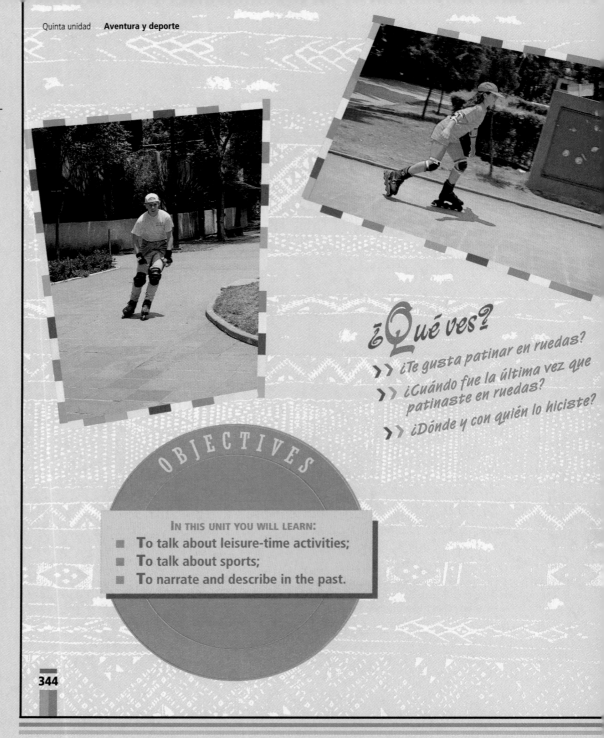

¿Qué ves?

>> ¿Te gusta patinar en ruedas?

>> ¿Cuándo fue la última vez que patinaste en ruedas?

>> ¿Dónde y con quién lo hiciste?

OBJECTIVES

IN THIS UNIT YOU WILL LEARN:
- **To talk about leisure-time activities;**
- **To talk about sports;**
- **To narrate and describe in the past.**

344

UNIDAD
cinco

Aventura y deporte

345

Planning Strategy

If you do not assign the Planning Strategy (Workbook, p. 237) for homework or if students have difficulty coming up with English expressions, you might ask several students to role play the situation. One person can play the Spanish speaker and another can play the American friend. You could also put students in groups to write a description of their country, their state, or their town. Then, as a class, they can make a list on the board of the words used in each type of description.

Chapter Objectives

Functions: Understanding short descriptions of warm-weather sports and pastimes; talking about the recent past; describing places and events in the past

Context: Sports and leisure activities in the Spanish-speaking world

Accuracy: Preterite of high frequency irregular verbs: **conducir, traer, decir, poder, saber, poner, leer, caer(se), creer, ver, oír;** various meanings of the verb **ponerse**

CAPÍTULO

13 EL VERANO PASADO

El esquí acuático es un buen ejercicio y una buena manera para divertirse con los amigos.

Objectives:

》》 **U**nderstanding short descriptions of warm-weather sports and pastimes

》》 **T**alking about the recent past

》》 **D**escribing places and events in the past

Strategies:

》》 **R**equesting and providing information

》》 **O**rganizing ideas

》》 **I**magining

346

Video/Laserdisc

Chapter 13 Video Program and Video Guide

PRIMERA ETAPA

Preparación

》》 **W**hat is one of your favorite activities?

》》 **W**hat did you do last summer?

》》 **D**o you like camping? Would you like to windsurf?

/./-/./-/./-/./-/./-/./

Learning Strategies:

Brainstorming, previewing

¿Qué hiciste?

Mi actividad favorita cuando voy a la playa es hacer windsurfing. Es buen ejercicio. En enero fui a Puerto Rico con la familia por una semana y me divertí mucho con los amigos. Una mañana salí temprano para correr en la playa y luego por la tarde hice windsurfing con mi amigo Raimundo. Esa noche fuimos a las discotecas. Pienso volver en el verano si puedo.

Antonio Salazar

Nos gusta mucho acampar. El verano pasado fuimos a Costa Rica donde hay muchos parques nacionales. Llevamos dos tiendas de campaña. Aprendimos mucho sobre los animales y las plantas tropicales. Fuimos a un parque donde vimos el cráter de un volcán y vimos que salía humo del cráter. Me gustó mucho el viaje.

Carmen Rivera

347

Etapa Support Materials

Workbook: **pp. 239–242**
Listening Activity masters: **p. 111**
Critical Thinking master: **Chapter 13, primera etapa, activity E**
Transparency: **#43**
Teacher Tape

Tapescript: **p. 147**
Quiz: **Testing Program, p. 186**

Support material, **¿Qué hiciste?**:
   Teacher Tape ◯ **, Transparency #43**

¡Aquí te toca a ti!

A. ¿Quién hizo qué? Indica las actividades que hizo cada persona (Carmen o Antonio) basándote en la página 347.

acampó en un parque nacional	vio un volcán
corrió en la playa	fue a Costa Rica
estuvo en Puerto Rico	llevó tiendas de campaña
aprendió mucho sobre la naturaleza	hizo windsurfing
viajó en el verano	viajó en enero
fue a una discoteca	vio humo saliendo de un cráter

ESTRUCTURA

Other verbs in the preterite: conducir, traer, decir

Conduje el coche a 55 millas por hora.	I *drove* the car at 55 miles per hour.
¿Quién **trajo** las bebidas?	Who *brought* the drinks?
Tus amigos lo **dijeron.**	Your friends *said* it.

These verbs change their stems in the preterite, but actually have a clear pattern of their own. Note that they all have **j** in the stem. In addition, the **yo** form does not have an accent on the last syllable, nor does the **él / ella / Ud.** form ending in **-o.** Also note that the **ellos / ellas / Uds.** form uses **-eron** (and not **-ieron**) after the **j.**

conducir (to drive)

yo	**conduje**	nosotros(as)	**condujimos**
tú	**condujiste**	vosotros(as)	**condujisteis**
él		ellos	
ella	**condujo**	ellas	**condujeron**
Ud.		Uds.	

traer (to bring)

yo	**traje**	nosotros(as)	**trajimos**
tú	**trajiste**	vosotros(as)	**trajisteis**
él		ellos	
ella	**trajo**	ellas	**trajeron**
Ud.		Uds.	

Ex. B: ✎ writing

*More-prepared students,
Ex. B:* Ask more-prepared students to give personal information about themselves, their family and friends, using the exercise as a model.

---

decir (to say)

yo	**dije**	nosotros(as)	**dijimos**
tú	**dijiste**	vosotros(as)	**dijisteis**
él		ellos	
ella }	**dijo**	ellas }	**dijeron**
Ud.		Uds.	

Note that the stem of the verb **decir** has the same vowel change in the preterite, **e** becoming **i,** as in the present tense.

Also, these verbs all have different **yo** forms in the present tense. All the other persons follow the standard present tense endings.

conducir → yo condu**z**co, tú conduces, él / ella / Ud. conduce, nosotros(as) conducimos, vosotros(as) conducís, ellos / ellas / Uds. conducen

decir (i) → yo di**g**o, tú dices, él / ella / Ud. dice, nosotros(as) decimos, vosotros(as) decís, ellos / ellas / Uds. dicen

traer → yo tra**ig**o, tú traes, él / ella / Ud. trae, nosotros(as) traemos, vosotros(as) traéis, ellos / ellas / Uds. traen

Aquí practicamos

B. Forma oraciones completas de una manera lógica, usando elementos de las columnas. Cambia los verbos a la forma apropiada del pretérito.

Modelo: Francisco   traer   los discos compactos
Francisco trajo los discos compactos.

A	B	C
Enrique y yo	conducir	los discos compactos
Carlos y José	traer	la verdad
María	decir	el coche de su papá
tú		su tabla vela
Esteban y tú		que vamos a la playa
vosotros		al centro

349

Ex. C: writing

Presentation: Aquí escuchamos

Ex. D: groups of three

C. ¿Qué pasó anoche en la fiesta? Contesta las preguntas sobre una fiesta. Usa el pretérito e inventa los detalles.

1. ¿Tú condujiste el coche de tus padres a la fiesta de Julián y José?
2. ¿A qué hora dijiste que terminó la fiesta?
3. ¿Qué tipo de cintas trajeron tus amigos?
4. ¿Quién dijo que fue aburrida la fiesta?
5. ¿Quiénes más condujeron anoche?

Aquí escuchamos:
"¿Qué hizo Lorenzo?"

Antes de escuchar

Think about what you usually tell your friends when you talk to them about a vacation you took. Now read the following questions to get a good idea of what to listen for in the conversation about what Lorenzo did during his vacation.

Después de escuchar

Contesta las preguntas sobre lo que hizo Lorenzo durante sus vacaciones.

1. ¿Adónde fue Lorenzo de vacaciones?
2. ¿Con quién fue de vacaciones?
3. ¿Qué hizo todos los días por la mañana? ¿Y por la tarde qué hizo con su hermano?
4. ¿Cuándo aprendió Lorenzo su nuevo deporte acuático?
5. ¿Qué le dijo Lorenzo a Roberto que le pasó varias veces al principio?
6. ¿Qué sabía hacer ya Lorenzo que le ayudó mucho?
7. ¿Cuál fue la reacción de Roberto a lo que le contó Lorenzo?

¡Aquí te toca a ti!

D. ¿Qué hizo? Talk with a classmate and (1) find out what three things he or she did last summer. Then (2) find a second classmate and tell him

350

or her what the first person you talked to said he or she did last summer. After doing this, (3) ask what three things your second partner did last summer and go on to repeat this process with a third student.

¡Adelante!

EJERCICIO ORAL

E. El verano pasado
(1) Talk with a partner about last summer. (2) Create a chart to compare your activities with those of your partner. (3) List at least five activities for each of you. Then (4) find at least two activities that you had in common and two in which only one of you participated. (Use the following list of suggestions to start you thinking.)

Yo		Mi amigo(a)
	ir a la playa	
	hacer windsurfing	
	ir a las discotecas	
	acampar	
	patinar en ruedas	
	ver un volcán	
	hablar por teléfono	
	leer	
	jugar al ténis	
	jugar al vólibol	
	pescar	
	estudiar en la universidad	

EJERCICIO ESCRITO

F. Una actividad fenomenal
Write an entry into your diary in which you tell about a memorable activity. Tell (1) who was involved, (2) your relationship to the principal characters, (3) where the action took place, (4) the goal of the main participants, (5) whether or not they achieved their goal, and (6) how you were affected. (Use several different verbs, paying special attention to the use of the preterite tense.)

Learning Strategy:

Organizing ideas in a paragraph

351

Ex. E: pair work

Suggestion, Ex. E: Instruct students to include at least two activities that are not on the list. Be sure to have students report back on their partners' activities or compare and contrast activities.

Ex. F: writing

Less-prepared students, Ex. F: Remind less-prepared students of the past time context. For each numbered item, help students come up with expressions they know in Spanish. For example, "who was involved" really means "who went"; "relationship" means "who went with you (friends, relatives, etc.)"; goals can be expressed with **para** + *infinitive* (**fuimos a la playa para nadar**) and so on.

More-prepared students, Ex. F: Begin to incorporate using both the preterite and imperfect tenses. Instruct more-prepared students to insert a description of what the place was like after item 3. Have them recall what tense is used to describe what a place was like in the past.

Variation, Ex. F: This is a good place to do a "tick mark" graph on the board to practice creating and reading a graph. You may be able to draw some interesting inferences from the graph.

Learning Strategy: Creating and reading a graph

Critical Thinking Strategy: Drawing inferences

Presentation: ¡Qué viaje!

Begin by asking students about memorable vacations. Poll the class to see how many students have traveled to a foreign country, where and when, where and when students have traveled in the U.S., and so on. Treat the passage as a reading exercise. Have students use prior knowledge, cognates, and the photos to help them comprehend. Then do Ex. A on p. 353.

Cultural Expansion

Cliff diving in Acapulco into the shallow channel below is a long-standing tradition in Mexico. In recent decades, regular international contests have been held at **La Quebrada,** drawing brave competitors and crowds of tourists. Some divers plunge from the amazing height at night, their shadows following behind on the lit wall of the cliff.

SEGUNDA ETAPA

Preparación

›› **W**hen was the last time you took a long trip?

›› **W**here did you go and with whom did you go?

›› **W**hat do you remember about that trip?

///-//-//-//-//-//-//-//-//
Learning Strategy:
Previewing

¡Qué viaje!

Un clavadista en Acapulco, México

dived

El año pasado fui de vacaciones con la familia a México. Fuimos a Acapulco donde vimos un espectáculo en "La Quebrada" donde unos hombres **se clavaron** al agua desde una altura de 55 metros. Una tarde alquilamos una lancha y mi hermano y yo esquiamos. Una noche fuimos a un excelente restaurante donde comimos mariscos y escuchamos música de mariachi. El último día compramos regalos en las tiendas para los amigos en los Estados Unidos. Fue un viaje **inolvidable**.

Miguel Martínez

unforgettable

352

Etapa Support Materials

Workbook: pp. 243–248
Transparencies: #43, #44
Teacher Tape
Quiz: Testing Program, p. 188

Support material, ¡Qué viaje!:
Teacher Tape , **Transparency #44**

¡Aquí te toca a ti!

A. ¿Qué hizo Miguel?
Indica las actividades que hizo Miguel durante sus vacaciones basándote en la página 352.

Miguel…

escuchó música de mariachi
hizo ciclismo
fue a la Ciudad de México
compró unos discos compactos
comió mariscos
fue a un museo
montó en bicicleta con su hermano
fue a un concierto de rock
se clavó desde una altura *(height)* de
   55 m
estuvo en Acapulco
esquió
fue de compras
vio a los clavadistas *(cliff divers)*

Repaso

B. Nuestras vacaciones
Imagina que tu familia fue de vacaciones a México el año pasado. Usa las pistas para hablar sobre tus vacaciones. Sigue el modelo.

Modelo: el año pasado / nosotros / ir de vacaciones a México
El año pasado nosotros fuimos de vacaciones a México.

1. nosotros / divertirse mucho
2. mis padres / decidir / ir a Acapulco
3. mi padre / reservar dos cuartos en el Hotel Presidente
4. el 5 de julio / nosotros / llegar al hotel
5. la familia / pasar dos semanas en Acapulco
6. yo / dar un paseo / todos los días
7. mis hermanos / ir a la playa / mucho
8. una tarde / mi papá / decir "¡Vamos a La Quebrada!"
9. en La Quebrada / nosotros / ver el espectáculo de los clavadistas
10. un experto valiente / clavarse al mar desde una altura de 55 m
11. esa noche / todos nosotros / acostarse muy tarde por la emoción
12. el último día / yo / levantarse temprano / para ir a la playa
13. nosotros / volver a los Estados Unidos / el 29 de julio
14. mi familia y yo / divertirse mucho / durante nuestras vacaciones

353

Suggestion, Ex. A: After students have read the passage on page 352, have them close their books. Do Ex. A as a listening exercise, with students writing **sí** or **no** after each statement you read. Afterwards have them open their books and check their accuracy.

Answers, Ex. A: Miguel escuchó música de mariachi, comió mariscos, estuvo en Acapulco, esquió, fue de compras y vió a los clavadistas.

Ex. B: writing

Suggestion, Ex. B: Because this exercise has a single story line, you may wish to do it with the entire class.

Answers, Ex. B: 1. Nosotros nos divertimos mucho.   2. Mis padres decidieron ir a Acapulco. 3. Mi padre reservó dos cuartos en el Hotel Presidente.   4. El 5 de julio (nosotros) llegamos al hotel. 5. La familia pasó dos semanas en Acapulco.   6. (Yo) Di un paseo todos los días.   7. Mis hermanos fueron a la playa mucho.   8. Una tarde mi papá dijo "¡Vamos a La Quebrada!"   9. En La Quebrada (nosotros) vimos el espectáculo de los clavadistas.   10. Un experto valiente se clavó al mar desde una altura de 55 metros.   11. Esa noche, todos nosotros nos acostamos muy tarde por la emoción. 12. El último día (yo) me levanté temprano para ir a la playa. 13. (Nosotros) Volvimos a los Estados Unidos el 29 de julio.   14. Mi familia y yo nos divertimos mucho durante nuestras vacaciones.

Presentation:
Estructura

This would be a good time to review the preterite of the verbs **tener** and **estar**. See Reteaching, Ex. A, p. T348.

ESTRUCTURA

Other verbs in the preterite: *poder, saber, poner*

Traté de hacerlo, pero no **pude**.	I tried to do it, but *I could* not.
Cuando llamó José, **supimos** lo que pasó.	When José called, *we found out* what happened.
Los niños **pusieron** los paquetes en la cocina.	The children *put* the packages in the kitchen.

These verbs are conjugated in a similar way. Note that the vowel in the stem of each verb changes to **u.** Here are the forms:

poder

pod- → pud-

yo	**pude**		nosotros(as)	**pudimos**
tú	**pudiste**		vosotros(as)	**pudisteis**
él			ellos	
ella	} **pudo**		ellas	} **pudieron**
Ud.			Uds.	

saber

sab- → sup-

yo	**supe**		nosotros(as)	**supimos**
tú	**supiste**		vosotros(as)	**supisteis**
él			ellos	
ella	} **supo**		ellas	} **supieron**
Ud.			Uds.	

poner

pon- → pus-

yo	**puse**		nosotros(as)	**pusimos**
tú	**pusiste**		vosotros(as)	**pusisteis**
él			ellos	
ella	} **puso**		ellas	} **pusieron**
Ud.			Uds.	

Aquí practicamos

C. Contesta las preguntas usando las formas apropiadas de los verbos en el pretérito. Compara tus respuestas con las de un(a) compañero(a). Anota cómo son semejantes o diferentes.

1. ¿Qué deporte pudiste hacer por fin después de practicar mucho?
2. ¿Qué supiste recientemente sobre algún atleta que no sabías antes?
3. ¿Qué deporte no pudiste hacer la primera vez que lo intentaste *(tried)*?
4. ¿Dónde pusieron los estudiantes sus bicicletas cuando llegaron a la escuela?

D. Dime... Create questions by combining the items in the left column with those in the right column, using the preterite of the verbs in the middle column. A classmate will give answers to your questions.

Modelo:

dónde	poner	las cintas

Estudiante A: *¿Dónde pusiste las cintas?*
Estudiante B: *Las puse en el coche.*

por qué (no)	poder	la bicicleta
cuándo	conducir	las cintas
quién	saber	salir de la casa
qué	dar	la propina *(tip)* a José
cuánto	poner	los precios del restaurante
dónde	decir	ir a la playa
	traer	el coche de su padre
		la verdad
		las bebidas
		el número de teléfono del hotel
		la silla
		lo que dijo el presidente

Nota gramatical

The verb *ponerse*

When the verb **poner** is used with a *reflexive pronoun,* it has two very different meanings:

1. to put on (an article of clothing)

Me puse el abrigo.	*I put on* my coat.

Ex. C: pair work

writing

Answers, Ex. C: 1. Pude hacer... 2. Supe... 3. No pude hacer... la primera vez que lo intenté. 4. Los estudiantes las pusieron...

Suggestion, Ex. C: As preparation and introduction to using the preterite and the imperfect together, point out and contrast the uses in questions 2 and 4.

Less-prepared students, Ex. C: Allow less-prepared students time to formulate answers before working with a partner.

More-prepared students, Ex. C: Have more-prepared students create three additional questions for their partners, using these same verbs.

Expansion, Ex. C: Poll the class informally to see which sports are most popular, which are considered the most difficult, and so on.

Expansion, Ex. C: List on the board all the sports named in response to question 1. Then make a "tick mark" graph to determine the sport that students think requires the most practice for success.

List on the board all the athletes named in response to question 2. Have students identify the sport associated with each one. Can any inferences be drawn here, such as which sports are in season that would explain why certain athletes are more in the media now?

Learning Strategies: Creating and reading a graph, identifying, expressing an opinion

Critical Thinking Strategies: Drawing inferences, categorizing, evaluating

Ex. D: pair work

Suggestion, Ex. D: Have students prepare their questions as homework in anticipation of the paired activity. Check for accuracy before having them do pair work.

Ex. E:  pair work

Less-prepared students,
Ex. E: Have less-prepared students scan the exercise to identify the time elements involved (present or immediate future) before working on any item. Have them do the same to identify reflexive and nonreflexive uses of **poner(se).**

More-prepared students,
Ex. E: Have more-prepared students create an additional question for each item in the past by adding an appropriate time expression. For example: **¿Cuándo te pones nervioso? ¿Te pusiste nervioso en el examen ayer?**

Presentation: Aquí escuchamos

Have students preview preliminary materials, then listen with books closed, taking notes on the monologue. After they have listened to the tape two or three times, call on volunteers for information and have them reconstruct the vacation in chronological order. Then have students answer the comprehension questions.

Answers, Aquí escuchamos: 1. a México con sus padres y su hermano   2. a sus abuelos   3. a la famosa Catedral de Guadalajara, al mercado "La libertad" y al museo   4. Fueron a un partido de fútbol profesional y a un concierto de rock.   5. al Lago de Chapala   6. Pasearon en un barco y comieron mariscos.   7. Sus abuelos pensaban visitarlos para la Navidad.   8. Pusieron contentos.

2. to get or become (an emotion, a state)

Jorge **se puso** furioso cuando perdió el partido de tenis.

Mis amigos siempre **se ponen** nerviosos cuando viajan por avión.

Jorge *became* furious when he lost the tennis match.

My friends always *get* nervous when they travel by plane.

E. Preguntas Alternando con otro(a) estudiante, usen las sugerencias para hacer preguntas. Sigan el modelo.

Modelo: cuándo / ponerse nervioso
—*¿Cuándo te pones nervioso(a)?*
—*Me pongo nervioso(a) cuando tengo un examen.*

1. cuándo / ponerse el suéter
2. dónde / poner las bebidas para la fiesta mañana
3. por qué / ponerse nervioso(a) cuando jugar al golf
4. cuándo / ponerse su ropa favorita
5. cuándo / ponerse furioso(a)

Antes de escuchar

Review the preterite forms of the verbs you have learned so far in this chapter. Then read the following questions to anticipate what María Elena might say about her trip to Mexico.

Después de escuchar

Ahora contesta las preguntas.

1. ¿Adónde y con quiénes fue de vacaciones María Elena?
2. ¿A quiénes visitó?
3. ¿A qué lugares fueron en la ciudad?
4. ¿Qué más hicieron para divertirse?
5. ¿Adónde condujeron en coche?
6. ¿Qué hicieron en este lugar a dos horas de la ciudad?
7. ¿Qué supieron al volver de su viaje en coche?
8. ¿Cuál fue la reacción ante estas noticias?

Learning Strategy:
Previewing

Learning Strategy:
Listening for details

356

¡Aquí te toca a ti!

F. *¿Qué pudiste hacer?*   Work with a classmate and ask each other about a memorable trip you each took or can pretend that you took. Ask each other about three things that you were able to do on the trip, using the correct preterite forms of the verb **poder** when asking and answering the questions.

¡Adelante!

EJERCICIO ORAL

G. *¿Qué hiciste la semana pasada?*   Use the cues as a starting point to describe at least five things you did last summer in each category. Report facts or make up the information, if you like, using a different verb for each activity you add after the cue. Make sure to relate the activities to the context of that particular cue. Follow the model.

> **Modelo:**   reunirse en la playa / mis amigos y yo
> *Mis amigos y yo nos reunimos en la playa. Nadamos, tomamos el sol, comimos mariscos, jugamos al vólibol y, por la noche, salimos a bailar.*

1. ir al cine / mi familia y yo
2. viajar en coche / con mi papá
3. ir de camping / con unos amigos
4. visitar a mis abuelos / mi familia
5. pasar una semana en la ciudad de México / yo

EJERCICIO ESCRITO

H. *Un viaje*   Write a letter to your grandmother about an interesting trip that you took, telling (1) where you went, (2) when, (3) how you got there, (4) with whom you went, (5) how long you stayed, and (6) at least four activities in which you participated. (You may base this letter on a real experience or on an imaginary trip.) (7) Don't forget to date and sign your letter.

> *Learning Strategies:*
> Expressing past time, listing, reporting based on personal experience
>
> *Critical Thinking Strategies:*
> Making associations, imagining

> *Learning Strategies:*
> Expressing past time, organizing details
>
> *Critical Thinking Strategy:*
> Imagining

357

Ex. F: pair work

Ex. G: pair work

Less-prepared students, Ex. G: Have less-prepared students create a list of infinitives for each item before beginning. They can refer to this list as they talk to their partners to help them organize their thoughts. Call on different students to give possibilities for each item.

More-prepared students, Ex. G: Do as a pair exercise and encourage more-prepared students to speak as conversationally as possible by adding comments (**yo también / yo tampoco**) or by repeating information before asking a question (**Así que fuiste a Nueva York, ¿viste la Estatua de la Libertad? ¿te gustó?**, etc.). Call on students to role play for the class.

Ex. H: writing

Less-prepared students, Ex. H: Remind less-prepared students to recycle ideas from Ex. F.

More-prepared students, Ex. H: Have more-prepared students exchange papers, read their partner's work, and write a reaction to it. For example, **Me gustó mucho el trabajo de mi compañero. Tuvo un verano más/ menos interesante que yo. Fue al cine tantas veces como yo pero vio más películas interesantes.**

TERCERA ETAPA

Preparación

>> **W**hat are some of the sports that you play?

>> **W**hat sports do you play in the summer?

>> **W**hich sport did you play the most last summer?

>> **W**hich sport would you like to learn to play?

/-/-/-/-/-/-/-/-/-/-/-/-/
Learning Strategy:
Previewing

¿A qué jugaste?

—¿A qué jugaste el verano pasado? ¿al tenis?
—No, jugué al béisbol. ¿Y tú?
—Ah, yo jugué mucho al baloncesto.

al golf

al fútbol americano

al béisbol

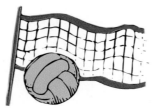

al vólibol

al tenis

al hockey sobre hierba

358

Etapa Support Materials

Workbook: **pp. 249–253**
Critical Thinking master: **Chapter 13, tercera etapa**, activity B
Transparency: **#45**
Teacher Tape ⌢

Quiz: **Testing Program, p. 191**
Chapter Test: **Testing Program, p. 195**

Support material: **¿A qué jugaste?:**
Teacher Tape ⌢, **Transparency #45**

al boliche

al dominó

a los naipes

al fútbol

al baloncesto

al ajedrez

a las damas

Ex. A: writing

Answers, Ex. A: 1. Mateo jugó al fútbol.   2. Enrique jugó al golf.   3. Susana jugó al hockey sobre hierba.   4. Alberto jugó al béisbol.   5. Gabriel jugó al vóli-bol.   6. Sara jugó al baloncesto. 7. Horacio y Elena jugaron al aje-drez.   8. Claudia jugó al tenis.

¡Aquí te toca a ti!

Learning Strategy:

Reporting in the past based on visual cues

A. ¿Qué hizo?   Indica lo que hizo cada una de las personas según los dibujos abajo y en la página 360.

1. Mateo

2. Enrique

3. Susana

4. Alberto

359

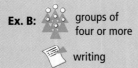

Ex. B: groups of
four or more

writing

Suggestion, Ex. B: Have students use the chart as a model to make their own charts, or use the corresponding Critical Thinking master.

Suggestion, Ex. B: Have students write a short questionnaire to use as they poll classmates. Afterward, have each group write up its findings in paragraph form.

5. Gabriel   **6.** Sara   **7.** Horacio y Elena   **8.** Claudia

Learning Strategies:

Polling, recording information in a chart

B. ¿Qué hiciste tú?   Your Spanish class has been asked by the school newspaper to participate in a survey to determine which sports and games were played the most last summer by the student body. Your task is to (1) poll five members of the class to find out who played what and (2) record the results of your poll in a chart like the following one. In the last column, (3) total the number of students who played that sport or game. The first column has been done for you.

	Nombre de estudiante: *Lupe*	Nombre: _____	Nombre: _____	Nombre: _____	Nombre: _____	Nombre: _____	Total que lo jugaron:
Deporte: golf	✓						
vólibol							
fútbol	✓						
béisbol	✓						
boliche	✓						
tenis	✓						
baloncesto							
ajedrez							
patinar en ruedas	✓						
esquiar	✓						
naipes							
equitación							
natación	✓						
acampar							

360

Now, in groups of four or five, (1) compare the results of your surveys. Together, (2) come up with some explanations as to (a) why you think certain activities were the most popular and (b) why the two with the fewest votes were not so popular. Consider geographical location, number of people required for a certain game, season, age of participants, gender of students surveyed, etc. (3) Be prepared to report this analysis to the class. Finally, (4) come up with a possible headline for the newspaper article on the student body's choices of summer activities. Your headline should reflect something about your findings.

Repaso

C. *La carta misteriosa*   Read the following brief passage, changing the underlined present tense verbs into the *preterite* tense. Then work with a group of three or four classmates to decide what happened next, creating your own ending to report back to the entire class.

A las 11:00 de la noche más o menos, Carolina <u>llega</u> a su casa después de un día muy ocupado. Cansada, <u>se sienta</u> por unos momentos. <u>Abre</u> su cartera y <u>saca</u> una carta. La <u>pone</u> sobre la mesita, al lado del sofá, pero luego la <u>mira</u> varias veces y, por fin, <u>decide</u> abrirla. Al principio, no lo <u>puede</u> hacer. <u>Se pone</u> nerviosa pero, por fin, <u>rompe</u> el sobre y <u>mira</u> la carta. Poco después, confundida (confused), <u>pone</u> la carta en el sobre y se <u>levanta</u> muy despacio del sofá. <u>Se da</u> cuenta del silencio total de la casa. Cuando <u>pone</u> el pie en el primer escalón (step) para subir a su cuarto, una voz <u>grita</u> (shouts) desde allí. No <u>puede</u> moverse. <u>Se queda</u> paralizada de terror, sin saber qué hacer.

ESTRUCTURA

Other verbs in the preterite: *leer, caer(se), creer, ver, oír*

Leíste la carta ayer.	*You read* the letter yesterday.
El niño llora porque **se cayó.**	The boy is crying because he *fell down.*
Creímos el cuento de Pablo.	*We believed* Paul's story.
Vi la película el sábado.	*I saw* the movie on Saturday.
Ellos **oyeron** las noticias.	They *heard* the news.

361

Ex. C: 👥 groups of three

Follow-up, Ex. C: Have a contest to see which group comes up with the most interesting, creative, or original ending. You might have an impartial third party (another teacher, perhaps) choose the winner. You could also have a student act out the story as a pantomime while another student narrates it.

Answers, Ex. C: llegó, se sentó, Abrió, sacó, puso, miró, decidió, pudo, Se puso, rompió, miró, puso, se levantó, Se dio, puso, gritó, pudo, Se quedó

Cooperative Learning

Learning Strategies:

Negotiating, reporting in the past

Critical Thinking Strategies:

Drawing inferences, making associations, generalizing, seeing cause-and-effect relationships

Learning Strategies:

Narrating in the past, negotiating

Critical Thinking Strategies:

Imagining, creating

The verbs **leer, caer(se), creer,** and **oír** are conjugated similarly in the preterite. They have in common a **y,** instead of an **i,** in the **él / ella / Ud.** and **ellos / ellas / Uds.** forms.

The other forms follow the normal pattern of **-er / -ir** verbs in the preterite tense.

leer

yo	leí	nosotros(as)	leímos
tú	leíste	vosotros(as)	leísteis
él		ellos	
ella	leyó	ellas	leyeron
Ud.		Uds	

caer(se)

yo	caí	nosotros(as)	caímos
tú	caíste	vosotros(as)	caísteis
él		ellos	
ella	cayó	ellas	cayeron
Ud.		Uds.	

oír

yo	oí	nosotros(as)	oímos
tú	oíste	vosotros(as)	oísteis
él		ellos	
ella	oyó	ellas	oyeron
Ud.		Uds.	

creer

yo	creí	nosotros(as)	creímos
tú	creíste	vosotros(as)	creísteis
él		ellos	
ella	creyó	ellas	creyeron
Ud.		Uds.	

362

The verb **ver** is conjugated similarly to the verb **dar** in the preterite. Its endings are exactly like those of **-er** and **-ir** verbs.

		ver		
yo	**vi**		nosotros(as)	**vimos**
tú	**viste**		vosotros(as)	**visteis**
él			ellos	
ella	**vio**		ellas	**vieron**
Ud.			Uds.	

Caer(se) and **oír** also have a special **yo** form in the present tense. **Oír** also changes its stem in the present tense.

caerse   →   me ca**ig**o, te caes, se cae, nos caemos, os caéis, se caen
oír   →   o**ig**o, oyes, oye, oímos, oís, oyen

Aquí practicamos

D. _Un espectáculo en Acapulco_   Sustituye las palabras en cursiva con las palabras entre paréntesis y haz los otros cambios necesarios.

1. _Yo_ leí sobre los clavadistas de Acapulco en la guía. (nosotros / ella / tú / mis amigos / vosotras)
2. _Mis padres_ no creyeron lo que dije sobre La Quebrada. (Uds. / él / mis hermanos / tú)
3. _Nosotros_ vimos, por fin, el espectáculo a la orilla del mar. (yo / ellos / tú / ella / vosotros)
4. _Un clavadista_ se cayó de la roca. (Uds. / mi hermano / yo / tú / nosotros)
5. _Yo_ oí que no se lastimó. (nosotros / ella / tú / Uds. / vosotros)
6. _Mi papá_ les dio una propina _(tip)_ a los clavadistas. (ellos / nosotros / yo / tú / Uds. / el Sr. Fuentes)

E. _México_   Usa los dibujos en la página 364 para decir lo que _(what)_ vieron diferentes estudiantes durante sus vacaciones en México y lo que piensan ver hoy y mañana. Sigue el modelo.

Modelo: nosotros
**Ayer** nosotros vimos las pirámides.
**Hoy** vemos las pirámides.
**Mañana** vamos a ver las pirámides.

las pirámides

//.//.//.//.//.//.//.//.//
Learning Strategies:
Reporting in the past, present, and immediate future based on visual cues

363

Ex. D: writing

Variation, Ex. D: Do this as an oral chain drill with a twist. Call on or go down the rows and have individual students give answers, but make it a rule from the beginning that any time the answer is going to be a stem-changer (**leyó, creyeron,** etc.), the whole class / row / all boys / all girls must say the answer together.

Answers, Ex. D: 1. Nosotros leímos / Ella leyó / Tú leíste / Mis amigos leyeron / Vosotras leísteis 2. Uds. no creyeron / Él no creyó / Mis hermanos no creyeron / Tú no creíste   3. Yo vi / Ellos vieron / Tú viste / Ella vio / Vosotros visteis 4. Uds. se cayeron / Mi hermano se cayó / Yo me caí / Tú te caíste / Nosotros nos caímos   5. Nosotros oímos / Ella oyó / Tú oíste / Uds. oyeron / Vosotros oísteis   6. Ellos les dieron / Nosotros les dimos / Yo les di / Tú les diste / Uds. les dieron / El Sr. Fuentes les dio

Ex. E: writing

los volcanes

1. yo

el monumento

2. ella

el clavadista

3. ellos

El Palacio de Bellas Artes

4. nosotros

La Catedral Nacional

5. ustedes

el centro

6. tú

El Museo Nacional de Antropología

7. nosotros

el zoológico Bosque de Chapultepec

8. yo

el mercado

9. ellos

364

F. El accidente Cambia los verbos en cursiva al pretérito.

1. Hoy *veo* un accidente en el lago.
2. *Puedo* ver el velero claramente desde el balcón del hotel.
3. El hombre *se cae* del velero y *grita* "¡Auxilio!" *("Help!")*.
4. El velero *da* una vuelta *(turns)* sin el hombre.
5. El hombre *puede* subir al velero cuando *pasa* cerca de él.
6. Al día siguiente *leo* del accidente en el periódico.
7. El hombre *dice* en el artículo que nunca *tiene* miedo durante el accidente.
8. ¡*Me río* cuando *leo* eso!
9. No *creo* al hombre porque lo *oigo* gritar tanto en el agua.

Aquí escuchamos:
"Un espectáculo en Acapulco"

Antes de escuchar

Review the preterite of the verbs you have learned in this chapter. Now read the following questions to focus your listening. You will hear a brief narration about Miguel's trip to Mexico and what happened to a cliff diver while he was in Acapulco.

Learning Strategy:
Previewing

Después de escuchar

Escucha el monólogo otra vez antes de contestar las preguntas.

Learning Strategy:
Listening for details

1. ¿Sobre qué leyó Miguel en la guía?
2. ¿Qué dice Miguel que no creyeron sus amigos?
3. ¿Quiénes vieron el espectáculo?
4. ¿Qué accidente tuvo uno de los hombres?
5. ¿Qué oyó Miguel después del accidente?
6. ¿Qué hizo el papá de Miguel al final?

¡Aquí te toca a ti!

G. ¿Qué jugaste? Work with a classmate to ask and answer each other's questions about three or four sports that you each played during the past year. Use the verb **jugar** each time you ask or answer a question.

365

Ex. F: writing

Less-prepared students, Ex. F: Have less-prepared students identify the subject of each verb by writing an appropriate subject pronoun in parentheses. Remind them to refer to these when they change to the preterite to be sure they maintain the same subject.

More-prepared students, Ex. F: Have more-prepared students create another accident scenario to describe in the preterite, using Ex. F as a model.

Answers, Ex. F: 1. vi
2. Pude   3. se cayó, gritó   4. dio
5. pudo, pasó   6. leí   7. dijo, tuvo
8. Me reí, leí   9. creí, oí

Presentation: Aquí escuchamos

Have students recall the basics of accident reporting (Ch. 10, p. 294): *who, what, when, where.* Then write the interrogatives in Spanish on the board. After students have previewed the materials to focus their listening, have them listen to the tape for these four key ideas. Play the tape several times. Afterwards ask students for the basic details of the accident. Then have them complete the comprehension questions.

Answers, Aquí escuchamos: 1. los famosos clavadistas   2. Los clavadistas se tiraron al agua desde una altura de 55 m.   3. Miguel, su padre y su hermano   4. El hombre se cayó de la roca.   5. Él no se lastimó seriamente.   6. Les dio una buena propina a los clavadistas.

Ex. G: pair work

Cooperative Learning

Ex. H: pair work

Less-prepared students, Ex. H: Have less-prepared students brainstorm a list of sports and board/card games. Remind them that they are going to talk about something that already happened. Have them recall what verb tense to use. Have students report back to the class on the content of their discussions.

More-prepared students, Ex. H: Have more-prepared students be prepared to report on their partners' activities as well as to compare and contrast them with their own.

Ex. I: writing

Less-prepared students, Ex. I: Have less-prepared students brainstorm a list of possible verbs to use in their writing.

More-prepared students, Ex. I: After they have prepared their paragraphs, have more-prepared students write an introduction, describing where the event occurred. Remind them to use the imperfect to tell what a thing, place, or person was like in the past.

Cooperative Learning

Group Itinerary, Ex. I

Learning Strategies: Planning an itinerary, negotiating

Critical Thinking Strategies: Sequencing, prioritizing

EJERCICIO ORAL

H. *Mis deportes y juegos favoritos* Talk with a classmate and (1) tell each other what sports and board games you generally like to play. Then think back to the last time you participated in a holiday gathering with some of your extended family (aunts, uncles, cousins, grandparents) where you played various sports and/or games. (2) Describe that event and (3) tell who was there. (4) Identify two things you and your partner can find in common and (5) one element that is different about the experiences you are describing.

EJERCICIO ESCRITO

I. *Una narración* Write about an interesting, dramatic, or funny incident that you remember from a trip you took at some point in the past. Use the preterite throughout your narration.

/-/-/-/-/-/-/-/-/-/-/-/

Cooperative Learning

Learning Strategies:

Reporting based on personal information, describing, organizing ideas, narrating in the past and present times

Critical Thinking Strategy:

Comparing and contrasting

/-/-/-/-/-/-/-/-/-/-/-/

Learning Strategies:

Reporting based on personal information, describing, organizing ideas in paragraphs, narrating in the past

366

- Put students into heterogeneous groups of four and tell them they are going to plan a trip to a Spanish-speaking country. They may get ideas from passages earlier in the Chapter on Acapulco (p. 352), Puerto Rico, and Costa Rica (p. 347). They may divide the planning as they wish, provided that each student participates equally. Explain that each team will share its itinerary with the class and that they may put it in any form they wish (an ad, a written report, a poster, an overhead transparency, a bulletin board display, etc.).

- Give students time to plan their itineraries.
- Direct each group to share their itinerary with another group.
- Call on students at random to describe another group's itinerary. Have the class decide which itinerary they like best and why.

Vocabulario

Temas y contextos

Las vacaciones

correr en la playa
los clavadistas
el concierto de rock
la discoteca
los mariscos
la música de mariachi
la naturaleza
el volcán

Las diversiones y los deportes

jugar...
al ajedrez
al boliche
a las damas
al dominó
a los naipes

Vocabulario general

Verbos

caer(se)   dividir
clavar(se)   traer
dar

Adjetivos

contento(a)
costoso(a)
feroz
furioso(a)
inolvidable
nervioso(a)
triste

Adverbios

al principio
por fin

- Then the student to his/her right adds to the story, using his/her vocabulary item(s), and so on.
- The last person in the circle must end the story.
- You may want to have the groups tell each other their stories afterwards.

Chapter Culminating Activity

You may want to arrange a "verb bee." Prepare ahead of time a master list of verbs and subjects. Divide the class into two teams. Create two grids on the board, each with four columns headed *present, preterite, imperfect,* and *future.* Send four members of each team to the board simultaneously. Then state a verb and a subject and team members will write the verbs in the correct form for their tense. There may be no coaching from the audience, but a team member in doubt can pass the chalk to a seated member, who can pinch hit for him/her. Each member can only pinch hit once! One student from each team records the other team's correct points. At the game's end, the team with the most points (correct verb forms) wins. You could also include a championship round with all irregular verbs.

Vocabulario

- Prepare ahead of time sets of cards with one or two items of vocabulary on each. Be sure there are proportionate numbers of nouns, verbs, adjectives, etc.
- Divide the class into groups of five and have each team sit in a circle.
- Distribute cards to the teams. Each team member gets one card.
- One student begins a story about his/her real or imaginary participation in a sport, using the word(s) on his/her card (plus any others he/she needs to make a complete thought).

Lectura cultural

Lectura
CULTURAL

LOS LLANOS VENEZOLANOS

Antes de leer

1. Look at the photos, map, and the title of the reading to form some impressions about its content.
2. If you were to take a trip to a rain forest in Latin America, what would you expect to see there?

Guía para la lectura

A. The following narrative by a young boy about his trip to Venezuela describes a series of sights and experiences that were memorable for him. Read the first sentence of each paragraph to get an idea of what he did. On a separate sheet of paper, summarize in your own words what the main idea is in each paragraph.

B. Now read the passage carefully and answer the following questions.

1. Make a list of all of the people identified in the reading. Who are they?
2. Make a list of all the animals identified in the reading. What are they?

C. Look over the following questions. Read the passage again and answer them.

1. ¿De dónde son los tíos de Miguel y adónde fueron de vacaciones?
2. En general, ¿cómo es la región del río Orinoco?
3. ¿Por qué no pudo nadar Miguel cuando hacía mucho calor?
4. ¿Qué pasó cuando Miguel y sus tíos trataron de comprar unas canastas?
5. ¿Qué recibían los indios a cambio de sus canastas?

368

Los llanos venezolanos

n septiembre mis tíos, que viven en Caracas, me invitaron a pasar unas semanas con ellos antes de empezar el colegio. Visité muchos lugares pero el fin de semana que fuimos a los llanos del Orinoco me pareció fantástico. Esta zona de prados que tiene 1.000 km de largo y 320 km de ancho, se extiende entre los Andes y el río Orinoco. Es una región muy plana, donde hay algunas pequeñas elevaciones. Tiene muchos ríos que fluyen del Orinoco.

Cruzamos varios de estos ríos durante el viaje. Tenía muchas ganas de nadar, porque hacía mucho calor, ¡pero había pirañas! Mis tíos me dijeron que también hay caimanes *(crocodiles)*, pero no vimos ninguno. Vi muchos pájaros rojos, blancos, rosados. En un árbol vi una iguana enorme.

Algo que nunca voy a olvidar de este viaje fue nuestro encuentro con una tribu de indios. Buscábamos un lugar para acampar y pasar la noche cuando vimos humo que salía de entre unos árboles. Nos acercamos. Y allí encontramos un pequeño pueblo indio. Aunque no hablábamos la misma lengua, inmediatamente pudimos entendernos. Coromoto, un chico de mi edad, me enseñó como hacían canastas, collares y pulseras. Yo quería tener una canasta de recuerdo y mi tía quería canastas para decorar la casa. No pudimos comprarlas porque los indios no usan el dinero. Finalmente las cambiamos por naranjas, una fruta que ellos no conocían.

Abajo: una iguana
Derecha: Un termitero inmenso en Venezuela

369

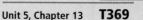

Chapter Objectives

Functions: Understanding short descriptions of outdoor sports; describing places and events in the past

Context: Outdoor sports, especially bicycling, rafting, and hiking

Accuracy: The imperfect and the preterite to talk about past actions, descriptions, and interrupted actions

CAPÍTULO

14

AL AIRE LIBRE

El ciclismo es un deporte de gran popularidad. Los ciclistas de países hispanos tienen mucho éxito en los campeonatos del mundo.

Objectives:

>>> **U**nderstanding short descriptions of outdoor sports

>>> **D**escribing places and events in the past

Strategies:

>>> **P**ersuading

>>> **S**upporting an opinion

>>> **D**rawing inferences

370

Video/Laserdisc

Chapter 14 Video Program and Video Guide

PRIMERA ETAPA

Preparación

>> **D**o you like to ride a bicycle? Why or why not?

>> **D**o you have a bicycle?

>> **D**id you have a bicycle when you were younger?

>> **I**s the bicycle that you have now different from the one you had as a child? in what ways?

/-/-/-/-/-/-/-/-/-/-/-/
Learning Strategy:
Brainstoming

El ciclismo

Cargarás con todo el equipo

Atleta urbano
Hombre o mujer que, sin castigarse el cuerpo, vive en la ciudad deportivamente.

Mochila
Para que te eches todo, incluso tus problemas, a las espaldas.

Camiseta
Imprecindible para el atleta urbano, porque con ella puedes hacer de todo: ir en mountain bike, correr, caminar y pasear.

Cámara fotográfica
Demuestra a tus amistades que eres un verdadero atleta urbano. Enséñales la foto.

Headphones
Ideal para hacer deporte sin perder el ritmo.

Botella de Trinaranjus
Todo atleta urbano se refresca de una manera natural y Trinaranjus sin burbujas es el refresco más natural e imprescindible para conseguir, entre otras cosas, el equipo del atleta urbano.

Mountain bike
Hay muchas maneras de practicar el atletismo urbano, pero hacerlo con una mountain bike es de las más cómodas.

Ahora, Trinaranjus te regala miles de camisetas, mochilas, headphones y cámaras de fotos. Y, además, sortea 50 mountain bikes. Todo, para que puedas tener el equipo de atleta urbano al completo. Las instrucciones las encontrarás en las botellas de Trinaranjus.

imprescindible: indispensable / mountain bike: *bicicleta de montaña* / headphones: *auriculares* / *sortea:* raffles off

371

Presentation, El ciclismo

Ask students what they think **Cargarás con todo el equipo** means. (Since they haven't learned the future tense yet, you may have to explain that **Cargarás** is the future of **cargar.**) Let students know that **Cargarás con todo el equipo** is a rather idiomatic way to say "You'll be carrying all the right equipment." Students may notice that some words in this ad have been borrowed from English. You may want to point out to students that a mountain bike is usually called a **bicicleta de montaña** and that headphones in Spanish is **auriculares.**

Reading Strategies

Have students think about the kind of information ads usually contain. Have them consider target audiences, etc. Then have them examine the ad in the text and draw conclusions: what is being advertised and to whom. Is this ad similar to or different from ads in the U.S.?

Etapa Support Materials

Workbook: pp. 255–259
Listening Activity masters: p. 115
Transparency: #46
Quiz: Testing Program, p. 200

Tapescript: p. 154

Support material, El ciclismo:
Transparency #46

Ex. A: writing

Answers, Ex. A: 1. a   2. a
3. a   4. b   5. b   6. b   7. b
8. a   9. a   10. b

Ex. B: writing

Answers, Ex. B: 1. leímos
2. oímos   3. se cayó   4. Supimos,
pudo   5. puso   6. creí

¡Aquí te toca a ti!

A. Un anuncio   Completa las oraciones con la opción que se corresponda mejor con el contenido del anuncio de la página 371.

1. Un atleta urbano es un hombre o una mujer que...
   a. vive en la ciudad deportivamente.
   b. vive en una ciudad.
2. La cámara es para demostrar a tus amigos que...
   a. eres un(a) buen(a) atleta.
   b. vas a pasear.
3. La manera más cómoda de practicar el atletismo urbano es
   a. con una bicicleta de montaña.
   b. caminando.
4. La camiseta es necesaria para...
   a. no tener frío.
   b. ir en bicicleta de montaña, correr, caminar y pasear.
5. Todo atleta urbano se refresca con...
   a. tres naranjas.
   b. Trinaranjus.
6. Trinaranjus te regala...
   a. cientos de camisetas, mochilas y cámaras de fotos.
   b. miles de camisetas, mochilas, auriculares y cámaras de fotos.
7. Trinaranjus es un refresco natural...
   a. con gas.
   b. sin gas.
8. Trinaranjus también...
   a. sortea cincuenta bicicletas de montaña.
   b. da cincuenta bicicletas de montaña.
9. En la mochila pones...
   a. de todo.
   b. tus problemas.
10. Las instrucciones para el sorteo están en...
    a. las tiendas donde compras Trinaranjus.
    b. las botellas de Trinaranjus.

Repaso

B. Cambia los verbos en cursiva, abajo y en la página 373, al pretérito.

1. En la escuela mi hermano y yo *leemos* sobre los volcanes de Centroamérica.
2. Poco después, *oímos* en la televisión de un accidente en un parque nacional costarricense.

372

3. Según las noticias, un turista *se cae* en un cráter.
4. *Sabemos* que un hombre *puede* ayudar al turista.
5. Lo *pone* sobre los hombros para salvarlo.
6. Yo *creo* que ese hombre *es* muy valiente.

C. *Nuestras vacaciones en Costa Rica* Cambia los verbos subrayados *(underlined)* al pretérito.

1. Nosotros <u>pasamos</u> una semana de vacaciones en Costa Rica. *(Begin with El año pasado...)*
2. Nuestro viaje <u>comienza</u> en San José, donde mi padre <u>hace</u> reservaciones en el famoso Hotel Cariari.
3. El primer día, <u>damos</u> un paseo por el mercado, donde <u>compramos</u> mucho café para llevar a nuestros amigos. También <u>visitamos</u> el Museo de Arte Costarricense, una fábrica de joyas *(jewel factory)* y el enorme Monumento a la Guerra de 1856.
4. El segundo día, <u>salimos</u> para Puntarenas. <u>Conducimos</u> a la costa en un coche que mi padre <u>alquila</u> para el viaje. En camino *(On the way)*, <u>conocemos</u> varios pueblos interesantes.
5. Por fin, <u>llegamos</u> a una hermosa playa de arenas *(sands)* blancas en el Pacífico. <u>Pedimos</u> ceviche *(marinated fish)* fresco y mariscos. Yo <u>como</u> un pescado grande.
6. Después de pasar unos días en la playa, toda la familia <u>va</u> a visitar el Parque Nacional Volcán Poás. A pesar de que *(Even though)* <u>empieza</u> a llover, <u>podemos</u> subir al enorme cráter de un volcán activo. Por suerte *(Luckily)*, <u>vemos</u> una pequeña erupción de vapores y gases.
7. Después, <u>volvemos</u> a San José, donde <u>vamos</u> a un concierto en el famoso Teatro Nacional en el centro de la ciudad.
8. Al día siguiente, <u>salimos</u> para los EE.UU. Todos <u>estamos</u> de acuerdo que el viaje a Costa Rica <u>es</u> muy interesante y que <u>aprendemos</u> mucho.

ESTRUCTURA

The imperfect and the preterite: Past actions

Antes, yo **iba** a México cada año.	In the past, I *used to go* to Mexico every year.
Pero el año pasado, yo **fui** a Costa Rica.	But last year, I *went* to Costa Rica.

In previous units you learned two past tenses, the preterite and the imperfect. When narrating or describing in the past, think of all actions as having a beginning, a middle, and an end. The preterite is used to report only *the beginning and the ending* of an action in the past. The middle stage or *continued process of an action*—and nothing more—is always described by the imperfect.

373

Suggestion, Ex. C: Divide the class into pairs. When each pair has finished the exercise, check verb forms by having several students tell the whole story.

Answers, Ex. C: 1. pasamos 2. comenzó, hizo 3. dimos, compramos, visitamos 4. salimos, Condujimos, alquiló, conocimos 5. llegamos, Pedimos, comí 6. fue, empezó, pudimos, vimos 7. volvimos, fuimos 8. salimos, estuvimos, fue, aprendimos

Presentation: Estructura

Because distinctions between the two tenses are often subtle, students are not expected to assimilate them the first time they are taught. This topic has many gray areas and only the most basic distinctions are presented at this point.

**Presentation:
Estructura
(cont'd)**

1. You may wish to begin your presentation with a review of the most common uses of the preterite: beginning of an action, completion of an action, definite time period.
2. Follow this with a quick transformation drill using familiar verbs.
3. Continue by reminding students of the contexts in which the imperfect is commonly used: ongoing actions, habitual actions, unspecified number of repetitions, indefinite time period.

Ex. D: pair work

Expansion, Ex. D: After students have completed this exercise, ask follow-up questions, such as, **¿Cuántos años tenías cuando recibiste tu primera bicicleta? ¿De qué marca era? ¿De qué color era? ¿Cómo era la bici de tu mejor amigo(a)?**

The main distinction between the use of the preterite and the imperfect has to do with certain *aspects* of actions in the past:

1. If an action is viewed as having been either begun or completed within any definite time period, occurs only once, or is repeated a specific number of times, the verb will be in the *preterite*.

   La semana pasada, yo **fui** a la casa de mis abuelos. *(single occurrence)*

   El sábado y el domingo pasado **fuimos** al cine juntos. *(specified number of repetitions)*

   Mi abuelo **jugó** al tenis tres veces en su vida. *(specified number of repetitions in a definite time period)*

2. If a past action is habitual, repeated an unspecified number of times, or performed in an indefinite time period, the verb will be in the *imperfect*.

   De joven, **iba** a la casa de mis abuelos todos los fines de semana. *(habitual occurrence)*

   Íbamos al cine juntos. *(unspecified number of repetitions)*

   Mi abuelo **jugaba** a menudo al tenis. *(indefinite time period)*

3. If an action is considered ongoing, or already in progress, the verb will be in the imperfect, whether or not the action takes place in either a definite or an indefinite period of time.

   Mi abuelo **jugaba** a las 5:00. *(in progress at definite time)*

4. As a general rule, the preterite moves a story's action forward in past time while the imperfect tends to be more descriptive.

Aquí practicamos

Learning Strategies:

Expressing past time, asking for information, reporting based on personal knowledge

D. *Cuando era niño(a)...* Alternando con otro(a) estudiante, hagan las siguientes preguntas. Presten atención *(Pay attention to)* al uso del imperfecto.

1. Cuando eras niño(a), ¿te gustaba montar en bicicleta? ¿Por qué sí o por qué no?
2. ¿Cuál era tu actividad favorita?
3. ¿Tenías una bicicleta? ¿Cómo era la bicicleta?
4. ¿Adónde ibas cuando montabas en bicicleta?
5. ¿Con quién montabas en bicicleta?
6. Cuando paseabas en bicicleta ¿de qué distancia eran tus recorridos?
7. ¿Ibas en bicicleta a la escuela cuando eras más joven?
8. ¿Jugabas algún tipo de juego con tu bicicleta? ¿Qué hacías?

E. *¿Tú lo hiciste?* Each time your parent asks you if you've done something you were supposed to do, you answer *Not yet* (**Todavía no**).

374

Then you say what you *were doing* instead. Use both the preterite and the imperfect to give your excuses.

 Modelo: ¿Lavaste la ropa? (hablar por teléfono)
Todavía no. No lavé la ropa porque hablaba por teléfono.

1. ¿Hiciste tu tarea? (jugar al tenis)
2. ¿Hablaste con tu padre? (estar en casa de mis amigos)
3. ¿Comiste? (escuchar cintas)
4. ¿Te duchaste? (mirar la televisión)
5. ¿Hiciste los mandados? (tocar la guitarra)
6. ¿Acompañaste a tu hermana al centro? (escribir una carta)
7. ¿Compraste el pan? (dar un paseo)
8. ¿Arreglaste tu cuarto? (echar una siesta)

¿Fuiste al centro con un(a) amigo(a)?

Aquí escuchamos:
"Una excursión en bicicleta"

Antes de escuchar

Before listening to the conversation about a bicycle excursion, look at the following questions to get an idea of which information to focus on as you listen.

Después de escuchar

1. ¿Cuántos kilómetros viajaron?
2. ¿Cuántos días duró el viaje?
3. ¿Dónde pasaron la noche?
4. ¿A qué hora comenzaban cada día?
5. ¿A qué hora terminaban cada día?

375

Ex. E: ✎ writing

More-prepared students, Ex. E: Have more-prepared students do this exercise orally, in pairs. Have them think of three additional situations or questions to add.

Answers, Ex. E: 1. Todavía no. No hice la tarea porque jugaba al tenis.   2. No hablé con mi padre porque estaba en casa de mis amigos.   3. No comí porque escuchaba cintas.   4. No me duché porque miraba la televisión.   5. No hice los mandados porque tocaba la guitarra.   6. No acompañé a mi hermana al centro porque escribía una carta.   7. No compré el pan porque daba un paseo.   8. No arreglé mi cuarto porque echaba una siesta.

Presentation: Aquí escuchamos

Be sure to have students preview materials. You may want them to jot down some information for each of the comprehension questions as they listen to the tape. You may also want to use all or part of the dialogue for dictation practice.

Answers, Aquí escuchamos: 1. 400 km   2. cuatro   3. Middlebury, Vermont   4. a las 7:00 de la mañana   5. a las 4:00 de la tarde

Ex. F: pair work

Ex. G: pair work

Ex. H: pair work

Less-prepared students,
Ex. H: Have less-prepared students read the instructions carefully. Ask them which items have the same time frame and which have a different one. Be sure to have them contrast the time context in items 1–4 (preterite) and item 5 (imperfect). You may want to brainstorm some of the information with students.

More-prepared students,
Ex. H: Remind more-prepared students that they need to convince someone and to make their activities as interesting and as exciting as possible.

Ex. I: writing

Less-prepared students,
Ex. I: Be sure to have less-prepared students decide on the time context of each item before beginning.

More-prepared students,
Ex. I: Look at the work of more-prepared students as they are writing to make sure they are using correct verb tenses. If you see they are not, point to a particular item and ask a relevant question to get the student to reconsider the time context. For example, did this happen many times or only once?

¡Aquí te toca a ti!

F. *Un fin de semana típico*   Work with a classmate and ask and answer each other's questions about what four activities you used to do on a typical weekend when you were in elementary school. Remember to use the *imperfect* tense in your questions and answers since you are talking about what you *used to do* on a regular basis (as part of a routine).

G. *El año pasado*   Now ask and answer questions about four things you did last year that are memorable. Remember to use the *preterite* tense since you are talking about specific, one-time events that happened in the past.

¡Adelante!

EJERCICIO ORAL

H. *El club de ciclismo*   Try to convince your partner to join the same bicycle club that you joined a year ago. In order to get him or her interested in the club, tell (1) what you did last year with the club, (2) how many excursions you took, (3) where you went, (4) with whom you went, and (5) what you usually did as opposed to what you did on one trip in particular. (Use the preterite and imperfect tenses appropriately.)

EJERCICIO ESCRITO

I. *Un viaje en bicicleta*   You are still trying to convince your partner to join your bicycle club. At the end of a bicycle trip, send your partner a postcard in which you describe the trip. Give several details about the excursion, such as (1) where you went, (2) how far, (3) when you left and returned, (4) how many bikers there were, (5) what the weather was like, (6) three interesting things that you saw, and (7) two exciting experiences. (8) Be sure to date and sign your card.

376

SEGUNDA ETAPA

Preparación

›› **H**ave you ever gone hiking? If so, when and where?

›› **I**s white-water rafting an activity that interests you or would interest you? Why, or why not?

El senderismo y el rafting

El senderismo es muy saludable y es una buena manera para apreciar la naturaleza.

EL SENDERISMO

El senderismo, o el montañismo, es una actividad muy de moda. También es divertido y saludable. Practicarlo significa caminar por un espacio natural generalmente montañoso. Se puede caminar hasta llegar a la **cima** de la montaña. Desde allí se ven **paisajes** maravillosos. Por medio del senderismo podemos **aumentar** nuestros **conocimientos** sobre la geografía, los animales, la vegetación, la historia y las costumbres de las zonas rurales.

El **equipo** necesario es muy simple. Los zapatos son muy importantes y deben ser **cómodos, ligeros** y apropiados al tipo de **terreno** en que se va a caminar. Otros elementos esenciales son una mochila fuerte, una **cantimplora,** un pequeño **botiquín** y un **bastón.**

En España hay más de 8.000 kilómetros de **senderos.** Algunos son muy largos, como el que va desde Valencia hasta Lisboa en Portugal. Otros **atraviesan** los hermosos paisajes montañosos de los Pirineos en la frontera con Francia. Si te gusta caminar por las montañas y te interesa la naturaleza, ¿qué mejor manera de conocer España durante las vacaciones?

El senderismo también se conoce como el andinismo y el alpinismo, nombres que vienen de las montañas llamadas los Andes en Sudamérica y los Alpes en Europa.
el senderismo: hiking

the top (of mountain)
landscapes

increase
knowledge

equipment
comfortable / light / terrain, land surface / canteen / first aid kit / walking stick, cane

paths

go across

377

Etapa Support Materials

Workbook: **pp. 260–264**
Critical Thinking master: **Chapter 14, segunda etapa, activity A**
Teacher Tape
Quiz: **Testing Program, p. 203**

Chapter Test: **Testing Program, p. 206**

Support material, **El senderismo y el rafting:**
    Teacher Tape   , **Transparency #47**

Ex. A: ✎ writing

Expansion, Ex. A: Are there any items that could be associated with both sports? If so, which ones? why? how?

El rafting es un deporte muy divertido y muy popular en España.

EL RAFTING

Si tienes interés en la aventura y en **disfrutar del** aire libre, deportes como el rafting, el **descenso de cañones** y el esquí acuático son los que te van a gustar. El rafting es un deporte muy popular en España. En Cataluña hay **campeonatos mundiales** de canookayak. Para practicarlo, sólo necesitas tener doce años, saber nadar y tener un espíritu muy **aventurero.**

El raft es una **balsa neumática** en la que pueden ir entre ocho y doce personas. Hay expediciones organizadas que duran cinco días. Tres días se hacen descensos de rafting. Otro día hay una excursión por un cañón y el otro hay práctica de esquí acuático.

disfrutar de: enjoy / *descenso de cañones:* climbing down canyons / *campeonatos mundiales:* world championships / *aventurero:* adventurous / *balsa neumática:* inflatable raft

¡Aquí te toca a ti!

/-//-//-//-//-//-//-//-//

Learning Strategies:

Reading for cultural information, reading for details

Critical Thinking Strategy:

Categorizing

A. ¿Qué va con qué? Decide which items go with which sport. Are there some that don't apply to either sport?

	El senderismo	El rafting
un río		
un esquí		
un bastón		
una canasta		
una bicicleta		
una mochila		
una cima		
un botiquín		
una raqueta		
una montaña		
una pelota		
una cantimplora		
unos animales		
unos zapatos		
un barco		

378

B. *Verdad o falso*   Indica si los comentarios son verdaderos o falsos según la información sobre el senderismo y el rafting en las páginas 377 y 378. Si es falso el comentario, explica por qué.

1. Es necesario tener mucho equipo para hacer senderismo.
2. Es importante saber nadar si vas a practicar el rafting.
3. En España hay muy pocos senderos para la persona que hace senderismo.
4. Normalmente hay expediciones de rafting que duran cincuenta días.
5. Es importante llevar una cantimplora cuando haces senderismo.
6. Los zapatos son importantes cuando estás en una balsa.
7. Aprendemos mucho sobre la naturaleza al hacer senderismo.
8. Para hacer rafting debemos llevar un buen bastón.
9. El rafting es para las personas que tienen un espíritu aventurero.

/././././././././././././

Learning Strategies:

Reading for details, supporting an opinion

Repaso

C. *El descubrimiento* (discovery) *de América*   Put the following sentences into the past, changing the underlined verbs to the imperfect or the preterite, according to the context and intended meaning.

1. Cristóbal Colón <u>sale</u> del puerto español de Palos el 3 de agosto de 1492.
2. En esa época, mucha gente <u>cree</u> que el mundo <u>es</u> plano *(flat)*.
3. Colón <u>quiere</u> probar *(to prove)* que <u>es</u> redondo y encontrar una ruta a las Indias.
4. Colón <u>cruza</u> el Atlántico en tres pequeñas carabelas *(sailing ships)*.
5. Muchos de sus hombres <u>tienen</u> miedo y <u>quieren</u> volver a España.
6. Pero Colón <u>insiste</u> en seguir adelante.
7. Por fin, después de diez semanas de viaje, <u>desembarcan</u> *(they step ashore)* en una isla del Caribe el 12 de octubre.
8. Colón ahora <u>está</u> en América, pero todavía <u>piensa</u> que el territorio <u>es</u> las Indias.
9. <u>Hace</u> otros tres viajes a América.
10. En su último viaje (1502–1504), Colón <u>explora</u> la costa de Centroamérica.
11. <u>Vuelve</u> a España donde <u>se enferma</u>, muriendo *(dying)* dos años después sin saber que América <u>es</u> un nuevo continente.

/././././././././././././

Learning Strategies:

Drawing meaning from context, expressing past time

Ex. B: writing

Variation, Ex. B: You may want to do this as a listening activity with students' books closed. Afterwards, students can check their accuracy by referring back to the text and writing sentences to correct false statements.

Answers, Ex. B: 1. falso. El equipo es muy símple.   2. verdadero   3. falso. Hay más de 8.000 km de senderos en España.   4. falso. Normalmente los expediciones duran cinco días.   5. verdadero   6. falso. Los zapatos son importantes cuando hace senderismo.   7. verdadero   8. falso. Para hacer senderismo debemos llevar un buen bastón.   9. verdadero

Suggestion, Ex. C: Have students explain their choice of verb tenses.

Answers, Ex. C: 1. salió   2. creía, era   3. quería, era   4. cruzó   5. tenían, querían   6. insistió   7. desembarcaron   8. estaba, pensaba, era   9. Hizo   10. exploró   11. Volvió, se enfermó, era

Presentation: Estructura

Give a short narrative that includes each of the four descriptive categories: **El fin de semana pasado fui a una fiesta. Allí me encontré con muchas personas interesantes. Había un hombre que era muy guapo. Tenía el pelo negro; tenía barba y bigote; era muy alto. Era muy simpático, pero siempre creía que sólo él tenía razón en todo. Era imposible tener una conversación con él. Tenía yo un dolor de cabeza después de tratar de hablar con ese hombre.** Do a quick analysis of what you said and ask students what they noticed about the verb tenses. Finally, do the same thing with the model paragraph in the **Estructura** box.

Reteaching: You may want to review formation of the imperfect tense and its three irregular verbs.

Ex. D: ✎ writing

Answers, Ex. D: 1. Un hombre era muy alto, tenía el pelo negro, tenía barba, llevaba una camisa verde, era delgado, hablaba en voz muy alta, parecía fuerte y llevaba una pistola grande.   2. El segundo hombre no era tan alto, era gordo, tenía bigote, llevaba una camiseta sucia, no hablaba, tenía el pelo rojo, llevaba una mochila y caminaba muy rápido.   3. La mujer era alta y era delgada, tenía el pelo rubio, tenía la cara redonda, llevaba pantalones y una camiseta, también llevaba sandalias amarillas, tenía una bolsa y era la conductora del coche.   4. El coche era un Fiat, era gris y era bastante nuevo.
5. Nosotros estábamos muy nerviosos y teníamos miedo.   6. Los empleados del banco eran muy valientes. Estaban bastante tranquilos.

ESTRUCTURA

The imperfect and the preterite: Descriptions

Ayer **fui** al centro. Allí **me encontré** con Juan y **fuimos** al Café Topo en la Avenida Central. **Conversamos** por tres horas. **Estábamos** muy contentos de estar juntos. **Hacía** mucho sol y yo **llevaba** un vestido ligero *(light)* y unas sandalias. Juan **llevaba** un sombrero amarillo y una chaqueta marrón muy bonita. **Estábamos** muy a la moda *(fashionable)* los dos.

Note that the preceding paragraph contains verbs in both the preterite and the imperfect. The first four verbs are in the preterite because they indicate actions that occurred at a very specific time in the past (yesterday). The remaining verbs are in the imperfect because they describe a state or a condition in the past.

The imperfect is generally used in four types of descriptions in the past:

1. Physical   La casa **era** grande. Nuestra casa **era** blanca.
2. Feelings   Nosotros **estábamos** contentos. Él **estaba** triste.
3. Attitudes and beliefs   Yo **creía** que ustedes **tenían razón.**
4. State of health   Mi hermano **estaba** enfermo.

Aquí practicamos

/./././././././././././

Learning Strategy:

Expressing past time

D. Los testigos (Witnesses)   You and your classmates were witnesses to a crime. You're now asked by the police to describe what you saw. Change the sentences into the imperfect tense.

Modelo: Dos hombres y una mujer están en el banco.
Dos hombres y una mujer estaban en el banco.

1. Un hombre es muy alto, tiene el pelo negro, tiene barba, lleva una camisa verde, es delgado, habla en voz *(voice)* muy alta, parece fuerte y lleva una pistola grande.
2. El segundo hombre no es tan alto, es gordo, tiene bigote, lleva una camiseta sucia, no habla, tiene el pelo rojo, lleva una mochila y camina muy rápido.
3. La mujer es alta y es delgada, tiene el pelo rubio, tiene la cara redonda *(round)*, lleva pantalones y una camiseta, también lleva sandalias amarillas, tiene una bolsa y es la conductora *(driver)* del coche.
4. El coche es un Fiat, es gris y es bastante nuevo.
5. Nosotros estamos muy nerviosos y tenemos miedo.
6. Los empleados del banco son muy valientes. Están bastante tranquilos.

380

Nota gramatical

The imperfect and the preterite: Interrupted actions

El Sr. Sosa trabajaba en Panamá cuando **nació** su hijo.
Mr. Sosa was working in Panamá when his son *was born.*

Estaba en su oficina cuando su esposa **llamó** por teléfono.
He was in his office when his wife *called.*

Hablaba con un amigo cuando **supo** la noticia.
He was talking with a friend when *he found out* the news.

Each model sentence contains a verb in the imperfect and another in the preterite. The imperfect describes what *was going on* when something else *happened.* The preterite is used to tell what *happened* to interrupt an action. Note that in Spanish the imperfect often corresponds to the progressive forms *was doing* or *were doing* in English.

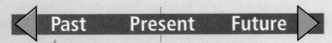

Past   Present   Future

Pretérito
Imperfecto →

381

Left margin (teacher's notes)

Ex. E: ✏ writing

Suggestion, Ex. E: It might help students to recognize that **cuando** is often an indicator of the preterite tense in sentences of this type.

Follow-up, Ex. E: To reinforce the concept of interrupted actions, you might redo the exercise by having volunteers mime certain selections while someone reads the sentence aloud. For example, in number 3, a student could mime clearing the table and a few seconds later Jorge could arrive. At the same time, someone could orally describe the scene by stating, **Cuando Jorge llegó, yo quitaba la mesa.** You could do this with a number of other sentences in this activity.

More-prepared students, Ex. E: Have more-prepared students prepare one or two more interrupted scenes to mime and describe to the class.

Answers, Ex. E: 1. Mi mamá se desayunaba cuando llegó la carta. 2. Nosotros dábamos una vuelta en el coche cuando ella tuvo el accidente. 3. Cuando Jorge llegó, yo quitaba la mesa. 4. Pablo y Marcos jugaban al vólibol cuando comenzó a llover. 5. Cuando Luis se puso mal, Sergio preparaba la comida. 6. Nosotros mirábamos la televisión cuando llegaron mis tíos. 7. Yo hacía los mandados cuando (yo) vi a mis amigos. 8. Cuando tu supiste la noticia tus padres estaban en el teatro.

Reteaching, Ex. F: You may want to review clothing vocabulary and descriptive adjectives with students briefly before having them do Ex. F.

Main content

Learning Strategy:
Expressing past time

E. Las interrupciones   The following people didn't get anything done because something always happened to interrupt them. Describe what happened in each case by putting together the elements provided to create a sentence in the past. Remember that the action in progress must be in the imperfect and the interrupting action must be in the preterite.

Modelo: yo / hacer / mi tarea / cuando / oír el teléfono
Yo hacía mi tarea cuando oí el teléfono.

1. mi mamá / desayunarse / cuando / llegar la carta
2. nosotros / dar una vuelta en el coche / cuando / ella / tener el accidente
3. cuando / Jorge / llegar / yo / quitar la mesa
4. Pablo y Marcos / jugar al vólibol / cuando / comenzar a llover
5. cuando / Luis / ponerse mal / Sergio / preparar la comida
6. nosotros / mirar / la televisión / cuando / llegar mis tíos
7. yo / hacer / los mandados / cuando / yo / ver a mis amigos
8. cuando / tú / saber / la noticia / tus padres / estar en el teatro

Learning Strategy:
Expressing past time

F. Una fiesta   Describe a las personas en el dibujo. Usa el imperfecto.

Modelo: *El muchacho tenía el pelo castaño, era delgado y llevaba una camiseta.*

Learning Strategies:
Expressing past time, reporting based on visual cues

Critical Thinking Strategy:
Comparing and contrasting

G. ¿Qué hacían ellos cuando... ?   Use the preterite and the imperfect to describe what the people in the drawings on page 383 were doing when something else happened. Follow the model.

Modelo: *María Luisa tocaba la guitarra cuando Pedro se cayó.*

María Luisa   Pedro

tocar / caerse

382

Ex. F: ✏ writing

Ex. G: ✏ writing

los Jiménez   Graciela

1. comer / llegar

los muchachos

2. jugar / empezar a llover

los jóvenes

Enrique

3. empezar a bailar / charlar

Vicente   Andrés   Antonio   ¡HOLA!

4. hablar / decir

los muchachos   Fernando

5. jugar / llegar

Elisa   Marlena   Federico

6. dar un paseo / encontrarse con

383

Answers, Ex. G: **1.** Los Jiménez comían cuando Graciela llegó.   **2.** Los muchachos jugaban cuando empezó a llover.   **3.** Los jóvenes charlaban cuando Enrique empezó a bailar.   **4.** Vicente y Andrés hablaban cuando Antonio dijo "¡Hola!"   **5.** Los muchachos jugaban cuando Fernando llegó. **6.** Elisa y Marlena daban un paseo cuando se encontraron con Federico.

Expansion, Ex. G: Have students recall their own activities last evening or yesterday afternoon and tell what or who interrupted them, using the exercise as a model.

Cultural Expansion

For item 5 in Ex. G, remind students that baseball is a very popular pastime in Latin America, particularly in the countries bordering on the Caribbean. Many of the top baseball players in the U.S., both current and past, come from Spanish-speaking countries or are Spanish-speakers born in the U.S. Ask students if they can name some of these current and former players (Bobby Bonilla, U.S.; Rubén Sierra, Puerto Rico; Roberto Clemente, Nicaragua; Juan Guzmán, Dominican Republic; John Candelaria, Puerto Rico; Juan Marichal, Dominican Republic; Fernando Valenzuela, Mexico; Dennis Martínez, Nicaragua; Rod Carew, Panama).

Presentation: Aquí escuchamos

Have students take out paper and pencil and make two columns headed *interviewer questions* and *answers*. Instruct them to write the key words they hear in the dialogue under the appropriate headings. Be sure to play the tape several times. Afterwards, create master lists on the board with students volunteering information. This should help them complete the comprehension exercise as well.

Answers, Aquí escuchamos: 1. Los Corre Caminos 2. 14   3. Hacen ciclismo de montaña.   4. Hacen turismo   5. No lleva nada más que lo necesario. 6. No, porque no se necesita gasolina, y los padres les compran los bicicletas.

Ex. H: pair work

 writing

Aquí escuchamos:
"Entrevista con un ciclista"

Antes de escuchar

Before listening to a short interview with a cyclist, think about some of the questions you might ask if you were doing the interview for your school paper. Then look at the following questions to get an idea of the content of the interview you'll hear between a **periodista** (*journalist*) and a student who is a member of a bicycle club.

Después de escuchar

Escucha la entrevista una vez más y después contesta las siguientes preguntas.

1. ¿Cómo se llama el club de ciclismo de los jóvenes?
2. ¿Cuántos miembros hay en el club ahora?
3. En general, ¿qué hacen los miembros del club los fines de semana?
4. ¿Qué hace el grupo durante las vacaciones?
5. ¿Qué dice el ciclista sobre el equipaje que lleva en una excursión?
6. ¿Cuesta mucho dinero el ciclismo? ¿Por qué?

¡Aquí te toca a ti!

H. *Nuestra aventura excelente* Work with a partner and make up a description of a bike trip you took last summer. Imagine that you took the trip together and include details from real life as well as your imagination about what happened during this trip to make it an unforgettable or unbelievable adventure. Use the preterite and imperfect tenses appropriately.

384

EJERCICIO ORAL

I. Mis fotos You've just returned from either a hiking trip or a bicycle trip in a national park and have lots of photos to show your friends. Imagine the scene on each photo (use the photo above as an example, but invent other scenes), and tell your classmates what they are seeing and what you did in each place. Follow the model.

 Modelo: *Aquí me ven con Mario en el Parque Nacional en _____. Estamos en una montaña muy grande. Caminamos por muchas horas. Llegamos a la cima de la montaña. Allí vimos un paisaje muy bonito.*

EJERCICIO ESCRITO

J. ¿Cuál prefieres? You have been selected to attend a camp next summer. Now you must choose which of the activities (**el ciclismo, el senderismo, el rafting**) you prefer as your "specialty," the one on which you will spend most of your time. Write a letter to the camp director explaining which activity you prefer over the others. Describe (1) what that activity involves; (2) when, where, and with whom you last participated in the activity; and (3) why you like it better than the other two. Give at last four reasons for your preference. Remember to date and sign your letter.

385

Para charlar

Para hablar del ciclismo	Para hablar del senderismo	Para hablar del rafting
la bicicleta	atravesar	aventurero(a)
la bicicleta de montaña	el bastón	la balsa neumática
	el botiquín	el barco
	la cantimplora	el canookayak
	la cima	el descenso de cañones
	cómodo(a)	el esquí acuático
	ligero(a)	el río
	la montaña	
	el montañismo	
	el paisaje	
	el sendero	
	el terreno	

Vocabulario general

Verbos	Sustantivos	Otras expresiones
refrescarse	los auriculares	con gas (sin gas)
	el (la) atleta	
	la cámara fotográfica	
	la camiseta	
	el campeonato mundial	
	la canasta	
	el equipo	
	la excursión	
	la mochila	

Lectura
CULTURAL

//-/-//-/-//-/-//-/-//
Learning Strategies:

Brainstorming, previewing

EN BICICLETA

Antes de leer

1. Look at the photos and the title of the reading to determine its content.
2. Think about what you know about bicycles. Do we use them for recreation, exercise, transportation?
3. Do you own a bicycle? Has the bicycle become more popular in recent years? Why, or why not?

Lectura cultural

Guía para la lectura

///-///-///-///-///-///
Learning Strategies:
Reading for main ideas, reading for details

///-///-///-///-///-///
Learning Strategy:
Reading for details

A. Read the first sentence of each paragraph and, on a separate sheet of paper, note the main idea of each one.

B. Look over the following questions. Read the passage again and then answer the questions.

1. Según el artículo, ¿cuántos años cumple la bicicleta este año?
2. ¿Cómo son las bicicletas de hoy en día?
3. ¿Qué tipos de bicicleta de los EE.UU. tienen mucha popularidad?
4. ¿Quiénes usan mucho la bicicleta en su vida diaria?
5. ¿Cuáles son algunos de los beneficios *(benefits)* de la bicicleta?
6. ¿Cuál es uno de los peligros *(dangers)* de montar en bicicleta?
7. ¿Quiénes tienen mucho éxito en los campeonatos de ciclismo?

En bicicleta

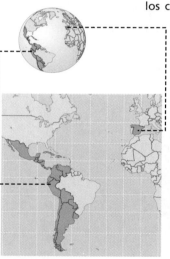

a bicicleta, que se usó por primera vez en el año 1840, perdió popularidad con la llegada de los primeros automóviles. Pero su nueva vida es una realidad, no sólo porque es un vehículo ecologista sino porque las bicicletas de hoy son ligeras y también rápidas.

El uso de la bicicleta de montaña, una especialidad importada de los Estados Unidos, y el peligro de las calles cambiaron las preferencias de los ciclistas. La bicicleta todo terreno también es preferida por montañeros y ecologistas. Es un deporte que, según sus aficionados, resulta menos aburrido y peligroso que pedalear en la ciudad.

Aunque las carreteras no son el lugar ideal para los ciclistas, los aficionados a este deporte crecen cada día en los países de habla española.

Son cada vez más los jóvenes que van al colegio o a la universidad en bicicleta, a pesar de que no hay carriles-bici en las ciudades. Cada fin de semana, chicos y chicas cambian los libros y los bolígrafos por el manillar y los pedales.

La llegada del buen tiempo y los éxitos de los ciclistas del mundo hispano en los campeonatos de ciclismo hacen de la bicicleta el vehículo de moda. Además, no contamina, no hace ruido, no gasta combustible y ayuda a estar en forma. ¡Viva la bicicleta!

388

15

DOS DEPORTES POPULARES

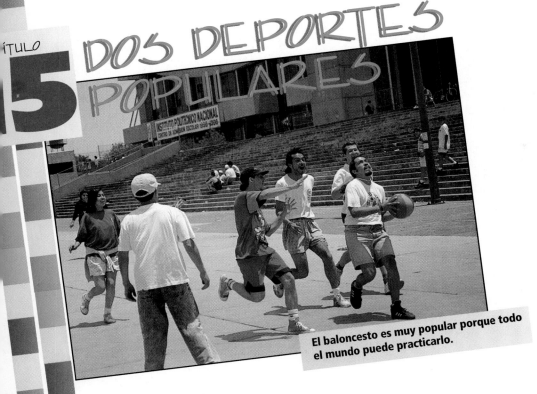

El baloncesto es muy popular porque todo el mundo puede practicarlo.

Objectives:

>>> **U**nderstanding short descriptions of team sports

>>> **D**escribing places and events in the past

>>> **T**alking about the recent past

Strategies:

>>> **D**rawing meaning from context

>>> **S**ummarizing

>>> **S**equencing

389

Chapter Objectives

Functions: Understanding short descriptions of team sports; describing places and events in the past; talking about the recent past

Context: Team sports, especially soccer and basketball

Accuracy: Imperfect and preterite: changes of meaning and translation; summary of uses

Video/Laserdisc

Chapter 15 Video Program and Video Guide

Presentation: El fútbol

Begin by asking students if they watched any of the World Cup games in '94, what cities they were played in (perhaps yours or one near yours), what countries participated, etc. If your school has a soccer team, ask if any students play on it, what positions, why they chose soccer, etc.

Reading Strategies

Have students use prior knowledge and information from photos as they scan the reading for cognates. Have them give some general ideas after scanning, then have them read for details and complete the comprehension exercises on pp. 391–392.

//-/-/-/-/-/-/-/-/-//

Learning Strategies:

Brainstorming, previewing, reporting based on personal knowledge

//-/-/-/-/-/-/-/-/-//

Learning Strategies:

Reading for cultural information, reading for main ideas

PRIMERA ETAPA

Preparación

》》 **D**o you like soccer?

》》 **D**o you know what "The World Cup" is?

》》 **H**ave you played soccer yourself? Have you watched a game?

》》 **W**hat are some of the differences between soccer and football, as they are called in the U.S.?

El fútbol

Los cinco principales jugadores hispanos de fútbol

aficionados: fans

La copa Mundial de fútbol tiene lugar cada cuatro años. Es el evento deportivo más grande del mundo, con millones y millones de aficionados. El fútbol es, sin duda, el deporte más popular en todos los países de habla española. "El Mundial" de 1994 tuvo lugar en los Estados Unidos y fue un gran éxito con el público norteamericano.

Cinco de los veinticuatro países que se clasificaron para el campeonato (después de la eliminación de casi 140 países que participaron en la competencia) eran hispanohablantes: Argentina, Bolivia, Colombia, España y México. Su país vecino, Brasil, ganó la prestigiosa Copa Mundial por cuarta vez, ahora el único equipo de fútbol en la historia con ese récord.

Hugo Sánchez (México)

No digas Hugo, di gol. Los años no pasan por él. Jugó en el Mundial de 1994 a la edad de 35 años. Todavía da mucho que hablar por su talento.

390

Etapa Support Materials

Workbook: pp. 265–271
Listening Activity masters: p. 119
Transparencies: #48A, #48B
Teacher Tape ⌒
Tapescript: p. 161

Quiz: Testing Program, p. 211

Support material, El fútbol:

Teacher Tape ⌒ **, Transparencies #48A, #48B**

Faustino Asprilla (Colombia)

La velocidad es su arma. Tiene mucha habilidad para anotar goles. En muchos partidos del Mundial fue la estrella de su equipo.

Andoni Zubizarreta (España)

Éste es uno de los mejores arqueros del mundo. Defiende con agilidad y fuerza. Los goles contra él son pocos.

arqueros: goalies
anotar: to make

Tab Ramos (Estados Unidos)

Es el mejor jugador estadounidense técnicamente hablando. Controla y avanza el balón con gran agilidad. Es fuerte y muy competitivo.

balón: pelota

Marco Antonio Etcheverry (Bolivia)

Sólo tiene 23 años. En ataque siempre es rápido. Su equipo cuenta con su entusiasmo y con sus goles.

¡Aquí te toca a ti!

A. *Su nacionalidad* Di de dónde son los equipos de estas estrellas de fútbol.

1. Zubizarreta 2. Ramos 3. Sánchez 4. Etcheverry 5. Asprilla

Learning Strategy:
Reading for details

391

Ask students what they know about Tab Ramos (for example, where the nickname Tab comes from). What about his last name? Obviously, Ramos is a Hispanic name. As a matter of fact, Tab's family is from Uruguay originally and his full name is Tabaré, a mythical hero from the past and a common first name in Uruguay.

Ex. A: pair work

writing

Answers, Ex. A: 1. España 2. Estados Unidos 3. México 4. Bolivia 5. Colombia

Variations, Exs. A and B: Do as listening exercises. Name a country and/or quality (i.e., **este jugador es rápido en el ataque**) and have students name the player.

B. *Su talento individual* Indica una de las cosas que cada jugador hace mejor cuando juega con su equipo, basándote en las páginas 390 y 391.

1. Etcheverry   2. Sánchez   3. Asprilla   4. Ramos   5. Zubizarreta

C. *La copa mundial* Contesta las preguntas sobre el Mundial basándote en la página 390.

1. ¿Qué importancia tiene el fútbol en los países de habla española?
2. ¿Con qué frecuencia juegan los países del mundo para el campeonato de fútbol?
3. ¿Dónde jugaron los equipos para el Mundial en 1994?
4. ¿Cuántos países hispanohablantes participaron en este campeonato?
5. ¿Quién ganó La Copa Mundial en 1994?

Repaso

D. *La historia de un crimen* Read the following account of a bank holdup. As you read, change the underlined present tense verbs to the imperfect or the preterite, according to the context.

Hay dos hombres y una mujer en un banco. Llegan a las 14:00. Yo estoy a la ventanilla. Uno de los hombres es muy alto, tiene el pelo negro, tiene barba y es muy delgado. Habla en una voz muy alta y parece impaciente. Lleva una pistola.

El otro hombre no es alto. Es gordo y tiene bigote. Lleva una camiseta con "Malibu" escrito en la espalda. Les pide a los clientes las carteras. Toma también nuestros relojes.

La mujer es alta. Tiene el pelo rubio. Lleva unos pantalones y una camiseta. Tiene una bolsa de mano. Pone nuestras cosas en una bolsa blanca. En seguida sale del banco. Es la conductora del coche.

El coche es un Fiat. Es gris y es bastante nuevo.

Hay muchos clientes en el banco. Nosotros estamos muy nerviosos. Tenemos miedo.

Los empleados del banco son muy valientes. Están tranquilos. Un empleado toca la alarma y los hombres corren del banco rápidamente. Afortunadamente, la policía llega unos pocos minutos después, pero los ladrones (robbers) ya no están allí.

392

ESTRUCTURA

The imperfect and the preterite: Changes of meaning and translation

As you have already learned, the decision to use one of the two past tenses with certain verbs in Spanish sometimes has a distinct effect on the overall message conveyed.

Carlos **estuvo** enfermo ayer.	Carlos *was* sick yesterday. *(He got sick and has recovered by now.)*
Carlos **estaba** enfermo ayer.	Carlos *was* sick yesterday. *(That was his condition at the time with no indication of the outcome.)*

Some verbs have different meanings in the preterite and the imperfect.

querer

Mi papá **quería** ayudarnos.	My dad *wanted* to help us. *(mental state; intention)*
Mi papá **quiso** ayudarnos.	My dad *tried* to help us. *(He actually did something.)*

no querer

Alicia **no quería** ver la película.	Alicia *didn't want* to see the movie. *(mental state; lack of desire)*
Alicia **no quiso** ver la película.	Alicia *refused* to see the movie. *(She truly refused.)*

poder

Él **podía** arreglar el coche.	He *was capable* of fixing the car.
Él **pudo** arreglar el coche.	He *succeeded* in fixing the car.

tener (que)

El diplomático **tenía** que aceptar la invitación a la ceremonia.	The diplomat *had* to accept the invitation to the ceremony. *(He was under obligation to do so but may not have done it.)*
El diplomático **tuvo** que aceptar la invitación a la ceremonia.	The diplomat *was compelled* to accept the invitation to the ceremony. *(He was compelled and he accepted it.)*

saber

¿Sabías que el avión llegaba tarde?	*Were you aware* that the plane was arriving late? *(Did you already know this?)*
Supe esta mañana que llegaba tarde.	*I found out* this morning that it was arriving late. *(first knowledge of this fact)*

conocer

¿Conocías a Carolina cuando eras niño?	*Did you know* Carolina when you were a child? *(Were you acquainted with her back then?)*
No, la **conocí** el año pasado.	No, *I met* her last year. *(I became acquainted with her for the first time.)*

393

Presentation: Estructura

Point out that there is always a difference in meaning between the preterite and imperfect, even though it is not always obvious in translation. With certain verbs this difference in meaning is more evident and consistent with the preterite concept of focusing on the beginning, completion, or end of an action (see pp. 373–374, Ch. 14). For example, the beginning of knowing someone **(conocer)** is the moment you met them (the preterite meaning of **conocer**). The beginning of knowing something **(saber)** is the moment you found out (preterite of **saber**).

   Querer, poder, and **tener** focus on the completion or failure to complete actions. You may review the contrastive meanings with the students before proceeding to the exercises.

Imperfect or Preterite?

To encourage students to focus on the ways the preterite and imperfect are used, ask them which tense they would expect to use most in the following situations: describing their childhood (imperfect), telling a funny story about something that happened last week (preterite), telling how their current habits differ from their old ones (imperfect), explaining to their teacher what happened yesterday that prevented them from doing their homework (preterite), describing how they found out that Santa Claus doesn't exist (preterite).

Learning Strategy:
Determining time frame and author intent

Critical Thinking Strategies: Analyzing, categorizing

Aquí practicamos

E. ¿Qué pasó? ¿Qué pasaba?   Choose one of the verb forms in italics, either the imperfect or the preterite tense, according to the meaning provided by the context in parentheses. Follow the model.

Modelo: Ramón y yo *nos conocimos / nos conocíamos /* en Montevideo. (for the first time)
Ramón y yo nos conocimos en Montevideo.

1. ¿Cómo *supiste / sabías* lo que pasó en el aeropuerto? (you found out right away)
2. Sus hermanas *decían / dijeron* que no les gustaban las películas de horror. (they would always say this)
3. El padre de Carlos no *quería / quiso* prestarle su coche. (that's why Carlos had to take a taxi)
4. ¿Cuándo *conociste / conocías* a Emilio Estévez? (for the first time)
5. *Tenía que ir / Tuve que ir* a la reunión porque soy presidente del grupo. (and that's why I finally went after all)
6. Ustedes no *supieron / sabían* cuánto dinero llevaron del banco los criminales. (you weren't able to get this information)
7. El profesor de matemáticas *pudo / podía* resolver el problema. (but he didn't do it because it was my homework assignment)
8. El perro *quería / quiso* salir de la casa mientras tú dormías. (he tried three times)
9. Roberto y yo nos *conocimos / conocíamos* en la escuela secundaria. (we were already friends back then)
10. La abuela *quiso / quería* besar al niño, pero él se fue corriendo. (so she didn't get to kiss him)

F. Entre amigos   Using the cues in parentheses, answer your friend's questions with the appropriate use of the imperfect or the preterite. Use the verb(s) in each question in your response. Follow the model.

Modelo: ¿Tú me llamaste por teléfono? (sí / hace media hora)
Sí, te llamé hace media hora.

1. ¿Me viste esta mañana? (sí / en el centro)
2. ¿Dónde estaba yo cuando me viste? (en una librería)
3. ¿Me buscabas? (no)
4. ¿Querías hablar conmigo? (sí / para invitarte al Café Topo)
5. ¿Por qué no entraste en la librería? (estar en el autobús)
6. ¿Me llamaste anoche? (sí / a las 8:00)
7. ¿Sabías que hoy es el cumpleaños de Eduardo Bolaños? (sí / ayer)
8. ¿Le compraste un regalo? (sí / esta mañana)
9. ¿Ya se lo diste? (no)

394

10. ¿Cuándo pensabas dárselo? (esta noche / en el Café Topo)
11. ¿Dijo Eduardo que podía salir esta noche? (sí / después de las 7:30)
12. ¿Pudiste reservar una mesa en el Café Topo? (sí / para las 8:00)
13. ¿A quién más invitaste? (Silvia y Marisol)
14. ¿Ah sí? ¿Dónde conociste a Marisol? (en la fiesta de Eduardo / el año pasado)
15. ¿A quién le pediste el coche? (a mi papá)
16. ¿Tuviste suerte? (sí / mucha)

G. *Las noticias del día* Working with two classmates, take turns adding some information to the part of the sentence that is provided. Invent the necessary details. Follow the model.

Modelo: Ayer, a las 10:00 de la mañana, un criminal…
Ayer, a las 10:00 de la mañana, un criminal entró en el banco. Afortunadamente, la policía llegó inmediatamente…

1. El presidente dice que cuando era niño, siempre…
2. La semana pasada, el actor Emilio Estévez…
3. Hoy supimos por primera vez que…
4. El representante de Nueva York dijo que él no era responsable, que él no…
5. El embajador *(ambassador)* conoció a la reina *(queen)* de Gran Bretaña cuando…
6. El sábado pasado, el equipo de fútbol de Colombia…
7. Ayer hizo tanto calor que todos nosotros…
8. En el último minuto del partido de fútbol, el equipo boliviano…
9. Cuando oyeron las noticias, los pobres muchachos…
10. Nadie sabe por qué, pero el sábado pasado, dos hombres…

Learning Strategy:

Expressing past time

Critical Thinking Strategies:

Seeing cause-and-effect relationships, imagining, creating

395

Ex. G: groups of three

More-prepared students, Ex. G: Have more-prepared students scan the text and decide from the context whether they will most likely need the preterite or the imperfect. Remind students that in some cases (items 3, 4, and 5 especially), the tense will depend entirely on the type of ending they create for the sentence. For example: **El embajador conoció a la reina… cuando fue al palacio / cuando estaba en Inglaterra.** Have them create both types of sentences.

Less-prepared students, Ex. G: Go through each item with less-prepared students, helping them analyze the time context (preterite or imperfect) and brainstorm a way to end each sentence accordingly.

Follow-up, Ex. G: Create two master lists of time expressions on the board, one for expressions that are most often used in a preterite context (**ayer, el año pasado, anoche, el miércoles pasado,** etc.) and one for expressions most often associated with the imperfect (**siempre, muchas veces, a menudo, a veces,** etc.). Have students write new sentences using the time expressions to help them choose the tense. Remind them, however, that no expression can be used exclusively with one or the other of the tenses—it's a matter of what you want to say. For example, **ayer a las 10:** did something happen? **(comí una pizza)** or was something already happening? **(estaba en la mesa y hacía la tarea).**

Aquí escuchamos:
"Los resultados de dos partidos de fútbol"

Antes de escuchar

What information do you usually expect when you listen to a brief report on a game between two teams? Read the following questions so that you will know what details to listen for as you listen to the sportscaster.

Después de escuchar

Escucha al reporte otra vez y luego contesta en español las siguientes preguntas.

1. ¿Quién ganó el partido entre Argentina y Bolivia?
2. ¿Qué pasaba cuando cada equipo trataba de anotar un gol?
3. ¿Quién anotó al final el gol para la victoria?
4. ¿Cómo anotó el gol este jugador?
5. ¿Cuál equipo ganó el partido entre los Estados Unidos y Colombia?
6. ¿Cómo jugó la defensa de los Estados Unidos?
7. ¿Qué pasaba cada vez que los colombianos se acercaban al arco?
8. ¿Quién anotó el gol para la victoria a los 40 minutos de la segunda mitad?

¡Aquí te toca a ti!

H. Un buen partido   Work with a classmate and take turns telling each other about an exciting soccer or football game you have seen recently. You can base your description on a real event or make up details about an imaginary one. Tell (1) who played, (2) when, (3) where, and (4) who won, including some information about (5) how specific players helped to win or lose the game.

396

Ex. I: pair work

Ex. J: writing

Less-prepared students, Ex. J: Brainstorm appropriate vocabulary with less-prepared students. Then have them analyze the time context of each item of information they need to give to decide on verb tenses.

Suggestion, Ex. J: Have students describe what the weather was like the day of the game, what some of the players looked like, and how they felt when a team scored, so that they have more "imperfect" contexts to include in their writing and to contrast with preterite uses (who won, who played, etc.).

A algunos minutos del final del partido, el equipo local anotó el gol de la victoria.

EJERCICIO ORAL

I. El fútbol y La Copa Mundial With your partner, discuss in Spanish the importance of soccer as a sport, particularly in the Spanish-speaking world. Based on the information in this chapter, mention (1) its popularity, (2) the World Cup, (3) how often this international competition takes place, (4) where it was held in 1994, and (5) who some of the stars of the game are. (6) Add any other details that you may know.

/-/-/-/-/-/-/-/-/-/-/
Learning Strategies:
Describing, organizing information, summarizing

EJERCICIO ESCRITO

J. ¿Quién ganó? Write about a soccer game to a Spanish-speaking pen pal. Indicate (1) who played, (2) when, (3) what the outcome was, (4) who scored, and (5) a detail or two about the game. You can base it on a real game or make up the information for this exercise. Use the preterite and imperfect tenses appropriately.

/-/-/-/-/-/-/-/-/-/-/
Learning Strategies:
Describing, identifying, reporting in the past

397

Reading Strategies

Ask students what they know about how the game of basketball is played: how many players, their objective, how they score points, etc. Remind them to keep this prior knowledge present as they read the passage. Before reading for details, you may also want to have them scan for cognates (perhaps making a list which could be checked by creating a master list from volunteer information on the board).

SEGUNDA ETAPA

Preparación

›› **D**o you play basketball? If so, when do you play?

›› **W**ho are some of the famous basketball players that you like to watch?

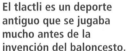

El tlactli es un deporte antiguo que se jugaba mucho antes de la invención del baloncesto.

Learning Strategies:

Brainstorming, previewing

"TLACTLI", UN DEPORTE AMERICANO ORIGINAL

El primer partido de baloncesto tuvo su origen en 1891 en los Estados Unidos, hace más de cien años. Pero ya existía un deporte similar que se jugaba entre las civilizaciones que vivían en México antes de la llegada de Cristobal Colón al continente americano. Se llamaba el juego de pelota, o "tlactli" en la lengua de los mayas.

Se jugaba en campos rectangulares que tenían paredes de una altura de unos 13 metros. En las paredes laterales había dos anillos de piedra. Cada anillo estaba colocado verticalmente a 10 metros de altura, uno frente al otro. El campo estaba dividido en dos partes y cada uno de los dos equipos ocupaba una parte del campo de juego.

Los jugadores tenían que pasar la pelota por uno de los anillos del campo del otro equipo. El equipo que podía hacerlo primero ganaba el

Etapa Support Materials

Workbook: **pp. 272–275**
Transparency: **#49**
Teacher Tape ⌒
Quiz: **Testing Program, p. 213**

Chapter Test: **Testing Program, p. 216**

Support materials: **El baloncesto:**
  Teacher Tape ⌒, **Transparency #49**

juego. Esto era muy difícil porque los jugadores sólo podían tocar la pelota con las rodillas o con las caderas. No podían usar las manos ni los pies. Además la pelota era muy dura.

Todavía se pueden ver muchos campos para el juego de pelota en las ruinas de las antiguas ciudades mayas.

¡Aquí te toca a ti!

A. ¿Verdad o falso?
Según el texto, decide si los comentarios son verdaderos o falsos. Si son falsos, da la información correcta.

1. "Tlactli" es un juego parecido al baloncesto.
2. El campo en el que se jugaba tenía paredes bajas y un anillo grande en cada una.
3. La pelota con la que se jugaba era dura.
4. Los jugadores podían tocar la pelota con los pies.
5. Ya no es posible ver los campos de este juego.

Learning Strategy:

Reading for details

B. ¿Cómo era el juego?
Completa las oraciones con la información apropiada basándote en el texto en las páginas 398–399.

1. "Tlactli" era un juego…
   a. fácil.   b. aburrido.   c. difícil.

2. El campo tenía la forma de un…
   a. rectángulo.   b. triángulo.   c. círculo.

3. Para ganar el juego los jugadores tenían que…
   a. correr con la pelota en la mano por 100 metros.
   b. pasar la pelota por el anillo en la pared.
   c. jugar por cuatro horas sin parar.

4. El campo en el que se jugaba estaba dividido en…
   a. dos partes.   b. tres partes.   c. cuatro partes.

Repaso

C. Una aventura en la naturaleza
Pair up with a classmate and tell him or her about something interesting that happened to you when you were younger while on a camping trip with your family. You may base this outdoor adventure on a real experience or make up the details for this exercise. Tell how old you were, where you went, with whom, for how long, and do your best to describe what happened that is so memorable. Use the preterite and imperfect tenses as accurately as you can.

Learning Strategies:

Organizing information, reporting based on personal knowledge, describing, expressing past time

399

Presentation: Estructura

As a review, it may be useful to have students listen to a short narrative in English and indicate the tense of the verbs. This exercise helps students focus on the contexts in which the imperfect and preterite tenses are used, even though there are several ways to express the past in English. In the following example, the tenses in parentheses should be identified by the students as you tell the story.

The man **arrived** (pret.) at the restaurant very early. He **walked** (pret.) in and **slammed** (pret.) the door. Everyone **looked** (pret.) at him. He **was wearing** (imp.) a fancy suit. The suit **was** (imp.) purple. He **looked** (pret.) around the room. People **were sitting** (imp.) at the bar and at the tables. The man **walked** (pret.) up to a table and **started** (pret.) yelling at a customer. He **threatened** (pret.) him. Someone **called** (pret.) the police. They **came** (pret.) and **asked** (pret.) the man to leave. When he **refused** (pret.), they **placed** (pret.) him under arrest. The customer at the table **looked / was looking** (imp.) very uncomfortable and **left** (pret.) quickly. Everyone **wondered / was wondering** (imp.) what this **was** (imp.) all about.

In lieu of this story, you might choose a fairy tale. You can retell the story in your own words and have the students identify the preterite or the imperfect, according to context.

ESTRUCTURA

The preterite and the imperfect: Summary

The following table outlines the various uses of the preterite and the imperfect. As you study it, keep in mind the following basic principles:

1. Both the preterite and the imperfect are past tenses.
2. Most Spanish verbs can be put into either tense, depending upon the aspect of the activity that is reported and the meaning that is to be conveyed.
3. As a general rule, the preterite narrates and moves a story's action forward in past time: **Me levanté, tomé** un café y **salí** de la casa.
4. As a general rule, the imperfect tends to be more descriptive: **Hacía** buen tiempo, los niños **jugaban** en el parque mientras yo **descansaba** tranquilamente sobre un banco.

Preterite	Imperfect
Actions that are begun or completed as single events	
Ella **corrió** hacia el parque. Ellos **llegaron** a las 7:00.	*Actions repeated habitually*
	Ella **desayunaba** conmigo todos los días. Siempre **salíamos** a bailar.
Actions that are repeated a specified number of times or that have a time limit	*Actions that occur simultaneously over an indefinite period of time*
Ayer **jugamos** al tenis tres veces. **Vivió** allí por diez años.	Todas las noches papá **leía** el periódico mientras mamá **preparaba** la cena.
	Ongoing activities, scenes, and conditions not regarding length of time involved or outcome
Actions that describe a chain of events	**Corría** por el parque central de la ciudad. La noche de la fiesta, **llevaba** un traje elegante. **Hacía** buen tiempo.
Compré una limonada, **me senté** en un banco en el parque y **descansé** un poco.	
	Telling time and age
	Eran las 5:00 de la tarde. El actor **tenía** diez años.

400

Ex. D:  writing

Suggestion, Ex. D: As students work through this exercise, have them give reasons for their choice of verb tense from the summary on pp. 400–401.

Possible answers, Ex. D:
1. Catalina se despertó a las 7:00, pero se quedó en cama quince minutos.   2. Ella se levantó aunque todavía estaba cansada. Se vistió, pero no estaba bien vestida.

Preterite	*Imperfect*
Sudden changes in mental states or conditions seen as completed (moods, feelings, opinions, illnesses, or other physical complaints)	General mental states
En ese momento, **tuve** miedo de subir al avión.	En esos días, **tenía** miedo de subir al avión.
Hasta ese día, **creí** que podía hacerlo.	**Creía** que podía hacerlo.
Estuve preparado para subir hasta que **me puse** tan nervioso que **fue** imposible seguir.	**Estaba** tan preparado para subir que **me sentía** valiente.
	Descriptions of characteristics of people, things, or physical conditions
	Era un muchacho fuerte y sano.
	El jardín **estaba** lleno de flores.
	Las sillas **estaban** pintadas de amarillo.

Aquí practicamos

D. *Un mal día* Basándote en los dibujos y las pistas en esta página y la página 402, describe el día de Catalina. Usa el imperfecto o el pretérito según el contexto. Sigue el modelo.

/-/-/-/-/-/-/-/-/-/-/-/
Learning Strategies:
Reporting based on visual cues, expressing past time

Modelo: despertarse
Catalina se despertó a las 7:00.

1. despertarse a las 7:00
   quedarse en cama quince minutos

2. levantarse
   estar cansada
   vestirse
   no estar bien vestida

401

3. salir de la casa
llover
darse prisa para llegar a la escuela

4. esperar
subir
no poder sentarse

5. entrar en
llegar tarde
no saber las respuestas
recibir una mala nota
estar descontenta

6. regresar a su casa
acostarse temprano

Learning Strategies:

Reporting based on personal knowledge, organizing details in a sequence, selecting and giving personal information

E. Ayer... Now tell a partner the story of your day yesterday. Use appropriate verbs from the following list or any other verbs you've learned. Use the imperfect or the preterite according to the context. Then your partner will tell you about his or her day.

despertarse	estar contento(a)	estar cansado(a)
levantarse	estar de mal humor	tener mucho trabajo
tener hambre	salir	comer
preparar	reunirse	practicar deportes
llegar	tener sed	acostarse
ir	llegar a tiempo / tarde	hablar con
hacer buen tiempo, etc.		
vestirse		

402

F. Otro descubridor (discoverer) Read the following historical passage, changing the underlined present tense verbs into either the preterite or the imperfect, according to the context.

En 1513, Vasco Núñez de Balboa _es_ el primer europeo que _ve_ el Océano Pacífico desde el este. Muchas personas creen que el escudo (coat of arms) de su familia representa el descubrimiento del Océano Pacífico, pero en realidad es mucho más antiguo. La historia dice que un señor de la familia de Balboa, que _está_ perdido (lost) en las montañas de Francia, _ve_ allí un león que _lucha_ contra una serpiente muy grande. Después de que el hombre _ayuda_ al león, éste _es_ su amigo hasta la muerte. El hombre le _da_ el león al rey de Francia, pero el noble animal _está_ triste y no _puede_ olvidar a su amigo. Un día, _sale_ del palacio para buscarlo. _Va_ al mar, al mismo punto donde había llegado con el hombre a la costa de Francia, y _entra_ en el agua, donde _muere_. Después de esto, la familia Balboa _manda_ hacer un escudo con el cuadro de un león entrando en el mar.

/·/·/·/·/·/·/·/·/·/·/·/·/

Learning Strategies:

Drawing meaning from context, expressing past time

403

Ex. F: ✎ writing

Suggestion, Ex. F: Have students tell why they made their verb tense choices.

Answers, Ex. F: En 1513, Vasco Nuñez de Balboa fue el primer europeo que vio el Océano Pacífico desde el este. Muchas personas creen que el escudo de su familia representa el descubrimiento del Océano Pacífico, pero en realidad es mucho más antiguo. La historia dice que un señor de la familia de Balboa, que estaba perdido en las montañas de Francia, vio allí un león que luchaba contra una serpiente muy grande. Después de que el hombre ayudó al león, éste fue su amigo hasta la muerte. El hombre le dio el león al rey de Francia, pero el noble animal estaba triste y no podía olvidar a su amigo. Un día, salió del palacio para buscarlo. Fue al mar, al mismo punto donde había llegado con el hombre a la costa de Francia, y entró en el agua, donde murió. Después de esto, la familia Balboa mandó hacer un escudo con el cuadro de un león entrando en el mar.

Presentation: Aquí escuchamos

Have students make two columns on their paper, one for Mark and one for Mario. Have them jot down the verbs each one uses as he talks. Afterwards, check for accuracy and note preterite and imperfect usages. Then have students do the comprehension exercise.

Answers, Aquí escuchamos: 1. verdadero
2. falso. Hay como treinta.
3. falso. Quería ir para ver a Michael Jordan.   4. verdadero

Ex. G: pair work

Learning Strategy:
Previewing

Critical Thinking Strategy:
Imagining

Learning Strategy:
Listening for details

Aquí escuchamos:
"El campamento de básquetbol"

Antes de escuchar

You will hear Mario and Mark talk about an experience at basketball camp.

Have you ever been to a basketball camp? If so, what was it like? If not, what do you think it might be like?

Después de escuchar

Según la información que escuchaste, decide si los comentarios son verdaderos o falsos. Si uno es falso, da la información correcta.

1. Mark dijo que después de los primeros días practicaba cinco horas cada día.
2. En el campamento hay unos veinte jugadores.
3. Mario quería ir al campamento para jugar en uno de los equipos.
4. Mark dijo que Mario podía quedarse en el dormitorio con él.

¡Aquí te toca a ti!

G. *Un partido de básquetbol* Work with a classmate and talk about a basketball game you have either played in or watched live or on television. You may base your information on a real event or make one up. Mention such details as (1) who played, (2) when and where the game took place, (3) the score, (4) why it was exciting, and (5) which player or players played well.

404

¡Adelante!

EJERCICIO ORAL

H. El básquetbol Discuss the sport of basketball with your partner, mentioning (1) what equipment you need, (2) where you can play, (3) whether you like to play or not, and (4) who some of the better known players are. Then (5) agree on who you think are the best five players (current and/or past)—the five that you would name to your "Dream Team."

EJERCICIO ESCRITO

I. Un deporte antiguo Using the information you have learned about "tlactli" on pages 398–399, write a paragraph describing it. Remember to use the imperfect tense.

405

Divide students into groups. Let each group decide on a sport. Then have each group research (if they don't have the necessary information) the last championship of that sport (football, basketball, tennis, hockey, etc.): where and when it took place, which teams and players participated, who won, final scores, exciting moments, star players, emotions, etc. Have each team present its report orally to other groups and/or in writing. You could distribute copies of all reports for the whole class to read. Then students could decide which championship was the most exciting / boring, and why.

Para charlar

Para hablar de los deportes

el (la) aficionado(a)
anotar goles
el (la) arquero(a)
el balón
el básquetbol / el baloncesto
el campo de juego
el éxito
el partido
el récord

Lectura cultural

Expansion, Lectura cultural: Have students make a list of sports played in the U.S. For each one, see how many Hispanic players they can name, starting with the ones mentioned in the reading. (This should be quite easy for a sport like baseball where Hispanic players abound.)

TODOS LOS DEPORTES

Antes de leer

1. Look at the photos and the title of the reading. What is the article about?
2. In which of the sports shown in the photos have you participated?
3. List in Spanish as many sports as you can.

Guía para la lectura

//-//-//-//-//-//-//-//
Learning Strategies:

Drawing meaning from key words, brainstorming

A. Now scan the article to see which sports are mentioned. Compare these words to the ones on your list, adding the sports from the article that are not already on your list.

//-//-//-//-//-//-//-//
Learning Strategies:

Reading for main ideas, reading for details

B. Read the first sentence of each paragraph to get an idea of its content. On a separate sheet of paper, write down your ideas for each paragraph.

407

C. Look over these questions. Read the passage again and answer them.

1. ¿Cuál es el deporte más popular en los países de habla española?
2. ¿Cuáles son dos deportes que se juegan a caballo?
3. ¿Qué deporte se jugaba hace siglos en México que se parece al básquetbol?
4. ¿En qué países hispanos se juega mucho el béisbol?
5. ¿Qué deporte que se juega en otros países es de origen español?
6. ¿Cómo se llaman algunas de las campeonas hispanas de tenis?

Todos los deportes

n el mundo hispano se practican todos los deportes más conocidos, junto con otros originarios de algunas de sus culturas. Entre éstos algunos han atravesado las fronteras, como *el jai-alai* o "pelota", un deporte de origen español que hoy se juega en otros países, especialmente en los Estados Unidos.

Los deportes ecuestres, o a caballo, tienen mucha difusión en el mundo hispano y los caballos españoles. Cada cultura fue adaptando los caballos y la equitación a sus propios usos y costumbres. *Las charreadas* son un evento ecuestre característico de México, mientras *el pato* se practica en Argentina desde principios del siglo XVII. *El polo*, originario de la India y difundido por los británicos, cuenta con excelentes jugadores en América Latina.

El fútbol es el deporte más popular en varios países latinoamericanos: Brasil, Argentina, Uruguay, Chile, Perú y México. Y en España, desde luego, es el deporte número uno. Pero también es cada vez mayor la popularidad del baloncesto, que tuvo su origen el siglo pasado en los Estados Unidos. En América Latina, donde se lo llama *básquetbol*, o *basket*, es también uno de los deportes más populares. Un juego muy similar existía ya en México antes de la conquista. En las ruinas de las antiguas ciudades hay canchas para el "juego de pelota", que consistía en pasar una pelota por un arco de piedra.

Otro juego estadounidense, el béisbol, es importante en varios países de Latinoamérica. Es el deporte nacional en Cuba y en la República Dominicana. También Puerto Rico, México, Nicaragua, Panamá y Venezuela cuentan con equipos excelentes.

Otro juego de pelota es el tenis. Son varios los campeones hispanos de tenis, y sobre todo, las campeonas: las españolas, Arantxa Sánchez Vicario y Conchita Martínez, la argentina Gabriela Sabatini y la estadounidense de origen dominicano Mary Joe Fernández.

408

Estrategia para la lectura

Reading Strategy:

Scanning

When reading interviews, keep the setting in mind: one person is there to ask questions, and the other to answer them. When reading an interview, concentrate on the questions first, then go to the answers. This particular interview is between a journalist and María Peláez, a 16-year-old Olympic swimmer. Notice that each person has a different style of speaking. The journalist is very direct, whereas María often says **"pues…"** to give herself time to think of an answer. María's language is also more informal than the journalist's. As you read what each person says, keep a mental picture of the speaker in mind.

Antes de leer

Before reading the interview with a swimmer, think about the kinds of questions you would ask if you were writing an article for your school paper. Then scan the text and read only the questions that the journalist asks. Think about likely answers to these questions.

Entrevista con María Peláez, una chica extraordinaria

Introducción

María, excelente nadadora de 16 años, es campeona de España y de Europa en 200 m mariposa. Fue finalista en los Juegos Olímpicos de Barcelona. Su colegio es miembro de la Federación Española de Natación, donde los mejores entrenadores preparan a los nadadores jóvenes españoles para la competencia internacional. Hablamos con ella cuando salía de la piscina.

Periodista: ¿Cuándo descubriste que te gustaba nadar?
María: Pues, cuando tenía cinco años, cuando empezaron mis hermanas y empecé yo también, en unos cursos de natación.
Periodista: ¿Y cuándo empezaste a practicar?
María: Pues… así más fuerte hace unos tres o cuatro años.
Periodista: ¿Cuántas horas al día practicas?
María: Ahora mismo como cuatro o cinco.
Periodista: ¿Qué es lo que encuentras más difícil de la natación?
María: Pues, depende… eso de ir a practicar todos los días es lo más duro.

409

Support Materials

Workbook: pp. 276–279
Unit Review Blackline Masters: **Unit 5 Review**
Listening Activity masters: **p. 126**
Tapescript: **p. 168**
Unit Exam: **Testing Program, p. 221**

Atajo, Writing Assistant Software supports ATAJO

Periodista:	¿Y el deporte te ayuda a estudiar?
María:	Hombre... hay que combinarlo. El deporte y los estudios son difíciles de llevar a la vez, pero sí que los llevo bien.
Periodista:	¿Practicas otros deportes?
María:	No, así en serio la natación nada más.
Periodista:	Tú fuiste a las Olimpiadas de Barcelona en el 92. Cuéntanos un poco cómo fue.
María:	Pues... fue algo muy especial, super emocionante. Eso de estar allí con los deportistas que nada más ves por la tele, y a lo mejor son tus ídolos...
Periodista:	¿Hiciste amistades con deportistas de otros países?
María:	Sí, con un argentino, con un estadounidense...
Periodista:	¿Piensas ir a Atlanta, para las próximas Olimpiadas?
María:	Sí, por supuesto, si es posible.

Actividad

A. Escoge la información correcta sobre María.

1. María empezó a practicar la natación cuando tenía...
   a. quince años.   **b.** ocho años.   **c.** cinco años.

2. La nadadora dijo que lo más difícil para ella era...
   a. no poder comer lo que quería.
   b. tener que ir a practicar cada día.
   c. la competencia con otros nadadores.

3. Según María, es importante...
   a. estudiar más que practicar.
   b. combinar la práctica con los estudios.
   c. practicar más que estudiar.

4. Cuando fue a las Olimpiadas de Barcelona, María conoció a...
   a. su novio.
   b. muchos deportistas famosos.
   c. actores de televisión.

410

Ya llegamos

Actividades orales

A. *Hablamos de nuestra niñez* (childhood). Imagine that you are a counselor-in-training at a summer camp. You and your fellow counselors are sitting around the campfire on a night off reminiscing about your childhood. Tell about (1) the sports you used to play in elementary school, mentioning your age when you played them; and (2) the sports and games you used to play in the summertime, including where you spent your summers. Then (3) recount one incident that happened to you or a close friend or family member while playing some game or sport.

Finally, determine experiences that some of you have in common, selecting (1) the most unexpected thing you have in common, (2) the experience(s) shared by the greatest number of you, and (3) the most unique experience mentioned. Be prepared to report these results to the class.

B. *Mi deporte favorito* Pair up with a classmate and tell each other about your favorite sport, why you like it, how often you play it, where and with whom.

C. *En mi tiempo libre* Talk to a classmate about the leisure-time activities you enjoyed last summer.

Actividades escritas

D. *Una aventura* Write about an interesting, strange, funny, or terrible experience you had in the past.

E. *Intercambio deportivo* Write a brief letter to a Spanish-speaking exchange student in which you describe two sports that are popular in the United States. Inquire about the sports that are most popular in his or her country.

F. *Mis vacaciones* You've just returned from an awesome vacation. Write a brief letter to a friend who lives in a Spanish-speaking country and tell him or her what you did.

/./././././././././

Cooperative Learning

Learning Strategies:

Selecting and reporting personal information, narrating in the past, organizing ideas

Critical Thinking Strategy:

Categorizing, evaluating

/./././././././././

Critical Thinking Strategies:

Expressing preferences, evaluating

/./././././././././

Learning Strategies:

Selecting and reporting personal information, describing, narrating in the past, organizing ideas in paragraphs

---

Ex. A: groups of three

Suggestion, Ex. A: Have students recall what "used to" implies for Spanish verbs (imperfect) and have them contrast this and item 3, recounting one incident in the past (preterite).

Exs. B and C: pair work

Writing Activities

Atajo, Writing Assistant Software

Functional vocabulary: Expressing time relationships; making transitions; planning a vacation; sequencing events; talking about daily routines

Topic vocabulary: Continents; countries; geography; leisure

Grammar: Verbs: preterite and imperfect

Exs. D, E, and F: writing

411

Conexión

Las estadísticas de béisbol

AL EMPEZAR

How do baseball fans decide which players on the All-Star ballot they should vote for? One way is to compare the players' statistics. What statistics do you think are important for measuring a batter's performance? Look at the following chart to see what statistics you will be learning about.

LOS SUPER-ESTRELLAS DE BÉISBOL

ESTADÍSTICAS

Nombre	Posición	TB	H	B	2B	3B	J	CI	PROM
Fielder, Cecil	1era base	624	163	78	25	0	44	133	0,261
Peña, Tony	Receptor	464	107	37	23	2	5	48	
Canseco, José	Jardín	572	152	78	32	1	44	122	
Carter, Joe	Jardín	638	174	49	42	3	33	108	
Griffey, Ken Jr.	Jardín	548	179	71	42	1	22	100	
Eisenreich, Jim	Jardín	375	113	20	22	3	2	47	
González, Juan	Jardín	545	144	42	34	1	27	102	

Clave

TB	= turnos de batear (**at bats**)	**3B**	= triples
H	= hits	**J**	= jonrones (**homeruns**)
B	= boletos (**walks**)	**CI**	= carreras impulsadas (**runs batted in**)
2B	= dobles	**PROM**	= promedio (**batting average**)

figures

na de las **cifras** más importantes es el número de hits que pega un jugador en relación con el número de turnos de batear que ha tenido. Esto se llama su promedio. Se considera bueno un promedio de 0,300 o más.

412

con las matemáticas

Answers, Actividad A:
1) .231   2) .266   3) .273
4) .327   5) .301   6) .264

Answers, Actividad B:
1. 592, 158, .266   2. 661, 180,
.272   3. 566, 182, .321   4. 395,
121, .306   5. 567, 149, .263

Expansion activity: Have
students do oral presentations
which include a brief biography
and statistical information on all-
time great batters, for example,
Babe Ruth, Hank Aaron, Roberto
Clemente, etc.

¿CÓMO SE CALCULA EL PROMEDIO?

Se divide el número de hits por el número de turnos de batear y se
redondea el número a tres dígitos después de la coma decimal.

Según el gráfico, Cecil Fielder tuvo 624 turnos de batear y pegó 163 hits.
Para calcular su promedio, se divide 163 por 624.

$$\frac{hits}{turnos\ de\ batear} = promedio$$

$$\frac{163}{624} = 0,261217 = 0,261$$

ACTIVIDAD A

You will notice that in the chart, the writers forgot to fill in the
averages for each player. Can you figure out what their averages should be?

1. El promedio de Tony Peña $107 \div 464 =$ _____
2. El promedio de José Canseco
3. El promedio de Joe Carter
4. El promedio de Ken Griffey, Jr.
5. El promedio de Jim Eisenreich
6. El promedio de Juan González

ACTIVIDAD B

Imagine that the season went just one week longer. Prepare the new chart in your
notebook based on the information about the players' performance for the week.

Cecil Fielder pegó 4 hits en 24 turnos de batear.
José Canseco pegó 6 hits en 20 turnos de batear.
Joe Carter pegó 6 hits en 23 turnos de batear.
Ken Griffey, Jr. pegó 3 hits en 18 turnos de batear.
Jim Eisenreich pegó 8 hits en 20 turnos de batear.
Juan González pegó 5 hits en 22 turnos de batear.

	Nombre	*TB*	*H*	*PROM*
	Fielder, Cecil	648	167	0.258
1.	Canseco, José			
2.	Carter, Joe			
3.	Griffey, Jr., Ken			
4.	Eisenreich, Jim			
5.	González, Juan			

413

esentation, Actividad B: Students may benefit
m the following hint: **Para calcular los totales nuevos,
ade las nuevas figuras a las anteriores.** See model.

Modelo:

Jugador	**turnos de batear**	**hits**
Fielder, Cecil		
Antes	624	163
Semana pasada	+24	+ 4
	648	167

Nuevo promedio = 167 ÷ 648 = .258

Critical Thinking Strategies

The numbers in parentheses on pages 415–418 refer to the chapter in which the strategy may be found.

Analysis

The separation of a whole into its identifiable parts

Analyzing

Examining an object or an idea, studying it from every angle to see what it is, how it works, how many similarities and differences it has from other objects or ideas, and how its parts relate or fit together
> Analyzing (2, 4, 5, 8, 11, 12, 14, 15)
> Analyzing time relationships (15)

Categorizing

Organizing information into groups with similar qualities or attributes
> Categorizing (PC, 1, 4, 13, 14, 15)

Comparing and contrasting

Looking for similarities and/or differences between ideas, people, places, objects, and situations
> Comparing and contrasting (PA, PC, 1, 2, 3, 4, 5, 6, 7, 8, 9, 10, 13, 14, 15)
> Comparing (PA, 4, 7)
> Contrasting (2, 7)

Making associations

Using an idea, person, event, or object to trigger the memory of another, seeing relationships between two or more things
> Making associations (PA, PB, 1, 2, 3, 4, 5, 6, 7, 8, 9, 10, 11, 12, 13, 14)

Sequencing

Arranging details in order according to specified criteria
> Ranking (4)
> Sequencing (2, 3, 7, 8, 9, 12, 15)

Creating

Producing an original product of human invention or imagination; originating; bringing about; dreaming up
> Creating (6, 8, 10, 12, 13, 15)
> Imagining (6, 8, 13, 15)

Synthesis

The combining of separate elements to form a unified, coherent whole

Drawing inferences

Guessing logical explanations or reasons for choices, actions, events, or situations
> Drawing inferences (PA, PC, 1, 12, 13, 14)

Hypothesizing

Making an assertion as a basis for reasoning or argument
> Hypothesizing (5, 12)

Predicting

Expecting behavior, actions, or events based on prior experience and/or available facts
> Predicting (1, 5, 6, 10, 11)

Seeing cause-and-effect relationships

Anticipating a logical result from an action or event
> Drawing conclusions (PA, PB)
> Problem solving (4)
> Seeing cause-and-effect relationships (1, 8, 9, 12, 13, 15)
> Solving problems (5)

Synthesizing

Pulling together pieces of information and ideas to create a new whole
> Generalizing (10, 13)

Evaluation

Determination of worth; judgment; appraisal

Determining preferences

Making personal value judgments
> Determining preferences (8, 14, 15)

Evaluating

Determining worth; judging
> Evaluating (PA, PB, PC, 1, 3, 9, 10, 12, 15)

Prioritizing

Establishing precedence in order of importance or urgency; determining relative value
> Prioritizing (6, 11)

Learning Strategies

Receptive Strategies

Active listening (PB, 5, 9, 12)
Asking for information (PC, 1, 4, 5, 10, 12, 14)
   Asking for personal information (PA, 1, 4, 7, 9, 11, 12)
   Asking questions (1, 2, 4, 5, 6, 7, 10, 12)
   Asking questions based on context (PC)
   Making requests (10)
   Requesting information (13)
   Requesting personal information (7)
Drawing meaning from context (14, 15)
   Drawing meaning from key words (15)
   Selecting appropriate meaning from context (7)
   Using cognates for meaning (2, 6)
Listening for details (PA, PB, 1, 2, 3, 4, 6, 7, 8, 9, 10, 11, 12, 13, 14, 15)
Listening for main ideas (6, 14)
Previewing (1, 2, 3, 4, 5, 6, 7, 8, 9, 10, 11, 12, 13, 14, 15)
Reading a calendar (PC)
Reading a chart (12)
Reading a map (PB, 4)
   Reading a weather map (1)
Reading a schedule (PB)
Reading a timetable (5)
Reading for cultural information (1, 2, 4, 5, 6, 7, 8, 9, 10, 11, 12, 13, 14, 15)
Reading for details (3, 4, 5, 6, 7, 8, 9, 10, 11, 12, 13, 14, 15)
   Reading for ideas (PC, 1, 8)
   Reading for information (7, 8, 12)
   Reading for relevant information (12)
   Reading for specific details (PC)
   Scanning for cognates (1, 3, 7, 8, 9)
   Scanning for details (8, 15)
Reading for main ideas (2, 7, 9, 10, 13, 14, 15)
   Reading for gist (2, 8)

Productive Strategies

Describing (PA, 1, 2, 3, 4, 6, 7, 8, 9, 10, 11, 13, 15)
   Describing and interpreting spatial relationships based on personal information (5)
   Describing based on personal information (1)
   Describing based on visual information (1, 5, 7, 10)
   Describing spatial relationships (PB)
Expressing past time (10, 11, 12, 13, 14, 15)
   Expressing future time (9)
   Expressing past and future time (5)
   Expressing present and future time (8)
   Expressing present and past time (10, 11, 12)
   Narrating in the past (4, 5, 10, 13, 15)
   Narrating in the past and present times (13)
   Narrating in the present, past, and future (5)
   Reporting in the past (10, 13)
   Reporting in the past based on visual cues (13)
   Reporting in the past, present, and immediate future based on visual cues (13)
Expressing preferences (4)
   Commenting on preferences (9, 10)
   Expressing opinion (1, 2, 12)
   Stating preferences (1)
Giving directions (PB)
Identifying (7, 13, 15)
   Identifying based on visual cues— Chapter 10
Listing (PB, PC, 1, 2, 3, 6, 7, 8, 9, 10, 11, 12, 15)
Providing information (8, 10, 11, 13, 14)
   Answering questions (4, 6, 7)
   Answering questions based on personal information (7)
   Answering questions based on visual cues (4)
Giving details (2)
Giving information (2, 5)
Giving information based on personal experience (13)
Giving personal information (7)
Inferring information based on visual cues (4)
Making suggestions (3)
Providing personal information (PB, PC, 3, 7, 10, 14)
Responding to questions (1)
Reporting (PA, 1, 2, 3, 7, 15)
   Reporting based on personal experience (12)
   Reporting based on personal knowledge (PA, PC, 1, 7, 8, 9, 11, 12, 13, 14, 15)
   Reporting based on visual information (PB, PC, 1, 5, 7, 9, 10, 11, 14, 15)
Selecting information (PA, 2, 3, 10)

Organizational Strategies

Brainstorming (8, 9, 10, 11, 12, 13, 14, 15)
Collecting information (PA)
   Collecting information in an article (1)
   Completing a chart (7)
   Creating a graph (12)
   Organizing notes in a chart (PB)
   Recording information on a chart (PB, 10, 13)
   Taking notes (PA, 1, 3, 9)
   Taking notes in a chart (7, 8, 10, 12)
   Taking notes on a calendar (7, 12)
   Tallying results in a poll (PB)
Determining time frame (4)
Interviewing (PA, 3, 4, 7, 10)
Making plans (PC)
Organizing (1, 3, 7, 8)
   Organizing a survey (12)
   Organizing details (3, 4, 5, 12, 13)
   Organizing details in a sequence (7, 10, 15)
   Organizing ideas (7, 10, 11, 13, 15)
   Organizing ideas in a paragraph (13, 14, 15)

Organizing information (PA, 1, 3, 4, 9, 14, 15)
Organizing information in a chart (4)
Scheduling (PB)

Multitasking Strategies

Calculating (5)
Calculating time conversions (6)
Making calculations (4)
Correcting (8)
Negotiating (1, 2, 4, 6, 8, 9, 10, 13)

Persuading (14)
Reaching an agreement (PB, PC)
Paraphrasing (1, 2, 3, 6)
Polling (PB, 4, 13)
Recommending (11)
Selecting and giving personal information (1, 7, 15)
Selecting and organizing information (PA, PB, 1)
Selecting and providing information (10)
Summarizing (6, 15)

Supporting choices (PB, 15)
Making decisions (4)
Supporting an opinion (PA, 1, 2, 3, 6, 8, 9, 14)
Supporting assertions (PC)
Supporting decisions (PC)
Using culturally appropriate language (PA)
Applying appropriate expressions (6)
Using appropriate journalistic tone (10)
Verifying (PB, PC)
Writing an invitation (8)

Reading Strategies

Predicting

When you predict, you use what you already know about a topic, person, or event. Using what you already know helps you make a logical prediction which, in turn, helps you to focus on the material you are reading. You make a prediction and then you read to check if your prediction is correct. (Unit 1)

Previewing

By looking over the whole reading before you start to read it, you begin to get a sense of what it may be about. There are several ways to do this.

Using the title to predict meaning

Look at the title and ask yourself questions about it. Then predict answers to your questions. (2, 3, 6, 7, 8, 9, 10, 11, 12, 13, 14, 15, Unit 2)

Activating background knowledge

Recall what you already know about the topic. (1, 2, 4, 5, 6, 7, 9, 10, 11, 12, 13, 14, 15, Unit 1)

Using photos, art work, and illustrations to predict meaning

Look at the pictures and predict what the reading is about. (2, 3, 4, 5, 6, 7, 8, 9, 10, 11, 12, 13, 14, 15)

Skimming

Look quickly at the reading to get the gist of its content, determining what kind of text it is. It may be a description, a narration, a comparison, a characterization, etc. (2, 3, 8, Unit 4)

Scanning

Look quickly for specific information, letting your eyes move quickly down the page. Don't worry about every word. Slow down when you see words or phrases that might be important to you. Look for clues in the text, such as names, dates, numbers, to help you see what kind of information is being presented. (1, 3, 4, 5, 6, 7, 8, 9, 10, 11, 12, 13, 14, 15; Units 2, 3, 5)

Cognate recognition

Cognates are words that look alike in two languages, for example, **hospital, universidad, moderno,** etc., shared by Spanish and English. There are cognates, however, whose meaning is not what it at first appears to be, for example **lectura** does not mean lecture but reading. (1, Unit 2)

Finding main ideas

Main ideas are the central or most important ideas contained in a reading. It may have many related ideas, but one or two ideas are usually the most important of all. (2, 10, 13, 14, 15; Units 2, 3)

Using context to guess meaning

Sometimes you can figure out the meaning of a difficult word by looking at the context—the other words and expressions in the sentence or nearby sentences. Look at these cues to help you. (Unit 2)

Paraphrasing

When you paraphrase, you put information and ideas into your own words. If you stop and paraphrase while you are reading, you can check your comprehension as you go along. Paraphrasing after you finish reading is a good way to check your understanding and help you to remember ideas and information. (3, 13)

Taking notes in a chart

Taking notes as you read helps you organize and remember important information. When you take notes, write down the most important information only. One type of chart you might use may have the main ideas in one column and the details in another column. (3, 8, 9)

Glossary of Functions

The numbers in parentheses refer to the chapter in which the word or phrase may be found.

Describing weather / climate

¿Qué tiempo hace? (1)
Hace buen tiempo. (1)
   mal tiempo. (1)
   sol. (1)
   calor. (1)
   frío. (1)
   viento. (1)
   fresco. (1)
Está despejado. (1)
   nublado. (1)
   resbaloso. (1)
Llueve. (1)
Llovizna. (1)
Nieva. (1)
Truena. (1)
Hay nubes. (1)
   niebla. (1)
   neblina. (1)
   hielo. (1)
   tormenta. (1)
La temperatura está
  en cinco grados. (1)

Talking about the date

¿Cuál es la fecha de hoy? (1)
¿Cuál es la fecha de… ? (1)
¿Qué fecha es hoy? (1)
¿A cuántos estamos? (1)
Hoy es el 5 de octubre. (1)
Yo nací el 5 de febrero. (1)

Describing people

Él / Ella tiene el pelo moreno. (3)
       los ojos azules. (3)
       la nariz pequeña. (3)
Él tiene bigote y barba. (3)
Él / Ella es fuerte. (3)
     alto(a). (3)
     alegre. (3)
     simpático(a). (3)
     impaciente. (3)
     serio(a). (3)
     generoso(a). (3)
     independiente. (3)
     optimista. (3)
     perezoso(a). (3)
     trabajador(a). (3)
¿Cuánto mides? (12)
Mido un metro. (12)
¿Cuánto pesas? (12)
Peso… kilos. (12)
Él / Ella se guarda la línea. (12)

Getting / Paying for a hotel room

Yo quisiera… (4)
Buscamos… (4)
Necesitamos una habitación…
   para dos personas. (4)
   por tres noches. (4)
   con una cama matrimonial. (4)
   con dos camas sencillas. (4)
   con (sin) baño. (4)
   en el primer piso. (4)
   con televisor. (4)
   con teléfono. (4)
Tenemos una reservación. (4)
¿Puede usted arreglar la cuenta? (4)
¿Tiene usted la cuenta
  para la habitación… ? (4)
Voy a pagar en efectivo. (4)
       con cheques de viajero. (4)
       con una tarjeta de crédito. (4)

Expressing time relationships

Yo llego a tiempo. (5)
     tarde. (5)
     temprano. (5)
En (veinte minutos, etc.) (5)
Por (una hora, etc.) (5)
Hace (un año, dos días, etc.). (5)

To talk about missing someone

Te extraño. (5)
Me extrañas. (5)

Los extrañan. *(5)*

Thanking someone

Les agradezco con todo el corazón
   su hospitalidad. *(5)*
Mil gracias por... *(5)*
Muchas gracias por... *(5)*

Asking for and making clarifications

¿Cómo se dice... ? *(6)*
¿Qué quiere decir... ? *(6)*
¿Qué dijiste? *(6)*
No sé como se dice... *(6)*

Finding an apartment

Yo prefiero un apartamento...
   pequeño. *(6)*
   amueblado. *(6)*
   cerca de la universidad. *(6)*
   con dos dormitorios. *(6)*

Talking about daily routines

Yo me despierto a... *(7)*
   me levanto a... *(7)*
   me baño a... *(7)*
   me cepillo los dientes. *(7)*
   me lavo (el pelo, las manos, etc.). *(7)*
   me maquillo. *(7)*
   me peino. *(7)*
   me afeito. *(7)*
   me ducho. *(7)*
   me acuesto a... *(7)*
   me duermo. *(7)*
   me visto. *(7)*

Inviting someone

Nos daría mucho gusto... *(8)*
Tenga la bondad de... *(8)*
Nos vemos a / en... *(8)*
¿Te parece bien? *(8)*
Contéstame cuanto antes. *(8)*

Talking about films

Es una comedia. *(8)*
   un drama psicológico. *(8)*
   un documental. *(8)*
   una película policíaca. *(8)*
      de terror. *(8)*
      de ciencia-ficción. *(8)*
      de aventura. *(8)*

¿A qué hora dan la película?
Dan la película a... *(8)*

Preparing for a party

Yo compro las bebidas. *(7)*
Yo lavo los platos. *(7)*
Yo pongo la mesa. *(7)*
Yo traigo los discos. *(8)*
Yo me encargo de la comida. *(8)*
               los refrescos. *(8)*
               las invitaciones. *(8)*
Yo invito a los amigos. *(8)*
La fiesta comienza a... *(8)*
Vamos a echar la casa por la ventana. *(9)*

Making plans for vacation

¿Qué vamos a hacer para las vacaciones? *(9)*
Vamos a visitar... *(9)*
      acampar. *(9)*
      esquiar. *(9)*
Vamos de viaje a... *(9)*
¿Por qué no acampamos? *(9)*
         dormimos en una tienda de campaña? *(9)*
         pasamos las vacaciones en... ? *(9)*
         tomamos el sol? *(9)*
         vamos a la costa? *(9)*
            a la orilla del mar? *(9)*
            a las montañas? *(9)*
         visitamos un centro ecuestre? *(9)*

Talking about health and fitness

Quiero bajar (subir) de peso. *(10)*
Ella se cayó. *(10)*
   se lastimó. *(10)*
   se cortó. *(10)*
Él se rompió (el brazo, la pierna, etc.). *(10)*
   se torció (la muñeca, el tobillo, etc.). *(10)*
   se lastimó (la mano, el dedo, etc.). *(10)*
   se cortó (la frente, el pie, etc.). *(10)*
¿Estás en forma? *(10)*
Yo me pongo en forma. *(10)*
Nosotros (no) nos sentimos bien (mal). *(10)*
Tengo dolor de cabeza. *(10)*
            garganta. *(10)*
            estómago. *(10)*
Él tuvo un accidente. *(10)*
¿Cómo te sientes? *(10)*
¿Te sientes bien (mal)? *(10)*
No te ves muy bien. *(10)*

420   GLOSSARY OF FUNCTIONS

¿Qué te pasa?   *(10)*
¿Qué te pasó?   *(10)*
¿Te lastimaste?   *(10)*
¿Tuviste un accidente?   *(10)*
Él tiene fiebre.   *(10)*
      escalofríos.   *(10)*
      catarro.   *(10)*
Ella tiene la gripe.   *(10)*
      una alergia.   *(10)*
      un virus.   *(10)*
      la tos.   *(10)*
      una infección.   *(10)*
Él tose.   *(11)*
Ella estornuda.   *(11)*
Me duele la cabeza.   *(11)*
      la garganta.   *(11)*
      el brazo.   *(11)*
      el estómago.   *(11)*
Estoy mareado(a).   *(11)*
¿Cuánto tiempo hace que te sientes así?   *(11)*

Identifying medicines

Quisiera algo para la garganta.   *(11)*
      los ojos.   *(11)*
      la tos.   *(11)*
      la alergia.   *(11)*
      la fiebre.   *(11)*
      la gripe.   *(11)*

Quisiera unas aspirinas.   *(11)*
      un antihistamínico.   *(11)*
      un antibiótico.   *(11)*
      unas pastillas para la garganta.   *(11)*
      unas gotas para los ojos.   *(11)*
      un jarabe para la tos.   *(11)*
El médico me dio la receta.   *(11)*
Tengo la medicina.   *(11)*

Talking about the past

¿Desde cuándo?   *(12)*
¿Cuánto tiempo hace?   *(12)*
Desde (que)…   *(12)*
Hace…   *(12)*

Verb Charts

SIMPLE TENSES

Infinitive	Present Indicative	Imperfect	Preterite	Commands
hablar	hablo	hablaba	hablé	habla
to speak	hablas	hablabas	hablaste	(no hables)
	habla	hablaba	habló	hable
	hablamos	hablábamos	hablamos	hablad
	habláis	hablabais	hablasteis	(no habléis)
	hablan	hablaban	hablaron	hablen
aprender	aprendo	aprendía	aprendí	aprende
to learn	aprendes	aprendías	aprendiste	(no aprendas)
	aprende	aprendía	aprendió	aprenda
	aprendemos	aprendíamos	aprendimos	aprended
	aprendéis	aprendíais	aprendisteis	(no aprendáis)
	aprenden	aprendían	aprendieron	aprendan
vivir	vivo	vivía	viví	vive
to live	vives	vivías	viviste	(no vivas)
	vive	vivía	vivió	viva
	vivimos	vivíamos	vivimos	vivid
	vivís	vivíais	vivisteis	(no viváis)
	viven	vivían	vivieron	vivan

COMPOUND TENSES

Present progressive	estoy	
	estás	
	está	hablando aprendiendo viviendo
	estamos	
	estáis	
	están	

SIMPLE TENSES

Infinitive Present Participle Past Participle	Present Indicative	Imperfect	Preterite	Commands
pensar	**pienso**	pensaba	pensé	**piensa**
to think	**piensas**	pensabas	pensaste	**no pienses**
e → ie	**piensa**	pensaba	pensó	**piense**
pensando	pensamos	pensábamos	pensamos	pensad
pensado	pensáis	pensabais	pensasteis	**no penséis**
	piensan	pensaban	pensaron	**piensen**
doler	**duelo**	dolía	dolí	
to hurt	**dueles**	dolías	dolió	
o → ue	**duele**	dolía	**dolió**	
doliendo	dolemos	dolíamos	dolimos	
dolido	doléis	dolíais	dolisteis	
	duelen	dolían	dolieron	
pedir	**pido**	pedía	pedí	**pide**
to ask	**pides**	pedías	pediste	**no pidas**
e → i, i	**pide**	pedía	**pidió**	**pida**
pidiendo	pedimos	pedíamos	pedimos	pedid
pedido	pedís	pedíais	pedisteis	**no pidáis**
	piden	pedían	**pidieron**	**pidan**
dormir	**duermo**	dormía	dormí	**duerme**
to sleep	**duermes**	dormías	dormiste	**no duermas**
o → ue, u	**duerme**	dormía	**durmió**	**duerma**
durmiendo	dormimos	dormíamos	dormimos	dormid
dormido	dormís	dormíais	dormisteis	**no durmáis**
	duermen	dormían	**durmieron**	**duerman**

SIMPLE TENSES

Infinitive Present Participle Past Participle	Present Indicative	Imperfect	Preterite	Commands
comenzar (e → ie) *to begin* z → c **before e** comenzando comenzado	comienzo comienzas comienza comenzamos comenzáis comienzan	comenzaba comenzabas comenzaba comenzábamos comenzabais comenzaban	**comencé** comenzaste comenzó comenzamos comenzasteis comenzaron	comienza (**no comiences)** **comience** comenzad (**no comencéis)** **comiencen**
conocer *to know* c → zc **before a, o** conociendo conocido	**conozco** conoces conoce conocemos conocéis conocen	conocía conocías conocía conocíamos conocíais conocían	conocí conociste conoció conocimos conocisteis conocieron	conoce (**no conozcas)** **conozca** conoced (**no conozcáis)** **conozcan**
pagar *to pay* g → gu **before e** pagando pagado	pago pagas paga pagamos pagáis pagan	pagaba pagabas pagaba pagábamos pagabais pagaban	**pagué** pagaste pagó pagamos pagasteis pagaron	paga (**no pagues)** **pague** pagad (**no paguéis)** **paguen**
tocar *to play* c → qu **before e** tocando tocado	toco tocas toca tocamos tocáis tocan	tocaba tocabas tocaba tocábamos tocabais tocaban	**toqué** tocaste tocó tocamos tocasteis tocaron	toca (**no toques)** **toque** tocad (**no toquéis)** **toquen**

SIMPLE TENSES

Infinitive Present Participle Past Participle	Present Indicative	Imperfect	Preterite	Commands
andar *to walk* andando andado	ando andas anda andamos andáis andan	andaba andabas andaba andábamos andabais andaban	**anduve** **anduviste** **anduvo** **anduvimos** **anduvisteis** **anduvieron**	anda (no andes) ande andad (no andéis) anden
caer(se) *to fall* **cayendo** caído	**caigo** caes cae caemos caéis caen	caía caías caía caíamos caíais caían	caí caíste **cayó** caímos caísteis **cayeron**	cae (no caigas) **caiga** caed **(no caigáis)** **caigan**
conducir *to drive* conduciendo conducido	**conduzco** conduces conduce conducimos conducís conducen	conducía conducías conducía conducíamos conducíais conducían	**conduje** **condujiste** **condujo** **condujimos** **condujisteis** **condujeron**	conduce **(no conduzcas)** **conduzca** conducid **(no conduzcáis)** **conduzcan**
creer *to believe* **creyendo** **creído**	creo crees cree creemos creéis creen	creía creías creía creíamos creíais creían	creí creíste **creyó** creímos creísteis **creyeron**	cree (no creas) crea creed (no creáis) crean

*Verbs with irregular **yo** forms in the present indicative

SIMPLE TENSES

Infinitive Present Participle Past Participle	Present Indicative	Imperfect	Preterite	Commands
*dar	**doy**	daba	**di**	da (**no des**)
to give	das	dabas	**diste**	**dé**
dando	da	daba	**dio**	dad (**no deis**)
dado	damos	dábamos	**dimos**	den
	dais	dabais	**disteis**	
	dan	daban	**dieron**	
*decir	**digo**	decía	**dije**	**di** (**no digas**)
to say, tell	**dices**	decías	**dijiste**	**diga**
diciendo	**dice**	decía	**dijo**	decid (**no digáis**)
dicho	decimos	decíamos	**dijimos**	**digan**
	decís	decíais	**dijisteis**	
	dicen	decían	**dijeron**	
*estar	**estoy**	estaba	**estuve**	**está** (**no estés**)
to be	**estás**	estabas	**estuviste**	**esté**
estando	**está**	estaba	**estuvo**	estad (**no estéis**)
estado	estamos	estábamos	**estuvimos**	**estén**
	estáis	estabais	**estuvisteis**	
	están	estaban	**estuvieron**	
*hacer	**hago**	hacía	**hice**	**haz** (**no hagas**)
to make, do	haces	hacías	**hiciste**	**haga**
haciendo	hace	hacía	**hizo**	haced (**no hagáis**)
hecho	hacemos	hacíamos	**hicimos**	**hagan**
	hacéis	hacíais	**hicisteis**	
	hacen	hacían	**hicieron**	

*Verbs with irregular **yo** forms in the present indicative

SIMPLE TENSES

Infinitive Present Participle Past Participle	Present Indicative	Imperfect	Preterite	Commands
ir	**voy**	**iba**	**fui**	**ve (no vayas)**
to go	**vas**	**ibas**	**fuiste**	**vaya**
yendo	**va**	**iba**	**fue**	**id (no vayáis)**
ido	**vamos**	**íbamos**	**fuimos**	**vayan**
	vais	**ibais**	**fuisteis**	
	van	**iban**	**fueron**	
leer	leo	leía	leí	lee (no leas)
to read	lees	leías	leíste	lea
leyendo	lee	leía	**leyó**	leed (no leáis)
leído	leemos	leíamos	leímos	lean
	leéis	leíais	leísteis	
	leen	leían	**leyeron**	
*oír	**oigo**	oía	oí	**oye (no oigas)**
to hear	**oyes**	oías	**oíste**	**oiga**
oyendo	**oye**	oía	**oyó**	oíd
oído	**oímos**	oíamos	**oímos**	**no oigáis**
	oís	oíais	**oísteis**	**oigan**
	oyen	oían	**oyeron**	
poder	**puedo**	podía	**pude**	
can, to be able	**puedes**	podías	**pudiste**	
pudiendo	**puede**	podía	**pudo**	
podido	podemos	podíamos	**pudimos**	
	podéis	podíais	**pudisteis**	
	pueden	podían	**pudieron**	

*Verbs with irregular **yo** forms in the present indicative

SIMPLE TENSES

Infinitive Present Participle Past Participle	Present Indicative	Imperfect	Preterite	Commands
*poner *to place, put* poniendo **puesto**	**pongo** pones pone ponemos ponéis ponen	ponía ponías ponía poníamos poníais ponían	**puse** **pusiste** **puso** **pusimos** **pusisteis** **pusieron**	**pon (no** **pongas)** **ponga** poned (no **pongáis)** **pongan**
*saber *to know* sabiendo sabido	**sé** sabes sabe sabemos sabéis saben	sabía sabías sabía sabíamos sabíais sabían	**supe** **supiste** **supo** **supimos** **supisteis** **supieron**	sabe (no **sepas**) **sepa** sabed (no **sepáis)** **sepan**
*salir *to go out* saliendo salido	**salgo** sales sale salimos salís salen	salía salías salía salíamos salíais salían	salí saliste salió salimos salisteis salieron	**sal (no salgas)** **salga** salid (no **salgáis)** **salgan**
ser *to be* siendo sido	**soy** eres es **somos** sois son	era eras era éramos erais eran	fui fuiste fue fuimos fuisteis fueron	sé (no seas) sea sed (no seáis) sean

*Verbs with irregular **yo** forms in the present indicative

SIMPLE TENSES

Infinitive Present Participle Past Participle	Present Indicative	Imperfect	Preterite	Commands
*tener	**tengo**	tenía	**tuve**	**ten (no tengas)**
to have	**tienes**	tenías	**tuviste**	**tenga**
teniendo	**tiene**	tenía	**tuvo**	tened **(no**
tenido	tenemos	teníamos	**tuvimos**	**tengáis)**
	tenéis	teníais	**tuvisteis**	**tengan**
	tienen	tenían	**tuvieron**	
traer	**traigo**	traía	**traje**	trae **(no traigas)**
to bring	traes	traías	**trajiste**	**traiga**
trayendo	trae	traía	**trajo**	traed **(no**
traído	traemos	traíamos	**trajimos**	**traigáis)**
	traéis	traíais	**trajisteis**	**traigan**
	traen	traían	**trajeron**	
ver	**veo**	**veía**	**vi**	ve **(no veas)**
to see	ves	**veías**	**viste**	**vea**
viendo	ve	**veía**	**vio**	ved **(no veáis)**
visto	vemos	**veíamos**	**vimos**	vean
	veis	**veíais**	**visteis**	
	ven	**veían**	**vieron**	

Spanish-English

The numbers in parentheses refer to the chapters in which active vocabulary words or phrases may be found.

A

a to, at (A)
abajo down, downwards
abogado(a) *m.(f.)* lawyer
abrazo *m.* hug (5)
abrigo *m.* coat
abril April (1)
¡No, en absoluto! Absolutely not!
abuela *f.* grandmother (A)
abuelo *m.* grandfather (A)
aburrido(a) bored, boring (2)
acabar de... to have just . . .
acampar to camp (9)
accidente *m.* accident (10)
acción *f.* action
aceite *m.* oil
aceituna *f.* olive (C)
acequia *f.* irrigation ditch
acerca de about
acercarse to approach
acostarse (ue) to go to bed (7)
activo(a) active (3)
además besides
adicional additional (12)
adiós good-bye (A)
admitir to admit (12)
¿adónde? where?
adorar to adore
aeropuerto *m.* airport (B)
afeitarse to shave (7)
aficionado(a) *m.(f.)* (sports) fan 15
afortunadamente fortunately
agilidad *f.* agility 15
agosto August (1)
agradable pleasant (10)
Les agradezco. I thank you. (5)
el agua *f.* water
    agua mineral (sin gas) mineral
    water (without carbonation) (C)
ahora now
    ahora mismo right now
ahorrar to save
aire acondicionado air-conditioned (6)

ajedrez *m.* chess 13
al to the
al aire libre in the open air
alboroto *m.* disturbance
alcanzar to reach, achieve (11)
alegre happy (2)
alemán(ana) German (A)
Alemania Germany
alentar to encourage
alergia *f.* allergy (11)
alfombra *f.* rug, carpet (A)
algo something
algodón *m.* cotton
algún día someday
alimento *m.* food
alma *f.* soul
almacén *m.* department store
almidón *m.* starch (12)
alquilar to rent
    alquilar un vídeo to rent a video
alquiler *m.* rent (6)
alrededor around
alto(a) tall
alumno(a) *m.(f.)* student
allá over there
allí there
amable friendly
amar to love
amarillo(a) yellow (2)
ambicioso(a) ambitious (3)
americano(a) American (A)
amigo(a) *m.(f.)* friend (A)
amistad *f.* friendship
(completamente) amueblado (fully)
    furnished (6)
anaranjado(a) orange (color) (2)
andar to go along, walk
anillo *m.* ring
animal *m.* animal (A)
ancho(a) wide
anoche last night (C)
anotar un gol make a goal, score (15)
ansiedad *f.* anxiety (12)
anterior previous (9)
antes before

antibiótico *m.* antibiotic (11)
antiguo(a) old
antihistamínico *m.* antihistamine
    (11)
antipático(a) disagreeable
anual annual (11)
anunciar to announce
año *m.* year (C)
aparentemente apparently (12)
apartamento *m.* apartment (A)
apellido *m.* last name (A)
aprender to learn (A)
aprovechar to take advantage of (8)
aquel(la) that
aquél(la) *m.(f.)* that one
aquí here
    Aquí tiene... Here you have . . . (C)
árbol *m.* tree
área de acampar *f.* campground (9)
Argentina Argentina
argentino(a) Argentine (A)
aro *m.* hoop
arquero(a) *m.(f.)* goaltender (15)
arquitecto(a) *m.(f.)* architect
arreglar to arrange, fix (6)
arriba up, above
arroz *m.* rice
arte *m.* or *f.* art (A)
artículo *m.* article (12)
ascensor *m.* elevator (4)
asegurar to assure (10)
¿Así es? Is that it?
asistir a to attend (A)
aspirina *f.* aspirin (11)
un atado de a bunch of (C)
ataque *m.* attack, offense (15)
atleta *m.(f.)* athlete (14)
atlético(a) athletic (3)
atún *m.* tuna
atravesar to cross (14)
atrever to dare
atrevido(a) *m.(f.)* daring
aunque although
auriculares *m.* headphones (14)
ausencia *f.* absence

autobús *m.* bus (B)
   estación de autobuses *f.* bus
     terminal
avanzar to advance (15)
¡Ave María! Good heavens!
avenida *f.* avenue (B)
aventurero(a) adventurous (14)
avión *m.* airplane
ayer yesterday
ayudar to help
azúcar *m.* sugar
azul blue (2)

B

bailar to dance (A)
baile *m.* dance
   baile folklórico folk dance
   baile popular popular dance
bajar to go down, lower
   bajar de peso to lose weight (10)
bajo(a) short (height)
balanceado(a) balanced (12)
balón *m.* ball (15)
baloncesto *m.* basketball (13)
balsa neumática *f.* inflatable raft
banana *f.* banana (C)
banco *m.* bank (B)
bañarse to bathe oneself (7)
baño *m.* bath (4)
bar de tapas *m.* tapas restaurant (C)
barato(a) cheap
barba *f.* beard (3)
barco *m.* boat (14)
barrio *m.* neighborhood
básquetbol *m.* basketball
bastante rather, enough (B)
bastón *m.* walking stick (14)
bebé *m.* or *f.* baby (12)
bebida *f.* drink
béisbol *m.* baseball
Belice Belize
belleza *f.* beauty
beneficiarse to benefit (5)
beso *m.* kiss
biblioteca *f.* library (B)
bicicleta *f.* bicycle (A)
   bicicleta de montaña *f.* mountain
     bike (14)
bidé *m.* bidet (4)
bien well, fine, very (A)
bigote *m.* mustache (3)
billete *m.* ticket
   billete de diez viajes ten-trip ticket

   billete de ida y vuelta roundtrip
     ticket
   billete sencillo one-way ticket
biología *f.* biology
blanco(a) white (2)
blusa *f.* blouse
boca *f.* mouth (10)
bocadillo *m.* sandwich (French bread)
   (C)
boda *f.* wedding (8)
boliche *m.* bowling (13)
bolígrafo *m.* ball-point pen (A)
Bolivia Bolivia
boliviano(a) Bolivian
bolsa *f.* purse
bomba *f.* pump
bonito(a) pretty (2)
borrador *m.* eraser (A)
bosque *m.* forest
bota *f.* boot
una botella de a bottle of (C)
botiquín *m.* first aid kid (14)
boutique *f.* boutique
Brasil Brazil
brazo *m.* arm (10)
brindis *m.* toast (salutation) (8)
bronceado(a) tan (3)
brusco(a) gruff
bucear to snorkel, dive
buceo *m.* snorkeling, diving
bueno(a) good (2)
   ¡Bueno! Hello! (telephone)
   Buenos días. Good morning. (A)
   Buenas noches. Good evening.,
     Good night.
   Buenas tardes. Good afternoon.
buscar to look for (4)

C

caballo *m.* horse
cabeza *f.* head (10)
cabina de teléfono *f.* telephone
   booth (4)
cacahuete *m.* peanut
cada every, each (10)
cadera *f.* hip
caerse to fall (10)
café *m.* café, coffee
   café *adj.* dark brown (2)
   café (con leche) coffee (with milk)
     (C)
caimán *m.* alligator
cajón *m.* drawer (5)

calamares *m.* squid (C)
calcetín *m.* sock
calcio *m.* calcium (12)
calculadora *f.* calculator (A)
calidad *f.* quality (4)
caliente warm, hot (7)
calle *f.* street (B)
¡Cálmate! Calm down! (9)
calor *m.* heat (1)
caloría *f.* calorie (12)
cama *f.* bed (A)
   cama (matrimonial / sencilla)
     (double / single) bed
cámara *f.* camera
camarero(a) *m.(f.)* waiter (waitress)
cambiar to change
cambio *m.* change, alteration
caminar to walk
camino *m.* road
camisa *f.* shirt
camiseta *f.* T-shirt
campeonato mundial *m.* world
   championship (14)
campo de juego *m.* field (sports) (15)
Canadá Canada (13)
canadiense Canadian
canasta *f.* basket (14)
cancha *f.* field (sports) (15)
canookayak canoe, kayak (14)
cansado(a) tired
cantar to sing (A)
cantidad *f.* quantity
cantimplora *f.* canteen (14)
cañón *m.* canyon (14)
capacidad *f.* capacity (10)
capital *f.* capital city (13)
cara *f.* face (10)
cariñoso(a) loving, affectionate
carne *f.* meat, beef (C)
carnicería *f.* butcher shop
caro(a) expensive (2)
carretera *f.* highway, road
carril-bici *m.* bike path
carrito *m.* shopping cart
cartel *m.* poster
cartera *f.* wallet (A)
casa *f.* house (A)
casado(a) married (A)
casi almost (7)
castaño(a) hazel (eyes), medium-brown
   (hair) (3)
castillo *m.* castle
catarro *m.* a cold (11)
catedral *f.* cathedral (B)

categoría *f.* category (4)
causa *f.* cause (12)
cebolla *f.* onion (C)
celebrar to celebrate
cenar to have supper
ceniza *f.* ash (14)
centenar *m.* hundred
centro *m.* downtown, the center (A)
   centro comercial shopping center
cepillarse (el pelo / los dientes) to brush (one's hair / teeth) (7)
cera *f.* wax
cerca de near (B)
cereal *m.* cereal (12)
cerrar(ie) to close
Chao. Good-bye. (A)
chaqueta *f.* jacket
charlar to chat (7)
cheque de viajero *m.* traveler's check (4)
chica *f.* girl
chico *m.* boy
chile *m.* hot pepper
Chile Chile
chileno(a) Chilean
China China
chino(a) Chinese (A)
chocolate *m.* chocolate (C)
chorizo *m.* Spanish sausage (C)
ciclismo *m.* cycling
cien(to) one hundred
ciencia *f.* science (A)
cima *f.* top (of a mountain) (14)
cincuenta fifty
cine *m.* movie theater (C)
cinta *f.* tape (recording) (A)
cinturón *m.* belt
cita *f.* date, appointment
cirugía *f.* surgery
ciudad *f.* city (A)
¡Claro! Of course!
   ¡Claro que no! Of course not! (4)
   ¡Claro que sí! Of course! (reaffirmed)
clásico(a) classic(al) (2)
clasificar to classify (4)
clavadista *m.* or *f.* diver
clavarse to dive (Mexico) (13)
clóset *m.* closet (5)
club *m.* club
cocina *f.* kitchen (6)
cocinar to cook (6)
coche *m.* car (A)
coche-caravana *m.* camper (9)

codo *m.* elbow (10)
colegio *m.* school
colina *f.* hill
collar *m.* necklace
Colombia Colombia
colombiano(a) Colombian
color *m.* color
   ¿De qué color es... ? What color is ... ? (2)
combustible *m.* fuel
comedor *m.* dining room (6)
comentar to comment
comenzar (ie) to begin (7)
comer to eat (C)
cómico(a) comical, funny (3)
comida *f.* meal, food
   comida mexicana Mexican food
como how, as, like
   como a around, about
   como de costumbre as usual
¿cómo? how?, what? (A)
   ¿Cómo se dice... ? How do you say ... ? (6)
   ¿Cómo es / son? How is it / are they?
   ¿Cómo está(s)? How are you?
   ¿Cómo te llamas? What's your name? (A)
   ¿Cómo te sientes? How do you feel? (10)
cómoda *f.* dresser (A)
cómodo(a) comfortable
compañía *f.* company
comparación *f.* comparison
compartir to share
competencia *f.* competition (15)
completo(a) complete (2)
comportamiento *m.* behavior
comprar to buy (A)
comprender to understand
comprensivo(a) understanding
comprobar(ue) to check
computadora *f.* computer (A)
con with (A)
   con frecuencia frequently (10)
   con regularidad regularly (10)
   con todo el corazón with all my heart (5)
concierto *m.* concert
concurso de poesía *m.* poetry contest
conducir to drive (13)
confort *m.* comfort (4)
confortable comfortable (4)
congelado(a) frozen

conjunto *m.* group, unit
conmigo with me
conocer to know (person, place) (3), met (15)
conocimiento *m.* knowledge
consecutivo(a) consecutive (10)
consejo *m.* advice
conserva *f.* preserve
constantemente constantly (11)
construir to build
contador(a) *m.(f.)* accountant
contar (ue) to count
   contar con count on, rely on
contento(a) content (13)
contestar to answer, respond
   Contéstame cuanto antes. Answer me as soon as possible. (8)
continuar to continue
continuo(a) continuous (10)
contra la pared against the wall
conveniente convenient (7)
conversación telefónica *f.* telephone conversation
convertirse en to become
corazón *m.* heart (5)
cordillera *f.* mountain range
corredor *m.* corridor, hallway (4)
correr to run (A)
cortar(se) to cut (oneself) (10)
cortina *f.* curtain (6)
corto(a) short (length) (3)
cosa *f.* thing
cosechar to harvest
costa *f.* coast (9)
Costa Rica Costa Rica
costar (ue) to cost (9)
costarricense Costa Rican
costoso(a) costly (13)
de costumbre customarily (C)
coyuntura *f.* joint (10)
crecer to grow
creer to believe (13)
crema *f.* cream
croissant *m.* croissant
crónica *f.* news chronicle
cruzar to cross (B)
cuaderno *m.* notebook (A)
cuadra *f.* city block
cuadro *m.* painting (2)
¿cuál? which?
   ¿Cuál es la fecha de hoy? What is the date today? (1)
cualquier any, whichever
cuando when (A)

¿cuánto(a)? how much / many?

    ¿Cuánto cuesta? How much does it cost? (C)

    ¿Cuánto tiempo hace? How long ago? (12)

    ¿Cuánto tiempo hace que te sientes así? How long have you felt this way?

    ¿Cuántos años tienes? How old are you? (A)

    ¿A cuántos estamos? What is the date? (1)

    ¿Cuántos hay? How many are there?

cuarenta forty

cuarto *m.* room (A), quarter (B)

    ... cuarto(s) de hora ... quarter(s) of an hour (5)

cuarto(a) fourth (4)

cuatrocientos(as) four hundred

Cuba Cuba

cubano(a) Cuban

cubierto(a) covered

cuchara *f.* spoon (6)

cuchillo *m.* knife (6)

cuello *m.* neck (10)

cuenta *f.* bill (4)

cuento contigo I'm counting on you (8)

cuero *m.* leather

cuesta it costs (C)

¡Cuidado! Careful! Watch out!

cuidar to care for (11)

    Cuídese. (Cuídate.) Take care of yourself. (A)

culpa *f.* fault (7)

cultivar to cultivate

cumbre *f.* summit

cumpleaños *m.* birthday (C)

curso de verano *m.* summer course

D

dar to give (11)

    dar una caminata to take a hike

    dar un paseo to take a walk (A)

    dar una película to show a movie (8)

    dar una vuelta to turn over (2)

    darles la despedida to say good-bye, give a going-away party (8)

    darse por satisfecho to have reason to feel satisfied with oneself

    darse prisa to hurry (7)

    Nos daría mucho gusto... It would give us great pleasure... (8)

de of (B)

    de acuerdo okay (C)

    de la / del of the

    de nada you're welcome

    ¿De qué color es... ? What color is ... ? (2)

    ¿De veras? Really?

deber to owe, must, should

débil weak (3)

décimo(a) tenth (4)

decir to say, tell (6)

    ¿Cómo se dice... ? How do you say ... ? (6)

    decir que sí (no) to say yes (no) (6)

    es decir that is to say

    lo que dice... what ... says (4)

    para decir la verdad to tell the truth (6)

    querer decir to mean (6)

    dedicarse a to devote oneself to (9)

dedo (de la mano) *m.* finger (10)

    dedo del pie toe (10)

defensa *f.* defense (15)

delante de in front of (B)

delgado(a) thin

delicioso(a) delicious (2)

demandar to demand (10)

demasiado too (much) (1)

¡Dense prisa! Hurry up! (7)

dentista *m.* or *f.* dentist

dentro de within (8)

depender de to depend on (1)

deporte *m.* sport (A)

derecha right (B)

    a la derecha to the right (B)

desafío *m.* challenge

desarrollar to develop (12)

desayunarse to eat breakfast (7)

desayuno *m.* breakfast (4)

descansar to rest (A)

descenso *m.* descent, the climb down (14)

desconocido(a) unknown

describir to describe

    le describe describes to him, her, you

Descríbeme... Describe ... for me. (2)

desde (que) since (12)

    ¿Desde cuándo? Since when? (12)

desear to want, wish for

    desearles to wish them (8)

desfile *m.* parade

deshonesto(a) dishonest (3)

desierto *m.* desert

despacio slowly, slow

despedirse (i, i) de to say good-bye to

despejado cloudy (1)

despertarse (ie) to wake up (7)

después after

detrás de behind, in back of (B)

día *m.* day (B)

    el Día de la Independencia Independence Day

    el Día de la Madre Mother's Day (C)

    el Día del Padre Father's Day (C)

diciembre December (1)

diente *m.* tooth (10)

dificultad *f.* difficulty (12)

difundir to spread

¡Diga / Dígame! Hello! (answering the phone)

¡No me digas! You don't say!

digestión *f.* digestion (12)

Dime. Tell me.

dinero *m.* money

¿en qué dirección? in which direction?

directamente directly (7)

disco compacto compact disc

discoteca *f.* discotheque (B)

discreto(a) discreet (3)

disculparse to apologize

discutir to argue

disfrutar de to enjoy (8)

divertido(a) enjoyable (2)

divertirse (ie,i) to have a good time (7)

dividir to divide (13)

divorciado(a) divorced (A)

doblar to turn (B)

una docena de a dozen (C)

doctor(a) *m.(f.)* doctor

doler (ue) to hurt (11)

dolor de (cabeza / espalda / estómago) *m.* (head / back / stomach)ache (11)

domingo *m.* Sunday (B)

dominicano(a) Dominican

dominó *m.* dominoes (13)

¿dónde? where?

    ¿De dónde es / eres? Where are you from?

    ¿Dónde está... ? Where is ... ?

    ¿Dónde hay... ? Where is / are there ... ?

dormilón(ona) *m.(f.)* sleepyhead (7)

dormir (ue, u) (la siesta) to sleep (take a nap) (4)

    dormirse to fall asleep (7)

dormitorio *m.* bedroom (6)

dos two (C)

los(las) dos the two, both

doscientos(as) two hundred

dosis *f.* dose (10)

ducha *f.* shower (4)

ducharse to take a shower (7)

duda *f.* doubt (12)

Me duele(n)... My ... hurt(s). (11)

dueño(a) *m.(f.)* owner

dulce *m.* sweet, candy

durante during (5)

durar to last (7)

duro(a) hard

E

echar una siesta to take a nap (1)

económico(a) economical (2)

Ecuador Ecuador (13)

ecuatoriano(a) Ecuadoran

edad *f.* age (5)

edificio *m.* building

en efectivo in cash (4)

eficiente efficient (10)

ejemplo *m.* example (7)

el *m.* the (A)

él he

El Salvador El Salvador

elegante elegant (2)

ella she

ellos(as) *m.(f.)* they

empacar to pack

empezar (ie) to begin

empleado(a) *m.(f.)* employee

empuje *m.* push

en in, on (A)

En (el mes de)... In (the month of) ... (1)

en... minutos in ... minutes (5)

ecabezar to head

Encantado(a). Delighted. (A)

encargarse de to take charge of (7)

encender (ie) to light

encerrarse (ie) to lock oneself in

enchilada *f.* enchilada (C)

encontrar (ue) to find

encuesta *f.* survey

energía *f.* energy (12)

enero January (1)

enfermero(a) *m.(f.)* nurse

enfermo(a) sick

enojado(a) angry, mad

ensalada *f.* salad (C)

ensalada de frutas fruit salad

ensalada de guacamole guacamole (C)

ensalada de vegetales (verduras) vegetable salad

enseñar to teach

entender to understand

entero(a) whole

entonces then

entrada *f.* entrance ticket

entre... y... between ... and ... (B)

entrenador coach, trainer

entrevista *f.* interview

envolverse to become involved

epidemia *f.* epidemic (11)

equipo *m.* equipment (14); team

equitación *f.* horseback riding (9)

es is

Es de... Is from ..., It belongs to ...

Es la una. It's one o'clock. (B)

escalofríos *m.* chills (11)

escaparate *m.* shop window

escribir to write

escribir a máquina to type (C)

escritorio *m.* desk (A)

escuchar to listen (to)

escuela *f.* school (A)

escuela secundaria high school

escultura *f.* sculpture (A)

ese(a) that

ése(a) *m.(f.)* that one

a eso de at about, around (7)

espacio *m.* space

espalda *f.* back (10)

España Spain

español(a) Spanish (A)

especial special

espectáculo *m.* spectacle, show

espejo *m.* mirror (4)

esperar to wait, hope (5)

los espera waits for them (7)

espero que Uds. puedan visitar I hope that you can visit (5)

Espero que no sea... I hope it's not ... (8)

esposa *f.* wife

esposo *m.* husband

esquí *m.* ski

esquí acuático *m.* waterskiing

esquiar to ski (A)

esquiar en agua to waterski (9)

en la esquina de... y... on the corner of ... and ... (B)

establecer to establish

estación *f.* station

estación de autobuses bus terminal

estación de metro subway station

estación de trenes railroad station

estacionamiento parking (6)

estacionar to park

estadio *m.* stadium (B)

estado *m.* state

los Estados Unidos United States (B)

estadounidense American, from the United States

estante *m.* bookshelf (5)

estar to be (A)

estar de mal humor to be in a bad mood

estar de visita to be visiting (12)

Está bien. Okay.

Está (despejado / nublado / resbaloso). It's a (clear / cloudy / slippery) day. (1)

¿Estás en forma? Are you in shape? (10)

¿Cómo está(s)? How are you? (A)

este *m.* east (B)

este(a) (mes / tarde) this (month / afternoon) (C)

éste(a) *m.(f.)* this one

estéreo *m.* stereo (A)

estilo *m.* style

estómago *m.* stomach (10)

estornudar to sneeze (11)

estrella *f.* star

estudiante *m.* or *f.* student

estudiar to study (A)

estufa *f.* stove (6)

evento social *m.* social event (10)

evitar to avoid

exactamente exactly (12)

Exacto. Exactly. (8)

exagerar to exaggerate

¡No te excites! Don't get excited!

excursión tour (14)

exigir to demand

éxito *m.* success (15)

experto(a) expert (10)

expresar to express

expresión *f.* expression

extrañar to miss (5)

Te (Los) extraño. I miss you (plural). (5)

extraño(a) strange

F

fácil easy

facilitar to facilitate (12)
falda *f.* skirt
falta *f.* lack (12)
familia *f.* family (A)
familiar *m.* relative, family member
famoso(a) famous
farmacia *f.* pharmacy, drugstore (B)
favorito(a) favorite
febrero February (1)
fecha *f.* date
   ¿Cuál es la fecha de hoy? What is the date today? (1)
felicidad *f.* happiness
feo(a) ugly (2)
feria *f.* fair
feroz ferocious (13)
fibra *f.* fiber (12)
fiebre *f.* fever (11)
   fiebre del heno hay fever (11)
fiesta *f.* party
   fiesta del pueblo religious festival honoring a town's patron saint
fin de semana *m.* weekend
al final de at the end of (B)
finalmente finally
finca *f.* farm
flan *m.* caramel custard
flauta *f.* flute (A)
florería *f.* flower shop
flotar to float (10)
al fondo de at the end of
formal formal (2)
formar to form (12)
formidable wonderful (2)
francés(esa) French (A)
Francia France
con frecuencia frequently (10)
frecuentemente frequently (B)
frente *f.* forehead (10)
frente a across from, facing
en frente de across from, facing (B)
fresa *f.* strawberry (C)
fresco(a) cool (1)
frijoles *m.* beans (C)
frío(a) cold (1)
frontera *f.* border (11)
fruta *f.* fruit (12)
fuego *m.* fire
fuegos artificiales *m.* fireworks
fuente *f.* fountain
fuera de outside of
fuerte strong (3)
fuerza *f.* force, strength
funcionar to function, work

furioso(a) furious (13)
fusilar to shoot
fútbol *m.* soccer
   fútbol americano football
futuro *m.* future

G

galleta *f.* biscuit, cookie
ganar to earn
garaje (para dos coches) *m.* (two-car) garage (6)
garganta *f.* throat (10)
gas
   con gas carbonated (14)
   sin gas not carbonated (14)
gastar to spend
gato *m.* cat
por lo general in general (C)
generoso(a) generous (3)
genial pleasant
gente *f.* people
geografía *f.* geography
gimnasio *m.* gym(nasium)
globo *m.* globe, sphere, balloon
gobierno *m.* government
gol *m.* goal (sports) (15)
golf *m.* golf (9)
gordo(a) fat
gotas para los ojos *f.* eyedrops (11)
grabadora *f.* tape recorder (A)
gracias thank you (A)
   mil gracias por... thanks a million for . . . (5)
   muchas gracias por... thank you very much (many thanks) for . . . (5)
grado *m.* degree (1)
(50) gramos de (50) grams of (C)
Gran Bretaña Great Britain
granadina *f.* grenadine
grande big, large (A)
grano *m.* bean
grasa *f.* fat (12)
grave grievous, grave (10)
gripe *f.* flu (11)
gris gray (2)
grupo *m.* group
guapo(a) handsome
guardar la línea to watch one's weight
Guatemala Guatemala
guatemalteco(a) Guatemalan
guisante *m.* pea (C)
guitarra *f.* guitar (A)
gustar to like (A)

   (No) (Me) gusta(n) (mucho)... (I) (don't) like . . . (very much). (A)
gusto *m.* taste
   con mucho gusto with pleasure
   Mucho gusto. Nice to meet you. (A)

H

habilidad *f.* ability (15)
habitación *f.* room (4)
hablar to talk
hacer to do, make
   hacer alpinismo to go mountain climbing
   hacer la cama to make the bed
   hacer ciclismo to bicycle (13)
   hacer ejercicio to exercise
   hacer ejercicios aeróbicos to do aerobics (10)
   hacer la equitación to go horse-back riding (9)
   hacer gimnasia to do exercises, gymnastics (10)
   hacer las maletas to pack suitcases
   hacer un mandado to do an errand (C)
   hacer un viaje to take a trip
   hacer windsurfing to windsurf (13)
   hace... . . . ago, it has been . . . (C)
   Hace (buen tiempo / calor / sol / viento). It's (nice / hot / sunny / windy) out. (1)
   ¿Cuánto tiempo hace? How long ago? (12)
   ¿Cuánto tiempo hace que te sientes así? How long have you felt this way? (11)
hamburguesa (con queso) *f.* hamburger (cheeseburger) (C)
harina *f.* flour
hasta until
   Hasta luego. See you later. (A)
hay there is / are (B)
   Hay (hielo / niebla / tormenta). It's (icy / foggy / stormy). (1)
   hay que pasar por... one must go through . . . (4)
   Hay que ser razonables. Let's be reasonable.
helado *m.* ice cream
hermana *f.* sister (A)
hermano *m.* brother (A)

hermoso(a) beautiful
hielo *m.* ice (1)
hierro *m.* iron (12)
hija *f.* daughter (A)
hijo *m.* son (A)
hijo(a) único(a) *m.(f.)* only child (A)
hispano(a) Hispanic
historia *f.* history (A)
histórico(a) historical (2)
hockey sobre hierba *m.* field hockey (13)
hoguera *f.* campfire, bonfire
hoja (de papel) *f.* sheet (of paper) (C)
Hola. Hello. (A)
hombre *m.* man
hombro *m.* shoulder (10)
Honduras Honduras
hondureño(a) Honduran
honesto(a) honest (3)
hora *f.* hour (B)
horario *m.* schedule
horno (de microondas) *m.* (microwave) oven (6)
horóscopo *m.* horoscope (2)
horrible horrible
hospital *m.* hospital (B)
hospitalidad *f.* hospitality (5)
hotel *m.* hotel (B)
hoy today (B)
   Hoy es el (día) de (mes). Today is the (day) of (month). (1)
hueso *m.* bone (12)
humo *m.* smoke

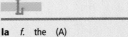

idealista idealist(ic) (3)
idioma *m.* language
iglesia *f.* church (B)
igualdad *f.* equality
Igualmente. Same here. (A)
impaciente impatient (3)
impermeable *m.* raincoat
incluido(a) included (4)
increíble incredible (6)
independiente independent (3)
indicación *f.* indication (12)
indígena *m.* or *f.* native
indiscreto(a) indiscreet (3)
infantil infantile, childish (2)
infección *f.* infection (11)
ingeniero(a) *m.(f.)* engineer
Inglaterra England
inglés(esa) English (A)

inolvidable unforgettable (13)
intelectual intellectual (3)
inteligente intelligent
interesante interesting (2)
invierno *m.* winter (1)
invitación *f.* invitation
ir to go (A)
   ir a... to be going to . . .
   ir de camping to go camping
   ir de compras to go shopping
   ir de pesca to go fishing
   irse to leave, go away (7)
Italia Italy
italiano(a) Italian (A)
izquierda left (B)
   a la izquierda to the left (B)

jabón *m.* soap (5)
jamón *m.* ham (C)
Japón Japan
japonés(esa) Japanese (A)
jarabe *m.* cough syrup (11)
jardín *m.* garden (6)
jazz *m.* jazz (A)
jinete *m.* rider, horseman
joven young
juego *m.* game
jueves *m.* Thursday (B)
jugador(a) *m.(f.)* player (15)
jugar (ue) to play (1)
   jugar a las damas to play checkers (13)
   jugar a los naipes to play cards (13)
   jugar al baloncesto to play basketball
   jugar al golf to play golf
   jugar al hockey to play hockey
   jugar al hockey sobre hierba to play field hockey
   jugar al (tenis / vólibol) to play (tennis / volleyball) (9)
jugo *m.* juice
julio July (1)
junio June (1)
junto(a) together

un kilo de a kilo(gram) of (C)
   medio kilo de half a kilo(gram) of (C)

kilómetro *m.* kilometer

la *f.* the (A)
lácteo dairy (12)
   producto lácteo *m.* dairy product (12)
lado *m.* side
   al lado de beside (B)
   del lado de mi padre (madre) on my father's (mother's) side (A)
lámpara *f.* lamp (4)
lancha *f.* (nav.) launch
lápiz *m.* pencil (A)
largo(a) long (2)
las *f. pl.* the (A)
lastimarse to hurt oneself (10)
   ¿Te lastimaste? Did you hurt yourself? (10)
una lata de a can of (C)
latido *m.* (heart) beat
latín *m.* Latin (7)
lavabo *m.* sink (4)
lavadora *f.* washing machine
lavar to wash (5)
   lavar la ropa to wash clothes (7)
   lavar los platos to wash dishes (7)
   lavarse (las manos, el pelo, los dientes) to wash (one's hands, hair, brush one's teeth) (7)
leche *f.* milk (C)
lechuga *f.* lettuce (C)
leer to read (A)
lejos de far from (B)
lengua *f.* language, tongue (A)
lesión *f.* injury
levantarse to get up (7)
   levantar pesas to lift weights
una libra de a pound of (C)
librería *f.* bookstore (B)
libro *m.* book (A)
licuado (de mango) *m.* (mango) milkshake (C)
ligero(a) light (2)
limón *m.* lemon (C)
limonada *f.* lemonade (C)
lindo(a) pretty
línea *f.* line
lípidos *m.* lipids (12)
listo(a) ready
literatura *f.* literature (A)
un litro de a liter of (C)

logro *m.* attainment, success
llamarse to be named (A)
  (Yo) me llamo... My name is . . .
llano *m.* plain (land)
llave *f.* key (A)
llegar (a / de) to arrive (at / from) (4)
lleno(a) full
llevar to carry, take (A)
  llevar a cabo to carry out
  lo lleva takes him
llorar to cry
llover (ue) a cántaros to rain cats and
  dogs (1)
Llovizna. It's drizzling. (1)
Llueve. It's raining. (1)
los *m. pl.* the (A)
luego later, afterwards
lugar *m.* place, location
  en primer lugar in the first place
lujo *m.* luxury (4)
luna *f.* moon
lunes *m.* Monday (B)

M

m² (metros cuadrados) square meters
  (6)
madrastra *f.* stepmother (A)
madre *f.* mother (A)
¡Magnífico! Magnificent! (9)
maíz *m.* corn (C)
mal poorly
maleta *f.* suitcase
malo(a) bad (2)
mandado *m.* errand (C)
mandar to give an order (11)
manejo *m.* management, handling
manera *f.* way, manner (10)
  de esa manera in that way
manija *f.* handle, clamp
manillar *m.* handle bar
mano *f.* hand (10)
mantenerse en condiciones óptimas
  to stay in top condition (10)
mantequilla *f.* butter
manzana *f.* apple (C)
mañana tomorrow (C)
  mañana (por la mañana / noche)
    tomorrow (morning / night) (C)
mañana *f.* morning (B)
  de la mañana in the morning
  por la mañana in the morning (C)
maquillarse to put on makeup (7)
máquina *f.* machine

máquina de escribir typewriter (A)
mar *m.* sea (1)
marcar un gol make a goal, score (15)
mariposa *f.* butterfly
marisco *m.* shellfish (13)
mármol *m.* marble
marrón maroon
martes *m.* Tuesday (B)
marzo March (1)
más more
  más o menos so-so
  más... que more . . . than
matemáticas *f.* mathematics (A)
máximo(a) maximum (10)
mayo May (1)
mayonesa *f.* mayonnaise
mayor older
mayoría *f.* majority (12)
mecánico(a) *m.(f.)* mechanic
media *f.* stocking
medianoche *f.* midnight
médico *m. or f.* doctor
medio *m.* middle, means
  medio de transporte means of
    transportation
medio(a) half
  media hora half hour (5)
  medio kilo de half a kilo of (C)
mediodía *m.* noon
medir (i, i) to measure (12)
mejor better
mejorar to improve (12)
melocotón *m.* peach
melón *m.* melon (C)
menor younger
menos less
  al menos at least (4)
  menos... que... less . . . than
  por lo menos at least (1)
a menudo often (10)
mercado *m.* market (C)
  mercado al aire libre open-air market
merienda *f.* snack
mermelada *f.* jam, jelly
mes *m.* month (C)
meseta *f.* high plain
mesita de noche *f.* night table (4)
meta *f.* goal
metro *m.* subway (B)
mexicano(a) Mexican (A)
México Mexico
mezcla *f.* mixture
mi my (A)
mí me

microbio *m.* microbe (11)
Mido... I am . . . tall. (12)
miedo *m.* fear (15)
miércoles *m.* Wednesday (B)
mil thousand
milla *f.* mile
millón million
mineral *m.* mineral (12)
minuto *m.* minute (B)
mirar to look at, watch
  mirar la televisión to watch televi-
    sion (A)
  mirarse to look at oneself (7)
  ¡Mira! Look!
misa de Acción de Gracias *f.*
  Thanksgiving mass
mismo(a) same (7)
  lo mismo the same (12)
mitad *f.* half; (5) middle
mochila *f.* backpack (A)
moda *f.* style
moderno(a) modern (2)
de todos modos at any rate (11)
en este momento at this moment
montaña *f.* mountain (1)
montañismo *m.* hiking (14)
montar a caballo to ride a horse (9)
montar en bicicleta to ride a bicycle
montículo *m.* mound
morado(a) purple (2)
moreno(a) dark-haired, brunet(te)
morir to die
motocicleta *f.* motorcycle, moped (A)
moverse (ue) to move (7)
movimiento *m.* movement (10)
  movimiento muscular muscle
    movement (12)
muchísimo very much
mucho(a) a lot
  muchas veces a lot of, many times
    (10)
muerto(a) dead (A)
lo muestra shows it (5)
mujer *f.* woman
mundo *m.* world
muñeca *f.* wrist (10)
músculo *m.* muscle (12)
museo *m.* museum (B)
música *f.* music
  música clásica classical music (A)
  música de mariachi mariachi
    music (13)
muslo *m.* thigh (10)
muy very (A)

Muy bien, gracias. Very well, thank you.

nacer to be born
(Él / Ella) nació... (He / She) was born . . . (1)
nacionalidad *f.* nationality
nada nothing
nadar to swim
naranja *f.* orange (C)
nariz *f.* nose (10)
natación *f.* swimming
naturaleza *f.* nature (A)
navegación a vela *f.* sailing (9)
navegar en velero (una tabla vela) to sail (to sailboard) (9)
neblina *f.* fog (1)
necesitar to need (4)
negocio *m.* business
   hombre (mujer) de negocios *m.(f.)* businessman(woman)
negro(a) black (2)
nervio *m.* nerve (12)
nervioso(a) nervous (13)
Nicaragua Nicaragua
nicaragüense Nicaraguan
nido *m.* nest
niebla *f.* fog (1)
nieto(a) *m.(f.)* grandson(daughter) (3)
Nieva. It's snowing. (1)
nieve *f.* snow (1)
niño(a) *m.(f.)* child
nivel *m.* level
no no
noche *f.* night (B)
   de la noche at night (B)
   por la noche at night (C)
nombre *m.* name (A)
normalmente normally (C)
norte *m.* north (B)
norteamericano(a) North American
nosotros(as) *m.(f.)* we
novato(a) *m.(f.)* beginner
novecientos(as) nine hundred
noveno(a) ninth (4)
noventa ninety
noviembre November (1)
novio(a) *m.(f.)* boy(girl)friend, fiance(é) (3)
nube *f.* cloud (1)
nublado cloudy (1)
nuestro(a) our

nuevo(a) new
   de nuevo again (7)
número *m.* number
nunca never (B)

o or
ochenta eighty
ochocientos(as) eight hundred
octavo(a) eighth (4)
octubre October (1)
ocuparse de to take care of (7)
odiar to hate
oeste *m.* west (B)
oferta *f.* sale
   ¿No está en oferta? It's not on sale?
oficina de correos post office
ofrecer to offer
oír to hear (13)
ojo *m.* eye (3)
optimista optimist(ic) (2)
oración *f.* sentence
orden *m.* order
   a sus órdenes at your service
oreja *f.* ear (10)
orgulloso(a) proud
orilla del mar *f.* seashore
oscuro(a) dark
otoño *m.* autumn, fall (1)
otro(a) other
   otra cosa another thing
   en otra oportunidad at some other time
oxígeno *m.* oxygen (10)

paciente patient (3)
padrastro *m.* stepfather (A)
padre *m.* father (A)
   padres *m. pl.* parents
pagar to pay (4)
país *m.* country (A)
paisaje *m.* countryside, landscape (14)
pájaro *m.* bird
palabra *f.* word
pálido(a) pale (3)
pan *m.* bread (C)
   pan dulce any sweet roll
   pan tostado toast
panadería *f.* bakery
Panamá Panama
panameño(a) Panamanian

pantalones *m.* pants, slacks
   pantalones de campana bell-bottom pants
papa *f.* potato (C)
papel *m.* paper (C)
   papel de avión air mail stationery (C)
   papel para escribir a máquina typing paper
papelería *f.* stationery store (C)
un paquete de a package of (C)
par *m.* pair
para for, in order to (B)
Paraguay Paraguay
paraguayo(a) Paraguayan
sin parar without stopping
pardo(a) brown (2)
parece it appears
   ¿Te parece bien? Is that okay with you? (8)
pared *f.* wall
parque *m.* park (B)
parque zoológico *m.* zoo
parte *f.* part
   en parte al menos at least in part (12)
   parte del cuerpo body part (11)
partido *m.* game (15)
(el lunes / la semana) pasado(a) last (Monday / week) (C)
pasar to pass (9)
   pasar tiempo to spend time (A)
   Lo pasamos bien. We have / had a good time.
paseo *m.* walk (A)
   dar un paseo to take a walk (A)
pasta *f.* pasta
pastel *m.* pastry, pie
pastilla *f.* pill (11)
patata *f.* potato (Spain) (C)
   patatas bravas potatoes in a spicy sauce (C)
patinar to skate
   patinar sobre ruedas to rollerskate
pecho *m.* chest (10)
un pedazo de a piece of (C)
pedir (i) to ask for, request (C)
peinarse to comb (7)
película *f.* movie (A)
   película de aventura adventure movie
   película de ciencia ficción science fiction movie
   película cómica comedy movie

película de horror   horror movie
peligro   *m.*   danger
peligroso(a)   dangerous
pelirrojo(a)   redheaded
pelo   *m.*   hair   (3)
pelota   *f.*   ball
  pelota de tenis   tennis ball
pensar (ie)   to think
peor   worse, worst
pepino   *m.*   cucumber   (C)
pequeño(a)   small   (A)
pera   *f.*   pear   (C)
perder (ie)   to lose
Perdón.   Excuse me.   (C)
perezoso(a)   lazy   (3)
perfeccionar   to perfect   (5)
perfecto(a)   perfect   (3)
periódico   *m.*   newspaper   (6)
periodista   *m.* or *f.*   journalist
período   *m.*   period (of time)   (2)
no permiten   do not permit, do not
  allow   (4)
pero   but
perro   *m.*   dog
persona   *f.*   person   (4)
Perú   Peru
peruano(a)   Peruvian
pesadilla   *f.*   nightmare   (12)
pesado(a)   heavy   (2)
pesar   to weigh   (12)
  Peso… kilos.   I weigh . . . kilos.
a pesar de   in spite of
pescado   *m.*   fish
pesimista   pessimist(ic)   (2)
piano   *m.*   piano   (A)
picante   spicy   (C)
pie   *m.*   foot   (B)
  a pie   on foot   (B)
pierna   *f.*   leg   (10)
pimienta   *f.*   pepper (spice)
pintor(a)   *m.(f.)*   painter
pintura   *f.*   painting   (A)
piscina   *f.*   swimming pool
piso   *m.*   floor   (4)
  (en el primer) piso   (on the first)
  floor   (4)
pizza   *f.*   pizza   (C)
plan   *m.*   floor plan   (6)
planear   to plan
plano(a)   flat
plano del metro   *m.*   subway map
planta   *f.*   floor, plant   (A)
  planta baja   ground floor   (4)
plátano   *m.*   banana

plata   *f.*   silver, money
plato   *m.*   dish, plate   (6)
playa   *f.*   beach
playa de estacionamiento   *f.*   parking
  lot
plaza   *f.*   square   (B)
pluma   *f.*   fountain pen
poco(a)   few, a little
poder   to be able (to)   (13), (preterite)
  made an attempt   (15)
  No puedo dormir.   I can't sleep.
  (11)
  ¿Puede Ud. arreglar la cuenta?
  Can you make up the bill?   (4)
  policía   *f.*   police, *m.*   police
  officer
  estación de policía   *f.*   police station
política   *f.*   politics   (A)
pollo   *m.*   chicken   (C)
poner   to put   (6)
  poner la mesa   to set the table   (7)
  ponerse   to put on   (7)
  ponerse en forma   to get in shape
  (10)
por   for, during   (4)
  por eso   that is why
  por eso mismo   for that very reason
  por favor   please   (C)
  por fin   finally   (13)
  por … horas   for … hours   (5)
  por lo general   in general   (C)
  por lo menos   at least
  por supuesto   of course
¿por qué?   why?   (C)
  ¿por qué no?   why not?   (C)
porque   because
portafolio   *m.*   briefcase   (A)
portero(a)   *m.(f.)*   goaltender   (15)
posesión   *f.*   possession
poste   *m.*   post
póster   *m.*   poster   (A)
practicar   to practice   (9)
  practicar el surfing   to surf
  practicar la vela   to sail
práctico(a)   practical   (2)
prado   *m.*   pasture
precio   *m.*   price   (4)
preferencia   *f.*   preference
preferir (ie, i)   to prefer
preguntar   to ask (a question)
premio   *m.*   prize
preocupado(a)   worried, preoccupied
preocupar   to worry
  No se preocupen.   Don't worry.   (8)

preparar   to prepare
  les voy a preparar…   I'm going to
  prepare, make . . . for you.
  prepararse   to get ready, prepare
  oneself   (7)
presentación   *f.*   presentation, introduction
presentar   to present, introduce   (12)
  Le (Te) presento a…   This is . . .
  (introduction)   (A)
presión   *f.*   pressure   (10)
prestar atención   to pay attention   (5)
primavera   *f.*   spring   (1)
primer(o/a)   first   (4)
primo(a)   *m.(f.)*   cousin   (A)
al principio   in, at the beginning   (13)
producto lácteo   *m.*   dairy product
  (12)
profesión   *f.*   profession
profesor(a)   *m.(f.)*   professor, teacher
programa de intercambio   *m.*
  exchange program   (5)
pronóstico   *m.*   forecast
propina   *f.*   tip
proteína   *f.*   protein   (12)
(el año / la semana) próximo(a)   next
  (year / week)   (C)
prueba   *f.*   test, quiz
pudo   he / she / it could   (2)
pueblo   *m.*   town   (9)
puente   *m.*   bridge
puerco   *m.*   pork   (C)
puerta   *f.*   door
Puerto Rico   Puerto Rico
puertorriqueño(a)   Puerto Rican
pues   then, well then
pulmón   *m.*   lung   (10)
pulsera   *f.*   bracelete
punto   *m.*   point   (11)

Q

que   that
¡Qué… !   How . . . !
  ¡Qué bueno(a)!   Great!
  ¡Qué comida más rica!   What deli-
  cious food!
  ¡Qué cosa!   Good grief!
  ¡Qué envidia!   I'm envious!   (12)
  ¡Qué horrible!   How awful!
  ¡Qué pena!   What a pity!
  ¡Qué va!   No way!
¿qué?   what?   (B)
  ¿Qué día es hoy?   What day is today?

¿Qué dijiste? What did you say? (6)

¿Qué fecha es hoy? What is the date today? (1)

¿Qué hay? What's new?

¿Qué hora es? What time is it? (B)

¿A qué hora... ? What time . . . ? (B)

¿Qué pasó? What's going on?

¿Qué te pasa? What's the matter with you? (10)

¿Qué te pasó? What happened to you? (10)

¿Qué tal? How are you? (A)

¿Qué tiempo hace? What's the weather like? (1)

quedarse en cama to stay in bed (7)

querer (ie) to want (C), tried (15)

no querer (preterite) refused (15)

querer decir to mean (6)

querido(a) dear (5)

quesadilla f. quesadilla, Mexican cheese turnover (C)

queso m. cheese (C)

¿quién? who?

¿De quién es? Whose is it?

Quiero presentarle(te) a... I want to introduce you to . . . (A)

química f. chemistry

quinceañera f. fifteenth birthday party (8)

quinientos(as) five hundred

quinto(a) fifth (4)

quiosco de periódicos m. newspaper kiosk

... quisiera... . . . would like . . . (C)

Quisiera algo (alguna cosa) para... I would like something for . . . (11)

Quisiera presentarle(te) a... I would like to introduce you to . . . (A)

(nosotros) quisiéramos... we would like . . . (C)

quitar la mesa to clear the table (7)

R

radio despertador m. clock radio (A)

raqueta f. racquet

rara vez rarely (B)

un buen rato a good while (7)

reacción f. reaction (2)

realista realist(ic) (3)

rebanada de pan f. slice of bread

recepción f. reception desk (4)

recibir to receive

recoger to pick up, harvest

lo recoge pick him / it up

reconocer to recognize

récord m. record (sports) (15)

recuerdo m. memory

recuperar to recuperate (12)

red f. network

refresco m. soft drink

refrigerador m. refrigerator (6)

regalo m. gift

regatear to bargain

regresar to return (7)

regular okay, regular, average (2); to regulate (12)

con regularidad regularly (10)

reírse (i, i) to laugh

remedio m. remedy (11)

renovar (ue) to renew (12)

de repente suddenly

repetir (i, i) to repeat (12)

la República Dominicana the Dominican Republic

res m. beef (C)

resbaloso(a) slippery (1)

reservación f. reservation (4)

resfrío m. a cold

respuesta f. answer, response (8)

restaurante m. restaurant (B)

resultado m. result (12)

reunirse to meet, get together (7)

revisar to review, check, look over

riesgo m. risk

río m. river (14)

riquísimo very delicious

ritmo cardíaco m. heart rate (12)

rock m. rock music (A)

rodilla f. knee (10)

rojo(a) red (2)

romántico(a) romantic (2)

romper(se) to break (a body part) (10)

roncar to snore (12)

ropa f. clothing (5)

rosado(a) pink (2)

rubio(a) blond(e) (3)

ruido m. noise

Rusia Russia

ruso(a) Russian (A)

S

sábado m. Saturday (B)

saber to know (a fact) (1); found out (15)

sabor m. flavor, taste

sabroso(a) tasty (A)

sacapuntas m. pencil sharpener (A)

sacar to get out something, obtain

sal f. salt

sala f. room

sala de baño bathroom (4)

sala de estar living room (6)

salida f. exit (5)

salir (con / de / para) to leave (with / from / for) (4)

salir con to go out with

salsa f. type of music

salsa picante hot, spicy sauce (C)

saltamontes m. grasshopper

salud f. health (12)

saludar to greet

saludo m. greeting

salvadoreño(a) Salvadoran

sandalia f. sandal

sandía f. watermelon (C)

sándwich (de jamón con queso) m. (ham and cheese) sandwich (C)

seco(a) dry (12)

secretario(a) m.(f.) secretary

en seguida right away, at once (9)

seguir (i, i) to continue, follow (B)

según according to

segundo(a) second (4)

seguro(a) sure

seiscientos(as) six hundred

semana f. week (C)

sencillo(a) simple (10)

sendero m. path (14)

senderismo m. hiking (14)

sensacional sensational (2)

sentarse (ie) to sit down (7)

sentido m. sense

sentirse (ie, i) bien (mal) to feel good (bad) (10)

señal f. signal, sign (12)

señor m. Mr., sir (A)

señora f. Mrs., ma'am (A)

señorita f. Miss (A)

septiembre September (1)

séptimo(a) seventh (4)

ser to be (A)

Será una sorpresa; no les digas nada. It will be a surprise; don't say anything to them. (8)

ser humano m. human being

serie f. series, sequence

serio(a) serious (2)

servicios sanitarios m. rest rooms

servilleta *f.* napkin (6)

servirse (i, i) to prepare for oneself, to serve oneself (7)

 ¿En qué puedo servirle(s)? How can I help you?

sesenta sixty

setecientos(as) seven hundred

setenta seventy

sexto(a) sixth (4)

si if

sí yes

siempre always (C)

 ¡Siempre lo hacemos! We always do it!

¿Cómo te sientes? How do you feel? (10)

¿Te sientes bien (mal)? Do you feel well (bad)? (10)

Lo siento. I'm sorry.

siglo *m.* century

significado *m.* meaning

lo siguiente the following (4)

silla *f.* chair (A)

sillón *m.* armchair (5)

simpático(a) nice

simple simple (4)

sin without (4)

 sin embargo nevertheless

 sin límite unlimited

 sin parar without stopping (11)

sistema *m.* system

 sistema cardiovascular cardiovascular system (10)

 sistema de clasificación classification system (4)

sitio *m.* place

situado(a) situated, located (B)

sobre *m.* envelope (C)

soda *f.* soda

sofá *m.* sofa, couch (6)

sol *m.* sun (1)

soledad *f.* solitude

sólo only (7)

soltero(a) single (3)

solución *f.* solution (10)

Son de... They are from . . . , They belong to . . .

Son las... It's . . . o'clock. (B)

sonreírse (i, i) to smile (12)

soñar to dream

sorpresa *f.* surprise (8)

sorteo *m.* raffle (14)

(Yo) (no) soy de... I am (not) from . . . (A)

(Yo) soy de origen... I am of . . . origin. (A)

su his, her, your, their (5)

subir to go up, climb, rise

 subir de peso to gain weight (12)

sucio(a) dirty (5)

sudar to sweat (10)

suéter *m.* sweater

suficiente sufficient, enough

sufrir to suffer (11)

¡Super! Super!

sur *m.* south (B)

T

taco (de carne) *m.* (beef) taco (C)

talento *m.* talent (15)

tal vez perhaps (8)

también also, too (A)

tampoco neither

tan so

 tan(to)... como... as much . . . as

tapa *f.* Spanish snack (C)

taquería *f.* taco stand (C)

taquilla *f.* booth

tardarse to take a long time (7)

 tarda... minutos it takes . . . minutes (B)

tarde late (5)

tarde *f.* afternoon

 por la tarde in the afternoon (C)

tarea *f.* homework (7)

tarjeta *f.* card (C)

 tarjeta de abono transportes commuter pass

 tarjeta de crédito credit card (4)

 tarjeta de cumpleaños birthday card (C)

 tarjeta del Día de la Madre Mother's Day card (C)

taxi *m.* taxi

taza *f.* cup (6)

té (helado) *m.* (iced) tea (C)

teatral theatrical (2)

teatro *m.* theater (A)

teléfono *m.* telephone (4)

televisor *m.* television set (A)

 televisor a colores color television set

temer to fear

temperatura *f.* temperature (1)

 La temperatura está en... grados (bajo cero). It's . . . degrees (below zero). (1)

temprano early (5)

tenedor *m.* fork (6)

tener to have (A)

 tener... años to be . . . years old (A)

 tener dolor de... to have a . . . ache (10)

 tener ganas de... to feel like…

 tener hambre to be hungry

 tener miedo to be afraid (15)

 tener que to be obligated, was compelled to (15)

 tener razón to be right (10)

 tener sed to be thirsty

 tener suerte to be lucky

Tenga la bondad de responder tan pronto como sea posible. Please be kind enough to respond as soon as possible. (8)

tenis *m.* tennis

tercer(o/a) third (4)

terraza *f.* terrace, porch (6)

terreno *m.* terrain, land surface (14)

territorio *m.* territory

tía *f.* aunt (A)

tiempo *m.* time, weather

 a tiempo on time (5)

 buen (mal) tiempo good (bad) weather (1)

 ¿Cuánto tiempo hace? How long ago? (12)

 ¿Cuánto tiempo hace que te sientes así? How long have you felt this way? (11)

tienda *f.* store

 tienda de campaña tent (9)

 tienda de deportes sporting goods store

 tienda de música music store

 tienda de ropa clothing store

tiene he / she / it has

 ¿Tiene Ud...? Do you have . . . ? (C)

 ¿Tiene Ud. cambio de... pesetas? Do you have change for . . . pesetas? (C)

 ¿Tiene Ud. la cuenta para...? Do you have the bill for . . . ? (4)

 ¿Cuántos años tienes? How old are you? (A)

tierra *f.* land

tímido(a) timid (3)

tío *m.* uncle (A)

tirarse   to dive, throw oneself   (10)
toalla   *f.*   towel   (5)
tobillo   *m.*   ankle   (10)
tocar   to touch, play (instrument)   (A)
todavía   still, yet
todo(a)   all
  en todo caso   in any event
  Es todo.   That's all.   (C)
  todos los días   every day   (C)
  de todos modos   at any rate
tomar   to take   (B)
  tomar el sol   to sunbathe
  tomar la temperatura   to take a
  temperature   (11)
tomate   *m.*   tomato   (C)
tonificar   to tone up   (10)
tono muscular   *m.*   muscle tone   (12)
tonto(a)   silly, stupid, foolish
torcerse   to twist (a body part)   (10)
tormenta   *f.*   storm   (1)
torneo   *m.*   tournament
torpe   clumsy
tortilla   *f.*   cornmeal pancake (Mexico)
  tortilla de patatas   Spanish
  omelette   (C)
tos   *f.*   cough   (11)
toser   to cough   (11)
pan tostado   *m.*   toast
tostador   *m.*   toaster   (6)
trabajador(a)   *m.(f.)*   worker, hard-
  working
trabajar   to work   (A)
tradicional   traditional   (A)
traer   to bring   (8)
tráigame...   bring me . . .   (C)
tratar de   to try to   (12)
trato   *m.*   treatment
tren   *m.*   train   (B)
trepar   to climb
tres   three   (C)
trescientos(as)   three hundred
triste   sad   (2)
trompeta   *f.*   trumpet   (A)
trotar   to jog   (10)
Truena.   There's thunder.   (1)
tu   your   (1)
tú   you (familiar)   (A)
turista   *m.* or *f.*   tourist
¿Tuviste algún accidente?   Did you
  have an accident?   (10)

U

ubicar   to locate

ubicado(a)   located
un(a)   *m.(f.)*   a, an   (A)
  Un(a)... , por favor.   One . . . , please.
  (C)
único(a)   only
universidad   *f.*   university   (B)
uno   one   (C)
unos(as)   some   (C)
Uruguay   Uruguay
uruguayo(a)   Uruguayan
usted/Ud.   you (formal)   (A)
usualmente   usually
útil   useful   (4)
uva   *f.*   grape   (C)

V

va a haber   there is going to be
vacaciones   *f.*   vacation   (9)
vacío(a)   vacant, empty   (6)
valiente   brave   (3)
¡Vamos!   Let's go!   (C)
  Vamos a...   Let's go . . .
  Vamos a ver.   Let's see.
  nos vamos   we're leaving
variado(a)   varied   (2)
varios(as)   various, several
vaso   *m.*   glass   (6)
a veces   sometimes   (B)
vecino(a)   *m.(f.)*   neighbor   (3)
vegetales   *m.*   vegetables   (12)
veinte   twenty
velocidad   *f.*   speed   (15)
vendedor(a)   *m.(f.)*   salesman(woman)
vender   to sell
venezolano(a)   Venezuelan
Venezuela   Venezuela
venir   to come   (B)
ventaja   *f.*   advantage   (10)
ventana   *f.*   window   (6)
ver   to see   (C)
  A ver.   Let's see.
  nos vemos   we'll see each other
verano   *m.*   summer   (1)
¿De veras?   Really?   (12)
verdad   *f.*   truth
  ¿verdad?   right?
verdaderamente   truly
verde   green   (2)
No te ves muy bien.   You don't look
  very well.   (10)
vestido   *m.*   dress
vestirse (i, i)   to get dressed   (7)
vez   *f.*   time, instance

de vez en cuando   from time to
  time   (B)
una vez   once
una vez al año   once a year
viajar   to travel   (A)
viaje   *m.*   trip
  agencia de viajes   *f.*   travel agency
viajero(a)   traveler
vida   *f.*   life
vídeo   *m.*   videocassette, VCR   (A)
viejo(a)   old   (2)
viento   *m.*   wind   (1)
viernes   *m.*   Friday   (B)
violeta   violet   (2)
violín   *m.*   violin   (A)
virus   *m.*   virus   (11)
visitar   to visit   (5)
vista nocturna   *f.*   night vision   (12)
vitamina   *f.*   vitamin   (12)
vivir   to live
  (Yo) vivo en...   I live in . . .   (A)
volcán   *m.*   volcano
vólibol   *m.*   volleyball
volver (ue)   to return   (1)
vosotros(as)   *m.(f.)*   you (familiar plural)
voy   I go   (A)
  (Yo) voy a hacerlo.   I'm going to do
  it.

W

WC   *m.*   toilet   (4)
waterpolo   *m.*   waterpolo
windsur   *m.*   windsurfing

Y

y   and   (A)
ya   already   (7)
  ya en casa   once home   (7)
  ¡Ya es hora!   It's about time!
yo   I   (A)
yogur   *m.*   yogurt

Z

zanahoria   *f.*   carrot   (C)
zapatería   *f.*   shoe store
zapato   *m.*   shoe
  zapato de tacón   high-heeled shoe
  zapato de tenis   tennis shoe

English-Spanish

The numbers in parentheses refer to the chapters in which active vocabulary words or phrases may be found.

a / an **un(a)** *m.(f.)* (A)
ability **habilidad** *f.* (15)
according to **según**
(to) be able to **poder** (13, 15)
about **como a**; (with regard to) **acerca de**
absence **ausencia** *f.*
Absolutely not! **¡No, en absoluto!** (9)
accident **accidente** *m.* (10)
    Did you have an accident? **¿Tuviste algún accidente?** (10)
accountant **contador(a)** *m.(f.)*
(head / back / stomach)ache **dolor de (cabeza / espalda / estómago)** *m.* (11)
(to) achieve **alcanzar** (11)
across from **frente a, en frente de** (B)
action **acción** *f.*
active **activo(a)** (3)
additional **adicional** (12)
(to) admit **admitir** (12)
(to) adore **adorar**
(to) advance **avanzar** (15)
advantage **ventaja** *f.* (10)
(to) take advantage of **aprovechar** (8)
adventure movie **película de aventura** *f.*
adventurous **aventurero(a)** (14)
advice **consejo** *m.* (3)
(to) do aerobics **hacer ejercicios aeróbicos** (10)
(to) be afraid **tener miedo** (15)
after **después**
afternoon **tarde** *f.*
    in the afternoon **por la tarde** (C)
afterwards **luego**
again **de nuevo** (7)
against the wall **contra la pared**
age **edad** *f.* (5)
agility **agilidad** *f.* (15)
. . . ago **hace...** (C)
air-conditioned **aire acondicionado** (6)
airplane **avión** *m.*

airport **aeropuerto** *m.* (B)
all **todo(a)**
allergy **alergia** *f.* (11)
alligator **caimán** *m.*
do not allow **no permiten** (4)
almost **casi** (7)
already **ya** (7)
also **también** (A)
alteration **cambio** *m.*
although **aunque**
always **siempre** (C)
ambitious **ambicioso(a)** (3)
American **americano(a)** (A)
    American, from the United States **estadounidense**
and **y** (A)
angry **enojado(a)**
animal **animal** *m.* (A)
ankle **tobillo** *m.* (10)
(to) announce **anunciar**
annual **anual** (11)
another thing **otra cosa**
(to) answer **contestar**
answer **respuesta** *f.* (8)
    Answer me as soon as possible.
    Contéstame cuanto antes. (8)
antibiotic **antibiótico** *m.* (11)
antihistamine **antihistamínico** *m.* (11)
anxiety **ansiedad** *f.* (12)
any **cualquier**
apartment **apartamento** *m.* (A)
(to) apologize **disculparse**
apparently **aparentemente** (12)
it appears **parece** (3)
apple **manzana** *f.* (C)
appointment **cita** *f.*
(to) approach **acercarse**
April **abril** (1)
architect **arquitecto(a)** *m.(f.)*
area **superficie** *f.*
Argentina **Argentina**
Argentine **argentino(a)** (A)
(to) argue **discutir**
arm **brazo** *m.* (10)
armchair **sillón** *m.* (5)

around **a eso de** (7); **alrededor** *adv.*
(to) arrange **arreglar** (6)
(to) arrive (at / from) **llegar (a / de)** (4)
art **arte** *m.* or *f.* (A)
article **artículo** *m.* (12)
as **como**
ash **ceniza** *f.*
(to) ask (a question) **preguntar**
(to) ask for **pedir (i)** (C)
(to) fall asleep **dormirse (ue)** (7)
aspirin **aspirina** *f.* (11)
(to) assure **asegurar** (10)
at **a** (A)
at about **a eso de** (7)
athlete **atleta** *m.(f.)* (14)
athletic **atlético(a)** (3)
attack **ataque** *m.* (15)
attainment **logro** *m.*
(to) attend **asistir a** (A)
August **agosto** (1)
aunt **tía** *f.* (A)
autumn **otoño** *m.* (1)
avenue **avenida** *f.* (B)
average **regular** (2)
(to) avoid **evitar**

baby **bebé** *m.* or *f.* (12)
back **espalda** *f.* (10)
    in back of **detrás de** (B)
backpack **mochila** *f.* (A)
bad **malo(a)** (2)
bakery **panadería** *f.*
balanced **balanceado(a)** (12)
ball **pelota** *f.;* **balón** *m.* (15)
balloon **globo** *m.*
ball-point pen **bolígrafo** *m.* (A)
banana **banana** *f.* (C); **plátano** *m.*
bank **banco** *m.* (B)
(to) bargain **regatear**
baseball **béisbol** *m.*
basket **canasta** *f.* (14)
basketball **básquetbol** *m.;* **baloncesto** *m.* (13)

bath **baño** *m.* (4)
(to) bathe oneself **bañarse** (7)
bathroom **sala de baño** *f.* (4)
(to) be **estar** (A); **ser** (A)
   (to) be in a bad mood **estar de mal humor**
   (to) be . . . years old **tener. . . años** (A)
beach **playa** *f.*
bean **grano** *m.*
beans **frijoles** *m.* (C)
beard **barba** *f.* (3)
beat (heart) **latido** *m.*
beautiful **hermoso(a)**
beauty **belleza** *f.*
because **porque**
(to) become **convertirse en**
   (to) become involved **envolverse**
bed **cama** *f.* (A)
   (double / single) bed **cama (matrimonial / sencilla)**
bedroom **dormitorio** *m.* (6)
beef **carne de res, carne** *f.* (C)
before **antes**
(to) begin **comenzar (ie)** (7); **empezar(ie)**
beginner **novato(a)** *m.(f.)*
in / at the beginning **al principio** (13)
behavior **comportamiento** *m.*
behind **detrás de** (B)
(to) believe **creer** (13)
Belize **Belice**
It belongs to . . . **Es de. . .**
   They belong to . . . **Son de. . .**
belt **cinturón** *m.*
(to) benefit **beneficiarse** (5)
beside **al lado de** (B)
besides **además**
better **mejor**
between . . . and . . . **entre. . . y. . .** (B)
bicycle **bicicleta** *f.* (A)
(to) bicycle **hacer ciclismo** (13)
bidet **bidé** *m.* (4)
big **grande** (A)
bike path **carril-bici** *m.*
bill **cuenta** *f.* (4)
   Can you make up the bill? **¿Puede Ud. arreglar la cuenta?** (4)
   Do you have the bill for . . . ? **¿Tiene Ud. la cuenta para. . . ?** (4)
biology **biología** *f.*
bird **pájaro** *m.*
birthday **cumpleaños** *m.* (C)
   birthday card **tarjeta de cumpleaños** *f.* (C)

biscuit **galleta** *f.*
black **negro(a)** (2)
block (city) **cuadra** *f.*
blond(e) **rubio(a)** (3)
blouse **blusa** *f.*
blue **azul** (2)
boat **banco** *m.* (14)
body part **parte del cuerpo** *f.* (11)
Bolivia **Bolivia**
Bolivian **boliviano(a)**
bone **hueso** *m.* (12)
book **libro** *m.* (A)
bookshelf **estante** *m.* (5)
bookstore **librería** *f.* (B)
boot **bota** *f.*
booth **taquilla** *f.*
border **frontera** *f.* (11)
bored, boring **aburrido(a)** (2)
(to) be born **nacer**
   (He / She) was born . . . **(Él / Ella) nació. . .** (1)
both **los (las) dos**
a bottle of **una botella de** (C)
boutique **boutique** *f.*
bowling **boliche** *m.* (13)
boy **chico** *m.*
boyfriend **novio** *m.* (3)
brave **valiente** (3)
Brazil **Brasil**
bread **pan** *m.* (C)
(to) break (a body part) **romper(se)** (10)
breakfast **desayuno** *m.* (4)
bridge **puente** *m.*
briefcase **portafolio** *m.* (A)
(to) bring **traer** (8)
bring me . . . **tráigame. . .** (C)
brother **hermano** *m.* (A)
brown **pardo(a)** (2)
   brown, dark **café** (2)
   medium-brown hair **castaño(a)** (3)
brunet(te) **moreno(a)**
(to) brush (one's hair / teeth) **cepillarse (el pelo / los dientes)** (7)
build **construir**
building **edificio** *m.*
a bunch of **un atado de** (C)
bus **autobús** *m.* (B)
   bus terminal **estación de autobuses** *f.*
business **negocio** *m.*
businessman(woman) **hombre (mujer) de negocios** *m.(f.)*
but **pero**
butcher shop **carnicería** *f.*

butter **mantequilla** *f.*
butterfly **mariposa** *f.*
(to) buy **comprar** (A)

café **café** *m.* (2)
calcium **calcio** *m.* (12)
calculator **calculadora** *f.* (A)
Calm down! **¡Cálmate!**
calorie **caloría** *f.* (12)
camera **cámara** *f.*
(to) camp **acampar** (9)
camper **coche-caravana** *m.* (9)
campfire **hoguera** *f.*
campground **área de acampar** *f.* (9)
a can of **una lata de** (C)
Canada **Canadá**
Canadian **canadiense**
candy **dulce** *m.*
canoe/kayak **canookayak** (14)
canteen **cantimplora** *f.* (14)
canyon **cañón** *m.*
capacity **capacidad** *f.* (10)
capital city **capital** *f.*
car **coche** *m.* (A)
caramel custard **flan** *m.*
carbonated **con gas** (14)
   not carbaonated **sin gas** (14)
card **tarjeta** *f.* (C)
cardiovascular system **sistema cardiovascular** (10)
(to) care for **cuidar** (11)
   (to) take care of **ocuparse de** (7)
   Take care of yourself. **Cuídese. (Cuídate.)** (A)
Careful! **¡Cuidado!**
carpet **alfombra** *f.* (A)
carrot **zanahoria** *f.* (C)
(to) carry **llevar** (A)
   (to) carry out **llevar a cabo**
in cash **en efectivo** (4)
castle **castillo** *m.*
cat **gato** *m.*
category **categoría** *f.* (4)
cathedral **catedral** *f.* (B)
cause **causa** *f.* (12)
(to) celebrate **celebrar**
center **centro** *m.* (A)
century **siglo** *m.*
cereal **cereal** *m.* (12)
chair **silla** *f.* (A)
   armchair **sillón** *m.* (5)
challenge **desafío** *m.*

(to) change **cambiar**

change **cambio** *m.*

    Do you have change for . . . pesetas?
¿Tiene Ud. cambio de… pesetas? (C)

(to) take charge of **encargarse de** (7)

(to) chat **charlar** (7)

cheap **barato(a)**

(to) check (go over) **revisar**; (verify) **comprobar**

cheese **queso** *m.* (C)

    cheeseburger **hamburguesa con queso** *f.* (C)

chemistry **química** *f.*

chess **ajedrez** (13)

chest **pecho** *m.* (10)

chicken **pollo** *m.* (C)

child **niño(a)** *m.(f.)*

childish **infantil** (2)

Chile **Chile**

Chilean **chileno(a)**

chills **escalofríos** *m.* (11)

China **China** (13)

Chinese **chino(a)** (A)

chocolate **chocolate** *m.* (C)

church **iglesia** *f.* (B)

city **ciudad** *f.* (A)

classic(al) **clásico(a)** (2)

classification system **sistema de clasificación** (4)

(to) classify **clasificar** (4)

(to) clear the table **quitar la mesa** (7)

It's a clear day. **Está despejado.** (1)

(to) climb **subir; trepar**

clock radio **radio despertador** *m.* (A)

(to) close **cerrar (ie)**

closet **clóset** *m.* (5)

clothing **ropa** *f.* (5)

    clothing store **tienda de ropa** *f.*

cloud **nube** *f.* (1)

cloudy **despejado, nublado** (1)

    It's a cloudy day. **Está nublado.** (1)

club **club** *m.*

clumsy **torpe**

coach **entrenador**

coast **costa** *f.* (9)

coat **abrigo** *m.*

coffee (with milk) **café (con leche)** *m.* (C)

a cold **catarro** *m.* (11); **resfrío** *m.*

cold **frío(a)** (1)

Colombia **Colombia**

Colombian **colombiano(a)**

color **color** *m.*

What color is . . . ? **¿De qué color es… ?** (2)

(to) comb **peinarse** (7)

(to) come **venir** (B)

comedy movie **película cómica** *f.*

comfort **confort** *m.* (4)

comfortable **cómodo(a)**, (14); **confortable**

comical **cómico(a)** (3)

(to) comment **comentar**

commuter pass **tarjeta de abono transportes** *m.*

compact disc **disco compacto** *m.*

company **compañía** *f.*

comparison **comparación** *f.*

competition **competencia** *f.* (15)

complete **completo(a)** (2)

computer **computadora** *f.* (A)

concert **concierto** *m.*

consecutive **consecutivo(a)** (10)

constantly **constantemente** (11)

content **contento(a)** (13)

contest **concurso** *m.*

(to) continue **continuar, seguir (i, i)** (B)

continuous **continuo(a)** (10)

convenient **conveniente** (7)

(to) cook **cocinar** (6)

cookie **galleta** *f.*

cool **fresco(a)** (1)

(to) cool off **refrescarse** (14)

corn **maíz** *m.* (C)

on the corner of . . . and . . . **en la esquina de… y…** (B)

cornmeal pancake (Mexico) **tortilla** *f.*

corridor **corredor** *m.* (4)

(to) cost **costar (ue)** (9)

Costa Rica **Costa Rica**

Costa Rican **costarricense**

costly **costoso(a)** (13)

(it) costs **cuesta** (C)

cotton **algodón** *m.*

couch **sofá** *m.* (6)

cough **tos** *f.* (11)

    cough syrup **jarabe** *m.* (11)

(to) cough **toser** (11)

(he / she / it) could **pudo** (2)

(to) count **contar (ue)**

    (to) count on **contar con**

    I'm counting on you **cuento contigo** (8)

country **país** *m.* (A)

countryside **paisaje** *m.* (14)

cousin **primo(a)** *m.(f.)* (A)

covered **cubierto(a)**

cream **crema** *f.*

credit card **tarjeta de crédito** *f.* (4)

croissant **croissant** *m.*

cross **cruz** *f.*

(to) cross **cruzar** (B); **atravesar** (14)

(to) cry **llorar**

Cuba **Cuba**

Cuban **cubano(a)**

cucumber **pepino** *m.* (C)

cup **taza** *f.* (6)

curtain **cortina** *f.* (6)

customarily **de costumbre** (C)

(to) cut (oneself) **cortar(se)** (10)

cycling **ciclismo**

D

dairy **lácteo** (12)

    dairy product **producto lácteo** *m.* (12)

dance **baile** *m.*

    popular dance **baile popular**

(to) dance **bailar** (A)

danger **peligro** *m.*

dangerous **peligroso(a)**

(to) dare **atrever**

daring **atrevido(a)**

dark **oscuro(a)**

dark-haired **moreno(a)**

date **fecha** *f.*; (appointment) **cita** *f.*

    What is the date? **¿A cuántos estamos?** (1)

    What is the date today? **¿Qué fecha es hoy?, ¿Cuál es la fecha de hoy?** (1)

daughter **hija** *f.* (A)

day **día** *m.* (B)

    What day is today? **¿Qué día es hoy?**

dead **muerto(a)** (A)

dear **querido(a)** (5)

December **diciembre** (1)

defense **defensa** *f.* (15)

degree **grado** *m.* (1)

    It's . . . degrees (below zero). **La temperatura está en… grados (bajo cero).** (1)

delicious **delicioso(a)** (2)

    very delicious **riquísimo**

    What delicious food! **¡Qué comida más rica!**

Delighted. **Encantado(a).** (A)

(to) demand **demandar** (10); **exigir**

dentist **dentista** *m.* or *f.*

deparment store **almacén** *m.*
(to) depend on **depender de** (1)
descent **decenso** *m.* (14)
(to) describe **describir**
    Describe . . . for me. **Descríbeme...**
    describes to him, her, you **le describe**
    (3)
desert **desierto** *m.*
desk **escritorio** *m.* (A)
(to) develop **desarrollar** (12)
(to) devote oneself to **dedicarse** (9)
(to) die **morir**
difficulty **dificultad** *f.* (12)
digestion **digestión** *f.* (12)
dining room **comedor** *m.* (6)
in which direction? **¿en qué dirección?**
directly **directamente** (7)
dirty **sucio(a)** (5)
disagreeable **antipático(a)**
discotheque **discoteca** *f.* (B)
discreet **discreto(a)** (3)
dish **plato** *m.* (6)
dishonest **deshonesto(a)** (3)
disturbance **alboroto** *m.*
(to) dive **tirarse** (10), **clavarse**
    (Mexico) (13)
diver **clavadista** *m.* or *f.* (13)
(to) divide **dividir** (13)
divorced **divorciado(a)** (A)
(to) do **hacer**
    I'm going to do it. **(Yo) voy a hacerlo.**
    We always do it! **¡Siempre lo hacemos!**
doctor **doctor(a)** *m.(f.);* **médico(a)** *m.(f.)*
dog **perro** *m.*
Dominican **dominicano(a)**
the Dominican Republic **la República**
    Dominicana
dominoes **dominó** *m.* (13)
door **puerta** *f.*
dose **dosis** *f.* (10)
doubt **duda** *f.* (12)
down **abajo**
(to) go down **bajar**
downtown **centro** *m.* (A)
a dozen **una docena de** (C)
drawer **cajón** *m.* (5)
(to) dream **soñar**
dress **vestido** *m.*
(to) get dressed **vestirse (i, i)** (7)
dresser **cómoda** *f.* (A)
drink **bebida** *f.*
(to) drive **conducir** (13)
It's drizzling. **Llovizna.** (1)
drugstore **farmacia** *f.* (B)

dry **seco(a)** (12)
during **durante** (5), **por** (4)

E

each **cada** (10)
ear **oreja** *f.* (10)
early **temprano** (5)
(to) earn **ganar**
east **este** *m.* (B)
(to) eat **comer** (C)
    (to) eat breakfast **desayunarse** (7)
    (to) eat supper **cenar**
easy **fácil**
economical **económico(a)** (2)
Ecuador **Ecuador**
Ecuadoran **ecuatoriano(a)**
efficient **eficiente** (10)
eight hundred **ochocientos(as)**
eighth **octavo(a)** (4)
eighty **ochenta**
El Salvador **El Salvador**
elbow **codo** *m.* (10)
elegant **elegante** (2)
elevator **ascensor** *m.* (4)
employee **empleado(a)** *m.(f.)*
empty **vacío(a)** (6)
enchilada **enchilada** *f.* (C)
(to) encourage **alentar**
at the end of **al final de** (B); **al fondo de**
energy **energía** *f.* (12)
engineer **ingeniero(a)** *m.(f.)*
England **Inglaterra**
English **inglés(esa)** (A)
(to) enjoy **disfrutar de** (8)
enjoyable **divertido(a)** (2)
enough **bastante, suficiente** (B)
entrance ticket **entrada** *f.*
envelope **sobre** *m.* (C)
I'm envious! **¡Qué envidia!** (12)
epidemic **epidemia** *f.* (11)
equality **igualdad** *f.*
equipment **equipo** *m.* (14)
eraser **borrador** *m.* (A)
errand **mandado** *m.* (C)
    (to) do an errand **hacer un mandado**
    (C)
(to) establish **establecer**
in any event **en todo caso**
every **cada** (10)
    every day **todos los días** (C)
exactly **exactamente** (12); **exacto** (8)
(to) exaggerate **exagerar**
example **ejemplo** *m.* (7)

exchange program **programa de inter-**
    cambio *m.* (5)
Don't get excited! **¡No te excites!**
Excuse me. **Perdón.** (C)
(to) do exercises **hacer gimnasia** (10)
(to) exercise **hacer ejercicio**
exit **salida** *f.* (5)
expensive **caro(a)** (2)
expert **experto(a)** (10)
(to) express **expresar**
expression **expresión** *f.*
eye **ojo** *m.* (3)
eyedrops **gotas para los ojos** *f.* (11)

F

face **cara** *f.* (10)
(to) facilitate **facilitar** (12)
facing **frente a, en frente de** (B)
fair **feria** *f.*
fall **otoño** *m.* (1)
(to) fall **caerse** (10)
family **familia** *f.* (A)
famous **famoso(a)**
fan (of sports) **aficionado(a)** *m.(f.)* (15)
far from **lejos de** (B)
farm **finca** *f.*
fat **gordo(a)** *adj.*
fat **grasa** *f.* (12)
father **padre** *m.* (A)
Father's Day **el Día del Padre** (C)
fault **culpa** *f.* (7)
favorite **favorito(a)**
fear **miedo** *m.* (15)
(to) fear **temer**
February **febrero** (1)
(to) feel good (bad) **sentirse (ie, i) bien**
    (mal) (10)
    Do you feel well (bad)? **¿Te sientes**
    bien (mal)? (10)
(to) feel like . . . **tener ganas de...**
ferocious **feroz** (13)
festival (religious) honoring a town's patron
    saint **fiesta del pueblo**
fever **fiebre** *f.* (11)
few **poco(a)**
fiance(é) **novio(a)** *m.(f.)* (3)
fiber **fibra** *f.* (12)
field (sports) **campo de juego** *m.;*
    cancha *f.* (15)
field hockey **hockey sobre hierba** *m.*
    (13)
fifteenth birthday party **quinceañera** *f.*
    (8)

fifth **quinto(a)** (4)
fifty **cincuenta**
finally **finalmente, por fin** (13)
(to) find **encontrar (ue)**
fine **bien** (A)
finger **dedo (de la mano)** *m.* (10)
fire **fuego** *m.*
fireworks **fuegos artificiales** *m.*
first **primer(o/a)** (4)
   in the first place **en primer lugar**
first aid kit **botiquín** *m.* (14)
fish **pescado** *m.*
five hundred **quinientos(as)**
(to) fix **arreglar** (6)
flat **plano(a)**
flavor **sabor** *m.*
(to) float **flotar** (10)
floor **planta** *f.* (A); **piso** *m.* (4)
   (on the first) floor **(en el primer) piso**
   (4)
   floor plan **plan** *m.* (6)
   ground floor **planta baja** (4)
flour **harina** *f.*
flower shop **florería** *f.*
flu **gripe** *f.* (11)
flute **flauta** *f.* (A)
fog **neblina** *f.;* **niebla** *f.* (1)
It's foggy. **Hay niebla.** (1)
folk dance **baile folklórico** *m.*
(to) follow **seguir (i, i)** (B)
the following **lo siguiente** (4)
food **alimento** *m.;* **comida** *f.*
foolish **tonto(a)**
foot **pie** *m.* (B)
   on foot **a pie** (B)
football **fútbol americano** *m.*
for **por** (4); **para** (B)
   for . . . hours **por... horas** (5)
forecast **pronóstico** *m.*
force **fuerza** *f.*
forehead **frente** *f.* (10)
forest **bosque** *m.*
fork **tenedor** *m.* (6)
(to) form **formar** (12)
formal **formal** (2)
fortunately **afortunadamente**
forty **cuarenta**
found out **saber** (preterite) (15)
fountain **fuente** *f.*
fountain pen **pluma** *f.*
four hundred **cuatrocientos(as)**
fourth **cuarto(a)** (4)
France **Francia**
French **francés(esa)** (A)

frequently **con frecuencia** (10); **frecuentemente** (B)
Friday **viernes** *m.* (B)
friend **amigo(a)** *m.(f.)* (A)
friendly **amable**
friendship **amistad** *f.*
Is from . . . **Es de...**
in front of **delante de** (B)
frozen **congelado(a)**
fruit **fruta** *f.* (12)
   fruit salad **ensalada de frutas** *f.*
full **lleno(a)**
(to) function **funcionar** (2)
funny **cómico(a)** (3)
furious **furioso(a)** (13)
(fully) furnished **(completamente) amueblado** (6)
future **futuro** *m.*

G

(to) gain weight **subir de peso** (12)
game **partido** *m.* (15); **juego** *m.*
(two-car) garage **garaje (para dos coches)** *m.* (6)
garden **jardín** *m.* (6)
in general **por lo general** (C)
generous **generoso(a)** (3)
geography **geografía** *f.*
German **alemán(ana)** (A)
Germany **Alemania**
(to) get out something **sacar**
(to) get together **reunirse** (7)
(to) get up **levantarse** (7)
gift **regalo** *m.*
girl **chica** *f.*
girlfriend **novia** *f.* (3)
(to) give **dar** (11)
   (to) give a going-away party **darles la despedida** (8)
(drinking) glass **vaso** *m.* (6)
globe **globo** *m.*
(to) go **ir** (A)
   I go **voy** (A)
   (to) go along **andar**
   (to) go away **irse** (7)
   (to) go to bed **acostarse (ue)** (7)
   (to) go camping **ir de camping**
   (to) go down **bajar**
   (to) go fishing **ir de pesca**
   (to) go up **subir** (4)
   (to) be going to . . . **ir a...**
goal (sport) **gol** *m.* (15); (objective)
   meta *f.*

goaltender **arquero(a)** *m.(f.);* **portero(a)** *m. (f.)* (15)
golf **golf** *m.* (9)
good **bueno(a)** (2)
   Good afternoon. **Buenas tardes.**
   Good evening. **Buenas noches.**
   Good grief! **¡Qué cosa!**
   Good heavens! **¡Ave María!**
   Good morning. **Buenos días.** (A)
   Good night. **Buenas noches.**
good-bye **adiós, chao** (A)
   (to) say good-bye **darles la despedida** (8)
   (to) say good-bye to **despedirse (i, i) de**
(50) grams of **(50) gramos de** (C)
granddaughter **nieta** *f.* (3)
grandfather **abuelo** *m.* (A)
grandmother **abuela** *f.* (A)
grandson **nieto** *m.* (3)
grape **uva** *f.* (C)
grasshopper **saltamontes** *m.*
grave **grave** *adj.* (10)
gray **gris** (2)
Great! **¡Qué bueno(a)!**
Great Britain **Gran Bretaña**
green **verde** (2)
(to) greet **saludar**
greeting **saludo** *m.*
grenadine **granadina** *f.*
grievous **grave** (10)
ground floor **planta baja** (4)
group **grupo** *m.;* (unit) **conjunto** *m.*
(to) grow **crecer**
guacamole **ensalada de guacamole** *f.* (C)
Guatemala **Guatemala**
Guatemalan **guatemalteco(a)**
guitar **guitarra** *f.* (A)
gym(nasium) **gimnasio** *m.* (10)

H

hair **pelo** *m.* (3)
half **medio(a); mitad** *f.*
hallway **corredor** *m.* (4)
ham **jamón** *m.* (C)
hamburger **hamburguesa** *f.* (C)
hand **mano** *f.* (10)
handle **manija** *f.*
handlebar **manillar** *m.*
handling **manejo** *m.*
handsome **guapo(a)**

What happened to you? **¿Qué te pasó?**
(10)
happiness **felicidad** *f.*
happy **alegre** (2)
hard **duro(a)** *f.* (C)
hard-working **trabajador(a)** (3)
(to) harvest **cosechar**
(he / she / it) has **tiene**
it has been . . . **hace...** (C)
(to) hate **odiar**
(to) have **tener** (A)
(to) have a . . . ache **tener dolor de...**
(10)
(to) have a good time **divertirse (ie, i)**
(7)
(to) have just . . . **acabar de...**
Do you have . . . ? **¿Tiene Ud... ?** (C)
We have / had a good time. **Lo**
pasamos bien. (9)
hay fever **fiebre del heno** (11)
hazel (eyes) **castaño(a)** (3)
he **él**
head **cabeza** *f.* (10)
headphones **auriculares** *m.* (14)
health **salud** *f.* (12)
(to) hear **oír** (13)
heart **corazón** *m.* (5)
heart rate **ritmo cardíaco** *m.* (12)
with all my heart **con todo el corazón**
(5)
heat **calor** *m.* (1)
heavy **pesado(a)** (2)
Hello. **Hola.** (A)
Hello! (answering the phone) **¡Bueno!,**
¡Diga / Dígame!
(to) help **ayudar**
her **su** (5)
here **aquí**
Here you have . . . **Aquí tiene...** (C)
high school **escuela secundaria**
high-heeled shoe **zapato de tacón**
highway **carretera** *f.*
(to) take a hike **dar una caminata**
hiking **montañismo** *m.* (14);
senderismo *m.* (14)
hill **colina** *f.*
hip **cadera** *f.*
his **su** (5)
Hispanic **hispano(a)**
historical **histórico(a)** (2)
history **historia** *f.* (A)
homework **tarea** *f.* (7)
Honduran **hondureño(a)**
Honduras **Honduras**

honest **honesto(a)** (3)
hoop **aro** *m.*
(to) hope **esperar** (5)
I hope it's not . . . **Espero que no**
sea... (8)
I hope that you can visit **espero que**
Uds. puedan visitar (5)
horoscope **horóscopo** *m.* (2)
horrible **horrible**
horror movie **película de horror**
horse **caballo** *m.*
horseback riding **equitación** *f.* (9)
(to) go horseback riding **hacer la equi-**
tación (9)
horseman **jinete** *m.*
hospital **hospital** *m.* (B)
hospitality **hospitalidad** *f.* (5)
hot **caliente** (7)
It's hot out. **Hace calor.** (1)
hot, spicy sauce **salsa picante** *f.* (C)
hotel **hotel** *m.* (B)
hour **hora** *f.* (B)
half hour **media hora** (5)
house **casa** *f.* (A)
how **como**
how? **¿cómo?**
How . . . ! **¡Qué... !**
How are you? **¿Cómo está(s)?, ¿Qué**
tal? (A)
How awful! **¡Qué horrible!**
How can I help you? **¿En qué puedo**
servirle(s)?
How do you feel? **¿Cómo te sientes?**
(10)
How do you say . . . ? **¿Cómo se**
dice... ? (6)
How is it / are they? **¿Cómo es / son?**
How long ago? **¿Cuánto tiempo**
hace? (12)
How long have you felt this way?
¿Cuánto tiempo hace que te sientes
así?
how much / many? **¿cuánto(a)?**
How many are there? **¿Cuántos hay?**
How much does it cost? **¿Cuánto**
cuesta? (C)
How old are you? **¿Cuántos años**
tienes? (A)
hug **abrazo** *m.* (5)
human being **ser humano** *m.*
(to) be hungry **tener hambre**
(to) hurry **darse prisa** (7)
Hurry up! **¡Dense prisa!** (7)
(to) hurt **doler (ue)** (11)

(to) hurt oneself **lastimarse** (10)
Did you hurt yourself? **¿Te lastimaste?**
(10)
My . . . hurt(s). **Me duele(n)...** (11)
husband **esposo** *m.*

I **yo** (A)
I am (not) from . . . **(Yo) (no) soy de...** (A)
I am of . . . origin. **(Yo) soy de**
origen... (A)
I am . . . tall. **Mido...** (12)
ice **hielo** *m.* (1)
ice cream **helado** *m.*
It's icy. **Hay hielo.** (1)
idealist(ic) **idealista** (3)
if **si**
impatient **impaciente** (3)
impossible **imposible**
(to) improve **mejorar** (12)
in **en** (A)
iIn (the month of). . . **en (el mes de)...**
(1)
included **incluido(a)** (4)
incredible **increíble** (6)
Independence Day **el Día de la**
Independencia
independent **independiente** (3)
indication **indicación** *f.* (12)
indiscreet **indiscreto(a)** (3)
infantile **infantil** (2)
infection **infección** *f.* (11)
inflatable raft **barco neumático** *m.* (14)
injury **lesión** *f.*
instance **vez** *f.*
intellectual **intelectual** (3)
intelligent **inteligente**
interesting **interesante** (2)
interview **entrevista** *f.*
(to) introduce **presentar** (12)
I want to introduce you to . . . **Quiero**
presentarle(te) a... (A)
I would like to introduce you to . . .
Quisiera presentarle(te) a... (A)
introduction **presentación** *f.*
invitation **invitación** *f.*
iron **hierro** *m.* (12)
irrigation ditch **acequia** *f.*
is **es**
Italian **italiano(a)** (A)
Italy **Italia**

J

jacket **chaqueta** f.
jam **mermelada** f.
January **enero** (1)
Japan **Japón**
Japanese **japonés(esa)** (A)
jazz **jazz** m. (A)
jeans **vaqueros** m.
jelly **mermelada** f.
(to) jog **trotar** (10)
joint **coyuntura** f. (10)
journalist **periodista** m. or f.
juice **jugo** m.
July **julio** (1)
June **junio** (1)
(to) have just . . . **acabar de...**

K

key **llave** f. (A)
a kilo(gram) of **un kilo de** (C)
    half a kilo(gram) of **medio kilo de** (C)
kilometer **kilómetro** m.
kiss **beso** m.
kitchen **cocina** f. (6)
knee **rodilla** f. (10)
knife **cuchillo** m. (6)
(to) know (a fact) **saber** (1); (a person, place) **conocer** (3)
knowledge (understanding) **conocimiento** m.

L

lack **falta** f. (12)
lamp **lámpara** f. (4)
land **tierra** f.
landscape **paisaje** m.
language **lengua** f. (A); **idioma** m.
large **grande** (A)
(to) last **durar** (7)
last (Monday / week) **(el lunes / la semana) pasado(a)** (C)
last night **anoche** (C)
late **tarde** (5)
later **luego**
Latin **latín** m. (7)
(to) laugh **reírse (i, i)**
lawyer **abogado(a)** m.(f.)
lazy **perezoso(a)** (3)
(to) learn **aprender** (A)
at least **al menos** (4); **por lo menos**

at least in part **en parte al menos** (12)
leather **cuero** m.
(to) leave **irse** (7)
    (to) leave (with / from / for) **salir (con / de / para)** (4)
    we're leaving **nos vamos**
left **izquierda** (B)
    to the left **a la izquierda** (B)
leg **pierna** f. (10)
lemon **limón** m. (C)
lemonade **limonada** f. (C)
less **menos**
    less . . . than **menos... que...**
Let's be reasonable. **Hay que ser razonables.**
Let's go! **¡Vamos!** (C)
    Let's go . . . **Vamos a...**
Let's see. **Vamos a ver.** (4), **A ver.**
lettuce **lechuga** f. (C)
level **nivel** m.
library **biblioteca** f. (B)
life **vida** f.
(to) lift weights **levantar pesas**
light **ligero(a)** (2)
(to) light **encender (ie)**
like **como**
(to) like **gustar** (A)
    (I) (don't) like . . . (very much). **(No) (Me) gusta(n) (mucho)...** (A)
line **línea** f.
lipids **lípidos** m. (12)
(to) listen (to) **escuchar**
a liter of **un litro de** (C)
literature **literatura** f. (A)
a little **poco(a)**
(to) live **vivir**
I live in . . . **(Yo) vivo en...** (A)
living room **sala de estar** f. (6)
located **situado(a)** (B); **ubicado(a)**
location **lugar** m.
(to) lock oneself in **encerrarse (ie)**
long **largo(a)** (2)
(to) look at **mirar**
    (to) look at oneself **mirarse** (7)
    Look! **¡Mira!**
    You don't look very well. **No te ves muy bien.** (10)
(to) look for **buscar** (4)
(to) look over **revisar**
(to) lose **perder (ie)**
(to) lose weight **bajar de peso** (10)
a lot **mucho(a)**
    a lot of times **muchas veces** (10)

(to) love **amar**
loving **cariñoso(a)**
(to) lower **bajar**
(to) be lucky **tener suerte**
lung **pulmón** m. (10)
luxury **lujo** m. (4)

M

ma'am **señora** f. (A)
machine **máquina** f.
mad **enojado(a)**
Magnificent! **¡Magnífico!** (9)
majority **mayoría** f. (12)
(to) make **hacer**
    I'm going to make . . . for you. **Les voy a preparar...**
    (to) make the bed **hacer la cama**
    (to) make a goal **anotar un gol, marcar un gol** (15)
man **hombre** m.
manner **manera** f. (10)
marble **mármol** m.
March **marzo** (1)
market **mercado** m. (C)
maroon **marrón**
married **casado(a)** (A)
mathematics **matemáticas** f. (A)
What's the matter with you? **¿Qué te pasa?** (10)
maximum **máximo(a)** (10)
May **mayo** (1)
mayonnaise **mayonesa** f.
me **mí**
meal **comida** f.
(to) mean **querer decir** (6)
meaning **significado** m.
means **medio** m.
    means of transportation **medio de transporte**
(to) measure **medir (i, i)** (12)
meat **carne** f. (C)
mechanic **mecánico(a)** m.(f.)
(to) meet **reunirse** (7)
melon **melón** m. (C)
memory **recuerdo** m.
square meters **m² (metros cuadrados)** (6)
Mexican **mexicano(a)** (A)
    Mexican food **comida mexicana** f.
Mexico **México**
microbe **microbio** m. (11)
microwave oven **horno de microondas** m. (6)

middle **medio** *m.*
midnight **medianoche** *f.*
mile **milla** *f.*
milk **leche** *f.* (C)
(mango) milkshake **licuado (de mango)** *m.* (C)
million **millón**
mineral **mineral** *m.* (12)
mineral water (without carbonation) **agua mineral (sin gas)** *f.* (C)
minute **minuto** *m.* (B)
in . . . minutes **en... minutos** (5)
mirror **espejo** *m.* (4)
Miss **señorita** *f.* (A)
(to) miss **extrañar** (5)
I miss you (plural). **Te (Los) extraño.** (5)
mixture **mezcla** *f.*
modern **moderno(a)** (2)
at this moment **en este momento**
Monday **lunes** *m.* (B)
money **dinero** *m.*
month **mes** *m.* (C)
moon **luna** *f.*
moped **motocicleta** *f.* (A)
more **más**
more . . . than **más... que**
morning **mañana** *f.* (B)
in the morning **de la mañana** (B); **por la mañana** (C)
mother **madre** *f.* (A)
Mother's Day **el Día de la Madre** *m.* (C)
Mothers' Day card **tarjeta del Día de la Madre** *f.* (C)
motorcycle **motocicleta** *f.* (A)
mound **montículo** *m.*
mountain **montaña** *f.* (1)
mountain range **cordillera** *f.*
mountain bike **bicicleta de montaña** *m.* (14)
mountain climbing **alpinismo** *m.*
(to) go mountain climbing **hacer alpinismo**
mouth **boca** *f.* (10)
(to) move **moverse (ue)** (7)
movement **movimiento** *m.* (10)
movie **película** *f.* (A)
movie theater **cine** *m.* (C)
Mr. **señor** *m.* (A)
Mrs. **señora** *f.* (A)
much **mucho(a)**
as much . . . as . . . **tan(to)... como...**
very much **muchísimo**

muscle **músculo** *m.* (12)
muscle movement **movimiento muscular** *m.* (12)
muscle tone **tono muscular** *m.* (12)
museum **museo** *m.* (B)
music **música** *f.*
classical music **música clásica** (A)
mariachi music **música de mariachi** (13)
music store **tienda de música** *f.*
must **deber**
mustache **bigote** *m.* (3)
my **mi** (A)

N

name **nombre** *m.* (A)
last name **apellido** *m.* (A)
My name is . . . **(Yo) me llamo...** (A)
What's your name? **¿Cómo te llamas?** (A)
(to) be named **llamarse** (A)
(to) take a nap **dormir la siesta** (4)
napkin **servilleta** *f.* (6)
nationality **nacionalidad** *f.*
native **indígena** *m.* or *f.*
nature **naturaleza** *f.* (A)
near **cerca de** (B)
neck **cuello** *m.* (10)
necklace **collar** *m.*
(to) need **necesitar** (4)
neighbor **vecino(a)** *m.(f.)* (3)
neighborhood **barrio** *m.*
neither **tampoco**
nerve **nervio** *m.* (12)
nervous **nervioso(a)** (13)
nest **nido** *m.*
network **red** *f.*
never **nunca** (B)
nevertheless **sin embargo**
new **nuevo(a)**
newspaper **periódico** *m.* (6)
newspaper kiosk **quiosco de periódicos** *m.*
next (year / week) **(el año / la semana) próximo(a)** (C)
Nicaragua **Nicaragua**
Nicaraguan **nicaragüense**
nice **simpático(a)**
Nice to meet you. **Mucho gusto.** (A)
It's nice out. **Hace buen tiempo.** (1)
night **noche** *f.* (B)
at night **de la noche** (B); **por la noche** (C)

last night **anoche** (C)
night table **mesita de noche** *f.* (4)
night vision **vista nocturna** *f.* (12)
nightmare **pesadilla** *f.* (12)
nine hundred **novecientos(as)**
ninety **noventa**
ninth **noveno(a)** (4)
no **no**
No way! **¡Qué va!**
noise **ruido** *m.*
noon **mediodía** *m.*
normally **normalmente** (C)
north **norte** *m.* (B)
North American **norteamericano(a)**
nose **nariz** *f.* (10)
notebook **cuaderno** *m.* (A)
nothing **nada**
November **noviembre** (1)
now **ahora**
right now **ahora mismo**
number **número** *m.*
nurse **enfermero(a)** *m.(f.)*

O

(to) be obligated **tener que** (15)
(to) obtain **sacar**
It's . . . o'clock. **Son las...** (B)
It's one o'clock. **Es la una.** (B)
October **octubre** (1)
of **de** (B)
of course **por supuesto**
Of course! **¡Claro!**
Of course!! (reaffirmed) **¡Claro que sí!**
Of course not! **¡Claro que no!** (4)
of the **de la / del**
(to) offer **ofrecer**
often **a menudo** (10)
oil **aceite** *m.*
okay **de acuerdo** (C); **regular** (2)
Okay. **Está bien.**
Is that okay with you? **¿Te parece bien?** (8)
old **viejo(a)**; **antiguo(a)**
older **mayor**
olive **aceituna** *f.* (C)
Spanish omelette **tortilla de patatas** (C)
on **en** (A)
on foot **a pie** (B)
on time **a tiempo** (5)
once **una vez**
at once **en seguida** (9)
once home **ya en casa** (7)

once a year **una vez al año**
one **uno** (C)
   One . . . , please. **Un(a)..., por favor.**
     (C)
one hundred **cien(to)**
one-way ticket **billete sencillo**
onion **cebolla** f. (C)
only **sólo** (7); adj. **único(a)**
only child **hijo(a) único(a)** m.(f.) (A)
open-air market **mercado al aire libre**
optimist(ic) **optimista** (2)
or **o**
orange (color) **anaranjado(a)** (2)
orange (fruit) **naranja** f. (C)
order **orden** m.
   (to) give an order **mandar** (11)
   in order to **para** (B)
other **otro(a)**
our **nuestro(a)**
(microwave) oven **horno (de microondas)**
   m. (6)
outside of **fuera de**
(to) owe **deber**
owner **dueño(a)** m.(f.)
oxygen **oxígeno** m. (10)

P

(to) pack **empacar** (14)
   (to) pack suitcases **hacer las maletas**
a package of **un paquete de** (C)
painter **pintor(a)** m.(f.) (2)
painting **cuadro** m. (2);
   pintura f. (A)
pair **par** m.
pale **pálido(a)** (3)
Panama **Panamá**
Panamanian **panameño(a)**
pants **pantalones** m.
paper **papel** m. (C)
   air mail stationery **papel de**
     avión (C)
   typing paper **papel para escribir a**
     máquina m.
parade **desfile** m.
Paraguay **Paraguay**
Paraguayan **paraguayo(a)**
parents **padres** m. (pl.)
park **parque** m. (B)
to park **estacionar**
parking **estacionamiento** m. (6)
   parking lot **playa de estaciona-**
     miento f.
part **parte** f.

party **fiesta** f.
(to) pass **pasar** (9)
pasta **pasta** f.
pastry **pastel** m.
pasture **prado** m.
path **sendero** m. (14)
patient **paciente** (3)
(to) pay **pagar** (4)
   (to) pay attention **prestar atención** (5)
pea **guisante** m. (C)
peach **melocotón** m.
peanut **cacahuete** m.
pear **pera** f. (C)
pen, ball-point **bolígrafo** m.; fountain
   pluma f.
pencil **lápiz** m. (A)
   pencil sharpener **sacapuntas** m. (A)
people **gente** f.
pepper (spice) **pimienta** f.
   hot pepper **chile** m.
perfect **perfecto(a)** (3)
(to) perfect **perfeccionar** (5)
perhaps **tal vez** (8)
period (of time) **período** m. (2)
do not permit **no permiten** (4)
person **persona** f. (4)
Peru **Perú**
Peruvian **peruano(a)**
pessimist(ic) **pesimista** (2)
pharmacy **farmacia** f. (B)
piano **piano** m. (A)
(to) pick up **recoger**
pie **pastel** m.
a piece of **un pedazo de** (C)
pill **pastilla** f. (11)
pink **rosado(a)** (2)
pizza **pizza** f. (C)
place **lugar** m.; **sitio** m.
high plain **meseta** f.
(to) plan **planear**
plant **planta** f. (A)
plate **plato** m. (6)
(to) play **jugar (ue)** (1)
   (to) play (golf / tennis / volleyball) **jugar**
     al (golf / tenis / vólibol) (9)
   (to) play cards **jugar a los naipes** (13)
   (to) play checkers **jugar a las damas**
     (13)
   (to) play (instrument) **tocar** (A)
player **jugador(a)** m.(f.) (15)
pleasant **agradable** (10); **genial**
please **por favor** (C)
   Please be kind enough to respond as soon
     as possible. **Tenga la bondad de**

     responder tan pronto como sea
     posible. (8)
with pleasure **con mucho gusto**
   It would give us great pleasure . . . **Nos**
     daría mucho gusto... (8)
poetry contest **concurso de poesía** m.
point **punto** m. (11)
police **policía** f.
   police officer **policía** m.
   police station **estación de policía** f.
politics **política** f. (A)
poorly **mal**
porch **terraza** f. (6)
pork **carne de puerco** m. (C)
possession **posesión** f.
post **poste** m.
post office **oficina de correos** f.
poster **póster** m. (A); **cartel** m.
potato **papa** f.; **patata** (Spain) f. (C)
   potatoes in a spicy sauce **patatas**
     bravas (C)
a pound of **una libra de** (C)
practical **práctico(a)** (2)
(to) practice **practicar** (9)
(to) prefer **preferir (ie, i)**
preference **preferencia** f.
preoccupied **preocupado(a)**
(to) prepare **preparar**
   (to) prepare oneself **prepararse** (7)
   (to) prepare for oneself **servirse (i, i)**
     (7)
   I'm going to prepare... **les voy a**
     preparar...
(to) present **presentar** (12)
presentation **presentación** f.
preserve **conserva** f.
pressure **presión** f. (10)
pretty **bonito(a)** (2); **lindo(a)**
previous **anterior** (9)
price **precio** m. (4)
prize **premio** m.
profession **profesión** f.
professor **profesor(a)** m.(f.)
protein **proteína** f. (12)
proud **orgulloso(a)**
Puerto Rican **puertorriqueño(a)**
Puerto Rico **Puerto Rico**
pump **bomba** f.
purple **morado(a)** (2)
purse **bolsa** f.
push **empuje** m.
(to) put **poner** (6)
(to) put on **ponerse** (7)
(to) put on makeup **maquillarse** (7)

Q

quality **calidad** *f.* (4)
quantity **cantidad** *f.*
quarter **cuarto** *m.* (B)
 . . . quarter(s) of an hour **. . . cuarto(s) de hora** (5)
quesadilla **quesadilla** *f.* (C)

R

racquet **raqueta** *f.*
raffle **sorteo** *m.* (14)
railroad station **estación de trenes**
(to) rain cats and dogs **llover (ue) a cántaros** (1)
raincoat **impermeable** *m.*
It's raining. **Llueve.** (1)
rarely **rara vez** (B)
at any rate **de todos modos**
rather **bastante** (B)
(to) reach **alcanzar** (11)
reaction **reacción** *f.* (2)
(to) read **leer** (A)
ready **listo(a)**
 (to) get ready **prepararse** (7)
realist(ic) **realista** (3)
Really? **¿De veras?**
for that very reason **por eso mismo**
Let's be reasonable **Hay que ser razonables.** (1)
(to) receive **recibir**
reception desk **recepción** *f.* (4)
(to) recognize **reconocer**
record (sports) **récord** *m.* (15)
(to) recuperate **recuperar** (12)
red **rojo(a)** (2)
redheaded **pelirrojo(a)**
refrigerator **refrigerador** *m.* (6)
(to) refuse **no querer** (preterite) (15)
regular **regular** (2)
regularly **con regularidad** (10)
(to) regulate **regular** (12)
relative (family) **familiar** *m.*
remedy **remedio** *m.* (11)
(to) renew **renovar (ue)** (12)
rent **alquiler** *m.* (6)
(to) rent **alquilar**
 (to) rent a video **alquilar un vídeo**
(to) repeat **repetir (i, i)** (12)
(to) request **pedir (i)** (C)
reservation **reservación** *f.* (4)
(to) respond **contestar**

response **respuesta** *f.* (8)
(to) rest **descansar** (A)
rest rooms **servicios sanitarios** *m.*
restaurant **restaurante** *m.* (B)
result **resultado** *m.* (12)
(to) return **regresar** (7); **volver (ue)** (1)
(to) review **revisar**
rice **arroz** *m.*
(to) ride a bicycle **montar en bicicleta**
(to) ride a horse **montar a caballo** (9)
right **derecha** (B)
 right? **¿verdad?**
 (to) be right **tener razón** (10)
 to the right **a la derecha** (B)
 right away **en seguida** (9)
 right now **ahora mismo**
ring **anillo** *m.*
(to) rise **subir** (14)
risk **riesgo** *m.*
river **río** *m.* (14)
road **camino** *m.*
rock music **rock** *m.* (A)
(to) rollerskate **patinar sobre ruedas**
romantic **romántico(a)** (2)
room **cuarto** *m.* (A);, **habitación** *f.* (4); **sala** *f.*
roundtrip ticket **billete de ida y vuelta**
rug **alfombra** *f.* (A)
(to) run **correr** (A)
Russia **Rusia**
Russian **ruso(a)** (A)

S

sad **triste** (2)
(to) sail (to sailboard) **navegar en velero (una tabla vela)** (9); **practicar la vela**
sailing **navegación a vela** *f.* (9)
salad **ensalada** *f.* (C)
 vegetable salad **ensalada de vegetales (verduras)** *f.*
sale **oferta** *f.*
 It's not on sale? **¿No está en oferta?**
salesman(woman) **vendedor(a)** *m.(f.)*
salsa (type of music) **salsa** *f.*
salt **sal** *f.*
Salvadoran **salvadoreño(a)**
same **mismo(a)** (7)
 Same here. **Igualmente.** (A)
 the same **lo mismo** (12)
sandal **sandalia** *f.*
sandwich (French bread) **bocadillo** *m.* (C)

(ham and cheese) sandwich **sándwich (de jamón con queso)** *m.* (C)
(to) have reason to feel satisfied with oneself **darse por satisfecho**
Saturday **sábado** *m.* (B)
sauce **salsa** *f.* (C)
Spanish sausage **chorizo** *m.* (C)
(to) save **ahorrar**
(to) say **decir** (6)
 (to) say yes (no) **decir que sí (no)** (6)
 what . . . says **lo que dice. . .** (4)
 What did you say? **¿Qué dijiste?** (6)
 You don't say! **¡No me digas!**
schedule **horario** *m.*
school **colegio** *m.*; **escuela** *f.* (A)
science **ciencia** *f.* (A)
 science fiction movie **película de ciencia-ficción** *f.*
(to) score (soccer) **anotar un gol, marcar un gol** (15)
sculpture **escultura** *f.* (A)
sea **mar** *m.* (1)
seashore **orilla del mar** *f.*
second **segundo(a)** (4)
secretary **secretario(a)** *m.(f.)*
(to) see **ver** (C)
 See you later. **Hasta luego.** (A)
 we'll see each other **nos vemos**
(to) sell **vender**
sensational **sensacional** (2)
sense **sentido** *m.*
sentence **oración** *f.*
September **septiembre** (1)
sequence, series **serie** *f.*
serious **serio(a)** (2)
(to) serve oneself **servirse (i, i)** (7)
at your service **a sus órdenes**
(to) set the table **poner la mesa** (7)
seven hundred **setecientos(as)**
seventh **séptimo(a)** (4)
seventy **setenta**
several **varios(as)**
(to) get in shape **ponerse en forma** (10)
 Are you in shape? **¿Estás en forma?** (10)
(to) share **compartir**
(to) shave **afeitarse** (7)
she **ella**
sheet (of paper) **hoja (de papel)** *f.* (C)
shellfish **marisco** *m.*
shirt **camisa** *f.*
shoe **zapato** *m.*
 shoe store **zapatería** *f.*

(to) shoot **fusilar**

(to) go shopping **ir de compras** (A)
   shopping cart **carrito** *m.*
   shopping center **centro comercial**

short (height) **bajo(a)**; (length) **corto(a)** (3)

should **deber**

shoulder **hombro** *m.* (10)

show **espectáculo** *m.*

(to) show a movie **dar una película** (8)

shower **ducha** *f.* (4)
   (to) take a shower **ducharse** (7)

shows it **lo muestra** (5)

sick **enfermo(a)**

side **lado** *m.*
   on my father's (mother's) side **del lado de mi padre (madre)** (A)

sign, signal **señal** *f.* (12)

silly **tonto(a)**

silver **plata** *f.*

simple **sencillo(a)** (10); **simple** (4)

since **desde (que)** (12)
   Since when? **¿Desde cuándo?** (12)

(to) sing **cantar** (A)

single **soltero(a)** (3)

sink **lavabo** *m.* (4)

sir **señor** *m.* (A)

sister **hermana** *f.* (A)

(to) sit down **sentarse (ie)** (7)

situated **situado(a)** (B)

six hundred **seiscientos(as)**

sixth **sexto(a)** (4)

sixty **sesenta**

(to) skate **patinar**

ski **esquí** *m.*

(to) ski **esquiar** (A)

skirt **falda** *f.*

slacks **pantalones** *m.*

(to) sleep **dormir (ue, u)** (4)}
   I can't sleep. **No puedo dormir.** (11)

sleepyhead **dormilón(ona)** *m.(f.)* (7)

slice of bread **rebanada de pan** *f.*

slippery **resbaloso(a)** (1)
   It's a slippery day. **Está resbaloso.** (1)

slow, slowly **despacio**

small **pequeño(a)** (A)

(to) smile **sonreírse (i, i)** (12)

smoke **humo** *m.*

snack **merienda** *f.*
   Spanish snack **tapa** *f.* (C)

(to) sneeze **estornudar** (11)

(to) snore **roncar** (12)

(to) snorkel **bucear**

snorkeling **buceo** *m.*

snow **nieve** *f.* (1)

It's snowing. **Nieva.** (1)

so **tan**
   so-so **más o menos**

soap **jabón** *m.* (5)

soccer **fútbol** *m.*

social event **evento social** *m.* (10)

sock **calcetín** *m.*

soda **soda** *f.*

sofa **sofá** *m.* (6)

soft drink **refresco** *m.*

solitude **soledad** *f.*

solution **solución** *f.* (10)

some **unos(as)** (C)

someday **algún día**

something **algo**

sometimes **a veces** (B)

son **hijo** *m.* (A)

I'm sorry. **Lo siento.**

soul **alma** *f.*

south **sur** *m.* (B)

space **espacio** *m.*

Spain **España**

Spanish **español(a)** (A)

special **especial**

speed **velocidad** *f.* (15)

spectacle **espectáculo** *m.* (13)

(to) spend **gastar**
   (to) spend time **pasar tiempo** (A)

sphere **globo** *m.*

spicy **picante** (C)
   spicy sauce **salsa picante** *f.* (C)

spoon **cuchara** *f.* (6)

sport **deporte** *m.* (A)

sporting goods store **tienda de deportes**

(to) spread **difundir**

spring **primavera** *f.* (1)

square **plaza** *f.* (B)
   square meters **m² (metros cuadrados)** (6)

squid **calamares** *m.* v

stadium **estadio** *m.* (B)

star **estrella** *f.*

starch **almidón** *m.* (12)

state **estado** *m.*

station **estación** *f.*

stationery store **papelería** *f.* (C)

(to) stay in bed **quedarse en cama** (7)

(to) stay in top condition **mantenerse en condiciones óptimas** (10)

stepfather **padrastro** *m.* (A)

stepmother **madrastra** *f.* (A)

stereo **estéreo** *m.* (A)

still **todavía**

stocking **media** *f.*

stomach **estómago** *m.* (10)

without stopping **sin parar** (11)

store **tienda** *f.*

storm **tormenta** *f.* (1)

It's stormy. **Hay tormenta.** (1)

stove **estufa** *f.* (6)

strange **extraño(a)**

strawberry **fresa** *f.* (C)

street **calle** *f.* (B)

strong **fuerte** (3)

student **alumno(a)** *m.(f.)*; **estudiante** *m.* or *f.*

(to) study **estudiar** (A)

stupid **tonto(a)**

style **estilo** *m.*; **moda** *f.*

subway **metro** *m.* (B)
   subway map **plano del metro** *m.*
   subway station **estación de metro**

success **éxito** *m.* (15)

suddenly **de repente**

(to) suffer **sufrir** (11)

sufficient **suficiente**

sugar **azúcar** *m.*

(to) suggest **sugerir (ie, i)**

suitcase **maleta** *f.*

summer **verano** *m.* (1)

summit **cumbre** *f.*

sun **sol** *m.* (1)

(to) sunbathe **tomar el sol**

Sunday **domingo** *m.* (B)

It's sunny out. **Hace sol.** (1)

Super! **¡Super!**

sure **seguro(a)**

(to) surf **practicar el surfing**

surgery **cirugía** *f.*

It will be a surprise; don't say anything to them. **Será una sorpresa; no les digas nada.** (8)

survey **encuesta** *f.*

(to) sweat **sudar** (10)

sweater **suéter** *m.*

sweet **dulce** *m.*
   sweet roll, any **pan dulce**

(to) swim **nadar**

swimming **natación** *f.*

swimming pool **piscina** *f.*

system **sistema** *m.*

T

T-shirt **camiseta** *f.*

(beef) taco **taco (de carne)** *m.* (C)
   taco stand **taquería** *f.* (C)

(to) take **tomar** (B)
  (to) take a long time **tardarse** (7)
  takes him **lo lleva**
  (it) takes … minutes **tarda… minutos** (B)
talent **talento** *m.* (15)
(to) talk **hablar**
tall **alto(a)**
tan **bronceado(a)** (3)
tapas restaurant **bar de tapas** *m.* (C)
tape (recording) **cinta** *f.* (A)
  tape recorder **grabadora** *f.* (A)
taste **gusto** *m.*
tasty **sabroso(a)**
taxi **taxi** *m.*
(iced) tea **té (helado)** *m.* (C)
(to) teach **enseñar**
teacher **profesor(a)** *m.(f.)*
team **equipo** *m.*
telephone **teléfono** *m.* (4)
  telephone booth **cabina de teléfono** *f.* (4)
  telephone conversation **conversación telefónica** *f.*
television set **televisor** *m.* (A)
  color television set **televisor a colores** *m.*
(to) tell **decir** (6)
  (to) tell the truth **para decir la verdad** (6)
  Tell me. **Dime.**
temperature **temperatura** *f.* (1)
  (to) take a temperature **tomar la temperatura** (11)
ten-trip ticket **billete de diez viajes**
tennis **tenis** *m.*
  tennis ball **pelota de tenis**
  tennis shoe **zapato de tenis**
tent **tienda de campaña** (9)
tenth **décimo(a)** (4)
terrace **terraza** *f.* (6)
terrain **terreno** *m.* (14)
territory **territorio** *m.*
test **prueba** *f.;* **examen** *m.*
thank you **gracias** (A)
  thank you very much (many thanks) for . . . **muchas gracias por...** (5)
  I thank you. **Les agradezco.** (5)
  thanks a million for . . . **mil gracias por...** (5)
Thanksgiving mass **misa de Acción de Gracias** *f.*
that **aquel(la), ese(a), que**
  Is that it? **¿Así es?**
  that is to say **es decir**

that is why **por eso**
that one **aquél(la)** *m.(f.),* **ése(a)** *m.(f.)*
That's all. **Es todo.** (C)
the **el** *m.,* **la** *f.,* **las** *f. pl.,* **los** *m. pl.* (A)
theater **teatro** *m.* (A)
theatrical **teatral** (2)
their **su** (5)
then **entonces, pues**
there **allí**
  there is / are **hay** (B)
  there is going to be **va a haber**
  over there **allá**
they **ellos(as)** *m.(f.)*
  They are from . . . **Son de...**
thigh **muslo** *m.* (10)
thin **delgado(a)**
thing **cosa** *f.*
(to) think **pensar (ie)**
third **tercer(o/a)** (4)
(to) be thirsty **tener sed**
this (month / afternoon) **este(a) (mes / tarde)** (C)
This is… (introduction) **Le (Te) presento a...** (A)
  this one **éste(a)** *m.(f.)*
thousand **mil**
three **tres** (C)
three hundred **trescientos(as)**
throat **garganta** *f.* (10)
one must go through . . . **hay que pasar por...** (4)
(to) throw oneself **tirarse** (10)
There's thunder. **Truena.** (1)
Thursday **jueves** *m.* (B)
ticket **billete** *m.*
time **tiempo** *m.,* **vez** *f.*
  at some other time **en otra oportunidad**
  on time **a tiempo** (5)
  from time to time **de vez en cuando** (B)
  It's about time! **¡Ya es hora!**
What time . . .? **¿A qué hora... ?** (B)
  What time is it? **¿Qué hora es?** (B)
  many times **muchas veces** (10)
timid **tímido(a)** (3)
tip **propina** *f.*
tired **cansado(a)**
to **a** (A)
  to the **al**
toast (salutation) **brindis** *m.* (8)
toast (food) **pan tostado** *m.*
toaster **tostador** *m.* (6)

today **hoy** (B)
  Today is the (day) of (month). **Hoy es el (día) de (mes).** (1)
toe **dedo del pie** *m.* (10)
together **junto(a)**
toilet **WC** *m.* (4)
tomato **tomate** *m.* (C)
tomorrow **mañana** (C)
tomorrow (morning / night) **mañana (por la mañana / noche)** (C)
(to) tone up **tonificar** (10)
tongue **lengua** *f.* (A)
too **también** (A)
  too (much) **demasiado** (1)
tooth **diente** *m.* (10)
top (of a mountain) **cima** *f.* (14)
(to) touch **tocar** (A)
tour **excursión** *f.* (14)
tourist **turista** *m.* or *f.*
tournament **torneo** *m.*
towel **toalla** *f.* (5)
town **pueblo** *m.* (9)
traditional **tradicional** (A)
train **tren** *m.* (B)
(to) travel **viajar** (A)
  travel agency **agencia de viajes** *f.*
traveler **viajero(a)**
  traveler's check **cheque de viajero** *m.* (4)
treatment **trato** *m.*
tree **árbol** *m.*
trip **viaje** *m.*
  (to) take a trip **hacer un viaje**
truly **verdaderamente**
trumpet **trompeta** *f.* (A)
truth **verdad** *f.*
(to) try to **tratar de** (12)
Tuesday **martes** *m.* (B)
tuna **atún** *m.*
(to) turn **doblar** (B)
(to) turn over **dar una vuelta** (2)
twenty **veinte**
(to) twist (a body part) **torcerse** (10)
two **dos** (C)
  the two **los(las) dos**
two hundred **doscientos(as)**
(to) type **escribir a máquina** (C)
typewriter **máquina de escribir** *f.* (A)

ugly **feo(a)** (2)
uncle **tío** *m.* (A)
(to) understand **comprender; entender**
understanding **comprensivo(a)**

unforgettable **inolvidable** (13)
United States **los Estados Unidos** (B)
university **universidad** f. (B)
unknown **desconocido(a)**
unlimited **sin límite**
until **hasta**
up **arriba** m. (1)
(to) go up **subir**
Uruguay **Uruguay** (13)
Uruguayan **uruguayo(a)**
useful **útil** (4)
as usual **como de costumbre**
usually **usualmente**

VCR **vídeo** m. (A)
vacant **vacío(a)** (6)
vacation **vacaciones** f. (9)
varied **variado(a)** (2)
various **varios(as)**
vegetable **vegetal** m. (12)
Venezuela **Venezuela**
Venezuelan **venezolano(a)**
very **muy, bien** (A)
   Very well, thank you. **Muy bien,
   gracias.**
videocassette **vídeo** m. (A)
violet **violeta** (2)
violin **violín** m. (A)
virus **virus** m. (11)
(to) visit **visitar** (5)
   (to) be visiting **estar de visita** (12)
vitamin **vitamina** f. (12)
volcano **volcán** m.
volleyball **vólibol** m.

(to) wait **esperar** (5)
   waits for them **los espera** (7)
waiter (waitress) **camarero(a)** m.(f.)
(to) wake up **despertarse (ie)** (7)
walk **paseo** m. (A)
   (to) take a walk **dar un paseo** (A)
(to) walk **caminar**
walking stick **bastón** m. (14)
wall **pared** f.
wallet **cartera** f. (A)
(to) want **desear, querer(ie)** (C, 15)
warm **caliente** (7)
(to) wash **lavar** (5)
   (to) wash (one's hands, hair, brush one's
   teeth) **lavarse (las manos, el pelo,
   los dientes)** (7)

(to) wash clothes **lavar la ropa** (7)
(to) wash dishes **lavar los platos** (7)
washing machine **lavadora** f.
(to) watch **mirar**
   (to) watch one's weight **guardar la
   línea**
   Watch out! **¡Cuidado!** (3)
   (to) watch television **mirar la televisión** (A)
water **el agua** f.
watermelon **sandía** f. (C)
(to) waterski **esquiar en agua** (9)
waterskiing **esquí acuático** m.
way **manera** f. (10)
in that way **de esa manera**
wax **cera** f.
we **nosotros(as)** m.(f.)
weak **débil** (3)
weather **tiempo** (1)
   What's the weather like? **¿Qué tiempo
   hace?** (1)
wedding **boda** f. (8)
Wednesday **miércoles** m. (B)
week **semana** f. (C)
weekend **fin de semana** m.
(to) weigh **pesar** (12)
   I weigh . . . kilos. **Peso... kilos.** (12)
you're welcome **de nada**
well **bien** (A)
   well then **pues**
west **oeste** m. (B)
what? **¿qué?, ¿cómo?** (B)
   What a pity! **¡Qué pena!**
   What's going on? **¿Qué pasó?**
   What's new? **¿Qué hay?**
when **cuando** (A)
where? **¿adónde?, ¿dónde?**
   Where are you from? **¿De dónde es /
   eres?**
   Where is . . .? **¿Dónde está... ?**
   Where is / are there . . . ? **¿Dónde
   hay... ?**
which? **¿cuál?**
whichever **cualquier**
a good while **un buen rato** (7)
white **blanco(a)** (2)
who? **¿quién?**
whole **entero(a)**
Whose is it? **¿De quién es?**
why? **¿por qué?** (C)
   why not? **¿por qué no?** (C)
wide **ancho(a)**
wife **esposa** f.
wind **viento** m. (1)
window **ventana** f. (6)

shop window **escaparate** m.
(to) windsurf **hacer windsurfing** (13)
It's windy out. **Hace viento.** (1)
winter **invierno** m. (1)
(to) wish for **desear**
   (to) wish them **desearles** (8)
with **con** (A)
   with all my heart **con todo el
   corazón** (5)
   with me **conmigo**
   with pleasure **con mucho gusto**
within **dentro de** (8)
without **sin** (4)
   without stopping **sin parar**
woman **mujer** f.
wonderful **formidable** (2)
word **palabra** f.
(to) work **trabajar, funcionar** (A)
worker **trabajador(a)** m.(f.)
world **mundo** m.)
world championship **campeonato mundial** m. (14)
(to) worry **preocupar**
   worried **preocupado(a)**
   Don't worry. **No se preocupen.** (8)
worse, worst **peor**
. . . would like... **quisiera...** (C)
   I would like something for . . . **Quisiera
   algo (alguna cosa) para...** (11)
   we would like . . . **(nosotros)
   quisiéramos...** (C)
wrist **muñeca** f. (10)
(to) write **escribir**

year **año** m. (C)
yellow **amarillo(a)** (2)
yes **sí**
yesterday **ayer**
yogurt **yogur** m.
you **(familiar) tú** (A), **(familiar plural)
   vosotros(as)** m.(f.), **(formal)
   usted/Ud.,** **(formal plural)
   ustedes/Uds.** (A)
young **joven**
younger **menor**
your **tu, su** (5)

zoo **parque zoológico** m.

Index

September 11
2002

2002

Pete Dohne!

To Barb

In appreciation for your organization
and hospitality of our visit
to LabVolt headquarters and CEC at
Newnan.

We hope to continue the association

Best wishes from the ASMS tour
party

Peter Crawford   Peter Sarb

James Sweeney   Yvonne Doherty

South Australia's Natural Landscapes

Photography and Text by Pete Dobré

Acknowledgements

I thank Jon Carr and the Bridgestone team who assisted us, during the last 9 years with their continuous support. We safely travelled over 500 000 kilometres with Bridgestone.

Thanks to Steve Lewis and the team at The Bureau for your tremendous help, encouragement and unhesitating involvement in this project. I appreciate your guidance in the changing field of technology. Special thanks to Rick Hurren and Dave Dobson for your attention to detail and your patience with a fussy person, while striving for excellence.

Thank you Greg Moore from T.J.M. Products for the support and the expert advice of your Adelaide Team, assisting us in our travels.

I appreciate John Atkins and the crew at Atkins -Technicolour for their high-class work which enabled me to confidently leave my films for processing. They readily received films from isolated parts of Australia and promptly returned them for evaluation.

I thank Fuji Australia for providing their superb, fine grain film and colour saturation for the Australian landscape.

I appreciate Nikon's support. The combination of Nikon cameras and lenses are a delight to use, displaying outstanding quality.

I am grateful for the meticulous maintenance of our Toyota vehicle by the Service Department and the mechanics at CMI-Toyota Southside, especially Trevor Short and Rick Pilkington.

I thank Dougie and Marg Sprigg at Arkaroola Wilderness Sanctuary for assisting us in our collection of images. We hope these photographs will help travellers see Arkaroola as a destination and not a stopover point.

My writing is enhanced by the editing skills of Gwenda Steward and my wife Cil. Your time is greatly appreciated.

To our close friends and family, in particular Mike and Viv Jeffs, thank you for your support, encouragement and interest.

National Library of Australia Cataloguing-in-Publication Data:
Dobré, Pete, 1958-
South Australia's Natural Landscapes
ISBN 0 9577063 0 8
1. Landscape Photography - South Australia. 2. Natural History - South Australia - Pictorial Works.
3. South Australia - Pictorial Works. I. Title.
779.369423

Published and distributed by Pete Dobré's Oz Scapes
P.O. Box 305, Happy Valley, South Australia, 5159, Australia
Email: ozscapes@cobweb.com.au
Phone/Fax: +61 8 8381 5895

Title Page: Sturt Desert Pea

Appreciation

To Cil, my special partner and best mate, who is extremely supportive. Together we share the same dreams, aspirations and passion for God.

To our two delightful children, Tess and Jed, who accompanied us camping in the wild places of Oz since they were 6 & 7 weeks old. Observing their growth and enthusiasm for this country and especially their affection for the Creator God is so special.

During the last 12 months some of my special memories have been when Tess, on her own initiative, joined me for sunrise. Since then my 10 year old daughter has photographed every sunrise with me. Together we climbed a variety of terrain to wait for that awesome scene. Climbing, stumbling and laughing through the dark to reach the top of the peaks remain treasured moments. Her zeal for photography displays a priceless desire to see the awesome creativity of God at dawn.

Young Jed continually suggests and advises the components of a good shot. He often says, "Dad I think you should come more on this angle." Quite often he is right. Perhaps his shorter height enables him to view scenes from a different perspective.

Jed's memory amazes me. Although only 6, he continually refers to the past, recalling our adventures in the wild places of Oz. He makes comparisons with features we have photographed. His inquisitive, exploring nature and delightful gestures are precious. In particular, sitting around the campfire at night, young Jed always finds a way to snuggle up on your lap, to recall the day's work. As a dad, I prize this intimate moment.

Around the campfire we experience a sense of peace and reflection, both on the day's work, and life in general. Cil and I treasure the campfire time of reflection and discussion. We have enjoyed many discussions with folk from all walks of life, about the God who created this wonderful earth.

I am forever thankful to Jesus for giving me the skill of photography and life. He took a kid from a broken home, who was heading in the wrong direction. Jesus' death and resurrection is a compelling event which changed my life. Death is no longer the end but the beginning.

Do you not know? Have you not heard? The Lord is the everlasting God, the Creator of the ends of the earth. Isaiah 40:28

Contents

Map of South Australia

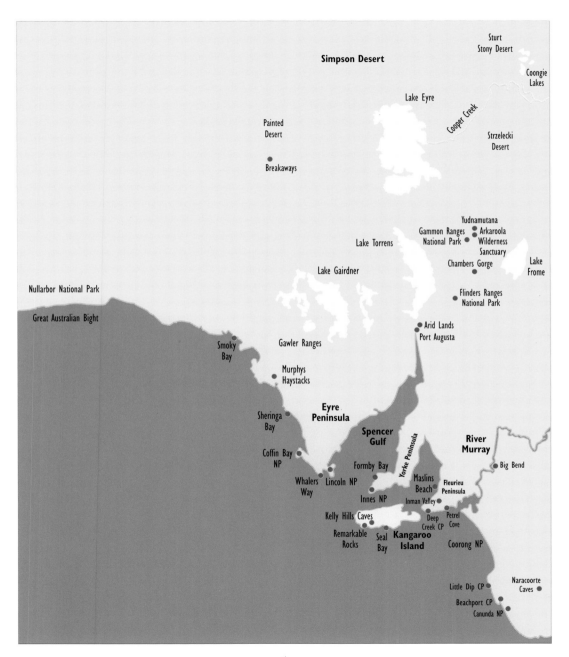

Simpson Desert

Sturt
Stony Desert

Coongie
Lakes

Lake Eyre

Cooper Creek

Painted
Desert

Strzelecki
Desert

Breakaways

Yudnamutana

Gammon Ranges
National Park

Arkaroola
Wilderness
Sanctuary

Lake Torrens

Chambers Gorge

Lake
Frome

Lake Gairdner

Flinders Ranges
National Park

Nullarbor National Park

Arid Lands
Port Augusta

Great Australian Bight

Smoky
Bay

Gawler Ranges

Murphys
Haystacks

Eyre
Peninsula

Sheringa
Bay

Spencer
Gulf

Yorke Peninsula

River
Murray

Coffin Bay
NP

Formby Bay

Big Bend

Whalers
Way

Lincoln NP

Maslins
Beach

Fleurieu
Peninsula

Innes NP

Inman Valley

Petrel
Cove

Kelly Hills Caves

Deep
Creek CP

Remarkable
Rocks

Seal
Bay

Kangaroo
Island

Coorong NP

Little Dip CP

Naracoorte
Caves

Beachport CP

Canunda NP

Cataloguing slides on South Australia's natural landscapes inspired me with the idea for this book. As I viewed the state's beauty, I realised that many South Australians and tourists may not venture into these breathtaking areas.

Records show that the majority of South Australians are yet to visit the magnificent Flinders Ranges, although this area is one of the state's best-known natural attractions. Because of this, I desire to display the rugged coastlines, the deserts, the mountain ranges, rock and sand formations, wildlife and all the stunning scapes of this state. The natural beauty is for everyone to share and enjoy.

This book overviews the majority of South Australia's natural landscapes, including those from the Outback Deserts, the Nullarbor Plain, the Great Australian Bight, the Southern and Northern Flinders Ranges, the Peninsulas- Eyre, Yorke and Fleurieu- Kangaroo Island, the River Murray, the Coorong and the South East.

It was difficult choosing transparencies for this book. For every photo chosen, there are others of equal beauty left out. Weather and unforeseen circumstances prevented me from photographing such areas as Bool Lagoon which, sadly, dried up over the last few years.

Enjoy the kaleidoscope of colours in the state's natural landscapes, as they vary from the reds of the Outback Desert, to the white towering dunes along the coastline. Rolling, iridescent green hills meet protected aqua bays and pristine beaches. Pounding blue seas hit rugged, towering cliffs of the Great Australian Bight, where you gaze in wonder at some of the most spectacular coastal scenery in Australia.

The Flinders Range's grandeur appears in the browns, blues, greens and purples, as well as in the rugged mountain ranges and tall river gums, glowing in the early morning and late afternoon light. Spectacular views from mountain tops provide wide colourful expanses. Rise at sunrise to appreciate the intense glowing colours. Savour the late afternoon light. It's a sheer delight to photograph the diversity of colours, which glow for a brief time and require quick action to capture them.

As I view the colours bleed into one in sunrises and sunsets, I hear God the Creator saying, "Hey I'm here. You are looking at my design." Often I say to myself, 'Surely this can't get any better.' I walk on and it does. Thanks God. I love it!

Although the deserts appear dry, barren and stony, rain transforms them. Stunning life springs up. Wildflowers in an array of pinks, purples and yellows protrude from the brown rocks and red dunes. Birds fly in to add beauty to the Outback. You must remind yourself that you are in a desert.

In the beginning God created nature for us to appreciate. He also entrusted men and women with the responsibility to care for the environment. We are not a product of time or matter plus chance, but the result of God's creation of people to be caretakers for the environment. Sadly, many who understand the wonder of creation have failed in this important responsibility.

With the moral, social and political obligation to respect and protect natural beauty for the enjoyment of future generations, let us keep a balance by opening these areas for all to enjoy.

A battle results when society bases its values on the dollar, as our natural areas erode, for financial gain. This wonderful planet provides our home, yet we slowly destroy it. Society shows little concern for caring, despite knowing the importance of the environment. It is foolish to sit back unconcerned for the future with a casual, 'She'll be right mate,' while neglecting to recognise the slow but certain warning signs.

The small word 'if' carries a huge burden when a mate, husband, wife or lover suddenly dies. Then we often hear, "If only I had said....If only I did...." We must learn from the past to prevent destruction to our natural landscapes so that future generations need not say of us, "If only they acted on...."

It is like a frog, sitting quietly in water. Gradually the water is heated to boiling point. The unresponsive frog sits there, until it is too late. Suddenly it panics when the water boils. Are we like the frog, allowing destruction in natural landscapes, until it is too late?

As I travel this state, I feel privileged and inspired. When I return to an area I see something new. Frequently I am asked, "Why do you return to the same places? Aren't you tired of regularly going back?" Venturing back to an area provides the opportunity to see the seasons with varying light effects, at different times of the day and in various months. Form, shape and light constantly change according to God's creativity. A complete picture of an area rewards me.

People ask, "What is your favourite area in this state?" Actually exciting scenes appear everywhere. A photographer appreciates the simplest aspects of the land, like the effect of wind on a dune, a dead tree against a stark background , or a pile of rocks engulfed with subtle light. From the Simpson Desert to the flat surface of a salt lake, some feature always adds a special delight. "Why would you want to go out there?" asks a friend. If they ventured out, they too could enjoy the magnificent complex structures and life forms, so dependent on each other.

Memorable Moments

The Wedge-tailed Eagle photographs on page 48 and 49 will remain my treasured moments. When I see an eagle's nest, I climb the tree to view it. On one particular day as we travelled through the Flinders with friends, my little mate Bryson spotted this nest. Climbing to the top of this tall tree became a mighty challenge. Cuts and bruises seemed insignificant as I looked into the nest. In the middle sat a baby eaglet. No words can describe my excitement.

My mind ticked over as I descended to get my cameras. Why not document the eaglet? For the next 10 weeks I travelled from Adelaide every weekend to photograph this bird, until its first flight. Each Saturday at 4.30 a.m. I left Adelaide, arriving at 10.00 a.m. to spend four hours with the bird, before heading home.

I was spell-bound as I became attached to the eagle over the ten weeks. I watched its amazing physical changes. Every time I left the bird, I felt sad wondering if it would be my last time with it. As I arrived on my tenth visit, I saw the bird balancing on a flimsy limb. Its wings were spread out for balance. At that moment I expected the eagle to fly. It didn't. I climbed the tree as a hot northerly wind blew. I was amazed to find a freshly killed rabbit in the nest. Out on the limb stood the bird. I wondered if the bird was use to my regular visits.

Unexpected and suddenly I lost my footing while taking a photograph and fell. My arm locked around the bough below and I dangled there, with cameras around my neck swinging to and fro. The top half of the tree swayed, dislodging the eagle. It plunged down, flapping its wings frantically to avoid contact with the ground.

A metre from the ground the bird levelled out and gradually flew skimming the top of the trees. I felt honoured to witness its inaugural flight. The bird made no attempt to return to the nest. Back on the ground, I wondered whether this was my last encounter with this eagle.

The following week I returned to the tree, but obviously the bird was no longer there. I climbed the tree to examine the empty nest. Eagles keep their nests clean and well preserved, daily lining the nest with new foliage. When I saw the dead leaves in the nest I knew the bird had gone.

As these birds sometimes use the same nest several times, I returned occasionally. The nest is still unused. I often reflect on my visits to that special bird. These photographs constantly remind me of the wonderful progression in creation.

*   *   *   *   *

I love sand dunes with their grandeur, shape, curvature, ripples and texture which constantly change with varying light. Lugging all my photographic gear, with my feet sinking in soft sand, is worth the effort to capture shots of dunes. Sometimes when I am so exhausted, I think , 'There has to be an easier way.'

Sand may also be a photographer's nightmare. Wind, sand and cameras do not mix. At a crucial moment, I'm often forced to change film in the middle of a dune system in gale force winds. Even one grain of sand entering the camera can have devastating results. My worst encounter and frightening moment with sand was the scariest event in my photographic experiences!

I visited the dunes at Sheringa Bay, on Eyre Peninsula, at sunrise. In excitement I planned my shots. Behind the dunes was a lake, so I thought that a shot from the middle would be stunning. With still water and no wind, reflections inspired me as soft morning light splashed across the dunes. I removed my boots and socks and entered the icy cold water.

Little did I realise what was ahead. A few steps took me two metres from the shore line. In another two steps I sank to my ankles. My next step was almost my undoing. I sank! In my right hand I held my tripod. On my back rested my pack of camera gear. In my left hand I held my panoramic camera. As a rush of adrenalin swept up my body I knew this was no ordinary feeling of sinking. I felt myself going down and sinking quickly. I called to my mate but he had walked off, so could not hear my cry for help.

I stood still, hoping to stop sinking which was ineffective, as in about 15 seconds I sank to my thighs, unable to free my legs. It became scary as I could not feel a hard bottom. Strangely the water across the lake was no deeper than the ankles. Yet one moment I stood on solid sand, the next I was going down like the Titanic! After about 20 seconds, the mud was up to my belly button. The weight of the camera gear on my back restricted me. I was only a few metres from the bank yet I couldn't grab anything solid. I felt my life disappearing before my eyes.

I threw my tripod to the shoreline and said, 'God, not now mate. This isn't the right time. There are still a few things I want to do for you.' By this stage I sank up to my nipples in mud. I tried to release my bag off my back. The more I moved the quicker I went down. Then a miracle from God occurred. I leaned to my left side, with my shoulder in the water and my camera bag wet.

Almost at right angles to my body I managed to lift out my right leg. Immediately I heard the squelch of the mud and water rushing down to fill the temporary gap left by my leg. With a mighty heave I manoeuvred my body to lie flat on top of the water. I could reach, grab the side and pull myself to shore. Through the ordeal I held the panoramic camera above the water line. My arm was sore and extremely painful. I had little strength left.

I was exhausted. Although the whole episode lasted about 30-45 seconds it seemed like a lifetime. Sitting on the bank, I pondered what might have been. I had heard about quicksand, but this was my first experience, I hope my last!

*   *   *   *   *

I was about to experience an unexpected once-in-a-lifetime event - yet again! We set off to the Simpson Desert to photograph for this book. As a photographer there are 3 situations I have longed for. I have asked God to show me the desert in flood. In July 1998 I was rewarded with that desire. I will always remember seeing the Simpson Desert change from an arid land to an inland sea, so quickly, in a matter of hours. My excitement grew as the desert came alive. The land transformed so quickly, with even a fresh smell.

We crossed the desert from west to east, pottering along. Light rain fell each night but it was not threatening. Awesome clouds complimented the landscape. Sunrises and sunsets with dramatic skies were tropical in appearance, with intense colours as though we were in the Northern Territory. Wildflowers bloomed in abundance, with the red dunes almost covered with an expanse of colour.

While we reached Birdsville with a sense of satisfaction, nothing prepared us for what occurred in the following days. Rain fell constantly for 24 hours in Birdsville. After a few days the Birdsville Police Station gave the all-clear for travel on the desert track. All other roads out of the town were closed. As we had planned to return through the desert, with the all-clear we set off to cross from east to west.

During our return travel on the track, heavy rain fell. Wherever we travelled the huge downpours formed enormous lakes and pools. When we drove over our last dune outside of Purnie Bore, we experienced the awesome sight of an inland sea (just like the early explorers hoped for.) To see this volume of water in the Simpson and its dramatic transformation of the landscape was a once-in-a-lifetime opportunity and a fulfilled dream. Standing on top of the dune, reflecting on the landscape before me, I chatted with God about His ability to change the entire scene so quickly.

We drove on to face inland seas and lakes so large that we debated whether to drive left, right or continue straight ahead. Binoculars allowed us to see green growth between the tracks, as a guide. The adventure with the rain did not conclude here. We continued on to experience numerous special and unforgettable moments in this desert crossing. Those days were certainly a highlight in my photographic career.

*   *   *   *   *

I hope this book inspires you to appreciate the amazing varieties of natural landscapes abounding in our wonderful state.

Our landscapes may be described by these wonderful words. For since the creation of the world God's invisible qualities – His eternal power and divine nature – have been clearly seen, being understood from what He has made. Romans 1:20

The Edge - Simpson Desert

Drifting Sands - Simpson Desert

Wind Swept – Simpson Desert

Flood Bound - Simpson Desert

Inspiring - Simpson Desert

Expanse – Simpson Desert

Approaching Storm – Simpson Desert

Fiery - Simpson Desert

Composed – Simpson Desert

Grasshoppers – Simpson Desert

Water-holding Frog – Simpson Desert

Deluge – Simpson Desert

Deluge – Simpson Desert

First Light – The Painted Desert

Sunrise - The Painted Desert

6.04 am – The Painted Desert

Provocative - The Painted Desert

Solitary - The Painted Desert

Fusion of Colours – The Painted Desert

Southern Right Whales

The Great Australian Bight

The Great Australian Bight

Nullarbor National Park

Day Break - The Nullarbor

Sheringa Bay - Eyre Peninsula

Sheringa Bay - Eyre Peninsula

Sheringa Bay - Eyre Peninsula

Coffin Bay National Park - Eyre Peninsula

Coffin Bay National Park - Eyre Peninsula

Coffin Bay National Park - Eyre Peninsula

Coffin Bay National Park - Eyre Peninsula

Coffin Bay National Park - Eyre Peninsula

Smoky Bay - Eyre Peninsula

Memory Cove – Lincoln National Park – Eyre Peninsula

Memory Cove – Lincoln National Park – Eyre Peninsula

Sleaford Dunes - Lincoln National Park - Eyre Peninsula

Sleaford Dunes - Lincoln National Park - Eyre Peninsula

Murphys Haystacks - Eyre Peninsula

Murphys Haystacks - Eyre Peninsula

Whalers Way - Eyre Peninsula

Barking Gecko

Yudnamutana - Northern Flinders Ranges

Chambers Gorge - Northern Flinders Ranges

Wedge-tailed Eagle - Flinders Ranges

A Ten Week Progression

Wilpena Pound – Flinders Ranges

Creek Bed – Flinders Ranges

Heysen Range - Flinders Ranges

Brachina Gorge - Flinders Ranges

Hucks Lookout - Flinders Ranges

Settler's Hut – Flinders Ranges

Contrast – Flinders Ranges

Contrast - Flinders Ranges

Sturt Stony Desert

Striking

Strzelecki Desert

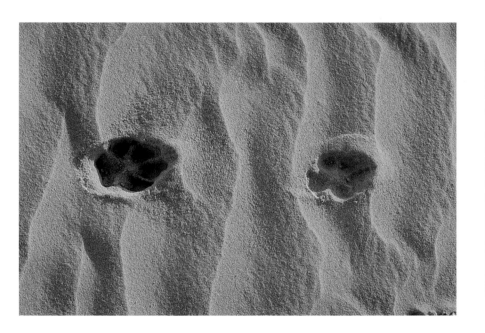

Strzelecki Desert

Innes National Park - Yorke Peninsula

Formby Bay - Yorke Peninsula

Spencer Gulf

Arid Lands - Port Augusta

Inman Valley - Fleurieu Peninsula

Deep Creek Conservation Park

Maslins Beach - Fleurieu Peninsula

Petrel Cove – Fleurieu Peninsula

Big Bend – River Murray

Big Bend – River Murray

Descending – Coorong National Park

Meeting Place – Coorong National Park

Sunrise – Coorong National Park

Serenity – Coorong National Park

Coorong National Park

Coorong National Park

Evening Light - Coorong National Park

Coorong National Park

Coongie Lakes - Strzelecki Desert

Coongie Lakes - Strzelecki Desert

Cooper Creek - Strzelecki Desert

Cooper Creek - Strzelecki Desert

Australian Pelican & Yellow-billed Spoonbill

Coongie Lakes – Strzelecki Desert

Naracoorte Caves - The South East

Naracoorte Caves – The South East

Canunda National Park - The South East

Canunda National Park - The South East

Little Dip Conservation Park – The South East

Beachport Conservation Park - The South East

Arkaroola - Northern Flinders Ranges

Arkaroola – Northern Flinders Ranges

93

Arkaroola Waterhole – Northern Flinders Ranges

Echo Camp Backtrack - Arkaroola - Northern Flinders Ranges

Stubbs Waterhole - Arkaroola - Northern Flinders Ranges

Echo Camp - Arkaroola - Northern Flinders Ranges

Spriggina Lookout - Arkaroola - Northern Flinders Ranges

Bararranna Gorge - Arkaroola - Northern Flinders Ranges

Lake Frome

Lake Frome

Gammon Ranges National Park

Bunyip Chasm – Gammon Ranges National Park

Lake Eyre

Seal Bay – Kangaroo Island

Remarkable Rocks - Kangaroo Island

Remarkable Rocks - Kangaroo Island

Remarkable Rocks - Kangaroo Island

Remarkable Rocks – Kangaroo Island

Kelly Hill Caves - Kangaroo Island

Kelly Hill Caves - Kangaroo Island

The Breakaways

The Breakaways

Rock Solid – Gawler Ranges

Dislodged – Gawler Ranges

Aged – Gawler Ranges

Life - Gawler Ranges

Peters Pillars - Mt Ive Station - Gawler Ranges

Peters Pillars - Mt Jve Station - Gawler Ranges

Lake Gairdner - Gawler Ranges

Lake Gairdner - Gawler Ranges

Lake Gairdner - Gawler Ranges

Lake Gairdner - Gawler Ranges

Lake Gairdner - Gawler Ranges